Bonus Chapters at www.dummies.com/extras/javaaio

Bonus Chapter 1: Using Eclipse

Bonus Chapter 2: Twiddling Your Bits

Bonus Chapter 3: Making Menus

Bonus Chapter 4: Using JavaBeans

Introduction

*W*elcome to *Java All-in-One For Dummies,* 4th Edition — the one
Java book that's designed to replace an entire shelf full of the dull,
tedious titles you'd otherwise have to buy. This book contains all the basic
information you need to know to get going with Java programming, starting
with writing statements and using variables and ending with techniques for
writing programs that use animation and play games. Along the way, you
find plenty of not-so-basic information about programming user interfaces,
working with classes and objects, creating web applications, and dealing
with files and databases.

You can (and probably should, eventually) buy separate books on each of
these topics. It won't take long before your bookshelf is bulging with 10,000
or more pages of detailed information about every imaginable nuance of
Java programming. But before you're ready to tackle each of those topics in
depth, you need to get a bird's-eye picture. That's what this book is about.

And if you already *own* 10,000 pages or more of Java information, you may
be overwhelmed by the amount of detail and wonder, "Do I really need to
read 1,200 pages about JSP just to create a simple web page? And do I really
need a six-pound book on Swing?" Truth is, most 1,200-page programming
books have about 200 pages of really useful information — the kind you use
every day — and about 1,000 pages of excruciating details that apply mostly
if you're writing guidance-control programs for nuclear missiles or trading
systems for the New York Stock Exchange.

The basic idea here is that I've tried to wring out the 100-or-so most useful
pages of information on these different Java programming topics: setup and
configuration, basic programming, object-oriented programming, programming techniques, Swing, file and database programming, web programming,
and animation and game programming. Thus you get a nice, trim book.

So whether you're just getting started with Java programming or you're
a seasoned pro, you've found the right book.

About this Book

Java All-in-One For Dummies, 4th Edition, is a reference for all the great things
(and maybe a few not-so-great things) that you may need to know when you're
writing Java programs. You can, of course, buy a huge 1,200-page book on each

of the programming topics covered in this book. But then, who would carry them home from the bookstore for you? And where would you find the shelf space to store them? And when will you find the time to read them?

In this book, all the information you need is conveniently packaged for you in-between one set of covers. And all of the information is current for the newest release of Java, known as JDK 8. This book doesn't pretend to be a comprehensive reference for every detail on every possible topic related to Java programming. Instead, it shows you how to get up and running fast so that you have more time to do the things you really want to do. Designed using the easy-to-follow *For Dummies* format, this book helps you get the information you need without laboring to find it.

Java All-in-One For Dummies, 4th Edition, is a big book made up of nine smaller books — minibooks, if you will. Each of these minibooks covers the basics of one key element of programming, such as installing Java and compiling and running programs, or using basic Java statements, or using Swing to write GUI applications.

Whenever one big thing is made up of several smaller things, confusion is always a possibility. That's why this book has multiple access points. At the beginning is a detailed table of contents that covers the entire book. Then each minibook begins with a minitable of contents that shows you at a mini-glance what chapters are included in that minibook. Useful running heads appear at the top of each page to point out the topic discussed on that page. And handy thumbtabs run down the side of the pages to help you find each minibook quickly. Finally, a comprehensive index lets you find information anywhere in the entire book.

Foolish Assumptions

You and I have never met, so it is difficult for me to make any assumptions about why you are interested in this book. However, let's start with a few basic assumptions:

✦ **You own or have access to a relatively modern computer.** The examples were created on a Windows computer, but you can learn to program in Java just as easily on a Mac or Linux computer.

✦ **You're an experienced computer user.** In other words, I assume that you know the basics of using your computer, such as starting programs and working with the file system.

✦ **You're interested in learning how to write programs in the Java language.** Since that's what this book teaches, it's a fair assumption.

I do *not* make any assumptions about any previous programming experience in Java or in any other programming language. Nor do I make any assumptions about *why* you want to learn about Java programming. There are all sorts of valid reasons for learning Java. Some want to learn Java for professional reasons; maybe you want to become a professional Java programmer, or maybe you are a C# or C++ programmer who occasionally needs to work in Java. On the other hand, maybe you think programming in Java would make an interesting hobby.

Regardless of your motivation, I *do* assume that you are a reasonably intelligent person. You don't have to have a degree in advanced physics, or a degree in anything at all for that matter, to master Java programming. All you have to be is someone who wants to learn and isn't afraid to try.

Icons Used in This Book

Like any *For Dummies* book, this book is chock-full of helpful icons that draw your attention to items of particular importance. You find the following icons throughout this book:

Danger, Will Robinson! This icon highlights information that may help you avert disaster.

Something new is aloft! I point it out with this icon.

One of the recent hot topics among programming gurus is the notion of *design patterns,* which provide predictable ways to do common things. This icon appears alongside text that describes such patterns.

Did I tell you about the memory course I took?

Pay special attention to this icon; it lets you know that some particularly useful tidbit is at hand.

When I mention bonus material that appears on this book's website (www. dummies.com/extras/javaaio), you'll see this icon. That includes code listings, which you can download directly.

Hold it — overly technical stuff is just around the corner. Obviously, because this is a programming book, almost every paragraph of the next 900 or so pages could get this icon. So I reserve it for those paragraphs that go into greater depth, down into explaining how something works under the covers — probably deeper than you really need to know to use a feature, but often enlightening.

Beyond the Book

There's much more to this book than the thousand or so pages you are holding in your hands. Go online to find the following:

✦ **The cheat sheet for this book is at**

    `www.dummies.com/cheatsheet/javaaio`

In the cheat sheet, you'll find helpful reference information for elements of Java you'll use all the time, such as `if` statements and `for` loops.

✦ **Online articles covering additional topics at**

    `www.dummies.com/extras/javaaio`

Here, you'll find interesting articles about topics ranging from why Java doesn't have a `goto` statement to solving classic puzzles or games such as The Towers of Hanoi or Nine Men's Morris.

✦ **Updates to this book, if we have any, are at**

    `www.dummies.com/extras/javaaio`

✦ **This book has an accompanying website at**

    `www.dummies.com/extras/javaaio`

The website includes even more goodies, including chapters about Eclipse, bit manipulation, menus, and JavaBeans. Plus, if you're looking for a way to save time, the page includes all the code listings used in this book.

Where to Go from Here

This isn't the kind of book you pick up and read from start to finish, as if it were a cheap novel. If I ever see you reading it at the beach, I'll kick sand in your face. Beaches are for reading romance novels or murder mysteries, not programming books. Although you could read straight through from start to finish, this book is a reference book, the kind you can pick up, open to just about any page, and start reading. You don't have to memorize anything in this book. It's a "need-to-know" book: You pick it up when you need to know something. Need a reminder on the constructors for the `ArrayList` class? Pick up the book. Can't remember the goofy syntax for anonymous inner classes? Pick up the book. After you find what you need, put the book down and get on with your life.

Book I

Getting Started with Java Basics

Getting Started
with
Java Basics

Visit www.dummies.com for great Dummies content online.

Contents at a Glance

Chapter 1: Welcome to Java

This chapter is a gentle introduction to the world of Java. In the next few pages, you find out what Java is, where it came from, and where it's going. You also discover some of the unique strengths of Java, as well as some of its weaknesses. Also, you see how Java compares with other popular programming languages, including C, C++, C#, and Visual Basic.

By the way, I assume in this chapter that you have at least enough background to know what computer programming is all about. That doesn't mean that I assume you're an expert or professional programmer. It just means that I don't take the time to explain such basics as what a computer program is, what a programming language is, and so on. If you have absolutely no programming experience, I suggest that you pick up a copy of *Java For Dummies*, 5th Edition, or *Beginning Programming with Java For Dummies*, 3rd Edition, both by Barry Burd (Wiley).

Throughout this chapter, you find little snippets of Java program code, plus a few snippets of code written in other languages, including C, C++, and Basic. If you don't have a clue what this code means or does, don't panic. I just want to give you a feel for what Java programming looks like and how it compares with programming in other languages.

All the code listings used in this book are available for download at www.dummies.com/extras/javaaio. Bonus chapters about Eclipse, JavaBeans, and other topics are at the site as well.

What Is Java, and Why Is It So Great?

Java is a programming language in the tradition of C and C++. As a result, if you have any experience with C or C++, you'll often find yourself in familiar territory as you discover the various features of Java. (For more information about the similarities and differences between Java and C or C++, see the section "Java versus Other Languages," later in this chapter.)

Java differs from other programming languages in a couple of significant ways, however. I point out the most important differences in the following sections.

Platform independence

One of the main reasons Java is so popular is its *platform independence,* which simply means that Java programs can be run on many types of computers. A Java program runs on any computer with a *Java Runtime Environment,* also known as a *JRE,* installed. A JRE is available for almost every type of computer you can think of: PCs running any version of Windows, Macintosh computers, Unix and Linux computers, huge mainframe computers, and even cellphones.

Before Java, other programming languages promised platform independence by providing compatible compilers for different platforms. (A *compiler* is the program that translates programs written in a programming language into a form that can actually run on a computer.) The idea was that you could compile different versions of the programs for each platform. Unfortunately, this idea never really worked. The compilers were never identical on each platform; each had its own little nuances. As a result, you had to maintain a different version of your program for each platform you wanted to support.

Java's platform independence isn't based on providing compatible compilers for different platforms. Instead, Java is based on the concept of a *virtual machine.* You can think of the Java Virtual Machine (sometimes called the *JVM*) as being a hypothetical computer platform — a design for a computer that doesn't exist as actual hardware. Instead, the JRE is an *emulator* — a program that sets aside part of your hard drive to act like a computer (namely, the JVM) that can execute Java programs.

The Java compiler doesn't translate Java into the machine language of the computer that the program is running on. Instead, the compiler translates Java into the machine language of the JVM, which is called *bytecode.* Then the JRE runs the bytecode in the JVM. Because of the JVM, you can execute a Java program on any computer that has a JRE installed without recompiling the program.

That's how Java provides platform independence — and believe it or not, it works pretty well. The programs you write run just as well on a PC running any version of Windows, a Macintosh, a Unix or Linux machine, or any other computer with a JRE installed — including smartphones or tablet computers.

While you lie awake tonight pondering the significance of Java's platform independence, here are a few additional thoughts to ponder:

✦ The JRE is separate from the Java compiler. As a result, you don't have to install a Java compiler to run compiled Java programs. All you need is the JRE.

✦ When someone asks whether your computer "has Java," he usually means to ask, "Have you installed the Java Runtime Environment?" (You need the JRE so that you can run Java programs.)

✦ Platform independence goes only so far. If you have some obscure type of computer system — such as an antique Olivetti Programma 101 — and a JRE isn't available for it, you can't run Java programs on it.

I didn't make up the Olivetti Programma 101. It was a desktop computer made in the early 1960s, and it happened to be my introduction to computer programming. (My junior high school math teacher had one in the back of his classroom, and he let me play with it during lunch.) Do a Google search for **Olivetti Programma 101** and you can find several interesting websites about it.

✦ Java's platform independence isn't perfect. Although the bytecode runs identically on every computer that has a JRE, some parts of Java use services provided by the underlying operating system. As a result, minor variations sometimes crop up, especially in applications that use graphical interfaces.

✦ Because a runtime system that emulates a JVM executes Java bytecode, some people mistakenly compare Java with interpreted languages such as Basic or Perl. Those languages aren't compiled at all, however. Instead, the interpreter reads and interprets each statement as it is executed. Java is a true compiled language; it's just compiled to the machine language of JVM rather than to the machine language of an actual computer platform.

✦ If you're interested, the JVM is completely *stack-oriented;* it has no registers for storing local data. (I'm not going to explain what that term means, so if it doesn't make sense to you, skip it. It's not important. It's just interesting to nerds who know about stacks, registers, and things of that ilk.)

Object orientation

Java is inherently *object-oriented,* which means that Java programs are made up from programming elements called objects. Simply put (don't you love it when you read *that* in a computer book?), an *object* is a programming entity that represents either some real-world object or an abstract concept.

All objects have two basic characteristics:

✦ Objects have data, also known as *state.* An object that represents a book, for example, has data such as the book's title, author, and publisher.

✦ Objects also have *behavior,* which means that they can perform certain tasks. In Java, these tasks are called *methods.* An object that represents a car might have methods such as `start`, `stop`, `drive`, and `crash`. Some methods simply allow you to access the object's data. A book object might have a `getTitle` method that tells you the book's title.

Classes are closely related to objects. A *class* is the program code you write to create objects. The class describes the data and methods that define the object's state and behavior. When the program executes, classes are used to create objects.

Suppose you're writing a payroll program. This program probably needs objects to represent the company's employees. So the program includes a class (probably named `Employee`) that defines the data and methods for each `Employee` object. When your program runs, it uses this class to create an object for each of your company's employees.

The Java API

The Java language itself is very simple, but Java comes with a library of classes that provide commonly used utility functions that most Java programs can't do without. This class library, called the *Java API* (short for *application programming interface*), is as much a part of Java as the language itself. In fact, the real challenge of finding out how to use Java isn't mastering the language; it's mastering the API. The Java language has only about 50 keywords, but the Java API has several thousand classes, with tens of thousands of methods that you can use in your programs.

The Java API has classes that let you do trigonometry, write data to files, create windows onscreen, and retrieve information from a database, among other things. Many of the classes in the API are general purpose and commonly used. A whole series of classes stores collections of data, for example. But many are obscure, used only in special situations.

Fortunately, you don't have to learn anywhere near all of the Java API. Most programmers are fluent with only a small portion of it: the portion that applies most directly to the types of programs they write. If you find a need to use some class from the API that you aren't yet familiar with, you can look up what the class does in the Java API documentation at `http://download.java.net/jdk8/docs/api`.

The Internet

Java is often associated with the Internet, and rightfully so, because Al Gore invented Java just a few days after he invented the Internet. Okay, Java wasn't really invented by Al Gore. It was developed right at the time the World Wide Web was becoming a phenomenon, and Java was specifically designed to take advantage of the web. In particular, the whole concept behind the JVM is to enable any computer connected to the Internet to run Java programs, regardless of the type of computer or the operating system it runs.

You can find two distinct types of Java programs on the Internet:

✦ **Applets:** *Applets* are Java programs that run directly within a web browser. To run an applet, the browser starts a JVM, and that virtual machine is given a portion of the web page to work with. Then the virtual machine runs the applet's bytecode.

✦ **Servlets:** *Servlets* are web-based Java programs that run on an Internet server computer rather than in an Internet user's web browser. Servlets are the real way that many, if not most, commercial websites work. A servlet generates a page of HTML that is sent to a user's computer to be displayed in the user's web browser. If you request information about a product from an online store, the store's web server runs a servlet to generate the HTML page containing the product information you requested.

You find out how to create both types of applications in Book VII.

Java versus Other Languages

Superficially, Java looks a lot like many of the programming languages that preceded it, most notably C and C++. For example, here's the classic Hello, World! program, written in the C programming language:

```
main()
{
    printf("Hello, World!");
}
```

This program simply displays the text "Hello, World!" on the computer's console. Here's the classic Hello, World! program written in Java:

```
public class HelloApp
{
    public static void main(String[] args)
    {
        System.out.println("Hello, World!");
    }
}
```

Although the Java version is a bit more verbose, the two have several similarities:

✦ Both require each executable statement to end with a semicolon (;).

✦ Both use braces ({}) to mark blocks of code.

✦ Both use a routine called main as the main entry point for the program.

Many other similarities aren't evident in these simple examples, but the examples bring the major difference between C and Java front and center: Object-oriented programming rears its ugly head even in simple examples. Consider the following points:

✦ In Java, even the simplest program is a class, so you have to provide a line that declares the name of the class. In this example, the class is named `HelloApp`. `HelloApp` has a method named `main`, which the JVM automatically calls when a program is run.

✦ In the C example, `printf` is a library function you call to print information to the console. In Java, you use the `PrintStream` class to write information to the console.

`PrintStream`? There's no `PrintStream` in this program! Wait a minute — yes, there is. Every Java program has available to it a `PrintStream` object that writes information to the console. You can get this `PrintStream` object by calling the `out` method of another class, named `System`. Thus `System.out` gets the `PrintStream` object that writes to the console. The `PrintStream` class in turn has a method named `println` that writes a line to the console. So `System.out.println` really does two things, in the following order:

1. It uses the `out` field of the `System` class to get a `PrintStream` object.

2. It calls the `println` method of that object to write a line to the console.

Confusing? You bet. Everything will make sense, however, when you read about object-oriented programming in Book III, Chapter 1.

✦ `void` looks familiar. Although it isn't shown in the C example, you could have coded `void` on the main function declaration to indicate that the main function doesn't return a value. `void` has the same meaning in Java. But `static`? What does that mean? That, too, is evidence of Java's object orientation. It's a bit early to explain what it means in this chapter, but you can find out in Book II, Chapter 7.

Important Features of the Java Language

If you believe the marketing hype put out by Oracle and others, you think that Java is the best thing to happen to computers since the invention of memory. Java may not be *that* revolutionary, but it does have many built-in features that set it apart from other languages (with the possible exception of Microsoft C#, which is basically a ripoff of Java). The following sections describe just three of the many features that make Java so popular.

Type checking

All programming languages must deal in one way or the other with *type checking* — the way that a language handles variables that store different types of data. Numbers, strings, and dates, for example, are commonly used *data types* available in most programming languages. Most programming languages also have several types of numbers, such as integers and real numbers.

All languages must check data types, so make sure that you don't try to do things that don't make sense (such as multiplying the gross national product by your last name). The question is, does the language require you to declare every variable's type so you can do type checking when it compiles your programs, or does the language do type checking only after it runs your program?

Some languages, such as Basic, do almost no type checking at compile time. In Microsoft's Visual Basic for Applications (VBA), for example, you can assign any type of data to a variable. Thus all of the following statements are allowed:

```
A = 5
A = "Strategery"
A = 3.14159
```

Here three different types of data — integer, string, and double — have been assigned to the same variable. This flexibility is convenient, but it comes with a price. The following sequence is perfectly legal in VBA:

```
A = 5
B = "Strategery"
C = A * B
```

Here an integer is assigned to variable A, and a string is assigned to variable B. Then the third statement attempts to multiply the string by the integer. You can't multiply strings, so the third statement fails.

Java, on the other hand, *does* complete type checking at runtime. As a result, you must declare all variables as a particular type so that the compiler can make sure you use the variables correctly. The following bit of Java code, for example, won't compile:

```
int a = 5;
String b = "Strategery";
String c = a * b;
```

If you try to compile these lines, you get an error message saying that Java can't multiply an integer and a string.

In Java, every class you define creates a new type of data for the language to work with. Thus, the data types you have available to you in Java aren't just simple predefined types, such as numbers and strings. You can create your own types. If you're writing a payroll system, you might create an Employee type. Then you can declare variables of type Employee that can hold only Employee objects. This capability prevents a lot of programming errors. Consider this code snippet:

```
Employee newHire;
newHire = 21;
```

This code creates a variable (newHire) that can hold only Employee objects. Then it tries to assign the number 21 to it. The Java compiler won't let you run this program because 21 is a number, not an employee.

An important object-oriented programming feature of Java called *inheritance* adds an interesting — and incredibly useful — twist to type checking. Inheritance is way too complicated to dive into just yet, so I'll be brief here: In Java, you can create your own data types that are derived from other data types. Employees are people, for example, and customers are people too, so you might create a Person class and then create Employee and Customer classes that both inherit the Person class. Then you can write code like this:

```
Person p;
Employee e;
Customer c;
p = e;   // this is allowed because an Employee is also a
    Person.
c = e;   // this isn't allowed because an Employee is not a
    Customer.
```

Confused yet? If so, that's my fault. Inheritance is a pretty heady topic for Chapter 1 of a Java book. Don't panic if it makes no sense just yet. It will all be clear by the time you finish reading Book III, Chapter 4, which covers all the subtle nuances of using inheritance.

Automatic memory management

Memory management is another detail that all programming languages have to deal with. All programming languages let you create variables. When you create a variable, the language assigns a portion of the computer's memory to store the data referred to by the variable. Exactly how this memory is allocated is a detail that you usually can safely ignore, no matter which language you're working with. But a detail that many languages do *not* let you safely ignore is what happens to that memory when you no longer need the data that was stored in it.

In C++ and similar languages, you must write code that explicitly releases that memory so that other programs can access it. If you don't do this, or if you do it wrong, your program might develop a memory leak. In a *memory leak,* your program slowly but surely sucks memory away from other programs until the operating system runs out of memory and the computer grinds to a halt.

In Java, you don't have to explicitly release memory when you're done with it; instead, memory is freed automatically when it's no longer needed. The JVM includes a special process called the *garbage collector* that snoops around the virtual machine's memory; determines when data is no longer being used; and automatically deletes that data, freeing the memory that it occupied.

A feature related to garbage collection is *bounds checking,* which guarantees that programs can't access memory that doesn't belong to them. Languages such as C and C++ don't have this type of safety net. As a result, programming errors in C or C++ can cause one program to trample over memory that's being used by another program, which in turn can cause your computer to crash.

Exception handling

As Robert Burns said, "The best-laid schemes o' mice an' men gang oft agley, an' lea'e us nought but grief an' pain, for promis'd joy!" When you tinker with computer programming, you'll quickly discover what he meant. No matter how carefully you plan and test your programs, errors happen, and when they do, they threaten to bring your whole program to a crashing halt.

Java has a unique approach to error handling that's superior to that of any other language (except C#, which just copies Java's approach, as I mention earlier in the chapter). In Java, the JRE intercepts and folds errors of all types into a special type of object called an *exception object.* After all, Java is object-oriented through and through, so why shouldn't its exception-handling features be object-oriented?

Java requires any statements that can potentially cause an exception to be bracketed by code that can catch and handle the exception. In other words, you, as the programmer, must anticipate errors that can happen while your program is running and make sure that those errors are dealt with properly. Although this necessity can be annoying, it makes the resulting programs more reliable.

On the Downside: Java's Weaknesses

So far, I've been tooting Java's horn pretty loudly. Lest you think that figuring out how to use it is a walk in the park, the following paragraphs point out some of Java's shortcomings (many of which have to do with the API rather than the language itself):

✦ **The API is way too big.** It includes so many classes and methods that you'll likely never use even half of them. Also, the sheer size of the Java API doesn't allow you to wander through it on your own, hoping to discover the one class that's perfect for the problem you're working on.

✦ **The API is overdesigned.** In some cases, it seems as though the Java designers go out of their way to complicate things that should be simple to use. The API class that defines a multiline text-input area doesn't have a scroll bar, for example. Instead, a separate class defines a panel that has a scroll bar. To create a multiline text area with a scroll bar, you have to use both classes. That's fine if you ever want to create a text area that *doesn't* have a scroll bar, but you never will. Java's designers complicated the design of the text area and scroll panel classes to provide for a case that no one ever uses or would want to use.

✦ **Some corners of the API are haphazardly designed.** Most of the problems can be traced back to the initial version of Java, which was rushed to market so that it could ride the crest of the World Wide Web wave in the late 1990s. Since then, many parts of the API have been retooled more thoughtfully, but the API is still riddled with remnants of Java's early days.

✦ **In my opinion, the biggest weakness of Java is that it doesn't directly support true decimal data.** This issue is a little too complicated to get into right now, but the implication is this: Without special coding (which few Java books explain and few Java programmers realize), Java doesn't know how to add. Consider this bit of code:

```
double x = 5.02;
double y = 0.01;
double z = x + y;
System.out.println(z);
```

This little program should print `5.03`, right? It doesn't. Instead, it prints `5.029999999999999`. This little error may not seem like much, but it can add up. If you ever make a purchase from an online store and notice that the sales tax is a penny off, this is why. The explanation for why these errors happen — and how to prevent them — is pretty technical, but it's something that every Java programmer needs to understand. You can find all the gory details in the BigDecimals chapter at `www.dummies.com/extras/javaaio`.

Java Version Insanity

Like most products, Java gets periodic upgrades and enhancements. Since its initial release in 1996, Java has undergone the following version updates:

✦ **Java 1.0:** This version was the original version of Java, released in 1996. Most of the language is still pretty much the same as it was in version 1.0, but the API has changed a lot since this release.

✦ **Java 1.1:** This version was the first upgrade to Java, released in 1997. This release is important because most Internet browsers include built-in support for applets based on Java 1.1. To run applets based on later versions of Java, in most cases you must download and install a current JRE.

✦ **Java 1.2:** This version, released in late 1998, was a huge improvement over the previous version — so much so, in fact, that Sun called it Java 2. It included an entirely new API called Swing for creating graphical user interfaces, as well as other major features.

✦ **Java 1.3:** This version, released in 2000, was mostly about improving performance by changing the way the runtime system works. Oddly, though this version is technically Java 1.3, it's also called Java 2 version 1.3. Go figure.

✦ **Java 1.4:** Released in 2001, this version offered a slew of improvements. As you might guess, it's called Java 2 version 1.4. Keep figuring . . . .

✦ **Java 1.5:** Released in 2004, this version included more changes and improvements than any other version. To add to Sun's apparent unpredictability in its version numbering, this version officially has *two* version numbers. Sun's official Java website explains it like this:

> Both version numbers "1.5.0" and "5.0" are used to identify this release of the Java 2 Platform Standard Edition. Version "5.0" is the *product version,* while "1.5.0" is the *developer version.*

That clears everything right up, doesn't it?

✦ **Java 1.6:** Released in December 2006 (just in time for the holidays!), this version of Java offered minor improvements and better efficiency.

For Java 1.6, the product version is 6 (not 6.0). Remember the extra 2 that appeared magically in 1998? Well, the 2 is gone in Java 1.6. So unlike the versions between 1998 and 2006, Java 1.6 is officially named the Java Platform (not the Java 2 Platform). Personally, I think someone at Sun has been talking to George Lucas. I fully expect the next version of Java to be a prequel called Java 0 Episode 1.

✦ **Java 1.7:** Released in mid-2011, this was a relatively minor upgrade that added a few enhancements to the API and a few tweaks to the language itself.

✦ **Java 1.8:** Released in February of 2014, Java 8 (as it is known) adds some significant and long-anticipated new features to Java. One of the most important is *lambda expressions,* a language feature that simplifies certain aspects of object-oriented programming. Other new features include a completely revamped API for working with dates and times, and a new framework for working with large collections of data in a way that can easily take advantage of multicore processors.

You may need to be aware of version differences if you're writing applications that you want to be able to run on earlier versions of Java. Bear in mind, however, that one of the chief benefits of Java is that the runtime system is free and can be easily downloaded and installed by end users. As a result, you shouldn't hesitate to use the features of Java 8 when you need them.

What's in a Name?

The final topic that I want to cover in this chapter is the names of the various pieces that make up Java's technology — specifically, the acronyms you constantly come across whenever you read or talk about Java, such as JVM, JRE, JDK, and J2EE. Here they are, in no particular order of importance:

✦ **JDK:** *Java Development Kit* — that is, the toolkit for developers that includes the Java compiler and the runtime environment. To write Java programs, you need the JDK. This term was used with the original versions of Java (1.0 and 1.1) and abandoned with version 1.2 in favor of SDK. But with versions 5.0, 6, and 7, the term *JDK* is officially back in vogue.

✦ **SDK:** *Software Development Kit* — what Sun called the JDK for versions 1.2, 1.3, and 1.4.

✦ **JRE:** *Java Runtime Environment* — the program that emulates the JVM so that users can run Java programs. To run Java programs, you need only download and install the JRE.

✦ **JVM:** *Java Virtual Machine* — the platform-independent machine that's emulated by the JRE. All Java programs run in a JVM.

✦ **Java SE:** *Java Standard Edition* — a term that describes the Java language and the basic set of API libraries that are used to create Java programs that can run on Windows, Linux, and other platforms, such as Macintosh. Java SE can also create programs, called *applets,* that run in a browser window. Most of this book focuses on Java SE.

✦ **J2SE:** *Java 2 Standard Edition* — an older term for the Java language and basic libraries (for Java versions 1.2 through 1.5).

✦ **Java EE:** *Java Enterprise Edition,* also known as J2EE (*Java 2 Enterprise Edition*) — an expanded set of API libraries that provide special functions such as servlets.

Chapter 2: Installing and Using Java Tools

In This Chapter

↙ **Downloading Java from the Oracle website**

↙ **Installing Java**

↙ **Using Java tools**

↙ **Getting help**

*J*ava development environments have two basic approaches. On the one hand, you can use a sophisticated integrated development environment (IDE) such as Oracle's Java Studio Creator, IntelliJ IDEA, or Eclipse. These tools combine a full-featured source editor that lets you edit your Java program files with integrated development tools, including visual development tools that let you create applications by dragging and dropping visual components onto a design surface.

At the other extreme, you can use just the basic command-line tools that are available free from Oracle's Java website (`http://java.Oracle.com`). Then you can use any text editor you want to create the text files that contain your Java programs (called *source files*), and compile and run your programs by typing commands at a command prompt.

As a compromise, you may want to use a simple development environment, such as TextPad. TextPad is an inexpensive text editor that provides some nice features for editing Java programs (such as automatic indentation) and shortcuts for compiling and running programs. It doesn't generate any code for you or provide any type of visual design aids, however. TextPad is the tool I used to develop all the examples shown in this book. For information about downloading and using TextPad, see Book I, Chapter 3.

Eclipse is another free open-source development environment that's gaining popularity; I describe it on the book's companion website at `www.dummies.com/extras/javaaio`.

Downloading and Installing the Java Development Kit

Before you can start writing Java programs, you have to download and install the correct version of the Java Development Kit (JDK) for the computer system you're using. Oracle's Java website provides versions for Windows, Solaris, and Unix. The following sections show you how to download and install the JDK.

Downloading the JDK

To get to the download page, point your browser to `http://java.oracle.com/technetwork/java`. Then follow the appropriate links to download the JDK 8 for your operating system.

When you get to the Java download page, you find links to download the JDK or the JRE. Follow the JDK link; the JRE link gets you only the Java Runtime Environment, not the complete Java Development Kit.

The JDK download comes in two versions: an online version that requires an active Internet connection to install the JDK and an offline version that lets you download the JDK installation file to your computer and install it later.

I recommend that you use the offline version. It installs faster, and you can reinstall the JDK later if you need to without having to download it again.

The exact size of the offline version depends on the platform, but most versions are between 50MB and 60MB. As a result, the download takes a few hours if you don't have a high-speed Internet connection. With a cable, DSL, or T1 connection, the download takes less than five minutes.

Legal mumbo jumbo

Before you can download the JDK, you have to approve of the Java license agreement — all 1,919 words of it, including all the *thereupon*s, *whereas*es, and *hitherto*s so finely crafted by Oracle's legal department. I'm not a lawyer (and I don't play one on TV), but I'll try to summarize the license agreement for you:

✔ The party of the first part (that's Oracle) grants you the right to use Java as is and doesn't promise that Java will do anything at all.

✔ The party of the second part (that's you) in turn promises to use Java only to write programs. You're not allowed to try to figure out how Java works and sell your secrets to Microsoft.

✔ You can't use Java to make a nuclear bomb or a missile delivery system. (I'm not making that up. It's actually in the license agreement.)

Installing the JDK

After you download the JDK file, you can install it by running the executable file you downloaded. The procedure varies slightly depending on your operating system, but basically, you just run the JDK installation program file after you download it, as follows:

✦ On a Windows system, open the folder in which you saved the installation program and double-click the installation program's icon.

✦ On a Linux or Solaris system, use console commands to change to the directory to which you downloaded the file and then run the program.

After you start the installation program, it prompts you for any information that it needs to install the JDK properly, such as which features you want to install and what folder you want to install the JDK in. You can safely choose the default answer for each option.

Perusing the JDK folders

When the JDK installs itself, it creates several folders on your hard drive. The locations of these folders vary depending on your system, but in all 32-bit versions of Windows, the JDK root folder is in the path `Program Files\Java` on your boot drive. On 64-bit versions of Windows, the root folder will be either `Program Files\Java` or `Program Files (x86)\Java`. The name of the JDK root folder also varies, depending on the Java version you've installed. For version 1.8, the root folder is named `jdk1.8.0`.

Table 2-1 lists the subfolders created in the JDK root folder. As you work with Java, you'll refer to these folders frequently.

Table 2-1	Subfolders of the JDK Root Folder
Folder	*Description*
`bin`	The compiler and other Java development tools.
`demo`	Demo programs you can study to see how to use various Java features.
`docs`	The Java API documentation.
`include`	This library contains files needed to integrate Java with programs written in other languages.
`jre`	The Runtime Environment files.
`lib`	Library files, including the Java API class library.
`Sample`	Sample code.

In addition to these folders, the JDK installs several files in the JDK root folder. I list these files in Table 2-2.

Table 2-2	Files in the JDK Root Folder
File	*Description*
README.html	The Java read-me file in HTML format.
README.txt	The read-me file again, this time in text format.
LICENSE	The Java license that you agreed to when you downloaded the JDK, on the outside chance that you enjoyed it so much the first time, you want to read it again. (If you work for Microsoft, you probably *should* read it again, at least twice.)
COPYRIGHT	The copyright notice. Most companies would be happy to just place © Oracle Microsystems, Inc., at the bottom of the read-me or license file. Not Oracle. It puts the copyright notice in a separate text file, along with information about all the copyright and export laws that apply.
Src.zip	The source code for the Java API classes. This folder is created only if you unpack the src.zip file (which may be named src.jar). After you get your feet wet with Java, looking at these source files can be a great way to find out more about how the API classes work.

Setting the path

After you install the JDK, you need to configure your operating system so that it can find the JDK command-line tools. To do that, you must set the Path environment variable — a list of folders that the operating system uses to locate executable programs. To do this on a Windows 7 or earlier system, follow these steps. You must be logged in as an administrator to make the changes described in this procedure. On Windows 8, Java installs as a desktop application that works like the Windows 7 configuration.

1. **Click the Start menu, then right-click Computer.**

This brings up the System Properties page.

2. **Click the Advanced System Settings link.**

3. **Click the Environment Variables button.**

The Environment Variables dialog box appears, as shown in Figure 2-1.

Figure 2-1:
The
Environment
Variables
dialog box.

4. **In the System Variables list, scroll to the Path variable, select it, and then click the Edit button.**

A little dialog box pops up to let you edit the value of the Path variable.

5. **Add the JDK bin folder to the beginning of the Path value.**

Use a semicolon to separate the bin folder from the rest of the information that may already be in the path.

Note: The name of the bin folder may vary on your system, as in this example:

```
c:\Program Files\Java\jdk1.8.0\bin;other directories...
```

6. **Click OK three times to exit.**

The first OK gets you back to the Environment Variables dialog box; the second OK gets you back to the System Properties dialog box; and the third OK closes the System Properties dialog box.

For Linux or Solaris, the procedure depends on which shell you're using. For more information, consult the documentation for the shell you're using.

Using Java's Command-Line Tools

Java comes with several command-line tools that you can run directly from a command prompt. The two most important are javac, the Java compiler used to compile a program, and java, the runtime command used to run a Java program. These tools work essentially the same way no matter what operating system you're using.

Compiling a program

You can compile a program from a command prompt by using the `javac` command. Before you can do that, however, you need a program to compile. Follow these steps:

1. **Using any text editor, type the following text in a file, and save it as `HelloApp.java`:**

```
public class HelloApp
{
    public static void main(String[] args)
    {
        System.out.println("Hello, World!");
    }
}
```

Pay special attention to capitalization. If you type `Public` instead of `public`, for example, the program won't work. (If you don't want to bother with typing, you can download the sample programs from this book's website at `www.dummies.com/extras/javaaio`.)

2. **Save the file in any directory you want.**

3. **Open a command prompt, use a `cd` command to change to the directory you saved the program file in, and then enter the command `javac HelloApp.java`.**

This command compiles the program (`javac`) and creates a class file named `HelloApp.class`.

Assuming that you typed the program exactly right, the `javac` command doesn't display any messages at all. If the program contains any errors, however, you get one or more error messages onscreen. If you typed `Public` instead of `public` despite my warning earlier in this section, the compiler displays the following error message:

```
C:\java\samples>javac HelloApp.java
HelloApp.java:1: error: class, interface, or enum expected
Public class HelloApp
      ^
1 error

C:\java\samples>
```

The compiler error message indicates that an error is in line 1 of the `HelloApp.java` file. If the compiler reports an error message like this one, your program contains a coding mistake. You need to find the mistake, correct it, and compile the program again.

Compiling more than one file

Normally, the `javac` command compiles only the file that you specify on the command line, but you can coax `javac` into compiling more than one file at a time by using any of the techniques I describe in the following paragraphs:

✦ If the Java file you specify on the command line contains a reference to another Java class that's defined by a `java` file in the same folder, the Java compiler automatically compiles that class too.

Suppose you have a `java` program named `TestProgram`, which refers to a class called `TestClass`, and the `TestClass.java` file is located in the same folder as the `TestProgram.java` file. When you use the `javac` command to compile the `TestProgram.java` file, the compiler automatically compiles the `TestClass.java` file too.

✦ You can list more than one filename in the `javac` command. The following command compiles three files:

```
javac TestProgram1.java TestProgram2.java TestProgram3.java
```

✦ You can use a wildcard to compile all the files in a folder, like this:

```
javac *.java
```

✦ If you need to compile a lot of files at the same time but don't want to use a wildcard (perhaps you want to compile a large number of files but not all the files in a folder), you can create an *argument file,* which lists the files to compile. In the argument file, you can type as many filenames as you want, using spaces or line breaks to separate them. Here's an argument file named `TestPrograms` that lists three files to compile:

```
TestProgram1.java
TestProgram2.java
TestProgram3.java
```

You can compile all the programs in this file by using an @ character followed by the name of the argument file on the `javac` command line, like this:

```
javac @TestPrograms
```

Using Java compiler options

The javac command has a gaggle of options that you can use to influence the way it compiles your programs. For your reference, I list these options in Table 2-3.

Table 2-3	Java Compiler Options
Option	*Description*
-g	Generates all debugging info.
-g:none	Generates no debugging info.
-g:{lines,vars,source}	Generates only some debugging info.
-nowarn	Generates no warnings.
-verbose	Outputs messages about what the compiler is doing.
-deprecation	Outputs source locations where deprecated APIs are used.
-classpath <path>	Specifies where to find user class files.
-cp <path>	Specifies where to find user class files.
-sourcepath <path>	Specifies where to find input source files.
-bootclasspath <path>	Overrides locations of bootstrap class files.
-extdirs <dirs>	Overrides locations of installed extensions.
-endorseddirs <dirs>	Overrides location of endorsed standards path.
-d <directory>	Specifies where to place generated class files.
-encoding <encoding>	Specifies character encoding used by source files.
-source <release>	Provides source compatibility with specified release.
-target <release>	Generates class files for specific virtual-machine version.
-version	Provides version information.
-help	Prints a synopsis of standard options.
-X	Prints a synopsis of nonstandard options.
-J<flag>	Passes <flag> directly to the runtime system.

To use one or more of these options, type the option before or after the source filename. Either of the following commands, for example, compiles the HelloApp.java file with the -verbose and -deprecation options enabled:

```
javac HelloWorld.java -verbose -deprecation
javac -verbose -deprecation HelloWorld.java
```

Don't get all discombobulated if you don't understand what all these options do. Most of them are useful only in unusual situations. The options you'll use the most are

✦ **-classpath or -cp:** Use this option if your program makes use of class files that you've stored in a separate folder.

✦ **-deprecation:** Use this option if you want the compiler to warn you whenever you use API methods that have been deprecated. (*Deprecated* methods are older methods that once were part of the Java standard API but are on the road to obsolescence. They still work but may not function in future versions of Java.)

✦ **-source:** Use this option to limit the compiler to previous versions of Java. Note, however, that this option applies only to features of the Java language itself, not to the API class libraries. If you specify -source 1.4, for example, the compiler won't allow you to use new Java language features that were introduced in a version later than 1.4, such as generics, enhanced for loops, or Lambda expressions. But you can still use the new API features that were added with version 1.5, such as the Scanner class.

✦ **-help:** Use this option to list the options that are available for the javac command.

Running a Java program

When you successfully compile a Java program, you can run the program by typing the java command followed by the name of the class that contains the program's main method. The JRE loads, along with the class you specify, and then runs the main method in that class. To run the HelloApp program, for example, type this command:

```
C:\java\samples>java HelloApp
```

The program responds by displaying the message "Hello, World!".

The class must be contained in a file with the same name as the class, and its filename must have the extension .class. You usually don't have to worry about the name of the class file because it's created automatically when you compile the program with the javac command. Thus, if you compile a program in a file named HelloApp.java, the compiler creates a class named HelloApp and saves it in a file named HelloApp.class.

Understanding error messages

If Java can't find a filename that corresponds to the class, you get a simple error message indicating that the class can't be found. Here's what you get if you type `JelloApp` instead of `HelloApp`:

```
C:\java\samples>java JelloApp
Exception in thread "main"
    java.lang.NoClassDefFoundError: JelloApp
```

This error message simply means that Java couldn't find a class named `JelloApp`.

Specifying options

Like the Java compiler, the Java runtime command lets you specify options that can influence its behavior. Table 2-4 lists the most commonly used options.

Table 2-4	Common Java Command Options
Option	*Description*
`-client`	Runs the client virtual machine.
`-server`	Runs the server virtual, which is optimized for server systems.
`-classpath` *directories and archives*	Lists the directories or JAR or Zip archive files used to search for class files.
`-cp <search path>`	Does the same thing as `-classpath`.
`-D` *name=value*	Sets a system property.
`-verbose`	Enables verbose output.
`-version`	Displays the JRE version number and then stops.
`-showversion`	Displays the JRE version number and then continues.
`-?` or `-help`	Lists standard options.
`-X`	Lists nonstandard options.
`-ea` or `-enableassertions`	Enables the `assert` command.
`-ea` *classes or packages*	Enables assertions for the specified classes or packages.
`-esa` or `-enablesystemas-sertions`	Enables system assertions.
`-dsa` or `-disablesystemas-sertions`	Disables system assertions.

TIP

Using other command-line tools

Java has many other command-line tools that come in handy from time to time. You can find a complete list of command-line tools at the following website:

```
http://download.java.net/jdk8/
    docs/technotes/tools/index.
    html#basic
```

I describe three of these additional tools elsewhere in this book:

✔ **applet viewer:** Runs a web applet application. For more information, see Book VII, Chapter 1.

✔ **javadoc:** Automatically creates HTML documentation for your Java classes. For more information, see Book III, Chapter 7.

✔ **jar:** Creates Java archive (JAR) files, which store classes in a compressed file that's similar to a Zip file. I cover this command in Book III, Chapter 7.

Using the javap command

The javap command is called the Java *disassembler* because it takes class files apart and tells you what's inside them. You won't use this command often, but using it to find out how a particular Java statement works is fun sometimes. You can also use it to find out what methods are available for a class if you don't have the source code that was used to create the class.

Here's the information you get when you run the javap HelloApp command:

```
C:\java\samples>javap HelloApp
Compiled from "HelloApp.java"
public class HelloApp{
    public HelloApp();
    public static void main(java.lang.String[]);
}
```

As you can see, the javap command indicates that the HelloApp class was compiled from the HelloApp.java file and that it consists of a HelloApp public class and a main public method.

You may want to use two options with the `javap` command. If you use the `-c` option, the `javap` command displays the actual Java bytecodes created by the compiler for the class. And if you use the `-verbose` option, the byte-codes (plus a ton of other fascinating information about the innards of the class) are displayed.

If you become a big-time Java guru, you can use this type of information to find out exactly how certain Java features work. Until then, you probably should leave the `javap` command alone except for those rare occasions when you want to impress your friends with your in-depth knowledge of Java. (Just hope that when you do, they don't ask you what the `aload` or `invokevirtual` instruction does.)

Using Java Documentation

Before you get too far into figuring out Java, don't be surprised if you find yourself wondering whether some class has some other method that I don't describe in this book — or whether some other class may be more appropriate for an application you're working on. When that time comes, you'll need to consult the Java help pages.

Complete documentation for Java is available on the Oracle Java website at `http://download.java.net/jdk8/docs`. Although this page contains many links to documentation pages, the two you'll use the most are the Java SE API documentation pages and the Developer's Guides pages. The following sections describe these two links.

Java SE API Docs

The API and documentation links at `http://download.java.net/jdk8/docs/api` take you to the complete documentation for all currently supported versions of the Java API, in English as well as Japanese. Figure 2-2 shows the English Java SE 8 API documentation page.

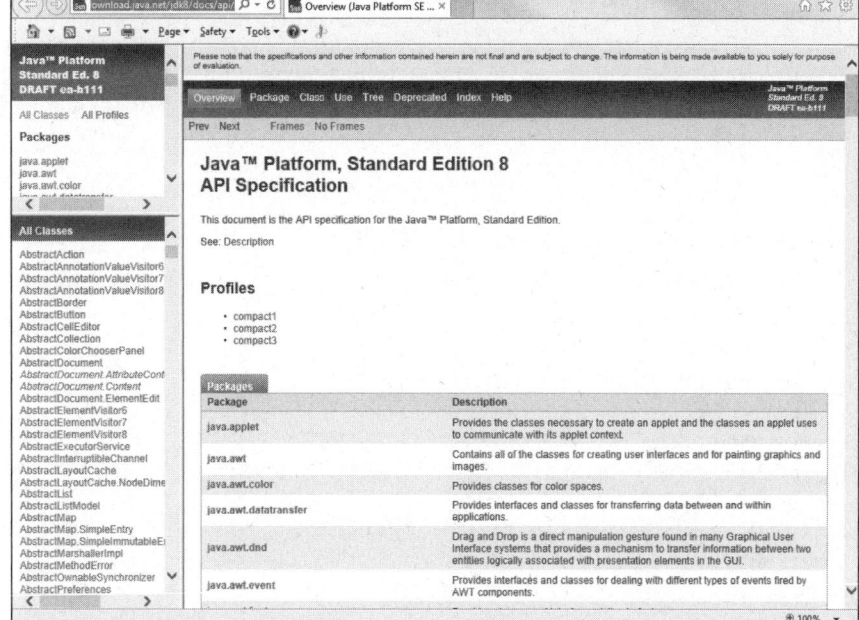

Book I
Chapter 2

Installing and Using
Java Tools

Figure 2-2:
The
documenta-
tion page for
Java SE
API 8
(English
version).

You can use this page to find complete information for any class in the API. By default, all the Java classes are listed in the frame that appears in the bottom-left corner of the page. You can limit this display to the classes in a particular package by choosing the package from the menu in the top-left corner of the page. (If you don't know what a Java package is, don't worry. You find out about packages at this book's companion website at www.dummies.com/extras/javaaio.)

Click the class you're looking for in the class list to call up its documentation page. Figure 2-3 shows the documentation page for the String class. If you scroll down this page, you find complete information about everything you can do with this class, including an in-depth discussion of what the class does, a list of the various methods it provides, and a detailed description of what each method does. In addition, you find links to similar classes.

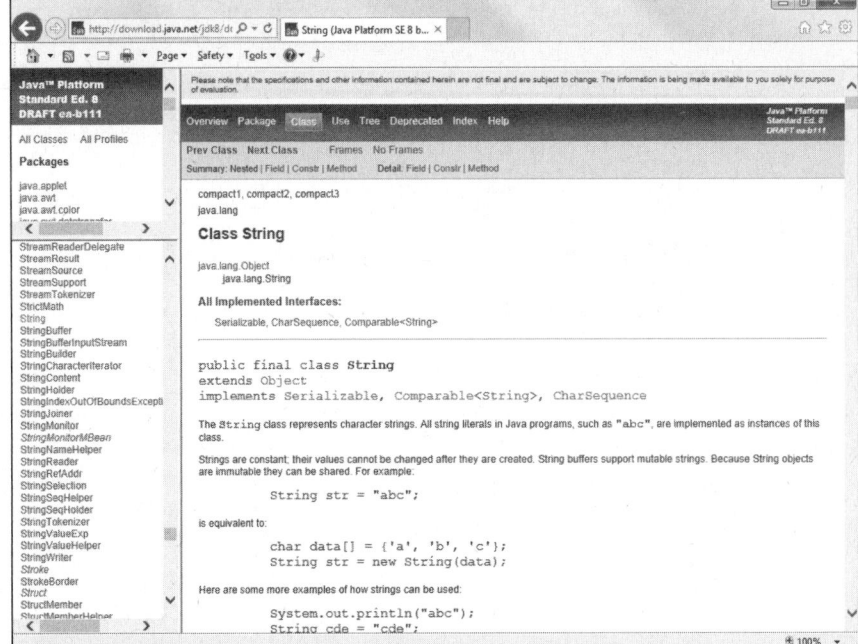

Figure 2-3:
The docu-
mentation
page for the
String class.

Java Language Specification

If you're interested in learning details about some element of the Java language itself (rather than the information about a class in the API class library),
visit the Java Programming Language reference page at `http://docs.`
`oracle.com/javase/specs/index.html`. That link takes you to a set of
pages that describes — in sometimes excruciating and obscure detail —
exactly how each element of the Java language works.

Frankly, this documentation isn't that much help for beginning programmers. It was written by computer scientists *for* computer scientists. You can
tell just by looking at the table of contents that it isn't for novices. The first
chapter is called "Introduction" (that's not so bad), but Chapters 2 and 3 are
titled "Grammars" and "Lexical Structure," respectively, and matters just get
more arcane from there.

That's why you're reading this book, after all. You won't even find a single
sentence more about lexical structure in this book (other than this one, of
course). Even so, at some time in your Java journeys, you may want to get
to the bottom of the rules that govern such strange Java features as anonymous inner classes. When that day arrives, grab a six-pack of Jolt Cola, roll
up your sleeves, and open the Java Language Specification pages.

Chapter 3: Working with TextPad

In This Chapter

✔ **Acquiring TextPad**

✔ **Using TextPad to edit source files**

✔ **Compiling Java programs**

✔ **Running Java programs**

TextPad is an inexpensive (\$33) text editor that you can integrate with the Java Development Kit (JDK) to simplify the task of coding, compiling, and running Java programs. It isn't a true integrated development environment (IDE), as it lacks features such as integrated debugging, code generators, and drag-and-drop tools for creating graphical user interfaces.

If you want to work with an IDE, I suggest that you skip this chapter and instead look to www.dummies.com/extras/javaaio, which offers a bonus chapter that covers a free IDE called Eclipse.

TextPad is a popular tool for developing Java programs because of its simplicity and speed. It's ideal for learning Java because it doesn't generate any code for you. Writing every line of code yourself may seem like a bother, but the exercise pays off in the long run because you have a better understanding of how Java works.

Downloading and Installing TextPad

You can download a free evaluation version of TextPad from Helios Software Systems at www.textpad.com. You can use the evaluation version free of charge, but if you decide to keep the program, you must pay for it. (Helios accepts credit card payment online.)

If the Java JDK is already installed on your computer when you install TextPad, TextPad automatically configures itself to compile and run Java programs. If you install the JDK after you install TextPad, you need to configure TextPad for Java by following these steps:

1. **Choose Configure⇨Preferences to open the Preferences dialog box.**

2. **Click Tools in the tree that appears on the left side of the dialog box.**

3. **Click the Add button to reveal a drop-down list of options and then click Java SDK Commands.**

Figure 3-1 shows how the Preferences dialog box appears when the Java tools are installed. As you can see, the Tools item in the tree on the left side of the dialog box includes three Java tools: Compile Java, Run Java Application, and Run Java Applet.

Figure 3-1:
Configuring
tools in
TextPad.

4. **Click OK.**

The commands you need to compile and run Java programs are added to TextPad's Tools menu.

Editing Source Files

Figure 3-2 shows a Java source file being edited in TextPad. If you've worked with a Windows text editor before, you'll have no trouble mastering the basics of TextPad. I won't go over such basic procedures as opening and saving files because they're standard; instead, I describe some TextPad features that are useful for editing Java program files.

When you first create a file (by clicking the New button on the toolbar or by choosing File⇨New), TextPad treats the file as a normal text file, not as a Java program file. After you save the file (by clicking the Save button or choosing File⇨Save) and assign .java as the file extension, TextPad's Java-editing features kick in.

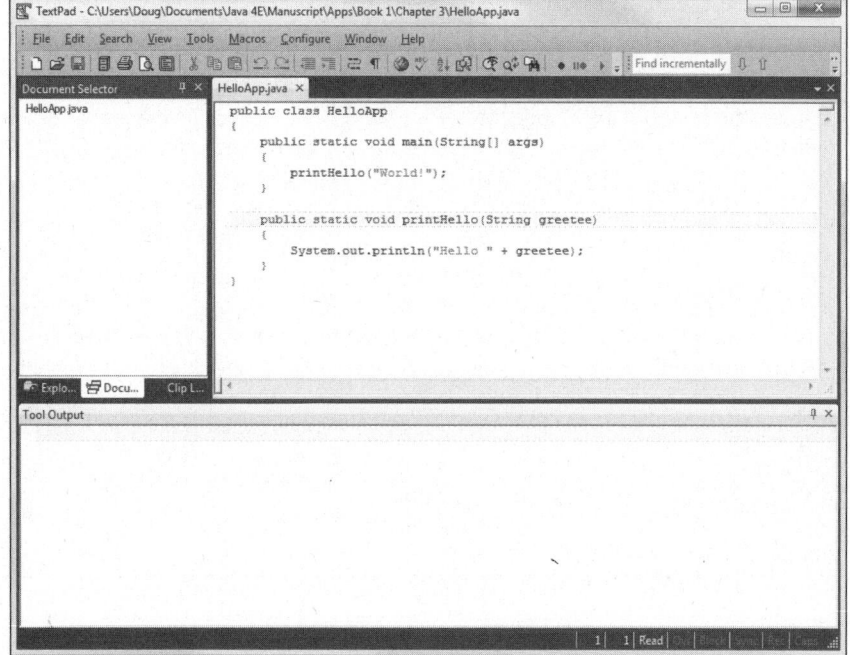

Figure 3-2:
Editing a
Java file in
TextPad.

The following paragraphs describe some of TextPad's most noteworthy features for working with Java files:

✦ You can't really tell from Figure 3-2, but TextPad uses different colors to indicate the function of each word or symbol in the program. Brackets are red so that you can spot them quickly and make sure that they're paired correctly. Keywords are blue. Comments and string literals are green. Other text, such as variable and method names, is black.

✦ TextPad automatically indents whenever you type an opening bracket and then reverts to the previous indent when you type a closing bracket. This feature makes keeping your code lined up easy.

✦ Line numbers display down the left edge of the editing window. You can turn these line numbers on or off by choosing View➪Line Numbers.

✦ To go to a particular line, press Ctrl+G to bring up the Go To dialog box. Make sure that Line is selected in the Go to What box, enter the line number in the text box, and click OK.

Using workspaces

In TextPad, a *workspace* is a collection of files that you work on together. Workspaces are useful for projects that involve more than just one file. When you open a workspace, TextPad opens all the files in the workspace.

To create a workspace, first open all the files that you want to include in the workspace. Then choose File⇨Workspace⇨Save As and, in the Save As dialog box, give the workspace a name. (The files that make up the workspace are saved in a single file with the .tws extension.)

To open a workspace, choose File⇨Workspace⇨Open to display the Open dialog box, select the workspace file that you previously saved, and click Open. Alternatively, you can choose the workspace from the list of recently used workspaces at the bottom of the File⇨Workspace submenu.

To configure TextPad to open the most recently used workspace automatically whenever you start TextPad, choose Configure⇨Preferences to open the Preferences dialog box, click General in the tree on the left side of the dialog box, select the Reload Last Workspace at Startup check box, and click OK to close the dialog box.

✦ If you have more than one file open, you can switch between the files by using the Document Selector — the pane on the left side of the TextPad window (refer to Figure 3-2). If the Document Selector isn't visible, choose View⇨Document Selector to summon it.

✦ Another way to switch between two (or more) files is to choose View⇨ Document Tabs. Tabs appear at the bottom of the document window, and you can click these tabs to switch documents.

✦ A handy Match Bracket feature lets you pair brackets, braces, and parentheses. To use this feature, move the insertion point to a bracket, brace, or parenthesis and then press Ctrl+M. TextPad finds the matching element.

✦ To search for text, press F5. In the Find dialog box, enter the text you're looking for, and click OK. To repeat the search, press Ctrl+F.

✦ To replace text, press F8.

Compiling a Program

To compile a Java program in TextPad, choose Tools⇨Compile Java or use the keyboard shortcut Ctrl + 1. The `javac` command compiles the program, and the compiler output is displayed in the Tool Results pane of the TextPad window. If the program compiles successfully, the message `Tool completed successfully` appears in the Tool Results pane. If the compiler finds something wrong with your program, one or more error messages are displayed, as shown in Figure 3-3.

Figure 3-3:
Error
messages
displayed
by the Java
compiler.

In this example, eight compiler error messages are displayed:

```
javac 1.8.0-ea
C:\Users\Doug\Documents\Java 4E\Manuscript\Apps\Book 1\Chapter 3\HelloApp.java:5:
    error: unclosed string literal
        printHello("World!);
                   ^
C:\Users\Doug\Documents\Java 4E\Manuscript\Apps\Book 1\Chapter 3\HelloApp.java:5:
    error: ';' expected
        printHello("World!);
                           ^
C:\Users\Doug\Documents\Java 4E\Manuscript\Apps\Book 1\Chapter 3\HelloApp.java:8:
    error: illegal start of expression
    public static void printHello(String greetee)
    ^
C:\Users\Doug\Documents\Java 4E\Manuscript\Apps\Book 1\Chapter 3\HelloApp.java:8:
    error: ';' expected
    public static void printHello(String greetee)
          ^
C:\Users\Doug\Documents\Java 4E\Manuscript\Apps\Book 1\Chapter 3\HelloApp.java:8:
    error: illegal start of expression
    public static void printHello(String greetee)
                 ^
C:\Users\Doug\Documents\Java 4E\Manuscript\Apps\Book 1\Chapter 3\HelloApp.java:8:
    error: ';' expected
    public static void printHello(String greetee)
                       ^
C:\Users\Doug\Documents\Java 4E\Manuscript\Apps\Book 1\Chapter 3\HelloApp.java:8:
    error: ';' expected
    public static void printHello(String greetee)
```

```
C:\Users\Doug\Documents\Java 4E\Manuscript\Apps\Book 1\Chapter 3\HelloApp.
    java:12: error: reached end of file while parsing
}
```

```
8 errors
```

```
Tool completed with exit code 1
```

If you double-click the first line of each error message, TextPad takes you to the spot where the error occurred. If you double-click the line with the `unclosed string literal` message, for example, you're taken to line 5, and the insertion point is positioned at the spot where the compiler found the error. Then you can correct the error and recompile the program.

Often, a single error can cause more than one error message to display, as is the case in Figure 3-3. The error is that I left off a closing quotation mark after the word `Hello` in line 5. That one error caused all eight error messages!

Running a Java Program

After you compile a Java program with no errors, you can run it by choosing Tools⇔Run Java Application or pressing Ctrl+2. A command window opens, in which the program runs. Figure 3-4 shows the `HelloApp` program running in a separate window atop the TextPad window.

Figure 3-4:
Running a
program.

When the program finishes, the message `Press any key to continue` appears in the command window. When you press a key, the window closes, and TextPad comes back to life.

In case you're wondering, TextPad actually runs your program by creating and running a *batch file* — a short text file that contains the commands necessary to run your program. This batch file is given a cryptic name, such as `tp02a11c.BAT`. Here's the batch file generated for the `HelloApp` program:

```
@ECHO OFF
C:
CD "\Users\Doug\Documents\Java 3E\Applications\Book 1\Chapter 3"
"C:\Program Files\Java\jdk1.6.0\bin\java.exe" HelloApp
PAUSE
```

Here's a closer look at these commands:

✦ The first command tells MS-DOS not to display the commands in the command window as the batch file executes.

✦ The next two commands switch to the drive and directory that contain the `java` program.

✦ Next, the `java.exe` program is called to run the `HelloApp` class.

✦ Finally, a `PAUSE` command executes. That command is what displays the `Press any key to continue` message when the program finishes.

Running an Applet

You can also run an applet directly from TextPad. First, compile the program. Then, if the program contains no errors, choose Tools➪Run Java Applet or press Ctrl+3. A command window appears, and the Java applet viewer starts. This viewer runs the applet in a separate window, without the need for a web browser. Figure 3-5 shows an applet in action. (You see how to write the code for this applet in Book VII, Chapter 1.)

When you quit the applet, the Applet Viewer window and the DOS command window close, and you return to TextPad.

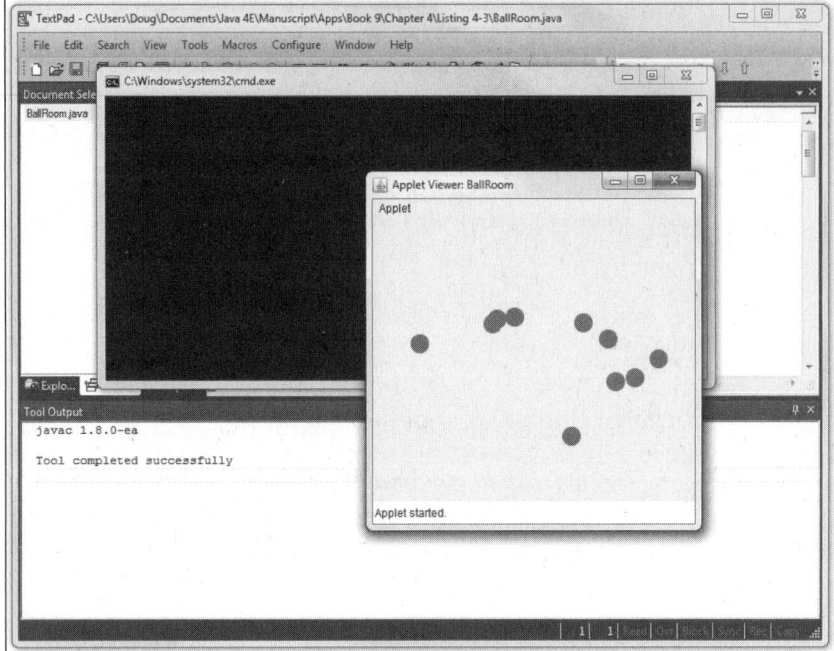

Figure 3-5:
Running an
applet.

Book II
Programming Basics

Contents at a Glance

Chapter 1: Java Programming Basics

In This Chapter

✔ The famous Hello, World! program

✔ Basic elements of Java programs such as keywords, statements, and blocks

✔ Different ways to add comments to your programs

✔ Basic information about object-oriented programming

✔ Ways to import classes

In this chapter, you find the basics of writing simple Java programs. The programs you see in this chapter are very simple: they just display simple information on a *console* (in Windows, that's a command-prompt window). You need to cover a few more chapters before you start writing programs that do anything worthwhile. But the simple programs you see in this chapter are sufficient to illustrate the basic structure of Java programs.

Be warned that in this chapter, I introduce you to several Java programming features that are explained in greater detail in later chapters. You see, for example, some variable declarations, a method, and even an `if` statement and a `for` loop. The goal of this chapter isn't to march you into instant proficiency with these programming elements, but just to introduce you to them.

You can find all the code listings used in this book at www.dummies.com/extras/javaaio.

Looking at the Infamous Hello, World! Program

Many programming books begin with a simple example program that displays the text `"Hello, World!"` on the console. In Book I, Chapter 1, I show you a Java program that does that to compare it with a similar program written in C. Now take a closer look at each element of this program, shown in Listing 1-1.

Listing 1-1:   The HelloApp Program

```
public class HelloApp                                          →1
{                                                             →2
    public static void main(String[] args)                    →3
    {                                                        →4
        System.out.println("Hello, World!");                  →5
    }                                                        →6
}                                                             →7
```

Later in this chapter, you discover in detail all the elements that make up this program. But first, I want to walk you through it word by word.

Lines 1 and 2 mark the declaration of a public class named HelloApp:

→ 1   **public:** A *keyword* of the Java language that indicates that the element that follows should be made available to other Java elements. In this case, what follows is a class named HelloApp. As a result, this keyword indicates that the HelloApp class is a *public class,* which means other classes can use it. (In Book III, Chapter 2, I cover the most common alternative to public: private. There are also other alternatives, but they're covered in later chapters.)

class: Another Java keyword that indicates that the element being defined here is a class. All Java programs are made up of one or more *classes.* A class definition contains code that defines the behavior of the objects created and used by the program. Although most real-world programs consist of more than one class, the simple programs you see in this minibook have just one class.

HelloApp: An *identifier* that provides the name for the class being defined here. Whereas keywords, such as public and class, are words that are defined by the Java programming language, identifiers are words that you create to provide names for various elements you use in your program. In this case, the identifier HelloApp provides a name for the public class being defined here. (Although *identifier* is the technically correct term, sometimes identifiers are called *symbols* or *names.*)

→ 2   **{:** The opening brace on line 2 marks the beginning of the *body* of the class. The end of the body is marked by the closing brace on line 7. Everything that appears within these braces belongs to the class. As you work with Java, you'll find that it uses these braces a lot. Pretty soon the third and fourth fingers on your right hand will know exactly where they are on the keyboard.

Lines 3 through 6 define a *method* of the HelloApp class named main:

→ 3   **public:** The public keyword is used again, this time to indicate that a method being declared here should have public access.

That means classes other than the `HelloApp` class can use it. All Java programs must have at least one class that declares a public method named `main`. The `main` method contains the statements that are executed when you run the program.

`static`: You find all about the `static` keyword in Book III, Chapter 3. For now, just take my word that the Java language requires that you specify `static` when you declare the `main` method.

`void`: In Java, a *method* is a unit of code that can calculate and return a value. For example, you could create a method that calculates a sales total. Then the sales total would be the return value of the method. If a method doesn't need to return a value, you must use the `void` keyword to indicate that no value is returned. Because Java requires that the `main` method not return a value, you must specify `void` when you declare the `main` method.

`main`: Finally, here's the *identifier* that provides the name for this method. As I've already mentioned, Java requires that this method be named `main`. Besides the `main` method, you can create additional methods with whatever names you want to use. You discover how to create additional methods in Book II, Chapter 7. Until then, the programs consist of just one method named `main`.

(`String[] args`): Oh, boy. This Java element is too advanced to thoroughly explain just yet. It's called a *parameter list,* and it's used to pass data to a method. Java requires that the `main` method must receive a single parameter that's an array of `String` objects. By convention, this parameter is named `args`. If you don't know what a parameter, a `String`, or an array is, don't worry about it. You can find out what a `String` is in the next chapter, and parameters are in Book II, Chapter 7; arrays are in Book IV. In the meantime, realize that you have to code (`String[] args`) on the declaration for the `main` methods in all your programs.

→ 4   **Another {:** Another set of braces begins at line 4 and ends at line 6. These braces mark the body of the `main` method. Notice that the closing brace in line 6 is paired with the opening brace in line 4, whereas the closing brace in line 7 is paired with the one in line 2. This type of pairing is commonplace in Java. In short, whenever you come to a closing brace, it's paired with the most recent opening brace that hasn't already been closed — that is, that hasn't already been paired with a closing brace.

→ 5   **`System.out.println("Hello, World!");`:** This is the only statement in the entire program. It calls a method named `println` that belongs to the `System.out` object. The `println` method displays a line of text on the console. The text to be displayed is passed to the `println` method as a parameter in parentheses following the word `println`. In this case, the text is the string literal `Hello, World!` enclosed in a set of quotation marks. As a result, this statement displays the text `Hello, World!` on the console.

Note that in Java, most (but not all) statements must end with a semicolon. Because this statement is the only one in the program, this line is the only one that requires a semicolon.

→ 6   `}`: Line 6 contains the closing brace that marks the end of the `main` method body that was begun by the brace on line 4.

→ 7   **Another** `}`: Line 7 contains the closing brace that marks the end of the `HelloApp` class body that was begun by the brace on line 2. Because this program consists of just one class, this line also marks the end of the program.

To run this program, you must first use a text editor such as Notepad or TextPad to enter it — exactly as it appears in Listing 1-1 — in a text file named `HelloApp.java`. Then you can compile it by running the following command at a command prompt:

```
javac HelloApp.java
```

This command creates a class file named `HelloApp.class` that contains the Java bytecodes compiled for the `HelloApp class`.

You can run the program by entering this command:

```
java HelloApp
```

Now that you've seen what a Java program actually looks like, you're in a better position to understand exactly what this command does. First, it loads the Java Virtual Machine (JVM) into memory. Then it locates the `HelloApp` class, which must be contained in a file named `HelloApp.class`. Finally, it runs the `main` method of the `HelloApp` class. The `main` method, in turn, displays the message `"Hello, World!"` on the console.

The rest of this chapter describes some of the basic elements of the Java programming language in greater detail.

Dealing with Keywords

A *keyword* is a word that has a special meaning defined by the Java programming language. The program shown earlier in Listing 1-1 uses four keywords: `public`, `class`, `static`, and `void`. In all, Java has 53 keywords. They're listed in alphabetical order in Table 1-1.

Table 1-1		Java's Keywords		
abstract	default	goto	package	synchronized
assert	do	if	private	this
boolean	double	implements	protected	throw
break	else	import	public	throws
byte	enum	instanceof	return	transient
case	extends	int	short	true
catch	false	interface	static	try
char	final	long	strictfp	void
class	finally	native	super	volatile
const	float	new	switch	while
continue	for	null		

Strangely enough, three keywords listed in Table 1-1 — true, false, and null — aren't technically considered to be keywords. Instead, they're called *literals*. Still, they're reserved for use by the Java language in much the same way that keywords are, so I lumped them in with the keywords.

Stranger still, two keywords — const and goto — are reserved by Java but don't do anything. Both are carryovers from the C++ programming language. The const keyword defines a constant, which is handled in Java by the final keyword. As for goto, it's a C++ statement that is considered anathema to object-oriented programming purists, so it isn't used in Java. Java reserves it as a keyword solely for the purpose of scolding you if you attempt to use it.

Like everything else in Java, keywords are case-sensitive. Thus, if you type If instead of if or For instead of for, the compiler complains about your error. Because Visual Basic keywords begin with capital letters, you'll make this mistake frequently if you've programmed in Visual Basic.

Considering the Java community's disdain for Visual Basic, it's surprising that the error messages generated when you capitalize keywords aren't more insulting. Accidentally capitalizing a keyword in Visual Basic style can really throw the Java compiler for a loop. Consider this program, which contains the single error of capitalizing the word For:

```java
public class CaseApp
{
    public static void main(String[] args)
    {
        For (int i = 0; i<5; i++)
            System.out.println("Hi");
    }
}
```

When you try to compile this program, the compiler generates a total of four error messages for this one mistake:

```
C:\Java AIO\CaseApp.java:5: '.class' expected
        For (int i = 0; i<5; i++)
                 ^
C:\Java AIO\CaseApp.java:5: illegal start of type
        For (int i = 0; i<5; i++)
                      ^
C:\Java AIO\CaseApp.java:5: not a statement
        For (int i = 0; i<5; i++)
                    ^
C:\Java AIO\CaseApp.java:5: ';' expected
        For (int i = 0; i<5; i++)
                          ^
4 errors        For (int i = 0; i<5; i++)
```

Even though this single mistake generates four error messages, not one of the messages actually points to the problem. The little arrow beneath the source line indicates what part of the line is in error, and none of these error messages has the arrow pointing anywhere near the word `For`! The compiler isn't smart enough to realize that you meant `for` instead of `For`. So it treats `For` as a legitimate identifier and then complains about everything else on the line that follows it. It would be much more helpful if the compiler generated an error message like this:

```
C:\Java AIO\CaseApp.java:5: 'For' is not a keyword
        For (int i = 0; i<5; i++)
```

Better yet, for those of us old enough to remember *Get Smart* on TV:

```
C:\Java AIO\CaseApp.java:5: Thees ees Java! Vee do not
    capitalize keyverds here!
        For (int i = 0; i<5; i++)
```

 The moral of the story is that keywords are case-sensitive, and if your program won't compile and the error messages don't make any sense, check for keywords that you've mistakenly capitalized.

Working with Statements

Like most programming languages, Java uses statements to build programs. Unlike most programming languages, Java doesn't use statements as its fundamental unit of code. Instead, it gives that honor to the class. However, every class must have a body, and the body of a class is made up of one or more statements. In other words, you can't have a meaningful Java program without at least one statement. The following sections describe the ins and outs of working with Java statements.

Types of statements

Java has many types of statements. Some statements simply create variables that you can use to store data. These types of statements are often called *declaration statements* and tend to look like this:

```
int i;
String s = "This is a string";
Customer c = new Customer();
```

Another common type of statement is an *expression statement,* which performs calculations. Here are some examples of expression statements:

```
i = a + b;
salesTax = invoiceTotal * taxRate;
System.out.println("Hello, World!");
```

Notice that the last statement in this group is the same as line 5 in Listing 1-1. Thus the single statement in the HelloApp program is an expression statement.

There are many kinds of statements besides these two. if-then statements, for example, execute other statements only if a particular condition has been met, and statements such as for, while, and do execute whole groups of statements one or more times.

It's often said that every Java statement must end with a semicolon. Actually, this isn't quite true. *Some* types of Java statements must end with semicolons — but others don't have to. The basic rule is that declaration and expression statements must end with a semicolon, but most other statement types do not. Where this rule gets tricky, however, is that most other types of statements include one or more declarations or expression statements that do use semicolons. Here's a typical if statement:

```
if (total > 100)
    discountPercent = 10;
```

Here, the variable named discountPercent is given a value of 10 if the value of the total variable is greater than 100. The expression statement ends with a semicolon, but the if statement itself doesn't. (The Java compiler lets you know if you use a semicolon when you shouldn't.)

White space

In Java, the term *white space* refers to one or more consecutive space characters, tab characters, or line breaks. All white space is considered the same.

Book II
Chapter 1

Java Programming Basics

In other words, a single space is treated the same as a tab or line break or any combination of spaces, tabs, and line breaks.

If you've programmed in Visual Basic, white space is different from what you're used to. In Visual Basic, line breaks mark the end of statements unless special continuation characters are used. In Java, you don't have to do anything special to continue a statement onto a second line. Thus the statement

```
x = (y + 5) / z;
```

is identical to this statement:

```
x =
(y + 5) / z;
```

In fact, you could write the preceding statement like this if you wanted:

```
x
=
(
y
+
5
)
/
z
;
```

I wouldn't advise it, but the statement does compile and execute properly.

Be advised, however, that you can't put white space in the middle of a keyword or identifier. The following example won't work:

```
p u b l i c   static   v o i d   main(String[] args)
```

Here the extra spaces between the letters in the words *public* and *void* will confuse the compiler.

Using white space liberally in your programs is a good idea. In particular, you should routinely use white space like this:

✦ **Line breaks:** Place each statement on a separate line.

✦ **Tabs:** Line up elements that belong together.

The compiler ignores the extra white space, so it doesn't affect the bytecode that's created for your program. As a result, using extra white space in your program doesn't affect your program's performance in any way, but it does make the program's source code easier to read.

Working with Blocks

A *block* is a group of one or more statements that's enclosed in braces. A block begins with an opening brace ({) and ends with a closing brace (}). Between the opening and closing braces, you can code one or more statements. Here's a block that consists of three statements:

```
{
    int i, j;
    i = 100;
    j = 200;
}
```

A block is itself a type of statement. As a result, any time the Java language requires a statement, you can substitute a block to execute more than one statement. In Book II, Chapter 4, you discover that the basic syntax of an `if` statement is this:

```
if ( expression ) statement
```

Here `statement` can be a single statement or a block. If you find this idea confusing, don't worry; it will make more sense when you turn to Book II, Chapter 4.

You can code the braces that mark a block in two popular ways. One is to place both braces on separate lines and then indent the statements that make up the block. For example:

```
if ( i > 0)
{
    String s = "The value of i is " + i;
    System.out.print(s);
}
```

The other style is to place the opening brace for the block on the same line as the statement the block is associated with, like this:

```
if ( i > 0) {
    String s = "The value of i is " + i;
    System.out.print(s);
}
```

Which style you use is a matter of personal preference. I prefer the first style, and that's the style I use throughout this book. But either style works — and many programmers prefer the second style because it's more concise.

Note that even though a block can be treated as a single statement, you should *not* end a block with a semicolon. The statements within the block may require semicolons, but the block itself does not.

Creating Identifiers

An *identifier* is a word that you make up to refer to a Java programming element by name. Although you can assign identifiers to many types of Java elements, they're most commonly used for the following elements:

✦ Classes, such as the `HelloApp` class in Listing 1-1

✦ Methods, such as the `main` method in Listing 1-1

✦ Variables and fields, which hold data used by your program

✦ Parameters, which pass data values to methods

Identifiers are also sometimes called *names*. Strictly speaking, a name isn't quite the same thing as an identifier; a name is often made up of two or more identifiers connected with periods (called *dots*). In line 5 of Listing 1-1, for example, `System` and `out` are both identifiers, but `System.out` is a name. In practice, the terms *name* and *identifier* are used interchangeably.

You must follow a few simple rules when you create identifiers:

✦ Identifiers are case-sensitive. As a result, `SalesTax` and `salesTax` are distinct identifiers.

✦ Identifiers can be made up of upper- or lowercase letters, numerals, underscore characters (_), and dollar signs ($). Thus, identifier names such as `Port1`, `SalesTax$`, and `Total_Sales`.

✦ All identifiers must begin with a letter. Thus, `a15` is a valid identifier, but `13Unlucky` isn't (because it begins with a numeral).

✦ An identifier can't be the same as any of the Java keywords listed in Table 1-1. Thus, you can't create a variable named `for` or a class named `public`.

✦ The Java language specification recommends that you avoid using dollar signs in names you create, because code generators use dollar signs to create identifiers. Thus, avoiding dollar signs helps you avoid creating names that conflict with generated names.

Crafting Comments

A *comment* is a bit of text that provides explanations of your code. The compiler ignores comments, so you can place any text you want in a comment. Using plenty of comments in your program is a good way to explain what your program does and how it works.

Java has three basic types of comments: *end-of-line comments, traditional comments,* and *JavaDoc comments.* More about that is coming right up.

End-of-line comments

An *end-of-line comment* begins with the sequence // (a pair of consecutive slashes) and ends at the end of the line. You can place an end-of-line comment at the end of any line. Everything you type after the // is ignored by the compiler. For example:

Book II
Chapter 1

Java Programming Basics

```
total = total * discountPercent; // calculate the discounted total
```

If you want, you can also place end-of-line comments on separate lines, like this:

```
// calculate the discounted total
total = total * discountPercent;
```

You can place end-of-line comments in the middle of statements that span two or more lines. For example:

```
total = (total * discountPercent)   // apply the discount first
      + salesTax;                   // then add the sales tax
```

Traditional comments

A *traditional comment* begins with the sequence /* , ends with the sequence */, and can span multiple lines. Here's an example:

```
/* HelloApp sample program.
   This program demonstrates the basic structure
   that all Java programs must follow. */
```

A traditional comment can begin and end anywhere on a line. If you want, you can even sandwich a comment between other Java programming elements, like this:

```
x = (y + /* a strange place for a comment */ 5) / z;
```

Usually, traditional comments appear on separate lines. One common use for traditional comments is to place a block of comment lines at the beginning of a class to indicate information about the class — such as what the class does, who wrote it, and so on. That type of comment, however, is usually better coded as a JavaDoc comment, as described in the next section.

You may be tempted to temporarily comment out a range of lines by placing /* in front of the first line in the range and */ after the last line in the range. That practice can get you in trouble, however, if the range of lines you try to comment out includes a traditional comment, because traditional comments can't be *nested.* The following code won't compile, for example:

```
/*
int x, y, z;
y = 10;
z = 5;
x = (y + /* a strange place for a comment */ 5) / z;
*/
```

Here, I tried to comment out a range of lines that already included a traditional comment. Unfortunately, the */ sequence near the end of the fifth line is interpreted as the end of the traditional comment that begins in the first line, so when the compiler encounters the */ sequence in line 6, it generates an error message.

JavaDoc comments

JavaDoc comments are actually special types of traditional comments that you can use to create web-based documentation for your programs — automatically. Because you'll have a better appreciation of JavaDoc comments when you know more about object-oriented programming, I devote a section in Book III, Chapter 8, to creating and using JavaDoc comments.

Introducing Object-Oriented Programming

Having presented some of the most basic elements of the Java programming language, most Java books would next turn to the important topics of variables and data types. Because Java is an inherently object-oriented programming language, however, and because classes are the heart of object-oriented programming, I look next at classes to explore the important role they play in creating objects. I get to variables and data types first thing in the next chapter.

Understanding classes and objects

As I've already mentioned, a *class* is code that defines the behavior of a Java programming element called an object. An *object* is an entity that has both state and behavior. The *state* of an object consists of any data that the object might be keeping track of, and the *behavior* consists of *actions* that the object can perform. The behaviors are represented in the class by one or more methods that can be called on to perform actions.

The difference between a class and an object is similar to the difference between a blueprint and a house. A blueprint is a plan for a house. A house is an implementation of a blueprint. One set of blueprints can be used to build many houses. Likewise, a class is a plan for an object, and an object is — in Java terms — an *instance* of a class. You can use a single class to create more than one object.

When an object is created, Java sets aside an area of computer memory that's sufficient to hold all the data that's stored by the object. As a result, each instance of a class has its own data, independent of the data used by other instances of the same class.

Understanding static methods

You don't necessarily have to create an instance of a class to use the methods of the class. If you declare a method with the `static` keyword, you can call the method without first creating an instance of the class, because `static` methods are called from classes, not from objects.

The `main` method of a Java application must be declared with the `static` keyword because when you start a Java program by using the `java` command from a command prompt, Java doesn't create an instance of the application class. Instead, it simply calls the program's static `main` method.

The difference between static and nonstatic methods will become more apparent when you look at object-oriented programming in more depth in Book III. But for now, consider this analogy. The blueprints for a house include the details about systems that actually perform work in a finished house, such as electrical and plumbing systems. To use those systems, you have to actually build a house. In other words, you can't turn on the hot water by using the blueprint alone; you have to have an actual house with an actual device to heat the water.

The blueprints do include detailed measurements of the dimensions of the house, however. As a result, you *can* use the blueprints to determine the square footage of the living room.

Now imagine that the blueprints actually have a built-in calculator that displays the size of the living room if you push the Living Room button. That button would be like a `static` method in a class: You don't actually have to build a house to use the button; you can activate it from the blueprints alone.

Many Java programs — in fact, many of the programs in the rest of Book II — are entirely made up of `static` methods. Most realistic programs, however, require that you create one or more objects that the program uses as it executes. As a result, knowing how to create simple classes and how to create objects from those classes are basic skills in Java programming.

Creating an object from a class

In Java, you can create an object from a class in several ways. The most straightforward way is to create a variable that provides a name you can use to refer to the object, use the `new` keyword to create an instance of the class, and then assign the resulting object to the variable. The general form of a statement that does that bit of magic looks like this:

```
ClassName variableName = new ClassName();
```

To create an object instance of a class named `Class1` and assign it to a variable named `myClass1Object`, you would write a statement like this:

```
Class1 myClass1Object = new Class1();
```

Why do you have to list the class name twice? The first time, you're providing a *type* for the variable. In other words, you're saying that the variable you're creating here can be used to hold objects created from the `Class1` class. The second time you list the class name, you're creating an object from the class. The `new` keyword tells Java to create an object, and the class name provides the name of the class to use to create the object.

The equal sign (=) is an *assignment operator*. It simply says to take the object created by the `new` keyword and assign it to the variable. Thus, this statement actually does *three* things:

✦ It creates a variable named `myClass1Object` that can be used to hold objects created from the `Class1` class. At this point, no object has been created — just a variable that can be used to store objects.

✦ It creates a new object in memory from the `Class1` class.

✦ It assigns this newly created object to the `myClass1Object` variable. That way, you can use the `myClassObject` variable to refer to the object that was created.

Viewing a program that uses an object

To give you an early look at what object-oriented programming really looks like, Listing 1-2 and Listing 1-3 show another version of the `HelloApp` application — this time using two classes, one of which is actually made into an object when the program is run. The first class, named `HelloApp2`, is shown in Listing 1-2. This class is similar to the `HelloApp` class shown in Listing 1-1 but uses an object created from the second class, named `Greeter`, to actually display the `"Hello, World!"` message on the console. The `Greeter` class is shown in Listing 1-3. It defines a method named `sayHello` that displays the message.

Both the `HelloApp` and the `Greeter` classes are public classes. Java requires that each public class be stored in a separate file with the same name as the class; the filename ends with the extension `.java`. As a result, the `HelloApp2` class is stored in a file named `HelloApp2.java`, and the `Greeter` class is stored in a file named `Greeter.java`.

The HelloApp2 class

The `HelloApp2` class is shown in Listing 1-2.

Book II
Chapter 1

Java Programming
Basics

Listing 1-2: The HelloApp2 Class

```
// This application displays a hello message on        →1
// the console by creating an instance of the
// Greeter class and then calling the Greeter
// object's sayHello method.

public class HelloApp2                                 →6
{
    public static void main(String[] args)            →8
    {
        Greeter myGreeterObject = new Greeter();      →10
        myGreeterObject.sayHello();                   →11
    }
}
```

The following paragraphs describe the key points:

→ 1   This class begins with a series of comment lines identifying the function of the program. For these comments, I used simple end-of-line comments rather than traditional comments. (For more on commenting, see the "Crafting Comments" section, earlier in this chapter.)

→ 6   The `HelloApp2` class begins on line 6 with the `public class` declaration. Because the `public` keyword is used, a file named `HelloApp2.java` must contain this class.

→ 8   The `main` method is declared, using the same form as the `main` method in the first version of this program (Listing 1-1). Get used to this form, because *all* Java applications must include a `main` method that's declared in this way.

→ **10**   The first line in the body of the main method creates a variable named `myGreeterObject` that can hold objects created from the `Greeter` class. Then it creates a new object using the `Greeter` class and assigns this object to the `myGreeterObject` variable.

→ **11**   The second line in the body of the `main` method calls the `myGreeterObject` object's `sayHello` method. As you'll see in a moment, this method simply displays the message `"Hello, World!"` on the console.

The Greeter class

The `Greeter` class is shown in Listing 1-3.

Listing 1-3:   The Greeter Class

```
// This class creates a Greeter object                    →1
// that displays a hello message on
// the console.

public class Greeter                                      →5
{
    public void sayHello()                                →7
    {
        System.out.println("Hello, World!");              →9
    }
}
```

The following paragraphs describe the key points:

→ **1**   This class also begins with a series of comment lines that identify the function of the program.

→ **5**   The class declaration begins on this line. The class is declared as public so other classes can use it. This declaration is required so that the `HelloApp2` class can access the `Greeter` class.

→ **7**   The `sayHello` method is declared using the `public` keyword so that it's available to other classes that use the `Greeter` class. The `void` keyword indicates that this method doesn't provide any data back to the class that calls it, and `sayHello` simply provides the name of the method.

→ **9**   The body of this method consists of just one line of code that displays the `"Hello, World!"` message on the console.

So what's the difference?

You may notice that the only line that actually does any real work in the `HelloApp2` program is line 9 in the `Greeter` class (Listing 1-3), and this line happens to be identical to line 5 in the original `HelloApp` class (Listing 1-1).

Other than the fact that the second version requires roughly twice as much code as the first version, what really *is* the difference between these two applications?

Simply put, the first version is procedural, and the second is object-oriented. In the first version of the program, the main method of the application class does all the work of the application by itself: It just says hello. The second version defines a class that knows how to say hello to the world and then creates an object from that class and asks that object to say hello. The application itself doesn't know (or even care) exactly how the Greeter object says hello. It doesn't know exactly what the greeting will be, what language the greeting will be in, or even how the greeting will be displayed.

To illustrate this point, consider what would happen if you used the Greeter class shown in Listing 1-4 rather than the one shown in Listing 1-3. This version of the Greeter class uses a Java library class called JOptionPane to display a message in a dialog box rather than in a console window. (I won't bother explaining in a list how this code works, but you can find out more about it in the next chapter.) If you were to run the HelloApp2 application using this version of the Greeter class, you'd get the dialog box shown in Figure 1-1.

Listing 1-4:   Another Version of the Greeter Class

```
// This class creates a Greeter object
// that displays a hello message
// in a dialog box.

import javax.swing.JOptionPane;                          →5

public class Greeter
{
    public void sayHello()
    {
        JOptionPane.showMessageDialog(null,              →11
            "Hello, World!", "Greeter",
            JOptionPane.INFORMATION_MESSAGE);
    }
}
```

Figure 1-1:
The class in
Listing 1-4
displays this
dialog box.

The important point to realize here is that the HelloApp2 class doesn't have to be changed to use this new version of the Greeter class. Instead, all you have to do is replace the old Greeter class with the new one, recompile the Greeter class, and the HelloApp2 class won't know the difference. That's one of the main benefits of object-oriented programming.

Importing Java API Classes

You may have noticed that the Greeter class in Listing 1-4 includes this statement:

```
import javax.swing.JOptionPane;
```

The purpose of the import statement is to let the compiler know that the program is using a class that's defined by the Java API called JOptionPane.

Because the Java API contains literally thousands of classes, some form of organization is needed to make the classes easier to access. Java does this by grouping classes into manageable groups called *packages.* In the previous example, the package that contains the JOptionPane class is named javax.swing.

Strictly speaking, import statements are never required. But if you don't use import statements to import the API classes your program uses, you must *fully qualify* the names of the classes when you use them by listing the package name in front of the class name. So if the class in Listing 1-4 didn't include the import statement in line 5, you'd have to code line 11 like this:

```
javax.swing.JOptionPane.showMessageDialog(null,
    "Hello, World!", "Greeter",
    javax.swing.JOptionPane.INFORMATION_MESSAGE);
```

In other words, you'd have to specify javax.swing.JOptionPane instead of just JOptionPane whenever you referred to this class.

Here are some additional rules for working with import statements:

✦ import statements must appear at the beginning of the class file, before any class declarations.

✦ You can include as many import statements as are necessary to import all the classes used by your program.

✦ You can import all the classes in a particular package by listing the package name followed by an asterisk wildcard, like this:

```
import javax.swing.*;
```

✦ Because many programs use the classes that are contained in the java.lang package, you don't have to import that package. Instead, those classes are automatically available to all programs. The System class is defined in the java.lang package. As a result, you don't have to provide an import statement to use this class.

Chapter 2: Working with Variables and Data Types

In This Chapter

✔ Creating proper variable declarations

✔ Discovering the difference between primitive and reference types

✔ Looking at Java's built-in data types

✔ Introducing strings

✔ Getting input from the console

✔ Getting input if you're using an older version of Java

*I*n this chapter, you find out the basics of working with variables in Java. Variables are the key to making Java programs general purpose. The `Hello, World!` programs in the previous chapter, for example, are pretty specific: The only thing they say is "Hello, World!" But with a variable, you can make this type of program more general. You could vary the greeting so that sometimes it would say "Hello, World!" and at other times it would say "Greetings, Foolish Mortals." Or you could personalize the greeting, so that it said "Hello, Bob!" or "Hello, Amanda!"

Variables are also the key to creating programs that can perform calculations. Suppose that you want to create a program that calculates the area of a circle, given the circle's radius. Such a program uses two variables: one to represent the radius of the circle and the other to represent the circle's area. The program asks the user to enter a value for the first variable. Then it calculates the value of the second variable.

Declaring Variables

In Java, you must explicitly declare all variables before using them. This rule is in contrast to some languages — most notably Basic and earlier versions of Visual Basic, which let you use variables that haven't been automatically declared.

Allowing you to use variables that you haven't explicitly declared might seem a pretty good idea at first glance, but it's a common source of bugs that result from misspelled variable names. Java requires that you explicitly declare variables so that if you misspell a variable name, the compiler can detect your mistake and display a compiler error.

The basic form of a variable declaration is this:

```
type name;
```

Here are some examples:

```
int x;
String lastName;
double radius;
```

In these examples, variables named x, lastName, and radius are declared. The x variable holds integer values, the lastName variable holds String values, and the radius variable holds double values. For more information about what these types mean, see the section "Working with Primitive Data Types" later in this chapter. Until then, just realize that int variables can hold whole numbers (such as 5, 1,340, or -34), double variables can hold numbers with fractional parts (such as 0.5, 99.97, or 3.1415), and String variables can hold text values (such as "Hello, World!" or "Jason P. Finch").

Notice that variable declarations end with semicolons. That's because a variable declaration is itself a type of statement.

Variable names follow the same rules as other Java identifiers, as I describe in Book II, Chapter 1, so see that chapter for details. In short, a variable name can be any combination of letters, numerals, or underscores and dollar signs – but must start with a letter. Most programmers prefer to start variable names with lowercase letters and capitalize the first letter of individual words within the name. firstName and salesTaxRate, for example, are typical variable names.

Declaring two or more variables in one statement

You can declare two or more variables of the same type in a single statement by separating the variable names with commas. For example:

```
int x, y, z;
```

Here three variables of type int are declared, using the names x, y, and z.

As a rule, I suggest that you avoid declaring multiple variables in a single statement. Your code is easier to read and maintain if you give each variable a separate declaration.

Declaring class variables

A *class variable* is a variable that any method in a class can access, including static methods such as main. When declaring a class variable, you have two basic rules to follow:

✦ You must place the declaration within the body of the class but not within any of the class methods.

✦ You must include the word static in the declaration. The word static comes before the variable type.

The following program shows the proper way to declare a class variable named helloMessage:

```
public class HelloApp
{
    static String helloMessage;

    public static void main(String[] args)
    {
        helloMessage = "Hello, World!";
        System.out.println(helloMessage);
    }
}
```

**Book II
Chapter 2**

Working with Variables and Data Types

As you can see, the declaration includes the word static and is placed within the HelloApp class body but not within the body of the main method.

You don't have to place class variable declarations at the beginning of a class. Some programmers prefer to place them at the end of the class, as in this example:

```
public class HelloApp
{
    public static void main(String[] args)
    {
        helloMessage = "Hello, World!";
        System.out.println(helloMessage);
    }

    static String helloMessage;
}
```

Here the helloMessage variable is declared *after* the main method.

I think classes are easier to read if the variables are declared first, so that's where you see them in this book.

Declaring instance variables

An *instance variable* is similar to a class variable but doesn't specify the word `static` in its declaration. As the name suggests, instance variables are associated with instances of classes. As a result, you can use them only when you create an instance of a class. Because static methods aren't associated with an instance of the class, you can't use an instance variable in a static method — and that includes the `main` method.

The following example program won't compile:

```
public class HelloApp
{
    String helloMessage;      // error -- should use static keyword

    public static void main(String[] args)
    {
        helloMessage = "Hello, World!";
        System.out.println(helloMessage);   // will not compile
    }
}
```

If you attempt to compile this program, you get the following error messages:

```
C:\Java\HelloApp.java:7: non-static variable helloMessage cannot be referenced
    from a static context
                helloMessage = "Hello, World!";
                ^
C:\Java\HelloApp.java:8: non-static variable helloMessage cannot be referenced
    from a static context
            System.out.println(helloMessage);
                               ^
```

Both of these errors occur because the `main` method is static, so it can't access instance variables.

Instance variables are useful whenever you create your own classes, but because I don't cover that topic until Book III, you won't see many examples of instance methods in the remainder of the chapters in Book II.

Declaring local variables

A *local variable* is a variable that's declared within the body of a method. Then you can use the variable only within that method. Other methods in the class aren't even aware that the variable exists.

Here's a version of the `HelloApp` class in which the `helloMessage` variable is declared as a local variable:

```
public class HelloApp
{
    public static void main(String[] args)
    {
        String helloMessage;
```

```
        helloMessage = "Hello, World!";
        System.out.println(helloMessage);
    }
}
```

Note that you don't specify `static` on a declaration for a local variable. If you do, the compiler generates an error message and refuses to compile your program. Local variables always exist in the context of a method, and they exist only while that method is executing. As a result, whether or not an instance of the class has been created is irrelevant.

Unlike class and instance variables, a local variable is fussy about where you position the declaration for it. In particular, you must place the declaration before the first statement that actually uses the variable. Thus the following program won't compile:

```
public class HelloApp
{
    public static void main(String[] args)
    {
        helloMessage = "Hello, World!";    // error -- helloMessage
        System.out.println(helloMessage);  // is not yet declared
        String helloMessage;
    }
}
```

When it gets to the first line of the `main` method, the compiler generates two error messages complaining that it can't find the symbol `"helloMessage"`. That's because the symbol hasn't been declared.

Although most local variables are declared near the beginning of a method's body, you can also declare local variables within smaller blocks of code marked by braces. This will make more sense to you when you read about statements that use blocks, such as `if` and `for` statements. But here's an example:

```
if (taxRate > 0)
{
    double taxAmount;
    taxAmount = subTotal * taxRate;
    total = subTotal + total;
}
```

Here the variable `taxAmount` exists only within the set of braces that belongs to the `if` statement.

Initializing Variables

In Java, local variables are not given initial default values. The compiler checks to make sure that you have assigned a value before you use a local variable. The following example program won't compile:

```
public class testApp
{
    public static void main(String[] args)
    {
        int i;
        System.out.println("The value of i is " + i);
    }
}
```

If you try to compile this program, you get the following error message:

```
C:\Java\testApp.java:6: variable i might not have been initialized
        System.out.println("The value of i is " + i);
                                                  ^
```

To avoid this error message, you must initialize local variables before you use them. You can do that by using an assignment statement or an initializer, as I describe in the following sections.

Unlike local variables, class variables and instance variables are given default values. Numeric types are automatically initialized to zero, and String variables are initialized to empty strings. As a result, you don't have to initialize a class variable or an instance variable, although you can if you want them to have an initial value other than the default.

Initializing variables with assignment statements

One way to initialize a variable is to code an *assignment statement* following the variable declaration. Assignment statements have this general form:

```
variable = expression;
```

Here, the expression can be any Java expression that yields a value of the same type as the variable. Here's a version of the main method from the previous example that correctly initializes the i variable before using it:

```
    public static void main(String[] args)
    {
        int i;
        i = 0;
        System.out.println("i is " + i);
    }
```

In this example, the variable is initialized to a value of zero before the println method is called to print the variable's value.

You find out a lot more about expressions in Book II, Chapter 3. For now, you can just use simple literal values, such as 0 in this example.

Initializing variables with initializers

Java also allows you to initialize a variable on the same statement that declares the variable. To do that, you use an *initializer,* which has the following general form:

```
type name = expression;
```

In effect, the initializer lets you combine a declaration and an assignment statement into one concise statement. Here are some examples:

```
int x = 0;
String lastName = "Lowe";
double radius = 15.4;
```

In each case, the variable is both declared and initialized in a single statement.

When you declare more than one variable in a single statement, each variable can have its own initializer. The following code declares variables named x and y, and initializes x to 5 and y to 10:

```
int x = 5, y = 10;
```

When you declare two class or instance variables in a single statement but use only one initializer, you can mistakenly think that the initializer applies to both variables. Consider this statement:

```
static int x, y = 5;
```

Here you might think that both x and y would initialize to 5. But the initializer applies only to y, so x is initialized to its default value, 0. (If you make this mistake with a local variable, the compiler displays an error message for the first statement that uses the x variable because it isn't properly initialized.)

Using Final Variables (Constants)

A *final variable,* also called a *constant,* is a variable whose value you can't change after it's been initialized. To declare a final variable, you add the final keyword to the variable declaration, like this:

```
final int WEEKDAYS = 5;
```

Although you can create final local variables, most final variables are class or instance variables. To create a final class variable (sometimes called a *class constant*), add static final (not final static) to the declaration, as follows:

```
static final WEEKDAYS = 5;
```

Although it isn't required, using all capital letters for final variable names is common. When you do so, you can easily spot the use of final variables in your programs.

Constants are useful for values that are used in several places throughout a program and that don't change during the course of the program. Suppose that you're writing a game that features bouncing balls, and you want the balls always to have a radius of 6 pixels. This program probably needs to use the ball diameter in several places — to draw the ball onscreen, to determine whether the ball has hit a wall, to determine whether the ball has hit another ball, and so on. Rather than just specify 6 whenever you need the ball's radius, you can set up a class constant named BALL_RADIUS, like this:

```
static final BALL_RADIUS = 6;
```

Using a class constant has two advantages:

✦ If you decide later that the radius of the balls should be 7, you make the change in just one place: the initializer for the BALL_RADIUS constant.

✦ The constant helps document the inner workings of your program. The operation of a complicated calculation that uses the ball's radius is easier to understand if it specifies BALL_RADIUS rather than 6, for example.

Working with Primitive Data Types

The term *data type* refers to the type of data that can be stored in a variable. Java is sometimes called a *strongly typed* language because when you declare a variable, you must specify the variable's type. Then the compiler ensures that you don't try to assign data of the wrong type to the variable. The following example code generates a compiler error:

```
int x;
x = 3.1415;
```

Because x is declared as a variable of type int (which holds whole numbers), you can't assign the value 3.1415 to it.

Java makes an important distinction between primitive types and reference types.

+ **Primitive types** are the data types defined by the language itself.

+ **Reference types** are types defined by classes in the Java application programming interface (API) or by classes you create rather than by the language itself.

A key difference between a primitive type and a reference type is that the memory location associated with a primitive-type variable contains the actual value of the variable. As a result, primitive types are sometimes called *value types.* By contrast, the memory location associated with a reference-type variable contains an address (called a *pointer*) that indicates the memory location of the actual object. I explain reference types more fully in the section "Using Reference Types," later in this chapter, so don't worry if this explanation doesn't make sense just yet.

It isn't quite true that reference types are defined by the Java API and not by the Java language specification. A few reference types, such as `Object` and `String`, are defined by classes in the API, but those classes are specified in the Java Language API. Also, a special type of variable called an *array,* which can hold multiple occurrences of primitive- or reference-type variables, is considered to be a reference type.

Java defines a total of eight primitive types, listed in Table 2-1. Of the eight primitive types, six are for numbers, one is for characters, and one is for true/false values.

**Book II
Chapter 2**

**Working with
Variables and
Data Types**

Table 2-1	Java's Primitive Types
Type	*Explanation*
`int`	A 32-bit (4-byte) integer value
`short`	A 16-bit (2-byte) integer value
`long`	A 64-bit (8-byte) integer value
`byte`	An 8-bit (1-byte) integer value
`float`	A 32-bit (4-byte) floating-point value
`double`	A 64-bit (8-byte) floating-point value
`char`	A 16-bit character using the Unicode encoding scheme
`boolean`	A `true` or `false` value

Integer types

An *integer* is a whole number — that is, a number with no fractional or decimal portion. Java has four integer types, which you can use to store numbers of varying sizes. The most commonly used integer type is int. This type uses 4 bytes to store an integer value that can range from about negative 2 billion to positive 2 billion.

If you're writing the application that counts how many hamburgers McDonald's has sold, an int variable may not be big enough. In that case, you can use a long integer instead. long is a 64-bit integer that can hold numbers ranging from about negative 9,000 trillion to positive 9,000 trillion. (That's a big number, even by federal deficit standards.)

In some cases, you may not need integers as large as the standard int type provides. For those cases, Java provides two smaller integer types. The short type represents a two-digit integer, which can hold numbers from –32,768 to +32,767, and the byte type defines an 8-bit integer that can range from –128 to +127.

Although the short and byte types require less memory than the int and long types, there's usually little reason to use them for desktop applications, where memory is usually plentiful. A few bytes here or there won't make any difference in the performance of most programs — so you should stick to int and long most of the time. Also, use long only when you know that you're dealing with numbers too large for int.

In Java, the size of integer data types is specified by the language and is the same regardless of what computer a program runs on. This is a huge improvement over the C and C++ languages, which let compilers for different platforms determine the optimum size for integer data types. As a result, a C or C++ program written and tested on one type of computer may not execute identically on another computer.

Java allows you to *promote* an integer type to a larger integer type. Java allows the following, for example:

```
int xInt;
long yLong;
xInt = 32;
yLong = xInt;
```

Here you can assign the value of the xInt variable to the yLong variable because yLong is larger than xInt. Java does not allow the converse, however:

```
int xInt;
long yLong;
yLong = 32;
xInt = yLong;
```

The value of the yLong variable cannot be assigned to the xInt because xInt is smaller than yLong. Because this assignment may result in a loss of data, Java doesn't allow it. (If you need to assign a long to an int variable, you must use explicit casting, as described in the "Type casting" section, later in this chapter.)

A feature that was new in Java 7 allows you to include underscores to make longer numbers easier to read. Thus, the following statements both assign the same value to the variables xLong1 and xLong2:

```
long xLong1 = 58473882;
long xLong2 = 58_473_882;
```

Book II
Chapter 2

Working with Variables and Data Types

Floating-point types

Floating-point numbers are numbers that have fractional parts (usually expressed with a decimal point). You should use a floating-point type whenever you need a number with a decimal, such as 19.95 or 3.1415.

Java has two primitive types for floating-point numbers: float, which uses 4 bytes, and double, which uses 8 bytes. In almost all cases, you should use the double type whenever you need numbers with fractional values.

The *precision* of a floating-point value indicates how many significant digits the value can have following its decimal point. The precision of a float type is only about six or seven decimal digits, which isn't sufficient for most types of calculations. If you use Java to write a payroll system, for example, you might get away with using float variables to store salaries for employees such as teachers or firefighters, but not for professional baseball players or corporate executives.

By contrast, double variables have a precision of about 15 digits, which is enough for most purposes.

Floating-point numbers actually use *exponential notation* (also called *scientific notation*) to store their values. That means that a floating-point number actually records two numbers: a base value (also called the *mantissa*) and an exponent. The actual value of the floating-point number is calculated by multiplying the mantissa by 2 raised to the power indicated by the exponent. For `float` types, the exponent can range from –127 to +128. For `double` types, the exponent can range from –1,023 to +1,024. Thus both `float` and `double` variables are capable of representing very large and very small numbers.

You can find more information about some of the nuances of working with floating-point values in Book II, Chapter 3.

When you use a floating-point literal, you should always include a decimal point, like this:

```
double period = 99.0;
```

If you omit the decimal point, the Java compiler treats the literal as an integer. Then, when it sees that you're trying to assign the integer literal to a double variable, the compiler converts the integer to a double value. This avoidable conversion step uses some precious processing time.

To save that time, you can add an F or D suffix to a floating-point literal to indicate whether the literal itself is of type `float` or `double`. For example:

```
float value1 = 199.33F;
double value2 = 200495.995D;
```

Getting scientific with floats and doubles

If you have a scientific mind, you may want to use scientific notation when you write floating-point literals. The equation

```
double e = 5.10e+6;
```

is equivalent to

```
double e = 5100000D;
```

The sign is optional if the exponent is positive, so you can also write

```
double e = 5.10e6;
```

Note that the exponent can be negative to indicate values smaller than 1. The equation

```
double impulse = 23e-7;
```

is equivalent to

```
double impulse = 0.0000023;
```

If you omit the suffix, D is assumed. As a result, you can usually omit the D suffix for double literals.

Interestingly, floating-point numbers have two distinct zero values: a negative zero and a positive zero. You don't have to worry about these much, because Java treats them as equal. Still, they would make for a good question on *Jeopardy!* ("I'll take Weird Numbers for $200, Alex.")

The char type

The char type represents a single character from the Unicode character set. It's important to keep in mind that a character is not the same as a string; you find out about strings later in this chapter, in the section "Working with Strings." For now, just realize that a char variable can store just one character, not a sequence of characters, as a string can.

To assign a value to a char variable, you use a character literal, which is always enclosed in apostrophes rather than quotes. Here's an example:

```
char code = 'X';
```

Here the character X is assigned to the variable named code.

The following statement won't compile:

```
char code = "X";   // error -- should use apostrophes, not quotes
```

That's because quotation marks are used to mark strings, not character constants.

Unicode is a 2-byte character code that can represent the characters used in most languages throughout the world. Currently, about 35,000 codes in the Unicode character set are defined, which leaves another 29,000 codes unused. The first 256 characters in the Unicode character set are the same as the characters of the ASCII character set, which is the most commonly used character set for computers with Western languages.

For more information about the Unicode character set, see the official Unicode website at www.unicode.org.

Character literals can also use special *escape sequences* to represent special characters. Table 2-2 lists the allowable escape sequences. These escape sequences let you create literals for characters that can't otherwise be typed within a character constant.

Table 2-2	Escape Sequences for Character Constants
Escape Sequence	*Explanation*
\b	Backspace
\t	Horizontal tab
\n	Line feed
\f	Form feed
\r	Carriage return
\"	Double quote
\'	Single quote
\\	Backslash

The Boolean type

A `boolean` type can have one of two values: `true` or `false`. Booleans are used to perform logical operations, most commonly to determine whether some condition is true. For example:

```
boolean enrolled = true;
boolean credited = false;
```

Here a variable named `enrolled` of type `boolean` is declared and initialized to a value of `true`, and another `boolean` named `credited` is declared and initialized to `false`.

In some languages, such as C or C++, integer values can be treated as Booleans, with `0` equal to `false` and any other value equal to `true`. Not so in Java. In Java, you can't convert between an `integer` type and a `boolean` type.

Wrapper classes

Every primitive type has a corresponding class defined in the Java API class library. This class is sometimes called a *wrapper class* because it wraps a primitive value with the object-oriented equivalent of pretty wrapping paper and a bow to make the primitive type look and behave like an object. Table 2-3 lists the wrapper classes for each of the eight primitive types.

As you find out later in this chapter, you can use these wrapper classes to convert primitive values to strings, and vice versa.

Table 2-3	Wrapper Classes for the Primitive Types
Primitive Type	*Wrapper Class*
int	Integer
short	Short
long	Long
byte	Byte
float	Float
double	Double
char	Character
boolean	Boolean

Book II
Chapter 2

Working with
Variables and
Data Types

Using Reference Types

In Book III, Chapter 1, you're introduced to some of the basic concepts of object-oriented programming. In particular, you see how all Java programs are made up of one or more classes, and how to use classes to create objects. In this section, I show how you can create variables that work with objects created from classes.

To start, a *reference type* is a type that's based on a class rather than on one of the primitive types that are built into the Java language. A reference type can be based on a class that's provided as part of the Java API class library or on a class that you write yourself. Either way, when you create an object from a class, Java allocates however much memory the object requires to store the object. Then, if you assign the object to a variable, the variable is actually assigned a *reference* to the object, not the object itself. This reference is the address of the memory location where the object is stored.

Suppose that you're writing a game program that involves balls, and you create a class named Ball that defines the behavior of a ball. To declare a variable that can refer to a Ball object, you use a statement like this:

```
Ball b;
```

Here, the variable b is a variable of type Ball.

To create a new instance of an object from a class, you use the new keyword along with the class name. This second reference to the class name is actually a call to a special routine of the class called a *constructor.* The constructor is responsible for initializing the new object. Here's a statement that declares a variable of type Ball, calls the Ball class constructor to create a new Ball object, and assigns a reference to the Ball object to the variable:

```
Ball b = new Ball();
```

One of the key concepts in working with reference types is the fact that a variable of a particular type doesn't actually contain an object of that type. Instead, it contains a reference to an object of the correct type. An important side effect is that two variables can refer to the same object.

Consider these statements:

```
Ball b1 = new Ball();
Ball b2 = b1;
```

Here I've declared two Ball variables, named b1 and b2, but I've created only one Ball object. In the first statement, the Ball object is created, and b1 is assigned a reference to it. Then, in the second statement, the variable b2 is assigned a reference to the same object that's referenced by b1. As a result, both b1 and b2 refer to the same Ball object.

If you use one of these variables to change some aspect of the ball, the change is visible to the ball no matter which variable you use. Suppose that the Ball class has a method called setSpeed that lets you set the speed of the ball to any int value and a getSpeed method that returns an integer value that reflects the ball's current speed. Now consider these statements:

```
b1.setSpeed(50);
b2.setSpeed(100);
int speed = b1.getSpeed();
```

When these statements complete, is the value of the speed variable 50 or 100? The correct answer is 100. Because b1 and b2 refer to the same Ball object, changing the speed by using b2 affects b1 as well.

This is one of the most confusing aspects of programming with an object-oriented language such as Java, so don't feel bad if you get tripped up from time to time.

Working with Strings

A *string* is a sequence of text characters, such as the message "Hello, World!" displayed by the HelloApp program illustrated in this chapter and the preceding chapter. In Java, strings are an interesting breed. Java doesn't define strings as a primitive type. Instead, strings are a *reference type* defined by the Java API String class. The Java language does have some built-in features for working with strings. In some cases, these features make strings appear to be primitive types rather than reference types.

Java's string-handling features are advanced enough to merit an entire chapter, so for the full scoop on strings, I refer you to Book IV, Chapter 1. The following sections present just the bare essentials of working with strings so that you can incorporate simple strings into your programs.

Declaring and initializing strings

Strings are declared and initialized much like primitive types. In fact, the only difference you may notice at first is that the word String is capitalized, unlike the keywords for the primitive types, such as int and double. That's because String isn't a keyword. Instead, it's the name of the Java API class that provides for string objects.

The following statements define and initialize a string variable:

```
String s;
s = "Hello, World!";
```

Here a variable named s of type String is declared and initialized with the *string literal* "Hello, World!". Notice that string literals are enclosed in quotation marks, not apostrophes. Apostrophes are used for character literals, which are different from string literals.

Like any variable declaration, a string declaration can include an initializer. Thus you can declare and initialize a string variable in one statement, like this:

```
String s = "Hello, World!";
```

Class variables and instance variables are automatically initialized to empty strings, but local variables aren't. To initialize a local string variable to an empty string, use a statement like this:

```
String s = "";
```

Combining strings

Combine two strings by using the plus sign (+) as a *concatenation operator*. (In Java-speak, combining strings is called *concatenation*.) The following statement combines the value of two string variables to create a third string:

```
String hello = "Hello, ";
String world = "World!";
String greeting = hello + world;
```

The final value of the greeting variable is "Hello, World!"

When Java concatenates strings, it doesn't insert any blank spaces between the strings. Thus, if you want to combine two strings and have a space appear between them, make sure that the first string ends with a space or the second string begins with a space. (In the preceding example, the first string ends with a space.)

Alternatively, you can concatenate a string literal along with the string variables. For example:

```
String hello = "Hello";
String world = "World!";
String greeting = hello + ", " + world;
```

Here the comma and the space that appear between the words Hello and World are inserted as a string literal.

Concatenation is one of the most commonly used string-handling techniques, so you see plenty of examples in this book. In fact, I've already used concatenation once in this chapter. Earlier, I showed you a program that included the following line:

```
System.out.println("The value of i is " + i);
```

Here the println method of the System.out object prints the string that's created when the literal "The value of i is " is concatenated with the value of the i variable.

Converting primitives to strings

Because string concatenation lets you combine two or more string values, and because primitive types such as int and double are *not* string types, you may be wondering how the last example in the preceding section can work. In other words, how can Java concatenate the string literal "The value of i is " with the integer value of i in this statement?:

```
System.out.println("The value of i is " + i);
```

The answer is that Java automatically converts primitive values to string values whenever you use a primitive value in a concatenation.

TIP

You can explicitly convert a primitive value to a string by using the `toString` method of the primitive type's wrapper class. To convert the `int` variable x to a string, for example, you use this statement:

```
String s = Integer.toString(x);
```

In the next chapter, you discover how to use a special class called the `NumberFormat` class to convert primitive types to strings while applying various types of formatting to the value, such as adding commas, dollar signs, or percentage marks.

Converting strings to primitives

Converting a primitive value to a string value is pretty easy. Going the other way — converting a string value to a primitive — is a little more complex, because it doesn't always work. If a string contains the value 10, for example, you can easily convert it to an integer. But if the string contains thirty-two, you can't.

To convert a string to a primitive type, you use a `parse` method of the appropriate wrapper class, as listed in Table 2-4. To convert a string value to an integer, you use statements like this:

```
String s = "10";
int x = Integer.parseInt(s);
```

Table 2-4	Methods That Convert Strings to Numeric Primitive Types	
Wrapper	*parse Method*	*Example*
Integer	parseInt(String)	int x = Integer. parseInt("100");
Short	parseShort(String)	short x = Short. parseShort("100");
Long	parseLong(String)	long x = Long. parseLong("100");
Byte	parseByte(String)	byte x = Byte. parseByte("100");

(continued)

Table 2-4 *(continued)*

Wrapper	parse Method	Example
Float	parseByte(String)	float x = Float.parseFloat("19.95");
Double	parseByte(String)	double x = Double.parseDouble("19.95");
Character	(none)	
Boolean	parseBoolean	boolean x = Boolean.parseBoolean
(String)	("true");	

You have no real reason to do this, of course, but as you see later in this chapter, you can use the parse methods to convert string values entered by the user to primitive types. That way, you can write programs that let the user enter numeric data via the console window.

Note that you don't need a parse method to convert a String to a Character. If you need to do that, you can find out how in Book IV, Chapter 1.

Converting and Casting Numeric Data

From time to time, you need to convert numeric data of one type to another. You may need to convert a double value to an integer, or vice versa. Some conversions can be done automatically; others are done using a technique called *casting*. I describe automatic type conversions and casting in the following sections.

Automatic conversions

Java can automatically convert some primitive types to others and do so whenever necessary. Figure 2-1 shows which conversions Java allows. Note that the conversions shown with dotted arrows in the figure may cause some of the value's precision to be lost. An int can be converted to a float, for example, but large int values won't be converted exactly because int values can have more digits than can be represented by the float type.

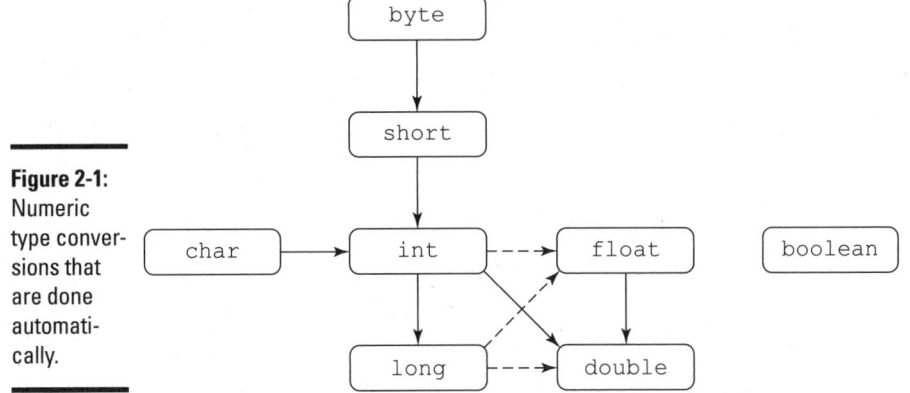

Figure 2-1:
Numeric type conversions that are done automatically.

Whenever you perform a mathematical operation on two values that aren't of the same type, Java automatically converts one of them to the type of the other. Here are the rules Java follows when doing this conversion:

✦ If one of the values is a `double`, the other value is converted to a `double`.

✦ If neither is a `double` but one is a `float`, the other is converted to a `float`.

✦ If neither is a `double` nor a `float` but one is a `long`, the other is converted to a `long`.

✦ If all else fails, both values are converted to `int`.

Type casting

Casting is similar to conversion but isn't done automatically. You use casting to perform a conversion that is *not* shown in Figure 2-1. If you want to convert a `double` to an `int`, for example, you must use casting.

When you use casting, you run the risk of losing information. A `double` can hold larger numbers than an `int`, for example. In addition, an `int` can't hold the fractional part of a `double`. As a result, if you cast a `double` to an `int`, you run the risk of losing data or accuracy, so `3.1415` becomes `3`, for example

To cast a primitive value from one type to another, you use a *cast operator,* which is simply the name of a primitive type in parentheses placed before the value you want to cast. For example:

```
double pi = 3.1314;
int iPi;
iPi = (int) pi;
```

Note that the fractional part of a double is simply discarded when cast to an integer; it isn't rounded. For example:

```
double price = 9.99;
int iPrice = (int) price;
```

Here iPrice is assigned the value 9. If you want to round the double value when you convert it, use the round method of the Math class, as I show you in the next chapter.

Thinking Inside the Box

Beginning with version 1.5, the Java language supports boxing and unboxing. *Boxing* occurs when Java converts a primitive value to its corresponding wrapped object, and *unboxing* occurs when Java goes the other way (converts from a wrapped object to the corresponding primitive value). Here's an example:

```
Integer wrap = 10;
System.out.println(wrap);

int prim = wrap;
System.out.println(prim);
```

The output of this code is 10 followed by another 10. In the first line, you assign a primitive value 10 to the wrapper object named wrap. Believe it or not, Java does a lot of work to put the little number 10 into a handsome Integer wrapper. In the third line of code, Java turns the big wrapped wrap object back into a primitive 10 (because the variable prim is of type int). Again, Java does some work behind the scenes.

Think of *boxing* and *unboxing* as nicknames for *wrapping* and *unwrapping.* The bottom line is, Java can wrap and unwrap values automatically. That's very handy.

Understanding Scope

The *scope* of a variable refers to which parts of a class the variable exists in. In the simplest terms, every variable exists only within the block in which the variable is declared, as well as any blocks that are contained within that block. That's why class and instance variables, which are declared in the class body, can be accessed by any methods defined by the class, but local variables defined within a method can be accessed only by the method in which they are defined.

In Java, a *block* is marked by a matching pair of braces. Java has many kinds of blocks, including class bodies, method bodies, and block statements that belong to statements such as `if` or `for` statements. But in each case, a block marks the scope boundaries for the variables declared within it.

The program in Listing 2-1 can help clarify the scope of class and local variables.

Book II
Chapter 2

Working with Variables and Data Types

Listing 2-1:   A Program That Demonstrates Scope for Class and Local Variables

```
public class ScopeApp
{                                                           →2

    static int x;

    public static void main(String[] args)
    {
        x = 5;
        System.out.println("main: x = " + x);
        myMethod();
    }

    public static void myMethod()
    {
        int y;
        y = 10;                                             →16
        if (y == x + 5)                                     →17
        {
            int z;
            z = 15;                                         →20
            System.out.println("myMethod: z = " + z);
        }                                                   →22
        System.out.println("myMethod: x = " + x);
        System.out.println("myMethod: y = " + y);
    }                                                       →25

}                                                           →27
```

The following paragraphs explain the scope of each of the variables used in this class:

→ **2**   The variable x is a class variable. Its scope begins in line 2 and ends in line 27. As a result, both the main method and the myMethod method can access it.

→ **16**   The variable y is a local variable that's initialized in line 16. As a result, its scope begins in line 16 and ends in line 25, which marks the end of the body of the myMethod method.

→ **17**   The variable z is a local variable that's declared and initialized in the statement block that belongs to the if statement in line 17.

→ **22**   The scope of variable z begins when the variable is initialized in line 20 and ends when the statement block ends in line 22.

When you run this program, you'll get the following output:

```
main: x = 5
myMethod: z = 15
myMethod: x = 5
myMethod: y = 10
```

Strictly speaking, the scope of a local variable begins when the variable is initialized and ends when the block that contains the variable's declaration ends. By contrast, the scope for a class or instance variable is the entire class in which the variable is declared. That means you can use a class or instance variable in a method that physically appears before the variable is declared, but you can't use a local variable before it's declared.

Shadowing Variables

A *shadowed variable* is a variable that would otherwise be accessible but is temporarily made unavailable because a variable with the same name has been declared in a more immediate scope. That's a mouthful, but the example in Listing 2-2 makes the concept clear. Here a class variable named x is declared. Then, in the main method, a local variable with the same name is declared.

Listing 2-2:   A Class That Demonstrates Shadowing

```
public class ShadowApp
{                                                              →2

    static int x;                                              →4

    public static void main(String[] args)
    {
        x = 5;                                                 →8
        System.out.println("x = " + x);                        →9
        int x;                                                 →10
        x = 10;                                                →11
        System.out.println("x = " + x);                        →12
        System.out.println("ShadowApp.x = " +
            ShadowApp.x);                                      →14
    }                                                          →15

}                                                              →17
```

Book II
Chapter 2

Working with Variables and Data Types

The following paragraphs explain the scoping issues in this program:

→ **2-4** The class variable x is declared in line 4. Its scope is the entire class body, from line 2 to line 17.

→ **8-9** The class variable x is assigned a value of 5 in line 8. Then this value is printed to the console in line 9.

→ **10** In line 10, a local variable named x is declared. The local variable shadows the class variable x, so any reference to x through the end of this method in line 15 refers to the local variable rather than the class variable.

→ **11** The local variable x is initialized in line 11. At that point, the local variable x comes into scope and remains in scope until the end of the method in line 15.

→ **12** The System.out.println statement in line 12 prints the value of the local variable x. Note that this statement is identical to the statement in line 9, which printed the class variable x because the class variable had not yet been shadowed.

→ **14** While a class variable is shadowed, you can access it by specifying the class name as shown in line 14. Here ShadowApp.x refers to the class variable.

→ **15** When the main method ends in line 15, the class variable x is no longer shadowed.

Here is the output you will get from this program:

```
x = 5
x = 10
ShadowApp.x = 5
```

The scope of a local variable that shadows a class variable doesn't necessarily begin at the same point that the local variable's scope begins. The shadowing begins when the local variable is declared, but the local variable's scope doesn't begin until the variable is initialized. If you attempt to access the variable between the declaration and the initialization, the Java compiler displays an error message.

Because shadowing is a common source of errors, I suggest that you avoid it as much as possible.

Printing Data with System.out

You've already seen several programs that use `System.out.println` to display output on the console. In the following sections, I officially show you how this method works, along with a related method called just `print`.

Using standard input and output streams

Java applications are designed to work in a terminal input/output (I/O) environment. Every Java application has at its disposal three *I/O streams* that are designed for terminal-based input and output, which simply sends or receives data one character at a time. The three streams are

✦ **Standard input:** A stream designed to receive input data. This stream is usually connected to the keyboard at the computer where the program is run. That way, the user can type characters directly into the standard input stream. In the section "Getting Input with the Scanner Class," later in this chapter, you connect this input stream to a class called `Scanner`, which makes it easy to read primitive data types from the standard input stream.

✦ **Standard output:** A stream designed to display text output onscreen. When you run a Java program under Windows, a special console window opens, and the standard output stream is connected to it. Then any text you send to standard output is displayed in that window.

✦ **Standard error:** Another stream designed for output. This stream is also connected to the console window. As a result, text written to the standard output stream is often intermixed with text written to the error stream.

Windows and other operating systems allow you to *redirect* standard output to some other destination — typically a file. When you do that, only the standard output data is redirected. Text written to standard error is still displayed in the console window.

To redirect standard output, you use a greater-than (>) sign on the command that runs the Java class, followed by the name of the file you want to save the standard output text to. Here's an example:

```
C:\Java>java TestApp >output.txt
```

Here the standard output created by the class TestApp is saved in a file named output.txt. Any text sent to the standard error stream still appears in the console window, however. As a result, the standard error stream is useful for programs that use output redirection to display status messages, error messages, or other information.

When you use a single > sign for redirection, Windows overwrites the redirected file if it already exists. If you prefer to add to the end of an existing file, use two greater-than signs, like this:

```
C:\Java>java TestApp >>output.txt
```

Then, if the output.txt file already exists, anything written to standard output by the TestApp class will be added to the end of the existing output.txt file.

All three standard streams are available to every Java program via the fields of the System class, described in Table 2-5.

Table 2-5	Static Fields of the System Object
Field	*Description*
System.in	Standard input
System.out	Standard output
System.err	Standard error

Using System.out and System.err

Both `System.out` and `System.err` represent instances of a class called `PrintWriter`, which defines the `print` and `println` methods used to write data to the console. You can use both methods with either a `String` argument or an argument of any primitive data type.

The only difference between the `print` and the `println` methods is that the `println` method adds a line-feed character to the end of the output, so the output from the next call to `print` or `println` begins on a new line.

Because it doesn't start a new line, the `print` method is useful when you want to print two or more items on the same line. Here's an example:

```
int i = 64;
int j = 23;
System.out.print(i);
System.out.print(" and ");
System.out.println(j);
```

The console output produced by these lines is

```
64 and 23
```

Note that you could do the same thing with a single call to `println` by using string concatenation, like this:

```
int i = 64;
int j = 23;
System.out.println(i + " and " + j);
```

Getting Input with the Scanner Class

Until Java 1.5, getting text input from the user in a console-based Java program wasn't easy. But with Java 1.5, a new class — called `Scanner` — was introduced to simplify the task of getting input from the user. In the following sections, you use the `Scanner` class to get simple input values from the user. The techniques that I present here are used in many of the programs shown in the rest of this book.

If you're using an older version of Java, you should still read this section, because many of the programs in this book use the Scanner class. However, you should also read the next section, "Getting Input with the JOptionPane Class," because that section describes a way of getting user input that works with earlier versions of Java.

Throughout the following sections, I refer to the program shown in Listing 2-3. This simple program uses the Scanner class to read an integer value from the user and then displays the value back to the console to verify that the program received the value entered by the user. Here's a sample of the console window for this program:

```
Enter an integer: 5
You entered 5.
```

The program begins by displaying the message Enter an integer: on the first line. Then it waits for you to enter a number. When you type a number and press the Enter key, it displays the confirmation message (You entered 5.) on the second line.

Listing 2-3:   A Program That Uses the Scanner Class

```
import java.util.Scanner;                                    →1

public class ScannerApp
{

    static Scanner sc = new Scanner(System.in);              →6

    public static void main(String[] args)
    {
        System.out.print("Enter an integer: ");             →10
        int x = sc.nextInt();                               →11
        System.out.println("You entered " + x + ".");       →12
    }

}
```

Importing the Scanner class

Before you can use the Scanner class in a program, you must import it. To do that, you code an import statement at the beginning of the program, before the class declaration, as shown in line 1 of Listing 2-3:

```
import java.util.Scanner;
```

Note that java and util aren't capitalized, but Scanner is.

If you're using other classes in the `java.util` package, you can import the entire package by coding the `import` statement like this:

```
import java.util.*;
```

Declaring and creating a Scanner object

Before you can use the `Scanner` class to read input from the console, you must declare a `Scanner` variable and create an instance of the `Scanner` class. I recommend that you create the `Scanner` variable as a class variable and create the `Scanner` object in the class variable initializer, as shown in line 6 of Listing 2-3:

```
static Scanner sc = new Scanner(System.in);
```

That way, you can use the `sc` variable in any method in the class.

To create a `Scanner` object, you use the `new` keyword followed by a call to the `Scanner` class constructor. Note that the `Scanner` class requires a parameter that indicates the *input stream* that the input comes from. You can use `System.in` here to specify standard keyboard console input.

Getting input

To read an input value from the user, you can use one of the methods of the `Scanner` class that are listed in Table 2-6. As you can see, the primitive data type has a separate method.

Table 2-6	Scanner Class Methods That Get Input Values
Method	*Explanation*
`boolean nextBoolean()`	Reads a `boolean` value from the user.
`byte nextByte()`	Reads a `byte` value from the user.
`double nextDouble()`	Reads a `double` value from the user.
`float nextFloat()`	Reads a `float` value from the user.
`int nextInt()`	Reads an `int` value from the user.
`String nextLine()`	Reads a `String` value from the user.
`long nextLong()`	Reads a `long` value from the user.
`short nextShort()`	Reads a `short` value from the user.

Notice in the first column of the table that each method listing begins with the type of the value that's returned by the method. The `nextInt` method, for example, returns an `int` value. Also, notice that each of the methods ends with an empty set of parentheses. That means that these methods don't require parameters. If a method does require parameters, the parameters are listed within these parentheses.

Because these methods read a value from the user and return the value, you most often use them in statements that assign the value to a variable. Line 11 in Listing 2-3, for example, reads an `int` and assigns it to a variable named `x`.

When the `nextInt` method is executed, the program waits for the user to enter a value in the console window. To let the user know what kind of input the program expects, usually you should call the `System.out.print` method before you call a `Scanner` method to get input. Line 10 in Listing 2-3 calls `System.out.print` to display the message `Enter an integer:` on the console. That way, the user knows that the program is waiting for input.

If the user enters a value that can't be converted to the correct type, the program *crashes*, which means that it terminates abruptly. As the program crashes, it displays a cryptic error message that indicates what caused the failure. If you enter `three` instead of an actual number, for example, the console window looks something like this:

```
Enter an integer: three Exception in thread "main" java.util.
    InputMismatchException
        at java.util.Scanner.throwFor(Scanner.java:819)
        at java.util.Scanner.next(Scanner.java:1431)
        at java.util.Scanner.nextInt(Scanner.java:2040)
        at java.util.Scanner.nextInt(Scanner.java:2000)
         at ScannerApp.main(ScannerApp.java:11)
```

This message indicates that an *exception* called `InputMismatchException` has occurred, which means that the program was expecting to see an integer but got something else instead. In Book II, Chapter 8, you find out how to provide for exceptions like these so that the program can display a friendlier message and give the user another shot at entering a correct value. Until then, you have to put up with the fact that if the user enters incorrect data, your program crashes ungracefully.

You can prevent the `nextInt` and similar methods from crashing with incorrect input data by first using one of the methods listed in Table 2-7 to test the next input to make sure it's valid. I haven't yet covered the Java statements you need to perform this test, but don't worry; in Book II, Chapter 8, I show you the solution.

Book II
Chapter 2

Working with
Variables and
Data Types

Table 2-7	Scanner Class Methods That Check for Valid Input Values
Method	*Explanation*
boolean hasNextBoolean()	Returns true if the next value entered by the user is a valid boolean value.
boolean hasNextByte()	Returns true if the next value entered by the user is a valid byte value.
boolean hasNextDouble()	Returns true if the next value entered by the user is a valid double value.
boolean hasNextFloat()	Returns true if the next value entered by the user is a valid float value.
boolean hasNextInt()	Returns true if the next value entered by the user is a valid int value.
boolean hasNextLong()	Returns true if the next value entered by the user is a valid long value.
boolean hasNextShort()	Returns true if the next value entered by the user is a valid short value.

Getting Input with the JOptionPane Class

If you're using a version of Java before Java 1.5, you don't have the luxury of using the Scanner class to read input directly from the user via a console window. You can use the JOptionPane class, however, to display simple dialog boxes such as the one shown in Figure 2-2 to get text input from the user. Then you can use the parse methods of the primitive-type wrapper classes to convert the text entered by the user to the appropriate primitive type.

Figure 2-2:
A dialog box
displayed
by the
JOptionPane
class.

Although the JOptionPane class has many methods, the only one you need to use to get simple text input is the showInputDialog method. This method uses a single parameter that specifies the prompting message that's displayed in the dialog box. It returns a string value that you can then parse to the proper type.

The JOptionPane class is a part of the javax.swing package, so you need to add an import javax.swing.JOptionPane statement to the beginning of any program that uses this class.

Listing 2-4 shows a simple program that uses the JOPtionPane class to get an integer value and display it on the console.

Listing 2-4:   A Program That Uses the JOptionPane Class to Get User Input

```
import javax.swing.JOptionPane;                            →1

public class DialogApp
{
    public static void main(String[] args)
    {
        String s;
        s = JOptionPane.showInputDialog                    →7
                ("Enter an integer:");                     →8
        int x = Integer.parseInt(s);                       →9
        System.out.println("You entered " + x + ".");      →10
    }
}
```

The following paragraphs describe the important lines in this program:

→ 1   This line imports the JOptionPane class.

→ 7-8   This statement displays an input dialog box with the prompt Enter an integer: and assigns the string entered by the user to the variable named s.

→ 9   This statement uses the parseInt method of the Integer class to convert the string entered by the user to an integer.

→ 10   This statement displays the integer value to confirm that the data entered by the user was converted properly to an integer.

This program terminates abruptly if the user enters anything other than an integer in the input dialog box. If the user enters ten, for example, the program terminates, and a cryptic message indicating that a NumberFormatException has occurred is displayed. In Book II, Chapter 8, you learn how to provide a more understandable message in this situation. Until then, just be careful to enter correct numbers when you use the JOptionPane class.

Using enum to Create Your Own Data Types

You will often find yourself using a String or int variable that you want to constrain to just a few different values. For example, suppose you're writing a program that plays a card game and you want a way to represent the suite of each card. You could do that with a String variable whose value should be Hearts, Spades, Clubs, or Diamonds. Or you might use an int and use the value 1 to represent Hearts, 2 for Spades, 3 for Clubs, or 4 for Diamonds. But such a scheme is error prone. What if you assign a value of 5 to the int variable?

A better way is to create an *enum*, which is basically a custom variable type which has a limited set of possible values. To define an enum, you use the enum keyword (usually modified by public) followed by a list of possible values enclosed in brackets:

```
public enum CardSuit {HEARTS, SPADES, CLUBS, DIAMONDS}
```

You can declare variables using the enum's name as the data type:

```
CardSuit suit;
```

Then, you can assign a value by using the enum name followed by a period and any of the enum values, as in this example:

```
suit = CardSuit.HEARTS;
```

Here's a complete program that defines an enum, creates a variable of the enum's type, assigns a value, and prints the result:

```
public class EnumTest
{
    public enum CardSuit {HEARTS, SPADES, CLUBS, DIAMONDS}

    public static void main(String[] args)
    {
        CardSuit suit;
        suit = CardSuit.HEARTS;
        System.out.println("The suit is " + suit);
    }
}
```

This program displays the following line on the console:

```
The suit is HEARTS
```

Chapter 3: Working with Numbers and Expressions

In This Chapter

✔ Dealing with operators, such as +, -, *, and /

✔ Creating finely crafted expressions

✔ Incrementing and decrementing

✔ Accepting an assignment

✔ Using the Math class

✔ Formatting your numbers

✔ Seeing strange things that can happen with numbers

In Book II, Chapter 2, you discover the various primitive numeric types that are supported by Java. In this chapter, you build on that knowledge by doing basic operations with numbers. Much of this chapter focuses on the complex topic of *expressions,* which combine numbers with operators to perform calculations. This chapter also covers performing advanced calculations using the Math class and techniques for formatting numbers when you display them. In addition, you find out why Java's math operations sometimes produce results you may not expect.

Working with Arithmetic Operators

An *operator* is a special symbol or keyword that's used to designate a mathematical operation or some other type of operation that can be performed on one or more values, called *operands.* In all, Java has about 40 operators. This chapter focuses on the operators that do arithmetic. These *arithmetic operators* — seven of them in all, summarized in Table 3-1 — perform basic arithmetic operations, such as addition, subtraction, multiplication, and division.

Table 3-1	Java's Arithmetic Operators
Operator	*Description*
+	Addition
-	Subtraction
*	Multiplication

(continued)

Table 3-1 *(continued)*

Operator	Description
/	Division
%	Remainder (Modulus)
++	Increment
--	Decrement

The following section of code can help clarify how these operators work for int types:

```
int a = 32, b = 5;
int c = a + b;      // c is 37
int d = a - b;      // d is 27
int e = a * b;      // e is 160
int f = a / b;      // f is 5 (32 / 5 is 6 remainder 2)
int g = a % b;      // g is 2  (32 / 5 is 6 remainder 2)
a++;                // a is now 33
b--;                // b is now 4
```

Notice that for division, the result is truncated. Thus 32 / 5 returns 6, not 6.4. For more information about integer division, see the section "Dividing Integers," later in this chapter.

Here's how the operators work for double values:

```
double x = 5.5, y = 2.0;
double m = x + y;      // m is 7.5
double n = x - y;      // n is 3.5
double o = x * y;      // o is 11.0
double p = x / y;      // p is 2.75
double q = x % y;      // q is 1.5
x++;                   // x is now 6.5
y--;                   // y is now 1.0
```

When you divide two int values, the result is an integer value, even if you assign it to a double variable. For example:

```
int a = 21, b = 6;
double answer = a / b;    // answer = 3.0
```

If that's not what you want, you can *cast* one of the operands to a double before performing the division. (*Casting an operand* means converting its value from one data type to another). Here's how:

```
int a = 21, b = 6;
double answer = (double)a / b;    // answer = 3.5
```

Categorizing operators by the number of operands

A common way to categorize Java's operators is to use the number of operands the operator works on. When the operators are categorized this way, you find three types:

✔ **Unary operators:** Operators that work on just one operand. Examples of unary operators are negation (`-x`, which returns the negative of `x`) and increment (`x++`, which adds 1 to `x`).

A unary operator can be a prefix operator or a postfix operator. A *prefix operator* is written before the operand, like this:

```
operator operand
```

A *postfix operator* is written after the operand, like this:

```
operand operator
```

✔ **Binary operators:** Operators that work on two operands. Examples of binary operators are addition (`x + y`), multiplication (`invoiceTotal * taxRate`), and comparison operators (`x < leftEdge`). In Java, all binary operators are *infix operators,* which means they appear between the operands, like this:

```
operand1 operator operand2
```

✔ **Ternary operators:** Operators that work on three operands. Java has only one ternary operator, called the *conditional operator* (`? :`). The conditional operator is also infix:

```
operand1 ? operand2 : operand3
```

The moral of the story is that if you want to divide `int` values and get an accurate `double` result, you must cast at least one of the `int` values to a `double`.

Here are a few additional things to think about tonight as you lie awake pondering the wonder of Java's arithmetic operators:

✦ In algebra, you can write a number right next to a variable to imply multiplication. In this case, *4x* means "four times *x*." Not so in Java. The following statement doesn't compile:

```
int x;
y = 4x;    // error, this line won't compile
```

✦ The remainder operator (`%`) is also called a *modulus* operator. It returns the remainder when the first operand is divided by the second operand. The remainder operator is often used to determine whether one number is evenly divisible by another, in which case the result is zero. For more information, see the next section, "Dividing Integers."

✦ All operators, including the arithmetic variety, are treated as separators in Java. As a result, any use of white space in an expression is optional. Thus the following two statements are equivalent:

```
a = ( (x + 4) * 7 ) / (y * x);
a=((x+4)*7)/(y*x);
```

Just remember that a little bit of white space never hurt anyone, and sometimes it helps make Java a little more readable.

Dividing Integers

When you divide one integer into another, the result is always another integer. Any remainder is simply discarded, and the answer is *not* rounded up. 5 / 4 gives the result 1, for example, and 3 / 4 gives the result 0. If you want to know that 5 / 4 is actually 1.25 or that 3 / 4 is actually 0.75, you need to use floats or doubles instead of integers.

If you need to know what the remainder is when you divide two integers, use the remainder operator (%). Suppose that you have a certain number of marbles to give away and a certain number of children to give them to. The program in Listing 3-1 lets you enter the number of marbles and the number of children. Then it calculates the number of marbles to give to each child and the number of marbles you have left over.

The remainder operator is also called the *modulus* operator.

Here's a sample of the console output for this program, where the number of marbles entered is 93 and the number of children is 5:

```
Welcome to the marble divvy-upper.
Number of marbles: 93
Number of children: 5
Give each child 18 marbles.
You will have 3 marbles left over.
```

Listing 3-1:   A Program That Divvies Up Marbles

```
import java.util.Scanner;                                          →1

public class MarblesApp
{
    static Scanner sc = new Scanner(System.in);                    →5

    public static void main(String[] args)
    {
        // declarations                                            →9
        int numberOfMarbles;
        int numberOfChildren;
        int marblesPerChild;
        int marblesLeftOver;

        // get the input data                                      →15
        System.out.println("Welcome to the marble divvy-upper.");
        System.out.print("Number of marbles: ");
        numberOfMarbles = sc.nextInt();
        System.out.print("Number of children: ");
        numberOfChildren = sc.nextInt();

        // calculate the results
        marblesPerChild = numberOfMarbles / numberOfChildren;      →23
        marblesLeftOver = numberOfMarbles % numberOfChildren;      →24
```

```
                                                              →26
    // print the results
    System.out.println("Give each child " +
        marblesPerChild + " marbles.");
    System.out.println("You will have " +
        marblesLeftOver + " marbles left over.");
    }

}
```

The following paragraphs describe the key lines in this program:

→ 1	Imports the `java.util.Scanner` class so that the program can use it to get input from the user.
→ 5	Creates the `Scanner` object and assigns it to a class variable so that it can be used in any method in the class.
→ 9-13	Declare the local variables used by the program.
→15-20	Get the input from the user.
→ 23	Calculates the number of marbles to give to each child by using integer division, which discards the remainder.
→ 24	Calculates the number of marbles left over.
→ 26-31	Print the results.

It's probably obvious if you think about it, but you should realize that if you use integer division to divide a by b, the result times b plus the remainder equals a. In other words:

```
int a = 29;          // any value will do
int b = 3;           // any value will do
int c = a / b;
int d = a % b;
int e = (c * b) + d;  // e will always equal a
```

Combining Operators

You can combine operators to form complicated expressions. When you do, the order in which the operations are carried out is determined by the *precedence* of each operator in the expression. The order of precedence for the arithmetic operators is

✦ Increment (++) and decrement (--) operators are evaluated first.

✦ Next, sign operators (+ or -) are applied.

✦ Then multiplication (*), division (/), and remainder (%) operators are evaluated.

✦ Finally, addition (+) and subtraction (-) operators are applied.

Book II
Chapter 3

Working with
Numbers and
Expressions

In the expression a + b * c, for example, multiplication has a higher precedence than addition. Thus b is multiplied by c first. Then the result of that multiplication is added to a.

If an expression includes two or more operators at the same order of precedence, the operators are evaluated left to right. Thus, in the expression a * b / c, a is multiplied by b and then the result is divided by c.

If you want, you can use parentheses to change the order in which operations are performed. Operations within parentheses are always performed before operations that aren't in parentheses. Thus, in the expression (a + b) * c, a is added to b first. Then the result is multiplied by c.

If an expression has two or more sets of parentheses, the operations in the innermost set are performed first. In the expression (a * (b + c)) / d, b is added to c. Then the result is multiplied by a. Finally, that result is divided by d.

Apart from the increment and decrement operators, these precedence rules and the use of parentheses are the same as they are for basic algebra. So if you were paying attention in the eighth grade, precedence should make sense.

With double or float values, changing the left to right order for operators with the same precedence doesn't affect the result. With integer types, however, it can make a huge difference if division is involved. Consider these statements:

```
int a = 5, b = 6, c = 7;
int d1 = a * b / c;    // d1 is 4
int d2 = a * (b / c);  // d2 is 0
```

This difference occurs because integer division always returns an integer result, which is a truncated version of the actual result. Thus, in the first expression, a is first multiplied by b, giving a result of 30. Then this result is divided by c. Truncating the answer gives a result of 4. But in the second expression, b is first divided by c, which gives a truncated result of 0. Then this result is multiplied by a, giving a final answer of 0.

Using the Unary Plus and Minus Operators

The unary plus and minus operators let you change the sign of an operand. Note that the actual operator used for these operations is the same as the binary addition and subtraction operators. The compiler figures out whether you mean to use the binary or the unary version of these operators by examining the expression.

The unary minus operator doesn't necessarily make an operand have a negative value. Instead, it changes whatever sign the operand has to start with. Thus, if the operand starts with a positive value, the unary minus operator changes it to negative. But if the operand starts with a negative value, the unary minus operator makes it positive. The following examples illustrate this point:

```
int a = 5;     // a is 5
int b = -a;    // b is -5
int c = -b;    // c is +5
```

Interestingly enough, the unary plus operator doesn't actually do anything. For example:

```
int a = -5;    // a is -5
int b = +a;    // b is -5
a = 5;         // a is now 5
int c = +a;    // c is 5
```

Notice that if a starts out positive, +a is also positive. But if a starts out negative, +a is still negative. Thus the unary plus operator has no effect. I guess Java provides the unary plus operator out of a need for balance.

You can also use these operators with more complex expressions, like this:

```
int a = 3, b = 4, c = 5;
int d = a * -(b + c);    // d is -27
```

Here, b is added to c, giving a result of 9. Then the unary minus operator is applied, giving a result of -9. Finally, -9 is multiplied by a, giving a result of -27.

Using Increment and Decrement Operators

One of the most common operations in computer programming is adding or subtracting 1 from a variable. Adding 1 to a variable is called *incrementing* the variable. Subtracting 1 is called *decrementing*. The traditional way to increment a variable is this:

```
a = a + 1;
```

Here the expression a + 1 is calculated, and the result is assigned to the variable a.

Java provides an easier way to do this type of calculation: the increment (++) and decrement (--) operators. These unary operators apply to a single variable. Thus, to increment the variable a, you can code just this:

```
a++;
```

Note that an expression that uses an increment or decrement operator is a statement by itself. That's because the increment or decrement operator is also a type of assignment operator, as it changes the value of the variable it applies to.

You can use the increment and decrement operators only on variables — not on numeric literals or other expressions. Java doesn't allow the following expressions, for example:

```
a = b * 5++;      // can't increment the number 5
a = (b * 5)++;    // can't increment the expression (b * 5)
```

Note that you can use an increment or decrement operator in an assignment statement. Here's an example:

```
int a = 5;
int b = a--;      // both a and b are set to 4
```

When the second statement is executed, the expression a-- is evaluated first, so a is set to 4. Then the new value of a is assigned to b. Thus both a and b are set to 4.

The increment and decrement operators are unusual because they are unary operators that can be placed either before *(prefix)* or after *(postfix)* the variable they apply to. Whether you place the operator before or after the variable can have a major effect on how an expression is evaluated. If you place an increment or decrement operator before its variable, the operator is applied before the rest of the expression is evaluated. As a result, the incremented value of the variable is used in the expression. By contrast, if you place the operator after the variable, the operator is applied after the expression is evaluated. Thus the original value of the variable is used in the expression.

Confused yet? A simple example can clear things up. First, consider these statements with an expression that uses a postfix increment:

```
int a = 5;
int b = 3;
int c = a * b++;    // c is set to 15
```

When the expression in the third statement is evaluated, the original value of b — 3 — is used in the multiplication. Thus c is set to 15. Then b is incremented to 4.

Now consider this version, with a prefix increment:

```
int a = 5;
int b = 3;
int c = a * ++b;    // c is set to 20
```

This time, b is incremented before the multiplication is performed, so c is set to 20. Either way, b ends up set to 4.

Similarly, consider this example:

```
int a = 5;
int b = --a;    // b is set to 5, a is set to 4.
```

This example is similar to an earlier example, but this time the prefix increment operator is used. When the second statement is executed, the value of a is assigned to b. Then a is decremented. As a result, b is set to 5, and a is set to 4.

Because the increment and decrement operators can be confusing when used with other operators in an expression, I suggest that you use them alone. Whenever you're tempted to incorporate an increment or decrement operator into a larger expression, pull the increment or decrement out of the expression, and make it a separate statement either before or after the expression. In other words, code

```
b++;
c = a * b;
```

instead of

```
c = a * ++b;
```

In the first version, it's crystal-clear that b is incremented before the multiplication is done.

Using the Assignment Operator

The standard assignment operator (=) is used to assign the result of an expression to a variable. In its simplest form, you code it like this:

```
variable = expression;
```

Here's an example:

```
int a = (b * c) / 4;
```

You've already seen plenty of examples of assignment statements like this one, so I won't belabor this point any further. I do want to point out — just for the record — that you *cannot* code an arithmetic expression on the left side of an equal sign. Thus the following statement doesn't compile:

```
int a;
a + 3 = (b * c);
```

In the rest of this section, I point out some unusual ways in which you can use the assignment operator. I don't recommend that you actually use any of these techniques, as they're rarely necessary and almost always confusing, but knowing about them can shed light on how Java expressions work and sometimes can help you find sneaky problems in your code.

The key to understanding the rest of this section is realizing that in Java, assignments are expressions, not statements. In other words, a = 5 is an assignment expression, not an assignment statement. It becomes an assignment statement only when you add a semicolon to the end.

The result of an assignment expression is the value that's assigned to the variable. The result of the expression a = 5, for example, is 5. Likewise, the result of the expression a = (b + c) * d is the result of the expression (b + c) * d.

The implication is that you can use assignment expressions in the middle of other expressions. The following example is legal:

```
int a;
int b;
a = (b = 3) * 2;    // a is 6, b is 3
```

As in any expression, the part of the expression inside the parentheses is evaluated first. Thus, b is assigned the value 3. Then the multiplication is performed, and the result (6) is assigned to the variable a.

Now consider a more complicated case:

```
int a;
int b = 2;
a = (b = 3) * b;    // a is 9, b is 3
```

What's happening here is that the expression in the parentheses is evaluated first, which means that b is set to 3 before the multiplication is performed.

The parentheses are important in the previous example because without parentheses, the assignment operator is the last operator to be evaluated in Java's order of precedence. Consider one more example:

```
int a;
int b = 2;
a = b = 3 * b;    // a is 6, b is 6
```

This time, the multiplication 3 * b is performed first, giving a result of 6. Then this result is assigned to b. Finally, the result of that assignment expression (6) is assigned to a.

Incidentally, the following expression is also legal:

```
a = b = c = 3;
```

This expression assigns the value 3 to all three variables. Although this code seems pretty harmless, you're better off just writing three assignment statements. (You might guess that clumping the assignments together is more efficient than writing them on three lines, but you'd be wrong. These three assignments require the same number of bytecode instructions either way.)

Using Compound Assignment Operators

A *compound assignment operator* is an operator that performs a calculation and an assignment at the same time. All of Java's binary arithmetic operators (that is, the ones that work on two operands) have equivalent compound assignment operators, which Table 3-2 lists.

Table 3-2	Compound Arithmetic Operators
Operator	*Description*
+=	Addition and assignment
-=	Subtraction and assignment
*=	Multiplication and assignment
/=	Division and assignment
%=	Remainder and assignment

The statement

```
a += 10;
```

is equivalent to

```
a = a + 10;
```

Also, the statement

```
z *=2;
```

is equivalent to

```
z = z * 2;
```

To prevent confusion, use compound assignment expressions by themselves, not in combination with other expressions. Consider these statements:

```
int a = 2;
int b = 3;
a *= b + 1;
```

Is a set to 7 or 8?

In other words, is the third statement equivalent to

```
a = a * b + 1;      // This would give 7 as the result
```

or

```
a = a * (b + 1);    // This would give 8 as the result
```

At first glance, you might expect the answer to be 7, because multiplication has a higher precedence than addition. But assignment has the lowest precedence of all, and the multiplication here is performed as part of the assignment. As a result, the addition is performed before the multiplication — and the answer is 8. (Gotcha!)

Using the Math Class

Java's built-in operators are useful, but they don't come anywhere near providing all the mathematical needs of most Java programmers. That's where the Math class comes in. It includes a bevy of built-in methods that perform a wide variety of mathematical calculations, from basic functions such as calculating an absolute value or a square root to trigonometry functions such as sin and cos (sine and cosine), to practical functions such as rounding numbers or generating random numbers.

I was going to make a joke here about how you'd have to take a math class to fully appreciate the Math class; or how you'd better stay away from the Math class if you didn't do so well in math class; or how if you're on the football team, maybe you can get someone to do the Math class for you. But these jokes seemed too easy, so I decided not to make them.

All the methods of the Math class are declared as static methods, which means you can use them by specifying the class name Math followed by a period and a method name. Here's a statement that calculates the square root of a number stored in a variable named y:

```
double x = Math.sqrt(y);
```

The Math class is contained in the java.lang package, which is automatically available to all Java programs. As a result, you don't have to provide an import statement to use the Math class.

The following sections describe the most useful methods of the Math class.

Using constants of the Math class

The `Math` class defines two constants that are useful for many mathematical calculations. Table 3-3 lists these constants.

Table 3-3	Constants of the Math Class	
Constant	*What It Is*	*Value*
PI	The constant pi (π), the ratio of a circle's radius and diameter	3.141592653589793
E	The base of natural logarithms	2.718281828459045

Note that these constants are only approximate values, because both π and *e* are irrational numbers.

The program shown in Listing 3-2 illustrates a typical use of the constant PI. Here, the user is asked to enter the radius of a circle. Then the program calculates the area of the circle in line 13. (The parentheses aren't really required in the expression in this statement, but they help clarify that the expression is the Java equivalent to the formula for the area of a circle, πr^2.)

Here's the console output for a typical execution of this program, in which the user entered 5 as the radius of the circle:

```
Welcome to the circle area calculator.
Enter the radius of your circle: 5
The area is 78.53981633974483
```

Listing 3-2: The Circle Area Calculator

```java
import java.util.Scanner;

public class CircleAreaApp
{
    static Scanner sc = new Scanner(System.in);

    public static void main(String[] args)
    {
        System.out.println(
            "Welcome to the circle area calculator.");
        System.out.print("Enter the radius of your circle: ");
        double r = sc.nextDouble();
        double area = Math.PI * (r * r);          →13
        System.out.println("The area is " + area);
    }
}
```

Working with mathematical functions

Table 3-4 lists the basic mathematical functions that are provided by the Math class. As you can see, you can use these functions to calculate such things as the absolute value of a number, the minimum and maximum of two values, square roots, powers, and logarithms.

Table 3-4	Mathematical Functions Provided by the Math Class
Method	*Explanation*
abs(argument)	Returns the absolute value of the argument. The argument can be an int, long, float, or double. The return value is the same type as the argument.
cbrt(argument)	Returns the cube root of the argument. The argument and return value are doubles.
exp(argument)	Returns *e* raised to the power of the argument. The argument and the return value are doubles.
hypot(arg1, arg2)	Returns the hypotenuse of a right triangle calculated according to the Pythagorean theorem — $\sqrt{x^2 + y^2}$. The argument and the return values are doubles.
log(argument)	Returns the natural logarithm (base *e*) of the argument. The argument and the return value are doubles.
log10(argument)	Returns the base 10 logarithm of the argument. The argument and the return value are doubles.
max(arg1, arg2)	Returns the larger of the two arguments. The arguments can be int, long, float, or double, but both must be of the same type. The return type is the same type as the arguments.
min(arg1, arg2)	Returns the smaller of the two arguments. The arguments can be int, long, float, or double, but both must be of the same type. The return type is the same type as the arguments.
pow(arg1, arg2)	Returns the value of the first argument raised to the power of the second argument. Both arguments and the return value are doubles.
random()	Returns a random number that's greater than or equal to 0.0 but less than 1.0. This method doesn't accept an argument, but the return value is a double.

Method	Explanation
`signum(argument)`	Returns a number that represents the sign of the argument: –1.0 if the argument is negative, 0.0 if the argument is zero, and 1.0 if the argument is positive. The argument can be a `double` or a `float`. The return value is the same type as the argument.
`sqrt(argument)`	Returns the square root of the argument. The argument and return value are `doubles`.

Book II
Chapter 3

The program shown in Listing 3-3 demonstrates each of these methods except `random`. When run, it produces output similar to this:

```
abs(b)      = 50
cbrt(x)     = 2.924017738212866
exp(y)      = 54.598150033144236
hypot(y,z)  = 5.0
log(y)      = 1.0986122886681096
log10(y)    = 0.47712125471966244
max(a, b)   = 100
min(a, b)   = -50
pow(a, c)   = 1000000.0
random()    = 0.8536014557793756
signum(b)   = -1.0
sqrt(x)     = 1.7320508075688772
```

Working with
Numbers and
Expressions

You can use this output to get an idea of the values returned by these Math class methods. You can see, for example, that the expression `Math.sqrt(y)` returns a value of `5.0` when `y` is `25.0`.

The following paragraphs point out a few interesting tidbits concerning these methods:

✦ You can use the `abs` and `signnum` methods to force the sign of one variable to match the sign of another, like this:

```
int a = 27;
int b = -32;
a = Math.abs(a) * Math.signum(b);   // a is now -27;
```

✦ You can use the `pow` method to square a number, like this:

```
double x = 4.0;
double y = Math.pow(x, 2);   // a is now 16;
```

Simply multiplying the number by itself, however, is often just as easy and just as readable:

```
double x = 4.0;
double y = x * x;   // a is now 16;
```

✦ In the classic movie *The Wizard of Oz,* when the Wizard finally grants the Scarecrow his brains, the Scarecrow suddenly becomes intelligent and quotes the Pythagorean theorem, which is (coincidentally) used by the `hypot` method of the `Math` class. Unfortunately, he quotes it wrong. What the Scarecrow actually says in the movie is this: "The sum of the square root of any two sides of an isosceles triangle is equal to the square root of the remaining side." Silly Scarecrow. What he should have said, of course, is "The square of the hypotenuse of any right triangle is equal to the sum of the squares of the other two sides."

✦ Every time you run the program in Listing 3-3, you get a different result for the `random` method call. The `random` method is interesting enough that I describe it separately in the next section, "Creating random numbers."

Listing 3-3: A Program That Uses the Mathematical Methods of the Math Class

```
public class MathFunctionsApp
{
    public static void main(String[] args)
    {
        int a = 100;
        int b = -50;
        int c = 3;
        double x = 25.0;
        double y = 3.0;
        double z = 4.0;

        System.out.println("abs(b)      = " + Math.abs(b));
        System.out.println("cbrt(x)     = " + Math.cbrt(x));
        System.out.println("exp(y)      = " + Math.exp(z));
        System.out.println("hypot(y,z)= " + Math.hypot(y,z));
        System.out.println("log(y)      = " + Math.log(y));
        System.out.println("log10(y)   = " + Math.log10(y));
        System.out.println("max(a, b)  = " + Math.max(a, b));
        System.out.println("min(a, b)  = " + Math.min(a, b));
        System.out.println("pow(a, c)  = " + Math.pow(a, c));
        System.out.println("random()   = " + Math.random());
        System.out.println("signum(b)  = " + Math.signum(b));
        System.out.println("sqrt(x)     = " + Math.sqrt(y));
    }
}
```

Creating random numbers

Sooner or later, you're going to want to write programs that play simple games. Almost all games have some element of chance built into them, so you need a way to create computer programs that don't work exactly the same every time you run them. The easiest way to do that is to use the `random` method of the `Math` class, which Table 3-4 lists later in this section, along with the other basic mathematical functions of the `Math` class.

The `random` method returns a `double` whose value is greater than or equal to 0.0 but less than 1.0. Within this range, the value returned by the `random` method is different every time you call it and is essentially random.

Strictly speaking, computers are not capable of generating *truly* random numbers, but over the years, clever computer scientists have developed ways to generate numbers that are random for all practical purposes. These numbers are called *pseudorandom numbers* because although they aren't completely random, they look random to most human beings.

Java has many methods and classes for generating random numbers. The `java.util.Random` class, for example, provides about ten specialized methods that generate random values. To generate a `double` with a value between 0.0 and 1.0, you can execute `new Random().nextDouble()`. In addition, the `java.security.SecureRandom` class provides random values for encrypting sensitive documents. And if size matters to you, the `java.math.BigInteger` class allows you to generate arbitrarily large random numbers (numbers with 1,000 digits, if that's what you need).

Book II
Chapter 3

Working with Numbers and Expressions

The `random` method generates a random `double` value between 0.0 (inclusive, meaning that it could be 0.0) and 1.0 (exclusive, meaning that it can't be 1.0). Most computer applications that need random values, however, need random integers between some arbitrary low value (usually 1, but not always) and some arbitrary high value. A program that plays dice needs random numbers between 1 and 6, whereas a program that deals cards needs random numbers between 1 and 52 (53 if jokers are used).

As a result, you need a Java expression that converts the `double` value returned by the `random` function to an `int` value within the range your program calls for. The following code shows how to do this, with the values set to `1` and `6` for a dice-playing game:

```
int low = 1;      // the lowest value in the range
int high = 6;     // the highest value in the range
int rnd = (int)(Math.random() * (high - low + 1)) + low;
```

This expression is a little complicated, so I show you how it's evaluated step by step:

1. The `Math.Random` method is called to get a random double value. This value is greater than 0.0 but less than 5.0.

2. The random value is multiplied by the high end of the range minus the low end, plus 1. In this example, the high end is 6 and the low end is 1, so you now have a random number that's greater than or equal to 0.0 but less than 6.0. (It could be 5.99999999999999, but it never is 6.0.)

3. This value is converted to an integer by the `(int)` cast. Now you have an integer that's 0, 1, 2, 3, 4, or 5. (Remember that when you cast a double to an `int`, any fractional part of the value is simply discarded. Because the number is less than 6.0, it never truncates to 6.0 when it is cast to an `int`.)

4. The `low` value in the range is added to the random number. Assuming that `low` is 1, the random number is now 1, 2, 3, 4, 5, or 6. That's just what you want: a random number between 1 and 6.

To give you an idea of how this random-number calculation works, Listing 3-4 shows a program that places this calculation in a method called `randomInt` and then calls it to simulate 100 dice rolls. The `randomInt` method accepts two parameters representing the low and high ends of the range, and it returns a random integer within the range. In the `main` method of this program, the `randomInt` method is called 100 times, and each random number is printed by a call to `System.out.print`.

The console output for this program looks something like this:

```
Here are 100 random rolls of the dice:
4 1 1 6 1 2 6 6 6 6 5 5 5 4 5 4 4 1 3 6 1 3 1 4 4 3 3 3 5 6 5 6 6 3 5 2 2 6 3 3
4 1 2 2 4 2 2 4 1 4 3 6 5 5 4 4 2 4 1 3 5 2 1 3 3 5 4 1 6 3 1 6 5 2 6 6 3 5 4 5
2 5 4 5 3 1 4 2 5 2 1 4 4 4 6 6 4 6 3 3
```

Every time you run this program, however, you see a different sequence of 100 numbers.

The program in Listing 3-4 uses several Java features that you haven't seen yet.

Listing 3-4:   Rolling the Dice

```java
public class DiceApp
{
    public static void main(String[] args)
    {
        int roll;
        String msg = "Here are 100 random rolls of the dice:";
        System.out.println(msg);
        for (int i=0; i<100; i++)                              →8
        {
            roll = randomInt(1, 6);                            →10
            System.out.print(roll + " ");                      →11
        }
        System.out.println();
    }

    public static int randomInt(int low, int high)            →16
    {
        int result = (int)(Math.random()                      →18
            * (high - low + 1)) + low;
        return result;                                         →20
    }

}
```

The following paragraphs explain how the program works, but don't worry if you don't get all the elements in this program. The main thing to see is the expression that converts the random `double` value returned by the `Math.double` method to an integer.

→ 8   The for statement causes the statements in its body (lines 10 and 11) to be executed 100 times. Don't worry about how this statement works for now; you find out about it in Book II, Chapter 5.

→ 10   This statement calls the randomInt method, specifying 1 and 6 as the range for the random integer to generate. The resulting random number is assigned to the roll variable.

→ 11   The System.out.print method is used to print the random number followed by a space. Because this statement calls the print method rather than the println method, the random numbers are printed on the same line rather than on separate lines.

→ 16   The declaration for the randomInt method indicates that the method returns an int value and accepts two int arguments: one named low and the other named high.

→ 18   This expression converts the random double value to an integer between low and high.

→ 20   The return statement sends the random number back to the statement that called the randomInt method.

Rounding functions

The Math class has four methods that round or truncate float or double values. Table 3-5 lists these methods. As you can see, each of these methods uses a different technique to calculate an integer value that's near the double or float value passed as an argument. Note that even though all four of these methods round a floating-point value to an integer value, only the round method actually returns an integer type (int or long, depending on whether the argument is a float or a double). The other methods return doubles that happen to be integer values.

Table 3-5	Rounding Functions Provided by the Math Class
Method	*Explanation*
ceil(argument)	Returns the smallest double value that is an integer and is greater than or equal to the value of the argument.
floor(argument)	Returns the largest double value that is an integer and is less than or equal to the value of the argument.
rint(argument)	Returns the double value that is an integer and is closest to the value of the argument. If two integer values are equally close, it returns the one that is even. If the argument is already an integer, it returns the argument value.
round(argument)	Returns the integer that is closest to the argument. If the argument is a double, it returns a long. If the argument is a float, it returns an int.

Listing 3-5 shows a program that uses each of the four methods to round three `double` values: `29.4`, `93.5`, and `-19.3`. Here's the output from this program:

```
round(x) = 29
round(y) = 94
round(z) = -19

ceil(x) = 30.0
ceil(y) = 94.0
ceil(z) = -19.0

floor(x) = 29.0
floor(y) = 93.0
floor(z) = -20.0

rint(x) = 29.0
rint(y) = 94.0
rint(z) = -19.0
```

Note that each of the four methods produces a different result for at least one of the values:

✦ All the methods except `ceil` return `29.0` (or `29`) for the value `29.4`. `ceil` returns `30.0`, which is the smallest integer that's greater than `29.4`.

✦ All the methods except `floor` return `94.0` (or `94`) for the value `93.5`. `floor` returns `93.0` because that's the largest integer that's less than `93.99`. `rint` returns `94.0` because it's an even number, and `93.5` is midway between `93.0` and `94.0`.

✦ All the methods except `floor` return `-19.0` (or `-19`) for `-19.3`. `floor` returns `-20` because –20 is the largest integer that's less than –19.3.

Listing 3-5: Program That Uses the Rounding Methods of the Math Class

```
public class RoundingApp
{
    public static void main(String[] args)
    {
        double x = 29.4;
        double y = 93.5;
        double z = -19.3;

        System.out.println("round(x) = " + Math.round(x));
        System.out.println("round(y) = " + Math.round(y));
        System.out.println("round(z) = " + Math.round(z));
        System.out.println();
        System.out.println("ceil(x) = " + Math.ceil(x));
        System.out.println("ceil(y) = " + Math.ceil(y));
        System.out.println("ceil(z) = " + Math.ceil(z));
```

```
System.out.println();
System.out.println("floor(x) = " + Math.floor(x));
System.out.println("floor(y) = " + Math.floor(y));
System.out.println("floor(z) = " + Math.floor(z));
System.out.println();
System.out.println("rint(x) = " + Math.rint(x));
System.out.println("rint(y) = " + Math.rint(y));
System.out.println("rint(z) = " + Math.rint(z));
    }
}
```

Formatting Numbers

Most of the programs you've seen so far have used the `System.out.println` or `System.out.print` method to print the values of variables that contain numbers. When you pass a numeric variable to one of these methods, the variable's value is converted to a string before it's printed. The exact format used to represent the value isn't very pretty: Large values are printed without any commas, and all the decimal digits for `double` or `float` values are printed whether you want them to be or not.

In many cases, you want to format your numbers before you print them — to add commas to large values and limit the number of decimal places printed, for example. Or, if a number represents a monetary amount, you may want to add a dollar sign (or whatever currency symbol is appropriate for your locale). To do that, you can use the `NumberFormat` class. Table 3-6 lists the `NumberFormat` class methods.

Table 3-6	Methods of the NumberFormat Class
Method	*Explanation*
`getCurrencyInstance()`	A static method that returns a `NumberFormat` object that formats currency values
`getPercentInstance()`	A static method that returns a `NumberFormat` object that formats percentages
`getNumberInstance()`	A static method that returns a `NumberFormat` object that formats basic numbers
`format(number)`	Returns a string that contains the formatted number
`setMinimumFraction Digits(int)`	Sets the minimum number of digits to display to the right of the decimal point
`setMaximumFraction Digits(int)`	Sets the maximum number of digits to display to the right of the decimal point

Like many aspects of Java, the procedure for using the `NumberFormat` class is a little awkward. It's designed to be efficient for applications that need to format a lot of numbers, but it's overkill for most applications.

The procedure for using the `NumberFormat` class to format numbers takes a little getting used to. First, you must call one of the static get*Xxx*Instance methods to create a `NumberFormat` object that can format numbers in a particular way. Then, if you want, you can call the `setMinimumFractionDigits` or `setMaximumFractionDigits` method to set the number of decimal digits to be displayed. Finally, you call that object's `format` method to actually format a number.

Note that the `NumberFormat` class is in the `java.text` package, so you must include the following `import` statement at the beginning of any class that uses `NumberFormat`:

```
import java.text.NumberFormat;
```

Here's an example that uses the `NumberFormat` class to format a `double` value as currency:

```
double salesTax = 2.425;
NumberFormat cf = NumberFormat.getCurrencyInstance();
System.out.println(cf.format(salesTax));
```

When you run this code, the following line is printed to the console:

```
$2.43
```

Note that the currency format rounds the value from `2.425` to `2.43`.

Here's an example that formats a number by using the general number format, with exactly three decimal places:

```
double x = 19923.3288;
NumberFormat nf = NumberFormat.getNumberInstance();
nf.setMinimumFractionDigits(3);
nf.setMaximumFractionDigits(3);
System.out.println(nf.format(x));
```

When you run this code, the following line is printed:

```
19,923.329
```

Here the number is formatted with a comma and the value is rounded to three places.

Here's an example that uses the percentage format:

```
double grade = .92;
NumberFormat pf = NumberFormat.getPercentInstance();
System.out.println(pf.format(grade));
```

When you run this code, the following line is printed:

```
92%
```

TIP

If your program formats several numbers, consider creating the `NumberFormat` object as a class variable. That way, the `NumberFormat` object is created when the program starts. Then you can use the `NumberFormat` object from any method in the program's class. Listing 3-6 is a simple example that shows how this process works. When this program is run, the following output is produced:

```
My allowance: $5.00
Cost of Paint Ball Gun: $69.95
```

Here the `cf` variable is created as a class variable. Then both the `print MyAllowance` and `printCostOfPaintBallGun` methods can use it in lines 19 and 27.

Listing 3-6:   A Program That Uses a NumberFormat Class Variable

```java
import java.text.NumberFormat;

public class NumberFormatClassApp
{

    static NumberFormat cf =                              →6
        NumberFormat.getCurrencyInstance();

    public static void main(String[] args)
    {
        printMyAllowance();
        printCostOfPaintBallGun();
    }

    public static void printMyAllowance()
    {
        double myAllowance = 5.00;
        cf = NumberFormat.getCurrencyInstance();
        System.out.println("My allowance: "              →19
            + cf.format(myAllowance));
    }

    public static void printCostOfPaintBallGun()
    {
        double costOfPaintBallGun = 69.95;
        cf = NumberFormat.getCurrencyInstance();
        System.out.println("Cost of Paint Ball Gun: "    →27
            + cf.format(costOfPaintBallGun));
    }
}
```

Recognizing Weird Things about Java Math

Believe it or not, computers — even the most powerful ones — have certain limitations when it comes to performing math calculations. These limitations are usually insignificant, but sometimes they sneak up and bite you. The following sections describe the things you need to watch out for when doing math in Java.

Integer overflow

The basic problem with integer types is that they have a fixed size. As a result, there is a limit to the size of the numbers that can be stored in variables of type short, int, or long. Although long variables can hold numbers that are huge, sooner or later you come across a number that's too big to fit in even a long variable.

Okay, consider this (admittedly contrived) example:

```
int a = 1000000000;
System.out.println(a);
a += 1000000000;
System.out.println(a);
a += 1000000000;
System.out.println(a);
a += 1000000000;
System.out.println(a);
```

Here you expect the value of a to get bigger after each addition. But here's the output that's displayed:

```
1000000000
2000000000
-1294967296
-294967296
```

The first addition seems to work, but after that, the number becomes negative! That's because the value has reached the size limit of the int data type. Unfortunately, Java doesn't tell you that this error has happened. It simply crams the int variable as full of bits as it can, discards whatever bits don't fit, and hopes that you don't notice. Because of the way int stores negative values, large positive values suddenly become large negative values.

The moral of the story is that if you're working with large integers, you should use long rather than int, because long can store much larger numbers than int. If your programs deal with numbers large enough to be a problem for long, consider using floating-point types instead. As you see in the next section, floating-point types can handle even larger values than long, and they let you know when you exceed their capacity.

Floating-point weirdness

Floating-point numbers have problems of their own. For starters, floating-point numbers are stored using the binary number system (base 2), but humans work with numbers in the decimal number system (base 10). Unfortunately, accurately converting numbers between these two systems is sometimes impossible. That's because in any number base, certain fractions can't be represented exactly. One example: Base 10 has no way to exactly represent the fraction 1/3. You can approximate it as 0.3333333, but eventually you reach the limit of how many digits you can store, so you have to stop. In base 2, it happens that one of the fractions you can't accurately represent is the decimal value 1/10. In other words, a `float` or `double` variable can't accurately represent `0.1`.

Don't believe me? Try running this code:

```
float x = 0.1f;
NumberFormat nf = NumberFormat.getNumberInstance();
nf.setMinimumFractionDigits(10);
System.out.println(nf.format(x));
```

The resulting output is this:

```
0.1000000015
```

Although `0.1000000015` is *close* to `0.1`, it isn't exact.

In most cases, Java's floating-point math is close enough not to matter. The margin of error is extremely small. If you're using Java to measure the size of your house, you'd need an electron microscope to notice the error. If you're writing applications that deal with financial transactions, however, normal rounding can sometimes magnify the errors to make them significant. You may charge a penny too much or too little sales tax. And in extreme cases, your invoices may actually have obvious addition errors.

I have much more to say about floating-point numbers in Book V, Chapter 6. For now, just realize that you can't use `float` or `double` to represent money unless you don't care whether your books are in balance.

Integer types are stored in binary too, of course. But integers aren't subject to the same errors that floating-point types are — because integers don't represent fractions at all — so you don't have to worry about this type of error for `integer` types.

Division by zero

According to the basic rules of mathematics, you can't divide a number by zero. The reason is simple: Division is the inverse of multiplication — which means that if `a * b = c`, it is also true that `a = c / b`. If you were to allow b to be zero, division would be meaningless, because any number times zero is zero. Therefore, both a and c would also have to be zero. In short, mathematicians solved this dilemma centuries ago by saying that division by zero is simply not allowed.

So what happens if you *do* attempt to divide a number by zero in a Java program? The answer depends on whether you're dividing integers or floating-point numbers. If you're dividing integers, the statement that attempts the division by zero chokes up what is called an *exception,* which is an impolite way of crashing the program. In Book II, Chapter 8, you find out how to intercept this exception to allow your program to continue. In the meantime, any program you write that attempts an integer division by zero crashes.

If you try to divide a floating-point type by zero, the results are not so abrupt. Instead, Java assigns to the floating-point result one of the special values listed in Table 3-7. The following paragraphs explain how these special values are determined:

+ If you divide a number by zero, and the sign of both numbers is the same, the result is positive infinity. 0.0 divided by 0.0 is positive infinity, as is -34.0 divided by -0.0.

+ If you divide a number by zero, and the signs of the numbers are different, the result is negative infinity. -40.0 divided by 0.0 is negative infinity, as is 34.0 divided by 0.0.

+ If you divide zero by zero, the result is not a number (NaN), regardless of the signs.

Floating-point zeros can be positive or negative. Java considers positive and negative zeros to be equal numerically.

If you attempt to print a floating-point value that has one of these special values, Java converts the value to an appropriate string. Suppose that you execute the following statements:

```
double i = 50.0;
double j = 0.0;
double k = i / j;
System.out.println(k);
```

The resulting console output is

```
Infinity
```

If i were -50.0, the console would display -Infinity, and if i were zero, the console would display NaN.

Table 3-7	Special Constants of the float and double Classes
Constant	*Meaning*
POSITIVE_INFINITY	Positive infinity
NEGATIVE_INFINITY	Negative infinity
NaN	Not a number

The following paragraphs describe some final bits of weirdness I want to sneak in before closing this chapter:

✦ NaN is not equal to itself, which can have some strange consequences. For example:

```
double x = Math.sqrt(-50);    // Not a number
double y = x;
if (x == y)
    System.out.println("x equals y");
```

Okay, I know that I jumped the gun here on the if statement, because I don't cover if statements until Book II, Chapter 4. So just assume, for the sake of argument, that the if statement tests whether the variable x is equal to the variable y. Because this test immediately follows an assignment statement that assigns the value of x to y, you can safely assume that x equals y, right?

Wrong. Because x is NaN, y also is NaN. NaN is never considered to be equal to any other value, including another NaN. Thus, the comparison in the if statement fails.

✦ Another strange consequence: You can't assume that a number minus itself is always zero. Consider this statement:

```
double z = x - x;    // not necessarily zero
```

Shouldn't this statement always set z to zero? Not if x is NaN. In that case, not a number minus not a number is still not a number.

✦ One more weirdness and then I'll stop: Any mathematical operation involving infinity results in either another infinity or NaN. Infinity + 5, for example, still equals infinity, so Buzz Lightyear's call "To infinity and beyond!" just isn't going to happen. But infinity minus infinity gives you . . . NaN.

Chapter 4: Making Choices

In This Chapter

✔ Boolean expressions for fun and profit (or is it for fun *or* profit?)

✔ Your basic, run-of-the-mill if statement

✔ else clauses and else-if statements

✔ Nested if statements

✔ Logical operators

✔ The weird ?: operator

✔ The proper way to do string comparisons

So far in this book, all the programs have run straight through from start to finish without making any decisions along the way. In this chapter, you discover two Java statements that let you create some variety in your programs. The if statement lets you execute a statement or a block of statements only if some conditional test turns out to be true. And the switch statement lets you execute one of several blocks of statements depending on the value of an integer variable.

The if statement relies heavily on the use of *Boolean expressions,* which are, in general, expressions that yield a simple true or false result. Because you can't do even the simplest if statement without a Boolean expression, this chapter begins by showing you how to code simple Java boolean expressions that test the value of a variable. Later, after looking at the details of how the if statement works, I revisit boolean expressions to show how to combine them to make complicated logical decisions. Then I get to the switch statement.

 You're going to have to put your thinking cap on for much of this chapter, as most of it plays with logic puzzles. Find yourself a comfortable chair in a quiet part of the house, turn off the TV, and pour yourself a cup of coffee.

Using Simple Boolean Expressions

All if statements, as well as several of the other control statements that I describe in Book II, Chapter 5 (while, do, and for), use boolean expressions to determine whether to execute or skip a statement (or a block of statements). A *boolean expression* is a Java expression that, when evaluated, returns a *Boolean value:* true or false.

As you discover later in this chapter, `boolean` expressions can be very complicated. Most of the time, however, you use simple expressions that compare the value of a variable with the value of some other variable, a literal, or perhaps a simple arithmetic expression. This comparison uses one of the *relational operators* listed in Table 4-1. All these operators are *binary operators,* which means that they work on two operands.

Table 4-1	Relational Operators
Operator	*Description*
==	Returns `true` if the expression on the left evaluates to the same value as the expression on the right.
!=	Returns `true` if the expression on the left does not evaluate to the same value as the expression on the right.
<	Returns `true` if the expression on the left evaluates to a value that is less than the value of the expression on the right.
<=	Returns `true` if the expression on the left evaluates to a value that is less than or equal to the expression on the right.
>	Returns `true` if the expression on the left evaluates to a value that is greater than the value of the expression on the right.
>=	Returns `true` if the expression on the left evaluates to a value that is greater than or equal to the expression on the right.

A basic Java `boolean` expression has this form:

```
expression relational-operator expression
```

Java evaluates a `boolean` expression by first evaluating the expression on the left, then evaluating the expression on the right, and finally applying the relational operator to determine whether the entire expression evaluates to `true` or `false`.

Here are some simple examples of relational expressions. For each example, assume that the following statements were used to declare and initialize the variables:

```
int i = 5;
int j = 10;
int k = 15;
double x = 5.0;
double y = 7.5;
double z = 12.3;
```

Here are the sample expressions, along with their results (based on the values supplied):

Expression	Value	Explanation
i == 5	true	The value of i is 5.
i == 10	false	The value of i is not 10.
i == j	false	i is 5, and j is 10, so they are not equal.
i == j - 5	true	i is 5, and j - 5 is 5.
i > 1	true	i is 5, which is greater than 1.
j == i * 2	true	j is 10, and i is 5, so i * 2 is also 10.
x = i	true	Casting allows the comparison, and 5.0 is equal to 5.
k < z	false	Casting allows the comparison, and 15 is greater than 12.3.
i * 2 < y	false	i * 2 is 10, which is not less than 7.5.

Note that the relational operator that tests for equality is two equal signs in a row (==). A single equal sign is the assignment operator. When you're first learning Java, you may find yourself typing the assignment operator when you mean the equals operator, like this:

```
if (i = 5)
```

Oops. But Java won't let you get away with this, so you have to correct your mistake and recompile the program. At first, doing so seems like a nuisance. The more you work with Java, the more you realize that it really *is* a nuisance, but one you can get used to.

Another important warning: Do *not* test strings by using any of the relational operators listed in Table 4-1, including the equals operator. You're probably going to feel tempted to test strings like this:

```
inputString == "Yes"
```

Note, however, that this is not the correct way to compare strings in Java. You find out the correct way in the section "Comparing Strings," later in this chapter.

Using if Statements

The if statement is one of the most important statements in any programming language, and Java is no exception. The following sections describe the ins and outs of using the various forms of Java's powerful if statement.

Simple if statements

In its most basic form, an `if` statement lets you execute a single statement or a block of statements only if a `boolean` expression evaluates to `true`. The basic form of the `if` statement looks like this:

```
if (boolean-expression)
    statement
```

Note that the `boolean` expression must be enclosed in parentheses. Also, if you use only a single statement, it must end with a semicolon. But the statement can also be a statement block enclosed by braces. In that case, each statement within the block needs a semicolon, but the block itself doesn't.

Here's an example of a typical `if` statement:

```
double commissionRate = 0.0;
if (salesTotal > 10000.0)
    commissionRate = 0.05;
```

In this example, a variable named `commissionRate` is initialized to `0.0` and then set to `0.05` if `salesTotal` is greater than `10000.0`.

Some programmers find it helpful to visualize the operation of an `if` statement as a flowchart, as shown in Figure 4-1. In this flowchart, the diamond symbol represents the condition test: If the sales total is greater than $10,000, the statement in the rectangle is executed. If not, that statement is bypassed.

Figure 4-1:
The flowchart for an if statement.

Indenting the statement under the `if` statement is customary because it makes the structure of your code more obvious. It isn't necessary, but it's always a good idea.

Here's an example that uses a block rather than a single statement:

```
double commissionRate = 0.0;
if (salesTotal > 10000.0)

{
    commissionRate = 0.05;
    commission = salesTotal * commissionRate;
}
```

In this example, the two statements within the braces are executed if `sales Total` is greater than $10,000. Otherwise neither statement is executed.

Here are a few additional points about simple `if` statements:

✦ Some programmers prefer to code the opening brace for the statement block on the same line as the `if` statement itself, like this:

```
if (salesTotal > 10000.0) {
    commissionRate = 0.05;
    commission = salesTotal * commissionRate;
}
```

This method is simply a matter of style, so either technique is acceptable.

✦ Indentation by itself doesn't create a block. Consider this code:

```
if (salesTotal > 10000.0)
    commissionRate = 0.05;
    commission = salesTotal * commissionRate;
```

Here I don't use the braces to mark a block but indent the last statement as though it were part of the `if` statement. Don't be fooled; the last statement is executed regardless of whether the expression in the `if` statement evaluates to `true`.

Some programmers like to code a statement block even for `if` statements that conditionally execute just one statement. Here's an example:

```
if (salesTotal > 10000.0)
{
    commissionRate = 0.05;
}
```

That's not a bad idea, because it makes the structure of your code a little more obvious by adding extra white space around the statement. Also, if you decide later that you need to add a few statements to the block, the braces are already there. (It's all too easy to later add extra lines to a conditional and forget to include the braces, which leads to a bug that can be hard to trace.)

✦ If only one statement needs to be conditionally executed, some programmers put it on the same line as the `if` statement, like this:

```
if (salesTotal > 10000.0) commissionRate = 0.05;
```

This method works, but I'd avoid it. Your classes are easier to follow if you use line breaks and indentation to highlight their structure.

if-else statements

An `if-else` statement adds an additional element to a basic `if` statement: a statement or block that's executed if the `boolean` expression is not `true`. Its basic format is

```
if (boolean-expression)
    statement
else
    statement
```

Here's an example:

```
double commissionRate;
if (salesTotal <= 10000.0)
    commissionRate = 0.02;
else
    commissionRate = 0.05;
```

In this example, the commission rate is set to 2 percent if the sales total is less than or equal to $10,000. If the sales total is greater than $10,000, the commission rate is set to 5 percent. Figure 4-2 shows a flowchart for this `if-else` statement.

Figure 4-2: The flow-chart for an if-else statement.

In some cases, you can avoid using the `else` part of an `if-else` statement by cleverly rearranging your code. This code has the same effect as the preceding `if-else` statement:

```
double commissionRate = 0.05;
if (salesTotal <= 10000.0)
    commissionRate = 0.02;
```

You can use blocks for either or both of the statements in an if-else statement. Here's an if-else statement in which both statements are blocks:

```
double commissionRate;
if (salesTotal <= 10000.0)
{
    commissionRate = 0.02;
    level1Count++;
}
else
{
    commissionRate = 0.05;
    level2Count++;
}
```

Nested if statements

The statement that goes in the if or else part of an if-else statement can be any kind of Java statement, including another if or if-else statement. This arrangement is called *nesting*, and an if or if-else statement that includes another if or if-else statement is called a *nested if statement*.

The general form of a nested if statement is this:

```
if (expression-1)
    if (expression-2)
        statement-1
    else
        statement-2
else
    if (expression-3)
        statement-3
    else
        statement-4
```

In this example, *expression-1* is first to be evaluated. If it evaluates to true, *expression-2* is evaluated. If that expression is true, *statement-1* is executed; otherwise *statement-2* is executed. But if *expression-1* is false, *expression-3* is evaluated. If *expression-3* is true, *statement-3* is executed; otherwise *statement-4* is executed.

An if statement that's contained within another if statement is called an *inner if statement*, and an if statement that contains another if statement is called an *outer if statement*. Thus, in the preceding example, the if statement that tests *expression-1* is an outer if statement, and the if statements that test *expression-2* and *expression-3* are inner if statements.

TIP

Nesting can be as complex as you want, but try to keep it as simple as possible. Also, be sure to use indentation to indicate the structure of the nested statements.

Suppose that your company has two classes of sales representatives (Class 1 and Class 2) and that these reps get different commissions for sales below $10,000 and sales above $10,000, according to this table:

Sales	Class 1	Class 2
$0 to $9,999	2%	2.5%
$10,000 and over	4%	5%

You could implement this commission structure with a nested `if` statement:

```
if (salesClass == 1)
    if (salesTotal < 10000.0)
        commissionRate = 0.02;
    else
        commissionRate = 0.04;
else
    if (salesTotal < 10000.0)
        commissionRate = 0.025;
    else
        commissionRate = 0.05;
```

This example assumes that if the `salesClass` variable isn't 1, it must be 2. If that's not the case, you have to use an additional `if` statement for Class 2 sales reps:

```
if (salesClass == 1)
    if (salesTotal < 10000.0)
        commissionRate = 0.02;
    else
        commissionRate = 0.04;
else if (salesClass == 2)
    if (salesTotal < 10000.0)
        commissionRate = 0.025;
    else
        commissionRate = 0.05;
```

Notice that I place this extra `if` statement on the same line as the `else` keyword. That's a common practice for a special form of nested `if` statements called *else-if statements*. You find more about this type of nesting in the next section.

You could just use a pair of separate `if` statements, of course, like this:

```
if (salesClass == 1)
    if (salesTotal < 10000.0)
        commissionRate = 0.02;
    else
        commissionRate = 0.04;
if (salesClass == 2)
    if (salesTotal < 10000.0)
        commissionRate = 0.025;
    else
        commissionRate = 0.05;
```

The result is the same. This particular technique, however, works only if the `if` statement itself doesn't change the variable being tested. If the first `if` statement does change the value of the `salesClass` variable, this statement doesn't work.

Note that you could also have implemented the commission structure by testing the sales level in the outer `if` statement and the sales representative's class in the inner statements:

```
if (salesTotal < 10000)
    if (salesClass == 1)
        commissionRate = 0.02;
    else
        commissionRate = 0.04;
else
    if (salesClass == 1)
        commissionRate = 0.025;
    else
        commissionRate = 0.05;
```

Be careful when you use nested `if` and `else` statements, as it is all too easy to end up with statements that don't work the way you expect them to. The key is knowing how Java pairs `else` keywords with `if` statements. The rule is actually very simple: Each `else` keyword is matched with the most previous `if` statement that hasn't already been paired with an `else` keyword.

Sorry — you can't coax Java into pairing the `if` and `else` keywords differently by using indentation. Suppose that Class 2 sales reps don't get any commission, so the inner `if` statements in the preceding example don't need `else` statements. You may be tempted to calculate the commission rate by using this code:

```
if (salesTotal < 10000)
    if (salesClass == 1)
        commissionRate = 0.02;
else
    if (salesClass == 1)
        commissionRate = 0.025;
```

Sorry — that won't work. The indentation creates the impression that the `else` keyword is paired with the first `if` statement, but in reality, it's paired with the second `if` statement. As a result, no sales commission rate is set for sales of $10,000 or more.

This problem has two solutions. The first, and preferred, solution is to use braces to clarify the structure:

```
if (salesTotal < 10000)
{
    if (salesClass == 1)
        commissionRate = 0.02;
}
else
{
    if (salesClass == 1)
        commissionRate = 0.025;
}
```

The other solution is to add an `else` statement that specifies an *empty statement* (a semicolon by itself) to the first inner `if` statement:

```
if (salesTotal < 10000)
    if (salesClass == 1)
        commissionRate = 0.02;
    else ;
else
    if (salesClass == 1)
        commissionRate = 0.025;
```

The empty `else` statement is paired with the inner `if` statement, so the second `else` keyword is properly paired with the outer `if` statement.

else-if statements

A common pattern for nested if statements is to have a series of if-else statements with another if-else statement in each else part:

```
if (expression-1)
    statement-1
else if (expression-2)
    statement-2
else if (expression-3)
    statement-3
```

These statements are sometimes called *else-if statements,* although that term is unofficial. Officially, all that's going on is that the statement in the else part happens to be another if statement — so this statement is just a type of a nested if statement. It's an especially useful form of nesting, however.

Suppose that you want to assign four commission rates based on the sales total, according to this table:

Sales	Commission
Over $10,000	5%
$5,000 to $9,999	3.5%
$1,000 to $4,999	2%
Under $1,000	0%

You can easily implement a series of else-if statements:

```
if (salesTotal >= 10000.0)
    commissionRate = 0.05;
else if (salesTotal >= 5000.0)
    commissionRate = 0.035;
else if (salesTotal >= 1000.0)
    commissionRate = 0.02;
else
    commissionRate = 0.0;
```

Figure 4-3 shows a flowchart for this sequence of else-if statements.

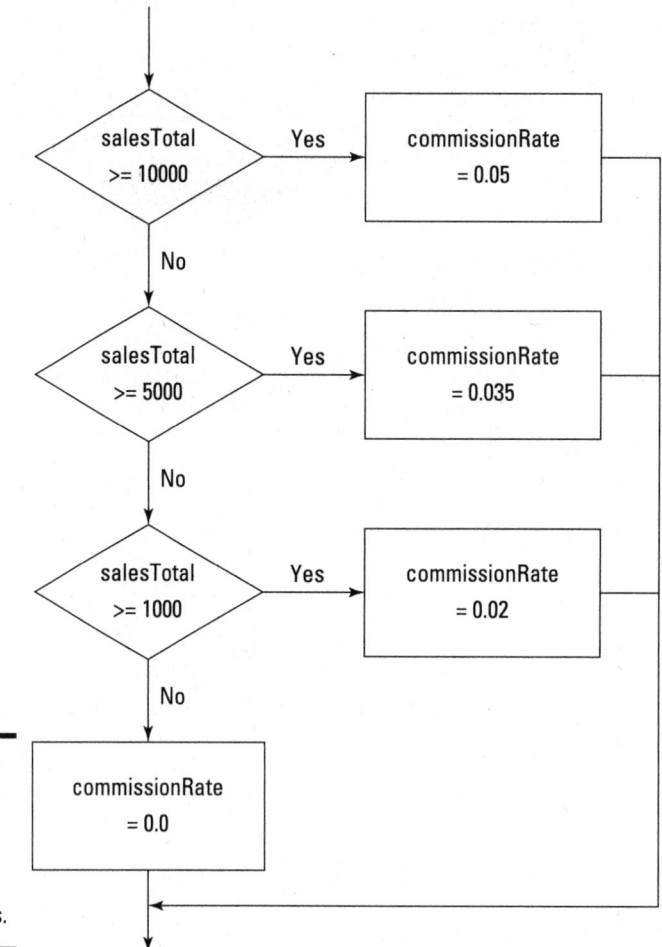

Figure 4-3:
The flow-
chart for a
sequence
of else-if
statements.

You have to think through carefully how you set up these else-if statements. At first glance, for example, this sequence looks as though it might work:

```
if (salesTotal > 0.0)
    commissionRate = 0.0;
else if (salesTotal >= 1000.0)
    commissionRate = 0.02;
else if (salesTotal >= 5000.0)
    commissionRate = 0.035;
else if (salesTotal >= 10000.0)
    commissionRate = 0.05;
```

Nice try, but this scenario won't work. These if statements always set the commission rate to 0 percent because the boolean expression in the first if statement always tests true (assuming that the salesTotal isn't zero or negative — and if it is, none of the other if statements matter). As a result, none of the other if statements are ever evaluated.

Using Mr. Spock's Favorite Operators (Logical Ones, of Course)

A *logical operator* (sometimes called a *Boolean operator*) is an operator that returns a Boolean result that's based on the Boolean result of one or two other expressions. Expressions that use logical operators are sometimes called *compound expressions* because the effect of the logical operators is to let you combine two or more condition tests into a single expression. Table 4-2 lists the logical operators.

Table 4-2			Logical Operators
Operator	*Name*	*Type*	*Description*
!	Not	Unary	Returns `true` if the operand to the right evaluates to `false`. Returns `false` if the operand to the right is `true`.
&	And	Binary	Returns `true` if both of the operands evaluate to `true`. Both operands are evaluated before the And operator is applied.
|	Or	Binary	Returns `true` if at least one of the operands evaluates to `true`. Both operands are evaluated before the Or operator is applied.
^	Xor	Binary	Returns `true` if one — and only one — of the operands evaluates to `true`. Returns `false` if both operands evaluate to `true` or if both operands evaluate to `false`.
&&	Conditional And	Binary	Same as &, but if the operand on the left returns `false`, returns `false` without evaluating the operand on the right.
||	Conditional Or	Binary	Same as |, but if the operand on the left returns `true`, returns `true` without evaluating the operand on the `right`.

The following sections describe these operators in excruciating detail.

Using the ! operator

The simplest of the logical operators is *Not* (!). Technically, it's a *unary* prefix operator, which means that you use it with one operand, and you code it immediately in front of that operand. (Technically, this operator is called the *complement operator,* not the *Not operator.* But in real life, most people call it *Not.* And many programmers call it *bang.*)

The Not operator reverses the value of a `boolean` expression. Thus, if the expression is `true`, Not changes it to `false`. If the expression is `false`, Not changes it to `true`.

Here's an example:

```
!(i = 4)
```

This expression evaluates to `true` if `i` is any value other than 4. If `i` is 4, it evaluates to `false`. It works by first evaluating the expression `(i = 4)`. Then it reverses the result of that evaluation.

Don't confuse the Not logical operator (`!`) with the Not Equals relational operator (`!=`). Although these operators are sometimes used in similar ways, the Not operator is more general. I could have written the preceding example like this:

```
i != 4
```

The result is the same. The Not operator can be applied to any expression that returns a `true-false` result, however, not just to an equality test.

You must almost always enclose the expression that the `!` operator is applied to in parentheses. Consider this expression:

```
! i == 4
```

Assuming that `i` is an integer variable, the compiler doesn't allow this expression because it looks like you're trying to apply the `!` operator to the variable, not to the result of the comparison. A quick set of parentheses solves the problem:

```
!(i == 4)
```

Using the & and && operators

The `&` and `&&` operators combine two `boolean` expressions and return `true` only if both expressions are `true`. This type of operation is called an *And operation,* because the first expression and the second expression must be `true` for the And operator to return `true`.

Suppose that the sales commission rate should be 2.5% if the sales class is 1 and the sales total is $10,000 or more. You could perform this test with two separate `if` statements (as I did earlier in this chapter), or you could combine the tests into one `if` statement:

```
if ((salesClass == 1) & (salesTotal >= 10000.0))
    commissionRate = 0.025;
```

Here the expressions `(salesClass == 1)` and `(salesTotal >= 10000.0)` are evaluated separately. Then the `&` operator compares the results. If they're both `true`, the `&` operator returns `true`. If one is `false` or both are `false`, the `&` operator returns `false`.

Notice that I use parentheses liberally to clarify where one expression ends and another begins. Using parentheses isn't always necessary, but when you use logical operators, I suggest that you always use parentheses to clearly identify the expressions being compared.

The `&&` operator is similar to the `&` operator, but it leverages your knowledge of logic a bit more. Because both expressions compared by the `&` operator must be `true` for the entire expression to be `true`, there's no reason to evaluate the second expression if the first one returns `false`. The `&` operator isn't aware of this fact, so it blindly evaluates both expressions before determining the results. The `&&` operator is smart enough to stop when it knows what the outcome is.

As a result, almost always use `&&` instead of `&`. Here's the preceding example, and this time it's coded smartly with `&&`:

```
if ((salesClass == 1) && (salesTotal >= 10000.0))
    commissionRate = 0.025;
```

Why do I say you should *almost* always use `&&`? Because sometimes the expressions themselves have side effects that are important. The second expression might involve a method call that updates a database, for example, and you want the database to be updated whether the first expression evaluates to `true` or to `false`. In that case, you want to use `&` instead of `&&` to ensure that both expressions get evaluated.

Relying on the side effects of expressions can be risky — and you can almost always find a better way to write your code to avert the side effects. In other words, placing an important call to a database-update method inside a compound expression that's buried in an `if` statement probably isn't a good idea.

Using the | and || operators

The `|` and `||` operators are called *Or operators* because they return `true` if the first expression is `true` or if the second expression is `true`. They also return `true` if both expressions are `true`. (You find the `|` symbol on your keyboard just above the Enter key.)

Suppose that sales representatives get no commission if total sales are less than $1,000 or if the sales class is 3. You could do that with two separate `if` statements:

```
if (salesTotal < 1000.0)
    commissionRate = 0.0;
if (salesClass == 3)
    commissionRate = 0.0;
```

With an Or operator, however, you can do the same thing with a compound condition:

```
if ((salesTotal < 1000.0) | (salesClass == 3))
    commissionRate = 0.0;
```

To evaluate the expression for this `if` statement, Java first evaluates the expressions on either side of the `|` operator. Then, if at least one of these expressions is `true`, the whole expression is `true`. Otherwise the expression is `false`.

In most cases, you should use the Conditional Or operator (`||`) instead of the regular Or operator (`|`), like this:

```
if ((salesTotal < 1000.0) || (salesClass == 3))
    commissionRate = 0.0;
```

Like the Conditional And operator (`&&`), the Conditional Or operator stops evaluating as soon as it knows what the outcome is. Suppose that the sales total is $500. Then there's no need to evaluate the second expression. Because the first expression evaluates to `true` and only one of the expressions needs to be `true`, Java can skip the second expression. If the sales total is $5,000, of course, the second expression must be evaluated.

As with the And operators, you should use the regular Or operator only if your program depends on some side effect of the second expression, such as work done by a method call.

Using the ^ operator

The `^` operator performs what in the world of logic is known as an *Exclusive Or,* commonly abbreviated as *Xor.* It returns `true` if one — and only one — of the two subexpressions is `true`. If both expressions are `true`, or if both expressions are `false`, the `^` operator returns `false`.

Most programmers don't bother with the `^` operator because it's pretty confusing. My feelings won't be hurt if you skip this section.

Put another way, the `^` operator returns `true` if the two subexpressions have different results. If they have the same result, it returns `false`.

Suppose that you're writing software that controls your model railroad set, and you want to find out whether two switches are set in a dangerous position that might allow a collision. If the switches are represented by simple `integer` variables named `switch1` and `switch2`, and 1 means the track is switched to the left and 2 means the track is switched to the right, you could easily test them like this:

```
if ( switch1 == switch2 )
    System.out.println("Trouble! The switches are the same");
else
    System.out.println("OK, the switches are different.");
```

Now, suppose that (for some reason) one of the switches is represented by an int variable where 1 means the switch goes to the left and *any* other value means the switch goes to the right — but the other switch is represented by an int variable where –1 means the switch goes to the left and any other value means the switch goes to the right. (Who knows — maybe the switches were made by different manufacturers.) You could use a compound condition like this:

```
if (((switch1==1)&&(switch2==-1)) ||
    ((switch1!=1)&&(switch2!=-1)))
    System.out.println("Trouble! The switches are the same");
else
    System.out.println("OK, the switches are different.");
```

But an Xor operator could do the job with a simpler expression:

```
if ((switch1==1)^(switch2==-1))
    System.out.println("OK, the switches are different.");
else
    System.out.println("Trouble! The switches are the same");
```

Book II
Chapter 4

Making Choices

Frankly, the ^ operator is probably one you consider avoiding. In fact, most of the Java books on my bookshelf (and believe me, I have a lot of them) don't even mention this operator except in its other, more useful application as a bitwise operator. (See the "Twiddling Your Bits" bonus chapter at www. dummies.com/extras/javaaio for information about bitwise operators.) That's probably because many applications don't use it as a logical operator, and the applications for which it is suitable can also be solved with the more traditional And and Or operators.

Combining logical operators

You can combine simple boolean expressions to create more complicated expressions. For example:

```
if ((salesTotal<1000.0)||((salesTotal<5000.0)&&
    (salesClass==1))||((salestotal < 10000.0)&&
    (salesClass == 2)))
    CommissionRate = 0.0;
```

Can you tell what the expression in this if statement does? It sets the commission to zero if any one of the following three conditions is true:

✦ The sales total is less than $1,000.

✦ The sales total is less than $5,000, and the sales class is 1.

✦ The sales total is less than $10,000, and the sales class is 2.

In many cases, you can clarify how an expression works just by indenting its pieces differently and spacing out its subexpressions. This version of the preceding `if` statement is a little easier to follow:

```
if ((salesTotal < 1000.0)
    || ( (salesTotal < 5000.0) && (salesClass == 1))
    || ( (salestotal < 10000.0) && (salesClass == 2))
  )
   commissionRate = 0.0;
```

Figuring out exactly what this `if` statement does, however, is still tough. In many cases, the better thing to do is skip the complicated expression and code separate `if` statements:

```
if (salesTotal < 1000.0)
   commissionRate = 0.0;
if ((salesTotal < 5000.0) && (salesClass == 1))
   commissionRate = 0.0;
if ((salestotal < 10000.0) && (salesClass == 2))
   commissionRate = 0.0;
```

In Java, `boolean` expressions can get a little complicated when you use more than one logical operator, especially if you mix And and Or operators. Consider this expression:

```
if ( a==1 && b==2 || c==3 )
    System.out.println("It's true!");
else
    System.out.println("No it isn't!");
```

What do you suppose this `if` statement does if a is 5, b is 7, and c = 3? The answer is that the expression evaluates to `true`, and `"It's true!"` is printed. That's because Java applies the operators from left to right. So the `&&` operator is applied to a==1 (which is `false`) and b==2 (which is also `false`). Thus, the `&&` operator returns `false`. Then the `||` operator is applied to that `false` result and the result of c==3, which is `true`. Thus the entire expression returns `true`.

Wouldn't this expression have been clearer if you had used a set of parentheses to clarify what the expression does? Consider this example:

```
if ((a==1 && b==2) || c==3 )
    System.out.println("It's true!");
else
    System.out.println("No it isn't!");
```

Here you can clearly see that the `&&` operator is evaluated first.

Using the Conditional Operator

Java has a special operator called the *conditional operator* that's designed to eliminate the need for if statements in certain situations. It's a *ternary operator,* which means that it works with three operands. The general form for using the conditional operator is this:

```
boolean-expression ? expression-1 : expression-2
```

The boolean expression is evaluated first. If it evaluates to true, *expression-1* is evaluated, and the result of this expression becomes the result of the whole expression. If the expression is false, *expression-2* is evaluated, and its results are used instead.

Suppose that you want to assign a value of 0 to an integer variable named salesTier if total sales are less than $10,000 and a value of 1 if the sales are $10,000 or more. You could do that with this statement:

```
int tier = salesTotal > 10000.0 ? 1 : 0;
```

Although not required, a set of parentheses helps make this statement easier to follow:

```
int tier = (salesTotal > 10000.0) ? 1 : 0;
```

One common use for the conditional operator is when you're using concatenation to build a text string, and you have a word that may need to be plural based on the value of an integer variable. Suppose that you want to create a string that says "You have x apples", with the value of a variable named appleCount substituted for x. But if apples is 1, the string should be "You have 1 apple", not "You have 1 apples".

The following statement does the trick:

```
String msg = "You have " + appleCount + " apple"
    + ((appleCount>1) ? "s." : ".");
```

When Java encounters the ? operator, it evaluates the expression (appleCount>1). If true, it uses the first string (s.). If false, it uses the second string (".").

Comparing Strings

Comparing strings in Java takes a little extra care, because the == operator really doesn't work the way it should. Suppose that you want to know whether a string variable named answer contains the value "Yes". You may be tempted to code an if statement like this:

```
if (answer == "Yes")
    System.out.println("The answer is Yes.");
```

Unfortunately, that's not correct. The problem is that in Java, strings are reference types, not primitive types; when you use the == operator with reference types, Java compares the references to the objects, not the objects themselves. As a result, the expression answer == "Yes" doesn't test whether the value of the string referenced by the answer variable is "Yes". Instead, it tests whether the answer string and the literal string "Yes" point to the same string object in memory. In many cases, they do — but sometimes they don't, and the results are difficult to predict.

The correct way to test a string for a given value is to use the equals method of the String class:

```
if (answer.equals("Yes"))
    System.out.println("The answer is Yes.");
```

This method actually compares the value of the string object referenced by the variable with the string you pass as a parameter and returns a Boolean result to indicate whether the strings have the same value.

The String class has another method, equalsIgnoreCase, that's also useful for comparing strings. It compares strings but ignores case, which is especially useful when you're testing string values entered by users. Suppose that you're writing a program that ends only when the user enters the word End. You could use the equals method to test the string:

```
if (input.equals("end"))
  // end the program
```

In this case, however, the user would have to enter end exactly. If the user enters End or END, the program won't end. It's better to code the if statement like this:

```
if (input.equalsIgnoreCase("end"))
  // end the program
```

Then the user could end the program by entering the word *end* spelled with any variation of upper- and lowercase letters, including end, End, END, or even eNd.

You can find much more about working with strings in Book IV, Chapter 1. For now, just remember that to test for string equality in an if statement (or in one of the other control statements presented in the next chapter), you must use the equals or equalsIgnoreCase method instead of the == operator.

Chapter 5: Going Around in Circles (Or, Using Loops)

In This Chapter

✔ The thrill of while loops

✔ The rapture of infinite loops

✔ The splendor of do loops

✔ The joy of validating input

✔ The wonder of for loops

✔ The ecstasy of nested loops

So far, all the programs in this book have started, run quickly through their main method, and then ended. If Dorothy from *The Wizard of Oz* were using these programs, she'd probably say, "My, programs come and go quickly around here!"

In this chapter, you find out how to write programs that don't come and go so quickly. They hang around by using *loops,* which let them execute the same statements more than once.

Loops are the key to writing one of the most common types of programs: programs that get input from the user, do something with it, get more input from the user and do something with that, and keep going this way until the user has had enough.

Put another way, loops are like the instructions on your shampoo: Lather. Rinse. *Repeat.*

Like if statements, loops rely on conditional expressions to tell them when to stop looping. Without conditional expressions, loops would go on forever, and your users would grow old watching them run. So if you haven't yet read Book II, Chapter 4, I suggest that you do so before continuing much further.

Using Your Basic while Loop

The most basic of all looping statements in Java is `while`. The `while` statement creates a type of loop that's called a *while loop*, which is simply a loop that executes continuously as long as some conditional expression evaluates to `true`. `while` loops are useful in all sorts of programming situations, so you use `while` loops a lot. (I tell you about other kinds of loops later in this chapter.)

The while statement

The basic format of the `while` statement is this:

```
while (expression)
    statement
```

The `while` statement begins by evaluating the expression. If the expression is `true`, *statement* is executed. Then the expression is evaluated again, and the whole process repeats. If the expression is `false`, *statement* is not executed, and the `while` loop ends.

Note that the statement part of the `while` loop can either be a single statement or a block of statements contained in a pair of braces. Loops that have just one statement aren't very useful, so nearly all the `while` loops you code use a block of statements. (Well, okay, sometimes loops with a single statement are useful. It isn't unheard of — just not all that common.)

A counting loop

Here's a simple program that uses a `while` loop to print the even numbers from 2 through 20 on the console:

```java
public class EvenCounter
{
    public static void main(String[] args)
    {
        int number = 2;
        while (number <= 20)
        {
            System.out.print(number + " ");
            number += 2;
        }
        System.out.println();
    }
}
```

If you run this program, the following output is displayed in the console window:

```
2 4 6 8 10 12 14 16 18 20
```

The conditional expression in this program's `while` statement is `number <= 20`. That means the loop repeats as long as the value of `number` is less than or equal to `20`. The body of the loop consists of two statements. The first prints the value of `number` followed by a space to separate this number from the next one. Then the second statement adds 2 to `number`.

Figure 5-1 shows a flowchart for this program. This flowchart can help you visualize the basic decision-making process of a loop.

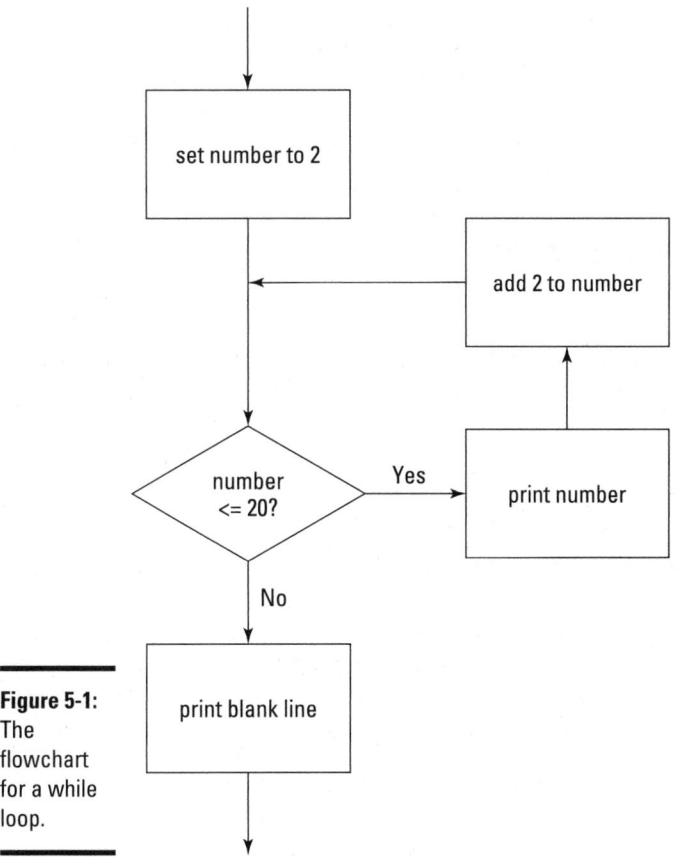

Figure 5-1: The flowchart for a while loop.

Breaking Out of a Loop

In many programs, you need to set up a loop that has some kind of escape clause. Java's escape clause is the `break` statement. When a `break` statement is executed in a `while` loop, the loop ends immediately. Any remaining statements in the loop are ignored, and the next statement executed is the statement that follows the loop.

Suppose that you're afraid of the number 12. (I'm not a doctor, and I don't play one on TV, but I think the scientific name for this condition would be *dodecaphobia*.) You could modify the counting program shown in the preceding section so that when it gets to the number 12, it panics and aborts the loop:

```java
public class Dodecaphobia

{
    public static void main(String[] args)
    {
        int number = 2;
        while (number <= 20)
        {
            if (number == 12)
                break;
            System.out.print(number + " ");
            number += 2;
        }
        System.out.println();
    }
}
```

When you run this program, the following line is displayed on the console:

```
2 4 6 8 10
```

Whew! That was close. Almost got to 12 there.

Looping Forever

One common form of loop is called an *infinite loop*. That's a loop that goes on forever. You can create infinite loops many ways in Java (not all of them intentional), but the easiest is to just specify `true` for the `while` expression.

Here's an example:

```java
public class CountForever
{
    public static void main(String[] args)
    {
        int number = 2;
        while (true)
        {
            System.out.print(number + " ");
            number += 2;
        }
    }
}
```

If you run this program, your console window quickly fills up with numbers and just keeps going. That's great if you *really like* even numbers, but eventually you'll tire of this loop and want it to stop. You can stop an infinite loop in any of three ways:

✦ Turn off your computer.

✦ Hit your computer with an ax or other heavy object.

✦ Close the console window.

The last one is probably the one you want to go with.

Obviously, infinite loops are something you want to avoid in your programs. So whenever you use a `while` expression that's always `true`, be sure to throw in a `break` statement to give your loop some way to terminate. You could use an infinite loop with a `break` statement in the Dodecaphobia program:

```
public class Dodecaphobia2
{
    public static void main(String[] args)
    {
        int number = 2;
        while (true)
        {
            if (number == 12)
                break;
            System.out.print(number + " ");
            number += 2;
        }
        System.out.println();
    }
}
```

Here the loop looks as though it might go on forever, but the `break` statement panics out of the loop when it hits 12.

Letting the user decide when to quit

It turns out that infinite loops are also useful when you want to let the user be in charge of when to stop the loop. Suppose that you don't know what numbers a user is afraid of, so you want to count numbers until the user says to stop. Here's a program that does that:

```
import java.util.Scanner;

public class NumberPhobia
{
    static Scanner sc = new Scanner(System.in);

    public static void main(String[] args)
```

```
    {
        int number = 2;
        String input;
        while (true)
        {
            System.out.println(number + " ");
            System.out.print
                ("Do you want to keep counting?"
                + " (Y or N)");
            input = sc.next();
            if (input.equalsIgnoreCase("N"))
                break;
            number += 2;
        }
        System.out.println("\nWhew! That was close.\n");
    }
}
```

Here's some typical console output from this program, for a user who has octophobia:

```
2
Do you want to keep counting? (Y or N)y
4
Do you want to keep counting? (Y or N)y
6
Do you want to keep counting? (Y or N)n
Whew! That was close.
```

Letting the user decide in another way

Another way to write a loop that a user can opt out of is to test the input string in the `while` condition. The only trick here is that you must first initialize the input string to the value that continues the loop. Otherwise, the loop doesn't execute at all!

Here's a variation of the `NumberPhobia` program named `NumberPhobia2` that uses this technique:

```
import java.util.Scanner;

public class NumberPhobia2
{
    static Scanner sc = new Scanner(System.in);

    public static void main(String[] args)
    {
        int number = 2;
        String input = "Y";
        while (input.equalsIgnoreCase("Y"))
        {
            System.out.println(number + " ");
            System.out.print
```

```
            ("Do you want to keep counting?"
            + " (Y or N)");
        input = sc.next();
        number += 2;
    }
    System.out.println("\nWhew! That was close.");
    }
}
```

This program works almost the same way as the preceding version, but with a subtle difference. In the first version, if the user says N after the program displays 6, the value of the number variable after the loop is 6 because the break statement bails out of the loop before adding 2 to number. But in this version, the value of number is 8.

Using the continue Statement

The break statement is rather harsh: It completely bails out of the loop. Sometimes that's what you need — but just as often, you don't really need to quit the loop; you just need to skip a particular iteration of the loop. The Dodecaphobia program presented earlier in this chapter stops the loop when it gets to 12. What if you just want to skip the number 12, so you go straight from 10 to 14?

To do that, you can use the break statement's kinder, gentler relative, the continue statement. The continue statement sends control right back to the top of the loop, where the expression is immediately evaluated again. If the expression is still true, the loop's statement or block is executed again.

Here's a version of the Dodecaphobia program that uses a continue statement to skip the number 12 rather than stop counting altogether when it reaches 12:

```
public class Dodecaphobia3
{
    public static void main(String[] args)
    {
        int number = 0;
        while (number < 20)
        {
            number += 2;
            if (number == 12)
                continue;
            System.out.print(number + " ");
        }
        System.out.println();
    }
}
```

Run this program, and you get the following output in the console window:

```
2 4 6 8 10 14 16 18 20
```

Notice that I had to make several changes in this program to get it to work with a `continue` statement instead of a `break` statement. If I had just replaced the word `break` with `continue`, the program wouldn't have worked, because the statement that added 2 to the number came after the `break` statement in the original version. As a result, if you just replace the `break` statement with a `continue` statement, you end up with an infinite loop when you reach 12, because the statement that adds 2 to `number` never gets executed.

To make this program work with a `continue` statement, I rearranged the statements in the loop body so that the statement that adds 2 to `number` comes before the `continue` statement. That way, the only statement skipped by the `continue` statement is the one that prints `number` to the console.

Unfortunately, this change affected other statements in the program. Because 2 is added to `number` before `number` is printed, I had to change the initial value of `number` from 2 to 0, and I had to change the `while` expression from `number <= 20` to `number < 20`.

Running do-while Loops

A *do-while loop* (sometimes just called a *do loop*) is similar to a `while` loop, but with a critical difference: In a `do-while` loop, the condition that stops the loop isn't tested until after the statements in the loop have executed. The basic form of a `do-while` loop is this:

```
do
     statement
while (expression);
```

Note that the `while` keyword and the expression aren't coded until *after* the body of the loop. As with a `while` loop, the body for a `do-while` loop can be a single statement or a block of statements enclosed in braces.

Also, notice that the expression is followed by a semicolon. `do-while` is the only looping statement that ends with a semicolon.

Here's a version of the `EvenCounter` program that uses a `do-while` loop instead of a `while` loop:

```
public class EvenCounter2

{
    public static void main(String[] args)
    {
        int number = 2;
        do
        {
            System.out.print(number + " ");
            number += 2;
```

```
        } while (number <= 20);

        System.out.println();
    }
}
```

Here's the most important thing to remember about `do-while` loops: The statement or statements in the body of a `do-while` loop *always* get executed at least once. By contrast, the statement or statements in the body of a `while` loop aren't executed at all if the `while` expression is `false` the first time it's evaluated.

Look at the flowchart in Figure 5-2 to see what I mean. You can see that execution starts at the top of the loop and flows through to the decision test after the loop's body has been executed once. Then, if the decision test is `true`, control flies back up to the top of the loop. Otherwise, it spills out the bottom of the flowchart.

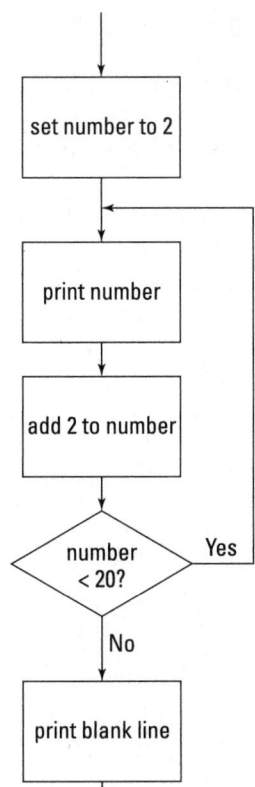

Figure 5-2:
The flowchart for a do-while loop.

Here are a few other things to be aware of concerning `do-while` loops:

✦ You often can skip initializing the variables that appear in the expression before the loop, because the expression isn't evaluated until the statements in the loop body have been executed at least once.

✦ You can use `break` and `continue` statements in a `do-while` loop, just as you can in a `while` loop.

✦ Some programmers like to place the brace that begins the loop body on the same line as the `do` statement and the `while` statement that ends the `do-while` loop on the same line as the brace that marks the end of the loop body. Whatever makes you happy is fine with me. Just remember that the compiler is agnostic when it comes to matters of indentation and spacing.

Validating Input from the User

`do-while` loops are especially useful for validating input by the user. Suppose you're writing a program that plays a betting game, and you want to get the amount of the user's bet from the console. The user can bet any dollar amount he wants (whole dollars only, though) but can't bet more than he has in the bank, and he can't bet a negative amount or zero. Here's a program that uses a `do-while` loop to get this input from the user:

```java
import java.util.Scanner;

public class GetABet
{

    static Scanner sc = new Scanner(System.in);

    public static void main(String[] args)
    {
        int bank = 1000;    // assume the user has $1,000
        int bet;            // the bet entered by the user

        System.out.println("You can bet between 1 and " +
            bank);
        do
        {
            System.out.print("Enter your bet: ");
            bet = sc.nextInt();
        } while ( (bet <= 0) || (bet > bank) );
        System.out.println("Your money's good here.");
    }
}
```

Here the expression used by the `do-while` loop validates the data entered by the user, which means that it checks the data against some set of criteria to make sure the data is acceptable.

The || operator performs an Or test. It returns `true` if at least one of the expressions on either side of the operator is true. So if the bet is less than or equal to zero (`bet <= 0`), or if the bet is greater than the money in the bank (`bet > bank`), this expression returns `true`.

This type of validation testing checks only whether the user entered a valid number in an acceptable range. If the user entered something that isn't a valid number, such as the word `Buttercup` or `Humperdinck`, the program chokes badly and spews forth a bunch of vile exception messages upon the console. You find out how to clean up that mess in Book II, Chapter 8.

(Actually, you can avoid this problem by using either a `do` loop or a `while` loop and the `hasNextDouble` method of the `Scanner` class, which I describe in Book II, Chapter 2.)

If you want to display an error message when the user enters incorrect input, you have to use an `if` statement inside the loop, and this `if` statement must duplicate the expression that validates the input data. Thus the expression that does the validation has to appear twice. For example:

```java
import java.util.Scanner;

public class GetABet2
{

    static Scanner sc = new Scanner(System.in);

    public static void main(String[] args)
    {
        int bank = 1000;    // assume the user has $1,000
        int bet;            // the bet entered by the user

        System.out.println
            ("You can bet between 1 and " + bank);
        do
        {
            System.out.print("Enter your bet: ");
            bet = sc.nextInt();
            if ( (bet <= 0) || (bet > bank) )
                System.out.println
                    ("What, are you crazy?");
        } while ( (bet <= 0) || (bet > bank) );
        System.out.println("Your money's good here.");
    }
}
```

Here, the `if` statement displays the message `"What, are you crazy?"` if the user tries to enter an inappropriate bet.

You can avoid duplicating the expression that does the data validation by adding a `boolean` variable that's set in the body of the `do-while` loop if the data is invalid, as in this example:

```
import java.util.Scanner;

public class GetABet3
{

    static Scanner sc = new Scanner(System.in);

    public static void main(String[] args)
    {
        int bank = 1000;    // assume the user has $1,000
        int bet;            // the bet entered by the user
        boolean validBet;   // indicates if bet is valid
        System.out.println
            ("You can bet between 1 and " + bank);
        do
        {
            System.out.print("Enter your bet: ");
            bet = sc.nextInt();
            validBet = true;
            if ( (bet <= 0) || (bet > bank) )
            {
                validBet = false;
                System.out.println
                    ("What, are you crazy?");
            }
        } while (!validBet);
        System.out.println("Your money's good here.");
    }
}
```

In this example, I use a `boolean` variable named `validBet` to indicate whether the user has entered a valid bet. After the user enters a bet, this variable is set to `true` before the `if` statement tests the validation criteria. Then, if the `if` statement finds that the bet is not valid, `validBet` is set to `false`.

Using the Famous for Loop

In addition to `while` and `do-while` loops, Java offers the *for loop*. You may have noticed that many of the loops presented so far in this minibook involve counting. It turns out that counting loops are quite common in computer programs, so the people who design computer programming languages (they're called computer programming language designers) long ago concocted a special kind of looping mechanism that's designed just for counting.

The basic principle behind a `for` loop is that the loop itself maintains a *counter variable* — that is, a variable whose value increases each time the body of the loop is executed. If you want a loop that counts from 1 to 10, you'd use a counter variable that starts with a value of 1 and is increased by 1 each time through the loop. Then you'd use a test to end the loop when the counter variable reaches 10. The `for` loop lets you set all this up in one convenient statement.

People who majored in computer science call the counter variable an *iterator*. They do so because they think that we don't know what it means. But we know perfectly well that the iterator is where you put your beer to keep it cold.

Understanding the formal format of the for loop

I would now like to inform you of the formal format of the `for` loop, so that you'll know how to form it from now on. The `for` loop follows this basic format:

```
for (initialization-expression; test-expression; count-expression)
    statement;
```

The three expressions in the parentheses following the keyword `for` control how the `for` loop works. The following paragraphs explain what these three expressions do:

✦ The *initialization expression* is executed before the loop begins. Usually, you use this expression to initialize the counter variable. If you haven't declared the counter variable before the `for` statement, you can declare it here too.

✦ The *test expression* is evaluated each time the loop is executed to determine whether the loop should keep looping. Usually, this expression tests the counter variable to make sure that it is still less than or equal to the value you want to count to. The loop keeps executing as long as this expression evaluates to `true`. When the test expression evaluates to `false`, the loop ends.

✦ The *count expression* is evaluated each time the loop executes. Its job is usually to increment the counter variable.

Figure 5-3 shows a flowchart to help you visualize how a `for` loop works.

Book II
Chapter 5

Going Around in
Circles (Or, Using
Loops)

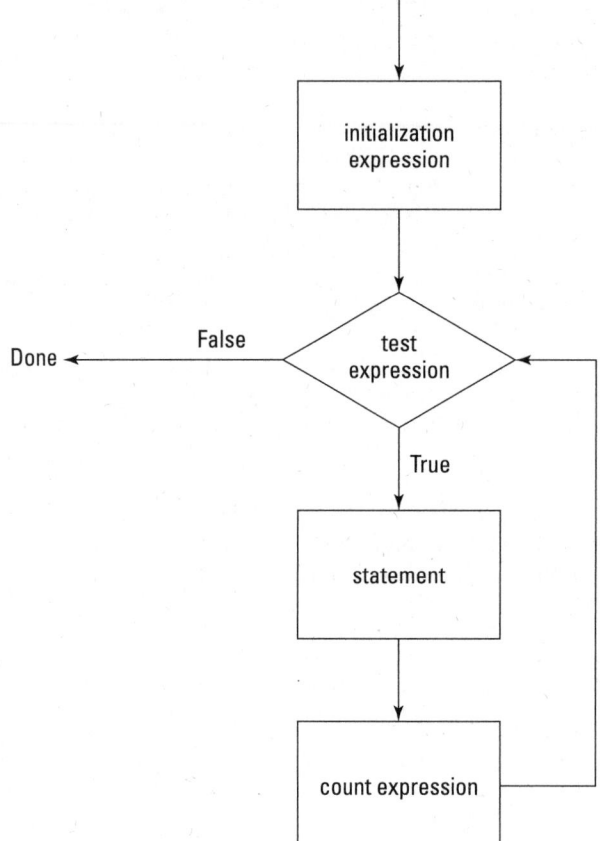

Figure 5-3:
The
flowchart
for a for
loop.

Here's a simple `for` loop that displays the numbers 1 to 10 on the console:

```
public class CountToTen
{
    public static void main(String[] args)
    {
        for (int i = 1; i <= 10; i++)
            System.out.println(i);
    }
}
```

Run this program, and here's what you see on the console:

```
1
2
3
4
5
6
```

```
7
8
9
10
```

This for loop has the following pieces:

✦ The initialization expression is int i = 1. This expression declares a variable named i of type int and assigns it an initial value of 1.

✦ The test expression is i <= 10. As a result, the loop continues to execute as long as i is less than or equal to 10.

✦ The count expression is i++. As a result, each time the loop executes, the variable i is incremented.

✦ The body of the loop is the single statement System.out.println(i). As a result, each time the loop executes, the value of the i variable is printed to the console.

**Book II
Chapter 5**

**Going Around in
Circles (Or, Using
Loops)**

I made up the terms I use to describe the three expressions in a for loop. Officially, Java calls them the *ForInit expression,* the *expression,* and the *ForUpdate expression.* Don't you think my terms are more descriptive?

Scoping out the counter variable

If you declare the counter variable in the initialization statement, the scope of the counter variable is limited to the for statement itself. Thus, you can use the variable in the other expressions that appear within the parentheses and in the body of the loop, but you can't use it outside the loop. This example code causes a compiler error:

```java
public class CountToTenError
{
    public static void main(String[] args)
    {
        for (int i = 1; i <=10; i++)
            System.out.println(i);
        System.out.println("The final value of i is " +
                            i);
    }
}
```

That's because the last statement in the main method refers to the variable i, which has gone out of scope because it was declared within the for loop.

You don't have to declare the counter variable in the for statement itself, however. The following program works:

```
public class CountToTenErrorFixed
{
    public static void main(String[] args)
    {
        int i;
        for (i = 1; i <=10; i++)
            System.out.println(i);
        System.out.println("The final value of i is " +
                                    i);
    }
}
```

Note that because the i variable is declared before the for statement, the initialization expression doesn't name the variable's data type. When you run this program, the following appears in the console window:

```
1
2
3
4
5
6
7
8
9
10
The final value of i is 11
```

Counting even numbers

Earlier in this chapter, you saw a program that counts even numbers up to 20. You can do that with a for loop too. All you have to do is adjust the count expression. Here's a version of the CountEven program that uses a for loop:

```
public class ForEvenCounter
{
    public static void main(String[] args)
    {
        for (int number = 2; number <= 20; number += 2)
            System.out.print(number + " ");
        System.out.println();
    }
}
```

Run this program, and sure enough, the console window displays the following:

```
2 4 6 8 10 12 14 16 18 20
```

Counting backward

No rule says `for` loops can only count forward. To count backward, you simply have to adjust the three `for` loop expressions. As usual, the initialization expression specifies the starting value for the counter variable. The test expression uses a greater-than test instead of a less-than test, and the count expression subtracts from the counter variable rather than adding to it.

For example:

```java
public class CountDown
{
    public static void main(String[] args)
    {
        for (int count = 10; count >= 1; count--)
        {
                System.out.println(count);
        }
    }
}
```

Run this program, and you see this result in the console window:

```
10
9
8
7
6
5
4
3
2
1
```

If you grew up in the 1960s watching NASA launches religiously, as I did, you'll appreciate this variation of the countdown program:

```java
public class LaunchControl
{
    public static void main(String[] args)
    {
        System.out.print
            ("We are go for launch in T minus ");
        for (int count = 10; count >= 0; count--)
        {
            if (count == 8)
                System.out.println
                    ("Ignition sequence start!");
            else
                System.out.println(count + "...");
        }
        System.out.println("All engines running!");
```

```
        System.out.println("Liftoff! We have a liftoff!");
    }
}
```

When you run it, here's the output that's displayed:

```
We are go for launch in T minus 10...
9...
Ignition sequence start!
7...
6...
5...
4...
3...
2...
1...
0...
All engines running!
Liftoff! We have a liftoff!
```

Can't you just hear the voice of Paul Haney, the famous "Voice of Mission Control" for NASA in the 1960s? If you can't, you're not nearly as nerdy (or as old) as I am.

Using for loops without bodies

Some programmers get a kick out of writing code that is as terse as possible. I think *Seinfeld* did an episode about that. Jerry had a girlfriend who was a "terse-coder," and he had to dump her because he couldn't understand her code.

Anyway, terse-coders sometimes like to play with for statements in an effort to do away with the body of a for loop altogether. To do that, they take advantage of the fact that you can code any expression you want in the count expression part of a for statement, including method calls. Here's a program that prints the numbers 1 to 10 on the console, using a for statement that has no body:

```
public class TerseCoder
{
    public static void main(String[] args)
    {
        for (int i = 1; i <=10; System.out.println(i++));
    }
}
```

Here the count expression is a call to System.out.println. The parameter to the println method cleverly uses the increment operator, so the variable is both printed and incremented in the same expression.

Stay away from terse-coders! Seinfeld was right to dump her.

Ganging up your expressions

An obscure aspect of `for` loops is the fact that the initialization and count expressions can actually be a list of expressions separated by commas. This can be useful if you need to keep track of two counter variables at the same time. Here's a program that counts from 1 to 10 and 10 to 1 at the same time, using two counter variables:

```
public class CountBothWays
{
    public static void main(String[] args)
    {
        int a, b;
        for (a = 1, b = 10; a <= 10; a++, b--)
            System.out.println(a + " " + b);
    }
}
```

If you run this program, here's what you see in the console window:

```
1 10
2 9
3 8
4 7
5 6
6 5
7 4
8 3
9 2
10 1
```

Keep in mind these rules when you use more than one expression for the initialization and counter expressions:

✦ In the initialization expression, you can't declare variables if you use more than one expression. That's why I declared the a and b variables before the `for` statement in the `CountBothWays` example.

✦ The expressions in an expression list can be assignment statements, increment or decrement statements (such as a++), method calls, or object creation statements that use the `new` keyword to create an object from a class. Other types of statements, such as `if` statements or loops, are not allowed.

✦ You can't list more than one expression in the test expression. You can use compound conditions created with boolean operators, however, so you don't need to use an expression list.

Here, just to prove that I can do it, is a version of the LaunchController
program that uses a bodiless for loop:

```java
public class ExpressionGanging
{
    public static void main(String[] args)
    {
        System.out.print
            ("We are go for launch in T minus ");
        for (int count = 10; count >= 0;
            System.out.println((count == 8) ?
                "Ignition sequence start!" :
                count + "..."),
            count--    );
        System.out.println("All engines running!");
        System.out.println
            ("Liftoff! We have a liftoff!");
    }
}
```

This program actually looks more complicated than it is. The count expression is a list of two expressions. First is a call to System.out.println
that uses the ternary ?: operator to determine what to print. The ?: operator first evaluates the count variable to see if it equals 8. If so, the string
"Ignition sequence start!" is sent to the println method. Otherwise,
count + ". . ." is sent. The second expression simply increments the
count variable.

I think you'll agree that coding the for statement like this example is way
out of line. It's better to keep the expressions simple and do the real work in
the loop's body.

Omitting expressions

Yet another oddity about for loops is that all three of the expressions are
optional. If you omit one or more of the expressions, you just code the semicolon as a placeholder so that the compiler knows what's going on.

Omitting the test expression or the iteration expression is not common,
but omitting the initialization expression is common. The variable you're
incrementing in the for loop may already be declared and initialized before
you get to the loop, for example. In that case, you can omit the initialization
expression, like this:

```java
Scanner sc = new Scanner(System.in);
System.out.print("Where should I start? ");
int a = sc.nextInt();
for ( ; a >= 0; a--)
    System.out.println(a);
```

This for loop simply counts down from whatever number the user enters
to zero.

If you omit the test expression, you'd better throw a break statement in the loop somewhere (as described earlier in the chapter in the "Breaking Out of a Loop" section). Otherwise you'll find yourself in an infinite loop.

You can omit all three of the expressions if you want to, as in this example:

```
for(;;)
    System.out.println("Oops");
```

This program also results in an infinite loop. There's little reason to do this, however, because while(true) has the same effect and is more obvious.

Breaking and continuing your for loops

You can use a break in a for loop just as you can in a while or do-while loop. Here I revisit the Dodecaphobia program from earlier in the chapter, this time with a for loop:

```
public class ForDodecaphobia
{
    public static void main(String[] args)
    {
        for (int number = 2; number <=20; number += 2)
        {
            if (number == 12)
                break;
            System.out.print(number + " ");
        }
        System.out.println();
    }
}
```

As before, this version counts by 2 until it gets to 20. When it hits 12, however, it panics and aborts the loop, so it never actually gets to 14, 16, 18, or 20. The console output looks like this:

```
2  4  6  8  10
```

And here's a version that uses a continue statement to skip 12 rather than abort the loop:

```
public class ForDodecaphobia2
{
    public static void main(String[] args)
    {
        for (int number = 2; number <=20; number += 2)
        {
            if (number == 12)
                continue;
            System.out.print(number + " ");
        }
```

```
        System.out.println();
    }
}
```

The console output from this version looks like this:

```
2 4 6 8 10 14 16 18 20
```

Nesting Your Loops

Loops can contain loops. The technical term for this is *loop-de-loop.* Just kidding. Actually, the technical term is *nested loop,* which is simply a loop that is completely contained inside another loop. The loop that's inside is called the *inner loop,* and the loop that's outside is called the *outer loop.*

A simple nested for loop

To demonstrate the basics of nesting, here's a simple little program that uses a pair of nested `for` loops:

```
public class NestedLoop
{
    public static void main(String[] args)
    {
        for(int x = 1; x < 10; x++)
        {
            for (int y = 1; y < 10; y++)
                System.out.print(x + "-" + y + "  ");
            System.out.println();
        }
    }
}
```

This program consists of two `for` loops. The outer loop uses x as its counter variable, and the inner loop uses y. For each execution of the outer loop, the inner loop executes 10 times and prints a line that shows the value of x and y for each pass through the inner loop. When the inner loop finishes, a call to `System.out.println` with no parameters forces a line break, thus starting a new line. Then the outer loop cycles so that the next line is printed.

When you run this program, the console displays this text:

```
1-1   1-2   1-3   1-4   1-5   1-6   1-7   1-8   1-9
2-1   2-2   2-3   2-4   2-5   2-6   2-7   2-8   2-9
3-1   3-2   3-3   3-4   3-5   3-6   3-7   3-8   3-9
4-1   4-2   4-3   4-4   4-5   4-6   4-7   4-8   4-9
5-1   5-2   5-3   5-4   5-5   5-6   5-7   5-8   5-9
6-1   6-2   6-3   6-4   6-5   6-6   6-7   6-8   6-9
7-1   7-2   7-3   7-4   7-5   7-6   7-7   7-8   7-9
8-1   8-2   8-3   8-4   8-5   8-6   8-7   8-8   8-9
9-1   9-2   9-3   9-4   9-5   9-6   9-7   9-8   9-9
```

A guessing game

Listing 5-1 shows a more complicated but realistic example of nesting. This program implements a simple guessing game in which the computer picks a number between 1 and 10, and you have to guess the number. After you guess, the computer tells you whether you're right or wrong and then asks whether you want to play again. If you enter Y or y, the game starts over.

The nesting comes into play because the entire game is written in a while loop that repeats as long as you say you want to play another game. Then — within that loop — each time the game asks for input from the user, it uses a do-while loop to validate the user's entry. Thus, when the game asks the user to guess a number between 1 and 10, it keeps looping until the number entered by the user is in that range. And when the game asks the user whether he or she wants to play again, it loops until the user enters Y, y, N, or n.

Here's a sample of the console output displayed by this program:

```
Let's play a guessing game!

I'm thinking of a number between 1 and 10.
What do you think it is? 5
You're wrong! The number was 8

Play again? (Y or N)y

I'm thinking of a number between 1 and 10.
What do you think it is? 32
I said, between 1 and 10. Try again: 5
You're wrong! The number was 6

Play again? (Y or N)maybe

Play again? (Y or N)ok

Play again? (Y or N)y

I'm thinking of a number between 1 and 10.
What do you think it is? 5
You're right!

Play again? (Y or N)n

Thank you for playing.
```

Listing 5-1:   The Guessing Game

```java
import java.util.Scanner;

public class GuessingGame
{

    static Scanner sc = new Scanner(System.in);

    public static void main(String[] args)
    {
        boolean keepPlaying = true;                             →10

        System.out.println("Let's play a guessing game!");
        while (keepPlaying)                                     →13
        {
            boolean validInput;                                →15
            int number, guess;
            String answer;

            // Pick a random number
            number = (int)(Math.random() * 10) + 1;            →20

            // Get the guess
            System.out.println("\nI'm thinking of a number "
                + "between 1 and 10.");
            System.out.print("What do you think it is? ");
            do                                                 →26
            {
                guess = sc.nextInt();
                validInput = true;
                if ( (guess < 1) || (guess > 10) )
                {
                    System.out.print
                        ("I said, between 1 and 10. "
                        + "Try again: ");
                    validInput = false;
                }
            } while (!validInput);                             →36

            // Check the guess
            if (guess == number)                               →39
                System.out.println("You're right!");
            else
                System.out.println("You're wrong! " +
                    "The number was " + number);

            // Play again?
            do                                                 →46
            {
                System.out.print("\nPlay again? (Y or N)");
                answer = sc.next();
                validInput = true;
                if (answer.equalsIgnoreCase("Y"));
                else if (answer.equalsIgnoreCase("N"))
                    keepPlaying = false;
```

```
        else
            validInput = false;
    } while (!validInput);                                    →57
    }                                                         →58
    System.out.println("\nThank you for playing!");           →59
    }
}
```

The following paragraphs describe some of the key lines in this program:

→ 10   Defines a `boolean` variable named `keepPlaying` that's initialized to `true` and changed to `false` when the user indicates that he or she has had enough of this silly game.

→ 13-58   Begins the main `while` loop for the game. The loop continues as long as `keepPlaying` is `true`. This loop ends on line 58.

→ 15   Defines a `boolean` variable named `validInput` that's used to indicate whether the user's input is valid. The same variable is used for both the entry of the user's guess and the `Y` or `N` string at the end of each round.

→ 20   Picks a random number between 1 and 10. For more information on random numbers, refer to Book II, Chapter 3.

→ 26-36   Begins the `do-while` loop that gets a valid guess from the user. This loop ends on line 36. The statements in this loop read the user's guess from the console and then test to make sure it is between 1 and 10. If so, `validInput` is set to `true`. Otherwise, `validInput` is set to `false`, an error message is displayed, and the loop repeats so that the user is forced to guess again. The loop continues as long as `validInput` is `false`.

→ 39   The `if` statement compares the user's guess with the computer's number. A message is displayed to indicate whether the user guessed right or wrong.

→ 46-57   Begins the `do-while` loop that asks whether the user wants to play again. This loop ends on line 57. The statements in this loop read a string from the user. If the user enters `Y` or `y`, `validInput` is set to `true`. (`keepPlaying` is already `true`, so it is left alone.) If the user enters `N` or `n`, `validInput` is set to `true`, and `keepPlaying` is set to `false`. And if the user enters anything else, `validInput` is set to `false`. The loop continues as long as `validInput` is `false`.

→ 59   This statement is executed after the program's main `while` loop finishes; it thanks the user for playing the game.

Chapter 6: Pulling a Switcheroo

In This Chapter

✔ Avoiding the trouble with big else-if statements

✔ Using the switch statement

✔ Creating case groups

✔ Using characters with case

*I*n Book II, Chapter 4, you find out about the workhorses of Java decision-making: `boolean` expressions and the mighty `if` statement. In this chapter, you discover another Java tool for decision-making: the `switch` statement. The `switch` statement is a pretty limited beast, but it excels at making one particular type of decision: choosing one of several actions based on a value stored in an integer variable. As it turns out, the need to do just that comes up a lot. You want to keep the `switch` statement handy for use when such a need arises.

Battling else-if Monstrosities

Many applications call for a simple logical selection of things to be done depending on some value that controls everything. As I describe in Book II, Chapter 4, such things are usually handled with big chains of `else-if` statements all strung together.

Unfortunately, these things can quickly get out of hand. `else-if` chains can end up looking like DNA double-helix structures or those things that dribble down from the tops of the computer screens in *The Matrix*, with hundreds of lines of code that string `else-if` after `else-if`. The `switch` statement provides a much more concise alternative.

Viewing an example else-if program

Listing 6-1 shows a bit of a program that might be used to decode error codes in a Florida or Ohio voting machine.

Listing 6-1:   The else-if Version of a Voting Machine Error Decoder

```
import java.util.Scanner;

public class VoterApp
{

  static Scanner sc = new Scanner(System.in);

  public static void main(String[] args)
  {

    System.out.println
      ("Welcome to the voting machine "
      + "error code decoder.\n\n"
      + "If your voting machine generates "
      + "an error code,\n"
      + "you can use this program to determine "
      + "the exact\ncause of the error.\n");
    System.out.print("Enter the error code: ");
    int err = sc.nextInt();

    String msg;
    if (err==1)
      msg = "Voter marked more than one candidate.\n"
        + "Ballot rejected.";
    else if (err==2)
      msg = "Box checked and write-in candidate "
        + "entered.\nBallot rejected.";
    else if (err==3)
      msg = "Entire ballot was blank.\n"
        + "Ballot filled in according to "
        + "secret plan.";
    else if (err==4)
      msg = "Nothing unusual about the ballot.\n"
        + "Voter randomly selected for tax audit.";
    else if (err==5)
      msg = "Voter filled in every box.\n"
        + "Ballot counted twice.";
    else if (err==6)
      msg = "Voter drooled in voting machine.\n"
        + "Beginning spin cycle.";
    else if (err==7)
      msg = "Voter lied to pollster after voting.\n"
        + "Voter's ballot changed "
        + "to match polling data.";
    else
      msg = "Voter filled out ballot correctly.\n"
        + "Ballot discarded anyway.";
    System.out.println(msg);
  }
}
```

Wow! And this program has to decipher just 7 error codes. What if the machine had 500 codes?

Creating a better version of the example program

Fortunately, Java has a special statement that's designed just for the kind of task represented by the voting machine error decoder program: the `switch` statement. Specifically, the `switch` statement is useful when you need to select one of several alternatives based on the value of an integer or character type variable.

Listing 6-2 shows a version of the voting machine error decoder program that uses a `switch` statement instead of a big `else-if` structure. I think you'll agree that this version of the program is a bit easier to follow. The `switch` statement makes it clear that all the messages are selected based on the value of the `err` variable.

Listing 6-2:   The switch Version of the Voting Machine Error Decoder

```java
import java.util.Scanner;

public class VoterApp2
{

  static Scanner sc = new Scanner(System.in);

  public static void main(String[] args)
  {

    System.out.println
      ("Welcome to the voting machine "
      + "error code decoder.\n\n"
      + "If your voting machine generates "
      + "an error code,\n"
      + "you can use this program to determine "
      + "the exact\ncause of the error.\n");
    System.out.print("Enter the error code: ");
    int err = sc.nextInt();

    String msg;

    switch (err)
    {
      case 1:
        msg = "Voter marked more than one "
          + "candidate.\nBallot rejected.";
        break;
      case 2:
        msg = "Box checked and write-in candidate "
          + "entered.\nBallot rejected.";
        break;
      case 3:
        msg = "Entire ballot was blank.\n"
          + "Ballot filled in according to "
          + "secret plan.";
        break;
      case 4:
        msg = "Nothing unusual about the ballot.\n"
          + "Voter randomly selected for tax audit.";
        break;
      case 5:
        msg = "Voter filled in every box.\n"
          + "Ballot counted twice.";
        break;
```

(continued)

Listing 6-2 *(continued)*

```
    case 6:
       msg = "Voter drooled in voting machine.\n"
          + "Beginning spin cycle.";
       break;
    case 7:
       msg = "Voter lied to pollster after voting.\n"
          + "Voter's ballot changed "
          + "to match polling data.";
       break;
    default:
       msg = "Voter filled out ballot correctly.\n"
          + "Ballot discarded anyway.";
       break;
    }
    System.out.println(msg);
  }
}
```

Using the switch Statement

The basic form of the switch statement is this:

```
switch (expression)
{
  case constant:
       statements;
       break;
  [ case constant-2:
       statements;
       break;  ]...
  [ default:
       statements;
       break;  ]...
}
```

The expression must evaluate to an int, short, byte, or char. It can't be a long or a floating-point type.

You can code as many case groups as you want or need. Each group begins with the word case, followed by a constant (usually, a simple numeric literal) and a colon. Then you code one or more statements that you want executed if the value of the switch expression equals the constant. The last line of each case group is a break statement, which causes the entire switch statement to end.

The default group, which is optional, is like a catch-all case group. Its statements are executed only if none of the previous case constants match the switch expression.

Note that the case groups are not true blocks marked with braces. Instead, each case group begins with the `case` keyword and ends with the `case` keyword that starts the next case group. All the case groups together, however, are defined as a block marked with a set of braces.

The last statement in each case group usually is a `break` statement. A `break` statement causes control to skip to the end of the `switch` statement. If you omit the `break` statement, control falls through to the next case group. Accidentally leaving out `break` statements is the most common cause of trouble with the `switch` statement.

Viewing a boring switch example, complete with flowchart

Okay, the voting machine error decoder was kind of fun. Here's a more down-to-earth example. Suppose that you need to set a commission rate based on a sales class represented by an integer (1, 2, or 3) according to this table:

Class	Commission Rate
1	2%
2	3.5%
3	5%
Any other value	0%

You could do this with the following `switch` statement:

```
double commissionRate;
switch (salesClass)
{
    case 1:
        commissionRate = 0.02;
        break;
    case 2:
        commissionRate = 0.035;
        break;
    case 3:
        commissionRate = 0.05;
        break;
    default:
        commissionRate = 0.0;
        break;
}
```

Figure 6-1 shows a flowchart that describes the operation of this `switch` statement. As you can see, this flowchart is similar to the flowchart in Figure 4-3 (Book II, Chapter 4), because the operation of the `switch` statement is similar to the operation of a series of `else-if` statements.

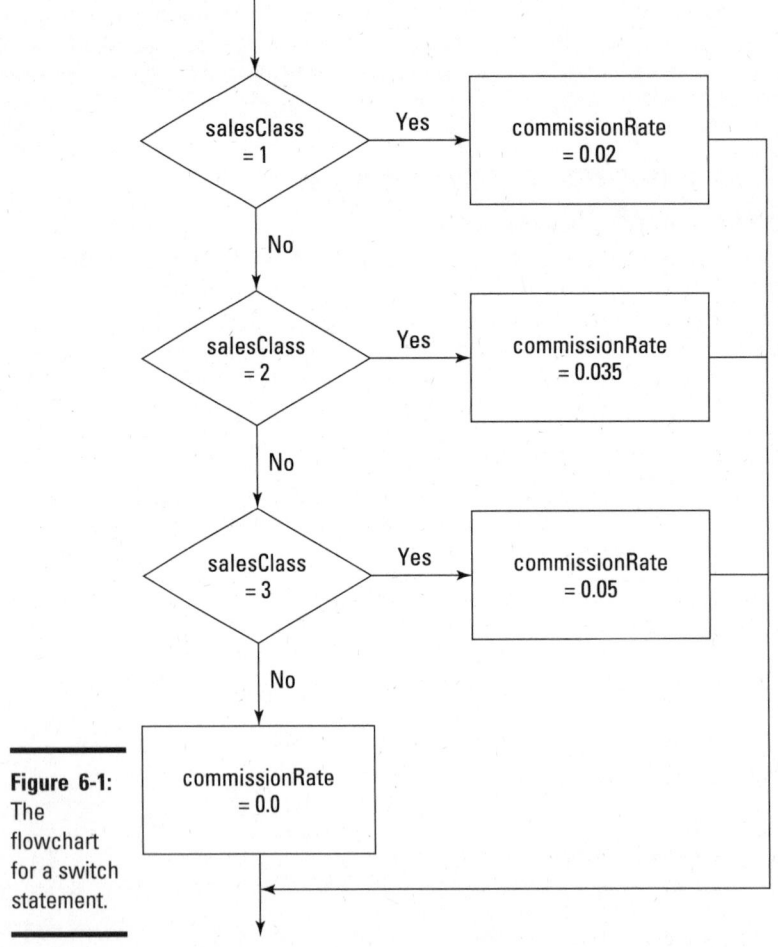

Figure 6-1: The flowchart for a switch statement.

Flowcharts remind me of the good old days, when many COBOL programming shops required their programmers to draw flowcharts for every program they wrote before they were allowed to write any code. The flowcharts didn't really help programmers write better programs, but they were fun to draw.

Putting if statements inside switch statements

You're free to include any type of statements you want in the case groups, including if statements. Suppose that your commission structure depends on total sales as well as sales class, as in this table:

Class	Sales < $10,000	Sales $10,000 and Above
1	1%	2%
2	2.5%	3.5%
3	4%	5%
Any other value	0%	0%

You can use the following switch statement:

```
double commissionRate;
switch (salesClass)
{
    case 1:
        if (salesTotal < 10000.0)
            commissionRate = 0.01;
        else
            commissionRate = 0.02;
        break;
    case 2:
        if (salesTotal < 10000.0)
            commissionRate = 0.025;
        else
            commissionRate = 0.035;
        break;
    case 3:
        if (salesTotal < 10000.0)
            commissionRate = 0.04;
        else
            commissionRate = 0.05;
        break;
    default:
        commissionRate = 0.0;
        break;
}
```

Here each case group includes an if statement. If necessary, these if statements could be complex nested if statements.

Other than the if statements within the case groups, there's nothing here to see, folks. Move along.

Creating Character Cases

Aside from having a nice alliterative title, this section shows how you can use a `char` variable rather than an integer in a `switch` statement. When you use a `char` type, providing two consecutive `case` constants for each case group is common, to allow for both lowercase and uppercase letters. Suppose that you need to set the commission rates for the sales class based on character codes rather than on integer values, according to this table:

Class	Commission Rate
A or a	2%
B or b	3.5%
C or c	5%
Any other value	0%

Here's a `switch` statement that can do the trick:

```
double commissionRate;
switch (salesClass)
{
    case 'A':
    case 'a':
        commissionRate = 0.02;
        break;
    case 'B':
    case 'b':
        commissionRate = 0.035;
        break;
    case 'C':
    case 'c':
        commissionRate = 0.05;
        break;
    default:
        commissionRate = 0.0;
        break;
}
```

The key to understanding this example is realizing that you don't have to code any statements at all for a case group — and that if you omit the `break` statement from a case group, control falls through to the next case group. Thus the `case 'A'` group doesn't contain any statements, but control falls through to the `case 'a'` group.

You use apostrophes, not quotation marks, to create character literals.

Intentionally Leaving Out a Break Statement

Although the most common cause of problems with the `switch` statement is accidentally leaving out a `break` statement at the end of a case group, sometimes you need to do it on purpose. Many applications have features that are progressively added based on a control variable. Your local car wash, for example, may sell several packages with different services, as in this table:

Package	Services
A	Wash, vacuum, and hand-dry
B	Package A + wax
C	Package B + leather/vinyl treatment
D	Package C + tire treatment
E	Package D + new-car scent

**Book II
Chapter 6**

**Pulling a
Switcheroo**

Listing 6-3 shows an application that displays all the products you get when you order a specific package. It works by testing the package codes in a `switch` statement in reverse order (starting with package E) and adding the products that come with each package to the `details` variable. None of the case groups except the last includes a `break` statement. As a result, control falls through each case group to the next group. Thus, once a case group has tested `true`, the rest of the case groups in the `switch` statement are executed.

Listing 6-3:   The Car Wash Application

```
import java.util.Scanner;

public class CarWashApp
{
  static Scanner sc = new Scanner(System.in);

  public static void main(String[] args)
  {
    System.out.println
      ("The car wash application!\n\n");
    System.out.print("Enter the package code: ");
    String s = sc.next();
    char p = s.charAt(0);

    String details = "";

    switch (p)
    {
      case 'E':
      case 'e':
        details += "\tNew Car Scent, plus . . . \n";
```

Listing 6-3 *(continued)*

```
      case 'D':
      case 'd':
        details += "\tTire Treatment, plus . . . \n";
      case 'C':
      case 'c':
      details +=
          "\tLeather/Vinyl Treatment, plus . . . \n";
      case 'B':
      case 'b':
        details += "\tWax, plus . . . \n";
      case 'A':
      case 'a':
        details += "\tWash, vacuum, and hand dry.\n";
        break;
      default:
        details = "That's not one of the codes.";
        break;
    }
    System.out.println("\nThat package includes:\n");
    System.out.println(details);
  }
}
```

Just between you and me, writing programs that depend on `switch` statements falling through the cracks (as in this example) isn't really a good idea. Instead, consider placing the statements for each case group in separate methods and then calling all the methods you need for each case group. Then you can use a `break` statement at the end of each group to prevent falling through. Listing 6-4 shows a version of the car wash application that uses this technique to prevent fall-throughs in the `switch` statement. (Using simple fall-throughs to treat uppercase and lowercase characters the same way isn't as confusing, so this program still uses that technique.)

Listing 6-4:   A Version of the Car Wash Program That Prevents Nasty Falls

```
import java.util.Scanner;

public class CarWashApp2
{
  static Scanner sc = new Scanner(System.in);

  public static void main(String[] args)
  {
    System.out.println
      ("The car wash application!\n\n");
    System.out.print("Enter the package code: ");
    String s = sc.next();
    char p = s.charAt(0);

    String details = "";
```

```
    switch (p)
    {
      case 'E':
      case 'e':
        details = packageE() + packageD() + packageC()
          + packageB() + packageA();
        break;
      case 'D':
      case 'd':
        details = packageD() + packageC()
          + packageB() + packageA();
        break;
      case 'C':
      case 'c':
        details = packageC() + packageB()
          + packageA();
        break;
      case 'B':
      case 'b':
        details = packageB() + packageA();
        break;
      case 'A':
      case 'a':
        details = packageA();
        break;
      default:
        details = "That's not one of the codes.";
        break;
    }
    System.out.println("\nThat package includes:\n");
    System.out.println(details);
  }

  public static String packageA()
  {
    return "\tWash, vacuum, and hand dry.\n";
  }

  public static String packageB()
  {
    return "\tWax, plus . . . \n";
  }

  public static String packageC()
  {
    return "\tLeather/Vinyl Treatment, plus . . . \n";
  }

  public static String packageD()
  {
    return "\tTire Treatment, plus . . . \n";
  }

  public static String packageE()
  {
    return "\tNew Car Scent, plus . . . \n";
  }
}
```

Switching with Strings

Beginning with Java 1.7, the expression in the `switch` statement can evaluate to a `String` value. Listing 6-5 shows a version of the car wash program that uses the string codes `PRESIDENTIAL`, `ELITE`, `DELUXE`, `SUPER`, and `STANDARD` as the car wash types, instead of the letters A through E. Notice that to allow for variations in how a user might capitalize these codes, the user's input is converted to all capital letters before it is tested against the string constants in the `switch` statement.

Listing 6-5:   A Version of the Car Wash Program That Uses a String

```java
import java.util.Scanner;

public class CarWashStringApp
{
    static Scanner sc = new Scanner(System.in);

    public static void main(String[] args)
    {
        System.out.println("The car wash application\n\n");
        System.out.print("Enter the package code: ");
        String s = sc.next();

        String details = "";

        switch (s.toUpperCase())
        {
            case "PRESIDENTIAL":
                details += "\tNew Car Scent, plus . . . \n";
            case "ELITE":
                details += "\tTire Treatment, plus . . . \n";
            case "DELUXE":
                details += "\tLeather/Vinyl Treatment, plus . . . \n";
            case "SUPER":
                details += "\tWax, plus . . . \n";
            case "STANDARD":
                details += "\tWash, vacuum, and hand dry.\n";
                break;
            default:
                details = "That's not one of the codes.";
                break;
        }
        System.out.println("\nThat package includes:\n");
        System.out.println(details);
    }
}
```

Chapter 7: Adding Some Methods to Your Madness

In This Chapter

✓ Introducing static methods

✓ Seeing some good reasons to use methods in your programs

✓ Creating methods that return values

✓ Creating methods that accept parameters

*I*n Java, a *method* is a block of statements that has a name and can be executed by *calling* (also called *invoking*) it from some other place in your program. You may not realize it, but you're already very experienced in using methods. To print text to the console, for example, you use the `println` or `print` method. To get an integer from the user, you use the `nextInt` method. To compare string values, you use the `equals` or `equalsIgnoreCase` method. Finally, the granddaddy of all methods — `main` — contains the statements that are executed when you run your program.

All the methods you've used so far (with the exception of `main`) have been defined by the Java API and belong to a particular Java class. The `nextInt` method belongs to the `Scanner` class, for example, and the `equalsIgnoreCase` method belongs to the `String` class. By contrast, the `main` method belongs to the class defined by your application.

In this chapter, you find out how to create additional methods that are part of your application's class. Then you can call these methods from your `main` method. As you'll see, this technique turns out to be very useful for all but the shortest Java programs.

The Joy of Methods

The use of methods can dramatically improve the quality of your programming life. Suppose that the problem your program is supposed to solve is complicated, and you need at least 1,000 Java statements to get 'er done. You could put all those 1,000 statements in the `main` method, but it would go on for pages and pages. It's better to break your program into a few well-defined sections of code and place each of those sections in a separate method. Then your `main` method can simply call the other methods in the right sequence.

Or suppose that your program needs to perform some calculation, such as how long to let the main rockets burn to make a midcourse correction on a moon flight, and the program needs to perform this calculation in several places. Without methods, you'd have to duplicate the statements that do this calculation. That approach is not only error-prone, but also makes your programs more difficult to test and debug. But if you put the calculation in a method, you can simply call the method whenever you need to perform the calculation. Thus methods help you cut down on repetitive code.

Another good use for methods is to simplify the structure of your code that uses long loops. Suppose you have a `while` loop that has 500 statements in its body. That structure makes it pretty hard to track down the brace that marks the end of the body. By the time you find it, you probably will have forgotten what the `while` loop does. You can simplify this `while` loop by placing the code from its body in a separate method. Then all the `while` loop has to do is call the new method.

At this point, the object-oriented programming zealots in the audience are starting to boo and hiss. A few of them have already left the auditorium. They're upset because I'm describing methods in traditional procedural-programming terms instead of modern object-oriented programming terms.

Well, phooey. They're right, but so what? I get to the object-oriented uses for methods in Book III. There, you find out that methods have a far greater purpose than simply breaking a long `main` method into smaller pieces. Even so, some of the most object-oriented programs I know use methods just to prevent repetitive code or to slice a large method into a couple of smaller ones. So there.

The Basics of Making Methods

All methods — including the `main` method — must begin with a *method declaration*. Here's the basic form of a method declaration, at least for the types of methods I talk about in this chapter:

```
public static return-type method-name (parameter-list)
{
        statements . . .
}
```

The following paragraphs describe the method declaration piece by piece:

✦ `public:` This keyword indicates that the method's existence should be publicized to the world and that any Java program that knows about your program (or, more accurately, the class defined for your Java program) should be able to use your method. That's not very meaningful for the types of programs you're dealing with at this point in the book, but it becomes more meaningful in Book III: There you find out more about what `public` means and see some alternatives to `public` that are useful in various and sundry situations.

✦ `static`: This keyword declares that the method is a *static method,* which means that you can call it without first creating an instance of the class in which it's defined. The `main` method must always be static, and any other methods in the class that contains the `main` method usually should be static as well.

✦ `return-type`: After the word `static` comes the *return type,* which indicates whether the method returns a value when it is called and, if so, what type the value is. If the method doesn't return a value, specify `void`. (I talk more about methods that return values later in this chapter, in the section "Methods That Return Values.")

✦ `method-name`: Now comes the name of your method. The rules for making up method names are the same as the rules for creating variable names: You can use any combination of letters and numbers, but the name has to start with a letter. Also, it can include the dollar sign ($) and underscore character (_). No other special characters are allowed.

When picking a name for your method, try to pick a name that's relatively short but descriptive. A method name such as `calculateThe TotalAmountOfTheInvoice` is a little long, but just `calc` is pretty ambiguous. Something along the lines of `calculateInvoiceTotal` seems more reasonable to me.

✦ `parameter list`: You can pass one or more values to a method by listing the values in parentheses following the method name. The parameter list in the method declaration lets Java know what types of parameters a method should expect to receive and provides names so that the statements in the method's body can access the parameters as local variables. You discover more about parameters in the section "Methods That Take Parameters," later in this chapter.

If the method doesn't accept parameters, you must still code the parentheses that surround the parameter list. You just leave the parentheses empty.

✦ **Method body:** The method body consists of one or more Java statements enclosed in a set of braces. Unlike Java statements such as `if`, `while`, and `for`, the method body requires you to use the braces even if the body consists of only one statement.

An example

Okay, all that was a little abstract. Now, for a concrete example, I offer a version of the `Hello, World!` program in which the message is displayed not by the `main` method, but by a method named `sayHello` that's called by the `main` method:

```
public class HelloWorldMethod

{
    public static void main(String[] args)
    {
```

```
        sayHello();
    }

    public static void sayHello()
    {
        System.out.println("Hello, World!");
    }

}
```

This program is admittedly trivial, but it illustrates the basics of creating and using methods in Java. Here, the statement in the `main` method calls the `sayHello` method, which in turn displays a message on the console.

The order in which methods appear in your Java source file doesn't matter. The only rule is that all the methods must be declared within the body of the class — that is, between the first left brace and the last right brace. Here's a version of the `HelloWorldMethod` program in which I reverse the order of the methods:

```
public class HelloWorldMethod
{
    public static void sayHello()
    {
        System.out.println("Hello, World!");
    }

    public static void main(String[] args)
    {
        sayHello();
    }

}
```

This version of the program works exactly like the preceding version.

Another example

Okay, the last example was kind of dumb. No one in his (or her) right mind would create a method that has just one line of code and then call it from another method that *also* has just one line of code. The `Hello, World!` program is too trivial to illustrate anything remotely realistic.

A program in Book II, Chapter 5, plays a guessing game. Most of this program's `main` method is a large `while` loop that repeats the game as long as the user wants to keep playing. This loop has 41 statements in its body. That's not so bad, but what if the game were 100 times more complicated, so that the `while` loop needed 4,100 statements to play a single cycle of the game? Do you really want a `while` loop that has 4,100 statements in its body? I should think not.

Listing 7-1 shows how you can simplify this game a bit just by placing the body of the main `while` loop in a separate method. I called this method `playARound`, because its job is to play one round of the guessing game. Now, instead of actually playing a round of the game, the `main` method of this program delegates that task to the `playARound` method.

Listing 7-1: A Version of the Guessing-Game Program That Uses a playARound Method

```
import java.util.Scanner;

public class GuessingGameMethod
{

    static Scanner sc = new Scanner(System.in);
    static boolean keepPlaying = true;                          →7
    public static void main(String[] args)
    {
        System.out.println("Let's play a guessing game!");
        while (keepPlaying)                                     →12
        {
            playARound();                                      →14
        }
        System.out.println("\nThank you for playing!");
    }

    public static void playARound()                            →19
    {
        boolean validInput;
        int number, guess;
        String answer;

        // Pick a random number
        number = (int)(Math.random() * 10) + 1;
        System.out.println("\nI'm thinking of a number "
            + "between 1 and 10.");

        // Get the guess
        System.out.print("What do you think it is? ");
        do
        {
            guess = sc.nextInt();
            validInput = true;
            if ((guess < 1) || (guess > 10))
            {
                System.out.print("I said, between 1 "
                    + "and 10. Try again: ");
                validInput = false;
            }
        } while (!validInput);

        // Check the guess
```

(continued)

Listing 7-1 *(continued)*

```
        if (guess == number)
            System.out.println("You're right!");
        else
            System.out.println("You're wrong!"
                + " The number was " + number);

        // Play again?
        do
        {
            System.out.print("\nPlay again? (Y or N)");
            answer = sc.next();
            validInput = true;
            if (answer.equalsIgnoreCase("Y"));
            else if (answer.equalsIgnoreCase("N"))
                keepPlaying = false;                       →60
            else
                validInput = false;
        } while (!validInput);
    }
}
```

Here are a few important details to notice about this method:

→ 7   Because both the `main` method (in line 12) and the `playARound` method (in line 60) must access the `keepPlaying` variable, I declare it as a class variable rather than as a local variable in the `main` method.

Class variables must be static if you intend to access them from static methods.

→ 14   The body of the `while` loop in the `main` method is just one line: a call to the `playARound` method. Thus, each time the loop repeats, the program plays one round of the game with the user.

→ 19   The declaration for the `playARound` method marks the method as `static` so that the static `main` method can call it.

The body of the `playARound` method is identical to the body of the `while` loop used in the single-method version of this program shown in Book II, Chapter 5. If you want a refresher on how this code works, I politely refer you to Listing 5-1, near the end of that chapter.

Methods That Return Values

Methods that just do work without returning any data are useful only in limited situations. The real utility of methods comes when they can perform some mundane task such as a calculation and then return the value of that calculation to the calling method so that the calling method can do something with the value. You find out how to do that in the following sections.

Declaring the method's return type

To create a method that returns a value, you simply indicate the type of the value returned by the method on the method declaration in place of the void keyword. Here's a method declaration that creates a method that returns an int value:

```
public static int getRandomNumber()
```

Here the getRandomNumber method calculates a random number and then returns the number to the caller.

The return type of a method can be any of Java's primitive return types (described in Book II, Chapter 2):

```
int
long
float
char
short
byte
double
boolean
```

Alternatively, the return type can be a *reference type*, including a class defined by the API such as String or a class you create yourself.

Using the return statement to return the value

When you specify a return type other than void in a method declaration, the body of the method must include a return statement that specifies the value to be returned. The return statement has this form:

```
return expression;
```

The expression must evaluate to a value that's the same type as the type listed in the method declaration. In other words, if the method returns an int, the expression in the return statement must evaluate to an int.

Here's a program that uses a method that determines a random number between 1 and 10:

```
public class RandomNumber

{
    public static void main(String[] args)
    {
        int number = getRandomNumber();
        System.out.println("The number is " + number);
    }
```

```
public static int getRandomNumber()
{
    int num = (int)(Math.random() * 10) + 1;
    return num;
}
}
```

In this program, the getRandomNumber method uses the Math.random method to calculate a random number from 1 to 10. (For more information about the Math.random method, see Book II, Chapter 3.) The return statement returns the random number that was calculated.

Because the return statement can specify an expression as well as a simple variable, I could just as easily have written the getRandomNumber method like this:

```
public static int getRandomNumber()
{
    return (int)(Math.random() * 10) + 1;
}
```

Here the return statement includes the expression that calculates the random number.

Using a method that returns a type

You can use a method that returns a value in an assignment statement, like this:

```
int number = getRandomNumber();
```

Here the getRandomNumber method is called, and the value it returns is assigned to the variable number.

You can also use methods that return values in expressions — such as

```
number = getRandomNumber() * 10;
```

Here the value returned by the getRandomNumber method is multiplied by 10, and the result is assigned to number.

You gotta have a proper return statement

If a method declares a return type other than void, it *must* use a return statement to return a value. The compiler doesn't let you get away with a method that doesn't have a correct return statement.

Things can get complicated if your `return` statements are inside `if` statements. Sometimes, the compiler gets fooled and refuses to compile your program. To explain this situation, I offer the following tale of multiple attempts to solve what should be a simple programming problem.

Suppose that you want to create a random-number method that returns random numbers between 1 and 20 but never returns 12 (because you have the condition known as dodecaphobia, which — as Lucy from *Peanuts* would tell you — is the fear of the number 12). Your first thought is to just ignore the 12s, like this:

```
public static int getRandomNumber()
{
    int num = (int)(Math.random() * 20) + 1;
    if (num != 12)
        return num;
}
```

The compiler isn't fooled by your trickery here, however. It knows that if the number is 12, the `return` statement won't get executed, so it issues the message `missing return statement` and refuses to compile your program.

Your next thought is to simply substitute 11 whenever 12 comes up:

```
public static int getRandomNumber()
{
    int num = (int)(Math.random() * 20) + 1;
    if (num != 12)
        return num;
    else
        return 11;
}
```

Later that day, you realize that this solution isn't a good one because the number isn't really random anymore. One of the requirements of a good random-number generator is that any number should be as likely as any other number to come up next. But because you're changing all 12s to 11s, you've made 11 twice as likely to come up as any other number.

To fix this error, you decide to put the random-number generator in a loop that ends only when the random number is not 12:

```
public static int getRandomNumber()
{
    int num;
```

```
do
{
    num = (int)(Math.random() * 20) + 1;
    if (num != 12)
        return num;
} while (num == 12);
}
```

But the compiler refuses to compile the method again. It turns out that the compiler is smart, but not very smart. It doesn't catch the fact that the condition in the do-while loop is the opposite of the condition in the if statement, meaning that the only way out of this loop is through the return statement in the if statement. So the compiler whines missing return statement again.

After thinking about it for a while, you come up with this solution:

```
public static int getRandomNumber()
{
    int num;
    while (true)
    {
        num = (int)(Math.random() * 20) + 1;
        if (num != 12)
            return num;
    }
}
```

Now everyone's happy. The compiler knows that the only way out of the loop is through the return statement, your duodecaphobic user doesn't have to worry about seeing the number 12, and you know that the random number isn't twice as likely to be 11 as any other number. Life is good, and you can move on to the next topic.

Trying another version of the guessing-game program

To illustrate the benefits of using methods that return values, Listing 7-2 presents another version of the guessing-game program that uses four methods in addition to main:

✦ **playARound:** This method plays one round of the guessing game. It doesn't return a value.

✦ **getRandomNumber:** This method returns a random number between 1 and 10.

✦ **getGuess:** This method gets the user's guess, makes sure that it is between 1 and 10, and returns the guess if it's within the acceptable range.

✦ **askForAnotherRound:** This method asks the user to play another round and returns a boolean value to indicate whether the user wants to continue playing.

Listing 7-2:   Another Version of the Guessing-Game Program

```
import java.util.Scanner;

public class GuessingGameMethod2
{

    static Scanner sc = new Scanner(System.in);

    public static void main(String[] args)
    {
        System.out.println("Let's play a guessing game!");
        do                                                      →11
        {
            playARound();                                       →13
        } while (askForAnotherRound());                         →14
        System.out.println("\nThank you for playing!");
    }

    public static void playARound()                             →18
    {
        boolean validInput;
        int number, guess;
        String answer;

        // Pick a random number
        number = getRandomNumber();                             →25

        // Get the guess
        System.out.println("\nI'm thinking of a number "
            + "between 1 and 10.");
        System.out.print("What do you think it is? ");
        guess = getGuess();                                     →31

        // Check the guess
        if (guess == number)
            System.out.println("You're right!");
        else
            System.out.println("You're wrong!"
                + " The number was " + number);
    }

    public static int getRandomNumber()                         →41
    {
        return (int)(Math.random() * 10) + 1;                   →43
    }

    public static int getGuess()                                →46
    {
        while (true)                                            →48
```

Book II
Chapter 7

Adding Some
Methods to Your
Madness

(continued)

Listing 7-2 *(continued)*

```
    {
        int guess = sc.nextInt();
        if ((guess < 1) || (guess > 10))
        {
            System.out.print("I said, between 1 and 10. "
                + "Try again: ");
        }
        else
            return guess;                                    →57
    }
}

public static boolean askForAnotherRound()                   →61
{
    while (true)                                             →63
    {
        String answer;
        System.out.print("\nPlay again? (Y or N) ");
        answer = sc.next();
        if (answer.equalsIgnoreCase("Y"))
            return true;                                     →69
        else if (answer.equalsIgnoreCase("N"))
            return false;                                    →71
    }
}
}
```

The following paragraphs point out the key lines of this program:

→ 11   The start of the do loop in the main method. Each cycle of this do loop plays one round of the game. The do loop continues until the user indicates that he or she wants to stop playing.

→ 13   Calls the playARound method to play one round of the game.

→ 14   Calls the askForAnotherRound method to determine whether the user wants to play another round. The boolean return value from this method is used as the expression for the do loop. Thus, the do loop repeats if the askForAnotherRound method returns true.

→ 18   The start of the playARound method.

→ 25   Calls the getRandomNumber method to get a random number between 1 and 10. The value returned by this method is stored in the number variable.

→ 31   Calls the getGuess method to get the user's guess. This method returns a number between 1 and 10, which is stored in the guess variable.

→ 41   The start of the getRandomNumber method, which indicates that this method returns an int value.

→ **43** The `return` statement for the `getRandomNumber` method. The random number is calculated using the `Math.random` method, and the result of this calculation is returned as the value of the `getRandomNumber` method.

→ **46** The start of the `getGuess` method, which indicates that this method returns an `int` value.

→ **48** The `getGuess` method uses a `while` loop, which exits only when the user enters a number between 1 and 10.

→ **57** The `return` statement for the `getGuess` method. Note that this `return` statement is in the `else` part of an `if` statement that checks whether the number is less than 1 or greater than 10. If the number is outside the acceptable range, the `return` statement isn't executed. Instead, the program displays an error message, and the `while` loop repeats.

→ **61** The start of the `askForAnotherRound` method, which returns a `boolean` value.

→ **63** The `askForAnotherRound` method, which uses a `while` loop that exits only when the user enters a valid `Y` or `N` response.

→ **69** The `askForAnotherRound` method, which returns `true` if the user enters `Y` or `y`.

→ **71** The `askForAnotherRound` method, which returns `false` if the user enters `N` or `n`.

Methods That Take Parameters

A *parameter* is a value that you can pass to a method. Then the method can use the parameter as though it were a local variable initialized with the value of the variable passed to it by the calling method.

The guessing-game application shown in Listing 7-2 has a method named `getRandomNumber` that returns a random number between 1 and 10:

```
public static int getRandomNumber()
{
    return (int)(Math.random() * 10) + 1;
}
```

This method is useful, but it would be even more useful if you could tell it the range of numbers you want the random number to fall in. It would be nice to call the method like this to get a random number between 1 and 10:

```
int number = getRandomNumber(1, 10);
```

Then, if your program needs to roll dice, you could call the same method:

```
int number = getRandomNumber(1, 6);
```

Or, to pick a random card from a deck of 52 cards, you could call it like this:

```
int number = getRandomNumber(1, 52);
```

You wouldn't have to start with 1, either. To get a random number between 50 and 100, you'd call the method like this:

```
int number = getRandomNumber(50, 100);
```

In the following sections, you write methods that accept parameters.

Declaring parameters

A method that accepts parameters must list the parameters in the method declaration. The parameters are placed in a *parameter list* inside the parentheses that follow the method name. For each parameter used by the method, you list the parameter type followed by the parameter name. If you need more than one parameter, you separate the parameters with commas.

Here's a version of the getRandomNumber method that accepts parameters:

```
public static int getRandomNumber(int min, int max)
{
    return (int)(Math.random()
        * (max - min + 1)) + min;
}
```

Here the method uses two parameters, both of type int, named min and max. Then, within the body of the method, these parameters can be used as though they were local variables.

The names you use for parameters can be the same as the names you use for the variables you pass to the method when you call it, but they don't have to be. You could call the getRandomNumber method like this:

```
int min = 1;
int max = 10;
int number = getRandomNumber(min, max);
```

Or you could call it like this:

```
int low = 1;
int high = 10;
int number = getRandomNumber(low, high);
```

Or you could dispense with the variables altogether and just pass literal values to the method:

```
int number = getRandomNumber(1, 10);
```

You can also specify expressions as the parameter values:

```
int min = 1;
int max = 10;
int number = getRandomNumber(min * 10, max * 10);
```

Here `number` is assigned a value between 10 and 100.

Scoping out parameters

The scope of a parameter is the method for which the parameter is declared. As a result, a parameter can have the same name as local variables used in other methods without causing any conflict. Consider this program:

```
public class ParameterScope
{
    public static void main(String[] args)
    {
        int min = 1;
        int max = 10;
        int number = getRandomNumber(min, max);
        System.out.println(number);
    }

    public static int getRandomNumber(int min, int max)
    {
        return (int)(Math.random()
            * (max - min + 1)) + min;
    }
}
```

Here the `main` method declares variables named `min` and `max`, and the `getRandomNumber` method uses `min` and `max` for its parameter names. This doesn't cause any conflict, because in each case the scope is limited to a single method.

Understanding pass-by-value

When Java passes a variable to a method via a parameter, the method itself receives a copy of the variable's value, not the variable itself. This copy is called a *pass-by-value,* and it has an important consequence: If a method changes the value it receives as a parameter, that change is *not* reflected in the original variable that was passed to the method. The following program can help clear this up:

```java
public class ChangeParameters
{
    public static void main(String[] args)
    {
        int number = 1;
        tryToChangeNumber(number);
        System.out.println(number);
    }

    public static void tryToChangeNumber(int i)
    {
        i = 2;
    }
}
```

Here a variable named `number` is set to 1 and then passed to the method named `tryToChangeNumber`. This method receives the variable as a parameter named `i` and then sets the value of `i` to 2. Meanwhile, back in the `main` method, `println` is used to print the value of `number` after the `tryToChangeNumber` method returns.

Because `tryToChangeNumber` gets only a copy of `number`, not the `number` variable itself, this program displays the following on the console (drum roll, please . . .): 1.

The key point is this: Even though the `tryToChangeNumber` method changes the value of its parameter, that change has no effect on the original variable that was passed to the method.

Trying yet another version of the guessing-game program

To show off the benefits of methods that accept parameters, Listing 7-3 shows one more version of the guessing-game program. This version uses the following methods in addition to `main`:

✦ **playARound:** This method plays one round of the guessing game. It doesn't return a value, but it accepts two arguments, `min` and `max`, that indicate the minimum and maximum values for the number to be guessed.

✦ **getRandomNumber:** This method returns a random number between min and max values passed as parameters.

✦ **getGuess:** This method also accepts two parameters, min and max, to limit the range within which the user must guess.

✦ **askForAnotherRound:** This method asks the user to play another round and returns a boolean value to indicate whether the user wants to continue playing. It accepts a String value as a parameter; this string is displayed on the console to prompt the user for a reply.

Listing 7-3:   Yet Another Version of the Guessing-Game Program

Book II
Chapter 7

Adding Some
Methods to Your
Madness

```java
import java.util.Scanner;

public class GuessingGameMethod3
{
    static Scanner sc = new Scanner(System.in);

    public static void main(String[] args)
    {
        System.out.println("Let's play a guessing game!");
        do
        {
            playARound(1, getRandomNumber(7, 12));              →13
        } while (askForAnotherRound("Try again?"));
        System.out.println("\nThank you for playing!");
    }

    public static void playARound(int min, int max)
    {
        boolean validInput;
        int number, guess;
        String answer;

        // Pick a random number
        number = getRandomNumber(min, max);                     →25

        // Get the guess
        System.out.println("\nI'm thinking of a number "
            + "between " + min + " and " + max + ".");          →29
        System.out.print("What do you think it is? ");
        guess = getGuess(min, max);                             →31

        // Check the guess
        if (guess == number)
            System.out.println("You're right!");
        else
            System.out.println("You're wrong!"
                + " The number was " + number);
    }

    public static int getRandomNumber(int min, int max)        →41
    {
        return (int)(Math.random()                             →43
            * (max - min + 1)) + min;
    }
```

(continued)

Listing 7-3 *(continued)*

```
public static int getGuess(int min, int max)                    →47
{
    while (true)
    {
        int guess = sc.nextInt();
        if ( (guess < min) || (guess > max) )                   →52
        {
            System.out.print("I said, between "
                + min + " and " + max
                + ". Try again: ");
        }
        else
            return guess;                                       →59
    }
}

public static boolean askForAnotherRound(String prompt)         →63
{
    while (true)
    {
        String answer;
        System.out.print("\n" + prompt + " (Y or N) ");
        answer = sc.next();
        if (answer.equalsIgnoreCase("Y"))
            return true;
        else if (answer.equalsIgnoreCase("N"))
            return false;
    }
}
}
```

The following paragraphs point out the key lines of this program:

→ 13   This line calls the `playARound` method to play one round of the game. The values for `min` and `max` are passed as literals. To add a small amount of variety to the game, the `getRandomNumber` method is called here to set the value for the `max` to a random number from 7 to 12.

→ 25   The call to the `getRandomNumber` method passes the values of `min` and `max` as parameters to set the range for the random numbers.

→ 29   The message that announces to the user that the computer has chosen a random number uses the `min` and `max` parameters to indicate the range.

→ 31   The call to the `getGuess` method now passes the range of acceptable guesses to the `getGuess` method.

→ 41   The declaration for the `getRandomNumber` method specifies the `min` and `max` parameters.

→ 43   The calculation for the random number is complicated a bit by the fact that `min` may not be 1.

→ 47   The declaration for the `getGuess` method accepts the `min` and `max` parameters.

→ 52   The `if` statement in the `getGuess` method uses the `min` and `max` values to validate the user's input.

→ 59   This line is the `return` statement for the `getGuess` method. Note that this `return` statement is in the `else` part of an `if` statement that checks whether the number is less than 1 or greater than 10. If the number is outside the acceptable range, the `return` statement isn't executed. Instead, the program displays an error message, and the `while` loop repeats.

→ 63   The `askForAnotherRound` method accepts a string variable to use as a prompt.

Chapter 8: Handling Exceptions

In This Chapter

✓ Seeing what to do when bad things happen to good programs

✓ Finding out all about exceptions

✓ Using try, catch, and finally

✓ Preventing exceptions from happening in the first place

*T*his chapter is about what happens when Java encounters an error situation that it can't deal with. Over the years, computer programming languages have devised many ways to deal with these types of errors. The earliest programming languages dealt with them rudely, by abruptly terminating the program and printing out the entire contents of the computer's memory in hexadecimal. This output was called a *dump.*

Later programming languages tried various ways to keep the program running when serious errors occurred. In some languages, the statements that could potentially cause an error had elements added to them that would provide feedback about errors. A statement that read data from a disk file, for example, might return an error code if an I/O error occurred. Still other languages let you create a special error processing section of the program to which control would be transferred if an error occurred.

Being an object-oriented programming language, Java handles errors by using special *exception objects* that are created when an error occurs. In addition, Java has a special statement called the `try` statement that you must use to deal with exception objects. In this chapter, you find all the gory details of working with exception objects and `try` statements.

Understanding Exceptions

An *exception* is an object that's created when an error occurs in a Java program and Java can't automatically fix the error. The exception object contains information about the type of error that occurred. The most important information — the cause of the error — is indicated by the name of the exception class used to create the exception. You usually don't have to do anything with an exception object other than figure out which one you have.

Each type of exception that can occur is represented by a different exception class. Here are some typical exceptions:

✦ **IllegalArgumentException:** You passed an incorrect argument to a method.

✦ **InputMismatchException:** The console input doesn't match the data type expected by a method of the Scanner class.

✦ **ArithmeticException:** You tried an illegal type of arithmetic operation, such as dividing an integer by zero.

✦ **IOException:** A method that performs I/O encountered an unrecoverable I/O error.

✦ **ClassNotFoundException:** A necessary class couldn't be found.

There are many other types of exceptions, and you find out about many of them in later chapters of this book.

You need to know a few other things about exceptions:

✦ When an error occurs and an exception object is created, Java is said to have *thrown an exception.* Java has a pretty good throwing arm, so the exception is always thrown right back to the statement that caused it to be created.

✦ The statement that caused the exception can *catch* the exception if it wants it, but it doesn't have to catch the exception if it doesn't want it. Instead, it can duck and let someone else catch the exception. That someone else is the statement that called the method that's currently executing.

✦ If everyone ducks and the exception is never caught by the program, the program ends abruptly and displays a nasty-looking exception message on the console (more on that in the next section).

✦ Two basic types of exceptions in Java are checked exceptions and unchecked exceptions:

   • A *checked exception* is an exception that the compiler requires you to provide for it one way or another. If you don't, your program doesn't compile.

   • An *unchecked exception* is an exception that you can provide for, but you don't have to.

✦ So far in this book, I've avoided using any Java API methods that throw checked exceptions, but I have used methods that can throw unchecked exceptions. The nextInt method of the Scanner class, for example, throws an unchecked exception if the user enters something other than a valid integer value. For more information, read on.

Witnessing an exception

Submitted for your approval is a tale of a hastily written Java program, quickly put together to illustrate certain Java programming details while ignoring others. Out of sight, out of mind, as they say. Said program played a guessing game with the user, accepting numeric input via a class called `Scanner`. Yet this same program ignored the very real possibility that the user may enter strange and unexpected data — data that could hardly be considered numeric, at least not in the conventional sense. The time: Now. The place: Here. This program is about to cross over into . . . the Exception Zone.

The program I'm talking about here is, of course, the guessing-game program that's appeared in several forms in recent chapters. (You can find the most recent version at the end of Book II, Chapter 7.) This program includes a validation routine that prevents the user from making a guess that's not between 1 and 10. That validation routine, however, assumes that the user entered a valid integer number. If the user enters something other than an integer value, the `nextInt` method of the `Scanner` class fails badly.

**Book II
Chapter 8**

Handling
Exceptions

Figure 8-1 shows an example of what the console looks like if the user enters text (such as `five`) instead of a number. The first line after the user enters the incorrect data says the program has encountered an exception named `InputMismatchException`. In short, this exception means that the data entered by the user couldn't be matched with the type of data that the `Scanner` class expected. The `nextInt` method expected to find an integer, and instead, it found the word `five`.

Figure 8-1:
This program has slipped into the Exception Zone.

Finding the culprit

You can find the exact statement in your program that caused the exception to occur by examining the lines that are displayed right after the line that indicates which exception was encountered. These lines, called the *stack trace,* list the methods that the exception passed through before your program was aborted. Usually, the first method listed is deep in the bowels of the Java API, and the last method listed is your application's `main` method. Somewhere in the middle, you find the switch from methods in the Java API to a method in your program. That's usually where you find the statement in your program that caused the error.

In Figure 8-1, the stack trace lines look like this:

```
at java.util.Scanner.throwFor(Scanner.java:909)
at java.util.Scanner.next(Scanner.java:1530)
at java.util.Scanner.nextInt(Scanner.java:2160)
at java.util.Scanner.nextInt(Scanner.java:2119)
at GuessingGameMethod3.getGuess(GuessingGameMethod3.java:51)
at GuessingGameMethod3.playARound(GuessingGameMethod3.java:31)
at GuessingGameMethod3.main(GuessingGameMethod3.java:13)
```

Each line lists not only a class and method name, but also the name of the source file that contains the class and the line number where the exception occurred. Thus, the first line in this stack trace indicates that the exception is handled in the `throwFor` method of the `Scanner` class at line 909 of the `Scanner.java` file. The next three lines also indicate methods in the `Scanner` class. The first line to mention the `GuessingGame` class (`GuessingGameMethod3`) is the fifth line. It shows that the exception happened at line 51 in the `GuessingGameMethod3.java` file. Sure enough, that's the line that calls the `nextInt` method of the `Scanner` class to get input from the user.

Catching Exceptions

Whenever you use a statement that might throw an exception, you should write special code to anticipate and catch the exception. That way, your program won't crash as shown in Figure 8-1 if the exception occurs.

You catch an exception by using a `try` statement, which has this general form:

```
try
{
    statements that can throw exceptions
}
catch (exception-type identifier)
{
    statements executed when exception is thrown
}
```

Here, you place the statements that might throw an exception within a *try block*. Then you catch the exception with a *catch block*.

Here are a few things to note about `try` statements:

✦ You can code more than one `catch` block. That way, if the statements in the `try` block might throw more than one type of exception, you can catch each type of exception in a separate `catch` block.

✦ For scoping purposes, the `try` block is its own self-contained block, separate from the `catch` block. As a result, any variables you declare in the `try` block are not visible to the `catch` block. If you want them to be, declare them immediately before the `try` statement.

✦ You can also code a special block (called a *finally block*) after all the `catch` blocks. For more information about coding `finally` blocks, see the section "Using a `finally` Block," later in this chapter.

✦ The various exception classes in the Java API are defined in different packages. If you use an exception class that isn't defined in the standard `java.lang` package that's always available, you need to provide an `import` statement for the package that defines the exception class.

A simple example

To illustrate how to provide for an exception, here's a program that divides two numbers and uses a `try/catch` statement to catch an exception if the second number turns out to be zero:

```
public class DivideByZero
{
    public static void main(String[] args)
    {
        int a = 5;
        int b = 0;                // you know this won't work
        try
        {
            int c = a / b;       // but you try it anyway
        }
        catch (ArithmeticException e)
        {
            System.out.println("Oops, you can't "
                + "divide by zero.");
        }
    }
}
```

Here, the division occurs within a `try` block, and a `catch` block handles `ArithmeticException`. `ArithmethicException` is defined by `java.lang`, so an `import` statement for it isn't necessary.

When you run this program, the following is displayed on the console:

```
Oops, you can't divide by zero.
```

There's nothing else to see here. The next section shows a more complicated example, though.

Another example

Listing 8-1 shows a simple example of a program that uses a method to get a valid integer from the user. If the user enters a value that isn't a valid integer, the catch block catches the error and forces the loop to repeat.

Listing 8-1:   Getting a Valid Integer

```java
import java.util.*;

public class GetInteger
{
    static Scanner sc = new Scanner(System.in);

    public static void main(String[] args)
    {
        System.out.print("Enter an integer: ");
        int i = GetAnInteger();
        System.out.println("You entered " + i);
    }

    public static int GetAnInteger()
    {
        while (true)
        {
            try
            {
                return sc.nextInt();
            }
            catch (InputMismatchException e)
            {
                sc.next();
                System.out.print("That's not "
                    + "an integer. Try again: ");
            }
        }
    }
}
```

Here the statement that gets the input from the user and returns it to the methods called is coded within the try block. If the user enters a valid integer, this statement is the only one in this method that gets executed.

If the user enters data that can't be converted to an integer, however, the `nextInt` method throws an `InputMismatchException`. Then this exception is intercepted by the `catch` block — which disposes of the user's incorrect input by calling the `next` method, as well as by displaying an error message. Then the `while` loop repeats.

Here's what the console might look like for a typical execution of this program:

```
Enter an integer: three
That's not an integer. Try again: 3.001
That's not an integer. Try again: 3
You entered 3
```

Here are a couple other things to note about this program:

✦ The `import` statement specifies `java.util.*` to import all the classes from the `java.util` package. That way, the `InputMismatchException` class is imported.

✦ The `next` method must be called in the `catch` block to dispose of the user's invalid input because the `nextInt` method leaves the input value in the `Scanner`'s input stream if an `InputMismatchException` is thrown. If you omit the statement that calls `next`, the `while` loop keeps reading it, throws an exception, and displays an error message in an infinite loop. If you don't believe me, look at Figure 8-2. I found this error out the hard way. (The only way to make it stop is to close the console window.)

Figure 8-2:
Why you
have to
call next to
discard the
invalid input.

```
G:\WINDOWS\System32\cmd.exe
teger. Try again: That's not an integer. Try again: That's not an integer. Try a
gain: That's not an integer. Try again: That's not an integer. Try again: That's
 not an integer. Try again: That's not an integer. Try again: That's not an inte
ger. Try again: That's not an integer. Try again: That's not an integer. Try aga
in: That's not an integer. Try again: That's not an integer. Try again: That's n
ot an integer. Try again: That's not an integer. Try again: That's not an intege
r. Try again: That's not an integer. Try again: That's not an integer. Try again
: That's not an integer. Try again: That's not an integer. Try again: That's not
an integer. Try again: That's not an integer. Try again: That's not an integer.
Try again: That's not an integer. Try again: That's not an integer. Try again:
That's not an integer. Try again: That's not an integer. Try again: That's not a
n integer. Try again: That's not an integer. Try again: That's not an integer. T
ry again: That's not an integer. Try again: That's not an integer. Try again: Th
at's not an integer. Try again: That's not an integer. Try again: That's not an
integer. Try again: That's not an integer. Try again: That's not an integer. Try
 again: That's not an integer. Try again: That's not an integer. Try again: That
's not an integer. Try again: That's not an integer. Try again: That's not an in
teger. Try again: That's not an integer. Try again: That's not an integer. Try a
gain: That's not an integer. Try again: That's not an integer. Try again: That's
 not an integer. Try again: That's not an integer. Try again: That's not an inte
ger. Try again: That's not an integer. Try again: That's not an integer. Try aga
in: That's not an integer. Try again: That's not an integer. Try again: That's n
ot an integer. Try again: That's not an integer. Try again: That's not an intege
r. Try again: That's not an integer. Try again: That's not an integer. Try again
: That's not an integer. Try again: That's not an integer. Try again:
```

Handling Exceptions with a Preemptive Strike

The `try` statement is a useful and necessary tool in any Java programmer's arsenal. The best way to handle exceptions, however, is to prevent them from happening in the first place. That's not possible all the time, but in many cases it is. The key is to test your data before performing the operation that can lead to an exception and then skipping or bypassing the operation of the data that is problematic. (One thing I really hate is problematic data.)

You can usually avoid the `ArithmethicException` that results from dividing integer data by zero by checking the data before performing the division:

```
if (b != 0)
    c = a / b;
```

This eliminates the need to enclose the division in a `try` block, because you know that the division by zero won't happen.

You can apply this same technique to input validation by using the `hasNextInt` method of the `Scanner` class. This method checks the next input value to make sure it's a valid integer. (The `Scanner` class calls the next input value a *token*, but that won't be on the test.) You can do this technique in several ways, and I've been encouraging you to ponder the problem since Book II, Chapter 2. Now behold the long-awaited answer: Listing 8-2 shows a version of the `GetInteger` method that uses a `while` loop to avoid the exception.

Listing 8-2:   Another Version of the GetInteger Method

```java
import java.util.*;

public class GetInteger2
{
    static Scanner sc = new Scanner(System.in);

    public static void main(String[] args)
    {
        System.out.print("Enter an integer: ");
        int i = GetAnInteger();
        System.out.println("You entered " + i);
    }

    public static int GetAnInteger()
    {
        while (!sc.hasNextInt())
        {
            sc.nextLine();
            System.out.print("That's not "
                + "an integer. Try again: ");
        }
        return sc.nextInt();
    }
}
```

This is a clever little bit of programming, don't you think? The conditional expression in the `while` statement calls the `hasNextInt` method of the `Scanner` to see whether the next value is an integer. The `while` loop repeats as long as this call returns `false`, indicating that the next value is not a valid integer. The body of the loop calls `nextLine` to discard the bad data and then displays an error message. The loop ends only when you know that you have good data in the input stream, so the `return` statement calls `nextInt` to parse the data to an integer and return the resulting value.

Catching All Exceptions at Once

Java provides a catch-all exception class called `Exception` that all other types of exceptions are based on. (Don't worry about the details of what I mean by that. When you read Book III, Chapter 4, it makes more sense.)

If you don't want to be too specific in a `catch` block, you can specify `Exception` instead of a more specific exception class. For example:

```
try
{
    int c = a / b;
}

catch (Exception e)
{
    System.out.println("Oops, you can't "
        + "divide by zero.");
}
```

In this example, the `catch` block specifies `Exception` rather than `ArithmeticException`.

If you have some code that might throw several types of exceptions, and you want to provide specific processing for some types but general processing for all the others, code the `try` statement this way:

```
try
{
    // statements that might throw several types of
    // exceptions
}
catch (InputMismatchException e)
{
    // statements that process InputMismatchException
}
catch (IOException e)
{
    // statements that process IOException
}
```

```
catch (Exception e)
{
    // statements that process all other exception types
}
```

In this example, imagine that the code in the try block could throw an InputMismatchException, an IOException, and perhaps some other type of unanticipated exception. Here the three catch blocks provide for each of these possibilities.

When you code more than one catch block on a try statement, always list the more specific exceptions first. If you include a catch block to catch Exception, list it last.

Displaying the Exception Message

In most cases, the catch block of a try statement won't do anything at all with the exception object passed to it. You may want to display an error message occasionally, however; exception objects have a few interesting methods that can come in handy from time to time. These methods are listed in Table 8-1.

Table 8-1	Methods of the Exception Class
Method	Description
String getMessage()	Describes the error in a text message.
void print StackTrace()	Prints the stack trace to the standard error stream.
String toString()	Returns a description of the exception. This description includes the name of the exception class followed by a colon and the getMessage message.

The following example shows how you could print the message for an exception in a catch block:

```
try
{
    int c = a / b;
}
catch (Exception e)
{
    System.out.println(e.getMessage());
}
```

This code displays the text / by zero on the console if b has a value of 0. You can get even more interesting output by using this line in the catch clause:

```
e.printStackTrace(System.out);
```

Using a finally Block

A finally block is a block that appears after all the catch blocks for a statement. It's executed whether or not any exceptions are thrown by the try block or caught by any catch blocks. Its purpose is to let you clean up any mess that might be left behind by the exception, such as open files or database connections.

The basic framework for a try statement with a finally block is this:

```
try
{
    statements that can throw exceptions
}
catch (exception-type identifier)
{
    statements executed when exception is thrown
}
finally
{
    statements that are executed whether or not
    exceptions occur
}
```

Listing 8-3 shows a contrived but helpful example that demonstrates how to use the finally clause. In this example, a method called divideThese Numbers tries to divide the numbers twice. If the division fails the first time (due to a divide-by-zero exception), it tries the division again. Completely irrational, I know. But persistent, like a teenager.

**Book II
Chapter 8**

**Handling
Exceptions**

Listing 8-3: A Program That Uses a finally Clause

```
public class CrazyWithZeros
{
    public static void main(String[] args)
    {
        try
        {
            int answer = divideTheseNumbers(5, 0);          →7
        }
        catch (Exception e)                                  →9
        {
            System.out.println("Tried twice, "
                + "still didn't work!");
        }
    }
```

```
public static int divideTheseNumbers(int a, int b)                    →16
    throws Exception
{
    int c;
    try
    {
        c = a / b;                                                    →22
        System.out.println("It worked!");                             →23
    }
    catch (Exception e)
    {
        System.out.println("Didn't work the first time.");            →27
        c = a / b;                                                    →28
        System.out.println("It worked the second time!");             →29
    }
    finally
    {
        System.out.println("Better clean up my mess.");               →33
    }
    System.out.println("It worked after all.");                       →35
    return c;                                                         →36
}
}
```

Here's the console output for the program:

```
Didn't work the first time.
Better clean up my mess.
Tried twice, still didn't work!
```

The following paragraphs explain what's going on, step by step:

→ 7   The main method calls the divideTheseNumbers method, passing 5 and 0 as the parameters. You already know that this method isn't going to work.

→ 9   The catch clause catches any exceptions thrown by line 7.

→ 16   The divideTheseNumbers method declares that it throws Exception.

→ 22   This line is the first attempt to divide the numbers.

→ 23   If the first attempt succeeds, this line is executed, and the message "It worked!" is printed. Alas, the division throws an exception, so this line never gets executed.

→ 27   Instead, the catch clause catches the exception, and the message "Didn't work the first time." is displayed. That's the first line in the console output.

→ 28   The divideTheseNumbers method stubbornly tries to divide the same two numbers again. This time, no try statement is there to catch the error.

→ 29   Because another exception is thrown for the second division, however, this line is never executed. Thus you don't see the message `"It worked the second time!"` on the console. (If you do, you're in an episode of *The Twilight Zone*.)

→ 33　This statement in the `finally` clause is always executed, no matter what happens. That's where the second line in the console output came from.

After the `finally` clause executes, the `ArithmeticException` is thrown back up to the calling method, where it is caught by line 9. That's where the last line of the console output came from.

→ 35　If the division did work, this line would be executed after the `try` block ends, and you'd see the message `"It worked after all."` on the console.

→ 36　Then the `return` statement would return the result of the division.

Handling Checked Exceptions

Checked exceptions are exceptions that the designers of Java feel that your programs absolutely must provide for, one way or another. Whenever you code a statement that could throw a checked exception, your program must do one of two things:

✦ Catch the exception by placing the statement within a `try` statement that has a `catch` block for the exception.

✦ Specify a `throws` clause on the method that contains the statement to indicate that your method doesn't want to handle the exception, so it's passing the exception up the line.

This is known as the *catch-or-throw* rule. In short, any method that includes a statement that might throw a checked exception must acknowledge that it knows the exception might be thrown. The method does this by handling it directly or by passing the exception up to its caller.

To illustrate the use of checked exceptions, I have to use some classes with methods that throw them. Up to now, I've avoided introducing classes that throw checked exceptions, so the following illustrations use some classes you aren't yet familiar with. Don't worry about what those classes do or how they work. The point is to see how to handle the checked exceptions they throw.

Viewing the catch-or-throw compiler error

Here's a program that uses a class called `FileInputStream`. To create an object from this class, you must pass the constructor a string that contains the path and name of a file that exists on your computer. If the file can't be found, the `FileInputStream` throws a `FileNotFoundException` that you must either catch or throw. This class is in the `java.io` package, so any program that uses it must include an `import java.io` statement.

Consider the following program:

```java
import java.io.*;

public class FileException1
{
    public static void main(String[] args)
    {
        openFile("C:\test.txt");
    }

    public static void openFile(String name)
    {
        FileInputStream f = new FileInputStream(name);
    }
}
```

This program won't compile. The compiler issues the following error message:

```
unreported exception java.io.FileNotFoundException; must be caught or declared to
    be thrown
```

This message simply means that you have to deal with the FileNotFoundException.

Catching FileNotFoundException

One way to deal with the FileNotFoundException is to catch it by using an ordinary try statement:

```java
import java.io.*;

public class FileException2
{
    public static void main(String[] args)
    {
        openFile("C:\test.txt");
    }

    public static void openFile(String name)
    {
        try
        {
            FileInputStream f =
                new FileInputStream(name);
        }
        catch (FileNotFoundException e)
        {
            System.out.println("File not found.");
        }
    }
}
```

In this example, the message `"File not found."` is displayed if the
`C:\test.txt` file doesn't exist.

Throwing the FileNotFoundException

Suppose that you don't want to deal with this error condition in the `openFile`
method, but would rather just pass the exception up to the method that calls
the `openFile` method.

To do that, you omit the `try` statement. Instead, you add a `throws` clause to
the `openFile` method's declaration. That clause indicates that the `open
File` method knows it contains a statement that might throw a `FileNot
FoundException` but doesn't want to deal with that exception here. Instead,
the exception is passed up to the caller.

**Book II
Chapter 8**

Here's the `openFile` method with the `throws` clause added:

```
public static void openFile(String name)
    throws FileNotFoundException
{
    FileInputStream f = new FileInputStream(name);
}
```

As you can see, the `throws` clause simply lists the exception or exceptions
that the method might throw. If more than one exception is in the list, separate the exceptions with commas:

```
public static void readFile(String name)
    throws FileNotFoundException, IOException
```

Adding a `throws` clause to the `openFile` method means that when the
`FileNotFoundException` occurs, it is simply passed up to the method
that called the `openFile` method. That means the calling method (in this
illustration, `main`) must catch or throw the exception. To catch the exception, the `main` method would have to be coded like this:

```
public static void main(String[] args)
{
    try
    {
        openFile("C:\test.txt");
    }
    catch (FileNotFoundException e)
    {
        System.out.println("File not found.");
    }
}
```

Then, if the file doesn't exist, the `catch` block catches the exception, and the error message is displayed.

Throwing an exception from main

If you don't want the program to handle the `FileNotFound` exception at all, you can add a `throws` clause to the `main` method, like this:

```
public static void main(String[] args)
    throws FileNotFoundException
{
    openFile("C:\test.txt");
}
```

Then the program abruptly terminates with an exception message and stack trace if the exception occurs.

Swallowing exceptions

What if you don't want to do anything if a checked exception occurs? In other words, you want to simply ignore the exception. You can do that by catching the exception in the `catch` block of a `try` statement but leaving the body of the `catch` block empty. Here's an example:

```
public static void openFile(String name)
{
    try
    {
        FileInputStream f = new FileInputStream(name);
    }
    catch (FileNotFoundException e)
    {
    }
}
```

Here the `FileNotFoundException` is caught and ignored. This technique is called *swallowing the exception.*

Swallowing an exception is considered to be bad programming practice. Simply swallowing exceptions that you know you should handle when working on a complicated program is tempting. Because you plan to get back to that exception handler after you iron out the basic functions of the program, a little exception-swallowing doesn't seem like that bad an idea. The problem is that inevitably, you never get back to the exception handler, so your program gets rushed into production with swallowed exceptions.

If you must swallow exceptions, at least write a message to the console indicating that the exception occurred. That way, you have a constant reminder that the program has some unfinished details you must attend to.

Note that not all exception swallowing is bad. Suppose you want the `openFile` method to return a `boolean` value to indicate whether the file exists, rather than throw an exception. Then you could code the method something like this:

```
public static boolean openFile(String name)
{
    boolean fileOpened = false;
    try
    {
        FileInputStream f = new FileInputStream(name);
        fileOpened = true;
    }
    catch (FileNotFoundException e)
    {
    }
    return fileOpened;
}
```

Here the exception isn't really swallowed. Instead, its meaning is converted to a `boolean` result that's returned from the method. As a result, the error condition indicated by the `FileNotFoundException` isn't lost.

**Book II
Chapter 8**

**Handling
Exceptions**

Throwing Your Own Exceptions

Although such methods are uncommon, you may want to write methods that throw exceptions all on their own. To do that, you use a `throw` statement. The `throw` statement has the following basic format:

```
throw new exception-class ();
```

The *exception-class* can be `Exception` or a class that's derived from `Exception`. You find out how to create your own classes — including exception classes — in Book III. For now, I just focus on writing a method that throws a general `Exception`.

Here's a program that demonstrates the basic structure of a method that throws an exception:

```
public class MyException
{
    public static void main(String[] args)
    {
        try
        {
            doSomething(true);
        }
        catch (Exception e)
```

```
        {
            System.out.println("Exception!");
        }
    }

    public static void doSomething(boolean t)
        throws Exception
    {
        if (t)
            throw new Exception();
    }
}
```

Here the doSomething method accepts a boolean value as a parameter. If this value is true, it throws an exception; otherwise it doesn't do anything.

Here are the essential points to glean from this admittedly trivial example:

✦ You throw an exception by executing a throw statement. The throw statement specifies the exception object to be thrown.

✦ If a method contains a throw statement, it must include a throws clause in its declaration.

✦ A method that calls a method that throws an exception must either catch or throw the exception.

✦ Yup, this example is pretty trivial. But it illustrates the essential points.

Catching Multiple Exceptions

A feature that was new in Java 7 lets you catch two or more exception types with a single catch statement. Suppose you have a bit of code that might throw two different exceptions — say, FileNotFoundException and IOException — and you want to handle both identically. One way to do that is to write two catch statements (one to catch each section), and then write the same code for both catch blocks, like this:

```
try
{
    // statements that might throw FileNotFoundException
    // or IOException
}
catch (FileNotFoundException e)
{
    System.out.println(e.getMessage());
}
catch (IOException e)
{
    System.out.println(e.getMessage());
}
```

This method works, but it's clumsy. Java lets you specify two or more exception types in the catch statement. You separate the exception types with a vertical bar, like this:

```
{
    // statements that might throw FileNotFoundException // or IOException
}
catch (FileNotFoundException | IOException e)
{
    System.out.println(e.getMessage());
}
```

This way, you can handle both exception types with just one block of code.

Book III

Object-Oriented Programming

You can find an interesting programming challenge that requires use of many of the programming techniques covered in this minibook at www.dummies.com/extras/javaaio. I challenge you to create an enhanced version of the Tic-Tac-Toe program you created for Book II so that it incorporates simple strategy into the computer's plays.

Contents at a Glance

Chapter 1: Understanding Object-Oriented Programming

In This Chapter

✔ **Looking at what object-oriented programming is**

✔ **Understanding objects and classes**

✔ **Investigating inheritance and interfaces**

✔ **Designing programs with objects**

✔ **Diagramming with UML**

*T*his chapter is a basic introduction to object-oriented programming. It introduces some of the basic concepts and terms you need to know as you get a handle on the specific details of how object-oriented programming works in Java.

If you're more of a hands-on type, you may want to skip this chapter and go straight to Book III, Chapter 2, where you find out how to create your own classes in Java. You can always return to this chapter later to review the basic concepts that drive object-oriented programming. Either way is okay by me. I get paid the same whether you read this chapter now or skip it and come back to it later.

What Is Object-Oriented Programming?

The term *object-oriented programming* means many different things. But at its heart, object-oriented programming is a type of computer programming based on the premise that all programs are essentially computer-based simulations of real-world objects or abstract concepts. For example:

✦ Flight-simulator programs attempt to mimic the behavior of real airplanes. Some do an amazingly good job; military and commercial pilots train on them. In the 1960s, the Apollo astronauts used a computer-controlled simulator to practice for their moon landings.

✦ Many computer games are simulations of actual games that humans play, such as baseball, NASCAR racing, and chess. But even abstract games such as Pac-Man and Final Fantasy IV attempt to model the behavior of creatures and objects that *could* exist somewhere. Those programs simulate a conceptual game — one that can't actually be played anywhere in the real world but *can* be simulated by a computer.

✦ Business programs can be thought of as simulations of business processes — such as order taking, customer service, shipping, and billing. An invoice, for example, isn't just a piece of paper; it's a paper that represents a transaction that has occurred between a company and one of its customers. Thus, a computer-based invoice is really just a simulation of that transaction.

The notion of a programming language having a premise of this sort isn't new. Traditional programming languages such as C (and its predecessors, including even COBOL) are based on the premise that computer programs are computerized implementations of actual procedures — the electronic equivalent of "Step 1: Insert Tab A into Slot B." The LISP programming language is based on the idea that all programming problems can be looked at as different ways of manipulating lists. And the ever-popular database-manipulation language SQL views programming problems as ways to manipulate mathematical sets.

Here are some additional thoughts about the notion of computer programs being simulations of real-world objects or abstract concepts:

✦ Sometimes the simulation is better than the real thing. Word-processing programs started out as simulations of typewriters, but a modern word-processing program is far superior to any typewriter.

✦ The idea that all computer programs are simulations of one type or another isn't a new one. In fact, the first object-oriented programming language (Simula) was developed in the 1960s. By 1967, this language had many of the features we now consider fundamental to object-oriented programming — including classes, objects, inheritance, and virtual methods.

✦ Come to think of it, manual business recordkeeping systems are simulations too. A file cabinet full of printed invoices doesn't hold actual orders; it holds written *representations* of those orders. A computer is a better simulation device than a file cabinet, but both are simulations.

Understanding Objects

All this talk of simulations is getting a little existential for me, so now I'm turning to the nature of the objects that make up object-oriented programming. *Objects* — both in the real world and in the world of programming — are entities that have certain basic characteristics. The following sections describe some of the most important of these characteristics: identity, type, state, and behavior.

Objects have identity

Every object in an object-oriented program has an *identity*. In other words, every occurrence of a particular type of object — called an *instance* — can be distinguished from every other occurrence of the same type of object, as well as from objects of other types.

In the real world, object identity is a pretty intuitive and obvious concept. Pick up two apples, and you know that although both of them are apples (that's the object type, described in the next section), you know that they aren't the same apple. Each has a distinct identity. Both are roughly the same color but not exactly. They're both roundish but have minor variations in shape. Either one (or both) could have a worm inside.

Open a file cabinet that's full of invoices, and you find page after page of papers that look almost identical, but each one has an invoice number printed somewhere near the top of the page. This number isn't what actually gives each of these invoices a unique identity, but it gives you an easy way to identify each individual invoice, just as your name gives other people an easy way to identify you.

In object-oriented programming, each object has its own location in the computer's memory. Thus, two objects, even though they may be of the same type, have their own distinct memory locations. The address of the starting location for an object provides a way of distinguishing one object from another, because no two objects can occupy the same location in memory.

Here are a few other important thoughts about object identity in Java:

✦ Java keeps each object's identity pretty much to itself. In other words, there's no easy way to get the memory address of an object; Java figures that it's none of your business, and rightfully so. If Java made that information readily available to you, you'd be tempted to tinker with it, which could cause all sorts of problems, as any C or C++ programmer can tell you.

✦ Java objects have something called a *hash code,* which is an `int` value that's automatically generated for every object and *almost* represents the object's identity. In most cases, the hash code for an object is based on the object's memory address, but not always. Java doesn't guarantee that two distinct objects won't have the same hash code.

✦ When used with objects, the equality operator (`==`) actually tests the object identity of two variables or expressions. If they refer to the same object instance, the two variables or expressions are considered equal.

Objects have type

I remember studying "Naming of Parts," a fine poem written by Henry Reed in 1942, back when I was an English major in college:

> Today we have naming of parts. Yesterday,
> We had daily cleaning. And tomorrow morning,
> We shall have what to do after firing. But today,
> Today we have naming of parts. Japonica
> Glistens like coral in all of the neighboring gardens,
>   And today we have naming of parts.

Sure, it's a fine antiwar poem and all that, but it's also a little instructive about object-oriented programming. After the first stanza, the poem goes on to name the parts of a rifle:

> This is the lower sling swivel. And this
> Is the upper sling swivel, whose use you will see,
> When you are given your slings. And this is the piling swivel,
> Which in your case you have not got.

Imagine a whole room of new soldiers taking apart their rifles, while the drill sergeant tells them, "This is the lower sling swivel. And this is the upper sling swivel. . . ." Each soldier's rifle has one of these parts — in object-oriented terms, an object of a particular type. The lower sling swivels in the soldiers' rifles are different objects, but all are of the type LowerSlingSwivel.

Like the drill sergeant in this poem, object-oriented programming lets you assign names to the different kinds of objects in a program. In Java, types are defined by classes. So when you create an object from a type, you're saying that the object is of the type specified by the class. The following example statement creates an object of type Invoice:

```
Invoice i = new Invoice();
```

In this case, the identity of this object (that is, its address in memory) is assigned to the variable i, which the compiler knows can hold references to objects of type Invoice.

Objects have state

Now switch gears to another literary genius:

> One fish, two fish,
> Red fish, blue fish

In object-oriented terms, Dr. Seuss here is enumerating a pair of objects of type Fish. The Fish type apparently has two attributes; call them Number and Color. These two objects have differing values for these attributes:

Attribute	Object 1	Object 2
Number	One	Two
Color	Red	Blue

The type of an object determines what attributes the object has. Thus all objects of a particular type have the same attributes. They don't necessarily have the same values for those attributes, however. In this example, all Fish have attributes named Number and Color, but the two Fish objects have different values for these attributes.

The combination of the values for all the attributes of an object is called the object's *state*. Unlike its identity, an object's state can — and usually does — change over its lifetime. Some fish can change colors, for example. The total sales for a particular customer changes each time the customer buys another product. The grade-point average for a student changes each time a new class grade is recorded. The address and phone number of an employee change if the employee moves.

Here are a few more interesting details about object state:

✦ Some of the attributes of an object are publicly known, but others can be private. The private attributes may be vital to the internal operation of the object, but no one outside the object knows that they exist. They're like your private thoughts: They affect what you say and do, but nobody knows them but you.

✦ In Java, the state of an object is represented by class variables, which are called *fields*. A *public field* is a field that's declared with the `public` keyword so that the variable can be visible to the outside world.

Objects have behavior

Another characteristic of objects is that they have *behavior,* which means that they can do things. Like state, the specific behavior of an object depends on its type. But unlike state, behavior isn't different for each instance of a type. Suppose that all the students in a classroom have calculators of the same type. Ask them all to pull out the calculators and add two numbers — any two numbers of their choosing. All the calculators display a different number, but they all add in the same way — that is, they all have a different state but the same behavior.

Another way to say that objects have behavior is to say that they provide services that can be used by other objects. You've already seen plenty of examples of objects that provide services to other objects. Objects created from the `NumberFormat` class, for example, provide formatting services that turn numeric values into nicely formatted strings such as $32.95.

In Java, the behavior of an object is provided by its methods. Thus the `format` method of the `NumberFormat` class is what provides the formatting behavior for `NumberFormat` objects.

Here are a few other notable points about object behavior:

✦ The *interface* of a class is the set of methods and fields that the class makes public so that other objects can access them.

✦ Exactly how an object does what it does can and should be hidden within the object. Someone who uses the object needs to know what the object does but doesn't need to know how it works. If you later find a better way for the object to do its job, you can swap in the new improved version without anyone knowing the difference.

Understanding the Life Cycle of an Object

As you work with objects in Java, understanding how objects are born, live their lives, and die is important. This topic is called the *life cycle* of an object, and it goes something like this:

1. Before an object can be created from a class, the class must be *loaded*. To do that, the Java runtime locates the class on disk (in a `.class` file) and reads it into memory. Then Java looks for any *static initializers* that initialize static fields — fields that don't belong to any particular instance of the class, but belong to the class itself and are shared by all objects created from the class.

   A class is loaded the first time you create an object from the class or the first time you access a static field or method of the class. When you run the `main` method of a class, for example, the class is initialized because the `main` method is static.

2. An object is created from a class when you use the `new` keyword. To initialize the class, Java allocates memory for the object and sets up a reference to the object so that the Java runtime can keep track of it. Then Java calls the class *constructor,* which is like a method but is called only once: when the object is created. The constructor is responsible for doing any processing required to initialize the object — initializing variables, opening files or databases, and so on.

3. The object lives its life, providing access to its public methods and fields to whoever wants and needs them.

4. When it's time for the object to die, the object is removed from memory, and Java drops its internal reference to it. You don't have to destroy objects yourself. A special part of the Java runtime called the *garbage collector* takes care of destroying all objects when they are no longer in use.

Working with Related Classes

So far, most of the classes you've seen in this book have created objects that stand on their own, each being a little island unto itself. The real power of object-oriented programming, however, lies in its ability to create classes that describe closely related objects.

Baseballs, for example, are similar to softballs. Both are specific types of balls. Each type has a diameter and a weight; both types can be thrown, caught, or hit. Baseballs and softballs, however, have different characteristics that cause them to behave differently when they're thrown, caught, or hit.

If you're creating a program that simulates the way baseballs and softballs work, you need a way to represent these two types of balls. One option is to create separate classes to represent each type of ball. These classes are similar, so you can just copy most of the code from one class to the other.

Another option is to use a single class to represent both types of balls. Then you pass a parameter to the constructor to indicate whether an instance of the class behaves like a baseball or like a softball.

Java has two object-oriented programming features that are designed specifically to handle classes that are related this way: inheritance and interfaces. I briefly describe these features in the following sections.

Inheritance

Inheritance is an object-oriented programming technique that lets you use one class as the basis for another. The existing class is called the *base class, superclass,* or *parent class;* the new class that's derived from it is called the *derived class, subclass,* or *child class.*

When you create a subclass, the subclass is automatically given all the methods and fields defined by its superclass. You can use these methods and fields as is, or you can override them to alter their behavior. In addition, you can add methods and fields that define data and behavior that's unique to the subclass.

You could use inheritance to solve the baseball/softball problem from the preceding section by creating a class named `Ball` that provides the basic features of all types of balls and then using it as the base class for separate classes named `BaseBall` and `SoftBall`. Then these classes could override the methods that need to behave differently for each type of ball.

One way to think of inheritance is as a way to implement *is-a-type-of* relationships. A softball is a type of ball, as is a baseball. Thus inheritance is an appropriate way to implement these related classes. (For more information about inheritance, see Book III, Chapter 4.)

Interfaces

An *interface* is a set of methods and fields that a class must provide to *implement* the interface. The interface itself is simply a set of public method and field declarations that are given a name. Note that the interface itself doesn't provide any code that implements those methods. Instead, it just provides the declarations. Then a class that *implements* the interface provides code for each of the methods the interface defines.

You could use an interface to solve the baseball/softball problem by creating an interface named `Ball` that specifies all the methods and fields that a ball should have. Then you could create the `SoftBall` and `BaseBall` classes so that they both implement the `Ball` interface.

Interfaces are closely related to inheritance but have two key differences:

✦ The interface itself doesn't provide code that implements any of its methods. An interface is just a set of method and field signatures. By contrast, a base class can provide the implementation for some or all of its methods.

✦ A class can have only one base class, but a class can implement as many interfaces as necessary.

You find out more about interfaces in Book III, Chapter 5.

Designing a Program with Objects

An object-oriented program usually isn't just a single object. Instead, it's a group of objects that work together to get a job done. The most important part of developing an object-oriented program is designing the classes that are used to create the program's objects. The basic idea is to break a large problem into a set of classes, each of which is manageable in size and complexity. Then you write the Java code that implements those classes.

So the task of designing an object-oriented application boils down to deciding what classes the application requires — and what the public interface to each of those classes should be. If you plan your classes well, implementing the application is easy. If you plan your classes poorly, you'll have a hard time getting your application to work.

One common way to design object-oriented applications is to divide the application into several distinct *layers* or *tiers* that provide distinct types of functions. Most common is a three-layered approach, as shown in Figure 1-1. Here the objects of an application are split into three basic layers:

✦ **Presentation:** The objects in this layer handle all the direct interaction with users. The HTML pages in a web application go in this layer, as do the Swing page and frame classes in a GUI-based application. (I cover Swing in Book VI.)

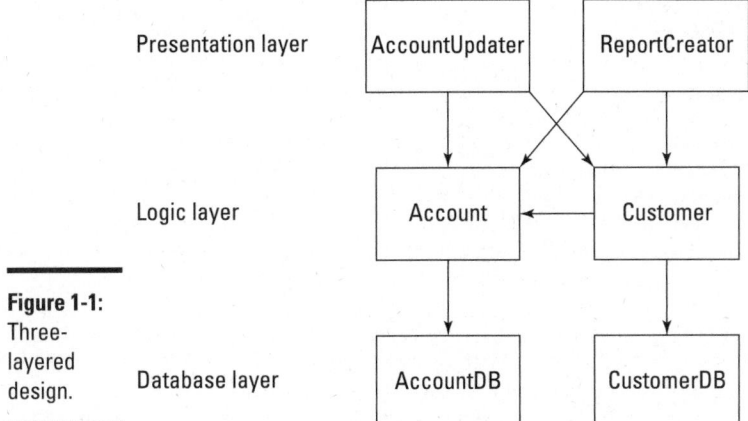

Figure 1-1:
Three-
layered
design.

Presentation layer — AccountUpdater, ReportCreator

Logic layer — Account, Customer

Database layer — AccountDB, CustomerDB

✦ **Logic:** The objects in this layer represent the core objects of the application. For a typical business-type application, this layer includes objects that represent business entities such as customer, products, orders, suppliers, and the like. This layer is sometimes called the *business rules layer* because the objects in this layer are responsible for carrying out the rules that govern the application.

✦ **Database:** The objects in this layer handle all the details of interacting with whatever form of data storage is used by the application. If the data is stored in a SQL database, for example, the objects in this layer handle all the SQL.

Diagramming Classes with UML

Since the very beginning of computer programming, programmers have loved to create diagrams of their programs. Originally, they drew flowcharts that graphically represented a program's procedural logic.

Flowcharts were good at diagramming procedures, but they were way too detailed. When the structured programming craze hit in the 1970s, and programmers started thinking about the overall structure of their programs, they switched from flowcharts to *structure charts,* which illustrated the organizational relationships among the modules of a program or system.

Now that object-oriented programming is the thing, programmers draw *class diagrams* to illustrate the relationships among the classes that make up an application. Figure 1-2 shows a class diagram of a simple system that has four classes. The rectangles represent the classes themselves, and the arrows represent the relationships among the classes.

**Book III
Chapter 1**

Understanding
Object-Oriented
Programming

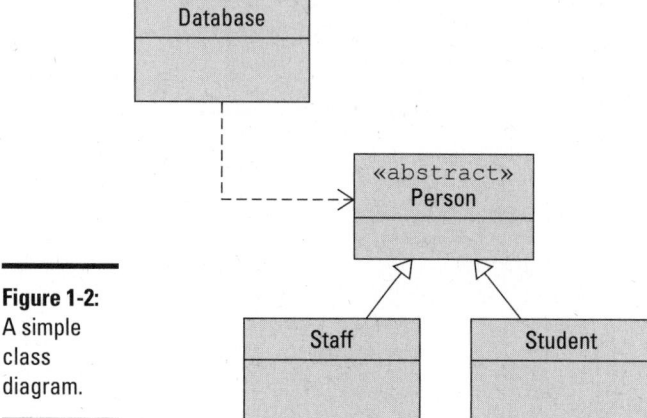

You can draw class diagrams in many ways. To add some consistency to their diagrams, most programmers use a standard called *UML,* which stands for *Unified Modeling Language*. The class diagram in Figure 1-2 is an example of a simple UML diagram, but UML diagrams can get much more complicated.

The following sections describe the details of creating UML class diagrams. Note that these sections don't even come close to explaining all the features of UML. I include just the basics of creating UML class diagrams so that you can make some sense of UML diagrams when you see them and so that you know how to draw simple class diagrams to design the class structure for your applications.

Drawing classes

The basic element in a class diagram is a class. In UML, each class is drawn as a rectangle. At minimum, the rectangle must include the class name. You can subdivide the rectangle into two or three compartments that can contain additional information about the class, as shown in Figure 1-3.

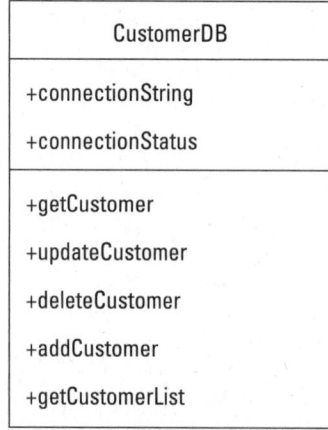

The middle compartment of a class lists the class variables, whereas the bottom compartment lists the class methods. The name of each variable or method can be preceded by a *visibility indicator,* which can be one of the symbols listed in Table 1-1. (In actual practice, it's common to omit the visibility indicator and list only those fields or methods that have public visibility.)

Table 1-1   Visibility Indicators for Class Variables and Methods

Indicator	Description
+	Public
–	Private
#	Protected

If you want, you can include type information for variables as well as for methods and parameters. The type of a variable is indicated by following the variable name with a colon and the type:

```
connectionString: String
```

A method's return type is indicated in the same way:

```
getCustomer(): Customer
```

Parameters are listed within the parentheses, and both the name and type are listed. For example:

```
getCustomer(custno: int): Customer
```

Note: Omitting the type and parameter information from UML diagrams is common.

Interfaces are drawn pretty much the same way as classes, but the class name is preceded by the word *interface*:

```
<<interface>>
 ProductDB
```

Note: The word *interface* is enclosed within a set of double-left and double-right arrows. These arrows aren't just two less-than or greater-than symbols typed in a row; they're a special combination of symbols. Fortunately, the double-arrow symbol is a standard part of the ASCII character set. You can access it in Microsoft Word via the Insert Symbol command.

Drawing arrows

Besides using rectangles to represent classes, class diagrams include arrows to represent relationships among classes. UML uses a variety of types of arrows, as I describe in the following paragraphs.

A solid line with a hollow closed arrow at one end represents inheritance:

The arrow points to the base class. A dashed line with a hollow closed arrow at one end indicates that a class implements an interface:

The arrow points to the interface. A solid line with an open arrow indicates an *association:*

An association simply indicates that two classes work together. It may be that one of the classes creates objects of the other class or that one class requires an object of the other class to perform its work. Or perhaps instances of one class contain instances of the other class.

You can add a name to an association arrow to indicate its purpose. If an association arrow indicates that instances of one class create objects of another class, you can place the word `Creates` next to the arrow.

Chapter 2: Making Your Own Classes

In This Chapter

✓ Creating your own class

✓ Looking at the pieces of a class declaration

✓ Finding out about class fields

✓ Constructing constructors

✓ Adding methods to your classes

✓ Using the this keyword

Okay, class, it's time to learn how to create your own classes.

In this chapter, you discover the basics of creating classes in Java. All Java programs are classes, so you've already seen many examples of classes. You've seen class headers such as `public class GuessingGame` and static methods such as `public static void main`. Now, in this chapter, I show you how to create programs that have more than one class.

Declaring a Class

All classes must be defined by a *class declaration* — lines of code that provide the name for the class and the body of the class. Here's the most basic form of a class declaration:

```
[public] class ClassName {class-body}
```

The `public` keyword indicates that this class is available for use by other classes. Although it's optional, you usually include it in your class declarations. After all, the main reason you write class declarations is so other classes can create objects from the class you're defining. (Find out more about using the `public` keyword in the section "Seeing where classes go," later in this chapter.)

In later chapters of this book, you find out about some additional elements that can go in a class declaration. The format I'm describing here is just the basic format used to create basic classes.

Picking class names

The `ClassName` is an identifier that provides a name for your class. You can use any identifier you want to name a class, but the following three guidelines can simplify your life:

+ **Begin the class name with a capital letter.** If the class name consists of more than one word, capitalize each word: for example, `Ball`, `RetailCustomer`, and `GuessingGame`.

+ **Whenever possible, use nouns for your class names.** Classes create objects, and nouns are the words you use to identify objects. Thus most class names should be nouns.

+ **Avoid using the name of a Java API class.** No rule says that you absolutely have to, but if you create a class that has the same name as a Java API class, you have to use fully qualified names (such as `java.util.Scanner`) to tell your class apart from the API class with the same name.

There are thousands of Java API classes, so avoiding them all is pretty hard. But at the least, you should avoid commonly used Java class names, as well as any API classes that your application is likely to use. Creating a class named `String` or `Math`, for example, is just asking for trouble.

Knowing what goes in the class body

The *class body* of a class is everything that goes within the braces at the end of the class declaration. The `public class ClassName` part of a class declaration takes just one line, but the body of the class declaration may take hundreds of lines (or thousands, if you get carried away).

The class body can contain the following elements:

+ **Fields:** Variable declarations define the public or private fields of a class.

+ **Methods:** Method declarations define the methods of a class.

+ **Constructors:** A *constructor* is a block of code that's similar to a method but is run to initialize an object when an instance is created. A constructor must have the same name as the class itself, and although it resembles a method, it doesn't have a return type.

+ **Initializers:** These stand-alone blocks of code are run only once, when the class is initialized. There are actually two types, called *static initializers* and *instance initializers*. Although you won't use them often, I talk about instance initializers later in this chapter, in the section "Using Initializers." (For information about static initializers, refer to Book III, Chapter 3.)

✦ **Other classes and interfaces:** A class can include another class, which is then called an *inner class* or a *nested class*. Classes can also contain interfaces. (For more information about inner classes, see Book III, Chapter 7. And for information about interfaces, refer to Book III, Chapter 5.)

Unlike some programming languages, Java doesn't care about the order in which items appear in the class body. Still, being consistent about the order in which you place things in your classes is a good idea. That way you know where to find them. I usually code all the fields together at the start of the class, followed by constructors and then methods. If the class includes initializers, I place them near the fields they initialize. And if the class includes inner classes, I usually place them after the methods that use them.

Some programmers like to place the fields at the end of the class rather than at the beginning. Whatever brings you happiness is fine with me.

The fields, methods, classes, and interfaces contained within a class are called the *members* of the class. Constructors and initializers aren't considered to be members, for reasons that are too technical to explain at this point. (You can find the explanation in Book III, Chapter 3.)

Seeing where classes go

A public class must be written in a source file that has the same name as the class, with the extension `java`. A public class named `Greeter`, for example, must be placed in a file named `Greeter.java`.

As a result, you can't place two public classes in the same file. The following source file (named `DiceGame.java`) won't compile:

```
public class DiceGame
{
    public static void main(String[] args)
    {
        Dice d = new Dice();
        d.roll();
    }
}

public class Dice
{
    public void roll()
    {
        // code that rolls the dice goes here
    }
}
```

The compiler coughs up a message indicating that `Dice` is a public class and must be declared in a file named `Dice.java`.

This problem has two solutions. The first is to remove the `public` keyword from the `Dice` class:

```
public class DiceGame
{
    public static void main(String[] args)
    {
        Dice d = new Dice();
        d.roll();
    }
}

class Dice
{
    public void roll()
    {
        // code that rolls the dice goes here
    }
}
```

The compiler gladly accepts this program.

An *inner class* is a class that's defined within the body of another class and is available only from within that class. (For more information about inner classes, see Book III, Chapter 7.)

When you code more than one class in a single source file, Java still creates a separate class file for each class. Thus, when you compile the `DiceGame.java` file, the Java compiler creates two class files: `DiceGame.class` and `Dice.class`.

Removing the `public` keyword from a class is acceptable for relatively small programs, but its limitation is that the `Dice` class is available only to the classes defined within the `DiceGame.java` file. If you want the `Dice` class to be more widely available, opt for the second solution: Place it, with the `public` keyword, in a separate file named `Dice.java`.

If you're going to create an application that has several public classes, create a separate folder for the application. Then save all the class files for the application to this folder. If you keep your class files together in the same folder, the Java compiler can find them. If you place them in separate folders, you may need to adjust your `ClassPath` environment variable to help the compiler find the classes.

Working with Members

The *members* of a class are the fields and methods defined in the class body. (Technically, classes and interfaces defined within a class are members too. I don't discuss them in this chapter, though, so you can ignore them for now.)

The following sections describe the basics of working with fields and methods in your classes.

Understanding fields

A *field* is a variable that's defined in the body of a class, outside any of the class's methods. Fields, which are also called *class variables,* are available to all the methods of a class. In addition, if the field specifies the `public` keyword, the field is visible outside the class. If you don't want the field to be visible outside the class, use the `private` keyword instead.

A field is defined the same as any other Java variable, but it can have a modifier that specifies whether the field is public or private. Here are some examples of public field declarations:

```
public int trajectory = 0;
public String name;
public Player player;
```

To create a private field, specify `private` instead of `public`:

```
private int x_position = 0;
private int y_position = 0;
private String error-message = "";
```

Fields can also be declared as `final`:

```
public final int MAX_SCORE = 1000;
```

The value of a `final` field can't be changed after it has been initialized. *Note:* Spelling `final` field names with all capital letters is customary (but not required).

Understanding methods

You define methods for a class by using the same techniques that I describe in Book II, Chapter 7. To declare a method that's available to users of your class, add the `public` keyword to the method declaration:

```
public boolean isActive()
{
    return this.isActive;
}
```

To create a private method that can be used within the class but isn't visible outside the class, use the `private` keyword:

```
private void calculateLunarTrajectory()
{
    // code to get the calculated lunar trajectory
}
```

Understanding visibility

In the preceding sections, I mention that both fields and methods can use the `public` or `private` keyword to indicate whether the field or method can be accessed from outside the class. This is called the *visibility* of the field or method.

The combination of all the members that have `public` access is sometimes called the *public interface* of your class. These members are the only means that other objects have to communicate with objects created from your class. As a result, carefully consider which public fields and methods your class declares.

The term *expose* is sometimes used to refer to the creation of public fields and methods. If a class has a public method named `isActive`, for example, you could say that the class exposes the `isActive` method. That simply means the method is available to other classes.

You can use private fields and methods within a class — but not from other classes. Private fields and methods provide implementation details that may be crucial to the operation of your class but that shouldn't be exposed to the outside world. Private fields and methods are sometimes called *internal members* because they're available only from within the class.

Using Getters and Setters

One of the basic goals of object-oriented programming is to hide the implementation details of a class inside the class while carefully controlling what aspects of the class are exposed to the outside world. As a general rule, you should avoid creating public fields. Instead, you can make all your fields private. Then you can selectively grant access to the data those fields contain by adding to the class special methods called *accessors*.

There are two types of accessors. A *get accessor* (also called a *getter*) is a method that retrieves a field value, whereas a *set accessor (setter)* is a method that sets a field value. These methods are usually named `get`*FieldName* and `set`*FieldName*, respectively. If the field is named `count`, for example, the getter and setter methods are named `getCount` and `setCount`.

Here's a class that uses a private field named `Health` to indicate the health of a player in a game program:

```
public class Player
{
    private int health;

    public int getHealth()
    {
        return health;
    }

    public void setHealth(int h)
    {
        health = h;
    }
}
```

Here the `health` field itself is declared as `private`, so it can't be accessed directly. Instead, it can be accessed only through the methods `getHealth` and `setHealth`.

Creating classes with accessors rather than simple public fields offers several benefits:

✦ You can create a read-only property by providing a `get` accessor but not a `set` accessor. Then other classes can retrieve the property value — but can't change it.

✦ Instead of storing the property value in a private field, you can calculate it each time the `get` accessor method is called. Suppose you have a class named `Order` that includes fields named `unitPrice` and `quantityOrdered`. This class might also contain a `getOrderTotal` method that looks like this:

```
public double getOrderTotal()
{
    return unitPrice * quantityOrdered;
}
```

Here, instead of returning the value of a class field, the `get` accessor calculates the value to be returned.

✦ You can protect the class from bad data by validating data in a property set accessor and either ignoring invalid data or throwing an exception if invalid data is passed to the method. Suppose that you have a set accessor for an `int` property named `Health` whose value can range from 0 to 100. Here's a set accessor that prevents the `Health` property from being set to an incorrect value:

```
public void setHealth(int h)
{
    if (h < 0)
```

```
                                 health = 0;
                      else if (h > 100)
                           health = 100;
                      else
                           health = h;
        }
```

Here, if the `setHealth` method is called with a value less than 0, `health` is set to 0. Likewise, if the value is greater than 100, `health` is set to 100.

For a little added insight on the use of accessors, see the nearby sidebar "The Accessor pattern."

Overloading Methods

A Java class can contain two or more methods with the same name, provided that those methods accept different parameters. This technique, called *overloading,* is one of the keys to building flexibility into your classes. With overloading, you can anticipate different ways that someone might want to invoke an object's functions and then provide overloaded methods for each alternative.

The Accessor pattern

The use of accessors (as described in the section "Using Getters and Setters" in this chapter) is an example of a design pattern that's commonly used by Java programmers. The *Accessor pattern* is designed to provide a consistent way to set or retrieve the value of class fields without having to expose the fields themselves to the outside world.

Most Java programmers quickly learn that one of the basic guidelines of object-oriented programming is to avoid public fields. Unfortunately, they often respond to this guideline by making all fields private and then providing get and set accessors for every field, whether they need them or not. So they write classes that look like this:

```
public class MyClass
{
    private int fieldX;
    private int fieldY;
```

```
    public int getX() { return x; }
    public void setX(int xValue) { this.x
        = xValue; }
    public int getY() { return y; }
    public void setY(int yValue) { this.y
        = yValue; }
}
```

Why not just make `fieldX` and `fieldY` public fields and skip the accessors?

If all your accessors do is set and return the values, without doing any data validation or other processing, you may as well skip them. The point of making your fields private is to carefully control access to them. If you're going to use accessors for all your fields, you might as well make the fields public.

Instead, carefully consider which fields really should be accessible to the outside world — and provide accessors only for those fields that really need them.

The term *overloading* is accurate but a little unfortunate. Normally, when you say that something is overloaded, there's a problem. I once saw a picture of a Volkswagen Jetta loaded down with 3,000 pounds of lumber. (You can find the picture courtesy of Snopes.com, the Urban Legend Reference Page website, at `www.snopes.com/photos/automobiles/lumber.asp`.) That's a classic example of overloading in the ordinary sense. Fortunately, you don't have to worry about Java collapsing under the weight of overloaded methods.

You're already familiar with several classes that have overloaded methods, though you may not realize it. The `PrintWriter` class, for example (which you access via `System.out`), defines 10 versions of the `println` method that allow you to print different types of data. The following lines show the method declaration for each of these overloads:

```
void println()
void println(boolean x)
void println(char x)
void println(char[] x)
void println(double x)
void println(float x)
void println(int x)
void println(long x)
void println(Object x)
void println(String x)
```

The basic rule in creating overloaded methods is that every method must have a unique signature. A method's *signature* is the combination of its name and the number and types of parameters it accepts. Thus, each of the `println` methods has a different signature, because although all the methods have the same name, each method accepts a different parameter type.

Two things that are *not* a part of a method's signature are

✦ **The method's return type:** You can't code two methods with the same name and parameters but with different return types.

✦ **The names of the parameters:** All that matters to the method signature are the types of the parameters and the order in which they appear. Thus the following two methods have the same signature:

```
double someMethodOfMine(double x, boolean y)
double someMethodOfMine(double param1, boolean param2)
```

Creating Constructors

A *constructor* is a block of code that's called when an instance of an object is created. In many ways, a constructor is similar to a method, but a few differences exist:

+ A constructor doesn't have a return type.

+ The name of the constructor must be the same as the name of the class.

+ Unlike methods, constructors are not considered to be members of a class. (That's important only when it comes to inheritance, which is covered in Book III, Chapter 4.)

+ A constructor is called when a new instance of an object is created. In fact, it's the `new` keyword that calls the constructor. After creating the object, you can't call the constructor again.

Here's the basic format for coding a constructor:

```
public ClassName (parameter-list) [throws exception...]
{
    statements...
}
```

The `public` keyword indicates that other classes can access the constructor. That's usually what you want, although in the next chapter, you see why you might want to create a `private` constructor. `ClassName` must be the same as the name of the class that contains the constructor. You code the parameter list the same way that you code it for a method.

Notice also that a constructor can throw exceptions if it encounters situations that it can't recover from. (For more information about throwing exceptions, refer to Book II, Chapter 8.)

Creating basic constructors

Probably the most common reason for coding a constructor is to provide initial values for class fields when you create the object. Suppose that you have a class named `Actor` that has fields named `firstName` and `lastName`. You can create a constructor for the `Actor` class:

```
public Actor(String first, String last)
{
    firstName = first;
    lastName = last;
}
```

Then you create an instance of the `Actor` class by calling this constructor:

```
Actor a = new Actor("Arnold", "Schwarzenegger");
```

A new `Actor` object for Arnold Schwarzenegger is created.

Like methods, constructors can be overloaded. In other words, you can provide more than one constructor for a class, provided that each constructor
has a unique signature. Here's another constructor for the `Actor` class:

```
public Actor(String first, String last, boolean good)
{
    firstName = first;
    lastName = last;
    goodActor = good;
}
```

This constructor lets you create an `Actor` object with information besides
the actor's name:

```
Actor a = new Actor("Arnold", "Schwarzenegger", false);
```

Creating default constructors

I grew up watching *Dragnet*. I can still hear Joe Friday reading some thug his
rights: "You have the right to an attorney during questioning. If you desire an
attorney and cannot afford one, an attorney will be appointed to you free of
charge."

Java constructors are like that. Every class has a right to a constructor. If
you don't provide a constructor, Java appoints one for you, free of charge.
This free constructor is called the *default constructor*. It doesn't accept any
parameters and doesn't do anything, but it does allow your class to be
instantiated.

Thus, the following two classes are identical:

```
public Class1
{
    public Class1() { }
}

public Class1 { }
```

In the first example, the class explicitly declares a constructor that doesn't accept any parameters and has no statements in its body. In the second example, Java creates a default constructor that works just like the constructor shown in the first example.

The default constructor is *not* created if you declare any constructors for the class. As a result, if you declare a constructor that accepts parameters and still want to have an empty constructor (with no parameters and no body), you must explicitly declare an empty constructor for the class.

An example might clear this point up. The following code does *not* compile:

```java
public class BadActorApp
{
    public static void main(String[] args)
    {
        Actor a = new Actor();    // error: won't compile
    }
}

class Actor
{
    private String lastName;
    private String firstName;
    private boolean goodActor;

    public Actor(String last, String first)
    {
        lastName = last;
        firstName = first;
    }

    public Actor(String last, String first, boolean good)
    {
        lastName = last;
        firstName = first;
        goodActor = good;
    }
}
```

This program won't compile because it doesn't explicitly provide a default constructor for the Actor class; because it does provide other constructors, the default constructor isn't generated automatically.

Calling other constructors

A constructor can call another constructor of the same class by using the special keyword this as a method call. This technique is commonly used when you have several constructors that build on one another.

Consider this class:

```
public class Actor
{
    private String lastName;
    private String firstName;
    private boolean goodActor;

    public Actor(String last, String first)
    {
        lastName = last;
        firstName = first;
    }

    public Actor(String last, String first, boolean good)
    {
        this(last, first);
        goodActor = good;
    }
}
```

Here the second constructor calls the first constructor to set the lastName and firstName fields. Then it sets the goodActor field.

You have a few restrictions in using the this keyword as a constructor call:

✦ You can call another constructor only in the very first statement of a constructor. Thus, the following code won't compile:

```
public Actor(String last, String first, boolean good)
{
    goodActor = good;
    this(last, first); // error: won't compile
}
```

If you try to compile a class with this constructor, you get a message saying call to this must be first statement in constructor.

✦ Each constructor can call only one other constructor, but you can chain constructors. If a class has three constructors, the first constructor can call the second one, which in turn calls the third one.

✦ You can't create loops in which constructors call one another. Here's a class that won't compile:

```
class CrazyClass
{
    private String firstString;
    private String secondString;

    public CrazyClass(String first, String second)
    {
        this(first);
        secondString = second;
    }

    public CrazyClass(String first)
    {
        this(first, "DEFAULT");  // error: won't
                                 // compile
    }
}
```

The first constructor starts by calling the second constructor, which calls the first constructor. The compiler complains that this error is a `recursive constructor invocation` and politely refuses to compile the class.

If you don't explicitly call a constructor in the first line of a constructor, Java inserts code that automatically calls the default constructor of the base class — that is, the class that this class inherits. (This little detail doesn't become too important until you get into inheritance, which is covered in Book III, Chapter 4, so you can conveniently ignore it for now.)

Finding More Uses for the this Keyword

As I describe in the preceding section, you can use the `this` keyword in a constructor to call another constructor for the current class. You can also use `this` in the body of a class constructor or method to refer to the current object — that is, the class instance for which the constructor or method has been called.

The this keyword is usually used to qualify references to instance variables of the current object. For example:

```
public Actor(String last, String first)
{
    this.lastName = last;
    this.firstName = first;
}
```

Here this isn't really necessary because the compiler can tell that lastName and firstName refer to class variables. Suppose, however, that you use lastName and firstName as the parameter names for the constructor:

```
public Actor(String lastName, String firstName)
{
    this.lastName = lastName;
    this.firstName = firstName;
}
```

Here the this keywords are required to distinguish among the parameters named lastName and firstName and the instance variables with the same names.

You can also use this in a method body. For example:

```
public String getFullName()
{
    return this.firstName + " " + this.lastName;
}
```

Because this example has no ambiguity, this isn't really required. Many programmers like to use this even when it isn't necessary, however, because it clarifies that they're referring to an instance variable.

Sometimes you use the this keyword all by itself to pass a reference to the current object as a method parameter. You can print the current object to the console by using the following statement:

```
System.out.println(this);
```

The println method calls the object's toString method to get a string representation of the object and then prints it to the console. By default, toString prints the name of the class that the object was created from and the object's hash code. If you want the println method to print something more meaningful, provide a toString method of your own for the class.

Using Initializers

An *initializer* (sometimes called an *initializer block*) is a lonely block of code that's placed outside any method, constructor, or other block of code. Initializers are executed whenever an instance of a class is created, regardless of which constructor is used to create the instance.

Initializer blocks are similar to variable initializers used to initialize variables. The difference is that with an initializer block, you can code more than one statement. Here's a class that gets the value for a class field from the user when the class is initialized:

```
class PrimeClass
{
    private Scanner sc = new Scanner(System.in);

    public int x;

    {
        System.out.print(
            "Enter the starting value for x: ");
        x = sc.nextInt();
    }

}
```

You can almost always achieve the same effect by using other coding techniques, which usually are more direct. You could prompt the user for the value in the constructor, for example, or you could call a method in the field initializer, like this:

```
class PrimeClass
{
    private Scanner sc = new Scanner(System.in);

    public int x = getX();

    private int getX()
    {
        System.out.print("Enter the starting value "
            + "for x: ");
        return sc.nextInt();
    }
}
```

Either way, the effect is the same.

Here are a few other tidbits of information concerning initializers:

✦ If a class contains more than one initializer, the initializers are executed in the order in which they appear in the program.

✦ Initializers are executed before any class constructors.

✦ A special kind of initializer block called a *static initializer* lets you initialize static fields. (For more information, see the next chapter.)

✦ Initializers are sometimes used with anonymous classes, as I describe in Book III, Chapter 6.

Chapter 3: Working with Statics

In This Chapter

✔ **Adding static fields to a class**

✔ **Creating static methods**

✔ **Creating classes that can be instantiated**

✔ **Working with static initializers**

A static method is a method that isn't associated with an instance of a class. (Unless you jumped straight to this chapter, you already knew that.) Instead, the method belongs to the class itself. As a result, you can call the method without first creating a class instance. In this chapter, you find out everything you need to know about creating and using static fields and methods.

Understanding Static Fields and Methods

According to my handy *Webster's* dictionary, the word *static* has several meanings, most of which relate to the idea of being stationary or unchanging. A *static display* is a display that doesn't move. *Static electricity* is an electrical charge that doesn't flow. A *static design* is a design that doesn't change.

As used by Java, however, the term *static* doesn't mean unchanging. You can create a static field, for example, and then assign values to it as a program executes. Thus, the value of the static field can change.

To confuse things further, the word *static* can also mean interference, as in radio static that prevents you from hearing music clearly on the radio. But in Java, the term *static* doesn't have anything to do with interference or bad reception.

So what does the term *static* mean in Java? It's used to describe a special type of field or method that isn't associated with a particular instance of a class. Instead, static fields and methods are associated with the class itself, which means that you don't have to create an instance of the class to access a static field or methods. Instead, you access a static field or method by specifying the class name, not a variable that references an object.

The value of a static field is the same across all instances of the class. In other words, if a class has a static field named CompanyName, all objects created from the class will have the same value for CompanyName.

Static fields and methods have many common uses. Here are but a few:

✦ **To provide constants or other values that aren't related to class instances:** A Billing class might have a constant named SALES_TAX_RATE that provides the state sales tax rate.

✦ **To keep count of how many instances of a class have been created:** A Ball class used in a game might have a static field that counts how many balls currently exist. This count doesn't belong to any one instance of the Ball class.

✦ **In a business application, to keep track of a reference or serial number that's assigned to each new object instance:** An Invoice class might maintain a static field that holds the invoice number that is assigned to the next Invoice object created from the class.

✦ **To provide an alternative way to create instances of the class:** An excellent example is the NumberFormat class, which has static methods such as getCurrencyInstance and getNumberInstance that return object instances to format numbers in specific ways. One reason you might want to use this technique is to create classes that can have only one object instance. This type of class, called a *singleton class*, is described in the sidebar "The Singleton pattern," later in this chapter.

✦ **To provide utility functions that aren't associated with an object at all:** A good example in the Java API library is the Math class, which provides a bunch of static methods to do math calculations. Examples that you might code yourself are a DataValidation class with static methods that validate input data and a database class with static methods that perform database operations.

Working with Static Fields

A *static field* is a field that's declared with the static keyword, like this:

```
private static int ballCount;
```

Note that the position of the static keyword is interchangeable with the positions of the *visibility keywords* (private and public, as well as protected, which I describe in the next chapter). As a result, the following statement works as well:

```
static private int ballCount;
```

As a convention, most programmers tend to put the visibility keyword first.

Note that you can't use the `static` keyword within a class method. Thus the following code won't compile:

```
private void someMethod()
{
    static int x;
}
```

In other words, fields can be static, but local variables can't.

You can provide an initial value for a static field. Here's an example:

```
private static String district = "Northwest";
```

Static fields are created and initialized when the class is first loaded. That happens when a static member of the class is referred to or when an instance of the class is created, whichever comes first.

Another way to initialize a static field is to use a *static initializer,* which I cover later in this chapter, in the section "Using Static Initializers."

Using Static Methods

A *static method* is a method declared with the `static` keyword. Like static fields, static methods are associated with the class itself, not with any particular object created from the class. As a result, you don't have to create an object from a class before you can use static methods defined by the class.

The best-known static method is `main`, which is called by the Java runtime to start an application. The `main` method must be static — which means that applications are run in a static context by default.

One of the basic rules of working with static methods is that you can't access a nonstatic method or field from a static method, because the static method doesn't have an instance of the class to use to reference instance methods or fields. The following code won't compile:

```
public class TestClass
{
    private int x = 5;        // an instance field
    public static void main(String[] args)
    {
        int y = x;            // error: won't compile
    }
}
```

Book III
Chapter 3

Working with
Statics

Here the `main` method is static, so it can't access the instance variable x.

Note: You *can* access static methods and fields from an instance method, however. The following code works fine:

```
public class Invoice
{
    private static double taxRate = 0.75;

    private double salesTotal;

    public double getTax()
    {
        return salesTotal * taxRate;
    }
}
```

Here the instance method named `salesTotal` has no trouble accessing the static field `taxRate`.

Counting Instances

One common use for static variables is to keep track of how many instances of a class have been created. To illustrate how you can do this, consider the program in Listing 3-1. This program includes two classes. The `CountTest` class is a simple class that keeps track of how many times its constructor has been called. Then the `CountTestApp` class uses a `for` loop to create 10 instances of the class, displaying the number of instances that have been created after it creates each instance.

Note that the instance count in this application is reset to zero each time the application is run. As a result, it doesn't keep track of how many instances of the `CountTest` class have ever been created — only of how many have been created *during a particular execution* of the program.

Listing 3-1:   The CountTest Application

```
public class CountTestApp                                          →1
{
    public static void main(String[] args)
    {
        printCount();
        for (int i = 0; i < 10; i++)
        {
            CountTest c1 = new CountTest();                        →8
            printCount();                                         →9
        }
    }
```

```
        private static void printCount()
        {
            System.out.println("There are now "            →15
                + CountTest.getInstanceCount()
                + "instances of the CountTest class.");
        }
    }

class CountTest                                            →21
{
    private static int instanceCount = 0;                  →23

    public CountTest()                                     →25
    {
        instanceCount++;
    }

    public static int getInstanceCount()                   →29
    {
        return instanceCount;
    }
}
```

The following paragraphs describe some of the highlights of this program:

→ 1   This line is the start of the CountTestApp class, which tests the CountTest class.

→ 8   This line creates an instance of the CountTest class. Because this code is contained in a for loop, 10 instances are created.

→ 9   This line calls the printCount method, which prints the number of CountTest objects that have been created so far.

→ 15 This line prints a message indicating how many CountTest objects have been created so far. It calls the static getInstanceCount method of the CountTest class to get the instance count.

→ 21 This line is the start of the CountTest class.

→ 23 The static instanceCount variable stores the instance count.

→ 25 This line is the constructor for the CountTest class. Notice that the instanceCount variable is incremented within the constructor. That way, each time a new instance of the class is created, the instance count is incremented.

→ 29 The static getInstanceCount method simply returns the value of the static instanceCount field.

DESIGN PATTERN

The Singleton pattern

A *singleton* is a class that you can use to create only one instance. When you try to create an instance, the class first checks to see whether an instance already exists. If so, the existing instance is used; if not, a new instance is created.

You can't achieve this effect by using Java constructors, because a class instance has already been created by the time the constructor is executed. (That's why you can use the `this` keyword from within a constructor.) As a result, the normal way to implement a singleton class is to declare all the constructors for the class as private. That way, the constructors aren't available to other classes. Then you provide a static method that returns an instance. This method either creates a new instance or returns an existing instance.

Here's a bare-bones example of a singleton class:

```
class SingletonClass
{
    private static SingletonClass
        instance;

    private SingletonClass()
    {
    }

    public static SingletonClass
        getInstance()
    {
        if (instance == null)
            instance = new
            SingletonClass();
```

```
        return instance;
    }
}
```

Here the `SingletonClass` contains a `private` instance variable that maintains a reference to an instance of the class. Then a default constructor is declared with private visibility to prevent the constructor from being used outside the class. Finally, the static `getInstance` method calls the constructor to create an instance if the `instance` variable is null. Then it returns the instance to the caller.

Here's a bit of code that calls the `getInstance` method twice and then compares the resulting objects:

```
SingletonClass s1 = SingletonClass.
        getInstance();
SingletonClass s2 = SingletonClass.
        getInstance();
if (s1 == s2)
    System.out.println("The objects are
        the same");
else
    System.out.println("The objects are
        not the same");
```

When this code is run, the first call to `getInstance` creates a new instance of the `SingletonClass` class. The second call to `getInstance` simply returns a reference to the instance that was created in the first call. As a result, the comparison in the `if` statement is true, and the first message is printed to the console.

Preventing Instances

Sometimes you want to create a class that can't be instantiated at all. Such a class consists entirely of static fields and methods. A good example in the Java API is the Math class. Its methods provide utility-type functions that aren't really associated with a particular object. You may need to create similar classes yourself occasionally. You might create a class with static methods for validating input data, for example, or a database access class that has static methods to retrieve data from a database. You don't need to create instances of either of these classes.

You can use a simple trick to prevent anyone from instantiating a class. To create a class instance, you have to have at least one public constructor. If you don't provide a constructor in your class, Java automatically inserts a default constructor, which happens to be public.

All you have to do to prevent a class instance from being created, then, is provide a single private constructor, like this:

```
public class Validation
{
    private Validation() {}        // prevents instances

    // static methods and fields go here
}
```

Book III
Chapter 3

Working with
Statics

Now, because the constructor is private, the class can't be instantiated.

Incidentally, the Math class uses this technique to prevent you from creating instances from it. Here's an actual snippet of code from the Math class:

```
public final class Math {

    /**
     * Don't let anyone instantiate this class.
     */
    private Math() {}
```

I figure that if this trick is good enough for the folks who wrote the Math class, it's good enough for me.

Using Static Initializers

In the preceding chapter, you discover *initializer blocks* that you can use to initialize instance variables. Initializer blocks aren't executed until an instance of a class is created, so you can't count on them to initialize static fields. After all, you might access a static field before you create an instance of a class.

Java provides a feature called a *static initializer* that's designed specifically to let you initialize static fields. The general form of a static initializer looks like this:

```
static
{
    statements...
}
```

As you can see, a static initializer is similar to an initializer block but begins with the word `static`. As with an initializer block, you code static initializers in the class body but outside any other block, such as the body of a method or constructor.

The first time you access a static member such as a static field or a static method, any static initializers in the class are executed — provided that you haven't already created an instance of the class. That's because the static initializers are also executed the first time you create an instance. In that case, the static initializers are executed *before* the constructor is executed.

If a class has more than one static initializer, the initializers are executed in the order in which they appear in the program.

Here's an example of a class that contains a static initializer:

```
class StaticInit
{
    public static int x;

    static
    {
        x = 32;
    }

// other class members such as constructors and
// methods go here...
}
```

This example is pretty trivial. In fact, you can achieve the same effect just by assigning the value 32 to the variable when it is declared. If, however, you had to perform a complicated calculation to determine the value of x — or if its value comes from a database — a static initializer could be very useful.

Chapter 4: Using Subclasses and Inheritance

In This Chapter

✔ **Explaining inheritance**

✔ **Creating subclasses**

✔ **Using protected access**

✔ **Creating final classes**

✔ **Demystifying polymorphism**

✔ **Creating custom exception classes**

As you find out in Book III, Chapter 1, a Java class can be based on another class. Then the class becomes like a child to the parent class: It inherits all the characteristics of the parent class, good and bad. All the fields and methods of the parent class are passed on to the child class. The child class can use these fields or methods as they are, or it can override them to provide its own versions. In addition, the child class can add fields or methods of its own.

In this chapter, you discover how this magic works, along with the basics of creating and using Java classes that inherit other classes. You also find out a few fancy tricks that help you get the most out of inheritance.

Introducing Inheritance

The word *inheritance* conjures up several noncomputer meanings:

✦ Children inherit certain characteristics from the parents. Two of my three children have red hair, for example. (Ideally, they won't be half bald by the time they're 30.)

✦ Children can also inherit behavior from their parents. As they say, the apple doesn't fall far from the tree.

✦ When someone dies, his heirs get his stuff. Some of it is good stuff, but some of it may not be. My kids are going to have a great time rummaging through my garage, deciding who gets what.

✦ You can inherit rights as well as possessions. You may be a citizen of a country by virtue of being born to parents who are citizens of that country.

In Java, *inheritance* refers to a feature of object-oriented programming that lets you create classes that are derived from other classes. A class that's based on another class is said to *inherit* the other class. The class that is inherited is called the *parent class,* the *base class,* or the *superclass.* The class that does the inheriting is called the *child class,* the *derived class,* or the *subclass.*

The terms *subclass* and *superclass* seem to be the preferred terms among Java gurus. So if you want to look like you know what you're talking about, use these terms. Also, be aware that the term *subclass* can be used as a verb. When you create a subclass that inherits a base class, for example, you are *subclassing* the base class.

You need to know a few important things about inheritance:

✦ A derived class automatically takes on all the behavior and attributes of its base class. Thus, if you need to create several classes to describe types that aren't identical but have many features in common, you can create a base class that defines all the common features. Then you can create several derived classes that inherit the common features.

✦ A derived class can add features to the base class it inherits by defining its own methods and fields. This is one way that a derived class distinguishes itself from its base class.

✦ A derived class can also change the behavior provided by the base class. A base class may provide that all classes derived from it have a method named `play`, for example, but each class is free to provide its own implementation of the `play` method. In this case, all classes that extend the base class provide their own implementation of the `play` method.

✦ Inheritance is best used to implement *is-a-type-of* relationships. Here are a few examples: Solitaire is a type of game; a truck is a type of vehicle; an invoice is a type of transaction. In each case, a particular kind of object is a specific type of a more general category of objects.

The following sections provide more examples that help illustrate these points.

Motorcycles, trains, and automobiles

Inheritance is often explained in terms of real-world objects such as cars and motorcycles or birds and reptiles. Consider various types of vehicles. Cars and motorcycles are two distinct types of vehicles. If you're writing software that represents vehicles, you could start by creating a class called `Vehicle` that would describe the features that are common to all types of vehicles, such as wheels; a driver; the ability to carry passengers; and the ability to perform actions such as driving, stopping, turning, and crashing.

A motorcycle is a type of vehicle that further refines the `Vehicle` class. The `Motorcycle` class would inherit the `Vehicle` class, so it would have wheels;

a driver; possibly passengers; and the ability to drive, stop, turn, and crash. In addition, it would have features that differentiate it from other types of vehicles, such as two wheels and handlebars used for steering control.

A car is also a type of vehicle. The Car class would inherit the Vehicle class, so it too would have wheels; a driver; possibly some passengers; and the ability to drive, stop, turn, and crash. Also, it would have some features of its own, such as four wheels, a steering wheel, seat belts and air bags, and an optional automatic transmission.

Game play

Because you're unlikely ever to write a program that simulates cars, motorcycles, and other vehicles, take a look at a more common example: games. Suppose that you want to develop a series of board games such as Life, Sorry!, and Monopoly. Most board games have certain features in common:

✦ They have a playing board with locations that players can occupy.

✦ They have players that are represented by objects.

✦ The game is played by each player taking a turn, one after the other. When the game starts, it keeps going until someone wins. (If you don't believe me, ask the kids who tried to stop a game of Jumanji before someone won.)

Each specific type of game has these basic characteristics but adds features of its own. The game Life adds features such as money, insurance policies, spouses, children, and a fancy spinner in the middle of the board. Sorry! has cards that you draw to determine each move and safety zones within which other players can't attack you. Monopoly has Chance and Community Chest cards, properties, houses, hotels, and money.

If you were designing classes for these games, you might create a generic BoardGame class that defines the basic features common to all board games and then use it as the base class for classes that represent specific board games, such as LifeGame, SorryGame, and MonopolyGame.

A businesslike example

If vehicles or games don't make the point clear enough, here's an example from the world of business. Suppose that you're designing a payroll system, and you're working on the classes that represent the employees. You realize that the payroll includes two types of employees: salaried employees and hourly employees. So you decide to create two classes, sensibly named SalariedEmployee and HourlyEmployee.

You quickly discover that most of the work done by these two classes is identical. Both types of employees have names, addresses, Social Security numbers, totals for how much they've been paid for the year, how much tax has been withheld, and so on.

The employee types also have important differences. The most obvious one is that the salaried employees have an annual salary, and the hourly employees have an hourly pay rate. Also, hourly employees have a schedule that changes week to week, and salaried employees may have a benefit plan that isn't offered to hourly employees.

Thus you decide to create three classes instead of just two. A class named `Employee` handles all the features that are common to both types of employees; then this class is the base class for the `SalariedEmployee` and `Hourly Employee` classes. These classes provide the additional features that distinguish salaried employees from hourly employees.

Inheritance hierarchies

One of the most important aspects of inheritance is that a class derived from a base class can in turn be used as the base class for another derived class. Thus you can use inheritance to form a hierarchy of classes.

You've already seen how an `Employee` class can be used as a base class to create two types of subclasses: a `SalariedEmployee` class for salaried employees and an `HourlyEmployee` class for hourly employees. Suppose that salaried employees fall into two categories: management and sales. Then you could use the `SalariedEmployee` class as the base class for two more classes: `Manager` and `SalesPerson`.

Thus, a `Manager` is a type of `SalariedEmployee`. Because a `Salaried Employee` is a type of `Employee`, a `Manager` is also a type of `Employee`.

All classes ultimately derive from a Java class named `Object`. Any class that doesn't specifically state what class it is derived from is assumed to derive from the `Object` class. This class provides some of the basic features that are common to all Java classes, such as the `toString` method. For more information, see Book III, Chapter 6.

Creating Subclasses

The basic procedure for creating a subclass is simple: You just use the `extends` keyword on the declaration for the subclass. The basic format of a class declaration for a class that inherits a base class is this:

```
public class ClassName extends BaseClass
{
    // class body goes here
}
```

The Delegation pattern

Inheritance is one of the great features of object-oriented programming languages such as Java, but it isn't the answer to every programming problem. Also, quite frankly, many Java programmers use it too much. In many cases, simply including an instance of one class in another class is easier than using inheritance. This technique is sometimes called the *Delegation pattern*.

Suppose that you need to create a class named `EmployeeCollection` that represents a group of employees. One way to create this class would be to extend one of the collection classes supplied by the Java API, such as the `ArrayList` class. Then your `EmployeeCollection` class would be a specialized version of the `ArrayList` class and would have all the methods that are available to the `ArrayList` class.

A simpler alternative, however, would be to declare a class field of type `ArrayList` within your `EmployeeCollection` class. Then you could provide methods that use this `ArrayList` object to add or retrieve employees from the collection.

Why is this technique called the *delegation?* Rather than write code that implements the functions of the collection, you *delegate* that task to an `ArrayList` object, because `ArrayList` objects already know how to perform these functions. (For more information about the `ArrayList` class, see Book IV, Chapter 3.)

Suppose that you have a class named `Ball` that defines a basic ball, and you want to create a subclass named `BouncingBall` that adds the ability to bounce:

```
public class BouncingBall extends Ball
{
    // methods and fields that add the ability to bounce
    // to a basic Ball object:

    public void bounce()
    {
        // the bounce method
    }
}
```

Here I'm creating a class named `BouncingBall` that extends the `Ball` class. (*Extends* is Java's word for *inherits.*)

The subclass automatically has all the methods and fields of the class it extends. Thus, if the `Ball` class has fields named `size` and `weight`, the `BouncingBall` class has those fields too. Likewise, if the `Ball` class has a method named `throw`, the `BouncingBall` class gets that method too.

You need to know some important details to use inheritance properly:

✦ A subclass inherits all the members from its base class. Constructors are *not* considered to be members, however. As a result, a subclass does *not* inherit constructors from its base class.

✦ The visibility (public or private) of any members inherited from the base class is the same in the subclass. That means that you can't access from the subclass methods or fields that are declared in the base class as private.

✦ You can *override* a method by declaring a new member with the same signature in the subclass. For more information, see the next section.

✦ A special type of visibility called protected hides fields and methods from other classes but makes them available to subclasses. For more information, see the section "Protecting Your Members," later in this chapter.

✦ You can add more methods or fields, private or protected, to a subclass. The BouncingBall class shown earlier in this section, for example, adds a public method named bounce.

Overriding Methods

If a subclass declares a method that has the same signature as a public method of the base class, the subclass version of the method *overrides* the base class version of the method. This technique lets you modify the behavior of a base class to suit the needs of the subclass.

Suppose you have a base class named Game that has a method named play. The base class, which doesn't represent any particular game, implements this method:

```
public class Game
{
    public void play()
    {
    }
}
```

Then you declare a class named Chess that extends the Game class but also provides an implementation for the play method:

```
public class Chess extends Game
{
    public void play()
    {
        System.out.println("I give up. You win.");
    }
}
```

Here, when you call the `play` method of a `Chess` object, the game announces that it gives up. (I was going to provide a complete implementation of an actual chess game program for this example, but it would have made this chapter about 600 pages long. So I opted for the simpler version here.)

Note that to override a method, three conditions have to be met:

✦ The class must extend the class that defines the method you want to override.

✦ The method must be declared in the base class with `public` access. You can't override a `private` method.

✦ The method in the subclass must have the same signature as the method in the base class. In other words, the name of the method and the parameter types must be the same.

Protecting Your Members

You're already familiar with the `public` and `private` keywords, which are used to indicate whether class members are visible outside the class or not. When you inherit a class, all the public members of the superclass are available to the subclass, but the private members aren't. They do become part of the derived class, but you can't access them directly in the derived class.

Java provides a third visibility option that's useful when you create subclasses: `protected`. A member with `protected` visibility is available to subclasses but not to other classes. Consider this example:

```
public class Ball
{
    private double weight;

    protected double getWeight()
    {
        return this.weight;
    }

    protected void setWeight(double weight)
    {
        this.weight = weight;
    }
}

public class BaseBall extends Ball
{
    public BaseBall()
    {
        setWeight(5.125);
    }
}
```

Here, the `getWeight` and `setWeight` methods are declared with `protected` access, which means that they're visible in the subclass `BaseBall`. These methods aren't visible to classes that don't extend `Ball`, however.

Using this and super in Your Subclasses

You already know about the `this` keyword: It provides a way to refer to the current object instance. It's often used to distinguish between a local variable or a parameter and a class field with the same name. For example:

```
public class Ball
{
    private int velocity;

    public void setVelocity(int velocity)
    {
        this.velocity = velocity;
    }
}
```

Here the `this` keyword indicates that the `velocity` variable referred to on the left side of the assignment statement is the class field named `velocity`, not the parameter with the same name.

But what if you need to refer to a field or method that belongs to a base class? To do that, you use the `super` keyword. It works similarly to `this` but refers to the instance of the base class rather than the instance of the current class.

Consider these two classes:

```
public class Ball
{
    public void hit()
    {
        System.out.println("You hit it a mile!");
    }
}

class BaseBall extends Ball
{
    public void hit()
    {
        System.out.println("You tore the cover off!");
        super.hit();
    }
}
```

Here the `hit` method in the `BaseBall` class calls the `hit` method of its base class object. Thus, if you call the `hit` method of a `BaseBall` object, the following two lines are displayed on the console:

```
You tore the cover off!
You hit it a mile!
```

You can also use the `super` keyword in the constructor of a subclass to explicitly call a constructor of the superclass. For more information, see the next section.

Understanding Inheritance and Constructors

When you create an instance of a subclass, Java automatically calls the default constructor of the base class before it executes the subclass constructor. Consider the following classes:

```
public class Ball
{
    public Ball()
    {
        System.out.println(
            "Hello from the Ball constructor");
    }
}

public class BaseBall extends Ball
{
    public BaseBall()
    {
        System.out.println(
            "Hello from the BaseBall constructor");
    }
}
```

If you create an instance of the `BaseBall` class, the following two lines are displayed on the console:

```
Hello from the Ball constructor
Hello from the BaseBall constructor
```

If you want, you can explicitly call a base class constructor from a subclass by using the `super` keyword. Because Java automatically calls the default constructor for you, the only reason to do this is to call a constructor of the base class that uses a parameter. Here's a version of the `Ball` and `BaseBall` classes in which the `BaseBall` constructor calls a `Ball` constructor that uses a parameter:

```
public class Ball
{
    private double weight;
```

```
    public Ball(double weight)
    {
        this.weight = weight;
    }
}

public class BaseBall extends Ball
{
    public BaseBall()
    {
        super(5.125);
    }
}
```

Here the `BaseBall` constructor calls the `Ball` constructor to supply a default weight for the ball.

You need to obey a few rules and regulations when working with superclass constructors:

+ If you use `super` to call the superclass constructor, you must do so in the very first statement in the constructor.

+ If you don't explicitly call `super`, the compiler inserts a call to the default constructor of the base class. In that case, the base class must have a default constructor. If the base class doesn't have a default constructor, the compiler refuses to compile the program.

+ If the superclass is itself a subclass, the constructor for its superclass is called in the same way. This continues all the way up the inheritance hierarchy until you get to the `Object` class, which has no superclass.

Using final

Java has a `final` keyword that serves three purposes. When you use `final` with a variable, it creates a constant whose value can't be changed after it has been initialized. Constants are covered in Book II, Chapter 2, so I won't describe this use of the `final` keyword more here. The other two uses of the `final` keyword are to create final methods and final classes. I describe these two uses of `final` in the following sections.

Final methods

A *final method* is a method that can't be overridden by a subclass. To create a final method, you simply add the keyword `final` to the method declaration. For example:

```
public class SpaceShip
{
    public final int getVelocity()
    {
```

```
        return this.velocity;
    }
}
```

Here the method `getVelocity` is declared as `final`. Thus, any class that uses the `SpaceShip` class as a base class can't override the `getVelocity` method. If it tries, the compiler issues the error message (`"Overridden method final"`).

Here are some additional details about final methods:

✦ You might think that a subclass wouldn't need to override a method, but there's no reason to be sure of that. Predicting how other people might use your class is difficult. As a result, usually you should avoid using final methods unless you have a compelling reason to do so.

✦ Final methods execute more efficiently than nonfinal methods because the compiler knows at compile time that a call to a final method won't be overridden by some other method. The performance gain isn't huge, but for applications in which performance is crucial, it can be noticeable.

✦ Private methods are automatically considered to be final because you can't override a method you can't see.

Final classes

A *final class* is a class that can't be used as a base class. To declare a class as final, just add the `final` keyword to the class declaration:

```
public final class BaseBall
{
    // members for the BaseBall class go here
}
```

Then no one can use the `BaseBall` class as the base class for another class.

When you declare a class to be final, all of its methods are considered to be final as well. That makes sense when you think about it. Because you can't use a final class as the base class for another class, no class can possibly be in a position to override any of the methods in the final class. Thus all the methods of a final class are final methods.

Casting Up and Down

An object of a derived type can be treated as though it were an object of its base type. If the `BaseBall` class extends the `Ball` class, for example, a `BaseBall` object can be treated as though it were a `Ball` object. This arrangement is called *upcasting,* and Java does it automatically, so you don't have to code a casting operator. Thus the following code is legal:

```
Ball b = new BaseBall();
```

Here an object of type `BaseBall` is created. Then a reference to this object is assigned to the variable b, whose type is `Ball`, not `BaseBall`.

Now suppose that you have a method in a ball-game application named `hit` that's declared like this:

```
public void hit(Ball b)
```

In other words, this method accepts a `Ball` type as a parameter. When you call this method, you can pass it either a `Ball` object or a `BaseBall` object, because `BaseBall` is a subclass of `Ball`. So the following code works:

```
BaseBall b1 = new BaseBall();
hit(b1);
Ball b2 = b1;
hit(b2);
```

Automatic casting doesn't work the other way, however. Thus you can't use a `Ball` object where a `BaseBall` object is called for. Suppose your program has a method declared like this:

```
public void toss(BaseBall b)
```

Then the following code does *not* compile:

```
Ball b = new BaseBall();
toss(b);      // error: won't compile
```

You can explicitly cast the b variable to a `BaseBall` object, however, like this:

```
Ball b = new BaseBall();
toss((BaseBall) b);
```

Note that the second statement throws an exception of type `ClassCast Exception` if the object referenced by the b variable isn't a `BaseBall` object. So the following code won't work:

```
Ball b = new SoftBall();
toss((BaseBall) b);           // error: b isn't a Softball
```

What if you want to call a method that's defined by a subclass from an object that's referenced by a variable of the superclass? Suppose that the SoftBall class has a method named riseBall that isn't defined by the Ball class. How can you call it from a Ball variable? One way to do that is to create a variable of the subclass and then use an assignment statement to cast the object:

```
Ball b = new SoftBall();
SoftBall s = (SoftBall)b;    // cast the Ball to a
                             // SoftBall
s.riseBall();
```

But there's a better way: Java lets you cast the Ball object to a SoftBall and call the riseBall method in the same statement. All you need is an extra set of parentheses, like this:

```
Ball b = new SoftBall();
((SoftBall) b).riseBall();
```

Here the expression ((SoftBall) b) returns the object referenced by the b variable, cast as a SoftBall. Then you can call any method of the SoftBall class by using the dot operator. (This operator throws a ClassCastException if b is not a SoftBall object.)

As a general rule, you should declare method parameters with types as far up in the class hierarchy as possible. Rather than create separate toss methods that accept BaseBall and SoftBall objects, for example, you can create a single toss method that accepts a Ball object. If necessary, the toss method can determine which type of ball it's throwing by using the instanceof operator, which is described in the next section.

Determining an Object's Type

As described in the preceding section, a variable of one type can possibly hold a reference to an object of another type. If SalariedEmployee is a subclass of the Employee class, the following statement is perfectly legal:

```
Employee emp = new SalariedEmployee();
```

Here the type of the emp variable is Employee, but the object it refers to is a SalariedEmployee.

Suppose you have a method named `getEmployee` whose return type is `Employee` but that actually returns either a `SalariedEmployee` or an `HourlyEmployee` object:

```
Employee emp = getEmployee();
```

In many cases, you don't need to worry about which type of employee this method returns, but sometimes you do. Suppose that the `Salaried Employee` class extends the `Employee` class by adding a method named `getFormattedSalary`, which returns the employee's salary formatted as currency. Similarly, the `HourlyEmployee` class extends the `Employee` class with a `getFormattedRate` method that returns the employee's hourly pay rate formatted as currency. Then you'd need to know which type of employee a particular object is, to know whether you should call the `getFormattedSalary` method or the `getFormattedRate` method to get the employee's pay.

To tell what type of object has been assigned to the `emp` variable, you can use the `instanceof` operator, which is designed specifically for this purpose. Here's the preceding code rewritten with the `instanceof` operator:

```
Employee emp = getEmployee();
String msg;
if (emp instanceof SalariedEmployee)
{
    msg = "The employee's salary is ";
    msg += ((SalariedEmployee) emp).getFormattedSalary();
}
else
{
    msg = "The employee's hourly rate is ";
    msg += ((HourlyEmployee) emp).getFormattedRate();
}
System.out.println(msg);
```

Here the `instanceof` operator is used in an `if` statement to determine the type of the object returned by the `getEmployee` method. Then the `emp` can be cast without fear of `CastClassException`.

Poly What?

The term *polymorphism* refers to the ability of Java to use base class variables to refer to subclass objects; to keep track of which subclass an object belongs to; and to use overridden methods of the subclass, even though the subclass isn't known when the program is compiled.

This sounds like a mouthful, but it's not hard to understand when you see an example. Suppose that you're developing an application that can play the venerable game Tic-Tac-Toe. You start by creating a class named `Player` that represents one of the players. This class has a public method named `move` that returns an `int` to indicate which square of the board the player wants to mark:

```
class Player
{
    public int move()
    {
        for (int i = 0; i < 9; i++)
        {
            System.out.println(
                "\nThe basic player says:");
            System.out.println(
                "I'll take the first open square!");
            return firstOpenSquare();
        }
        return -1;
    }

    private int firstOpenSquare()
    {
        int square = 0;
        // code to find the first open square goes here
        return square;
    }
}
```

This basic version of the `Player` class uses a simple strategy to determine what its next move should be: It chooses the first open square on the board. This strategy stokes your ego by letting you think you can beat the computer every time. (To keep the illustration simple, I omit the code that actually chooses the move.)

Now you need to create a subclass of the `Player` class that uses a more intelligent method to choose its next move:

```
class BetterPlayer extends Player
{
    public int move()
    {
        System.out.println("\nThe better player says:");
        System.out.println(
            "I'm looking for a good move...");
        return findBestMove();
    }

    private int findBestMove()
    {
        int square;
        // code to find the best move goes here
        return square;
    }
}
```

As you can see, this version of the Player class overrides the move method and uses a better algorithm to pick its move. (Again, to keep the illustration simple, I don't show the code that actually chooses the move.)

The next thing to do is write a short class that uses these two Player classes to play a game. This class contains a method named playTheGame that accepts two Player objects. It calls the move method of the first player and then calls the move method of the second player:

```java
public class TicTacToeApp
{
    public static void main(String[] args)
    {
        Player p1 = new Player();
        Player p2 = new BetterPlayer();
        playTheGame(p1, p2);
    }

    public static void playTheGame(Player p1, Player p2)
    {
        p1.move();
        p2.move();
    }
}
```

Notice that the playTheGame method doesn't know which of the two players is the basic player and which is the better player. It simply calls the move method for each Player object.

When you run this program, the following output is displayed on the console:

```
Basic player says:
I'll take the first open square!

Better player says:
I'm looking for a good move...
```

When the move method for p1 is called, the move method of the Player class is executed. But when the move method for p2 is called, the move method of the BetterPlayer class is called.

Java knows to call the move method of the BetterPlayer subclass because it uses a technique called late binding. *Late binding* simply means that when the compiler can't tell for sure what type of object a variable references, it doesn't hard-wire the method calls when the program is compiled. Instead, it waits until the program is executing to determine exactly which method to call.

Creating Custom Exceptions

The last topic I want to cover in this chapter is how to use inheritance to create your own custom exceptions. I cover most of the details of working with exceptions in Book II, Chapter 8, but I hadn't explored inheritance, so I couldn't discuss custom exception classes in that chapter. I promised that I'd get to it in this minibook. The following sections deliver on that long-awaited promise.

Tracing the Throwable hierarchy

As you know, you use the try/catch statement to catch exceptions and the `throw` statement to throw exceptions. Each type of exception that can be caught or thrown is represented by a different exception class. What you may not have realized is that those exception classes use a fairly complex inheritance chain, as shown in Figure 4-1.

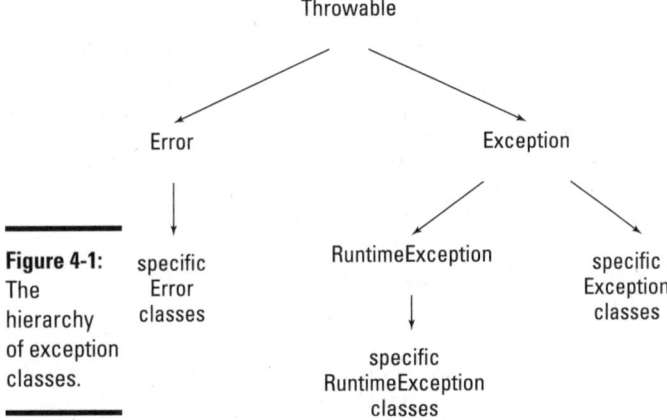

Figure 4-1: The hierarchy of exception classes.

The following paragraphs describe the classes in this hierarchy:

✦ **Throwable:** The root of the exception hierarchy is the `Throwable` class. This class represents any object that can be thrown with a `throw` statement and caught with a `catch` clause.

✦ **Error:** This subclass of `Throwable` represents serious error conditions that reasonable programs can't recover from. The subclasses of this class represent the specific types of errors that can occur. If the Java Virtual

Machine runs out of memory, for example, a `VirtualMachineError` is thrown. You don't have to worry about catching these errors in your programs.

✦ **Exception:** This subclass of `Throwable` represents an error condition that most programs should try to recover from. Thus, `Exception` is effectively the top of the hierarchy for the types of exceptions you catch with `try/catch` statements.

With the exception (sorry) of `RuntimeException`, the subclasses of `Exception` represent specific types of checked exceptions that must be caught or thrown. Note that some of these subclasses have subclasses of their own. The exception class named `IOException`, for example, has more than 25 subclasses representing different kinds of I/O exceptions that can occur.

✦ **RuntimeException:** This subclass of `Exception` represents unchecked exceptions. You don't have to catch or throw unchecked exceptions, but you can if you want to. Subclasses of `RuntimeException` include `NullPointerException` and `ArithmeticException`.

If your application needs to throw a custom exception, you can create an exception class that inherits any of the classes in this hierarchy. Usually, however, you start with the `Exception` class to create a custom checked exception. The next section explains how to do that.

Creating an exception class

To create a custom exception class, you just define a class that extends one of the classes in the Java exception hierarchy. Usually you extend `Exception` to create a custom checked exception.

Suppose that you're developing a class that retrieves product data from a file or database, and you want methods that encounter I/O errors to throw a custom exception rather than the generic `IOException` that's provided in the Java API. You can do that by creating a class that extends the `Exception` class:

```
public class ProductDataException extends Exception
{
}
```

Unfortunately, constructors aren't considered to be class members, so they aren't inherited when you extend a class. As a result, the `ProductDataException` has only a default constructor. The `Exception` class itself and most other exception classes have a constructor that lets you pass a string message that's stored with the exception and can be retrieved via the `getMessage` method. Thus you want to add this constructor to your class, which means that you want to add an explicit default constructor too. So now the `ProductDataException` class looks like this:

```
public class ProductDataException extends Exception
{
    public ProductDataException
    {
    }

    public ProductDataException(String message)
    {
        super(message);
    }
}
```

Although it's possible to do so, adding fields or methods to a custom exception class is unusual.

Throwing a custom exception

As for any exception, you use a `throw` statement to throw a custom exception. You usually code this `throw` statement in the midst of a `catch` clause that catches some other, more generic exception. Here's a method that retrieves product data from a file and throws a `ProductDataException` if an `IOException` occurs:

```
public class ProductDDB
{
    public static Product getProduct(String code)
        throws ProductDataException
    {
        try
        {
            Product p;
            // code that gets the product from a file
            // and might throw an IOException
            p = new Product();
            return p;
        }
        catch (IOException e)
        {
            throw new ProductDataException(
                "An IO error occurred.");
        }
    }
}
```

Here's some code that calls the get Product method and catches the exception:

```
try
{
    Product p = ProductDB.getProduct(productCode);
}
catch (ProductDataException e)
{
    System.out.println(e.getMessage());
}
```

Here the message is simply displayed on the console if a ProductData Exception is thrown. In an actual program, you want to log the error, inform the user, and figure out how to continue the program gracefully even though this data exception has occurred.

Chapter 5: Using Abstract Classes and Interfaces

In This Chapter

- ✔ Understanding abstract methods and classes
- ✔ Using basic interfaces
- ✔ Using interfaces as types
- ✔ Adding constants to an interface
- ✔ Inheriting interfaces
- ✔ Working with callbacks
- ✔ Using default methods

*I*n this chapter, you find out how to use two similar but subtly distinct features: abstract classes and interfaces. Both let you declare the signatures of the methods and fields that a class implements separately from the class itself. Abstract classes accomplish this by way of inheritance. Interfaces do it without using inheritance, but the effect is similar.

This chapter also covers a new feature of Java 1.8 called *default methods*, which are designed to make interfaces easier to work with.

Using Abstract Classes

Java lets you declare that a method or an entire class is *abstract*, which means that the method has no body. An *abstract method* is just a prototype for a method: a return type, a name, a list of parameters, and (optionally) a `throws` clause.

To create an abstract method, you specify the modifier `abstract` and replace the method body with a semicolon:

```
public abstract int hit(int batSpeed);
```

Here the method named `hit` is declared as an abstract method that returns an `int` value and accepts an `int` parameter.

The Abstract Factory pattern

One common use for abstract classes is to provide a way to obtain an instance of one of several subclasses when you don't know which subclass you need in advance. To do this, you can create an *Abstract Factory class* that has one or more methods that return subclasses of the abstract class.

Suppose that you want to create a `Ball` object, but you want to let the user choose whether to create a `SoftBall` or a `BaseBall`. To use the Abstract Factory pattern, you create a class (I call it `BallFactory`) that has a method named `getBallInstance`. This method accepts a `String` parameter that's set to `"BaseBall"` if you want a `BaseBall` object or `"SoftBall"` if you want a `SoftBall` object.

Here's the factory class:

```
class BallFactoryInstance
{
```

```
public static Ball getBall(String t)
{
    if (s.equalsIgnoreCase("BaseBall"))
        return new BaseBall();
    if (s.equalsIgnoreCase("SoftBall"))
        return new SoftBall();
    return null;
}
}
```

Then, assuming that the `String` variable `userChoice` has been set according to the user's choice, you can create the selected type of `Ball` object like this:

```
Ball b = BallFactory.getBallInstance
            (userChoice);
```

In an actual application, using an `enum` variable is better than using a `String` variable to indicate the type of object to be returned.

A class that contains at least one abstract method is called an *abstract class* and must be declared with the `abstract` modifier on the class declaration. For example:

```
public abstract class Ball
{
    public abstract int hit(int batSpeed);
}
```

If you omit the `abstract` modifier from the class declaration, the Java compiler coughs up an error message to remind you that the class must be declared `abstract`.

An abstract class can't be instantiated. Thus, given the preceding declaration, the following line doesn't compile:

```
Ball b = new Ball();    // error: Ball is abstract
```

The problem here isn't with declaring the variable b as a Ball; it's using the new keyword with the Ball class in an attempt to create a Ball object. Because Ball is an abstract class, you can use it to create an object instance.

You can create a subclass from an abstract class like this:

```
public class BaseBall extends Ball
{
    public int hit(int batSpeed)
    {
        // code that implements the hit method goes here
    }
}
```

When you subclass an abstract class, the subclass must provide an implementation for each abstract method in the abstract class. In other words, it must override each abstract method with a nonabstract method. (If it doesn't, the subclass is also abstract, so it can't be instantiated either.)

Abstract classes are useful when you want to create a generic type that is used as the superclass for two or more subclasses, but the superclass itself doesn't represent an actual object. If all employees are either salaried or hourly, for example, it makes sense to create an abstract Employee class and then use it as the base class for the SalariedEmployee and HourlyEmployee subclasses.

Here are a few additional points to ponder concerning abstract classes:

✦ Not all the methods in an abstract class have to be abstract. A class can provide an implementation for some of its methods but not others. In fact, even if a class doesn't have any abstract methods, you can still declare it as abstract. (In that case, the class can't be instantiated.)

A private method can't be abstract. That makes sense, because a subclass can't override a private method, and abstract methods must be overridden.

✦ Although you can't create an instance of an abstract class, you can declare a variable by using an abstract class as its type. Then use the variable to refer to an instance of any of the subclasses of the abstract class.

✦ A class can't specify both abstract and final. That would cause one of those logical paradoxes that result in the annihilation of the universe. Well, ideally, the effect would be localized. But the point is that because an abstract class can be used only if you subclass it, and because a final class can't be subclassed, letting you specify both abstract and final for the same class doesn't make sense.

Abstract classes are used extensively in the Java API. Many of the abstract classes have names that begin with `Abstract` — such as `AbstractBorder`, `AbstractCollection`, and `AbstractMap` — but most of the abstract classes don't. The `InputStream` class (used by `System.in`) is abstract, for example.

Using Interfaces

An *interface* is similar to an abstract class, but an interface can include only abstract methods and final fields (constants), and an interface can't be used as a base class. A class *implements* an interface by providing code for each method declared by the interface.

Interfaces have two advantages over inheritance:

✦ Interfaces are easier to work with than an abstract class, because you don't have to worry about providing any implementation details in the interface.

✦ A class can extend only one other class, but it can implement as many interfaces as you need.

The following sections describe the details of creating and using interfaces.

Creating a basic interface

Here's a basic interface that defines a single method, named `Playable`, that includes a single method named `play`:

```
public interface Playable
{
    void play();
}
```

This interface declares that any class that implements the `Playable` interface must provide an implementation for a method named `play` that accepts no parameters and doesn't return a value.

This interface has a few interesting details:

✦ The interface itself is declared as `public` so that it can be used by other classes. Like a public class, a public interface must be declared in a file with the same name. Thus this interface must be in a file named `Playable.java`.

✦ The name of the interface (`Playable`) is an adjective. Most interfaces are named with adjectives rather than nouns because they describe some additional capability or quality of the classes that implement the interface. Thus classes that implement the `Playable` interface represent objects that can be played.

In case you haven't been to English class in a while, an *adjective* is a word that modifies a noun. You can convert many verbs to adjectives by adding *-able* to the end of the word — *playable, readable, drivable,* and *stoppable,* for example. This type of adjective is commonly used for interface names.

✦ Another common way to name interfaces is to combine an adjective with a noun to indicate that the interface adds some capability to a particular type of object. You could call an interface that provides methods unique to card games `CardGame`, and this interface might have methods such as `deal`, `shuffle`, and `getHand`.

✦ All the methods in an interface are assumed to be public and abstract. If you want, you can code the `public` and `abstract` keywords on interface methods. That kind of coding is considered to be bad form, however, because it might indicate that you think the default is private and not abstract.

Implementing an interface

To implement an interface, a class must do two things:

✦ It must specify an `implements` clause on its class declaration.

✦ It must provide an implementation for every method declared by the interface.

Here's a class that implements the `Playable` interface:

```
public class TicTacToe implements Playable
{
    // additional fields and methods go here

    public void play()
    {
        // code that plays the game goes here
    }

    // additional fields and methods go here

}
```

Here the declaration for the `TicTacToe` class specifies `implements Playable`. Then the body of the class includes an implementation of the `play` method.

A class can implement more than one interface:

```
public class Hearts implements Playable, CardGame
{
    // must implement methods of the Playable
    // and CardGame interfaces
}
```

Here, the `Hearts` class implements two interfaces: `Playable` and `CardGame`.

A class can possibly inherit a superclass and implement one or more interfaces. Here's an example:

```
public class Poker extends Game
    implements Playable, CardGame
{
    // inherits all members of the Game class
    // must implement methods of the Playable
    // and CardGame interfaces
}
```

Using an interface as a type

In Java, an interface is a kind of type, just like a class. As a result, you can use an interface as the type for a variable, parameter, or method return value.

Consider this snippet of code:

```
Playable game = getGame();
game.play();
```

Here I assume that the `getGame` method returns an object that implements the `Playable` interface. This object is assigned to a variable of type `Playable` in the first statement. Then the second statement calls the object's `play` method.

For another (slightly more complex) example, suppose that you have an interface named `Dealable` defining a method named `deal` that accepts the number of cards to deal as a parameter:

```
public interface Dealable
{
    void deal(int cards);
}
```

Now suppose that you have a method called `startGame` that accepts two parameters: a `Dealable` object and a `String` that indicates what game to play. This method might look something like this:

```
private void startGame(Dealable deck, String game)
{
    if (game.equals("Poker"))
        deck.deal(5);
```

```
        else if (game.equals("Hearts"))
            deck.deal(13);
        else if (game.equals("Gin"))
            deck.deal(10);
    }
```

Assuming that you also have a class named `CardDeck` that implements the `Dealable` interface, you might use a statement like this example to start a game of Hearts:

```
Dealable d = new CardDeck();
startGame(d, "Hearts");
```

Notice that the variable d is declared as a `Dealable`. You could just as easily declare it as a `CardDeck`:

```
CardDeck d = new CardDeck();
startGame(d, "Hearts");
```

Because the `CardDeck` class implements the `Dealable` interface, it can be passed as a parameter to the `startGame` method.

More Things You Can Do with Interfaces

Book III
Chapter 5

There's more to interfaces than just creating abstract methods. The following sections describe some additional interesting things you can do with interfaces. Read on. . . .

Using Abstract Classes and Interfaces

Adding fields to an interface

Besides abstract methods, an interface can include final fields — that is, constants. Interface fields are used to provide constant values that are related to the interface. For example:

```
public interface GolfClub
{
    int DRIVER = 1;
    int SPOON = 2;
    int NIBLICK = 3;
    int MASHIE = 4;
}
```

Here any class that implements the `GolfClub` interface has these four fields (that is, constants) available.

Note that interface fields are automatically assumed to be static, final, and public. You can include these keywords when you create interface constants, but you don't have to.

Extending interfaces

You can extend interfaces by using the extends keyword. An interface that extends an existing interface is called a *subinterface,* and the interface being extended is called the *superinterface.*

When you use the extends keyword with interfaces, all the fields and methods of the superinterface are effectively copied into the subinterface. Thus the subinterface consists of a combination of the fields and methods in the superinterface *plus* the fields and methods defined for the subinterface.

Here's an example:

```
public interface ThrowableBall
{
    void throwBall();
    void catchBall();
}

public interface KickableBall
{
    void kickBall();
    void catchBall();
}

public interface PlayableBall
    extends ThrowableBall, KickableBall
{
    void dropBall();
}
```

Here three interfaces are declared. The first, named ThrowableBall, defines two methods: throwBall and catchBall. The second, named KickableBall, also defines two methods: kickBall and catchBall. The third, named PlayableBall, extends ThrowableBall and KickableBall, and adds a method of its own named dropBall.

Thus any class that implements the PlayableBall interface must provide an implementation for four methods: throwBall, catchBall, kickBall, and dropBall. Note that because the catchBall methods defined by the ThrowableBall and KickableBall interfaces have the same signature, only one version of the catchBall method is included in the PlayableBall interface.

The Marker Interface pattern

A *marker interface* is an interface that doesn't have any members. Its sole purpose in life is to identify a class as belonging to a set of classes that possess some capability or have some characteristic in common.

The best-known example of a marker interface is the Java API `Cloneable` interface, which marks classes that can be cloned. The `Object` class, which all classes ultimately inherit, provides a method named `clone` that can be used to create a copy of the object. You're allowed to call the `clone` method only if the object implements the `Cloneable` interface, however. If you try to call `clone` for an object that doesn't implement `Cloneable`,

`CloneNotSupportedException` is thrown. (For more information about the `clone` method, refer to Book III, Chapter 6.)

Here's the actual code for the `Cloneable` interface:

```
public interface Cloneable {
}
```

In some cases, you might find a use for marker interfaces in your own application. If you're working on a series of classes for creating games, you might create a marker interface named `Winnable` to distinguish games that have a winner from games that you just play for enjoyment.

Using interfaces for callbacks

In the theater, a callback is when you show up for an initial audition, they like what they see, and they tell you that they want you to come back so they can have another look.

In Java, a *callback* is sort of like that. It's a programming technique in which an object lets another object know that the second object should call one of the first object's methods whenever a certain event happens. The first object is called an *event listener* because it waits patiently until the other object calls it. The second object is called the *event source* because it's the source of events that result in calls to the listener.

Okay, my theater analogy was a bit of a stretch. Callbacks in Java aren't really that much like callbacks when you're auditioning for a big part. A callback is more like when you need to get hold of someone on the phone, and you call him when you know he isn't there and leave your phone number on his voice-mail so he can call you back.

Callbacks are handled in Java by a set of interfaces designed for this purpose. The most common use of callbacks is in graphical applications built with Swing, where you create event listeners that handle user-interface events, such as mouse clicks.

You find out all about Swing in Book VI. For now, I look at callbacks by using the Timer class, which is part of the javax.Swing package. This class implements a basic timer that generates events at regular intervals — and lets you set up a *listener object* to handle these events. The listener object must implement the ActionListener interface, which defines a method named actionPerformed that's called for each timer event.

The Timer class constructor accepts two parameters:

✦ The first parameter is an int value that represents how often the timer events occur.

✦ The second parameter is an object that implements the Action Listener interface. This object's actionPerformed method is called when each timer event occurs.

The ActionListener interface is defined in the java.awt.event package. It includes the following code:

```
public interface ActionListener extends EventListener {

    /**
     * Invoked when an action occurs.
     */
    public void actionPerformed(ActionEvent e);

}
```

As you can see, the ActionListener interface consists of a single method named actionPerformed. It receives a parameter of type ActionEvent, but you don't use this parameter here. (You do use the ActionEvent class in Book VI.)

The Timer class has about 20 methods, but I talk about only one of them here: start, which sets the timer in motion. This method doesn't require any parameters and doesn't return a value.

Listing 5-1 shows a program that uses the Timer class to alternately display the messages Tick... and Tock... on the console at 1-second intervals. The JOptionPane class is used to display a dialog box; the program runs until the user clicks the OK button in this box. Figure 5-1 shows the Tick Tock program in action. (Actually it takes a while for the JOptionPane class to shut down the timer, so you'll see a few extra tick-tocks after clicking OK.)

Listing 5-1: The Tick Tock Program

```java
import java.awt.event.*;                                          →1
import javax.swing.*;                                             →2

public class TickTock
{
    public static void main(String[] args)
    {
        // create a timer that calls the Ticker class
        // at one second intervals
        Timer t = new Timer(1000, new Ticker());                  →10
        t.start();                                                →11

        // display a message box to prevent the
        // program from ending immediately
        JOptionPane.showMessageDialog(null,                       →15
            "Click OK to exit program");
    }
}

class Ticker implements ActionListener                            →20
{
    private boolean tick = true;                                  →22

    public void actionPerformed(ActionEvent event)               →24
    {
        if (tick)
        {
            System.out.println("Tick...");                        →28
        }
        else
        {
            System.out.println("Tock...");                        →32
        }
        tick = !tick;                                             →34
    }
}
```

Book III
Chapter 5

Using Abstract
Classes and
Interfaces

Figure 5-1:
The Tick
Tock appli-
cation in
action.

The following paragraphs describe the important details of this program's operation:

→ **1**   The `ActionListener` interface is part of the `java.awt.event` package, so this `import` statement is required.

→ **2**   The `Timer` class is part of the `javax.swing` package, so this `import` statement is required.

→ **10**   This statement creates a new `Timer` object. The timer's interval is set to 1,000 milliseconds — which is equivalent to 1 second. A new instance of the `Ticker` class is passed as the second parameter. The timer calls this object's `actionPerformed` method at each timer tick — in other words, once per second.

→ **11**   This statement calls the `start` method to kick the timer into action.

→ **15**   The `JOptionPane` class is used to display a dialog box that tells the user to click the OK button to stop the application. You might think I include this dialog box to give the user a way to end the program. In reality, I use it to give the timer some time to run. If I just end the `main` method after starting the timer, the application ends, which kills the timer. Because I use `JOptionPane` here, the application continues to run as long as the dialog box is displayed. (For more information about `JOptionPane`, see Book II, Chapter 2.)

→ **20**   This line is the declaration of the `Ticker` class, which implements the `ActionListener` interface.

→ **22**   This line is a private boolean class field that's used to keep track of whether the `Ticker` displays `Tick...` or `Tock...` Each time the `actionPerformed` method is called, this field is toggled.

→ **24**   This line is the `actionPerformed` method, which is called at each timer interval.

→ **28**   This line prints `Tick...` on the console if `tick` is true.

→ **32**   This line prints `Tock...` on the console if `tick` is false.

→ **34**   This line toggles the value of the `tick` variable. In other words, if `tick` is true, it's set to `false`. If `tick` is false, it's set to `true`.

Using Default Methods

Although interfaces are an incredibly useful feature of Java, they have an inherent limitation: After you define an interface and then build classes that implement the interface, there's no easy way to modify the interface by adding additional methods to it.

For example, suppose you have created the following interface:

```
public interface Playable
{
    void play();
}
```

You then build several classes that implement this interface. Here's a simple example:

```
class Game implements Playable
{
    public void play()
    {
        System.out.println("Good luck!");
    }
}
```

This is a pretty pointless game, of course; it simply prints the message "Good luck!" whenever the play method is called.

Now suppose that you decide that the Playable interface should have an additional features — specifically, you want to add the ability to end the game by calling a method named quit.

You'd be tempted to just add the new method to the existing interface, like this:

```
public interface Playable
{
    void play();
    void quit();
}
```

Unfortunately, however, doing so will break the Game class because it doesn't provide an implementation of the quit method.

You could, of course, modify the Game class by adding an implementation of the quit method. But what if you have written dozens, or even hundreds, of classes that implement Playable? As you can imagine, once an interface has become popular, it becomes nearly impossible to modify.

To alleviate this problem, Java 1.8 introduces a new type of interface method called a *default method*, which supplies code that will be used as the implementation of the method for any classes that implement the interface but do not themselves provide an implementation for the default method.

Thus, Java 8 allows you to safely add the `quit` method to the `Playable` interface by specifying it as a default method, like this:

```
interface Playable
{
    void play();

    default void quit()
    {
        System.out.println("Sorry, quitting is not allowed.");
    }
}
```

Here the `Playable` interface specifies that if an implementing class does not provide an implementation of the `quit` method, the default method will be used. In this case, the default method simply prints the message `"Sorry, quitting is not allowed."`

Note that the preceding example won't compile on versions of Java prior to 1.8. If you get an error message when you try to compile an interface that uses the `default` keyword, check your Java version to make sure you're running version 1.8 or later.

Here's a complete example that uses the `Playable` interface and its default method:

```
public class TestLambdaCollection
{

    public static void main(String[] args)
    {
        Game g = new Game();
        g.play();
        g.quit();
    }
}

interface Playable
{
    void play();

    default void quit()
    {
        System.out.println("Sorry, quitting is not allowed.");
    }
}
```

```
class Game implements Playable
{
    public void play()
    {
        System.out.println("Good luck!");
    }
}
```

When you run this program, the following will be displayed on the console:

```
Good luck!
Sorry, quitting is not allowed.
```

Chapter 6: Using the Object and Class Classes

In This Chapter

✔ Using the toString method

✔ Implementing the equals method

✔ Trying out the clone method

✔ Understanding the Class class

In this chapter, you find out how to use two classes of the Java API that are important to object-oriented programming:

✦ The Object class, which every other class inherits — including all the classes in the Java API and any classes you create yourself

✦ The Class class, which is used to get information about an object's type

 If I could, I'd plant a huge Technical Stuff icon on this entire chapter. All this stuff is a bit on the technical side, and many Java programmers get by for years without understanding or using it. Still, I recommend that you read this chapter carefully. Even if it all doesn't sink in, it may help explain why some things in Java don't work quite the way you think they should, and the information in this chapter may someday help you program your way out of a difficult corner.

The Mother of All Classes: Object

Object is the mother of all classes. In Java, every class ultimately inherits the Object class. This class provides a set of methods that is available to every Java object.

Every object is an Object

Any class that doesn't have an extends clause implicitly inherits Object. Thus you never have to code a class like this:

```
public class Product extends Object...
```

If a subclass has an `extends` clause that specifies a superclass other than `Object`, the class still inherits `Object`. That's because the inheritance hierarchy eventually gets to a superclass that doesn't have an `extends` clause, and that superclass inherits `Object` and passes it down to all its subclasses.

Suppose you have these classes:

```
public class Manager extends SalariedEmployee...

public class SalariedEmployee extends Employee...

public class Employee extends Person...

public class Person...
```

Here the `Manager` class inherits the `Object` class indirectly because it inherits `SalariedEmployee`, which inherits `Employee`, which inherits `Person`, which inherits `Object`.

In Java, creating a class that *doesn't* inherit `Object` is not possible.

Object as a type

If you don't know or care about the type of an object referenced by a variable, you can specify its type as `Object`. The following example is perfectly legal:

```
Object emp = new Employee();
```

You can't do anything useful with the `emp` variable, however, because the compiler doesn't know that it's an `Employee`. If the `Employee` class has a method named `setLastName`, the following code doesn't work:

```
Object emp = new Employee();
emp.setLastName("Smith");      // error: won't compile
```

Because `emp` is an `Object`, not an `Employee`, the compiler doesn't know about the `setLastName` method.

Note that you could still cast the object to an `Employee`:

```
Object emp = new Employee();
((Employee)emp).setLastName("Smith");  // this works
```

But what's the point? You may as well make `emp` an `Employee` in the first place.

Declaring a variable, parameter, or return type as `Object` in certain situations, however, does make perfect sense. The Java API provides a set of classes designed to maintain collections of objects. One of the most commonly used of these classes is the `ArrayList` class, which has a method named `add` that accepts an `Object` as a parameter. This method adds the specified object to the collection. Because the parameter type is `Object`, you can use the `ArrayList` class to create collections of any type of object. (For more information about the `ArrayList` class and other collection classes, see Book IV.)

Methods of the Object class

Table 6-1 lists all the methods of the `Object` class. Ordinarily, I wouldn't list all the methods of a class; I'd just list the ones that I think are most useful. Because `Object` is such an important player in the game of object-oriented programming, however, I thought it best to show you all its capabilities, even though some of them are a bit obscure.

I warned you — this entire chapter should have a Technical Stuff icon.

Table 6-1	Methods of the Object Class
Method	*What It Does*
`protected Object clone()`	Returns a copy of this object.
`boolean equals(Object obj)`	Indicates whether this object is equal to the `obj` object.
`protected void finalize()`	Is called by the garbage collector when the object is destroyed.
`Class getClass()`	Returns a `Class` object that represents this object's runtime class.
`int hashCode()`	Returns this object's hash code.
`void notify()`	Is used with threaded applications to wake up a thread that's waiting on this object.
`void notifyAll()`	Is used with threaded applications to wake up all threads that are waiting on this object.
`String toString()`	Returns a String representation of this object.
`void wait()`	Causes this object's thread to wait until another thread calls `notify` or `notifyAll`.
`void wait(Long timeout)`	Is a variation of the basic `wait` method.
`void wait(Long timeout, int nanos)`	Is yet another variation of the `wait` method.

Note: Almost half of these methods (`notify`, `notifyAll`, and the three `wait` methods) are related to threading. You find complete information about those five methods in Book V, Chapter 1. Here's the rundown on the remaining six methods:

✦ **clone:** This method is commonly used to make copies of objects, and overriding it in your own classes is not uncommon. I explain this method in detail later in this chapter, in the section "The `clone` Method."

✦ **equals:** This method is commonly used to compare objects. Any class that represents an object that can be compared with another object should override this method. Turn to the section "The `equals` Method," later in this chapter, for more info.

✦ **finalize:** This method is called when the garbage collector realizes that an object is no longer being used and can be discarded. The intent of this method is to let you create objects that clean up after themselves by closing open files and performing other cleanup tasks before being discarded. But because of the way the Java garbage collector works, there's no guarantee that the `finalize` method is ever actually called. As a result, this method isn't commonly used.

✦ **getClass:** This method is sometimes used in conjunction with the `Class` class, which I describe later in this chapter, in the section "The `Class` Class."

✦ **hashCode:** Every Java object has a *hash code,* which is an `int` representation of the class that's useful for certain operations. This method isn't terribly important until you start to work with hash tables — which is a pretty advanced technique, best left to people with pocket protectors and tape holding their glasses together.

✦ **toString:** This method is one of the most commonly used methods in Java. I describe it in the section "The `toString` Method," later in this chapter.

Primitives aren't objects

I need to note that primitive types, such as `int` and `double`, are not objects. As a result, they do not inherit the `Object` class and don't have access to the methods listed in the preceding section.

As a result, the following code won't work:

```
int x = 50;
String s = x.toString();  // error: won't compile
```

If you really want to convert an `int` to a string in this way, you can use a wrapper class such as `Integer` to create an object from the value and then call its `toString` method:

```
String s = new Integer(x).toString();  // OK
```

Each of the wrapper classes also defines a static `toString` method, which you can use like this:

```
String s = Integer.toString(x);
```

Sometimes, using the compiler shortcut that lets you use primitive types in string concatenation expressions is easier:

```
String s = "" + x;
```

Here the `int` variable x is concatenated with an empty string.

The point of all this is that primitive types aren't objects, so they don't inherit anything from `Object`. If you want to treat a primitive value as an object, you can use the primitive type's wrapper class (as I describe in Book II, Chapter 2).

The toString Method

The `toString` method returns a `String` representation of an object. By default, the `toString` method returns the name of the object's class plus its hash code. In the sections that follow, I show you how to use the `toString` method and how to override it in your own classes to create more useful strings.

Using toString

Here's a simple program that puts the `toString` method to work:

```
public class TestToString
{
    public static void main(String[] args)
    {
        Employee emp = new Employee("Martinez",
            "Anthony");
        System.out.println(emp.toString());
    }
}

class Employee
{
    private String lastName;
    private String firstName;

    public Employee(String lastName, String firstName)
    {
        this.lastName = lastName;
        this.firstName = firstName;
    }
}
```

This code creates a new Employee object; then the result of its toString method is printed to the console. When you run this program, the following line is printed on the console:

```
Employee@82ba41
```

Note: The hash code — in this case, 82ba41 — will undoubtedly be different on your system.

It turns out that the explicit call to toString isn't really necessary in this example. I could just as easily have written the second line of the main method like this:

```
System.out.println(emp);
```

That's because the println method automatically calls the toString method of any object you pass it.

Overriding toString

The default implementation of toString isn't very useful in most situations. You don't really learn much about an Employee object by seeing its hash code, for example. Wouldn't it be better if the toString method returned some actual data from the object, such as the employee's name?

To do that, you must override the toString method in your classes. In fact, one of the basic guidelines of object-oriented programming in Java is to *always* override toString. Here's a simple program with an Employee class that overrides toString:

```
public class TestToString
{
    public static void main(String[] args)
    {
        Employee emp = new Employee("Martinez",
            "Anthony");
        System.out.println(emp.toString());
    }
}

class Employee
{
    private String lastName;
    private String firstName;

    public Employee(String lastName, String firstName)
    {
        this.lastName = lastName;
        this.firstName = firstName;
    }
```

```
    public String toString()
    {
        return "Employee["
            + this.firstName + " "
            + this.lastName + "]";
    }
}
```

When you run this program, the following line is displayed on the console:

```
Employee[Anthony Martinez]
```

Note that the output consists of the class name followed by some data from the object in brackets. This convention is common in Java programming.

The only problem with the preceding example is that the class name is hard-coded into the `toString` method. You can use the `getClass` method to retrieve the actual class name at runtime:

```
    public String toString()
    {
        return this.getClass().getName() + "["
            + this.firstName + " "
            + this.lastName + "]";
    }
```

Here the `getClass` method returns a `Class` object that represents the class of the current object. Then the `Class` object's `getName` method is used to get the actual class name. (You discover more about the `Class` object later in this chapter.)

The equals Method

Testing objects to see whether they are equal is one of the basic tasks of any object-oriented programming language. Unfortunately, Java isn't very good at it. Consider this program:

```
public class TestEquality1
{
    public static void main(String[] args)
    {
        Employee emp1 = new Employee(
            "Martinez", "Anthony");
        Employee emp2 = new Employee(
            "Martinez", "Anthony");
        if (emp1 == emp2)
            System.out.println(
                "These employees are the same.");
        else
            System.out.println(
                "These are different employees.");
    }
}
```

```
class Employee
{
    private String lastName;
    private String firstName;

    public Employee(String lastName, String firstName)
    {
        this.lastName = lastName;
        this.firstName = firstName;
    }
}
```

Here the `main` method creates two `Employee` objects with identical data and then compares them. Alas, the comparison returns `false`. Even though the `Employee` objects have identical data, they're not considered to be equal because the equality operator (`==`) compares the object references, not the data contained by the objects. Thus the comparison returns `true` only if both `emp1` and `emp2` refer to the same instance of the `Employee` class.

If you want to create objects that are considered to be equal if they contain identical data, you have to do two things:

✦ Compare them with the `equals` method rather than the equality operator.

✦ Override the `equals` method in your class to compare objects based on their data.

The following sections describe both of these steps.

Using equals

To test objects using the `equals` method rather than the equality operator, you simply rewrite the comparison expression like this:

```
if (emp1.equals(emp2))
    System.out.println("These employees are the same.");
else
    System.out.println
        ("These are different employees.");
```

Here, the `equals` method of `emp1` is used to compare `emp1` with `emp2`.

By default, the `equals` operator returns the same result as the equality operator. So just replacing `==` with the `equals` method doesn't have any effect unless you also override the `equals` method, as explained in the next section.

Which object's `equals` method you use shouldn't matter. Thus the `if` statement shown here returns the same result:

```
if (emp2.equals(emp1))
    System.out.println("These employees are the same.");
else
    System.out.println
        ("These are different employees.");
```

Note that I said it *shouldn't* matter. Whenever you override the `equals` method, you're supposed to make sure that comparisons work in both directions. Sloppy programming, however, sometimes results in `equals` methods where a equals b but b doesn't equal a. Be on your toes.

Overriding the equals method

You can override the `equals` method so that objects can be compared based on their values. At the surface, you might think this is easy to do. You could be tempted to write the `equals` method for the `Employee` class like this:

```
// warning -- there are several errors in this code!
public boolean equals(Employee emp)
{
    if (this.getLastName().equals(emp.getLastName())
      && this.getFirstName().equals(emp.getFirstName()))
        return true;
    else
        return false;
}
```

The basic problem with this code — and the challenge of coding a good `equals` method — is that the parameter passed to the `equals` method must be an `Object`, not an `Employee`. That means that the `equals` method must be prepared to deal with anything that comes its way. Someone might try to compare an `Employee` object with a `Banana` object, for example, or with a null. The `equals` method must be prepared to deal with all possibilities.

Specifically, the Java API documentation says that whenever you override the `equals` method, you must ensure that the `equals` method meets five specific conditions. Here they are, quoted right out of the API documentation:

+ **It is *reflexive.*** For any non-null reference value x, `x.equals(x)` should return `true`.

+ **It is *symmetric.*** For any non-null reference values x and y, `x.equals(y)` should return `true` if — and only if — `y.equals(x)` returns `true`.

✦ **It is *transitive*.** For any non-null reference values x, y, and z, if x.equals(y) returns true and y.equals(z) returns true, x.equals(z) should return true.

✦ **It is *consistent*.** For any non-null reference values x and y, multiple invocations of x.equals(y) consistently return true or consistently return false, provided that no information used in equals comparisons on the objects is modified.

✦ For any non-null reference value x, x.equals(null) should return false.

Sound confusing? Fortunately, it's not as complicated as it seems at first. You can safely ignore the transitive rule, because if you get the other rules right, this one happens automatically. The consistency rule basically means that you return consistent results. As long as you don't throw a call to Math.random into the comparison, that shouldn't be a problem.

Here's a general formula for creating a good equals method (assume that the parameter is named obj):

1. **Test the reflexive rule.**

   Use a statement like this:

   ```
   if (this == obj)
       return true;
   ```

   In other words, if someone is silly enough to see whether an object is equal to itself, it returns true.

2. **Test the non-null rule.**

   Use a statement like this:

   ```
   if (this == null)
       return false;
   ```

   Null isn't equal to anything.

3. **Test that obj is of the same type as this.**

   You can use the getClass method to do that, like this:

   ```
   if (this.getClass() != obj.getClass())
       return false;
   ```

   The two objects can't possibly be the same if they aren't of the same type. (It may not be apparent at first, but this test is required to fulfill the symmetry rule — that if x equals y, y must also equal x.)

4. **Cast `obj` to a variable of your class; then compare the fields you want to base the return value on, and return the result.**

Here's an example:

```
Employee emp = (Employee) obj;
return this.lastName.equals(emp.getLastName())
    && this.firstname.equals(emp.getFirstName());
```

Notice that the field comparisons for the String values use the `equals` method rather than `==`. This is because you can't trust `==` to compare strings. If you need to compare primitive types, you can use `==`. But you should use `equals` to compare strings and any other reference types.

Putting it all together, Listing 6-1 shows a program that compares two `Employee` objects by using a properly constructed `equals` method.

Listing 6-1:   Comparing Objects

```
public class TestEquality2
{
    public static void main(String[] args)
    {
        Employee emp1 = new Employee(                    →5
            "Martinez", "Anthony");
        Employee emp2 = new Employee(                    →7
            "Martinez", "Anthony");
        if (emp1.equals(emp2))                           →9
            System.out.println(
                "These employees are the same.");
        else
            System.out.println(
                "These are different employees.");
    }
}

class Employee                                           →18
{
    private String lastName;
    private String firstName;

    public Employee(String lastName, String firstName)
    {
        this.lastName = lastName;
        this.firstName = firstName;
    }

    public String getLastName()
    {
        return this.lastName;
    }
```

(continued)

Listing 6-1 *(continued)*

```
public String getFirstName()
{
    return this.firstName;
}

public boolean equals(Object obj)                            →39
{
    // an object must equal itself
    if (this == obj)                                         →42
        return true;

    // no object equals null
    if (this == null)                                        →46
        return false;

    // objects of different types are never equal
    if (this.getClass() != obj.getClass())                   →50
        return false;

    // cast to an Employee, then compare the fields
    Employee emp = (Employee) obj;                           →54
    return this.lastName.equals(emp.getLastName())           →55
        && this.firstName.equals(emp.getFirstName());
}
}
```

Following are some noteworthy points in this listing:

→ 5   Creates an Employee object with the name Anthony Martinez.

→ 7   Creates another Employee object with the name Anthony Martinez.

→ 9   Compares the two Employee objects by using the equals method.

→ 18   The Employee class.

→ 39   The overridden equals method.

→ 42   Returns true if the same object instances are being compared. This meets the first equality test: that an object must always be equal to itself.

→ 46   Returns false if the object being compared is null. This meets the last equality test: that nothing is equal to null.

→ 50   Returns false if the object being compared isn't of the correct type. This helps ensure the symmetry test: that if x equals y, y must equal x.

→ 54   Having slid through the other tests, you can assume that you're comparing two different Employee objects, so the next step is to cast the other object to an Employee.

→ 55   Having cast the other object to an Employee, the two fields (lastName and firstName) are compared, and the result of the compound comparison is returned.

The clone Method

Cloning refers to the process of making an exact duplicate of an object. Unfortunately, this process turns out to be a pretty difficult task in an object-oriented language such as Java. You'd think that cloning would be as easy as this:

```
Employee emp1 = new Employee("Stewart", "Martha");
Employee emp2 = emp1;
```

This code doesn't make a copy of the Employee object at all, however. Instead, you now have two variables that refer to the same object, which usually isn't what you want. Suppose that you execute these statements:

```
emp1.setLastName("Washington");
emp2.setLastName("Graham");
String lastName = emp1.getLastName();
```

After these statements execute, does lastName return Washington or Graham? The correct answer is Graham, because both emp1 and emp2 refer to the same Employee object.

By contrast, a *clone* is an altogether new object that has the same values as the original object. Often you can create a clone manually by using code like this:

```
Employee emp1 = new Employee("Stewart", "Martha");
Employee emp2 = new Employee();
emp2.setLastName(emp1.getLastName());
emp2.setFirstName(emp1.getFirstName());
emp2.setSalary(emp1.getSalary());
```

Here a new Employee object is created, and its fields are set to the same values as the original object.

 Java provides a more elegant way to create object copies: the clone method, which is available to all classes because it's inherited from the Object class. As you discover in the following sections, however, the clone method can be difficult to create and use. For this reason, you want to implement it only for those classes that you think can really benefit from cloning.

Implementing the clone method

The clone method is defined by the Object class, so it's available to all Java classes, but clone is declared with protected access in the Object class. As a result, the clone method for a given class is available only within that class. If you want other objects to be able to clone your object, you must override the clone method and give it public access.

Note that the clone method defined by the Object class returns an Object type. That makes perfect sense, because the Object class doesn't know the type of the class in which you'll be overriding the clone method. An inconvenient side effect of returning an Object is that whenever you call the clone method for a class that overrides clone, you must cast the result to the desired object type.

Listing 6-2 gives a simple example of a program that clones Employee objects. In a nutshell, this program overrides the clone method for the Employee class: It creates an Employee object, clones it, changes the name of the original Employee object, and prints out both objects to the console.

Listing 6-2:   A Cloning Example

```
public class CloneTest
{
    public static void main(String[] args)
    {
        Employee emp1 = new Employee(                    →5
            "Martinez", "Anthony");
        emp1.setSalary(40000.0);                          →7
        Employee emp2 = (Employee)emp1.clone();           →8
        emp1.setLastName("Smith");                        →9
        System.out.println(emp1);                        →10
        System.out.println(emp2);                        →11
    }
}

class Employee                                           →15
{
    private String lastName;
    private String firstName;
    private Double salary;

    public Employee(String lastName,
                    String firstName)
    {
        this.lastName = lastName;
        this.firstName = firstName;
    }

    public String getLastName()
    {
        return this.lastName;
    }

    public void setLastName(String lastName)
    {
        this.lastName = lastName;
    }
```

```
public String getFirstName()
{
    return this.firstName;
}

public void setFirstName(String firstName)
{
    this.firstName = firstName;
}

public Double getSalary()
{
    return this.salary;
}

public void setSalary(Double salary)
{
    this.salary = salary;
}

public Object clone()                              →57
{
    Employee emp;
    emp = new Employee(                            →60
        this.lastName, this.firstName);
    emp.setSalary(this.salary);                    →62
    return emp;                                    →63
}

public String toString()
{
    return this.getClass().getName() + "["
        + this.firstName + " "
        + this.lastName + ", "
        + this.salary + "]";
}
}
```

**Book III
Chapter 6**

Using the Object
and Class Classes

When you run this program, the following lines appear on the console:

```
Employee[Anthony Smith, 40000.0]
Employee[Anthony Martinez, 40000.0]
```

As you can see, the name of the second Employee object was successfully changed without affecting the name of the first Employee object.

The following paragraphs draw your attention to some of the highlights of this program:

→ 5   Creates the first Employee object for an employee named Anthony Martinez.

→ 7   Sets Mr. Martinez's salary.

→ 8   Creates a clone of the `Employee` object for Mr. Martinez. Notice that the return value must be cast to an `Employee`, because the return value of the `clone` method is `Object`.

→ 9   Changes the last name for the second `Employee` object.

→ 10   Prints the first `Employee` object.

→ 11   Prints the second `Employee` object.

→ 15   The `Employee` class. This class defines private fields to store the last name, first name, and salary, as well as getter and setter methods for each field.

→ 57   Overrides the `clone` method. Notice that its return type is `Object`, not `Employee`.

→ 60   Creates a new `Employee` object, using the last name and first name from the current object.

→ 62   Sets the new employee's salary to the current object's salary.

→ 63   Returns the cloned `Employee` object.

Using clone to create a shallow copy

In the preceding example, the `clone` method manually creates a copy of the original object and returns it. In many cases, this is the easiest way to create a clone. But what if your class has a hundred or more fields that need to be duplicated? The chance of forgetting to copy one of the fields is high, and if you add a field to the class later on, you may forget to modify the `clone` method to include the new field.

Fortunately, you can solve this problem by using the `clone` method of the `Object` class directly in your own `clone` method. The `clone` method of the `Object` class can automatically create a copy of your object that contains duplicates of all the fields that are primitive types (such as `int` and `double`), as well as copies of immutable reference types — most notably, strings. So if all the fields in your class are either primitives or strings, you can use the `clone` method provided by the `Object` class to clone your class.

This type of clone is known as a *shallow copy,* for reasons that I explain in the next section.

To call the `clone` method from your own `clone` method, just specify `super.clone()`. Before you can do that, however, you must do two things:

✦ Declare that the class supports the `Cloneable` interface. The `Cloneable` interface is a tagging interface that doesn't provide any methods. It simply marks a class as being appropriate for cloning.

✦ Enclose the call to `super.clone()` in a `try/catch` statement that catches the exception `CloneNotSupportedException`. This exception is thrown if you try to call `clone` on a class that doesn't implement the

Cloneable interface. Provided that you implement Cloneable, this exception won't ever happen, but because CloneNotSupportedException is a checked exception, you must catch it.

Here's an example of an Employee class with a clone method that uses super.clone() to clone itself:

```
class Employee implements Cloneable
{
    // Fields and methods omitted...

    public Object clone()
    {
        Employee emp;
        try
        {
            emp = (Employee) super.clone();
        }
        catch (CloneNotSupportedException e)
        {
            return null;    // will never happen
        }
        return emp;
    }
}
```

Notice that this method doesn't have to be aware of any of the fields declared in the Employee class. This clone method, however, works only for classes whose fields are all either primitive types or immutable objects such as strings.

Creating deep copies

It's not uncommon for some fields in a class actually to be other objects. The Employee class, for example, might have a field of type Address that's used to store each employee's address:

```
class Employee
{
    public Address address;

    // other fields and methods omitted
}
```

If that's the case, the super.clone() method won't make a complete copy of the object. The clone won't get a clone of the address field. Instead, it has a reference to the same address object as the original.

To solve this problem, you must do a deep copy of the Employee object. A *deep copy* is a clone in which any subobjects within the main object are also cloned. To accomplish this feat, the clone method override first calls super.clone() to create a shallow copy of the object. Then it calls the clone method of each of the subobjects contained by the main object to create clones of those objects. (For a deep copy to work, of course, those objects must also support the clone methods.)

Listing 6-3 shows an example. Here, an Employee class contains a public field named address, which holds an instance of the Address class. As you can see, the clone method of the Employee class creates a shallow copy of the Employee object and then sets the copy's address field to a clone of the original object's address field. To make this example work, the Address class also overrides the clone method. Its clone method calls super.clone() to create a shallow copy of the Address object.

Listing 6-3: Creating a Deep Copy

```
public class CloneTest2
{
    public static void main(String[] args)
    {
        Employee emp1 = new Employee(                    →5
            "Martinez", "Anthony");
        emp1.setSalary(40000.0);
        emp1.address = new Address(                      →8
            "1300 N. First Street",
            "Fresno", "CA", "93702");
        Employee emp2 = (Employee)emp1.clone();          →11

        System.out.println(                              →13
            "**** after cloning ****\n");
        printEmployee(emp1);
        printEmployee(emp2);

        emp2.setLastName("Smith");                       →18
        emp2.address = new Address(                      →19
            "2503 N. 6th Street",
            "Fresno", "CA", "93722");

        System.out.println(                              →23
            "**** after changing emp2 ****\n");
        printEmployee(emp1);
        printEmployee(emp2);

    }

    private static void printEmployee(Employee e)        →30
    {
        System.out.println(e.getFirstName()
            + " " + e.getLastName());
        System.out.println(e.address.getAddress());
```

```
            System.out.println("Salary: " + e.getSalary());
            System.out.println();
        }
    }

    class Employee implements Cloneable                          →40
    {
        private String lastName;
        private String firstName;
        private Double salary;

        public Address address;                                  →46

        public Employee(String lastName, String firstName)
        {
            this.lastName = lastName;
            this.firstName = firstName;
            this.address = new Address();
        }

        public String getLastName()
        {
            return this.lastName;
        }

        public void setLastName(String lastName)
        {
            this.lastName = lastName;
        }

        public String getFirstName()
        {
            return this.firstName;
        }

        public void setFirstName(String firstName)
        {
            this.firstName = firstName;
        }

        public Double getSalary()
        {
            return this.salary;
        }

        public void setSalary(Double salary)
        {
            this.salary = salary;
        }
```

(continued)

**Book III
Chapter 6**

**Using the Object
and Class Classes**

Listing 6-3 *(continued)*

```
public Object clone()                                          →85
{
    Employee emp;
    try
    {
        emp = (Employee) super.clone();                        →90
        emp.address = (Address)address.clone();                →91
    }
    catch (CloneNotSupportedException e)                       →93
    {
        return null;    // will never happen
    }
    return emp;                                                →97
}

public String toString()
{
    return this.getClass().getName() + "["
        + this.firstName + " "
        + this.lastName + ", "
        + this.salary + "]";
}
}

class Address implements Cloneable                             →109
{
    private String street;
    private String city;
    private String state;
    private String zipCode;

    public Address()
    {
        this.street = "";
        this.city = "";
        this.state = "";
        this.zipCode = "";
    }

    public Address(String street, String city,
                String state, String zipCode)
    {
        this.street = street;
        this.city = city;
        this.state = state;
        this.zipCode = zipCode;
    }

    public Object clone()                                      →133
    {
        try
        {
```

```
        return super.clone();                          →137
    }
    catch (CloneNotSupportedException e)
    {
        return null;    // will never happen
    }
}

public String getAddress()
{
    return this.street + "\n"
        + this.city + ", "
        + this.state + " "
        + this.zipCode;
}
}
```

The main method in the CloneTest2 class creates an Employee object and
sets its name, salary, and address. Then it creates a clone of this object and
prints the data contained in both objects. Next, it changes the last name and
address of the second employee and prints the data again. Here's the output
that's produced when this program is run:

```
**** after cloning ****

Anthony Martinez
1300 N. First Street
Fresno, CA 93702
Salary: 40000.0

Anthony Martinez
1300 N. First Street
Fresno, CA 93702
Salary: 40000.0

**** after changing emp2 ****

Anthony Martinez
1300 N. First Street
Fresno, CA 93702
Salary: 40000.0

Anthony Smith
2503 N. 6th Street
Fresno, CA 93722
Salary: 40000.0
```

As you can see, the two Employee objects have identical data after they are
cloned, but they have different data after the fields for the second employee
have been changed. Thus, you can safely change the data in one of the objects
without affecting the other object.

The following paragraphs describe some of the highlights of this program:

→ 5   Creates an employee named Anthony Martinez.

→ 8   Sets the employee's address.

→ 11   Clones the employee (okay, just the object, not the co-worker).

→ 13   Prints the two Employee objects after cloning. They should have identical data.

→ 18   Changes the second employee's name.

→ 19   Changes the second employee's address.

→ 23   Prints the two Employee objects after changing the data for the second employee. The objects should now have different data.

→ 30   A utility method that prints the data for an Employee object.

→ 40   The Employee class. Notice that this class implements Cloneable.

→ 46   The address field, which holds an object of type Address.

→ 85   The clone method in the Employee class.

→ 90   Creates a shallow copy of the Employee object.

→ 91   Creates a shallow copy of the Address object and assigns it to the address field of the cloned Employee object.

→ 93   Catches CloneNotSupportedException, which won't ever happen because the class implements Cloneable. The compiler requires the try/catch statement here because CloneNotSupportedException is a checked exception.

→ 97   Returns the cloned Employee object.

→ 109   The Address class, which also implements Cloneable.

→ 133   The clone method of the Address class.

→ 137   Returns a shallow copy of the Address object.

The Class Class

Okay, class, it's time for one last class in this chapter: the Class class. The wording might get confusing, so put your thinking cap on.

Every class used by a Java application is represented in memory by an object of type Class. If your program uses Employee objects, for example, there's also a Class object for the Employee class. This Class object has information not about specific employees but about the Employee class itself.

You've already seen how you can get a Class object by using the getClass method. This method is defined by the Object class, so it's available to every object. Here's an example:

```
Employee emp = new Employee();
Class c = emp.getClass();
```

Note that you have to initialize a variable with an object instance before you can call its getClass method. That's because the getClass method returns a Class object that corresponds to the type of object the variable refers to, not the type the variable is declared as.

Suppose that an HourlyEmployee class extends the Employee class. Then consider these statements:

```
HourlyEmployee emp = new Employee();
Class c = emp.getClass();
```

Here c refers to a Class object for the HourlyEmployee class, not the Employee class.

The Class class has more than 50 methods, but only 2 of them are worthy of your attention:

✦ getName(): Returns a String representing the name of the class

✦ getSuperclass(): Returns another Class object representing this Class object's superclass

If you're interested in the other capabilities of the Class class, you can always check it out in the Java API documentation.

One of the most common uses of the getClass method is to tell whether two objects are of the same type by comparing their Class objects. This works because Java guarantees that the Class object has only one instance for each different class used by the application. So even if your application instantiates 1,000 Employee objects, there is only one Class object for the Employee class.

As a result, the following code can determine whether two objects are both objects of the same type:

```
Object o1 = new Employee();
Object o2 = new Employee();
if (o1.getClass() == o2.getClass())
    System.out.println("They're the same.");
else
    System.out.println("They are not the same.");
```

In this case, the type of both objects is Employee, so the comparison is true.

To find out whether an object is of a particular type, use the object's `getClass` method to get the corresponding `Class` object. Then use the `getName` method to get the class name, and use a string comparison to check the class name. Here's an example:

```
if (emp.getClass().getName().equals("Employee"))
    System.out.println("This is an employee object.");
```

If all the strung-out method calls give you a headache, you can break the code apart:

```
Class c = emp.getClass();
String s = c.getName();
if (s.equals("Employee"))
    System.out.println("This is an employee object.");
```

The result is the same.

Chapter 7: Using Inner Classes, Anonymous Classes, and Lambda Expressions

In This Chapter

✔ Using inner classes

✔ Creating static inner classes

✔ Implementing anonymous classes

✔ Adding Lambda expressions

*I*n this chapter, you find out how to use three advanced types of classes: inner classes, static inner classes, and anonymous inner classes. All three types are useful in certain circumstances. In particular, inner classes and anonymous inner classes are commonly used with graphical applications created with Swing. For more information about Swing, refer to Book VI. In this chapter, I concentrate on the mechanics of creating these types of classes.

You'll also learn about a new feature of Java 8 called *lambda expressions,* which simplify the task of creating and using anonymous classes.

Once again, this chapter could have a Technical Stuff icon pasted next to every other paragraph. The immediate usefulness of some of the information I present in this chapter may seem questionable. But trust me — you need to know this stuff when you start writing Swing applications. If you want to skip this chapter for now, that's okay. You can always come back to it when you're learning Swing and need to know how inner classes and anonymous inner classes work.

Declaring Inner Classes

An *inner class* is a class that's declared inside another class. Thus the basic structure for creating an inner class is as follows:

```
class outerClassName
{
    private class innerClassName
    {
        // body of inner class
    }
}
```

The class that contains the inner class is called an *outer class.* You can use a visibility modifier with the inner class to specify whether the class should be public, protected, or private. This visibility determines whether other classes can see the inner class.

Understanding inner classes

At the surface, an inner class is simply a class that's contained inside another class, but there's more to it than that. Here are some key points about inner classes:

✦ An inner class automatically has access to all the fields and methods of the outer class, even to private fields and methods. Thus an inner class has more access to its outer class than a subclass has to its superclass. (A subclass can access public and protected members of its superclass, but not private members.)

✦ An inner class carries with it a reference to the current instance of the outer class that enables it to access instance data for the outer class.

✦ Because of the outer-class instance reference, you can't create or refer to an inner class from a static method of the outer class. You can, however, create a *static inner class,* as I describe in the section "Using Static Inner Classes," later in this chapter.

✦ One of the main reasons for creating an inner class is to create a class-that's of interest only to the outer class. As a result, you usually declare inner classes to be private so that other classes can't access them.

✦ Occasionally, code in an inner class needs to refer to the instance of its outer class. To do that, you list the name of the outer class followed by the dot operator and this. If the outer class is named MyOuterClass, for example, you would use MyOuterClass.this to refer to the instance of the outer class.

Viewing an example

Book III, Chapter 5 introduces an application that uses the Timer class in the Swing package (javax.swing.Timer) that displays the lines Tick... and Tock... on the console at one-second intervals. It uses a class named Ticker that implements the ActionListener interface to handle the Timer object's clock events.

In this chapter, you see three versions of this application. You may want to quickly review Book III, Chapter 5 if you're unclear on how this application uses the Timer class to display the Tick... and Tock... messages or why the JOptionPane dialog box is required.

Listing 7-1 shows a version of this application that implements the Ticker class as an inner class.

Listing 7-1: Tick Tock with an Inner Class

```
import java.awt.event.*;
import javax.swing.*;

public class TickTockInner
{
    private String tickMessage = "Tick...";              →6
    private String tockMessage = "Tock...";              →7

    public static void main(String[] args)
    {
        TickTockInner t = new TickTockInner();           →11
        t.go();                                          →12
    }

    private void go()                                    →15
    {
        // create a timer that calls the Ticker class
        // at one second intervals
        Timer t = new Timer(1000, new Ticker());         →19
        t.start();

        // display a message box to prevent the
        // program from ending immediately
        JOptionPane.showMessageDialog(null,              →24
            "Click OK to exit program");
        System.exit(0);                                  →26
    }

    class Ticker implements ActionListener               →29
    {
        private boolean tick = true;

        public void actionPerformed(ActionEvent event)   →33
        {
            if (tick)
            {
                System.out.println(tickMessage);         →37
            }
            else
            {
                System.out.println(tockMessage);         →41
            }
            tick = !tick;
        }
    }
}
```

The Observer pattern

Event listeners in Java are part of a Java model called the *Delegation Event Model,* which is an implementation of a more general design pattern called the Observer pattern. This pattern is useful when you need to create objects that interact with one another when a change in the status of one of the objects occurs. The object whose changes are being monitored is called the *observable object,* and the object that monitors those changes is called the *observer object.* The observer object registers itself with the observable object, which then notifies the observer object when its status changes.

You discover more about how Java implements this pattern for event handling in Book VI. But if you're interested, you may want to investigate the Observer and Observable interfaces that are part of the Java API. They provide a standard way to create simple implementations of the Observer pattern.

The following paragraphs describe some of the highlights of this program:

→ 6　　The String variables named tickMessage and tockMessage (line 7) contain the messages to be printed on the console. Note that these variables are defined as fields of the outer class. As you'll see, the inner class Ticker is able to access these fields directly.

→ 11　　Because an inner class can be used only by an instantiated object, you can't use it directly from the static main method. As a result, the main method in this program simply creates an instance of the application class (TickTockInner).

→ 12　　This line executes the go method of the new instance of the TickTockInner class.

The technique used in lines 11 and 12 is a fairly common programming technique that lets an application get out of a static context quickly and into an object-oriented mode.

→ 15　　This line is the go method, called from line 12.

→ 19　　This line creates an instance of the Timer class with the timer interval set to 1,000 milliseconds (1 second) and the ActionListener set to a new instance of the inner class named Ticker.

→ 24　　Here, the JOptionPane class is used to display a dialog box. This dialog box is necessary to give the timer a chance to run. The application ends when the user clicks OK.

→ 26　　This line calls the exit method of the System class, which immediately shuts down the Java Virtual Machine. This method call isn't strictly required here, but if you leave it out, the timer continues to run for a few seconds after you click OK before the JVM figures out that it should kill the timer.

→ 29   This line is the declaration for the inner class named `Ticker`. Note that this class implements the `ActionListener` interface.

→ 33   The `actionPerformed` method is called by the `Timer` object every 1,000 milliseconds.

→ 37   In this line and in line 41, the inner class directly accesses a field of the outer class.

Using Static Inner Classes

A *static inner class* is similar to an inner class but doesn't require an instance of the outer class. Its basic form is the following:

```
class outerClassName
{
    private static class innerClassName
    {
        // body of inner class
    }
}
```

Like a static method, a static inner class can't access any nonstatic fields or methods in its outer class. It can access static fields or methods, however.

Listing 7-2 shows a version of the `Tick Tock` application that uses a static inner class rather than a regular inner class.

Book III
Chapter 7

Using Inner Classes,
Anonymous Classes,
and Lambda
Expressions

Listing 7-2:   Tick Tock with a Static Inner Class

```
import java.awt.event.*;
import javax.swing.*;

public class TickTockStatic
{
    private static String tickMessage = "Tick...";        →6
    private static String tockMessage = "Tock...";        →7

    public static void main(String[] args)
    {
        TickTockStatic t = new TickTockStatic();
        t.go();
    }
```

(continued)

Listing 7-2 *(continued)*

```
private void go()
{
    // create a timer that calls the Ticker class
    // at one second intervals
    Timer t = new Timer(1000, new Ticker());
    t.start();

    // display a message box to prevent the
    // program from ending immediately
    JOptionPane.showMessageDialog(null,
        "Click OK to exit program");
    System.exit(0);
}

static class Ticker implements ActionListener        →29
{
    private boolean tick = true;

    public void actionPerformed(
        ActionEvent event)
    {
        if (tick)
        {
            System.out.println(tickMessage);
        }
        else
        {
            System.out.println(tockMessage);
        }
        tick = !tick;
    }
}
}
```

This version of the application and the Listing 7-1 version have only three differences:

- → 6   The `tickMessage` field is declared as static. This is necessary so that the static class can access it.

- → 7   The `tockMessage` field is also declared as static.

- → 29   The `Ticker` class is declared as static.

Using Anonymous Inner Classes

Anonymous inner classes (usually just called *anonymous classes*) are probably the strangest feature of the Java programming language. The first time you see an anonymous class, you'll almost certainly think that someone made a mistake and that the code can't possibly compile. But compile it does, and it even works. When you get the hang of working with anonymous classes, you'll wonder how you got by without them.

An anonymous class is a class that's defined on the spot, right at the point where you want to instantiate it. Because you code the body of the class right where you need it, you don't have to give it a name. (That's why it's called an *anonymous* class.)

Creating an anonymous class

The basic form for declaring and instantiating an anonymous class is this:

```
new ClassOrInterface() { class-body }
```

As you can see, you specify the `new` keyword followed by the name of a class or interface that specifies the type of the object created from the anonymous class. This class or interface name is followed by parentheses, which may include a parameter list that's passed to the constructor of the anonymous class. Then you code a class body enclosed in braces. This class body can include anything that a regular class body can include: fields, methods, and even other classes or interfaces.

Here's an example of a simple anonymous class:

```
public class AnonClass
{
    public static void main(String[] args)
    {
        Ball b = new Ball()
            {
                public void hit()
                {
                    System.out.println("You hit it!");
                }
            };
        b.hit();
    }

    interface Ball
    {
        void hit();
    }
}
```

In this example, I create an interface named `Ball` that has a single method named `hit`. Then, back in the `main` method, I declare a variable of type `Ball` and use an anonymous class to create an object. The body of the anonymous class consists of an implementation of the `hit` method that simply displays the message `You hit it!` on the console. After the anonymous class is instantiated and assigned to the `b` variable, the next statement calls the `hit` method.

Book III
Chapter 7

**Using Inner Classes,
Anonymous Classes,
and Lambda
Expressions**

When you run this program, the single line You hit it! is displayed on the console.

Here are some things to ponder when you work with anonymous classes:

✦ You can't create a constructor for an anonymous class, because the anonymous class doesn't have a name. What would you call the constructor, anyway?

✦ You can't pass parameters if the anonymous class is based on an interface. That makes sense; interfaces don't have constructors, so Java wouldn't have anything to pass the parameters to.

✦ An assignment statement can use an anonymous class as shown in this example. In that case, the anonymous class body is followed by a semicolon that marks the end of the assignment statement. Note that this semicolon is part of the assignment statement, not the anonymous class. (In the next section, you see an example of an anonymous class that's passed as a method parameter. In that example, the body isn't followed by a semicolon.)

✦ An anonymous class is a special type of inner class; like any inner class, it automatically has access to the fields and methods of its outer class.

✦ An anonymous class can't be static.

Creating a program with an anonymous class

Listing 7-3 shows a more complex example of an anonymous class: a version of the Tick Tock application that uses an anonymous class as the action listener for the timer.

Listing 7-3:   Tick Tock with an Anonymous Class

```
import java.awt.event.*;
import javax.swing.*;

public class TickTockAnonymous
{
    private String tickMessage = "Tick...";
    private String tockMessage = "Tock...";

    public static void main(String[] args)                    →9
    {
        TickTockAnonymous t = new TickTockAnonymous();
        t.go();
    }

    private void go()
    {
        // create a timer that calls the Ticker class
        // at one second intervals
        Timer t = new Timer(1000,                             →19
```

```
        new ActionListener()                              →20
        {                                                 →21
            private boolean tick = true;

            public void actionPerformed(                  →24
                ActionEvent event)
            {
                if (tick)
                {
                    System.out.println(tickMessage);
                }
                else
                {
                    System.out.println(tockMessage);
                }
                tick = !tick;
            }
        } );                                              →37

    t.start();

    // display a message box to prevent the
    // program from ending immediately
    JOptionPane.showMessageDialog(null,
        "Click OK to exit program");
    System.exit(0);
    }
}
```

By now, you've seen enough versions of this program that you should understand how it works. The following paragraphs explain how this version uses an anonymous class as the ActionListener parameter supplied to the Timer constructor:

→ 9   Anonymous classes won't work in a static context, so the main method creates an instance of the TickTockAnonymous class and executes the go method.

→ 19   In the go method, an instance of the Timer class is created.

→ 20   The second parameter of the TimerClass constructor is an object that implements the ActionListener interface. This object is created here via an anonymous class. ActionListener is specified as the type for this class.

→ 21   This left brace marks the beginning of the body of the anonymous class.

→ 24   The actionPerformed method is called every 1,000 milliseconds by the timer. Note that this method can freely access fields defined in the outer class.

→ 37   The right brace on this line marks the end of the body of the anonymous class. Then the right parenthesis marks the end of the parameter list for the `Timer` constructor. The left parenthesis that's paired with this right parenthesis is on line 19. Finally, the semicolon marks the end of the assignment statement that started on line 19.

Using Lambda Expressions

Java 8 introduces a new feature that in some ways is similar to anonymous classes, but with more concise syntax. More specifically, a lambda expression lets you create an anonymous class that implements a specific type of interface called a *functional interface* — which has one and only one abstract method.

The `Ball` interface that was presented in the previous section meets that definition:

```
interface Ball
{
    void hit();
}
```

Here the only abstract method is the `hit` method.

A functional interface can contain additional methods, provided they are not abstract. Until Java 8, this was not possible because an interface could contain *only* abstract methods. However, in Java 8 you can create default methods which provide a default implementation. Thus a functional interface can contain one or more default methods, but can contain only one abstract method. (For more information about default methods, refer to Chapter 5 of this minibook.)

A lambda expression is a concise way to create an anonymous class that implements a functional interface. Instead of providing a formal method declaration that includes the return type, method name, parameter types, and method body, you simply define the parameter types and the method body. The Java compiler infers the rest based on the context in which you use the lambda expression.

The parameter types are separated from the method body by a new operator, called the *arrow operator,* which consists of a hyphen followed by a greater-than symbol. Here's an example that implements the `Ball` interface:

```
() -> { System.out.println("You hit it!");}
```

Here the lambda expression implements a functional interface whose single method does not accept parameters. When the method is called, the text `"You hit it!"` is printed.

You can use a lambda expression anywhere you can use a normal Java expression. You'll use them most in assignment statements or as passed parameters. The only restriction is that you can use a lambda expression only in a context that requires an instance of a functional interface. For example, here's a complete program that uses a lambda expression to implement the `Ball` interface:

```java
public class LambdaBall
{
    public static void main(String[] args)
    {
        Ball b = () -> { System.out.println("You hit it!"); };
        b.hit();
    }

    interface Ball
    {
        void hit();
    }
}
```

The general syntax for a lambda expression is this:

```
(parameters) -> expression
```

or this:

```
(parameters) -> { statement; ... }
```

If you use an expression, a semicolon is not required. If you use one or more statements, the statements must be enclosed in curly braces and a semicolon is required at the end of each statement.

Don't forget that the statement in which you use the lambda expression must itself end with a semicolon. Thus, the lambda expression in the previous example has two semicolons in close proximity:

```
Ball b = () -> { System.out.println("You hit it!"); };
```

The first semicolon marks the end of the statement that calls `System.out.println`; the second semicolon marks the end of the assignment statement that assigns the lambda expression to the variable b.

**Book III
Chapter 7**

**Using Inner Classes,
Anonymous Classes,
and Lambda
Expressions**

Chapter 8: Packaging and Documenting Your Classes

In This Chapter

✔ Creating packages for your classes

✔ Archiving your packages in JAR files

✔ Documenting your classes with JavaDocs

This chapter shows you what to do with the classes you create. Specifically, I show you how to organize classes into neat packages. Packages enable you to keep your classes separate from classes in the Java API, allow you to reuse your classes in other applications, and even let you distribute your classes to others, assuming other people might be interested in your classes. If that's the case, you probably won't want to send those people all your separate class files. Instead, bundle them into a single file called a JAR file. That's covered in this chapter too.

Finally, you find out how to use a feature called JavaDocs that lets you add documentation comments to your classes. With JavaDocs, you can build professional-looking documentation pages automatically. Your friends will think you're a real Java guru when you post your JavaDoc pages to your website.

Working with Packages

A *package* is a group of classes that belong together. Without packages, the entire universe of Java classes would be a huge, unorganized mess. Imagine the thousands of classes that are available in the Java API combined with millions of Java classes created by Java programmers throughout the world and all thrown into one big pot. Packages let you organize this mass into smaller, manageable collections of related classes.

Importing classes and packages

When you use `import` statements at the beginning of a Java source file, you make classes from the packages mentioned in the `import` statements available throughout the file. (I cover `import` statements in Book II, Chapter 1, but it doesn't hurt to repeat it here.)

An `import` statement can import all the classes in a package by using an asterisk wildcard. Here all the classes in the `java.util` package are imported:

```
import java.util.*;
```

Alternatively, you can import classes one at a time. Here just the `ArrayList` class is imported:

```
import java.util.ArrayList;
```

Note: You don't have to use an `import` statement to use a class from a package. But if you don't use an `import` statement, you must *fully qualify* any references to the class. For example, you can use the `ArrayList` class without importing `java.util`:

```
java.util.ArrayList = new java.util.ArrayList();
```

Because fully qualified names are a pain to always spell out, you should always use `import` statements to import the packages or individual classes your application uses.

You never have to explicitly import two packages:

✦ **`java.lang`:** This package contains classes that are so commonly used that the Java compiler makes them available to every program. Examples of the classes in this package are `String`, `Exception`, and the various wrapper classes, such as `Integer` and `Boolean`. (For complete documentation on this package and all of the other Java packages described in this book, refer to `http://download.java.net/jdk8/docs/api`.)

✦ **The default package:** This package contains classes that aren't specifically put in some other package. All the programs I show in this book up to this point rely on the default package.

For simple program development and experimentation, using the default package is acceptable. However, if you start work on a serious Java application, create a separate package for it and place all of the application's classes there. You find out how to do that in the next section.

You can't import the default package, even if you want to. Suppose you have two packages — the default package and the `com.lowewriter.util` package. The default package's code contains the statement `import com.lowewriter.util.*`. That's okay. But the default package doesn't have a

name — at least it has no name that you can use inside a program. The
`com.lowewriter.util` package's code can't contain a statement like
this one:

```
import that_default_package.you_know.the_one_with_no_name
```

Creating your own packages

Creating your own packages to hold your classes is easy. Well, relatively
easy, anyway. You must go through a few steps:

1. Pick a name for your package.

You can use any name you wish, but I recommend you follow the established convention of using your Internet domain name (if you have one),
only backwards. I own a domain called `LoweWriter.com`, so I use the
name `com.lowewriter` for all my packages. (Using your domain name
backwards ensures that your package names are unique.)

Notice that package names are in all-lowercase letters. That's not an
absolute requirement, but it's a Java convention that you ought to stick
to. If you start using capital letters in your package names, you'll be
branded a rebel for sure. And since Java is case-sensitive, a package
named `com.lowewriter` is a different package from one named `com.
LoweWriter`.

You can add additional levels beyond the domain name if you want. For
example, I put my utility classes in a package named `com.lowewriter.
util`.

If you don't have a domain all to yourself, try using your e-mail
address backwards. For example, if your e-mail address is `SomeBody@
SomeCompany.com`, use `com.somecompany.somebody` for your pack-
age names. That way they are still unique. (If you ever want to distribute
your Java packages, you should register a domain name. Nothing says
"Amateur" like a package name that starts with `com.aol`. And, although
a package name created from a backwards e-mail address is almost sure
to be unique, there is a small chance that it won't be.)

**2. Choose a directory on your hard drive to be the root of your class
library.**

You need a place on your hard drive to store your classes. I suggest you
create a directory such as `c:\javaclasses`.

This folder becomes the *root directory* for your Java packages.

**3. Create subdirectories within the root directory for your package
name.**

For example, for the package named `com.lowewriter.util`, create a
directory named `com` in the `c:\javaclasses` directory (assuming that's

the name of your root). Then, in the com directory, create a directory named lowewriter. Then, in lowewriter, create a directory named util. Thus, the complete path to the directory that contains the classes for the com.lowewriter.util package is c:\javaclasses\com\lowewriter\util.

4. Add the root directory for your package to the ClassPath environment variable.

The exact procedure for doing this depends on your operating system. You can set the ClassPath by double-clicking System from the Control Panel. Click the Advanced tab, and then click Environment Variables.

Be careful not to disturb any directories already listed in the ClassPath. To add your root directory to the ClassPath, add a semicolon followed by the path to your root directory to the end of the ClassPath value. For example, suppose your ClassPath is already set to this:

```
.;c:\util\classes
```

Then you modify it to look like this:

```
.;c:\util\classes;c:\javaclasses
```

Here I added ;c:\javaclasses to the end of the ClassPath value.

5. Save the files for any classes you want to be in a particular package in the directory for that package.

For example, save the files for a class that belongs to the com.lowewriter.util package in c:\javaclasses\com\lowewriter\util.

6. Add a package statement to the beginning of each source file that belongs in a package.

The package statement simply provides the name for the package that any class in the file is placed in. For example:

```
package com.lowewriter.util;
```

The package statement must be the first non-comment statement in the file.

An example

Suppose you've developed a utility class named Console that has a bunch of handy static methods for getting user input from the console. For example, this class has a static method named askYorN that gets a Y or N from the user and returns a boolean value to indicate which value the user entered. You decide to make this class available in a package named

`com.lowewriter.util` so you and other like-minded programmers can use
it in their programs.

Here's the source file for the `Console` class:

```
package com.lowewriter.util;

import java.util.Scanner;

public class Console
{

    static Scanner sc = new Scanner(System.in);

    public static boolean askYorN(String prompt)
    {
        while (true)
        {
            String answer;
            System.out.print("\n" + prompt
                + " (Y or N) ");
            answer = sc.next();
            if (answer.equalsIgnoreCase("Y"))
                return true;
            else if (answer.equalsIgnoreCase("N"))
                return false;
        }
    }
}
```

Okay, so far this class has just the one method (`askYorN`), but one of these
days you'll add a bunch of other useful methods to it. In the meantime, you
want to get it set up in a package so you can start using it right away.

So you create a directory named `c:\javaclasses\com\lowewriter\`
`util` (as described in the preceding section) and save the source file to
this directory. Then you compile the program so the `Console.class` file
is stored in that directory too. And you add `c:\javaclasses` to your
ClassPath environment variable.

Now you can use the following program to test that your package is alive
and well:

```
import com.lowewriter.util.*;

public class PackageTest
{
    public static void main(String[] args)
```

```
    {
        while (Console.askYorN("Keep going?"))
        {
            System.out.println("D'oh!");
        }
    }
}
```

Here the `import` statement imports all the classes in the `com.lowewriter.util` package. Then, the `while` loop in the `main` method repeatedly asks the user if he or she wants to keep going.

Putting Your Classes in a JAR File

A *JAR file* is a single file that can contain more than one class in a compressed format that the Java Runtime Environment can access quickly. (*JAR* stands for *Java archive.*) A JAR file can have just a few classes in it, or thousands. In fact, the entire Java API is stored in a single JAR file named `rt.java`. (The `rt` stands for *runtime.*) It's a pretty big file — over 35MB — but that's not bad, considering that it contains more than 12,000 classes.

JAR files are created by the `jar` utility, which you find in the Java `bin` directory along with the other Java command-line tools, such as `java` and `javac`. JAR files are similar in format to Zip files, a compressed format made popular by the PKZIP program. The main difference is that JAR files contain a special file, called the *manifest file,* that contains information about the files in the archive. This manifest is automatically created by the `jar` utility, but you can supply a manifest of your own to provide additional information about the archived files.

JAR files are the normal way to distribute finished Java applications. After finishing your application, you run the `jar` command from a command prompt to prepare the JAR file. Then, another user can copy the JAR file to his or her computer. The user can then run the application directly from the JAR file.

JAR files are also used to distribute class libraries. You can add a JAR file to the ClassPath environment variable. Then the classes in the JAR file are automatically available to any Java program that imports the package that contains the classes.

jar command-line options

The `jar` command is an old-fashioned Unix-like command, complete with arcane command-line options that you have to get right if you expect to coax `jar` into doing something useful.

The basic format of the jar command is this:

```
jar options jar-file [manifest-file] class-files...
```

The options specify the basic action you want jar to perform and provide additional information about how you want the command to work. Table 8-1 lists the options.

Table 8-1	Options for the jar Command
Option	*Description*
c	Creates a new jar file.
u	Updates an existing jar file.
x	Extracts files from an existing jar file.
t	Lists the contents of a jar file.
f	Indicates that the jar file is specified as an argument. You almost always want to use this option.
v	Verbose output. This option tells the jar command to display extra information while it works.
0	Doesn't compress files when it adds them to the archive. This option isn't used much.
m	Specifies that a manifest file is provided. It's listed as the next argument following the jar file.
M	Specifies that a manifest file should not be added to the archive. This option is rarely used.

Note that you must specify at least the c, u, x, or t option to tell jar what action you want to perform.

Archiving a package

The most common use for the jar utility is to create an archive of an entire package. The procedure for doing that varies slightly depending on what operating system you're using. However, the jar command itself is the same regardless of your operating system. Here's the procedure for archiving a package on a PC running any version of Windows:

1. **Open a command window.**

The easiest way to do that is to choose Start➪Run, type cmd in the Open text box, and click OK. On Windows 8, right-click the Start button, and then choose Command Prompt on the menu that appears.

If you have trouble running the jar command in Step 3, you may need to open the command prompt in Administrator mode. To do so, click the Start menu, type cmd, right-click cmd.exe at the top of the Start menu, and choose Run as Administrator.

2. **Use a cd command to navigate to your package root.**

   For example, if your packages are stored in c:\javaclasses, use this command:

   ```
   cd \javaclasses
   ```

3. **Use a jar command that specifies the options cf, the name of the jar file, and the path to the class files you want to archive.**

   For example, to create an archive named utils.jar that contains all the class files in the com.lowewriter.util package, use this command:

   ```
   jar cf utils.jar com\lowewriter\util\*.class
   ```

4. **To verify that the jar file was created correctly, use the jar command that specifies the options tf and the name of the jar file.**

   For example, if the jar file is named utils.jar, use this command:

   ```
   jar tf utils.jar
   ```

   This lists the contents of the jar file so you can see what classes were added. Here's some typical output from this command:

   ```
   META-INF/
   META-INF/MANIFEST.MF
   com/lowewriter/util/Console.class
   ```

   As you can see, the utils.jar file contains the Console class, which is in my com.lowewriter.util package.

5. **That's all!**

   You're done. You can leave the jar file where it is, or you can give it to your friends so they can use the classes it contains.

Adding a jar to your classpath

To use the classes in an archive, you must add the jar file to your ClassPath environment variable. I describe the procedure for modifying the ClassPath variable in Windows XP earlier in this chapter, in the section "Creating your own packages." So I won't repeat the details here.

To add an archive to the ClassPath variable, just add the complete path to the archive, making sure to separate it from any other paths already in the ClassPath with a semicolon. Here's an example:

```
.;c:\javaclasses\utils.jar;c:\javaclasses
```

Here I added the path `c:\javaclasses\utils.jar` to my `ClassPath` variable.

Starting with Java 1.6, you can add all the `jar` files from a particular directory to the `ClassPath` in one fell swoop. For example, imagine that your `c:\javaclasses` directory contains two `jar` files — `utils.jar` and `extras.jar`. To add both `jar` files to the ClassPath, use a forward slash (/) followed by an asterisk:

```
.;c:\javaclasses/*
```

The forward slash looks strange, especially when combined with the backslash in `c:\javaclasses`. But that's the way you use a `ClassPath` wildcard.

The first path in a `ClassPath` variable is always a single dot (`.`), which allows Java to find classes in the current directory.

Also, be aware that Java searches the various paths and archive files in the `ClassPath` variable in the order in which you list them. Thus, with the `ClassPath .;c:\javaclasses\utils.jar;c:\javaclasses`, Java searches for classes first in the current directory, then in the `utils` archive, and finally in the `c:\javaclasses` directory.

Running a program directly from an archive

With just a little work, you can set up an archive so that a Java program can be run directly from it. All you have to do is create a *manifest file* before you create the archive. Then, when you run the `jar` utility to create the archive, you include the manifest file on the `jar` command line.

A *manifest file* is a simple text file that contains information about the files in the archive. Although it can contain many lines of information, it needs just one line to make an executable `jar` file:

```
Main-Class: ClassName
```

The `ClassName` is the fully qualified name of the class that contains the `main` method that is executed to start the application. It isn't required, but it's typical to use the extension `.mf` for manifest files.

For example, suppose you have an application whose main class is `GuessingGame`, and all the class files for the application are in the package `com.lowewriter.game`. First, create a manifest file named `game.mf` in the `com\lowewriter\game` directory. This file contains the following line:

```
Main-Class: com.lowewriter.game.GuessingGame
```

Then run the `jar` command with the options `cfm`, the name of the archive to create, the name of the manifest file, and the path for the class files. Here's an example:

```
jar cfm game.jar com\lowewriter\game\game.mf com\lowewriter\game\*.class
```

Now you can run the application directly from a command prompt by using the `java` command with the `-jar` switch and the name of the archive file. Here's an example:

```
java -jar game.jar
```

This command starts the JRE and executes the `main` method of the class specified by the manifest file in the `game.jar` archive file.

If your operating system is configured properly, you can also run the application by double-clicking an icon for the `jar` file.

Using JavaDoc to Document Your Classes

One last step remains before you can go public with your hot new class library or application: preparing the documentation for its classes. Fortunately, Java provides a tool called *JavaDoc* that can automatically create fancy HTML-based documentation based on comments in your source files. All you have to do is add a comment for each public class, field, and method; then run the source files through the `javadoc` command; *voilà!* you have professional-looking, web-based documentation for your classes.

The following sections show you how to add JavaDoc comments to your source files, how to run the source files through the `javadoc` command, and how to view the resulting documentation pages.

Adding JavaDoc comments

The basic rule for creating JavaDoc comments is that they begin with `/**` and end with `*/`. You can place JavaDoc comments in any of three different locations in a source file:

✦ Immediately before the declaration of a public class

✦ Immediately before the declaration of a public field

✦ Immediately before the declaration of a public method or constructor

A JavaDoc comment can include text that describes the class, field, or method. Each subsequent line of a multiline JavaDoc comment usually begins with an asterisk. JavaDoc ignores this asterisk and any white space between it and the first word on the line.

The text in a JavaDoc comment can include HTML markup if you want to apply fancy formatting. You should avoid using heading tags (`<h1>` and so on) because JavaDoc creates those, and your heading tags just confuse things. But you can use tags for boldface and italics (`<b>` and `<i>`) or to format code examples (use the `<pre>` tag).

In addition, you can include special *doc tags* that provide specific information used by JavaDoc to format the documentation pages. Table 8-2 summarizes the most commonly used tags.

Table 8-2	Commonly Used JavaDoc Tags
Tag	**Explanation**
`@author`	Provides information about the author, typically the author's name, e-mail address, website information, and so on.
`@version`	Indicates the version number.
`@since`	Used to indicate the version with which this class, field, or method was added.
`@param`	Provides the name and description of a method or constructor.
`@return`	Provides a description of a method's return value.
`@throws`	Indicates exceptions that are thrown by a method or constructor.
`@deprecated`	Indicates that the class, field, or method is deprecated and shouldn't be used.

To give you an idea of how JavaDoc comments are typically used, Listing 8-1 shows a class named `Employee` with JavaDoc comments included.

Note that for the `Employee` class to compile, you must also provide a class named `Address`, which represents a street address. The following simple class will suffice:

```
public class Address implements Cloneable
{
    public String street;
    public String city;
    public String state;
    public String zipCode;
}
```

Listing 8-1:   An Employee Class with JavaDoc Comments

```java
package com.lowewriter.payroll;

/** Represents an employee.
 * @author Doug Lowe
 * @author www.LoweWriter.com
 * @version 1.5
 * @since 1.0
 */
public class Employee
{
    private String lastName;
    private String firstName;
    private Double salary;

/** Represents the employee's address.
 */
    public Address address;

/** Creates an employee with the specified name.
 * @param lastName The employee's last name.
 * @param firstName The employee's first name.
 */
    public Employee(String lastName, String firstName)
    {
        this.lastName = lastName;
        this.firstName = firstName;
        this.address = new Address();
    }

/** Gets the employee's last name.
 * @return A string representing the employee's last
 *                  name.
 */
    public String getLastName()
    {
        return this.lastName;
    }

/** Sets the employee's last name.
 * @param lastName A String containing the employee's
 *                  last name.
 */
    public void setLastName(String lastName)
    {
        this.lastName = lastName;
    }
```

```
/** Gets the employee's first name.
 * @return A string representing the employee's first
 *                   name.
 */
   public String getFirstName()
   {
       return this.firstName;
   }

/** Sets the employee's first name.
 * @param firstName A String containing the
 *                   employee's first name.
 */
   public void setFirstName(String firstName)
   {
       this.firstName = firstName;
   }

/** Gets the employee's salary.
 * @return A double representing the employee's salary.
 */
   public double getSalary()
   {
       return this.salary;
   }

/** Sets the employee's salary.
 * @param lastName A double containing the employee's
 *                   salary.
 */
   public void setSalary(double salary)
   {
       this.salary = salary;
   }
}
```

Using the javadoc command

The javadoc command has a few dozen options you can set, making it a complicated command to use. However, you can ignore all these options to create a basic set of documentation pages. Just specify the complete path to all the Java files you want to create documentation for, like this:

```
javadoc com\lowewriter\payroll\*.java
```

The `javadoc` command creates the documentation pages in the current directory, so you may want to switch to the directory where you want the pages to reside first.

For more complete information about using this command, refer to the `javadoc` documentation at the Sun website. You can find it here:

`java.sun.com/j2se/javadoc`

Viewing JavaDoc pages

After you run the `javadoc` command, you can access the documentation pages by starting with the `index.html` page. To quickly display this page, just type `index.html` at the command prompt after you run the `javadoc` command. Or you can start your browser, navigate to the directory where you created the documentation pages, and open the `index.html` page. Either way, Figure 8-1 shows an index page that lists two classes.

Figure 8-1:
A JavaDocs
index page.

If you think this page looks familiar, that's because the documentation for the Java API was created using JavaDocs. So you should already know how to find your way around these pages.

To look at the documentation for a class, click the class name's link. A page with complete documentation for the class comes up. For example, Figure 8-2 shows part of the documentation page for the `Employee` class. JavaDocs generated this page from the source file shown in Listing 8-1.

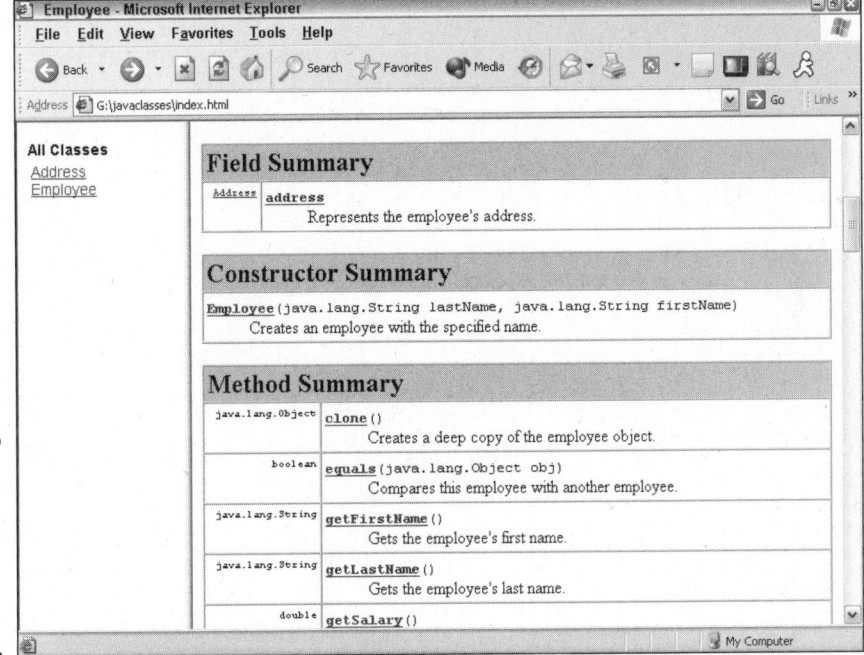

Figure 8-2: Docu-mentation for the Employee class.

Book IV
Strings, Arrays, and Collections

a8	b8	c8	d8	e8	f8	g8	h8
a7	b7	c7	d7	e7	f7	g7	h7
a6	b6	c6	d6	e6	f6	g6	h6
a5	b5	c5	d5	e5	f5	g5	h5
a4	b4	c4	d4	♘	f4	g4	h4
a3	b3	c3	d3	e3	f3	g3	h3
a2	b2	c2	d2	e2	f2	g2	h2
a1	b1	c1	d1	e1	f1	g1	h1

web extras

You can find an interesting programming challenge that requires use of many of the programming techniques covered in this minibook at www.dummies.com/extras/javaaio. The challenge is to enhance the Tic-Tac-Toe program you've created for Books II and III so that it plays with even better strategy. You will also use an array for the program's internal representation of the game board.

Contents at a Glance

Chapter 1: Working with Strings

In This Chapter

✔ **Quickly reviewing what you already know about strings**

✔ **Examining string class methods**

✔ **Working with substrings**

✔ **Splitting strings**

✔ **Using the StringBuilder and StringBuffer classes**

✔ **Using the CharSequence interface**

Strings are among the most common types of objects in Java. Throughout this book are various techniques for working with strings. You've seen how to create string variables, how to concatenate strings, and how to compare strings. But so far, I've only scratched the surface of what you can do with strings. In this chapter, I dive deeper into what Java can do with string.

I start with a brief review of what I've covered so far about strings, so that you don't have to go flipping back through the book to find basic information. Then I look at the `String` class itself and some of the methods it provides for working with strings. Finally, I examine two almost identical classes named `StringBuilder` and `StringBuffer` that offer features not available in the basic `String` class as well as an interface named `CharSequence` that is implemented by `String`, `StringBuilder`, and `StringBuffer`.

Reviewing Strings

To save you the hassle of flipping back through this book, the following paragraphs summarize what I present about strings in earlier chapters:

✦ Strings are reference types, not value types, such as `int` or `boolean`. As a result, a string variable holds a reference to an object created from the `String` class, not the value of the string itself.

✦ Even though strings aren't primitive types, the Java compiler has some features designed to let you work with strings almost as though they were primitive types. Java lets you assign string literals to string variables, for example, like this:

```
String line1 = "Oh what a beautiful morning!";
```

The Immutable pattern

Many applications can benefit from classes that describe immutable objects. An *immutable object* is an object that, once created, can never be changed. The `String` class is the most common example of an immutable object. After you create a `String` object, you can't change it.

Suppose that you're designing a game in which the playing surface has fixed obstacles, such as trees. You can create the `Tree` class by using the Immutable pattern. The constructor for the `Tree` class could accept parameters that define the size, type, and location of the tree. But after you create the tree, you can't move it.

Follow these three simple rules for creating an immutable object:

1. Provide one or more constructors that accept parameters to set the initial state of the object.

2. Don't allow any methods to modify any instance variables in the object. Set instance variables with constructors and then leave them alone.

3. Any method that modifies the object should do so by creating a new object with the modified values. Then this method returns the new object as its return value.

✦ Strings can include *escape sequences* that consist of a slash followed by another character. The most common escape sequences are \n for new line and \t for tab. If you want to include a slash in a string, you must use the escape sequence \\. Here is a complete list of all the escape sequences you can use:

Escape Sequence	Explanation
\n	Newline
\t	Tab
\b	Backspace
\r	Carriage return
\f	Form feed
\'	Apostrophe
\"	Quotation mark
\\	Backslash

✦ Strings and characters are different. String literals are marked by quotation marks; character literals are marked by apostrophes. Thus, "a" is a string literal that happens to be one character long. By contrast, 'a' is a character literal.

✦ You can combine, or *concatenate,* strings by using the + operator, like this:

```
String line2 = line1 + "\nOh what a beautiful day!";
```

✦ You can also use the += operator with strings, like this:

```
line2 += "\nI've got a beautiful feeling";
```

✦ When a primitive type is used in a concatenation expression, Java automatically converts the primitive type to a string. Thus Java allows the following:

```
int empCount = 50;
String msg = "Number of employees: " + empCount;
```

✦ The various primitive wrapper classes (such as integer and double) have parse methods that can convert string values to numeric types. Here's an example:

```
String s = "50";
int i = Integer.parseInt(s);
```

✦ You can't compare strings by using the equality operator (==). Instead, you should use the equals method. Here's an example:

```
if (lastName.equals("Lowe"))
    System.out.println("This is me!");
```

✦ The String class also has an equalsIgnoreCase method that compares strings without considering case. Here's an example:

```
if (lastName.equalsIgnoreCase("lowe"))
    System.out.println("This is me again!");
```

Using the String Class

The String class is the class you use to create string objects. It has a whole gaggle of methods that are designed to let you find out information about the string that's represented by the String class. Table 1-1 lists the most useful of these methods.

Table 1-1	String Class Methods
Method	**Description**
char charAt(int)	Returns the character at the specified position in the string.
int compareTo(String)	Compares this string to another string, using alphabetical order. Returns -1 if this string comes before the other string, 0 if the strings are the same, and 1 if this string comes after the other string.
int compareToIgnoreCase(String)	Similar to compareTo but ignores case.

(continued)

Table 1-1 *(continued)*

Method	Description
boolean contains(CharSequence)	Returns true if this string contains the parameter value. The parameter can be a String, StringBuilder, or StringBuffer.
boolean endsWith(String)	Returns true if this string ends with the parameter string.
boolean equals(String)	Returns true if this string has the same value as the parameter string.
boolean equalsIgnoreCase(String)	Similar to equals but ignores case.
int indexOf(char)	Returns the index of the first occurrence of the char parameter in this string. Returns -1 if the character isn't in the string.
int indexOf(String)	Returns the index of the first occurrence of the String parameter in this string. Returns -1 if the string isn't in this string.
int indexOf(String, int start)	Similar to indexOf, but starts the search at the specified position in the string.
int lastIndexOf(char)	Returns the index of the last occurrence of the char parameter in this string. Returns -1 if the character isn't in the string.
int lastIndexOf(String)	Returns the index of the last occurrence of the String parameter in this string. Returns -1 if the string isn't in this string.
int lastIndexOf(String, int)	Similar to lastIndexOf, but starts the search at the specified position in the string.
int length()	Returns the length of this string.
String replace(char, char)	Returns a new string that's based on the original string, but with every occurrence of the first parameter replaced by the second parameter.
String replaceAll(String old, String new)	Returns a new string that's based on the original string, but with every occurrence of the first string replaced by the second parameter. Note that the first parameter can be a regular expression.

Method	Description
`String replaceFirst(String old, String new)`	Returns a new string that's based on the original string, but with the first occurrence of the first string replaced by the second parameter. Note that the first parameter can be a regular expression.
`String[] split(String)`	Splits the string into an array of strings, using the string parameter as a pattern to determine where to split the strings.
`boolean startsWith(String)`	Returns `true` if this string starts with the parameter string.
`boolean startsWith(String, int)`	Returns `true` if this string contains the parameter string at the position indicated by the `int` parameter.
`String substring(int)`	Extracts a substring from this string, beginning at the position indicated by the int parameter and continuing to the end of the string.
`String substring(int, int)`	Extracts a substring from this string, beginning at the position indicated by the first parameter and ending at the position one character before the value of the second parameter.
`char[] toCharArray()`	Converts the string to an array of individual characters.
`String toLowerCase()`	Converts the string to lowercase.
`String toString()`	Returns the string as a `String` (pretty pointless, if you ask me, but all classes must have a `toString` method).
`String toUpperCase()`	Converts the string to uppercase.
`String trim()`	Returns a copy of the string with all leading and trailing white spaces removed.
`String valueOf(primitiveType)`	Returns a string representation of any primitive type.

The most important thing to remember about the String class is that in spite of the fact that it has a bazillion methods, none of those methods let you alter the string in any way. A String object is *immutable,* which means that it can't be changed.

Although you can't change a string after you create it, you can use methods of the String class to create new strings that are variations of the original string. The following sections describe some of the more interesting things you can do with these methods.

Finding the length of a string

One of the most basic string operations is determining the length of a string. You do that with the length method. For example:

```
String s = "A wonderful day for a neighbor.";
int len = s.length();
```

Here len is assigned a value of 31 because the string s consists of 30 characters.

Getting the length of a string usually isn't very useful by itself, but the length method often plays an important role in other string manipulations, as you see throughout the following sections.

Making simple string modifications

Several of the methods of the String class return modified versions of the original string. toLowerCase, for example, converts a string to all-lowercase letters:

```
String s1 = "Oompa Loompa";
String s2 = s1.toLowerCase();
```

Here s2 is set to the string oompa loompa. The toUpperCase method works the same way but converts strings to all-uppercase letters.

The trim method removes white-space characters (spaces, tabs, newlines, and so on) from the start and end of a word. Here's an example:

```
String s = "   Oompa Loompa   ";
s = s.trim();
```

Here the spaces before and after Oompa Loompa are removed. Thus, the resulting string is 10 characters long.

Bear in mind that because strings are immutable, these methods don't actually change the String object. Instead, they create a new String with the modified value. A common mistake — especially for programmers who are new to Java but experienced in other languages — is to forget to assign the return value from one of these methods. The following statement has no effect on s:

```
s.trim();
```

Here the `trim` method trims the string — but then the program discards the result. The remedy is to assign the result of this expression back to s, like this:

```
s = s.trim();
```

Extracting characters from a string

You can use the `charAt` method to extract a character from a specific position in a string. When you do, keep in mind that the index number for the first character in a string is 0, not 1. Also, you should check the length of the string before extracting a character. If you specify an index value that's beyond the end of the string, the exception `StringIndexOutOfBounds Exception` is thrown. (Fortunately, this is an unchecked exception, so you don't have to enclose the `charAt` method in a `try/catch` statement.)

Here's an example of a program that uses the `charAt` method to count the number of vowels in a string entered by the user:

```java
import java.util.Scanner;

public class CountVowels
{
    static Scanner sc = new Scanner(System.in);

    public static void main(String[] args)
    {
        System.out.print("Enter a string: ");
        String s = sc.nextLine();

        int vowelCount = 0;

        for (int i = 0; i < s.length(); i++)
        {
            char c = s.charAt(i);
            if (    (c == 'A') || (c == 'a')
                || (c == 'E') || (c == 'e')
                || (c == 'I') || (c == 'i')
                || (c == 'O') || (c == 'o')
                || (c == 'U') || (c == 'u') )
                vowelCount++;
        }
        System.out.println("That string contains "
            + vowelCount + " vowels.");
    }
}
```

Here the `for` loop checks the length of the string to make sure that the index variable i doesn't exceed the string length. Then each character is extracted and checked with an `if` statement to see whether it is a vowel. The condition expression in this `if` statement is a little complicated because it must check for five different vowels, both uppercase and lowercase.

Following is an example that shows the output created by this program if you enter a string listing all of the letters of the alphabet:

```
Enter a string: abcdefghijklmnopqrstuvwxyz
That string contains 5 vowels.
```

Extracting substrings from a string

The `substring` method lets you extract a portion of a string. This method has two forms. The first version accepts a single integer parameter. It returns the substring that starts at the position indicated by this parameter and extends to the rest of the string. (Remember that string positions start with 0, not 1.) Here's an example:

```
String s = "Baseball";
String b = s.substring(4);        // "ball"
```

Here b is assigned the string `ball`.

The second version of the `substring` method accepts two parameters to indicate the start and end of the substring you want to extract. Note that the substring actually ends at the character that's immediately before the position indicated by the second parameter. So, to extract the characters at positions 2 through 5, specify 1 as the start position and 6 as the ending position. For example:

```
String s = "Baseball";
String b = s.substring(2, 6);     // "seba"
```

Here b is assigned the string `seba`.

The following program uses substrings to replace all the vowels in a string entered by the user with asterisks:

```
import java.util.Scanner;

public class MarkVowels
{
    static Scanner sc = new Scanner(System.in);

    public static void main(String[] args)
    {
        System.out.print("Enter a string: ");
        String s = sc.nextLine();
        String originalString = s;
```

```
        int vowelCount = 0;

        for (int i = 0; i < s.length(); i++)
        {
            char c = s.charAt(i);
            if (    (c == 'A') || (c == 'a')
                 || (c == 'E') || (c == 'e')
                 || (c == 'I') || (c == 'i')
                 || (c == 'O') || (c == 'o')
                 || (c == 'U') || (c == 'u') )
            {
                String front = s.substring(0, i);
                String back = s.substring(i+1);
                s = front + "*" + back;
            }
        }
        System.out.println();
        System.out.println(originalString);
        System.out.println(s);
    }
}
```

This program uses a `for` loop and the `charAt` method to extract each character from the string. Then, if the character is a vowel, a string named `front` is created that consists of all the characters that appear before the vowel. Next, a second string named `back` is created with all the characters that appear after the vowel. Finally, the s string is replaced by a new string that's constructed from the `front` string, an asterisk, and the `back` string.

Here's some sample console output from this program so that you can see how it works:

```
Enter a string: Where have all the vowels gone?

Where have all the vowels gone?
Wh*r* h*v* *ll th* v*w*ls g*n*?
```

Splitting a string

The `split` command is especially useful for splitting a string into separate strings based on a delimiter character. Suppose you have a string with the parts of an address separated by colons, like this:

```
1500 N. Third Street:Fresno:CA:93722
```

With the `split` method, you can easily separate this string into four strings. In the process, the colons are discarded.

Unfortunately, the use of the split method requires that you use an array, and arrays are covered in the next chapter. I'm going to plow ahead with this section anyway on a hunch that you already know a few basic things about arrays. (If not, you can always come back to this section after you read the next chapter.)

The split method carves a string into an array of strings separated by the delimiter character passed via a string parameter. Here's a routine that splits an address into separate strings and then prints out all the strings:

```
String address =
    "1500 N. Third Street:Fresno:CA:93722";

String[] parts = address.split(":");

for (int i = 0; i < parts.length; i++)
    System.out.println(parts[i]);
```

If you run this code, the following lines are displayed on the console:

```
1500 N. Third Street
Fresno
CA
93722
```

The string passed to the split method is actually a special type of string used for pattern recognition, called a *regular expression*. You discover regular expressions in Book V. For now, here are a few regular expressions that might be useful when you use the split method:

Regular Expression	Explanation
\\t	A tab character
\\n	A newline character
\\|	A vertical bar
\\s	Any white-space character
\\s+	One or more occurrences of any white-space character

The last regular expression in this table, \\s+, is especially useful for breaking a string into separate words. The following program accepts a string from the user, breaks it into separate words, and then displays the words on separate lines:

```
import java.util.Scanner;

public class ListWords
```

```
{
    static Scanner sc = new Scanner(System.in);

    public static void main(String[] args)
    {
        System.out.print("Enter a string: ");
        String s = sc.nextLine();
        String[] word = s.split("\\s+");
        for (String w : word)
            System.out.println(w);
    }
}
```

Here's a sample of the console output for a typical execution of this program:

```
Enter a string: This string    has    several    words
This
string
has
several
words
```

Notice that some of the words in the string entered by the user are preceded by more than one space character. The \\s+ pattern used by the split method treats any consecutive white-space character as a single delimiter when splitting the words.

Replacing parts of a string

You can use the replaceFirst or replaceAll method to replace a part of a string that matches a pattern you supply with some other text. Here's the main method of a program that gets a line of text from the user and then replaces all occurrences of the string cat with dog:

```
public static void main(String[] args)
{
    Scanner sc = new Scanner(System.in);
    System.out.print("Enter a string: ");
    String s = sc.nextLine();

    s = s.replaceAll("cat", "dog");

    System.out.println(s);
}
```

And here's the console for a typical execution of this program:

```
Enter a string: I love cats.
I love dogs.
```

As with the `split` methods, the first parameter of `replace` methods can be a regular expression that provides a complex matching string. (For more information, see Book V, Chapter 3.)

Once again, don't forget that strings are immutable. As a result, the `replace` methods don't actually modify the `String` object itself. Instead, they return a new `String` object with the modified value.

Using the StringBuilder and StringBuffer Classes

The `String` class is powerful, but it's not very efficient for programs that require heavy-duty string manipulation. Because `String` objects are immutable, any method of the `String` class that modifies the string in any way must create a new `String` object and copy the modified contents of the original string object to the new string. That's not so bad if it happens only occasionally, but it can be inefficient in programs that do it a lot.

Even string concatenation is inherently inefficient. Consider these statements:

```
int count = 5;
String msg = "There are ";
String msg += count;
String msg += " apples in the basket.";
```

These four statements actually create five `String` objects:

- ✦ **"There are "**: Created for the literal in the second statement. The `msg` variable is assigned a reference to this string.

- ✦ **"5"**: Created to hold the result of `count.toString()`. The `toString` method is implicitly called by the third statement, so `count` is concatenated with `msg`.

- ✦ **"There are 5"**: Created as a result of the concatenation in the third statement. A reference to this object is assigned to `msg`.

- ✦ **"apples in the basket."**: Created to hold the literal in the fourth statement.

- ✦ **"There are 5 apples in the basket."**: Created to hold the result of the concatenation in the fourth statement. A reference to this object is assigned to `msg`.

For programs that do only occasional string concatenation and simple string manipulations, these inefficiencies aren't a big deal. For programs that do extensive string manipulation, however, Java offers two alternatives to the `String` class: the `StringBuilder` and `StringBuffer` classes.

The `StringBuilder` and `StringBuffer` classes are mirror images. Both have the same methods and perform the same string manipulations. The only difference is that whereas the `StringBuffer` class is safe to use in applications that work with multiple threads, `StringBuilder` is not safe for threaded applications but is more efficient than `StringBuffer`. As a result, you should use the `StringBuilder` class unless your application uses threads. (Find out how to work with threads in Book V, Chapter 1.)

Note: The `StringBuilder` class was introduced in Java version 1.5. If you're using an older Java compiler, you have to use `StringBuffer` instead.

Creating a StringBuilder object

You can't assign string literals directly to a `StringBuilder` object, as you can with a `String` object. The `StringBuilder` class, however, has a constructor that accepts a `String` as a parameter. So to create a `StringBuilder` object, you use a statement such as this:

```
StringBuilder sb = new StringBuilder("Today is the day!");
```

Internally, a `StringBuilder` object maintains a fixed area of memory where it stores a string value. This area of memory is called the *buffer*. The string held in this buffer doesn't have to use the entire buffer. As a result, a `StringBuilder` object has both a length and a capacity. The *length* represents the current length of the string maintained by the `StringBuilder`, and the *capacity* represents the size of the buffer itself. Note that the length can't exceed the capacity.

When you create a `StringBuilder` object, initially the capacity is set to the length of the string plus 16. The `StringBuilder` class automatically increases its capacity whenever necessary, so you don't have to worry about exceeding the capacity.

Using StringBuilder methods

Table 1-2 lists the most useful methods of the `StringBuilder` class. Note that the `StringBuffer` class uses the same methods. If you have to use `StringBuffer` instead of `StringBuilder`, just change the class name and use the same methods.

Table 1-2	**StringBuilder Methods**
Method	*Description*
append(*primitiveType*)	Appends the string representation of the primitive type to the end of the string.
append(Object)	Calls the object's toString method and appends the result to the end of the string.
append(CharSequence)	Appends the string to the end of the StringBuilder's string value. The parameter can be a String, StringBuilder, or StringBuffer.
char charAt(int)	Returns the character at the specified position in the string.
delete(int, int)	Deletes characters starting with the first int and ending with the character before the second int.
deleteCharAt(int)	Deletes the character at the specified position.
ensureCapacity(int)	Ensures that the capacity of String-Builder is at least equal to the int value; increases the capacity if necessary.
int capacity()	Returns the capacity of this StringBuilder.
int indexOf(String)	Returns the index of the first occurrence of the specified string. If the string doesn't appear, returns -1.
int indexOf(String, int)	Returns the index of the first occurrence of the specified string, starting the search at the specified index position. If the string doesn't appear, returns -1.
insert(int, *primitiveType*)	Inserts the string representation of the primitive type at the point specified by the int argument.
insert(int, Object)	Calls the toString method of the Object parameter and then inserts the resulting string at the point specified by the int argument.

Method	Description
`insert(int, CharSequence)`	Inserts the string at the point specified by the `int` argument. The second parameter can be a `String`, `StringBuilder`, or `StringBuffer`.
`int lastIndexOf(String)`	Returns the index of the last occurrence of the specified string. If the string doesn't appear, returns `-1`.
`int lastIndexOf(String, int)`	Returns the index of the last occurrence of the specified string, starting the search at the specified index position. If the string doesn't appear, returns `-1`.
`int length()`	Returns the length of this string.
`replace(int, int, String)`	Replaces the substring indicated by the first two parameters with the string provided by the third parameter.
`reverse()`	Reverses the order of characters.
`setCharAt(int, char)`	Sets the character at the specified position to the specified character.
`setLength(int)`	Sets the length of the string. If that length is less than the current length, the string is truncated; if it's greater than the current length, new characters — hexadecimal zeros — are added.
`String substring(int)`	Extracts a substring, beginning at the position indicated by the `int` parameter and continuing to the end of the string.
`String substring(int, int)`	Extracts a substring, beginning at the position indicated by the first parameter and ending at the position one character before the value of the second parameter.
`String toString()`	Returns the current value as a `String`.
`String trimToSize()`	Reduces the capacity of the `StringBuffer` to match the size of the string.

Viewing a StringBuilder example

To illustrate how the `StringBuilder` class works, here's a `StringBuilder` version of the `MarkVowels` program from earlier in this chapter:

```java
import java.util.Scanner;

public class StringBuilderApp
{
    static Scanner sc = new Scanner(System.in);

    public static void main(String[] args)
    {
        System.out.print("Enter a string: ");
        String s = sc.nextLine();

        StringBuilder sb = new StringBuilder(s);

        int vowelCount = 0;

        for (int i = 0; i < s.length(); i++)
        {
            char c = s.charAt(i);
            if (    (c == 'A') || (c == 'a')
                || (c == 'E') || (c == 'e')
                || (c == 'I') || (c == 'i')
                || (c == 'O') || (c == 'o')
                || (c == 'U') || (c == 'u') )
            {
                sb.setCharAt(i, "*");
            }
        }
        System.out.println();
        System.out.println(s);
        System.out.println(sb.toString());
    }
}
```

This program uses the `setCharAt` method to directly replace any vowels it finds with asterisks. That's much more efficient than concatenating substrings (which is the way the `String` version of this program worked).

Using the CharSequence Interface

The Java API includes a useful interface called `CharSequence`. All three of the classes discussed in this chapter — `String`, `StringBuilder`, and `StringBuffer` — implement this interface. This method exists primarily to let you use `String`, `StringBuilder`, and `StringBuffer` interchangeably.

Toward that end, several of the methods of the `String`, `StringBuilder`, and `StringBuffer` classes use `CharSequence` as a parameter type. For those methods, you can pass a `String`, `StringBuilder`, or `StringBuffer` object. Note that a string literal is treated as a `String` object, so you can use a string literal anywhere a `CharSequence` is called for.

In case you're interested, the `CharSequence` interface defines four methods:

✦ `char charAt(int)`: Returns the character at the specified position.

✦ `int length()`: Returns the length of the sequence.

✦ `subSequence(int start, int end)`: Returns the substring indicated by the start and end parameters.

✦ `toString()`: Returns a `String` representation of the sequence.

If you're inclined to use `CharSequence` as a parameter type for a method so that the method works with a `String`, `StringBuilder`, or `StringBuffer` object, be advised that you can use only these four methods.

Chapter 2: Using Arrays

In This Chapter

✔ Working with basic one-dimensional arrays

✔ Using array initializers to set the initial values of an array

✔ Using for loops with arrays

✔ Working with two-dimensional arrays

✔ Working with the Arrays class

I could use a raise. . . .

Oh, *arrays*. Sorry.

Arrays are an important aspect of any programming language, and Java is no exception. In this chapter, you discover just about everything you need to know about using arrays. I cover run-of-the-mill one-dimensional arrays; multidimensional arrays; and two classes that are used to work with arrays, named Array and Arrays.

Understanding Arrays

An *array* is a set of variables that is referenced by using a single variable name combined with an index number. Each item of an array is called an *element*. All the elements in an array must be of the same type. Thus the array itself has a type that specifies what kind of elements it can contain. An int array can contain int values, for example, and a String array can contain strings.

The index number is written after the variable name and enclosed in brackets. So if the variable name is x, you could access a specific element with an expression like x[5].

You might think that x[5] would refer to the fifth element in the array. But index numbers start with zero for the first element, so x[5] actually refers to the sixth element. This little detail is one of the chief causes of problems when working with arrays — especially if you cut your array-programming teeth in a language in which arrays are indexed from one instead of from zero. So, in Java, get used to counting from zero instead of from one.

The real power of arrays comes from the simple fact that you can use a variable or even a complete expression as an array index. So (for example) instead of coding x[5] to refer to a specific array element, you can code x[i] to refer to the element indicated by the index variable i. You see plenty of examples of index variables throughout this chapter.

Here are a few additional tidbits of array information to ponder before you get into the details of creating and using arrays:

✦ An array is itself an object. You can refer to the array object as a whole, rather than to a specific element of the array, by using the array's variable name without an index. Thus, if x[5] refers to an element of an array, x refers to the array itself.

✦ An array has a fixed length that's set when the array is created. This length determines the number of elements that can be stored in the array. The maximum index value you can use with any array is one less than the array's length. Thus, if you create an array of 10 elements, you can use index values from 0 to 9.

✦ You can't change the length of an array after you create the array.

✦ You can access the length of an array by using the length field of the array variable. x.length, for example, returns the length of the array x.

Creating Arrays

Before you can create an array, you must declare a variable that refers to the array. This *variable declaration* should indicate the type of elements that are stored by the array followed by a set of empty brackets, like this:

```
String[] names;
```

Here a variable named names is declared. Its type is an array of String objects.

Just to make sure that you're confused as much as possible, Java also lets you put the brackets on the variable name rather than on the type. The following two statements both create arrays of int elements:

```
int[] array1;    // an array of int elements
int array2[];    // another array of int elements
```

Both of these statements have exactly the same effect. Most Java programmers prefer to put the brackets on the type rather than on the variable name.

By itself, that statement doesn't create an array; it merely declares a variable that can refer to an array. You can actually create the array in two ways:

✦ Use the `new` keyword followed by the array type, this time with the brackets filled in to indicate how many elements the array can hold. For example:

```
String[] names;
names = new String[10];
```

Here, an array of `String` objects that can hold 10 strings is created. Each of the strings in this array is initialized to an empty string.

✦ As with any other variable, you can combine the declaration and the creation into one statement:

```
String[] names = new String[10];
```

Here the array variable is declared and an array is created in one statement.

TIP

If you don't know how many elements the array needs at compile time, you can use a variable or an expression for the array length. Here's a routine from a method that stores player names in an array of strings. It starts by asking the user how many players are on the team. Then it creates an array of the correct size:

```
System.out.print("How many players? ");
int count = sc.nextInt();            // sc is a Scanner
String[] players = new String[count];
```

Initializing an Array

One way to initialize the values in an array is to simply assign them one by one:

```
String[] days = new Array[7];
Days[0] = "Sunday";
Days[1] = "Monday";
Days[2] = "Tuesday";
Days[3] = "Wednesday";
Days[4] = "Thursday";
Days[5] = "Friday";
Days[6] = "Saturday";
```

Java has a shorthand way to create an array and initialize it with constant values:

```
String[] days = { "Sunday", "Monday", "Tuesday",
                  "Wednesday", "Thursday",
                  "Friday", "Saturday" };
```

**Book IV
Chapter 2**

Using Arrays

Here each element to be assigned to the array is listed in an *array initializer*. Here's an example of an array initializer for an int array:

```
int[] primes = { 2, 3, 5, 7, 11, 13, 17 };
```

Note: The length of an array created with an initializer is determined by the number of values listed in the initializer.

An alternative way to code an initializer is this:

```
int[] primes = new int[] { 2, 3, 5, 7, 11, 13, 17 };
```

To use this type of initializer, you use the new keyword followed by the array type and a set of empty brackets. Then you code the initializer.

Using for Loops with Arrays

One of the most common ways to process an array is with a for loop. In fact, for loops were invented specifically to deal with arrays. Here's a for loop that creates an array of 100 random numbers, with values ranging from 1 to 100:

```
int[] numbers = new int[100];
for (int i = 0; i < 100; i++)
    numbers[i] = (int)(Math.random() * 100) + 1;
```

And here's a loop that fills an array of player names with strings entered by the user:

```
String[] players = new String[count];
for (int i = 0; i < count; i++)
{
    System.out.print("Enter player name: ");
    players[i] = sc.nextLine();      // sc is a Scanner
}
```

For this example, assume that count is an int variable that holds the number of players to enter.

You can also use a for loop to print the contents of an array. For example:

```
for (int i = 0; i < count; i++)
    System.out.println(players[i]);
```

Here the elements of a String array named players are printed to the console.

The previous example assumes that the length of the array was stored in a variable before the loop was executed. If you don't have the array length handy, you can get it from the array's length property:

```
for (int i = 0; i < players.length; i++)
    System.out.println(players[i]);
```

Solving Homework Problems with Arrays

Every once in a while, an array and a `for` loop or two can help you solve your kids' homework problems for them. I once helped my daughter solve a tough homework assignment for a seventh-grade math class. The problem was stated something like this:

> Bobo (these problems always had a character named Bobo in them) visits the local high school on a Saturday and finds that all the school's 1,000 lockers are neatly closed. So he starts at one end of the school and opens them all. Then he goes back to the start and closes every other locker (lockers 2, 4, 6, and so on). Then he goes back to the start and hits every third locker: If it's open, he closes it; if it's closed, he opens it. Then he hits every fourth locker, every fifth locker, and so on. He keeps doing this all weekend long, walking the hallways opening and closing lockers 1,000 times. Then he gets bored and goes home. How many of the school's 1,000 lockers are left open, and which ones are they?

Sheesh!

This problem presented a challenge, and being the computer-nerd father I am, I figured that this was the time to teach my daughter about `for` loops and arrays. So I wrote a little program that set up an array of 1,000 booleans. Each represented a locker: `true` meant open, and `false` meant closed. Then I wrote a pair of nested `for` loops to do the calculation.

My first attempt told me that 10,000 of the 1,000 lockers were opened, so I figured that I'd made a mistake somewhere. And while I was looking at the code, I realized that the lockers were numbered 1 to 1,000, but the elements in my array were numbered 0 to 999, and that was part of what led to the confusion that caused my first answer to be ridiculous.

So I decided to create the array with 1,001 elements and ignore the first one. That way, the indexes corresponded nicely to the locker numbers.

After a few hours of work, I came up with the program in Listing 2-1.

Listing 2-1:   The Classic Locker Problem Solved

```
public class BoboAndTheLockers
{
    public static void main(String[] args)
    {
        // true = open; false = closed
        boolean[] lockers = new boolean[1001];          →6

        // close all the lockers
        for (int i = 1; i <= 1000; i++)                 →9
            lockers[i] = false;
```

(continued)

Listing 2-1: *(continued)*

```
for (int skip = 1; skip <= 1000; skip++)          →12
{
    System.out.println("Bobo is changing every "
        + skip + " lockers.");
    for (int locker = skip; locker < 1000;        →16
            locker += skip)
        lockers[locker] = !lockers[locker];       →18
}

System.out.println("Bobo is bored"
    + " now so he's going home.");

// count and list the open lockers
String list = "";
int openCount = 0;
for (int i = 1; i <= 1000; i++)                   →27
    if (lockers[i])
    {
        openCount++;
        list += i + " ";
    }

System.out.println("Bobo left " + openCount
    + " lockers open.");
System.out.println("The open lockers are: "
    + list);
    }
}
```

Here are the highlights of how this program works:

→ 6   This line sets up an array of booleans with 1,001 elements. I created one more element than I needed so I could ignore element 0.

→ 9   This `for` loop closes all the lockers. This step isn't really necessary because booleans initialize to `false`, but being explicit about initialization is good.

→ 12   Every iteration of this loop represents one complete trip through the hallways opening and closing lockers. The `skip` variable represents how many lockers Bobo skips on each trip. First he does every locker, then every second locker, and then every third locker. So this loop simply counts from 1 to 1,000.

→ 16   Every iteration of this loop represents one stop at a locker on a trip through the hallways. This third expression in the `for` statement (on the next line) adds the `skip` variable to the `index` variable so that Bobo can access every *n*th locker on each trip through the hallways.

→ **18**   This statement uses the not operator (`!`) to reverse the setting of each locker. Thus, if the locker is open (`true`), it's set to closed (`false`), and vice versa.

→ **27**   Yet another `for` loop spins through all the lockers and counts the ones that are open. It also adds the locker number for each open locker to the end of a string so that all the open lockers can be printed.

This program produces more than 1,000 lines of output, but only the last few lines are important. Here they are:

```
Bobo is bored now so he's going home.
Bobo left 31 lockers open.
The open lockers are: 1 4 9 16 25 36 49 64 81 100 121 144 169
    196 225 256 289 324 361 400 441 484 529 576 625 676 729
    784 841 900 961
```

So there's the answer: 31 lockers are left open. I got an A. (I mean, my daughter got an A.)

By the way, did you notice that the lockers that were left open were the ones whose numbers are perfect squares? Or that 31 is the largest number whose square is less than 1,000? I didn't, either — until my daughter told me after school the next day.

Using the Enhanced for Loop

Java 1.5 introduced a new type of `for` loop called an *enhanced for loop* that's designed to simplify loops that process arrays and collections (which I cover in the next chapter). When it's used with an array, the enhanced `for` loop has this format:

```
for (type identifier : array)
{
    statements...
}
```

The *type* identifies the type of the elements in the array, and the *identifier* provides a name for a local variable that is used to access each element. *array* names the array you want to process.

Here's an example:

```
String[] days = { "Sunday", "Monday", "Tuesday",
                  "Wednesday", "Thursday",
                  "Friday", "Saturday" };
for (String day : days)
{
    System.out.println(day);
}
```

**Book IV
Chapter 2**

Using Arrays

This loop prints the following lines to the console:

```
Sunday
Monday
Tuesday
Wednesday
Thursday
Friday
Saturday
```

In other words, it prints each of the strings in the array on a separate line.

Using Arrays with Methods

You can write methods that accept arrays as parameters and return arrays as return values. You just use an empty set of brackets to indicate that the parameter type or return type is an array.

Here's a static method that creates and returns a `String` array with the names of the days of the week:

```
public static String[] getDaysOfWeek()
{
    String[] days = { "Sunday", "Monday", "Tuesday",
                      "Wednesday", "Thursday",
                      "Friday", "Saturday" };
    return days;
}
```

And here's a static method that prints the contents of any `String` array to the console, one string per line:

```
public static void printStringArray(String[] strings)
{
    for (String s : strings)
        System.out.println(s);
}
```

Finally, here are two lines of code that call these methods:

```
String[] days = getDaysOfWeek();
printStringArray(days);
```

The first statement declares a `String` array and then calls `getDaysOfWeek` to create the array. The second statement passes the array to the `printString Array` method as a parameter.

Using Two-Dimensional Arrays

The elements of an array can be any type of object you want, including another array. In the latter case, you have a *two-dimensional array,* sometimes called an *array of arrays.*

Two-dimensional arrays are often used to track data in column-and-row format, much the way that a spreadsheet works. Suppose that you're working on a program that tracks five years' worth of sales (2004 through 2008) for a company, with the data broken down for each of four sales territories (North, South, East, and West). You could create 20 separate variables, with names such as `sales2001North`, `sales2001South`, `sales2001East`, and so on. But that gets a little tedious.

Alternatively, you could create an array with 20 elements, like this:

```
double[] sales = new sales[20];
```

But then how would you organize the data in this array so that you know the year and sales region for each element?

With a two-dimensional array, you can create an array with an element for each year. Each of those elements in turn is another array with an element for each region.

Thinking of a two-dimensional array as a table or spreadsheet is common, like this:

Year	North	South	East	West
2004	23,853	22,838	36,483	31,352
2005	25,483	22,943	38,274	33,294
2006	24,872	23,049	39,002	36,888
2007	28,492	23,784	42,374	39,573
2008	31,932	23,732	42,943	41,734

Here each row of the spreadsheet represents a year of sales, and each column represents one of the four sales regions.

Creating a two-dimensional array

To declare a two-dimensional array for this sales data, you simply list two sets of empty brackets, like this:

```
double sales[][];
```

Here `sales` is a two-dimensional array of type `double`. To put it another way, `sales` is an array of `double` arrays.

To create the array, you use the new keyword and provide lengths for each set of brackets, as in this example:

```
sales = new double[5][4];
```

Here the first dimension specifies that the sales array has five elements. This array represents the rows in the table. The second dimension specifies that each of those elements has an array of type double with four elements. This array represents the columns in the table.

A key point to grasp here is that one instance is of the first array, but a separate instance of the second array for each element is in the first array. So this statement actually creates five double arrays with four elements each. Then those five arrays are used as the elements for the first array.

Note that as with a one-dimensional array, you can declare and create a two-dimensional array in one statement, like this:

```
double[][] sales = new double[5][4];
```

Here the sales array is declared and created all in one statement.

Accessing two-dimensional array elements

To access the elements of a two-dimensional array, you use two indexes. This statement sets the 2004 sales for the North region:

```
sales[0][0] = 23853.0;
```

As you might imagine, accessing the data in a two-dimensional array by hard-coding each index value can get tedious. No wonder for loops are normally used instead. The following bit of code uses a for loop to print the contents of the sales array to the console, separated by tabs. Each year is printed on a separate line, with the year at the beginning of the line. In addition, a line of headings for the sales regions is printed before the sales data. Here's the code:

```
NumberFormat cf = NumberFormat.getCurrencyInstance();
System.out.println("\tNorth\t\tSouth\t\tEast\t\tWest");
int year = 2004;
for (int y = 0; y < 5; y++)
{
    System.out.print(year + "\t");
    for (int region = 0; region < 4; region++)
    {
        System.out.print(cf.format(sales[y][region]));
        System.out.print("\t");
    }
    year++;
    System.out.println();
}
```

Assuming that the `sales` array has already been initialized, this code produces the following output on the console:

```
        North        South        East         West
2004    $23,853.00   $22,838.00   $36,483.00   $31,352.00
2005    $25,483.00   $22,943.00   $38,274.00   $33,294.00
2006    $24,872.00   $23,049.00   $39,002.00   $36,888.00
2007    $28,492.00   $23,784.00   $42,374.00   $39,573.00
2008    $31,932.00   $23,732.00   $42,943.00   $41,734.00
```

The order in which you nest the `for` loops that access each index in a two-dimensional array is crucial! The preceding example lists the sales for each year on a separate line, with the sales regions arranged in columns. You can print a listing with the sales for each region on a separate line, with the years arranged in columns, by reversing the order in which the `for` loops that index the arrays are nested:

```
for (int region = 0; region < 4; region++)
{
    for (int y = 0; y < 5; y++)
    {
        System.out.print(cf.format(sales[y][region]));
        System.out.print("    ");
    }
    System.out.println();
}
```

Here the outer loop indexes the region and the inner loop indexes the year:

```
$23,853.00    $25,483.00    $24,872.00    $28,492.00    $31,932.00
$22,838.00    $22,943.00    $23,049.00    $23,784.00    $23,732.00
$36,483.00    $38,274.00    $39,002.00    $42,374.00    $42,943.00
$31,352.00    $33,294.00    $36,888.00    $39,573.00    $41,734.00
```

Initializing a two-dimensional array

The technique for initializing arrays by coding the array element values in curly braces works for two-dimensional arrays too. You just have to remember that each element of the main array is actually another array. So you have to nest the array initializers.

Here's an example that initializes the sales array:

```
double[][] sales =
    { {23853.0, 22838.0, 36483.0, 31352.0},      // 2004
      {25483.0, 22943.0, 38274.0, 33294.0},      // 2005
      {24872.0, 23049.0, 39002.0, 36888.0},      // 2006
      {28492.0, 23784.0, 42374.0, 39573.0},      // 2007
      {31932.0, 23732.0, 42943.0, 41734.0} };    // 2008
```

Here I added a comment to the end of each line to show the year that the line initializes. Notice that the left brace for the entire initializer is at the beginning of the second line, and the right brace that closes the entire initializer is at the end of the last line. Then the initializer for each year is contained in its own set of braces.

Using jagged arrays

When you create an array with an expression such as new int [5] [3], you're specifying that each element of the main array is actually an array of type int with three elements. Java, however, lets you create two-dimensional arrays in which the length of each element of the main array is different. This is sometimes called a *jagged array* because the array doesn't form a nice rectangle. Instead, its edges are jagged.

Suppose that you need to keep track of four teams, each consisting of two or three people. The teams are as follows:

Team	Members
A	Henry Blake, Johnny Mulcahy
B	Benjamin Pierce, John McIntyre, Jonathan Tuttle
C	Margaret Houlihan, Frank Burns
D	Max Klinger, Radar O'Reilly, Igor Straminsky

The following code creates a jagged array for these teams:

```
String[] [] teams
    = { {"Henry Blake", "Johnny Mulcahy"},
        {"Benjamin Pierce", "John McIntyre",
            "Jonathan Tuttle"},
        {"Margaret Houlihan", "Frank Burns"},
        {"Max Klinger", "Radar O'Reilly",
            "Igor Straminsky"} };
```

Here each nested array initializer indicates the number of strings for each subarray. The first subarray has two strings, the second has three strings, and so on.

You can use nested for loops to access the individual elements in a jagged array. For each element of the main array, you can use the length property to determine how many entries are in that element's subarray. For example:

```
for (int i = 0; i < teams.length; i++)
{
    for (int j = 0; j < teams[i].length; j++)
        System.out.println(teams[i][j]);
    System.out.println();
}
```

Notice that the length of each subarray is determined with the expression `teams[i].length`. This `for` loop prints one name on each line, with a blank line between teams, like this:

```
Margaret Houlihan
Frank Burns

Max Klinger
Radar O'Reilly
Igor Straminsky

Henry Blake
Johnny Mulcahy

Benjamin Pierce
John McIntyre
Jonathan Tuttle
```

If you don't want to fuss with keeping track of the indexes yourself, you can use an enhanced `for` loop and let Java take care of the indexes. For example:

```
for (String[] team : teams)
{
    for (String player : team)
        System.out.println(player);
    System.out.println();
}
```

Here the first enhanced `for` statement specifies that the type for the `team` variable is `String[]`. As a result, each cycle of this loop sets `team` to one of the subarrays in the main `teams` array. Then the second enhanced `for` loop accesses the individual strings in each subarray.

Going beyond two dimensions

Java doesn't limit you to two-dimensional arrays. Arrays can be nested within arrays, to as many levels as your program needs. To declare an array with more than two dimensions, you just specify as many sets of empty brackets as you need. For example:

```
int[][][] threeD = new int[3][3][3];
```

Here a three-dimensional array is created, with each dimension having three elements. You can think of this array as a cube. Each element requires three indexes to access.

You can access an element in a multidimensional array by specifying as many indexes as the array needs. For example:

```
threeD[0][1][2] = 100;
```

This statement sets element 2 in column 1 of row 0 to `100`.

You can nest initializers as deep as necessary, too. For example:

```
int [] [] [] threeD =
     {  {  {1,    2,   3},  { 4,   5,   6},  { 7,   8,   9} },
        {  {10, 11, 12},  {13, 14, 15},  {16, 17, 18} },
        {  {19, 20, 21},  {22, 23, 24},  {25, 26, 27} } };
```

Here a three-dimensional array is initialized with the numbers 1 through 27.

You can also use multiple nested if statements to process an array with three or more dimensions. Here's another way to initialize a three-dimensional array with the numbers 1 to 27:

```
int [] [] [] threeD2 = new int [3] [3] [3];
int value = 1;
for (int i = 0; i < 3; i++)
    for (int j = 0; j < 3; j++)
        for (int k = 0; k < 3; k++)
            threeD2 [i] [j] [k] = value++;
```

Working with a Fun but Complicated Example: A Chessboard

Okay, so much for the business examples. Here's an example that's more fun — assuming you think chess is fun. The program in Listing 2-2 uses a two-dimensional array to represent a chessboard. Its sole purpose is to figure out the possible moves for a knight (that's the horsey, for the non-chess players among us), given its starting position. The user is asked to enter a starting position (such as f1), and the program responds by displaying the possible squares. Then the program prints out a crude-but-recognizable representation of the board, with the knight's position indicated with an X and each possible move indicated with a question mark (?).

In case you're not familiar with chess, it's played on a board that's 8 by 8 squares, with alternating light and dark squares. The normal way to identify each square is to use a letter and a number, where the letter represents the column (called a *file*) and the number represents the row (called a *rank*), as shown in Figure 2-1. The knight has an interesting movement pattern: He moves two squares in one direction and then makes a 90-degree turn and moves one square to the left or right. The possible moves for the knight, given a starting position of e4, are shaded dark. As you can see, this knight has eight possible moves: c3, c5, d6, f6, g5, g3, f2, and d2.

a8	b8	c8	d8	e8	f8	g8	h8
a7	b7	c7	d7	e7	f7	g7	h7
a6	b6	c6	d6	e6	f6	g6	h6
a5	b5	c5	d5	e5	f5	g5	h5
a4	b4	c4	d4	♘	f4	g4	h4
a3	b3	c3	d3	e3	f3	g3	h3
a2	b2	c2	d2	e2	f2	g2	h2
a1	b1	c1	d1	e1	f1	g1	h1

Figure 2-1:
A classic
chessboard.

Here's a sample of what the console looks like if you enter e4 for the knight's position:

```
Welcome to the Knight Move calculator.

Enter knight's position: e4

The knight is at square e4
From here the knight can move to:
c5
d6
f6
g5
g3
f2
d2
c3
 -  -  -  -  -  -  -  -
 -  -  -  -  -  -  -  -
 -  -  -  ?  -  ?  -  -
 -  -  ?  -  -  -  ?  -
 -  -  -  -  X  -  -  -
 -  -  ?  -  -  -  ?  -
 -  -  -  ?  -  ?  -  -
 -  -  -  -  -  -  -  -
Do it again? (Y or N) n
```

As you can see, the program indicates that the knight's legal moves from e4 are c5, d6, f6, g5, g3, f2, d2, and c3. Also, the graphic representation of the board indicates where the knight is and where he can go.

Listing 2-2: Playing Chess in a *For Dummies* Book

```java
import java.util.Scanner;

public class KnightMoves
{

    static Scanner sc = new Scanner(System.in);

    // the following static array represents the 8
    // possible moves a knight can make
    // this is an 8 x 2 array
    static int[][] moves = { {-2, +1},                            →10
                             {-1, +2},
                             {+1, +2},
                             {+2, +1},
                             {+2, -1},
                             {+1, -2},
                             {-1, -2},
                             {-2, -1} };

    public static void main(String[] args)
    {
        System.out.println("Welcome to the "
            + "Knight Move calculator.\n");
        do
        {
            showKnightMoves();                                   →26
        }
        while (getYorN("Do it again?"));
    }

    public static void showKnightMoves()                        →31
    {
        // The first dimension is the file (a, b, c, etc.)
        // The second dimension is the rank (1, 2, 3, etc.)
        // Thus, board[3][4] is square d5.
        // A value of 0 means the square is empty
        // 1 means the knight is in the square
        // 2 means the knight could move to the square
        int[][] board = new int[8][8];                          →39

        String kSquare; // the knight's position as a square
        Pos kPos;       // the knight's position as a Pos

        // get the knight's initial position
        do                                                      →45
        {
            System.out.print("Enter knight's position: ");
            kSquare = sc.nextLine();
            kPos = convertSquareToPos(kSquare);
        } while (kPos == null);

        board[kPos.x][kPos.y] = 1;                              →52
        System.out.println("\nThe knight is at square "
            + convertPosToSquare(kPos));
        System.out.println(
            "From here the knight can move to:");
```

```
        for (int move = 0; move < moves.length; move ++)        →59
        {
            int x, y;
            x = moves[move][0];   // the x for this move
            y = moves[move][1];   // the y for this move
            Pos p = calculateNewPos(kPos, x, y);
            if (p != null)
            {
                System.out.println(convertPosToSquare(p));
                board[p.x][p.y] = 2;
            }
        }

        printBoard(board);                                       →72

    }

    // this method converts squares such as a1 or d5 to
    // x, y coordinates such as [0][0] or [3][4]              →78
    public static Pos convertSquareToPos(String square)
    {
        int x = -1;
        int y = -1;
        char rank, file;

        file = square.charAt(0);
        if (file == 'a') x = 0;
        if (file == 'b') x = 1;
        if (file == 'c') x = 2;
        if (file == 'd') x = 3;
        if (file == 'e') x = 4;
        if (file == 'f') x = 5;
        if (file == 'g') x = 6;
        if (file == 'h') x = 7;

        rank = square.charAt(1);
        if (rank == '1') y = 0;
        if (rank == '2') y = 1;
        if (rank == '3') y = 2;
        if (rank == '4') y = 3;
        if (rank == '5') y = 4;
        if (rank == '6') y = 5;
        if (rank == '7') y = 6;
        if (rank == '8') y = 7;

        if (x == -1 || y == -1)
        {
            return null;
        }
        else
            return new Pos(x, y);
    }

    // this method converts x, y coordinates such as
    // [0][0] or [3][4] to squares such as a1 or d5.        →114
    public static String convertPosToSquare(Pos p)
    {
        String file = "";

        if (p.x == 0) file = "a";
        if (p.x == 1) file = "b";
        if (p.x == 2) file = "c";
```

Book IV
Chapter 2

Using Arrays

(continued)

Listing 2-2 *(continued)*

```java
        if (p.x == 3) file = "d";
        if (p.x == 4) file = "e";
        if (p.x == 5) file = "f";
        if (p.x == 6) file = "g";
        if (p.x == 7) file = "h";

        return file + (p.y + 1);
    }

    // this method calculates a new Pos given a

    // starting Pos, an x move, and a y move
    // it returns null if the resulting move would
    // be off the board.
    public static Pos calculateNewPos(Pos p, int x, int y)      →134
    {
        // rule out legal moves
        if (p.x + x < 0)
            return null;
        if (p.x + x > 7)
            return null;
        if (p.y + y < 0)
            return null;
        if (p.y + y > 7)
            return null;

        // return new position
        return new Pos(p.x + x, p.y + y);
    }

    public static void printBoard(int[][] b)                     →150
    {
        for (int y = 7; y >= 0; y--)
        {
            for (int x = 0; x < 8; x++)
            {
                if (b[x][y] == 1)
                    System.out.print(" X ");
                else if (b[x][y] == 2)
                    System.out.print(" ? ");
                else
                    System.out.print(" - ");
            }
            System.out.println();
        }
    }

    public static boolean getYorN(String prompt)                 →167
    {
        while (true)
        {
            String answer;
            System.out.print("\n" + prompt + " (Y or N) ");
            answer = sc.nextLine();
            if (answer.equalsIgnoreCase("Y"))
                return true;
            else if (answer.equalsIgnoreCase("N"))
                return false;
        }
    }
}
```

```
// this class represents x, y coordinates on the board
class Pos                                                        →183
{
    public int x;
    public int y;

    public Pos(int x, int y)
    {
        this.x = x;
        this.y = y;
    }
}
```

You have to put your thinking cap on to make your way through this program, which is a bit on the complicated side. The following paragraphs can help clear up the more complicated lines:

→ 10   This line declares a two-dimensional array that's used to store the possible moves for a knight in terms of x and y. The knight's move of two squares left and one square up, for example, is represented as {–2, 1}. There are a total of eight possible moves, and each move has two values (x and y). So this two-dimensional array has eight rows and two columns.

→ 26   The code that gets the user's starting position for the knight and does all the calculations is complicated enough that I didn't want to include it in the main method, so I put it in a separate method named showNightMoves. That way, the do loop in the main method is kept simple. It just keeps going until the user enters N when getYorN is called.

→ 31   The showNightMoves method begins here.

→ 39   The board array represents the chessboard as a two-dimensional array with eight rows for the ranks and eight columns for the files. This array holds int values. A value of 0 indicates that the square is empty. The square where the knight resides gets a 1, and any square that the knight can move to gets a 2.

→ 45   This do loop prompts the user for a valid square to plant the knight in. The loop includes a call to the method convertSquareToPos, which converts the user's entry (such as e4) to a Pos object. (The Pos class is defined later in the program; it represents a board position as an x, y pair.) This method returns null if the user enters an incorrect square, such as a9 or x4. So to get the user to enter a valid square, the loop just repeats if the converSquareToPos returns null.

→ 52   The board position entered by the user is set to 1 to indicate the position of the knight.

→ 59   A for loop is used to test all the possible moves for the knight to see whether they're valid from the knight's current position, using the moves array that was created way back in line 10. In the body of this loop, the calculateNewPos method is called. This

**Book IV
Chapter 2**

Using Arrays

method accepts a board position and x and y values to indicate where the knight can be moved. If the resulting move is legal, it returns a new `Pos` object that indicates the position the move leads to. If the move is not legal (that is, it takes the knight off the board), the `calculateNewPos` method returns null.

Assuming that `calculateNewPos` returns a non-null value, the body of this loop prints the square (it calls `convertPosTosquare` to convert the `Pos` object to a string, such as c3). Then it marks the board position represented by the move with 2 to indicate that the knight can move to this square.

→ 72   After all the moves are calculated, the `printBoard` method is called to print the board array.

→ 78   This is the `convertSquareToPos` method. It uses a pair of brute-force if statements to convert a string such as a1 or e4 to a `Pos` object representing the same position. I probably could have made this method a little more elegant by converting the first letter in the string to a `Char` and then subtracting the offset of the letter a to convert the value to a proper integer. But I think the brute-force method is clearer, and it requires only a few more lines of code.

Note that if the user enters an incorrect square (such as a9 or x2), null is returned.

→ 114   This is the `convertPosToSquare` method, which does the opposite of the `convertSquareToPos` method. It accepts a `Pos` argument and returns a string that corresponds to the position. It uses a series of brute-force if statements to determine the letter that corresponds to the file but does a simple addition to calculate the rank. (The `Pos` object's y member is an array for the y position. Array indexes are numbered starting with 0, but chess rank numbers start with 1. That's why 1 is added to the y position to get the rank number.)

→ 134   The `calculateNewPos` method accepts a starting position, an x offset, and a y offset. It returns a new position if the move is legal; otherwise it returns null. To find illegal moves, it adds the x and y offsets to the starting x and y position and checks to see whether the result is less than 0 or greater than 7. If the move is legal, it creates a new `Pos` object whose position is calculated by adding the x and y offsets to the x and y values of the starting position.

→ 150   The `printBoard` method uses a nested for loop to print the board. The outer loop prints each rank. Notice that it indexes the array backward, starting with 7 and going down to 0. That's necessary so that the first rank is printed at the bottom of the console output. An inner for loop is used to print the squares for each rank. In this loop, an if statement checks the value of the board array element that corresponds to the square to determine whether it prints an X, a question mark, or a hyphen.

→ 167　The `getYorN` method simply displays a prompt on-screen and asks the user to enter `Y` or `N`. It returns `true` if the user enters `Y` or `false` if the user enters `N`. If the user enters anything else, this method prompts the user again.

→ 183　The `Pos` class simply defines two public fields, `x` and `y`, to keep track of board positions. It also defines a constructor that accepts the `x` and `y` positions as parameters.

Using the Arrays Class

The final topic for this chapter is the `Arrays` class, which provides a collection of `static` methods that are useful for working with arrays. The `Arrays` class is in the `java.util` package, so you have to use an `import` statement for the `java.util.Arrays` class or the entire `java.util.*` package to use this class. Table 2-1 lists the most commonly used methods of the `Arrays` class.

Table 2-1	Handy Methods of the Arrays Class
Method	*Description*
`static int binarySearch(array, key)`	Searches for the specified key value in an array. The return value is the index of the element that matches the key. The method returns -1 if the key couldn't be found. The array and the key must be of the same type and can be any primitive type or an object.
`static array copyOf(arrayOriginal, newLength)`	Returns an array that's a copy of `arrayOriginal`. The `newLength` parameter need not equal the original array's length. If `newLength` is larger, the method pads the new array with zeros. If `newLength` is smaller, the method doesn't copy all of the original array's values.
`static array copyOfRange(arrayOriginal, from, to)`	Does basically what the `copyOf` method does, but copies only a selected slice of values (from one index to another) of the original array.
`boolean deepEquals(array1, array2)`	Returns `true` if the two arrays have the same element values. This method works for arrays of two or more dimensions.

(continued)

Book IV
Chapter 2

Using Arrays

Table 2-1 *(continued)*

Method	Description
boolean equals(*array1,* *array2*)	Returns true if the two arrays have the same element values. This method checks equality only for one-dimensional arrays.
static void fill(*array,* *value*)	Fills the array with the specified value. The value and array must be of the same type and can be any primitive type or an object.
static void fill(*array,* *from, to, value*)	Fills the elements indicated by the *from* and *to* int parameters with the specified value. The value and array must be of the same type and can be any primitive type or an object.
static void sort(*array*)	Sorts the array in ascending sequence.
static void sort(*array,* *from, to*)	Sorts the specified elements of the array in ascending sequence.
static String toString(*array*)	Formats the array values in a string. Each element value is enclosed in brackets, and the element values are separated with commas.

Filling an array

The fill method can be handy if you want to prefill an array with values other than the default values for the array type. Here's a routine that creates an array of integers and initializes each element to 100:

```
int[] startValues = new int[10];
Arrays.fill(startValues, 100);
```

Although you can code a complicated expression as the second parameter, the fill method evaluates this expression only once. Then it assigns the result of this expression to each element in the array.

You might think that you could fill an array of 1,000 integers with random numbers from 1 to 100, like this:

```
int[] ran = new int[1000]
Arrays.fill(ran, (int)(Math.random() * 100) + 1);
```

Unfortunately, this code won't work. What happens is that the expression is evaluated once to get a random number; then all 1,000 elements in the array are set to that random number.

Copying an array

In Java 1.6, the `Arrays` class has some useful new methods. Using the new `copyOf` and `copyOfRange` methods, you can copy a bunch of elements from an existing array into a brand-new array. If you start with something named `arrayOriginal`, for example, you can copy the `arrayOriginal` elements to something named `arrayNew`, as shown in Listing 2-3.

Listing 2-3:   The Copycat

```java
import java.util.Arrays;

class CopyDemo
{
    public static void main(String args[])
    {
        int arrayOriginal[] = {42, 55, 21};
        int arrayNew[] =
            Arrays.copyOf(arrayOriginal, 3);          →9
        printIntArray(arrayNew);
    }

    static void printIntArray(int arrayNew[])
    {
        for (int i : arrayNew)
        {
            System.out.print(i);
            System.out.print(' ');
        }
        System.out.println();
    }
}
```

The output of the `CopyDemo` program looks like this:

```
42 55 21
```

→ **9**   This is the line where you can change the number 3 to something smaller.

You can do the following, for example:

```java
int arrayNew[] = Arrays.copyOf(arrayOriginal, 2);
```

If you do, `arrayNew` has fewer than three elements:

```
42 55
```

You can also change the number 3 to something larger:

```
int arrayNew[] = Arrays.copyOf(arrayOriginal, 8);
```

Then `arrayNew` has more than three elements:

```
42 55 21 0 0 0 0 0
```

The `copyOfRange` method is even more versatile. If you execute the instructions

```
int arrayOriginal[] = {42, 55, 21, 16, 100, 88};
int arrayNew[] = Arrays.copyOfRange(arrayOriginal, 2, 5);
```

the values in `arrayNew` are

```
21 16 100
```

Sorting an array

The `sort` method is a quick way to sort an array in sequence. These statements create an array with 100 random numbers and then sort the array in sequence so that the random numbers are in order:

```
int[] lotto = new int[6];
for (int i = 0; i < 6; i++)
    lotto[i] = (int)(Math.random() * 100) + 1;
Arrays.sort(lotto);
```

Searching an array

The `binarySearch` method is an efficient way to locate an item in an array by its value. Suppose you want to find out whether your lucky number is in the `lotto` array created in the preceding example. You could just use a `for` loop, like this:

```
int lucky = 13x;
int foundAt = -1;
for (int i = 0; i < lotto.length; i++)
    if (lotto[i] == lucky)
        foundAt = i;
if (foundAt > -1)
    System.out.println("My number came up!");
else
    System.out.println("I'm not lucky today.");
```

Here the `for` loop compares each element in the array with your lucky number. This code works fine for small arrays, but what if the array had 1,000,000 elements instead of 6? In that case, it would take a while to look at each element. If the array is sorted in sequence, the `binarySearch` method can find your lucky number more efficiently and with less code:

```
int lucky = 13;
int foundAt = Arrays.binarySearch(lotto, lucky);
if (foundAt > -1)
    System.out.println("My number came up!");
else
    System.out.println("I'm not lucky today.");
```

The `binarySearch` method uses a technique similar to the strategy for guessing a number. If I say that I'm thinking of a number between 1 and 100, you don't start guessing the numbers in sequence starting with 1. Instead, you guess 50. If I tell you that 50 is low, you guess 75. Then if I tell you 75 is high, you guess halfway between 50 and 75, and so on until you find the number. The `binarySearch` method uses a similar technique, but it works only if the array is sorted first.

Comparing arrays

If you use the equality operator (==) to compare array variables, the array variables are considered to be equal only if both variables point to exactly the same array instance. To compare two arrays element by element, you should use the `Arrays.equal` method instead. For example:

```
if (Arrays.equal(array1, array2))
    System.out.println("The arrays are equal!");
```

Here the arrays `array1` and `array2` are compared element by element. If both arrays have the same number of elements, and all elements have the same value, the `equals` method returns `true`. If the elements are not equal, or if one array has more elements than the other, the `equals` method returns `false`.

If the array has more than one dimension, you can use the `deepEquals` method instead. It compares any two subarrays, element by element, to determine whether they're identical.

Converting arrays to strings

The `toString` method of the `Arrays` class is handy if you want to quickly dump the contents of an array to the console to see what it contains. This method returns a string that shows the array's elements enclosed in brackets, with the elements separated by commas.

Here's a routine that creates an array, fills it with random numbers, and then uses the `toString` method to print the array elements:

```
int[] lotto = new int[6];
for (int i = 0; i < 6; i++)
    lotto[i] = (int)(Math.random() * 100) + 1;
System.out.println(Arrays.toString(lotto));
```

Here's a sample of the console output created by this code:

```
[4, 90, 65, 84, 99, 81]
```

Note that the toString method works only for one-dimensional arrays. To print the contents of a two-dimensional array with the toString method, use a for loop to call the toString method for each subarray.

Chapter 3: Using the ArrayList Class

In This Chapter

✔ **Working with the ArrayList class**

✔ **Creating an array list**

✔ **Introducing generics**

✔ **Adding elements to an array list**

✔ **Deleting elements from or modifying elements in an array list**

Some people love to collect things: nick-knacks, baseball cards, postage stamps, dolls — you name it, someone collects it.

If I were a collector of some random thing — say, old tin advertising signs — an array would be a poor choice for storing the data. That's because on any given day, I may find another tin sign at a yard sale. So if I had 87 tin signs before, and I had created an array big enough to hold all 87 signs, I'd have to change the array declaration to hold 88 signs.

Java's *collection classes* are designed to simplify the programming for applications that have to keep track of groups of objects. These classes are very powerful and surprisingly easy to use — at least the basics, anyway. The more advanced features of collection classes take some serious programming to get right, but for most applications, a few simple methods are all you need to use collection classes.

Unfortunately, Java's collection classes are organized according to a pretty complicated inheritance hierarchy that can be very confusing for beginners. Most of the Java books I have on my shelf start by explaining this inheritance scheme and showing how each of the various collection classes fits into this scheme, and why.

I'm not going to do that. I think it's very confusing for newcomers to collections to have to wade through a class hierarchy that doesn't make sense until they know some of the details of how the basic classes work. Instead, I just show you how to use two of the best of these classes.

In this chapter, you find out how to use the `ArrayList` class. Then, in the next chapter, you find out how to use its first cousin, the `LinkedList`. When you know how to use these two classes, you shouldn't have any trouble figuring out how to use the other collection classes from the API documentation.

Java 1.5 introduced a major new language feature called *generics* that is aimed specifically at making collections easier to work with. Specifically, the generics feature lets you create list objects, such as `ArrayList` or `LinkedList`, that are bound to a specific data type, such as strings or integers.

Because generics are an integral part of how collections work in Java 1.5 and subsequent versions, I incorporate the generics feature into this chapter from the very start. I point out the differences for using `ArrayList` without generics along the way, just in case you're using an older version of Java or are working with programs that were written before Java 1.5 became available. (For a complete explanation of how the generics feature works, you can move ahead to Book IV, Chapter 5.)

I have even more good news about new features: the major new feature of Java 8, *lambda expressions,* introduces an entirely new way of working with collections that is especially useful for efficiently dealing with collections that have a large number of items. For more information about working with these new collection features, see Chapter 6 of this minibook. And for more information about lambda expressions, see Book III, Chapter 7.

Understanding the ArrayList Class

An *array list* is the most basic type of Java collection. You can think of an array list as being an array on steroids. It's similar to an array but averts many of the most common problems of working with arrays, specifically the following:

+ **An array list automatically resizes itself whenever necessary.** If you create an array with 100 elements, and then fill it up and need to add a 101st element, you're out of luck. The best you can do is create a new array with 101 elements, copy the 100 elements from the old array to the new one, and then put the new data in the 101st element. With an array list, there's never a limit to how many elements you can create. You can keep adding elements as long as you want.

+ **An array list lets you insert elements into the middle of the collection.** With an array, inserting elements is pretty hard to do. Suppose that you have an array that can hold 100 elements, but only the first 50 have data. If you need to insert a new element after the 25th item, you first must make a copy of elements 26 through 50 to make room for the new element. With an array list, you just tell the array list you want to insert the new element after the 25th item; the array list takes care of shuffling things around.

+ **An array list lets you delete items.** If you delete an item from an array, the deleted element becomes null, but the empty slot that was occupied by the item stays in the array. When you delete an item from an array list, any subsequent items in the array are automatically moved forward one position to fill the spot that was occupied by the deleted item.

✦ **The `ArrayList` class actually uses an array internally to store the data you add to the array list.** The `ArrayList` class takes care of managing the size of this array. When you add an item to the array list, and the underlying array is full, the `ArrayList` class automatically creates a new array with a larger capacity and copies the existing items to the new array before it adds the new item.

The `ArrayList` class has several constructors and a ton of methods. For your reference, Table 3-1 lists the constructors and methods of the `ArrayList` class.

Table 3-1	The ArrayList Class
Constructor	*Explanation*
`ArrayList()`	Creates an array list with an initial capacity of 10 elements.
`ArrayList(int capacity)`	Creates an array list with the specified initial capacity.
`ArrayList(Collection c)`	Creates an array list and copies all the elements from the specified collection into the new array list.
Method	*Explanation*
`add(Object element)`	Adds the specified object to the array list. If you specified a type when you created the array list, the object must be of the correct type.
`add(int index, Object element)`	Adds the specified object to the array list at the specified index position. If you specified a type when you created the array list, the object must be of the correct type.
`addAll(Collection c)`	Adds all the elements of the specified collection to this array list.
`addAll(int index, Collection c)`	Adds all the elements of the specified collection to this array list at the specified index position.
`clear()`	Deletes all elements from the array list.
`clone()`	Returns a shallow copy of the array list. The elements contained in the copy are the same object instances as the elements in the original.
`contains(Object elem)`	Returns a `boolean` that indicates whether the specified object is in the array list.

**Book IV
Chapter 3**

Using the ArrayList Class

(continued)

Table 3-1 *(continued)*

Constructor	Explanation
containsAll(Collection c)	Returns a boolean that indicates whether this array list contains all the objects that are in the specified collection.
ensureCapacity(int minCapacity)	Increases the array list's capacity to the specified value. (If the capacity is already greater than the specified value, this method does nothing.)
get(int index)	Returns the object at the specified position in the list.
indexOf(Object elem)	Returns the index position of the first occurrence of the specified object in the array list. If the object isn't in the list, it returns -1.
isEmpty()	Returns a boolean value that indicates whether the array list is empty.
iterator()	Returns an iterator for the array list.
lastIndexOf(Object elem)	Returns the index position of the last occurrence of the specified object in the array list. If the object isn't in the list, it returns -1.
remove(int index)	Removes the object at the specified index and returns the element that was removed.
remove(Object elem)	Removes an object from the list. Note that more than one element refers to the object; this method removes only one of them. It returns a boolean that indicates whether the object was in the list.
remove(int fromIndex, int toIndex)	Removes all objects whose index values are between the values specified. Note that the elements at the fromIndex and toIndex positions are not themselves removed.
removeAll(Collection c)	Removes all the objects in the specified collection from this array list.
retainAll(Collection c)	Removes all the objects that are not in the specified collection from this array list.

Constructor	Explanation
set(int *index*, Object *elem*)	Sets the specified element to the specified object. The element that was previously at that position is returned as the method's return value.
size()	Returns the number of elements in the list.
toArray()	Returns the elements of the array list as an array of objects (Object []).
toArray(type[] array)	Returns the elements of the array list as an array whose type is the same as the array passed via the parameter.

The rest of this chapter shows you how to use these constructors and methods to work with ArrayList objects.

Creating an ArrayList Object

To create an array list, you first declare an ArrayList variable and then call the ArrayList constructor to instantiate an ArrayList object and assign it to the variable. You can do this on separate lines:

```
ArrayList signs;
signs = new ArrayList();
```

Alternatively, you can do it on a single line:

```
ArrayList signs = new ArrayList();
```

Here are a few things to note about creating array lists:

Book IV
Chapter 3

Using the ArrayList Class

✦ The ArrayList class is in the java.util package, so your program must import either java.util.ArrayList or java.util.*.

✦ Unlike an array, an array list doesn't make you specify a capacity — though you can if you want. Here's a statement that creates an array list with an initial capacity of 100:

```
ArrayList signs = new ArrayList(100);
```

If you don't specify a capacity for the array list, the initial capacity is set to 10. Providing at least a rough estimate of how many elements each array list can hold when you create it is a good idea.

✦ The capacity of an array list is not a fixed limit. The ArrayList class automatically increases the list's capacity whenever necessary.

TIP

- If you're using Java 1.5 or later, you can also specify the type of elements the array list is allowed to contain. This statement creates an array list that holds String objects:

    ```
    ArrayList<String> signs = new ArrayList<String>();
    ```

    The advantage of specifying a type when you declare an array list is that the compiler complains if you then try to add an object of the wrong type to the list. (This feature is called *generics* because it lets the Java API designers create generic collection classes that can be used to store any type of object. For more information, see Book IV, Chapter 5.)

- The ArrayList class also has a constructor that lets you specify another collection object (typically, another array list) whose items are copied into the new array list. This provides an easy way to make a copy of an array list, but you can also use it to convert any other type of collection to an array list.

Adding Elements

After you create an array list, you can use the add method to add objects to the array list. Here's code that adds strings to an array list:

```
signs.add("Drink Pepsi");
signs.add("No minors allowed");
signs.add("Say Pepsi, Please");
signs.add("7-Up: You Like It, It Likes You");
signs.add("Dr. Pepper 10, 2, 4");
```

If you specified a type when you created the array list, the objects you add via the add method must be of the correct type.

You can insert an object at a specific position in the list by listing the position in the add method. Consider these statements:

```
ArrayList<String> nums = new ArrayList<String>();
nums.add("One");
nums.add("Two");
nums.add("Three");
nums.add("Four");
nums.add(2, "Two and a half");
```

After these statements execute, the nums array list contains the following strings:

```
One
Two
Two and a half
Three
Four
```

Here are some important points to keep in mind when you add elements to array lists:

❖ If an array list is already at its capacity when you add an element, the array list automatically expands its capacity. Although this capacity is flexible, it's also inefficient. Whenever possible, you should anticipate how many elements you're adding to an array list and set the list's initial capacity accordingly. (You can also change the capacity at any time by calling the *ensureCapacity* method.)

❖ Like arrays, array lists are indexed starting with zero. Keep this in mind when you use the version of the add method that accepts an index number.

❖ The add method that inserts elements at a specific index position throws the unchecked exception IndexOutOfBoundsException if an object isn't already at the index position you specify.

Accessing Elements

To access a specific element in an array list, you can use the get method, which specifies the index value of the element you want to retrieve. Here's a for loop that prints all the strings in an array list:

```
for (int i = 0; i < nums.size(); i++)
    System.out.println(nums.get(i));
```

Here the size method is used to set the limit of the for loop's index variable.

The easiest way to access all the elements in an array list is to use an enhanced for statement, which lets you retrieve the elements without bothering with indexes or the get method. For example:

```
for (String s : nums)
    System.out.println(s);
```

Here each String element in the nums array list is printed to the console.

If you need to know the index number of a particular object in an array list, and you have a reference to the object, you can use the indexOf method. Here's an enhanced for loop that prints the index number of each string along with the string:

```
for (String s : nums)
{
    int i = nums.indexOf(s);
    System.out.println("Item " + i + ": " + s);
}
```

Depending on the contents of the array list, the output from this loop may look something like this:

```
Item 0: One
Item 1: Two
Item 2: Three
Item 3: Four
```

Printing an ArrayList

The toString method of the ArrayList class (as well as other collection classes) is designed to make it easy to quickly print out the contents of the list. It returns the contents of the array list enclosed in a set of brackets, with each element value separated by commas. The toString method of each element is called to obtain the element value.

Consider these statements:

```
ArrayList<String> nums = new ArrayList<String>();
nums.add("One");
nums.add("Two");
nums.add("Three");
nums.add("Four");
System.out.println(nums);
```

When you run these statements, the following is displayed on the console:

```
[One, Two, Three, Four]
```

Although this output isn't very useful for actual applications, it's convenient for testing purposes or for debugging problems in programs that use array lists.

Using an Iterator

Another way to access all the elements in an array list (or any other collection type) is to use an iterator. An *iterator* is a special type of object whose sole purpose in life is to let you step through the elements of a collection.

The enhanced for statement introduced with Java 1.5 is designed to simplify programs that use iterators. As a result, if you're using Java 1.5 or later, you can use the enhanced for statement instead of iterators. Still, you'll probably encounter existing programs that use iterators, so you need to know how they work.

An iterator object implements the Iterator interface, which is defined as part of the java.util package. As a result, to use an iterator, you must import either java.util.Iterator or java.util.*. The Iterator interface defines just three methods, as listed in Table 3-2. These methods are all you need to access each element of a collection. (Actually, you need only the hasNext and next methods. The remove method is gravy.)

Table 3-2	The Iterator Interface
Method	*Explanation*
hasNext()	Returns true if the collection has at least one element that hasn't yet been retrieved
next()	Returns the next element in the collection
remove()	Removes the most recently retrieved element

The Iterator pattern

Java's iterators follow a common design pattern called the *Iterator pattern,* which is useful whenever you need to provide sequential access to a collection of objects. The Iterator pattern relies on interfaces so that the code that's using the iterator doesn't have to know what actual class is being iterated. As long as the class implements the iterator interface, it can be iterated.

The Iterator interface itself defines the methods used for sequential access. The common pattern is for this interface to provide at least two methods:

✔ **hasNext:** Returns a boolean value that indicates whether another item is available.

✔ **next:** Returns the next item.

Java also defines a third method for its Iterator interface: remove, which removes the most recently retrieved object.

In addition to the Iterator interface, the collection class itself needs a way to get an iterator object. It does so via the iterator method, which simply returns an iterator object for the collection. The iterator method is defined by the Iterable interface. Thus, any object that implements Iterable has an iterator method that provides an iterator for the object.

**Book IV
Chapter 3**

Using the ArrayList
Class

To use an iterator, you first call the array list's `iterator` method to get the iterator. Then you use the iterator's `hasNext` and `next` methods to retrieve each item in the collection. The normal way to do that is with a `while` loop. Here's an example:

```
ArrayList<String> nums = new ArrayList<String>();
nums.add("One");
nums.add("Two");
nums.add("Three");
nums.add("Four");

String s;
Iterator e = nums.iterator();
while (e.hasNext())
{
    s = (String)e.next();
    System.out.println(s);
}
```

Here the first five statements create an array list and add four strings to it. Next, the `iterator` method is called to get an iterator for the `nums` array list. The `hasNext` method is called in the `while` statement, and the `next` method is called to get the element to be printed.

Note that the object returned by the `next` method must be cast to a `String`. That's because the `Iterator` interface has no knowledge of the type of objects stored in the collection. As a result, it simply returns an `Object`. You must cast this object to the correct type before you can use it.

Updating Elements

You can use the `set` method to replace an existing object with another object. Consider this example:

```
ArrayList<String> nums = new ArrayList<String>();
nums.clear();
nums.add("One");
nums.add("Two");
nums.add("Three");
System.out.println(nums);
nums.set(0, "Uno");
nums.set(1, "Dos");
nums.set(2, "Tres");
System.out.println(nums);
```

Here an array list is created with three strings, and the contents of the array list are printed to the console. Then each of the three strings is replaced by another string, and the contents print to the console again. When you run this code, the following is what you see printed on the console:

```
[One, Two, Three]
[Uno, Dos, Tres]
```

Because array lists contain references to objects, not the objects themselves, any changes you make to an object in an array list are automatically reflected in the list. As a result, you don't often have to use the set method.

For example:

```
ArrayList<Employee> emps = new ArrayList<Employee>();

// add employees to array list
emps.add(new Employee("Addams", "Gomez"));
emps.add(new Employee("Taylor", "Andy"));
emps.add(new Employee("Kirk", "James"));

// print array list
System.out.println(emps);

// change one of the employee's names
Employee e = emps.get(1);
e.changeName("Petrie", "Robert");

// print the array list again
System.out.println(emps);
```

This example uses the Employee class, whose constructor accepts an employee's last name and first name to create a new employee object, as well as a changeName method that also accepts a last name and a first name. In addition, the Employee class overrides the toString method to return the employee's first name and last name.

The main method begins by creating an ArrayList object and adding three employees. Then it prints out the contents of the array list. Next, it retrieves the employee with index number 1 and changes that employee's name. Finally, it prints the contents of the array list again.

Here's what this code produces on the console:

```
[Gomez Addams, Andy Taylor, James Kirk]
[Gomez Addams, Robert Petrie, James Kirk]
```

Notice that the second employee's name was changed, even though the program doesn't use the set method to replace the changed Employee object in the collection. That's because the array list merely stores references to the Employee objects.

Deleting Elements

The ArrayList class provides several methods that let you remove elements from the collection. To remove all the elements, use the clear method, like this:

```
emps.clear();
```

To remove a specific element, use the remove method. It lets you remove an element based on the index number, like this:

```
emps.remove(0);
```

Here the first element in the array list is removed.

Alternatively, you can pass the actual object you want removed. This is useful if you don't know the index of the object you want to remove, but you happen to have a reference to the actual object, as in this example:

```
ArrayList<Employee> emps = new ArrayList<Employee>();

// create employee objects
Employee emp1 = new Employee("Addams", "Gomez");
Employee emp2 = new Employee("Taylor", "Andy");
Employee emp3 = new Employee("Kirk", "James");

// add employee objects to array list
emps.add(emp1);
emps.add(emp2);
emps.add(emp3);

// print the array list
System.out.println(emps);

// remove one of the employees
emps.remove(emp2);

// print the array list again
System.out.println(emps);
```

Here's what this code produces on the console:

```
[Gomez Addams, Andy Taylor, James Kirk]
[Gomez Addams, James Kirk]
```

As you can see, the program was able to remove `Andy Taylor` from the list without knowing his index position.

Here are a few important details to keep in mind:

✦ The `clear` and `remove` methods don't actually delete objects; they simply remove the references to the objects from the array list. Like any other objects, the objects in a collection are deleted automatically by the garbage collector — and then only if the objects are no longer being referenced by the program.

✦ You can remove more than one element at the same time by using the `removeRange` method. On it, you specify the starting and ending index numbers. (Note that this method removes all elements between the elements you specify, but the elements you specify aren't themselves removed. `removeRange(5, 8)`, for example, removes elements 6 and 7, but elements 5 and 8 aren't removed.)

✦ You can also use the `removeAll` method to remove all the objects in one collection from another collection. A similar method, `retainAll`, removes all the objects that are *not* in another collection.

Chapter 4: Using the LinkedList Class

In This Chapter

✔ **Introducing linked lists**

✔ **Comparing linked lists with array lists**

✔ **Creating linked lists**

✔ **Adding items to a linked list**

✔ **Retrieving items from a linked list**

✔ **Updating and deleting items in a linked list**

The `ArrayList` class, which I cover in the preceding chapter, is a collection class that's based on an array. Arrays have their strengths and their weaknesses. The strength of an array is that it's very efficient — at least until you fill it up or try to reorganize it by inserting or deleting elements. Then it suddenly becomes very inefficient.

Over the years, computer scientists have developed various alternatives to arrays that are more efficient for certain types of access. One of the oldest of these alternatives is the linked list. A linked list is less efficient than an array for tasks such as directly accessing an element based on its index number, but linked lists run circles around arrays when you need to insert or delete items in the middle of the list.

In this chapter, you find out how to use Java's `LinkedList` class, which provides a collection that's based on a linked list rather than an array. You'll find that although the `LinkedList` class provides many of the same features as the `ArrayList` class, it also has some tricks of its own.

Java 1.5 introduced a major new language feature called *generics* that is aimed specifically at making collections easier to work with. Specifically, the generics feature makes it possible for you to create list objects, such as `ArrayList` or `LinkedList`, that are bound to a specific data type, such as strings or integers.

Because generics are an integral part of how collections work in Java 1.5 and up, I incorporate the generics feature into this chapter from the very start. I point out the differences for using `ArrayList` without generics along the way, just in case you're using an older version of Java or are working with programs that were written before Java 1.5 became available. (For a complete explanation of how the generics feature works, you can read Book IV, Chapter 5.)

Also, be aware that lambda expressions, introduced with Java 8, provide an alternative method for working with collections, including the LinkedList class. For more information about working with these new collection features, see Chapter 6 of this minibook. And for more information about lambda expressions, see Book III, Chapter 7.

Understanding the LinkedList Class

A *linked list* is a collection in which every object in the list maintains with it a pointer to the following object in the list and another pointer to the preceding object in the list. No array is involved at all in a linked list. Instead, the list is managed entirely by these pointers.

Don't worry — you don't have to do any of this pointer management yourself. It's all taken care of for you by the LinkedList class.

This arrangement has some compelling advantages over arrays:

✦ Because the ArrayList class uses an array to store list data, the ArrayList class frequently has to reallocate its array when you add items to the list. Not so with the LinkedList class. Linked lists don't have any size issues. You can keep adding items to a linked list until your computer runs out of memory.

✦ Like the ArrayList class, the LinkedList class lets you insert items into the middle of the list. With the ArrayList class, however, this operation is pretty inefficient. It has to copy all the items past the insertion point one slot over to free a slot for the item you're inserting. Not so with the LinkedList class. To insert an item into the middle of a linked list, all you have to do is change the pointers in the preceding and the following objects.

✦ With an array list, removing items from the list is pretty inefficient. The ArrayList class has to copy every item after the deleted item one slot closer to the front of the array to fill the gap left by the deleted item. Not so with the LinkedList class. To remove an item from a linked list, all that's necessary is to update the pointers in the items that were before and after the item to be removed.

If you want to remove the third item from a list that has 10,000 items in it, for example, the ArrayList class has to copy 9,997 items. By contrast, the LinkedList class does it by updating just two of the items. By the time the ArrayList class is done, the LinkedList class has had time to mow the lawn, read a book, and go to Disneyland.

✦ Linked lists are especially well suited for creating two common types of lists:

- *Stacks:* A *stack* is a list in which items can be added to and retrieved from only the front of the list.

- *Queues:* A *queue* is a list in which items are always added to the back of the list and always retrieved from the front.

Arrays are terribly inefficient for the sort of processing required by stacks and queues. (You see examples of how to use linked lists to create stacks and queues in Book IV, Chapter 5.)

✦ The `ArrayList` class actually uses an array internally to store the data you add to the array list. The `ArrayList` class takes care of managing the size of this array. When you add an item to the array list, and the underlying array is full, the `ArrayList` class automatically creates a new array with a larger capacity and copies the existing items to the new array before it adds the new item.

There's no such thing as a free lunch, however. The flexibility of a linked list comes at a cost: Linked lists require more memory than arrays and are slower than arrays when it comes to simple sequential access.

Like the `ArrayList` class, the `LinkedList` class has several constructors and a ton of methods. For your reference, Table 4-1 lists the constructors and methods of the `LinkedList` class.

Table 4-1	The LinkedList Class
Constructor	*Explanation*
`LinkedList()`	Creates an empty linked list.
`LinkedList (Collection c)`	Creates a linked list and copies all the elements from the specified collection into the new linked list.
Method	*Explanation*
`add(Object element)`	Adds the specified object to the end of the linked list. If you specified a type when you created the linked list, the object must be of the correct type.
`add(int index, Object element)`	Adds the specified object to the linked list at the specified index position. If you specified a type when you created the linked list, the object must be of the correct type.
`addAll (Collection c)`	Adds all the elements of the specified collection to this linked list.

(continued)

Book IV
Chapter 4

Using the
LinkedList Class

Table 4-1 *(continued)*

Constructor	Explanation
addAll(int *index*, Collection *c*)	Adds all the elements of the specified collection to this linked list at the specified index position.
addFirst (Object *element*)	Inserts the specified object at the beginning of the list. If you specified a type when you created the linked list, the object must be of the correct type.
addLast (Object *element*)	Adds the specified object to the end of the list. This method performs the same function as the add method. If you specified a type when you created the linked list, the object must be of the correct type.
clear()	Deletes all elements from the linked list.
clone()	Returns a copy of the linked list. The elements contained in the copy are the same object instances as the elements in the original.
contains (Object *elem*)	Returns a boolean that indicates whether the specified object is in the linked list.
containsAll (Collection *c*)	Returns a boolean that indicates whether this linked list contains all the objects that are in the specified collection.
descendingIterator()	Returns an iterator that steps backward from the end to the beginning of the linked list.
element()	Retrieves the first element from the list. (The element is not removed.)
get(int *index*)	Returns the object at the specified position in the list.
getFirst()	Returns the first element in the list. If the list is empty, it throws NoSuchElementException.
getLast()	Returns the last element in the list. If the list is empty, it throws NoSuchElementException.
indexOf (Object *elem*)	Returns the index position of the first occurrence of the specified object in the list. If the object isn't in the list, it returns -1.
isEmpty()	Returns a boolean value that indicates whether the linked list is empty.
iterator()	Returns an iterator for the linked list.

Constructor	Explanation
`lastIndexOf` `(Object elem)`	Returns the index position of the last occurrence of the specified object in the linked list. If the object isn't in the list, it returns `-1`.
`offer` `(Object elem)`	Adds the specified object to the end of the list. This method returns a `boolean` value, which is always `true`.
`offerFirst` `(Object elem)`	Adds the specified object to the front of the list. This method returns a `boolean` value, which is always `true`.
`offerLast` `(Object elem)`	Adds the specified object to the end of the list. This method returns a `boolean` value, which is always `true`.
`peek()`	Returns (but does not remove) the first element in the list. If the list is empty, it returns `null`.
`peekFirst()`	Returns (but does not remove) the first element in the list. If the list is empty, it returns `null`.
`peekLast()`	Returns (but does not remove) the last element in the list. If the list is empty, it returns `null`.
`poll()`	Retrieves the first element and removes it from the list. It returns the element that was retrieved or, if the list is empty, `null`.
`pollFirst()`	Retrieves the first element and removes it from the list. It returns the element that was retrieved or, if the list is empty, `null`.
`pollLast()`	Retrieves the last element and removes it from the list. It returns the element that was retrieved or, if the list is empty, `null`.
`pop()`	Pops an element from the stack represented by this list.
`push(Object elem)`	Pushes an element onto the stack represented by this list.
`remove()`	Retrieves the first element and removes it from the list. It returns the element that was retrieved. If the list is empty, it throws `NoSuchElementException`.
`remove(int index)`	Removes the object at the specified index and returns the element that was removed.

(continued)

Table 4-1 (continued)

Constructor	Explanation
remove(Object *elem*)	Removes an object from the list. Note that if more than one element refers to the object, this method removes only one of them. It returns a boolean that indicates whether the object was in the list.
removeAll (Collection *c*)	Removes all the objects in the specified collection from this linked list.
removeFirst()	Retrieves the first element and removes it from the list. It returns the element that was retrieved. If the list is empty, it throws NoSuchElementException.
removeFirstOccurrence (Object *elem*)	Finds the first occurrence of elem in the list and removes this occurrence from the list. It returns false if the list has no such occurrence.
removeLast()	Retrieves the last element and removes it from the list. It returns the element that was retrieved. If the list is empty, it throws NoSuchElementException.
removeLastOccurrence (Object *elem*)	Finds the last occurrence of elem in the list and removes this occurrence from the list. It returns false if the list has no such occurrence.
retainAll (Collection *c*)	Removes all the objects that are not in the specified collection from this linked list.
set(int index, Object *elem*)	Sets the specified element to the specified object. The element that was previously at that position is returned as the method's return value.
size()	Returns the number of elements in the list.
toArray()	Returns the elements of the linked list as an array of objects (Object []).
toArray(type[] array)	Returns the elements of the linked list as an array whose type is the same as the array passed via the parameter.

As you look over these methods, you'll find several that seem to do the same thing. These similar methods usually have subtle differences. The getFirst and peek methods, for example, both return the first element from the list without removing the element. The only difference is what happens if the list is empty. In that case, getFirst throws an exception, but peek returns null.

In some cases, however, the methods are identical, such as the remove and removeFirst methods. In fact, if you're crazy enough to look at the source code for the LinkedList class, you'll find that the remove method consists of a single line: a call to the removeFirst method.

Creating a LinkedList

As with any other kind of object, creating a linked list is a two-step affair. First, you declare a LinkedList variable; then you call one of the LinkedList constructors to create the object, as in this example:

```
LinkedList officers = new LinkedList();
```

Here a linked list is created and assigned to the variable officers.

If you're using Java 1.5 or later, you can use the generics feature to specify a type when you declare the linked list. Here's a statement that creates a linked list that holds strings:

```
LinkedList<String> officers = new LinkedList<String>();
```

Then you can add only String objects to this list. If you try to add any other type of object, the compiler balks. (Base runners advance.)

Adding Items to a LinkedList

The LinkedList class gives you many ways to add items to the list. The most basic is the add method, which works pretty much the same way that it does for the ArrayList class. Here's an example:

```
LinkedList<String> officers = new LinkedList<String>();
officers.add("Blake");
officers.add("Burns");
officers.add("Houlihan");
officers.add("Pierce");
officers.add("McIntyre");
for (String s : officers)
    System.out.println(s);
```

The add method adds these items to the end of the list. So the resulting output is this:

```
Blake
Burns
Houlihan
Pierce
McIntyre
```

The `addLast` method works the same way, but the `addFirst` method adds items to the front of the list. Consider these statements:

```
LinkedList<String> officers = new LinkedList<String>();
officers.addFirst("Blake");
officers.addFirst("Burns");
officers.addFirst("Houlihan");
officers.addFirst("Pierce");
officers.addFirst("McIntyre");
for (String s : officers)
    System.out.println(s);
```

Here the resulting output shows the officers in reverse order:

```
McIntyre
Pierce
Houlihan
Burns
Blake
```

To insert an object into a specific position into the list, specify the index in the add method, as in this example:

```
LinkedList<String> officers = new LinkedList<String>();
officers.add("Blake");
officers.add("Burns");
officers.add("Houlihan");
officers.add("Pierce");
officers.add("McIntyre");
officers.add(2, "Tuttle");
for (String s : officers)
    System.out.println(s);
```

The console output from these statements is this:

```
Blake
Burns
Tuttle
Houlihan
Pierce
McIntyre
```

(In case you're not a *M*A*S*H* fan, Tuttle was a fictitious officer that Hawkeye and Trapper made up in one episode so that they could collect his paychecks and donate the money to the local orphanage. Unfortunately, the ruse got out of hand. When Tuttle won a medal, and a general wanted to present it in person, they arranged for "Tuttle" to "die" in an unfortunate helicopter accident.)

Here are some other thoughts to consider when you ponder how to add elements to linked lists:

✦ If you specified a type for the list when you created it, the items you add must be of the correct type. The compiler kvetches if they aren't.

✦ Like arrays and everything else in Java, linked lists are indexed starting with zero.

✦ If you specify an index that doesn't exist, the add method throws IndexOutOfBoundsException. This is an unchecked exception, so you don't have to handle it.

✦ LinkedList also has weird methods named offer, offerFirst, and offerLast. The offer method adds an item to the end of the list and has a return type of boolean, but it always returns true. The offer method is defined by the Queue interface, which LinkedList implements. Some classes that implement Queue can refuse to accept an object added to the list via offer. In that case, the offer method returns false. But because a linked list never runs out of room, the offer method always returns true to indicate that the object offered to the list was accepted.

Retrieving Items from a LinkedList

As with the ArrayList class, you can use the get method to retrieve an item based on its index. If you pass it an invalid index number, the get method throws the unchecked IndexOutOfBoundsException.

You can also use an enhanced for loop to retrieve all the items in the linked list. The examples in the preceding section use this enhanced for loop to print the contents of the officers linked list:

```
for (String s : officers)
    System.out.println(s);
```

If you want, you can also use the iterator method to get an iterator that can access the list. (For more information about iterators, refer to Book IV, Chapter 3.)

The LinkedList class also has a variety of other methods that retrieve items from the list. Some of these methods remove the items as they are retrieved; some throw exceptions if the list is empty; others return null.

Nine methods retrieve the first item in the list:

✦ **getFirst:** Retrieves the first item from the list. This method doesn't delete the item. If the list is empty, NoSuchElement-Exception is thrown.

- ✦ **element:** Identical to the getFirst method. This strangely named method exists because it's defined by the Queue interface, and the LinkedList class implements Queue.

- ✦ **peek:** Similar to getFirst but doesn't throw an exception if the list is empty. Instead, it just returns null. (The Queue interface also defines this method.)

- ✦ **peekFirst:** Identical to peek. Only the name of the method is changed to protect the innocent.

- ✦ **remove:** Similar to getFirst but also removes the item from the list. If the list is empty, it throws NoSuchElementException.

- ✦ **removeFirst:** Identical to remove. If the list is empty, it throws NoSuchElementException.

- ✦ **poll:** Similar to removeFirst but returns null if the list is empty. (This method is yet another method that the Queue interface defines.)

- ✦ **pollFirst:** Identical to poll (well, identical except for the name of the method).

- ✦ **pop:** Identical to removeFirst (but with a catchier name).

Four methods also retrieve the last item in the list:

- ✦ **getLast:** Retrieves the last item from the list. This method doesn't delete the item. If the list is empty, NoSuchElement-Exception is thrown.

- ✦ **peekLast:** Similar to getLast but doesn't throw an exception if the list is empty. Instead, it just returns null.

- ✦ **removeLast:** Similar to getLast but also removes the item. If the list is empty, it throws NoSuchElementException.

- ✦ **pollLast:** Similar to removeLast but returns null if the list is empty.

Updating LinkedList Items

As with the ArrayList class, you can use the set method to replace an object in a linked list with another object. In that *M*A*S*H* episode in which Hawkeye and Trapper made up Captain Tuttle, they quickly found a replacement for him when he died in that unfortunate helicopter accident. Here's how Java implements that episode:

```
LinkedList<String> officers = new LinkedList<String>();

// add the original officers
officers.add("Blake");
officers.add("Burns");
officers.add("Tuttle");
```

```
officers.add("Houlihan");
officers.add("Pierce");
officers.add("McIntyre");
System.out.println(officers);

// replace Tuttle with Murdock
officers.set(2, "Murdock");
System.out.println("\nTuttle is replaced:");
System.out.println(officers);
```

The output from this code looks like this:

```
[Blake, Burns, Tuttle, Houlihan, Pierce, McIntyre]


Tuttle is replaced:
[Blake, Burns, Murdock, Houlihan, Pierce, McIntyre]
```

 As with an `ArrayList`, any changes you make to an object retrieved from a linked list are automatically reflected in the list. That's because the list contains references to objects, not the objects themselves. (For more information about this issue, refer to Book IV, Chapter 3.)

Removing LinkedList Items

You've already seen that several of the methods that retrieve items from a linked list also remove the items. In particular, the `remove`, `removeFirst`, and `poll` methods remove the first item from the list, and the `removeLast` method removes the last item.

You can also remove any arbitrary item by specifying either its index number or a reference to the object you want to remove on the `remove` method. To remove item 3, for example, use a statement like this:

```
officers.remove(3);
```

If you have a reference to the item that you want to remove, use the `remove` method, like this:

```
officers.remove(tuttle);
```

To remove all the items from the list, use the `clear` method:

```
officers.clear();      // Goodbye, Farewell, and Amen.
```

Chapter 5: Creating Generic Collection Classes

In This Chapter

✔ Discovering why the generics feature was invented

✔ Using generics in your own classes

✔ Working with wildcards in a generic class

✔ Examining a pair of classes that demonstrate generics

*I*n the previous two chapters, you've seen how you can specify the type for an `ArrayList` or a `LinkedList` so the compiler can prevent you from accidentally adding the wrong type of data to the collection. The `ArrayList` and `LinkedList` classes can do this because they take advantage of a feature called *generics*. Generics first became available in Java 1.5.

In this chapter, I show you how the generics feature works and how to put it to use in your own classes. Specifically, you see examples of two classes that use the `LinkedList` class to implement a specific kind of collection. The first is a *stack*, a collection in which items are always added to the front of the list and retrieved from the front of the list. The second is a *queue*, a collection in which items are added to the end of the list and retrieved from the front.

This is one of those chapters where the entire chapter could get a Technical Stuff icon. Frankly, generics is on the leading edge of object-oriented programming. You can get by without knowing any of the information in this chapter, so feel free to skip it if you're on your way to something more interesting. However, this chapter is worth looking at, even if you just want to get an idea of how the `ArrayList` and `LinkedList` classes use the new generics feature. And you might find that someday you want to create your own generic classes. Your friends will surely think you're a genius.

To be sure, I won't be covering all the intricacies of programming with generics. If your next job happens to be writing Java class libraries for Oracle, you'll need to know a lot more about generics than this chapter covers. I focus just on the basics of writing simple generic classes.

Why Generics?

Before Java 1.5, collection classes could hold any type of object. For example, the add method for the ArrayList class had this declaration:

```
public boolean add(Object o)
{
    // code to implement the add method
}
```

Thus, you could pass any type of object to the add method — and the array list gladly accepted it.

When you retrieved an item from a collection, you had to cast it to the correct object type before you could do anything with it. For example, if you had an array list named empList with Employee objects, you'd use a statement like this one to get the first Employee from the list:

```
Employee e = (Employee)empList.get(0);
```

The trouble is, what if the first item in the list isn't an Employee? Because the add method accepts any type of object, there was no way to guarantee that only certain types of objects could be added to the collection.

That's why generics were invented. Now you can declare the ArrayList like this:

```
ArrayList<Employee> empList = new ArrayList<Employee>();
```

Here empList is declared as an ArrayList that can hold only Employee types. Now the add method has a declaration that is the equivalent of this:

```
public boolean add(Employee o)
{
    // code to implement the add method
}
```

Thus you can only add Employee objects to the list. And the get method has a declaration that's equivalent to this:

```
public Employee get(int index)
{
    // code to implement the get method
}
```

Thus the get method returns Employee objects. You don't have to cast the result to an Employee because the compiler already knows the object is an Employee.

Creating a Generic Class

Generics let you create classes that can be used for any type specified by the programmer at compile time. To accomplish that, the Java designers introduced a new feature to the language, called *formal type parameters*. To create a class that uses a formal type parameter, you list the type parameter after the class name in angle brackets. The type parameter has a name — Sun recommends you use single uppercase letters for type parameter names — that you can then use throughout the class anywhere you'd otherwise use a type.

For example, here's a simplified version of the class declaration for the `ArrayList` class:

```
public class ArrayList<E>
```

I left out the `extends` and `implements` clauses to focus on the formal type parameter: `<E>`. The E parameter specifies the type of the elements that are stored in the list. Oracle recommends the type parameter name E (for Element) for any parameter that specifies element types in a collection.

So consider this statement:

```
ArrayList<Employee> empList;
```

Here the E parameter is `Employee`, which simply means that the element type for this instance of the `ArrayList` class is `Employee`.

Now take a look at the declaration for the `add` method for the `ArrayList` class:

```
public boolean add(E o)
{
    // body of method omitted (thank you)
}
```

Where you normally expect to see a parameter type, you see the letter E. Thus, this method declaration specifies that the type for the o parameter is the type specified for the formal type parameter E. If E is `Employee`, that means the add method only accepts `Employee` objects.

So far, so good. Now take a look at how you can use a formal type parameter as a return type. Here's the declaration for the `get` method:

```
public E get(int index)
{
    // body of method omitted (you're welcome)
}
```

Here E is specified as the return type. That means that if E is Employee, this method returns Employee objects.

One final technique you need to know before moving on: You can use the formal type parameter within your class to create objects of any other class that accepts formal type parameters. For example, the clone method of the ArrayList class is written like this:

```
public Object clone()
{
    try
    {
        ArrayList<E> v = (ArrayList<E>) super.clone();
        v.elementData = (E[])new Object[size];
        System.arraycopy(elementData, 0,
            v.elementData, 0, size);
        v.modCount = 0;
        return v;
    }
    catch (CloneNotSupportedException e)
    {
        // this shouldn't happen since we're Cloneable
        throw new InternalError();
    }
}
```

You don't need to look much at the details in this method; just notice that the first statement in the try block declares an ArrayList of type <E>. In other words, the ArrayList class uses its own formal type parameter to create another array list object of the same type. If you think about it, that makes perfect sense. After all, that's what the clone method does: It creates another array list just like this one.

The key benefit of generics is that this typing happens at compile time. Thus, after you specify the value of a formal type parameter, the compiler knows how to do the type checking implied by the parameter. That's how it knows not to let you add String objects to an Employee collection.

A Generic Stack Class

Now that you've seen the basics of creating generic classes, in this section you look at a simple generic class that implements a stack. A *stack* is a simple type of collection that lets you add objects to the top of the collection and remove them from the top. I name this Stack class in this section GenStack, and it has five methods:

✦ **push:** This method adds an object to the top of the stack.

✦ **pop:** This method retrieves the top item from the stack. The item is removed from the stack in the process. If the stack is empty, this method returns null.

✦ `peek:` This method lets you peek at the top item on the stack. In other words, it returns the top item without removing it. If the stack is empty, it returns `null`.

✦ `hasItems:` This method returns a `boolean` value of `true` if the stack has at least one item in it.

✦ `size:` This method returns an `int` value that indicates how many items are in the stack.

The `GenStack` class uses a `LinkedList` to implement the stack. For the most part, this class simply exposes the various methods of the `LinkedList` class using names that are more appropriate for a stack. The complete code for the `GenStack` class is shown in Listing 5-1.

Listing 5-1:   The GenStack Class

```
import java.util.*;

public class GenStack<E>                                    →3
{
    private LinkedList<E> list = new LinkedList<E>();       →5

    public void push(E item)                                →7
    {
        list.addFirst(item);
    }

    public E pop()                                          →12
    {
        return list.poll();
    }

    public E peek()                                         →17
    {
        return list.peek();
    }

    public boolean hasItems()                               →22
    {
        return !list.isEmpty();
    }

    public int size()                                       →27
    {
        return list.size();
    }
}
```

The following paragraphs highlight the important details in this class:

→ 3   The class declaration specifies the formal type parameter <E>. Thus users of this class can specify the type for the stack's elements.

→ 5   This class uses a private LinkedList object list to keep the items stored in the stack. The LinkedList is declared with the same type as the GenStack class itself. Thus, if the E type parameter is Employee, the type for this LinkedList is Employee.

→ 7   The push method accepts a parameter of type E. It uses the linked list's addFirst method to add the item to the beginning of the list.

→ 12   The pop method returns a value of type E. It uses the linked list's poll method, which removes and returns the first element in the linked list. If the list is empty, the poll method — and therefore the pop method — returns null.

→ 17   The peek method also returns a value of type E. It simply returns the result of the linked list's peek method.

→ 22   The hasItems method returns the opposite of the linked list's isEmpty method.

→ 27   The size method simply returns the result of the linked list's size method.

That's all there is to it. The following program gives the GenStack class a little workout to make sure it functions properly:

```
public class GenStackTest
{
    public static void main(String[] args)
    {
        GenStack<String> gs = new GenStack<String>();

        System.out.println(
            "Pushing four items onto the stack.");
        gs.push("One");
        gs.push("Two");
        gs.push("Three");
        gs.push("Four");

        System.out.println("There are "
            + gs.size() + " items in the stack.\n");

        System.out.println("The top item is: "
            +gs.peek() + "\n");

        System.out.println("There are still "
            + gs.size() + " items in the stack.\n");
```

```
System.out.println("Popping everything:");
while (gs.hasItems())
    System.out.println(gs.pop());

System.out.println("There are now "
    + gs.size() + " items in the stack.\n");

System.out.println("The top item is: "
    +gs.peek() + "\n");

    }
}
```

This program creates a GenStack object that can hold String objects.
It then pushes four strings onto the stack and prints the number of items
in the stack. Next, it uses the peek method to print the top item and again
prints the number of items in the stack, just to make sure the peek method
doesn't accidentally remove the item. Next, it uses a while loop to pop
each item off the stack and print it. Then, once again, it prints the number
of items (which should now be zero), and it peeks at the top item (which
should be null).

Here's the output that results when you run this program:

```
Pushing four items onto the stack.
There are 4 items in the stack.

The top item is: Four

There are still 4 items in the stack.

Popping everything:
Four
Three
Two
One
There are now 0 items in the stack.

The top item is: null
```

Notice that when the program pops the items off the stack, they come out in
reverse order in which they were pushed onto the stack. That's normal behavior for stacks. In fact, stacks are sometimes called *Last-In, First-Out* lists, or
LIFO lists, for this very reason.

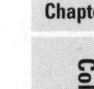

**Book IV
Chapter 5**

**Creating Generic
Collection Classes**

Using Wildcard-Type Parameters

Suppose you have a method that's declared like this:

```
public void addItems(ArrayList<Object> list)
{
    // body of method not shown
}
```

Thought question: Does the following statement compile?

```
addItems(new ArrayList<String>());
```

Answer: Nope.

That's surprising because `String` is a subtype of `Object`. So you'd think that a parameter that says it accepts an `ArrayList` of objects accepts an `ArrayList` of strings.

Unfortunately, inheritance doesn't work quite that way when it comes to formal type parameters. Instead, you have to use another feature of generics, called *wildcards*.

In short, if you want to create a method that accepts any type of `ArrayList`, you have to code the method like this:

```
public void addItems(ArrayList<?> list)
```

In this case, the question mark indicates that you can code any kind of type here.

That's almost as good as inheritance, but what if you want to actually limit the parameter to collections of a specific superclass? For example, suppose you're working on a payroll system that has an `Employee` superclass with two subclasses named `HourlyEmployee` and `SalariedEmployee`, and you want this method to accept an `ArrayList` of `Employee` objects, `HourlyEmployee` objects, or `SalariedEmployee` objects?

In that case, you can add an `extends` clause to the wildcard, like this:

```
public void addItems(ArrayList<? extends Employee> list)
```

Then you can call the `addItems` method with an `ArrayList` of type `Employee`, `HourlyEmployee`, or `SalariedEmployee`.

Now, before you call it a day, take this example one step further: Suppose this `addItems` method appears in a generic class that uses a formal type parameter `<E>` to specify the type of elements the class accepts, and you want the addItems method to accept an ArrayList of type E or any of its subclasses. To do that, you'd declare the addItems method like this:

```
public void addItems(ArrayList<? extends E> list)
```

Here the wildcard type parameter <? extends E> simply means that the ArrayList can be of type E or any type that extends E.

A Generic Queue Class

Now that you've seen how to use wildcards in a generic class, this section presents a generic class that implements a queue. A *queue* is another type of collection that lets you add objects to the end of the collection and remove them from the top. Queues are commonly used in all sorts of applications, from data processing applications to sophisticated networking systems.

This queue class is named GenQueue and has the following methods:

✦ **enqueue:** This method adds an object to the end of the queue.

✦ **dequeue:** This method retrieves the first item from the queue. The item is removed from the queue in the process. If the queue is empty, this method returns null.

✦ **hasItems:** This method returns a boolean value of true if the queue has at least one item in it.

✦ **size:** This method returns an int value that indicates how many items are in the stack.

✦ **addItems:** This method accepts another GenQueue object as a parameter. All the items in that queue are added to this queue. In the process, all the items from the queue passed to the method are removed. The GenQueue parameter must be of the same type as this queue or a subtype of this queue's type.

The GenQueue class uses a LinkedList to implement its queue. The complete code for the GenQueue class is shown in Listing 5-2.

Book IV
Chapter 5

Creating Generic Collection Classes

Listing 5-2:   The GenQueue Class

```
import java.util.*;

public class GenQueue<E>                                    →3
{
    private LinkedList<E> list = new LinkedList<E>();        →5

    public void enqueue(E item)                             →7
```

(continued)

Listing 5-2 *(continued)*

```
    {
        list.addLast(item);
    }

    public E dequeue()                                          →12
    {
        return list.poll();
    }

    public boolean hasItems()                                   →17
    {
        return !list.isEmpty();
    }

    public int size()                                           →22
    {
        return list.size();
    }

    public void addItems(GenQueue<? extends E> q)               →27
    {
        while (q.hasItems())
            list.addLast(q.dequeue());
    }
}
```

The following paragraphs point out the highlights of this class:

→ 3   The class declaration specifies the formal type parameter <E>. Thus, users of this class can specify the type for the elements of the queue.

→ 5   Like the GenStack class, this class uses a private LinkedList object list to keep its items.

→ 7   The enqueue method accepts a parameter of type E. It uses the linked list's addLast method to add the item to the end of the queue.

→ 12   The dequeue method returns a value of type E. Like the pop method of the GenStack class, this method uses the linked list's poll method to return the first item in the list.

→ 17   The hasItems method returns the opposite of the linked list's isEmpty method.

→ 22   The size method returns the result of the linked list's size method.

→ 27   The addItems method accepts a parameter that must be another GenQueue object whose element type is either the same type as this GenQueue object's elements or a subtype of this GenQueue object's element type. This method uses a while loop to remove all the items from the q parameter and add them to this queue.

The following program exercises the GenQueue class:

```java
public class GenQueueTest
{
    public static void main(String[] args)
    {
        GenQueue<Employee> empList;
        empList = new GenQueue<Employee>();

        GenQueue<HourlyEmployee> hList;
        hList = new GenQueue<HourlyEmployee>();
        hList.enqueue(new HourlyEmployee(
            "Trump", "Donald"));
        hList.enqueue(new HourlyEmployee(
            "Gates", "Bill"));
        hList.enqueue(new HourlyEmployee(
            "Forbes", "Steve"));

        empList.addItems(hList);

        while (empList.hasItems())
        {
            Employee emp = empList.dequeue();
            System.out.println(emp.firstName
                + " " + emp.lastName);
        }
    }
}

class Employee
{
    public String lastName;
    public String firstName;

    public Employee() {}

    public Employee(String last, String first)
    {
        this.lastName = last;
        this.firstName = first;
    }

    public String toString()
    {
        return firstName + " " + lastName;
    }
}
```

```
class HourlyEmployee extends Employee
{
    public double hourlyRate;

    public HourlyEmployee(String last, String first)
    {
        super(last, first);
    }
}
```

This program begins by creating a GenQueue object that can hold Employee objects. This queue is assigned to a variable named empList.

Next, the program creates another GenQueue object. This one can hold HourlyEmployee objects (HourlyEmployee is a subclass of Employee) and is assigned to a variable named hList.

Then three rookie employees are created and added to the hList queue. The addItems method of the empList queue is then called to transfer these employees from the hList queue to the empList queue. Because HourlyEmployee is a subclass of Employee, the addItems method of the empList queue accepts hList as a parameter.

Finally, a while loop is used to print the employees that are now in the empList queue.

When this program is run, the following is printed on the console:

```
Donald Trump
Bill Gates
Steve Forbes
```

Thus the addItems method successfully transferred the employees from the hlist queue, which held HourlyEmployee objects, to the empList queue, which holds Employee objects.

Using the Diamond Operator

One of the more annoying things about working with generics is that you have to specify the types twice when you create a variable of a generic type, and then use the constructor to instantiate an object. For example, to create an ArrayList of type String, you must code this:

```
ArrayList<String> nums = new ArrayList<String>();
```

Here the type String must be specified twice: once in the type declaration for the variable, and again in the call to the constructor.

Java 7 introduced a new feature called the *diamond operator* that lets you skip the type when you call the constructor, like this:

```
ArrayList<String> nums = new ArrayList<>();
```

Here's another example:

```
ArrayList<String> nums;
nums = new ArrayList<>();
```

The diamond operator simply deduces the correct type based on the variable's type.

Chapter 6: Using Bulk Data Operations with Collections

In This Chapter

✓ **Understanding basic stream operations**

✓ **Examining the `stream` interface**

✓ **Filtering and sorting streams**

✓ **Computing sums, averages, and other values**

*O*ne of the most common things to do with a collection is to iterate over it, performing some type of operation on all of its elements. For example, you might use a `foreach` loop to print all of the elements. The body of the `foreach` loop might contain an if statement to select which elements to print. Or it might perform a calculation such as accumulating a grand total or counting the number of elements that meet a given condition.

In Java, `foreach` loops are easy to create and can be very powerful. However, they have one significant drawback: They iterate over the collection's elements one at a time, beginning with the first element and proceeding sequentially to the last element. As a result, a `foreach` loop must be executed sequentially within a single tread.

That's a shame, since modern computers have multicore processors that are capable of doing several things at once. Wouldn't it be great if you could divide a `foreach` loop into several parts, each of which can be run independently on one of the processor cores? For a small collection, the user probably wouldn't notice the difference. But if the collection is extremely large (say, a few million elements), unleashing the power of a multicore processor could make the program run much faster.

While you can do that with earlier versions of Java, the programming is tricky: You have to master one of the more difficult aspects of programming in Java: working with threads, which are like separate sections of your program that can be executed simultaneously. You'll learn the basics of working with threads in Book V, Chapter 1. For now, take my word for it: Writing programs that work with large collections of data and take advantage of multiple threads is a difficult undertaking. At least until Java 8.

Java 8 introduces a new feature called *bulk data operations* that's designed specifically to attack this very problem. When you use bulk data operations, you do not directly iterate over the collection data using a `foreach` loop. Instead, you simply provide the operations that will be done on each of the collection's elements and let Java take care of the messy details required to spread the work over multiple threads.

At the heart of the bulk data operations feature is a new type of object called a *stream*, defined by the `stream` interface. A stream is simply a sequence of elements of any data type which can be processed sequentially or in parallel. The `stream` interface provides methods that let you perform various operations such as filtering the elements or performing an operation on each of the elements.

Don't confuse the type of stream I describe in this chapter with the file streams that are described in Book VIII, Chapter 2. File streams are used to read and write data to disk files. The streams described in this chapter are used to process data extracted from collection classes.

Streams rely on the use of Lambda expressions to pass the operations that are performed on stream elements. In fact, the primary reason Java's developers introduced Lambda expressions into the Java language was to facilitate streams. If you haven't yet read Book III, Chapter 7, I suggest you do so now, before reading further into this chapter. Otherwise you'll find yourself hopelessly confused by the peculiar syntax of the Lambda expressions used throughout this chapter.

In this chapter, you learn the basics of using streams to perform simple bulk data operations.

Looking At a Basic Bulk Data Operation

Suppose you have a list of spells used by a certain wizard who, for copyright purposes, we'll refer to simply as HP. The spells are represented by a class named `Spell`, which is defined as follows:

```java
public class Spell
{
    public String name;
    public SpellType type;
    public String description;

    public enum SpellType {SPELL, CHARM, CURSE}

    public Spell(String spellName, SpellType spellType,
        String spellDescription)
    {
        name = spellName;
        type = spellType;
        description = spellDescription;
    }
}
```

```
public String toString()
{
    return name;
}
}
```

As you can see, the `Spell` class has three public fields that represent the spell's name, type (SPELL, CHARM, or CURSE), and description, as well as a constructor that lets you specify the name, type, and description for the spell. Also, the `toString()` method is overridden to return simply the spell name.

Let's load a few of HP's spells into an `ArrayList`:

```
ArrayList<Spell> spells = new ArrayList<>();
spells.add(new Spell("Aparecium", Spell.SpellType.SPELL,
    "Makes invisible ink appear."));
spells.add(new Spell("Avis", Spell.SpellType.SPELL,
    "Launches birds from your wand."));
spells.add(new Spell("Engorgio", Spell.SpellType.CHARM,
    "Enlarges something."));
spells.add(new Spell("Fidelius", Spell.SpellType.CHARM,
    "Hides a secret within someone."));
spells.add(new Spell("Finite Incatatum",
    Spell.SpellType.SPELL,
    "Stops all current spells."));
spells.add(new Spell("Locomotor Mortis",
    Spell.SpellType.CURSE,
    "Locks an opponent's legs."));
```

Now, suppose you want to list the name of each spell on the console. You could do that using a `foreach` loop like this:

```
for (Spell spell : spells)
    System.out.println(spell.name);
```

The equivalent code using the streams looks like this:

```
spells.stream().forEach(s -> System.out.println(s));
```

Here, I first use the `stream` method of the `ArrayList` class to convert the `ArrayList` to a stream. All of the classes that inherit from `java.Collection` implement a stream method that returns a `Stream` object. That includes not only `ArrayList`, but also `LinkedList` and `Stack`.

Next, I use the stream's `forEach` method to iterate the stream, passing a Lambda expression that calls `System.out.println` for each item in the stream. The `forEach` method processes the entire stream, writing each element to the console.

Suppose you want to list just the spells, not the charms or curses. Using a traditional `foreach` loop, you'd do it like this:

```
for (Spell spell : spells)
{
    if (spell.type == Spell.SpellType.SPELL)
        System.out.println(spell.name);
}
```

Here an `if` statement selects just the spells so that the charms and curses aren't listed.

Here's the same thing using streams:

```
spells.stream()
    .filter(s -> s.type == Spell.SpellType.SPELL)
    .forEach(s -> System.out.println(s));
```

In this example, the `stream` method converts the `ArrayList` to a stream. Then the stream's `filter` method is used to select just the `SPELL` items. Finally, the `forEach` method sends the selected items to the console. Notice that Lambda expressions are used in both the `forEach` method and the `filter` method.

The `filter` method of the `Stream` class returns a `Stream` object. Thus, it is possible to apply a second filter to the result of the first filter, like this:

```
spells.parallelStream()
    .filter(s -> s.type == Spell.SpellType.SPELL)
    .filter(s -> s.name.toLowerCase().startsWith("a"))
    .forEach(s -> System.out.println(s));
```

In this example, just the spells that start with the letter A are listed.

The term *pipeline* is often used to describe a sequence of method calls that start by creating a stream, then manipulate the stream in various ways by calling methods such as `filter`, and finally end by calling a method that does not return another stream object, such as `forEach`.

Looking Closer at the Stream Interface

The `Stream` interface defines about 40 methods. In addition, three related interfaces — `DoubleStream`, `IntStream`, and `LongStream` — extend the `Stream` interface to define operations that are specific to a single date type: double, int, and long. Table 6-1 lists the most commonly used methods of these interfaces.

Table 6-1	The Stream and Related Interfaces
Methods that Return Streams	*Explanation*
`Stream distinct()`	Returns a stream consisting of distinct elements of the input stream. In other words, duplicates are removed.
`Stream limit(long maxSize)`	Returns a stream having no more than `maxSize` elements derived from the input stream.
`Stream filter(Predicate<? super T> predicate)`	Returns a stream consisting of those elements in the input stream that match the conditions of the predicate.
`Stream sorted()`	Returns the stream elements in sorted order using the natural sorting method for the stream's data type.
`Stream sorted(Comparator<? super T> comparator)`	Returns the stream elements in sorted order using the specified `Comparator` function. The `Comparator` function accepts two parameters and returns a negative value if the first is less than the second, zero if they are equal, and a positive value if the first is greater than the second.
Mapping Methods	*Explanation*
`<R> Stream<R> map(Function<? super T,? extends R> mapper`	Returns a stream created by applying the `mapper` function to each element of the input stream.
`DoubleStream mapToDouble(ToDouble Function<? super T> mapper)`	Returns a `DoubleStream` created by applying the `mapper` function to each element of the input stream.
`IntStream mapToInt(ToIntFunction<? super T> mapper)`	Returns an `IntStream` created by applying the `mapper` function to each element of the input stream.
`LongStream mapToLong(ToLongFunction<? super T> mapper)`	Returns a `LongStream` created by applying the `mapper` function to each element of the input stream.
Terminal and Aggregate Methods	*Explanation*
`void forEach(Consumer<? super T> action)`	Executes the action against each element of the input stream.

(continued)

Table 6-1 *(continued)*

Terminal and Aggregate Methods	Explanation

`void forEachOrdered`
`(Consumer<? super T>`
`action)`
	Executes the action against each element of the input stream, ensuring that the elements of the input stream are processed in order.

`long count()`	Returns the number of elements in the stream.

`Optional<T>`
`max(Comparator<? super T>`
`comparator)`
	Returns the largest element in the stream.

`Optional<T>`
`min(Comparator<? super T>`
`comparator)`
	Returns the smallest element in the stream.

`OptionalDouble average()`	Returns the average value of the elements in the stream. Valid only for `DoubleStream`, `IntStream`, and `Longstream`.
`resultType sum()`	Returns the sum of the elements in the stream. Result type is `double` for `DoubleStream`, int for `IntStream`, and long for `LongStream`.
`resultType` `summaryStatistics()`	Returns a summary statistics object that includes property methods named `getCount`, `getSum`, `getAverage`, `getMax`, and `getMmin` of the elements in the stream. The result type is `IntSummaryStatistics` for an `IntStream`, `DoubleSummaryStatistics` for a `DoubleStream`, and `LongSummaryStatistics` for a `LongStream`.

The first group of methods in Table 6-1 define methods that return other `Stream` objects. Each of these methods manipulates the stream in some way, then passes the altered stream down the pipeline to be processed by another operation.

The `filter` method is one of the most commonly used stream methods. It's argument, called a *predicate,* is a function that returns a boolean value. The function is called once for every element in the stream and is passed a single argument that contains the element under question. If the method returns `true`, the element is passed on to the result stream. If it returns `false`, the element is *not* passed on.

The easiest way to implement a filter predicate is to use a Lambda expression that specifies a conditional expression. For example, the following Lambda expression inspects the name field of the stream element and returns `true` if it begins with the letter *a* (upper- or lowercase):

```
s -> s.name.toLowerCase().startsWith("a")
```

The other methods in the first group let you limit the number of elements in a stream or sort the elements of the stream. To sort a stream, you can use either the element's natural sorting order, or you can supply your own comparator function.

The second group of methods in Table 6-1 are called *mapping methods* because they convert a stream whose elements are of one type to a stream whose elements are of another type. The mapping function, which you must pass as a parameter, is responsible for converting the data from the first type to the second.

One common use for mapping methods is to convert a stream of complex types to a stream of simple numeric values of type `double`, `int`, or `long`, which you can then use to perform an aggregate calculation such as `sum` or `average`. For example, suppose HP's spells were for sale and the `Spell` class included a public field named `price`. To calculate the average price of all the spells, you would first have to convert the stream of `Spell` objects to a stream of doubles. To do that, you use the `mapToDouble` method. The mapping function would simply return the `price` field:

```
.mapToDouble(s -> s.price)
```

Methods in the last group in Table 6-1 are called *terminal methods* because they do not return another stream. As a result, they are always the last methods called in stream pipelines.

You have already seen the `forEach` method in action; it provides a function that is called once for each element in the stream. Note that in the examples so far, the function to be executed on each element has consisted of just a single method call, so I've included it directly in the Lambda expression. If the function is more complicated, you can isolate it in its own method. Then the Lambda expression should call the method that defines the function.

Aggregate methods perform a calculation on all of the elements in the stream, then return the result. Of the aggregate methods, `count` is straightforward: It simply returns the number of elements in the stream. The other aggregate methods need a little explanation because they return an optional data type. An *optional data type* is an object that might contain a value, or it might not.

For example, the `average` method calculates the average value of a stream of integers, longs, or doubles and returns the result as an `OptionalDouble`. If the stream was empty, the average is undefined, so the `OptionalDouble` contains no value. You can determine if the `OptionalDouble` contains a value by calling its `isPresent` method, which returns true if there is a value present. If there is a value, you can get it by calling the `getAsDouble` method.

Note that `getAsDouble` will throw an exception if no value is present, so you should always call `isPresent` before you call `getAsDouble`.

Here's an example that calculates the average price of spells:

```
OptionalDouble avg = spells.stream()
            .mapToDouble(s -> s.price)
            .average();
```

Here is how you would write the average price to the console:

```
if (avg.isPresent())
{
    System.out.println("Average = "
        + avg.getAsDouble());
}
```

Using Parallel Streams

Streams come in two basic flavors: *sequential* and *parallel*. Elements in a sequential stream are produced by the `stream` method and create streams that are processed one element after the next. Parallel streams, in contrast, can take full advantage of multicore processors by breaking its elements into two or more smaller streams, performing operations on them, and then recombining the separate streams to create the final result stream. Each of the intermediate streams can be processed by a separate thread, which can improve performance for large streams.

By default, streams are sequential. But creating a parallel stream is easy: Just use the `parallelStream` method instead of the `stream` method at the beginning of the pipeline.

For example, to print all of HP's spells using a parallel stream, use this code:

```
spells.parallelStream()
    .forEach(s -> System.out.println(s));
```

Note that when you use a parallel stream, you can't predict the order in which each element of the stream is processed. That's because when the stream is split and run on two or more threads, the order in which the processor executes the threads is not predictable.

To demonstrate this point, consider this simple example:

```
System.out.println("First Parallel stream: ");
spells.parallelStream()
    .forEach(s -> System.out.println(s));
System.out.println("\nSecond Parallel stream: ");
spells.parallelStream()
    .forEach(s -> System.out.println(s));
```

When you execute this code, the results will look something like this:

```
First parallel stream:
Fidelius
Finite Incatatum
Engorgio
Locomotor Mortis
Aparecium
Avis

Second parallel stream:
Fidelius
Engorgio
Finite Incatatum
Locomotor Mortis
Avis
Aparecium
```

Notice that although the same spells are printed for each of the streams, they are printed in a different order.

Book V
Programming Techniques

```
G:\WINDOWS\System32\cmd.exe                          _ □ ×
Welcome to the Bart Client

What server do you want to connect to?localhost
Connected on port 1234
I will not hide behind the Fifth Amendment.
I will not hide behind the Fifth Amendment.
I will not hide behind the Fifth Amendment.
I will not hide behind the Fifth Amendment.
I will not hide behind the Fifth Amendment.
I will not hide behind the Fifth Amendment.
I will not hide behind the Fifth Amendment.
I will not hide behind the Fifth Amendment.
I will not hide behind the Fifth Amendment.
I will not hide behind the Fifth Amendment.
I will not hide behind the Fifth Amendment.
I will not hide behind the Fifth Amendment.
I will not hide behind the Fifth Amendment.
I will not hide behind the Fifth Amendment.
I will not hide behind the Fifth Amendment.
I will not hide behind the Fifth Amendment.
I will not hide behind the Fifth Amendment.
I will not hide behind the Fifth Amendment.
I will not hide behind the Fifth Amendment.
I will not hide behind the Fifth Amendment.
I will not hide behind the Fifth Amendment.
Press any key to continue . . .
```

You can find an interesting programming challenge that requires use of many of the programming techniques covered in this minibook at www.dummies.com/extras/javaaio. This challenge tasks you with creating a program that solves the classic Towers of Hanoi game.

Contents at a Glance

Chapter 1: Programming Threads

In This Chapter

✔ Examining threads

✔ Creating threads from the Thread class

✔ Working with the Runnable interface

✔ Creating threads that cooperate

✔ Executing threads

✔ Making methods cooperate

✔ Using a lock

✔ Interrupting threads

Remember the guy from the old *Ed Sullivan Show* who used to spin plates? Somehow, he managed to keep all those plates spinning, running from pole to pole to give each plate a little nudge — just enough to keep it going.

In Java, *threads* are the equivalent of the spinning-plate guy. Threads let you divide the work of an application into separate pieces, all of which then run simultaneously. The result is a faster and more efficient program, but along with the increased speed come more difficult programming and debugging.

Truthfully, the subtleties of threaded programming are a topic for computer science majors, but the basics of working with threads aren't all that difficult to understand. In this chapter, I focus on those basics and leave the advanced techniques for the grad students.

The main application I use to illustrate threading in this chapter simulates the countdown clock for the spacecraft. Working with threads isn't really rocket science, but threading is used to solve difficult programming problems. You invariably find yourself trying to get two or more separate pieces of code to coordinate their activities, and that's not as easy as you might think at first guess. As a result, I can't possibly talk about threading without getting into some challenging mental exercises, so be prepared to spend some mental energy figuring out how it works.

The listings in this chapter, as well as throughout the book, are available at www.dummies.com/extras/javaaio.

Understanding Threads

A *thread* is a single sequence of executable code within a larger program. All the programs shown so far in this book have used just one thread — the *main thread* that starts automatically when you run the program — but Java lets you create programs that start additional threads to perform specific tasks.

You're probably familiar with programs that use threads to perform several tasks at the same time. Here are some common examples:

✦ Web browsers can download files while letting you view web pages. When you download a file in a web browser, the browser starts a separate thread to handle the download.

✦ E-mail programs don't make you wait for all your messages to download before you can read the first message. Instead, these programs use separate threads to display and download messages.

✦ Word processors can print long documents in the background while you continue to work. These programs start a separate thread to handle print jobs.

✦ Word processors can also check your spelling as you type. Depending on how the word processor is written, it may run the spell check in a separate thread.

✦ Game programs commonly use several threads to handle different parts of the game to improve the overall responsiveness of the game.

✦ All GUI-based programs use at least two threads — one thread to run the application's main logic and another thread to monitor mouse and keyboard events. You find out about creating GUI programs in Java in Book VI.

✦ Indeed, the Java Virtual Machine itself uses threading for some of its housekeeping chores. The garbage collector, for example, runs as a separate thread so it can constantly monitor the state of the VM's memory and decide when it needs to create some free memory by removing objects that are no longer being used.

Creating a Thread

Suppose you're developing software for NASA, and you're in charge of the program that controls the final 31 seconds of the countdown for a manned spacecraft. Your software has to coordinate several key events that occur when the clock reaches certain points:

✦ **T minus 16 seconds:** Flood launch pad. This event releases 350,000 gallons of water onto the launch pad, which helps protect the spacecraft systems during launch.

✦ **T minus 6 seconds:** Start the main engines. Huge clamps hold the spacecraft in place while the engines build up thrust.

✦ **T minus 0:** Lift off! The the clamps are released, and the spacecraft flies into space.

For this program, I don't actually start any rocket engines or release huge amounts of water. Instead, I just display messages on the console to simulate these events. But I do create four separate threads to make everything work. One thread manages the countdown clock. The other three threads fire off their respective events at T minus 16 seconds (flood the pad), T minus 6 seconds (fire the engines), and T minus 0 (launch).

For the first attempt at this program, I just get the countdown clock up and running. The countdown clock is represented by a class named `CountDown-Clock`. All this class does is count down from 20 to 0 at 1-second intervals, displaying messages such as `T minus 20` on the console as it counts. This version of the program doesn't do much of anything, but it does demonstrate how to get a thread going. We'll start by looking at the `Thread` class.

Understanding the Thread class

The `Thread` class lets you create an object that can be run as a thread in a multithreaded Java application. The `Thread` class has quite a few constructors and methods, but for most applications, you need to use only the ones listed in Table 1-1. (Note that this table is here to give you an overview of the `Thread` class and to serve as a reference. Don't worry about the details of each constructor and method just yet. By the end of this chapter, I explain each of the constructors and methods.)

Table 1-1 Constructors and Methods of the Thread Class

Constructor	Explanation
`Thread()`	Creates an instance of the `Thread` class. This constructor is the basic `Thread` constructor without parameters.
`Thread(String name)`	Creates a `Thread` object and assigns the specified name to the thread.
`Thread(Runnable target)`	Turns any object that implements an API interface called `Runnable` into a thread. You see how this more-advanced constructor is used later in this chapter.
`Thread(Runnable target, String name)`	Creates a thread from any object that implements `Runnable` and assigns the specified name to the thread.
`static int activeCount()`	Returns the number of active threads.
`static int enumerate(Thread[] t)`	Fills the specified array with a copy of each active thread. The return value is the number of threads added to the array.
`String getName()`	Returns the name of the thread.
`int getPriority()`	Returns the thread's priority.
`void interrupt()`	Interrupts this thread.
`boolean isInterrupted()`	Checks whether the thread has been interrupted.
`void setPriority(int priority)`	Sets the thread's priority.
`void setName(String name)`	Sets the thread's name.
`static void Sleep`	Causes the currently executing thread `(int milliseconds)` to sleep for the specified number of milliseconds.
`void run()`	Is called when the thread is started. Place the code that you want the thread to execute inside this method.
`void start()`	Starts the thread.
`static void yield()`	Causes the currently executing thread to yield to other threads that are waiting to execute.

Extending the Thread class

The easiest way to create a thread is to write a class that extends the
Thread class. Then all you have to do to start a thread is create an instance
of your thread class and call its start method.

Listing 1-1 is a version of the CountDownClock class that extends the
Thread class.

Listing 1-1:   The CountDownClock Class (Version 1)

```
public class CountDownClock extends Thread               →1
{
    public void run()                                    →3
    {
        for (int t = 20; t >= 0; t--)                    →5
        {
            System.out.println("T minus " + t);
            try
            {
                Thread.sleep(1000);                      →10
            }
            catch (InterruptedException e)
            {}
        }
    }
}
```

Here are a few key points to notice in this class:

→ 1   The CountDownClock class extends the Thread class. Thread
       is defined in the java.language package, so you don't have to
       provide an import statement to use it.

→ 3   The CountDownClock class has a single method, named run.
       This method is called by Java when the clock thread has been
       started. All the processing done by the thread must either be
       in the run method or in some other method called by the run
       method.

→ 5   The run method includes a for loop that counts down from 20 to 0.

→ 10   The CountDownClock class uses the sleep method to pause for
       1 second. Because the sleep method throws Interrupted
       Exception, a try/catch statement handles this exception. If the
       exception is caught, it is simply ignored.

REMEMBER

At some point in its execution, the run method must either call sleep or
yield to give other threads a chance to execute.

Creating and starting a thread

After you define a class that defines a `Thread` object, you can create and start the thread. Here's the main class for the first version of the countdown application:

```
public class CountDownApp
{
    public static void main(String[] args)
    {
        Thread clock = new CountDownClock();
        clock.start();
    }
}
```

Here a variable of type `Thread` is declared, and an instance of the `Count DownClock` is created and assigned to it. This creates a `Thread` object, but the thread doesn't begin executing until you call its `start` method.

When you run this program, the thread starts counting down in 1-second increments, displaying messages such as the following on the console:

```
T minus 20
T minus 19
T minus 18
```

And so on, all the way to zero. So far, so good.

Implementing the Runnable Interface

For the threads that trigger specific countdown events such as flooding the launch pad, starting the events, and lifting off, I create another class called `LaunchEvent`. This class uses another technique for creating and starting threads — one that requires a few more lines of code but is more flexible.

The problem with creating a class that extends the `Thread` class is that a class can have one superclass. What if you'd rather have your thread object extend some other class? In that case, you can create a class that implements the `Runnable` interface rather than extends the `Thread` class. The `Runnable` interface marks an object that can be run as a thread. It has only one method, `run`, that contains the code that's executed in the thread. (The `Thread` class itself implements `Runnable`, which is why the `Thread` class has a `run` method.)

Using the Runnable interface

To use the Runnable interface to create and start a thread, you have to do the following:

1. **Create a class that implements Runnable.**

2. **Provide a run method in the Runnable class.**

3. **Create an instance of the Thread class and pass your Runnable object to its constructor as a parameter.**

A Thread object is created that can run your Runnable class.

4. **Call the Thread object's start method.**

The run method of your Runnable object is called and executes in a separate thread.

The first two of these steps are easy. The trick is in the third and fourth steps, because you can complete them in several ways. Here's one way, assuming that your Runnable class is named RunnableClass:

```
RunnableClass rc = new RunnableClass();
Thread t = new Thread(rc);
t.start();
```

Java programmers like to be as concise as possible, so you often see this code compressed to something more like

```
Thread t = new Thread(new RunnableClass());
t.start();
```

or even just this:

```
new Thread(new RunnableClass()).start();
```

This single-line version works — provided that you don't need to access the thread object later in the program.

Creating a class that implements Runnable

To sequence the launch events for the NASA application, I create a Runnable object named LaunchEvent. The constructor for this class accepts two parameters: the countdown time at which the event fires and the message that is displayed when the time arrives. The run method for this class uses Thread.sleep to wait until the desired time arrives. Then it displays the message.

Listing 1-2 shows the code for this class.

Listing 1-2:   The LaunchEvent Class (Version 1)

```
public class LaunchEvent implements Runnable                    →1
{
    private int start;
    private String message;

    public LaunchEvent(int start, String message)               →6
    {
        this.start = start;
        this.message = message;
    }

    public void run()
    {
        try
        {
            Thread.sleep(20000 - (start * 1000));               →16
        }
        catch (InterruptedException e)
        {}
        System.out.println(message);                            →20
    }
}
```

The following paragraphs draw your attention to the listing's key lines:

→ 1   This class implements the `Runnable` interface.

→ 6   The constructor accepts two parameters: an integer representing the start time (in seconds) and a string message that's displayed when the time arrives. The constructor simply stores these parameter values in private fields.

→ 16   In the `run` method, the `Thread.sleep` method is called to put the thread to sleep until the desired countdown time arrives. The length of time that the thread should sleep is calculated by the expression `20000 - (start * 1000)`. The countdown clock starts at 20 seconds, which is 20,000 milliseconds. This expression simply subtracts the number of milliseconds that corresponds to the desired start time from 20,000. Thus, if the desired start time is 6 seconds, the `sleep` method sleeps for 14,000 milliseconds — that is, 14 seconds.

→ 20   When the thread wakes up, it displays the message passed via its constructor on the console.

Using the CountDownApp class

Now that you've seen the code for the `LaunchEvent` and `CountDownClock` classes, Listing 1-3 shows the code for a `CountDownApp` class that uses these classes to launch a space spacecraft.

Listing 1-3:   The CountDownApp Class (Version 2)

```
public class CountDownApp
{
   public static void main(String[] args)
   {
      Thread clock = new CountDownClock();            →5

      Runnable flood, ignition, liftoff;              →7
      flood = new LaunchEvent(16, "Flood the pad!");
      ignition = new LaunchEvent(6, "Start engines!");
      liftoff = new LaunchEvent(0, "Liftoff!");

      clock.start();                                  →12

      new Thread(flood).start();                      →14
      new Thread(ignition).start();
      new Thread(liftoff).start();
   }
}
```

The following paragraphs summarize how this program works:

→ 5   The main method starts by creating an instance of the Count DownClock class and saving it in the clock variable.

→ 7   Next, it creates three LaunchEvent objects to flood the pad at 16 seconds, start the engines at 6 seconds, and lift off at 0 seconds. These objects are assigned to variables of type Runnable named flood, ignition, and liftoff.

→ 12   The clock thread is started. The countdown starts ticking.

→ 14   Finally, the program starts the three LaunchEvent objects as threads. It does this by creating a new instance of the Thread class, passing the LaunchEvent objects as parameters to the Thread constructor, and then calling the start method to start the thread.

Note that because this program doesn't need to do anything with these threads after they're started, it doesn't bother creating variables for them.

When you run this program, output similar to the following is displayed on the console:

```
T minus 20
T minus 19
T minus 18
T minus 17
T minus 16
Flood the pad!
T minus 15
```

```
T minus 14
T minus 13
T minus 12
T minus 11
T minus 10
T minus 9
T minus 8
T minus 7
T minus 6
Start engines!
T minus 5
T minus 4
T minus 3
T minus 2
T minus 1
Liftoff!
T minus 0
```

As you can see, the `LaunchEvent` messages are interspersed with the `CountDownClock` messages. Thus, the launch events are triggered at the correct times.

Note that the exact order in which some of the messages appear may vary slightly. For example, `"Flood the pad!"` might sometimes come before `"T minus 16."` because of slight variations in the precise timing of these independently operating threads. Later in this chapter, the section "Creating Threads That Work Together" shows you how to avoid such inconsistencies.

You can improve the `main` method for this class by using an `ArrayList` to store the `Runnable` objects. Then you can start all the `LaunchEvent` threads by using an enhanced `for` loop. Here's what the improved code looks like:

```java
public static void main(String[] args)
{
    Thread clock = new CountDownClock();

    ArrayList<Runnable> events
        = new ArrayList<Runnable>();
    events.add(new LaunchEvent(16, "Flood the pad!"));
    events.add(new LaunchEvent(6, "Start engines!"));
    events.add(new LaunchEvent(0, "Liftoff!"));

    clock.start();

    for (Runnable e : events)
        new Thread(e).start();
}
```

The advantage of this technique is that you don't need to create a separate variable for each `LaunchEvent`. (Don't forget to add an `import` statement for the `java.util.*` to gain access to the `ArrayList` class.)

Creating Threads That Work Together

Unfortunately, the countdown application presented in the preceding section has a major deficiency: The CountDownClock and LaunchEvent threads depend strictly on timing to coordinate their activities. After these threads start, they run independently of one another. As a result, random variations in their timings can cause the thread behaviors to change. If you run the program several times in a row, you'll discover that sometimes the Start engines! message appears after the T minus 6 message, and sometimes it appears *before* the T minus 6 message. That might not seem like a big deal to you, but it probably would be disastrous for the astronauts on the spacecraft. What these classes really need is a way to communicate.

Listing 1-4 shows an improved version of the countdown application that incorporates several enhancements. The CountDownClock class in this version adds a new method named getTime that gets the current time in the countdown. Then the LaunchEvent class checks the countdown time every 10 milliseconds and triggers the events only when the countdown clock actually says that it's time. This version of the application runs consistently.

In addition, you want to enable the LaunchEvent class to monitor the status of the CountDownClock, but you don't want to couple the LaunchEvent and CountDownClock classes too closely. Suppose that later, you develop a better countdown clock. If the LaunchEvent class knows what class is doing the counting, you have to recompile it if you use a different countdown class.

The solution is to use an interface as a buffer between the classes. This interface defines a method that gets the current status of the clock. Then the CountDownClock class can implement this interface, and the LaunchEvent class can use any object that implements this interface to get the time.

Listing 1-4:   The Coordinated CountDown Application

```
import java.util.ArrayList;

// version 2.0 of the Countdown application
public class CountDownApp
{
    public static void main(String[] args)
    {
        CountDownClock clock = new CountDownClock(20);      →8
        ArrayList<Runnable> events =
            new ArrayList<Runnable>();                      →10

        events.add(new LaunchEvent(16,                      →12
            "Flood the pad!", clock));
        events.add(new LaunchEvent(6,
            "Start engines!", clock));
```

(continued)

Listing 1-4 *(continued)*

```
        events.add(new LaunchEvent(0,
            "Liftoff!", clock));

        clock.start();                                    →19

        for (Runnable e : events)                         →21
            new Thread(e).start();
    }
}

interface TimeMonitor                                     →26
{
    int getTime();
}

class CountDownClock extends Thread
    implements TimeMonitor                                →31
{
    private int t;                                        →33

    public CountDownClock(int start)                      →35
    {
        this.t = start;
    }

    public void run()
    {
        for (; t >= 0; t--)                               →42
        {
            System.out.println("T minus " + t);
            try
            {
                Thread.sleep(1000);
            }
            catch (InterruptedException e)
            {}
        }
    }

    public int getTime()                                  →54
    {
        return t;
    }
}

class LaunchEvent implements Runnable                     →60
{
    private int start;
    private String message;
    TimeMonitor tm;                                       →64
```

```
    public LaunchEvent(int start, String message,
        TimeMonitor monitor)
    {
        this.start = start;
        this.message = message;
        this.tm = monitor;
    }

    public void run()
    {
      boolean eventDone = false;
      while (!eventDone)
      {
          try
          {
              Thread.sleep(10);                           →81
          }
          catch (InterruptedException e)
          {}
          if (tm.getTime() <= start)                       →85
          {
              System.out.println(this.message);
              eventDone = true;
          }
      }
    }
}
```

The following paragraphs describe the high points of this version:

→ 8 As you see in line 35, the constructor for the CountDownClock class now accepts a parameter to specify the starting time for the countdown. As a result, this line specifies 20 as the starting time for the CountDownClock object.

→ 10 An ArrayList of LaunchEvent objects is used to store each launch event.

→ 12 The lines that create the LaunchEvent objects pass the Count DownClock object as a parameter to the LaunchEvent constructor. That way the LaunchEvent objects can call the clock's abort method if necessary.

→ 19 The clock is started!

→ 21 An enhanced for loop starts threads to run the LaunchEvent objects.

→ 26 The TimeMonitor interface defines just one method, named getTime. This method returns an integer that represents the number of seconds left on the countdown timer.

→ 31 The CountDownClock class implements the TimeMonitor interface.

→ **33**   A private field named `t` is used to store the current value of the countdown clock. That way, the current clock value can be accessed by the constructor, the `run` method, and the `getTime` method.

→ **35**   The constructor for the `CountDownClock` class accepts the starting time for the countdown as a parameter. Thus, this countdown clock doesn't have to start at 20 seconds. The value passed via this parameter is saved in the `t` field.

→ **42**   The `for` loop in the `run` method tests and decrements the `t` variable. But because this variable is already initialized, it doesn't have an initialization expression.

→ **54**   The `getTime()` method simply returns the value of the `t` variable.

→ **60**   This line is the start of the `LaunchEvent` class.

→ **64**   A private field of type `TimeMonitor` is used to access the countdown clock. A reference to this object is passed to the `LaunchEvent` class via its constructor. The constructor simply stores that reference in this field.

→ **81**   The `while` loop includes a call to `Thread.sleep` that sleeps for just 10 milliseconds. Thus, this loop checks the countdown clock every 10 milliseconds to see whether its time has arrived.

→ **85**   This statement calls the `getTime` method of the countdown clock to see whether it's time to start the event. If so, a message is displayed, and `eventDone` is set to true to terminate the thread.

Using an Executor

The countdown application in Listings 1-1 through 1-4 uses Java's original threading mechanisms — tools that were available in the mid-1990s, when Java was in diapers. Since then, Java programmers have longed for newer, more sophisticated threading techniques. The big breakthrough came in 2004, with the release of Java 1.5. The Java API gained a large assortment of classes for fine-grained control of the running of threads. Since then, subsequent releases of Java have added even more classes to give you even better control over how threads execute.

A full discussion of Java threading would require another 850 pages. (How about *Java Threading All-in-One For Masochists*?) This chapter presents only a small sampling of these Java threading features.

Listings 1-5 through 1-7 repeat the work done by Listings 1-1 through 1-4, but Listings 1-5 through 1-7 use Java 1.5 threading classes.

Listing 1-5: A New CountDownClock

```java
public class CountDownClockNew implements Runnable
{
    int t;

    public CountDownClockNew(int t)
    {
        this.t = t;
    }

    public void run()
    {
        System.out.println("T minus " + t);
    }
}
```

Listing 1-6: A New Event Launcher

```java
public class LaunchEventNew implements Runnable
{
    private String message;

    public LaunchEventNew(String message)
    {
        this.message = message;
    }

    public void run()
    {
        System.out.println(message);
    }
}
```

Listing 1-7: A New CountDown Application

```java
import java.util.concurrent.ScheduledThreadPoolExecutor;
import java.util.concurrent.TimeUnit;

class CountDownAppNew
{
    public static void main(String[] args)
    {
        ScheduledThreadPoolExecutor pool =
            new ScheduledThreadPoolExecutor(25);
        Runnable flood, ignition, liftoff;
        flood = new LaunchEventNew("Flood the pad!");
        ignition = new LaunchEventNew("Start engines!");
        liftoff = new LaunchEventNew("Liftoff!");
        for (int t = 20; t >= 0; t--)
```

(continued)

Listing 1-7 *(continued)*

```
            pool.schedule(new CountDownClockNew(t),
                (long) (20 - t), TimeUnit.SECONDS);
        pool.schedule(flood, 3L, TimeUnit.SECONDS);
        pool.schedule(ignition, 13L, TimeUnit.SECONDS);
        pool.schedule(liftoff, 19L, TimeUnit.SECONDS);
        pool.shutdown();
    }
}
```

In the new version of the countdown application, Listing 1-7 does all the busywork. The listing uses the `ScheduledThreadPoolExecutor` class. The class's long name tells much of the story:

✦ **Scheduled:** Using this class, you can schedule a run of code for some future time.

✦ **ThreadPool:** This class typically creates several threads (a pool of threads) at the same time. When you want to run some code, you grab an available thread from the pool and use that thread to run your code.

✦ **Executor:** An `Executor` executes something. No big surprise here!

The loop in Listing 1-7 spawns 20 threads, each with its own initial delay. The fifth loop iteration, for example, calls

```
pool.schedule(new CountDownClockNew(16),
    (long) (20 - 16), TimeUnit.SECONDS);
```

In the `pool.schedule` method call, the number `(long) (20 - 16)` tells Java to wait 4 seconds before running the `T minus 16` thread. Each of the `T minus` threads has a different delay, so each thread runs at the appropriate time. The same is true of the `flood`, `ignition`, and `liftoff` events.

Synchronizing Methods

Whenever you work on a program that uses threads, you have to consider the nasty issue of concurrency. In particular, what if two threads try to access a method of an object at precisely the same time? Unless you program carefully, the result can be disastrous. A method that performs a simple calculation returns inaccurate results. In an online banking application, you might discover that some deposits are credited twice and some withdrawals aren't credited at all. In an online ordering system, one customer's order might get recorded in a different customer's account.

The key to handling concurrency issues is recognizing methods that update data and that might be called by more than one thread. After you identify those methods, the solution is simple. You just add the `synchronized` keyword to the method declaration, like this:

```
public synchronized void someMethod()...
```

This code tells Java to place a *lock* on the object so that no other methods can call any other synchronized methods for the object until this method finishes. In other words, it temporarily disables multithreading for the object. (I discuss locking in the section "Creating a Lock," later in this chapter.)

The next several listings present some concrete examples. Listing 1-8 creates an instance of the CountDownClock class (the class in Listing 1-1).

Listing 1-8: Creating Two CountDownClock Threads

```
import java.util.concurrent.ScheduledThreadPoolExecutor;

public class DoTwoThings
{
    ScheduledThreadPoolExecutor pool =
        new ScheduledThreadPoolExecutor(2);

    CountDownClock clock = new CountDownClock(20);

    public static void main(String[] args)
    {
        new DoTwoThings();
    }

    DoTwoThings()
    {
        pool.execute(clock);
        pool.execute(clock);
        pool.shutdown();
    }
}
```

The resulting output is an unpredictable mishmash of two threads' outputs, with some of the counts duplicated and others skipped altogether, like this:

```
T minus 20
T minus 20
T minus 19
T minus 19
T minus 18
T minus 17
T minus 16
T minus 15
T minus 13
T minus 13
T minus 12
T minus 12
T minus 11
T minus 11
```

```
T minus 10
T minus 9
T minus 7
T minus 7
T minus 6
T minus 5
T minus 4
T minus 3
T minus 2
T minus 2
T minus 1
T minus 0
```

The two threads execute their loops simultaneously, so after one thread displays its T minus 20, the other thread displays its own T minus 20. The same thing happens for T minus 19, T minus 18, and so on.

Then Listing 1-9 spawns two threads, each of which runs a copy of the CountDownClock instance's code.

Listing 1-9:   Creating Two More CountDownClock Threads

```java
import java.util.concurrent.ScheduledThreadPoolExecutor;

public class DoTwoThingsSync
{
    ScheduledThreadPoolExecutor pool =
        new ScheduledThreadPoolExecutor(2);

    CountDownClockSync clock =
        new CountDownClockSync(20);

    public static void main(String[] args)
    {
        new DoTwoThingsSync();
    }

    DoTwoThingsSync()
    {
        pool.execute(clock);
        pool.execute(clock);
        pool.shutdown();
    }
}
```

In Listing 1-10, Java's synchronized keyword ensures that only one thread at a time calls the run method. The resulting output shows one complete execution of the run method followed by another.

Listing 1-10:   Using the synchronized Keyword

```
class CountDownClockSync extends Thread
{
    private int start;

    public CountDownClockSync(int start)
    {
        this.start = start;
    }

    synchronized public void run()
    {
        for (int t = start; t >= 0; t--)
        {
            System.out.println("T minus " + t);
            try
            {
                Thread.sleep(1000);
            }
            catch (InterruptedException e)
            {}
        }
    }
}
```

The two threads' calls to the run method are not interleaved, so the output counts down from 20 to 0 and then counts down a second time from 20 to 0:

```
T minus 20
T minus 19
T minus 18
```

And so on, down to

```
T minus 2
T minus 1
T minus 0
T minus 20
T minus 19
T minus 18
```

And so on, down to

```
T minus 2
T minus 1
T minus 0
```

The tough part is knowing which methods to synchronize. When I said that any method that updates data can be synchronized, I didn't mean just any method that updates a database. Any method that updates instance variables is at risk — and needs to be synchronized. That's because when two or more threads run a method at the same time, the threads have a common copy of the method's instance variables.

Even methods that consist of just one line of code are at risk. Consider this method:

```
int sequenceNumber = 0;
public int getNextSequenceNumber()
{
    return sequenceNumber++;
}
```

You'd think that because this method has just one statement, some other thread could not interrupt it in the middle. Alas, that's not the case. This method must get the value of the sequenceNumber field, add 1 to it, save the updated value back to the sequenceNumber field, and return the value. In fact, this single Java statement compiles to 11 bytecode instructions. If the thread is preempted between any of those bytecodes by another thread calling the same method, the serial numbers get munged.

For safety's sake, why not just make all the methods synchronized? You have two reasons not to do so:

✦ Synchronizing methods takes time. Java has to acquire a lock (see the next section) on the object being synchronized, run the method, and then release the lock. But before it can do that, it has to check to make sure that some other thread doesn't already have a lock on the object. All this work takes time.

✦ More important, synchronizing all your methods defeats the purpose of multithreading, so you should synchronize only those methods that require it.

The synchronized keyword doesn't block all access to an object. Other threads can still run unsynchronized methods of the object while the object is locked.

The Object class provides three methods that can let synchronized objects coordinate their activities. The wait method puts a thread in the waiting state until some other thread calls either the object's notify or (more commonly) notifyAll method. These methods are useful when one thread has to wait for another thread to do something before it can proceed. The classic example is a banking system in which one thread makes withdrawals and the other makes deposits. If a customer's account balance drops to zero, the thread that makes withdrawals can call wait; then the thread that makes deposits can call notifyAll. That way, each time a deposit is made, the withdrawal thread can recheck the customer's account balance to see whether it now has enough money for the customer to make a withdrawal.

Creating a Lock

A few years back, Java version 1.5 introduced many new threading features. One such feature was the introduction of locks. A lock can take the
place of Java's `synchronized` keyword, but a lock is much more versatile.
Listings 1-11 and 1-12 illustrate the use of a lock.

Listing 1-11:   Creating CountDownClock Threads (Again)

```
import java.util.concurrent.ScheduledThreadPoolExecutor;

public class DoTwoThingsLocked {
    ScheduledThreadPoolExecutor pool =
        new ScheduledThreadPoolExecutor(2);
    CountDownClockLocked clock =
        new CountDownClockLocked();

    public static void main(String[] args)
    {
        new DoTwoThingsLocked();
    }

    DoTwoThingsLocked()
    {
        pool.execute(clock);
        pool.execute(clock);
        pool.shutdown();
    }
}
```

Listing 1-12:   Using a Lock

```
import java.util.concurrent.locks.ReentrantLock;

public class CountDownClockLocked extends Thread
{
    ReentrantLock lock = new ReentrantLock();

    public void run()
    {
        lock.lock();
        for (int t = 20; t >= 0; t--)
        {
            System.out.println("T minus " + t);
            try
            {
                Thread.sleep(1000);
            }
```

(continued)

Listing 1-12 *(continued)*

```
            catch (InterruptedException e)
            {}
        }
        lock.unlock();
    }
}
```

Listing 1-12 is remarkably similar to Listing 1-10. The only significant difference is the replacement of the `synchronized` keyword by calls to `ReentrantLock` methods.

At the start of Listing 1-12, the code declares the variable `lock` — an instance of the `ReentrantLock` class. This `lock` object is like a gas station's restroom key: Only one thread at a time can have the `lock` object. When one thread gets the `lock` object — by calling `lock.lock()` at the start of the `run` method — no other thread can get past the `lock.lock()` call. A second thread must wait at the `lock.lock()` call until the "restroom key" becomes available. In Listing 1-12, the key becomes available only when the first thread reaches the `lock.unlock()` statement. After the first thread calls `lock.unlock()`, the second thread proceeds into the method's `for` loop.

The overall result is the same as the output of Listings 1-9 and 1-10. In this example, using a lock is no better than using Java's `synchronized` keyword. But Java 1.5 has several kinds of locks, and each kind of lock has its own useful features.

Coping with Threadus Interruptus

You can interrupt another thread by calling its `interrupt` method, provided that you have a reference to the thread, as in this example:

```
t.interrupt();
```

Here the thread referenced by the `t` variable is interrupted. Now all the interrupted thread has to do is find out that it has been interrupted and respond accordingly. That's the topic of the following sections.

Finding out whether you've been interrupted

As you've already seen, several methods of the `Thread` class, including `sleep` and `yield`, throw `InterruptedException`. Up until now, I've told you to simply ignore this exception — and in many cases, that's appropriate. Many (if not most) threads, however, should respond to `InterruptedException` in one way or another. In most cases, the thread should terminate when it's interrupted.

Unfortunately, finding out whether a thread has been interrupted isn't as easy as it sounds. `InterruptedException` is thrown when another thread calls the `interrupt` method on this thread while the thread is not executing. That's why the methods that can cause the thread to give up control to another thread throw this exception. That way, when the thread resumes execution, you know that it was interrupted.

The `yield` and `sleep` methods aren't the only way for control to be wrested away from a thread, however. Sometimes the thread scheduler just steps in and says, "You've had enough time; now it's someone else's turn to play." If that happens and then some other thread calls your thread's `interrupt` method, `InterruptedException` isn't thrown. Instead, a special flag called the *interrupted flag* is set to indicate that the thread was interrupted. You can test the status of this flag by calling the static `interrupted` method.

Unfortunately, that means your threads have to check twice to see whether they have been interrupted. The usual way to do that is to follow this form:

```
public void run()
{
    boolean done = false
    boolean abort = false;
    while(!done)
    {
        // do the thread_s work here
        // set done to true when finished
        try
        {
            sleep(100);   // sleep a bit
        }
        catch(InterruptedException e)
        {
            abort = true;
        }
        if (Thread.interrupted())
            abort = true;
        if (abort)
            break;
    }
}
```

Here the `boolean` variable `abort` is set to `true` if `InterruptedException` is thrown or if the `interrupted` flag is set. Then, if `abort` has been set to `true`, a `break` statement is executed to leave the `while` loop. This scheme has a million variations, of course, but this one works in most situations.

Aborting the countdown

To illustrate how you can interrupt threads, Listing 1-13 shows yet another version of the countdown application. This version aborts the countdown if something goes wrong with any of the launch events.

To simplify the code a bit, I assume that things aren't going well at NASA, so every launch event results in a failure that indicates a need to abort the countdown. Thus, whenever the start time for a `LaunchEvent` arrives, the `LaunchEvent` class attempts to abort the countdown. It goes without saying that in a real launch-control program, you wouldn't want to abort the launch unless something actually *does* go wrong.

Listing 1-13: The Countdown Application with Aborts

```java
import java.util.ArrayList;

public class CountDownApp
{
    public static void main(String[] args)
    {
        CountDownClock clock = new CountDownClock(20);

        ArrayList<Runnable> events =
            new ArrayList<Runnable>();
        events.add(new LaunchEvent(16,
            "Flood the pad!", clock));
        events.add(new LaunchEvent(6,
            "Start engines!", clock));
        events.add(new LaunchEvent(0,
            "Liftoff!", clock));

        clock.start();

        for (Runnable e : events)
            new Thread(e).start();
    }
}

interface TimeMonitor
{
    int getTime();
    void abortCountDown();
}

class CountDownClock extends Thread
    implements TimeMonitor
{
    private int t;

    public CountDownClock(int start)
    {
        this.t = start;
    }

    public void run()
    {
```

→3

→26

```
        boolean aborted = false;                          →40
        for (; t >= 0; t--)
        {
            System.out.println("T minus " + t);
            try
            {
                Thread.sleep(1000);
            }
            catch (InterruptedException e)
            {
                aborted = true;                            →50
            }
            if (Thread.interrupted())
                aborted = true;                            →53
            if (aborted)                                   →54
            {
                System.out.println(
                    "Stopping the clock!");
                break;
            }
        }
    }

    public int getTime()
    {
        return t;
    }

    public synchronized void abortCountDown()             →67
    {
        Thread[] threads =
            new Thread[Thread.activeCount()];              →69
        Thread.enumerate(threads);                         →70
        for(Thread t : threads)                            →71
            t.interrupt();
    }
}

class LaunchEvent implements Runnable
{
    private int start;
    private String message;
    TimeMonitor tm;

    public LaunchEvent(int start, String message,
        TimeMonitor monitor)
    {
        this.start = start;
        this.message = message;
        this.tm = monitor;
    }
```

(continued)

Listing 1-13 *(continued)*

```
public void run()
{
    boolean eventDone = false;
    boolean aborted = false;                                    →92
    while (!eventDone)
    {
        try
        {
            Thread.sleep(10);
        }
        catch (InterruptedException e)
        {
            aborted = true;                                     →101
        }
        if (tm.getTime() <= start)
        {
            System.out.println(this.message);
            eventDone = true;
            System.out.println("ABORT!!!!");                    →107
            tm.abortCountDown();                                →108
        }
        if (Thread.interrupted())
            aborted = true;                                     →111
        if (aborted)                                            →112
        {
            System.out.println(
                "Aborting " + message);
            break;
        }
    }
}
```

The following paragraphs point out the highlights of this program:

→ 3   The CountDownApp class itself hasn't changed. That's the beauty of object-oriented programming. Although I changed the implementations of the CountDownClock and LaunchEvent classes, I didn't change the public interfaces for these classes. As a result, no changes are needed in the CountDownApp class.

→ 26   The LaunchEvent class needs a way to notify the CountDown Timer class that the countdown should be aborted. To do that, I added an abortCountDown method to the TimeMonitor interface.

→ 40   The run method of the CountDownClass uses a boolean variable named aborted to indicate whether the thread has been interrupted. This variable is set to true in line 50 if InterruptedException is caught. It's also set to true in line 53 if Thread.interrupted() returns true.

→ 54 If the `aborted` field has been set to `true`, it means that the thread has been interrupted, so the message `Stopping the clock!` is displayed, and a `break` statement exits the loop. Thus the thread is terminated.

→ 67 The `abortCountDown` method is synchronized. That happens because any of the `LaunchEvent` objects can call it, and there's no guarantee that they won't all try to call it at the same time.

→ 69 The `abortCountDown` method starts by creating an array of `Thread` objects that's large enough to hold all the active threads. The number of active threads is provided by the `activeCount` method of the `Thread` class.

→ 70 The `abortCountDown` method calls the `enumerate` method of the `Thread` class to copy all the active threads into this array. Note that this method is static, so you don't need a reference to any particular thread to use it. (The `activeCount` method used in line 69 is static too.)

→ 71 An enhanced `for` loop is used to call the `interrupt` method on all the active threads. That method shuts down everything.

→ 92 Like the `CountDownClock` class, the `LaunchEvent` class uses a `boolean` variable to indicate whether the thread has been interrupted. This variable is set if `InterruptedException` is caught in line 101 or if `Thread.interrupted()` returns `true` in line 111; then it's tested in line 112. If the `aborted` variable has been set to `true`, the thread prints a message indicating that the launch event has been aborted, and a `break` statement is used to exit the loop and (therefore) terminate the thread.

→ 101 When the launch event's start time arrives, the `LaunchEvent` class displays the message `ABORT!` and calls the `abortCountDown` method. Thus the countdown is aborted the first time any launch event occurs.

When you run this version of the countdown application, the console output will appear something like this (minor variations might occur because of the synchronization of the threads):

```
T minus 20
T minus 19
T minus 18
T minus 17
T minus 16
Flood the pad!
ABORT!!!!
Stopping the clock!
Aborting Flood the pad!
Aborting Start engines!
Aborting Liftoff!
```

Chapter 2: Network Programming

In This Chapter

✔ IP addresses, DNS names, and other fun stuff

✔ The InetAddress class

✔ The Socket class

✔ The ServerSocket class

✔ A simple client/server program

✔ A server program that uses threads

The term *network programming* can mean a lot of different things. Applets are a form of network programming — as are Java Server Pages and servlets. I cover these network programming features in detail in Book VII.

File and database programming can also be thought of as a form of network programming; files and databases can be located on a server computer rather than on the computer where the application is run. Book VIII covers the networking aspects of file and database programming.

In this chapter, you discover how to use Java's *sockets interface,* which lets you set up input and output streams between programs on client and server computers. In fact, I show you how to create a simple server program that can be accessed over the Internet.

Along the way, you find out about the TCP/IP networking protocol, IP addresses and ports, and other useful networking topics.

Understanding Network Programming

Network programming usually involves two types of programs: client programs and server programs. A *server program* is a program that provides services to one or more users who run *client programs* to access those services. These client and server computers communicate with each other through well-established *protocols,* which dictate the nature of the communications between clients and servers.

Examples of client and server programs abound:

✦ The World Wide Web uses *web servers* that provide services. The clients in the World Wide Web are web browsers, such as Internet Explorer and Navigator. The protocol used to communicate between web servers and browsers is called *HTTP*.

✦ E-mail is made possible by a protocol called *Simple Mail Transfer Protocol,* or SMTP. The servers are mail servers, such as Sendmail and Microsoft Exchange; the clients are e-mail programs, such as Microsoft Outlook.

✦ The Internet system that converts human-friendly addresses such as www.dummies.com to numeric IP addresses such as 208.215.179.139 is managed by a protocol called DNS, which stands for *Domain Name System*. Your own computer serves as a DNS client, requesting address lookup from DNS servers. When you type **www.dummies.com** in your web browser, for example, the browser first asks a DNS server to get the correct IP address for the website.

I could go on and on.

IP addresses and ports

An *IP address* is a number that uniquely identifies every computer on an IP network. IP addresses are 32-bit binary numbers, which means that theoretically, a maximum of something in the neighborhood of 4 billion unique host addresses can exist throughout the Internet.

IP addresses are usually represented in a format known as *dotted-decimal notation*. In dotted-decimal notation, each group of 8 bits, known as an *octet,* is represented by its decimal equivalent, as in this example:

```
192.168.136.28
```

You usually see IP addresses represented in this format.

Besides having an IP address, you must use a port to access data from a computer over the Internet. The various services that a server computer might provide are assigned well-known port numbers. The port number for the web protocol HTTP, for example, is 80. As a result, a computer that wants to access a web server HTTP must do so over port 80.

Port numbers are often specified with a colon following an IP address. The HTTP service on a server whose IP address is 192.168.10.133 is 192.168.10.133:80.

Literally thousands of established ports are in use. If you need to make up a port number for an application, pick one that's greater than 49151 but less than 65,535 (the maximum allowable port number). Port numbers above 49151 are available for private use. (You can find a list of commonly used port numbers by searching **common IP ports** on a search engine such as Google.)

Host names, DNS, and URLs

A *host name* is a name that's associated with a particular IP address. Host names are created according to the DNS naming standard. If it weren't for DNS, you'd buy books from 205.251.242.54 instead of from www.amazon.com, you'd sell your used furniture at 66.135.205.14 instead of on www.ebay.com, and you'd search the web at 74.125.224.70 instead of at www.google.com.

The Internet has an entire network of DNS server computers throughout the world that look up host names and provide the corresponding IP address. When you enter **www.dummies.com** in the address bar of a web browser, your browser consults a DNS server to find out the IP address for www.dummies.com; then it displays the home page for that address.

Closely related to DNS is URL, which stands for *Uniform Resource Locator*. URL is a naming scheme that can uniquely identify any resource on the Internet. By *resource,* I usually mean *file*. Thus URLs turn the DNS naming system into a huge file system that lets you access any file that's available anywhere on the Internet. It does this by appending file path information to the end of a host name, like this:

```
ftp.someserver.com/pub/myfile.txt
```

This URL refers to a file named myfile.txt in a directory named pub on a computer identified by the host name ftp.someserver.com. I won't deal with URLs in this chapter, but they play a big role in web programming, so be prepared to revisit them in Book VII.

Every computer has a special host name and IP address that's used to identify itself to itself. This host name is localhost, and the IP address is 127.0.0.1. This it's-all-about-me address is sometimes called the *loopback address*. localhost is an invaluable testing feature because it lets you test networking programs without requiring that you use separate computers. In other words, you can run a client and server program on the same computer by having them both use localhost to refer to each other.

telnet

The handy debugging tool telnet can let you check out network programs interactively. It comes free with just about every operating system, though it may not be installed automatically. If you don't have it, you may have to retrieve it from your operating system's discs.

Using telnet is easy. From a command prompt, just type **telnet** followed by the name of the host (or its IP address) and the port number you want to connect to. Here's an example:

```
telnet somecomputer.com 80
```

This command connects to port 80 of somecomputer.com.

To connect to a network server program running on the same computer you're running telnet on, just use `localhost` as the host name. Here's a command that connects to a server program using port 1234:

```
telnet localhost 1234
```

After telnet fires up, anything you type is sent to the port, and anything received from the port is displayed in the telnet window.

You may have to configure telnet to echo characters that you type so you can see what you're typing. Each telnet program has a different way to do this, so you have to consult the program's help to find out. (Try running `telnet -?` from the command prompt to get help.)

On Windows Vista and later systems, telnet is disabled by default. To enable it, follow these steps:

1. **Open the Control Panel.**

   On Windows 7 (and prior systems), choose Start⇨Control Panel⇨Programs and Features.

   On Windows 8, call up the Apps screen by swiping the Start screen and then scroll to the right to reveal the Windows System category. Tap the Control Panel icon.

2. **Click Turn Windows Features On or Off.**

3. **Check the Telnet Client option.**

4. **Click OK.**

After a few moments, your computer will be ready to run telnet.

Telnet is a notoriously insecure protocol. It sends all of its information, including usernames and passwords, in plain text that can be easily intercepted by an intruder listening in on your network. The telnet client is perfectly safe to use for the examples described in this chapter, but I recommend you do *not* use the telnet client to communicate with applications that require password authentication. Instead, use a more secure program, such as PuTTY (www. putty.org).

Getting Information about Internet Hosts

One of the most useful Java API classes for network programming is the `InetAddress` class. In the following sections, you discover what this class does and how to use it in a simple program that displays the IP address used for any domain name.

The InetAddress class

As you know, an IP address is simply a number that corresponds to a particular host computer on the Internet. The designers of Java could simply have represented IP addresses as `long` numbers. Instead, they created a powerful class called `InetAddress` that represents an IP address.

The `InetAddress` includes several useful methods that let you create `Inet Address` objects from strings that represent IP addresses or host names, or perform useful lookups to find out the IP address for a given host name (or vice versa). Table 2-1 lists the most commonly used methods.

Table 2-1	Methods of the InetAddress Class
Method	*Description*
`byte[] getAddress()`	Returns the raw IP address as an array of bytes.
`static InetAddress[] getAllByName(String host)`	Returns an array of Internet addresses for the specified host name. This method performs a DNS query to get the addresses. It throws `UnknownHostException` if the specified host doesn't exist.
`static InetAddress getByName(String host)`	Returns the Internet address for the specified host name or IP address. This method performs a DNS query to get the address. It throws `UnknownHostException` if the specified host doesn't exist.
`String getCannonicalHostName()`	Returns the fully qualified host name for this IP address.
`String getHostAddress()`	Returns the IP address as a formatted string.
`String getHostName()`	Performs a reverse DNS lookup to get the host name for this IP address.
`boolean isReachable (int timeout)`	Determines whether the IP address can be reached. The attempt fails if no response is reached before the timeout period (in milliseconds) elapses.
`String toString()`	Converts the IP address to a string. The result includes both the host name and the IP address.

Here are a few additional points about this class:

✦ This class doesn't have a constructor. Instead, the normal way to create it is to call one of its static methods, such as `getByName`.

✦ The `isReachable`, `getAllByName`, and `getByName` methods throw exceptions.

✦ Several of these methods perform DNS queries to determine their return values. These methods use the DNS server configured for your system to perform these queries.

✦ This class is part of the `java.net` package, so any program that uses it must import either `java.net.InetAddress` or `java.net.*`.

A program that looks up host names

Listing 2-1 presents a program that uses the `InetAddress` class to look up the IP addresses associated with any given host name. This program uses the `getAllByName` method of the `InetAddress` class to do this lookup. Here's a sample of what this handy little program can do:

```
Welcome to the IP lookup application.

Enter a host name: www.wiley.com
www.wiley.com/208.215.179.146

Look up another? (Y or N) y

Enter a host name: www.dummies.com
www.dummies.com/208.215.179.139

Look up another? (Y or N) y

Enter a host name: www.amazon.com
www.amazon.com/72.21.215.232

Look up another? (Y or N) n
```

Note that your output will vary, as the IP address for any of these websites may change at any time.

As you can see, this program prompts the user for a host name. Then it looks up the IP address or addresses for the host name, displays the results, and asks the user whether he wants to look up another host.

The Façade pattern

The `InetAddress` class is an example of a commonly used design pattern called the *Façade pattern*. In this pattern, you use a single class to hide the details of a complex object or set of related classes. The `InetAddress` class combines the representation of an IP address with a variety of tasks that are commonly associated with IP addresses, such as using DNS to get the IP address based on a host name. (An even better example of the Façade pattern is the `URL` class, which provides a single class to access the complex features of URLs.)

The Façade pattern is commonly used in Java programming, especially in systems that need to incorporate access to complicated existing systems. Suppose that you have a fully integrated order-handling system in place, and you want to provide a way for web users to order directly from your company via this system. Unfortunately, the existing system is way too complicated for your customers to use directly. It's designed to be used by trained sales personnel and provides access to many sales features that your customers don't need and shouldn't be exposed to.

One way to do this is to create a facade for the ordering system. This facade includes an interface that provides just the classes and methods needed to implement your ordering system online, hiding as much of the complexity of the real ordering system as possible.

Listing 2-1: The HostLookup Application

```
import java.util.Scanner;
import java.net.*;                                           →2

public class HostLookup
{
    static Scanner sc = new Scanner(System.in);

    public static void main(String[] args)
    {
        System.out.println(
            "Welcome to the IP lookup application.");
        String host;
        do                                                   →11
        {
            System.out.print("\nEnter a host name: ");
            host = sc.nextLine();                            →14
            try
            {
                InetAddress[] addresses                      →17
                    = InetAddress.getAllByName(host);
                for (InetAddress ip : addresses)             →19
                    System.out.println(ip.toString());       →20
            }
            catch (UnknownHostException e)
```

(continued)

Listing 2-1 *(continued)*

```
        {
            System.out.println("Unknown host.");
        }
    } while (doAgain());                                          →26
}

private static boolean doAgain()
{
    System.out.println();
    String s;
    while (true)
    {
        System.out.print("Look up another? "
        + "(Y or N) ");
        s = sc.nextLine();
        if (s.equalsIgnoreCase("Y"))
            return true;
        else if (s.equalsIgnoreCase("N"))
            return false;
    }
}
}
```

The following paragraphs describe the key lines in this program:

→ 2   The InetAddress class lives in the java.net package, so an
        import statement is required to use it.

→ 11   This do loop lets the user look up as many host names as she
        wants. The loop ends in line 26, which calls the doAgain method
        to ask the user whether she wants to look up another host.

→ 14   This line gets the host name the user wants to look up and saves it
        in the string variable host.

→ 17   This statement creates an array variable named addresses whose
        type is InetAddress. In other words, this variable holds an array
        of Internet addresses. Then it calls the static getAllByName
        method of the InetAddress class, passing the host name entered
        in line 14 as the parameter. This method performs a DNS lookup on
        the host name and returns an array that contains all the Internet
        addresses for the name.

→ 19   An enhanced for loop is used to process each InetAddress
        object in the addresses array.

→ 20   This line calls the toString method to convert an Internet address
        to a string. The string returned by the toString method includes
        both the host name and the IP address.

Creating Network Server Applications

One popular form of network programming is creating client and server programs that work together to perform specific tasks. These programs communicate by sending information over the network. The format of this information is governed by a *protocol,* which is merely an agreement on the types of messages the clients and servers can send and receive.

A few hundred well-established protocols already exist for such things as sending e-mail and web pages, looking up DNS names, sharing files, and so on. For specialized networking applications, however, you may find yourself developing your own protocol to coordinate your clients and servers.

Each protocol usually has a unique port assigned to it. Port 80 is reserved for the HTTP protocol used to exchange web pages, for example, and port 25 is used for the standard Internet e-mail protocol known as SMTP (Simple Mail Transfer Protocol). If you end up creating your own protocol, you need to pick a port that doesn't conflict with any of the known ports or with any ports that the users of your application may already be using for other purposes.

Client and server computers establish a connection on a port by means of a special object called a *socket.* In the following sections, I talk about two Java classes that are designed to work with sockets. Then you see an example of a simple server program and a client that's designed to work with the server.

In this section, I look at two classes that are designed for communicating through sockets. The first, `Socket`, represents a basic socket object. The second, `ServerSocket`, is used to help servers establish socket connections with clients.

The Socket class

The `Socket` class represents a socket connection between two programs. Although the programs can be running on the same computer, they don't have to be. In fact, any two computers that are connected to the Internet can communicate via a socket. Table 2-2 lists the most commonly used constructors and methods of this class.

Table 2-2	Constructors and Methods of the Socket Class
Constructor	*Description*
`Socket()`	Creates an unconnected socket.
`Socket(InetAddress address, int port)`	Creates a socket and connects it to the specified address and port.
`Socket(String host, int port)`	Creates a socket and connects it to the specified host and port.

(continued)

Table 2-2 *(continued)*

Method	Description
`void Close()`	Closes the socket.
`void connect (InetSocketAddress endpoint)`	Connects the socket to the specified address.
`InetAddress getInetAddress()`	Gets the address to which the socket is connected.
`InputStream getInputStream()`	Gets an input stream that can be used to receive data sent through this socket.
`OutputStream getOutputstream()`	Gets an output stream that can be used to send data through this socket.
`int getPort()`	Gets the port to which this socket is connected.
`boolean isBound()`	Indicates whether the socket is bound to a port.
`boolean isClosed()`	Indicates whether the socket is closed.

Here are a few important details about the `Socket` class:

+ Although the `Socket` class has constructors that let you connect to a specific address, the normal way to create a socket is to use the `attach` method of the `ServerSocket` class.

+ The `InputStream` object returned by the `getInputStream` method can be passed to a constructor of the `Scanner` class. Then you can use the resulting `Scanner` object to retrieve data from the socket.

+ The `getOutputStream` method returns an object of the `OutputStream` class. This is the same class used by `System.out`. As a result, you can use the familiar `print` and `println` methods to send data to the socket.

+ All the constructors and methods of this class except the default constructor and the `getInetAddress`, `getPort`, `isBound`, and `isClosed` methods throw exceptions. As a result, you need to enclose calls to these methods in a `try/catch` statement.

The ServerSocket class

A *server socket* is a socket that lets clients connect with your application. When a client connects, the server socket creates a `Socket` object, which the application can use to communicate with the client. Table 2-3 lists the most commonly used constructors and methods of this class.

Table 2-3   Constructors and Methods of the ServerSocket Class

Constructor	Description
`ServerSocket()`	Creates a server socket that isn't bound to any port.
`ServerSocket(int port)`	Creates a server socket and binds it to the specified port. Then the server socket listens for connection attempts on this port.

Method	Description
`Socket attach()`	Listens for connection attempts via the port this socket is bound to. The thread that calls this method waits until a connection is made. Then this method exits, returning a `Socket` object that can be used to communicate with the client.
`void bind (InetSocketAddress endpoint)`	Binds this server socket to the specified address.
`void close()`	Closes the server socket.
`InetAddress getInetAddress()`	Gets the address to which the server socket is connected.
`boolean isBound()`	Indicates whether the server socket is bound to a port.
`boolean isClosed()`	Indicates whether the server socket is closed.

Here are some important points to remember about the `ServerSocket` class:

✦ When you call the `attach` method, the thread is suspended until a connection is made.

✦ The second constructor and the `attach`, `bind`, and `close` methods throw exceptions. As a result, you need to enclose calls to these methods in a `try/catch` statement.

Introducing BART

In this section, I create a simple network-server program that provides clients with a randomly selected quote from a well-known television program called *The Shrimpsons.* It seems that a certain young boy on this program, whose name shall remain unknown, frequently has to write sentences on the blackboard as punishment. The sentences that he has been known to write have some minor amusement value.

I call the server the BartServer and the protocol used to communicate with the BartServer BART — short for *Blackboard Assignment Retrieval Transaction,* because it allows you to randomly retrieve blackboard assignments. The protocol itself is simple:

1. When you connect to the BartServer, it displays a greeting line and a line of instructions.

2. If you send the command `get`, the BartServer replies by sending you a randomly selected sentence from one of the young man's blackboard assignments.

3. If you send the command `bye`, the BartServer disconnects you.

4. If you send anything else, the BartServer replies `Huh?`

The BartServer communicates over port 1234. After you get the BartServer up and running on your computer, you can test it by running the `telnet` command from a command prompt. Type the command **telnet localhost 1234**, and you're greeted by a message indicating that you have connected successfully. Here's a typical telnet session with the BartServer:

```
Welcome to BartServer 1.0
Enter GET to get a quote or BYE to exit.
get
I will not waste chalk.
get
I will not instigate a revolution.
get
I will not conduct my own fire drills.
gte
Huh?
bye
So long, suckers!
Connection to host lost.
```

Don't forget — it's *The Shrimp-sons*. We don't want to get sued, now, do we?

The BartQuote class

Before you roll up your sleeves and look at the network programming required to implement the BartServer, take a look at the supporting class, named `BartQuote`. This class has a single method named `getQuote` that returns one of 20 randomly selected blackboard sentences. The code for this class is shown in Listing 2-2.

Note that the sentences are hard-coded into this program. That's not the way you'd do it if you really wanted to use the BartServer. Instead, you'd put the sentences in a file and read the file each time you start up the server. (I don't cover file I/O until Book VIII, though, and I don't want to introduce any code here that you couldn't follow, because the network programming in the rest of this chapter is complicated enough. Don't have a cow, man.)

Listing 2-2:   The BartQuote Class

```java
import java.util.ArrayList;

public class BartQuote
{
    ArrayList<String> q = new ArrayList<String>();              →5

    public BartQuote()                                         →7
    {
        q.add("I will not waste chalk.");
        q.add("I will not skateboard in the halls.");
        q.add("I will not burp in class.");
        q.add("I will not instigate a revolution.");
        q.add("It's potato, not potatoe.");
        q.add("I will not encourage others to fly.");
        q.add("Tar is not a plaything.");
        q.add("I will not sell school property.");
        q.add("I will not get very far with this "
            + "attitude.");
        q.add("I will not sell land in Florida.");
        q.add("I will not grease the monkey bars.");
        q.add("I will not hide behind the Fifth "
            + "Amendment.");
        q.add("I am not a dentist.");
        q.add("I will finish what I sta");
        q.add("Hamsters cannot fly.");
        q.add("I will not aim for the head.");
        q.add("I will not expose the ignorance "
            + "of the faculty.");
        q.add("I will not conduct my own fire "
            + "drills.");
        q.add("I will not fake seizures.");
        q.add("This punishment is not boring "
            + "and meaningless.");
    }

    public String getQuote()                                  →33
    {
        int i = (int)(Math.random() * q.size());
        return q.get(i);
    }
}
```

Here are the key points of this class:

→ 5   The sentences are kept in an `ArrayList` object named q. If
       you haven't read about the `ArrayList` class, run (don't walk) to
       Book IV, Chapter 3.

→ 7   The `BartQuote` constructor uses the `add` method of the
       `ArrayList` class to add 20 sentences to the array list.

→ 33   The `getQuote` method returns a sentence randomly selected from the array list. `Math.random` is used to calculate the random number. (For more information about `Math.random`, refer to Book II, Chapter 3.)

The BartServer program

The `BartServer` program is the program you run on a server computer to provide randomly selected blackboard sentences for clients that want them. This program is shown in Listing 2-3.

Listing 2-3:   The BartServer Program

```
import java.net.*;                                           →1
import java.util.*;
import java.io.*;

public class BartServer
{
    public static void main(String[] args)
    {
        int port = 1234;                                    →9

        BartQuote bart = new BartQuote();                   →11

        try
        {
            System.out.println("BartServer 1.0");
            System.out.println("Listening on port " + port);
            ServerSocket ss;                                →17
            ss = new ServerSocket(port);
            Socket s;                                       →20
            s = ss.accept();

            String client;
            client = s.getInetAddress().toString();         →24
            System.out.println("Connected to " + client);

            Scanner in;
            in = new Scanner(s.getInputStream());           →28
            PrintWriter out;
            out = new PrintWriter(s.getOutputStream(),
                true);                                      →31

            out.println("Welcome to BartServer 1.0");       →33
            out.println("Enter GET to get a quote "
                + "or BYE to exit.");

            while (true)                                    →37
            {
```

```
        String input = in.nextLine();                    →39
        if (input.equalsIgnoreCase("bye"))
            break;
        else if (input.equalsIgnoreCase("get"))
        {
            out.println(bart.getQuote());
            System.out.println("Serving " + client);
        }
        else
            out.println("Huh?");
    }
    out.println("So long, suckers!");
    s.close();                                            →51
    System.out.println(
        "Closed connection to " + client);
    }
    catch (Exception e)                                   →55
    {
        e.printStackTrace();
    }
    }
}
```

The following paragraphs walk you through the key parts of this program:

→ 1   This program begins with an `import` statement to import the
       `java.net` package. Notice also that the `java.io` package is
       imported. Later in this program, you'll see that this program uses
       the `PrintWriter` class. You're already familiar with this class:
       `System.out` is a `PrintWriter` object.

→ 9   The `port` variable stores the port that the server communicates
       on. This variable is hard-coded with the value `1234`, but you could
       just as easily ask the user to enter the port number or read it from
       a configuration file.

→ 11   This line creates a new instance of the `BartQuote` class and
       assigns it to a variable named `bart`.

→ 17   This line and the next line declare a `ServerSocket` variable and
       create a new `ServerSocket` object using the `port` variable. As a
       result, this `ServerSocket` object can be used to establish client
       connections on port 1234.

→ 20   This line declares a `Socket` variable. Then the next line uses the
       `accept` method of the `ServerSocket` object to wait for a client
       to connect to port 1234. When a client connects, a `Socket` object
       is created and assigned to the variable s.

→ 24   This statement uses the `getInetAddress` method of the `Socket`
       object to get an `InetAddress` object that represents the client's
       IP address. Then it uses the `InetAddress` object's `toString`

method to create a string that shows the client's address. This string is saved to the `client` variable.

→ **28**   The `BartServer` program uses a `Scanner` object to read data sent from the client over the socket. In this line, it uses the socket's `getInputStream` method to get a standard input stream for the socket. Next, it uses this input stream as a parameter to the `Scanner` constructor, which in turn creates a `Scanner` object that works over the socket's input stream. Then you can use the `Scanner` object referenced by the `in` variable to get commands sent to the server from clients.

→ **31**   You do a similar thing to get a `PrintWriter` object that can send data to a client through the socket. The `getOutputStream` method gets a standard output stream, which is used as a parameter to the `PrintWriter` constructor. Then this `PrintWriter` is assigned to a variable named `out`.

→ **33**   These lines send the greeting messages to the client.

→ **37**   The `while` loop processes commands from the client until the `bye` command is entered. That way, the client can request as many blackboard sentences as it wants.

→ **39**   The `Scanner` object is used to get a line of input from the client. Then the client input is checked with nested `if` statements. If the client sent `bye`, the `break` statement breaks the `while` loop. If the client sent `get`, the `getQuote` method of the `BartQuote` object is called to get a random quote, and the quote is sent to the client via a `println` command. If the user enters anything else, the server sends back `Huh?`.

→ **51**   When the loop ends, the program displays a farewell message and closes the socket connection.

→ **55**   Most of the `Socket` class methods throw an exception if something goes wrong with the socket connection. That's why most of the statements for the `main` method are contained in a `try` block. If an exception is thrown, `e.printStackTrace` is called to print detailed information about the exception on the console.

You may have noticed that the BartServer program displays various status messages in its console window as it runs. When a client connects, it displays a message showing the IP address of the client, and when a client requests a quote, it displays a message on the console. Here's a typical console screen for BartServer that shows a client connecting, requesting three quotes, and then disconnecting:

```
BartServer 1.0
Listening on port 1234
Connected to /127.0.0.1
Serving /127.0.0.1
```

```
Serving /127.0.0.1
Serving /127.0.0.1
Closed connection to /127.0.0.1
```

This program is pretty simple as network-server programs go. Still, it illustrates the basic techniques of network-server programming. Many server programs consist mostly of a big `while` loop that gets input from the client, inspects the input to see what the client wants to do, does what the client asks, and then sends some output back to the client.

Note: You may get a firewall warning message when you run this program. If you get a warning from your firewall when you run the BartServer program, you can safely dismiss the warning message.

The BartClient program

The preceding section shows you how to connect to the `BartServer` program with telnet to interact with the server. This section presents a client program that communicates with a `BartServer` server. The program starts by asking the user for a host name; then it connects to `BartServer` at that host, requests a quote, and displays that result on the computer's console 20 times (as though the console were a blackboard).

Figure 2-1 shows a typical execution of this program. Here I entered `localhost` as the `BartServer` host. `localhost` is useful for testing clients and servers together on the same computer system. The Java code for this program is shown in Listing 2-4.

```
G:\WINDOWS\System32\cmd.exe                              _ □ ×
Welcome to the Bart Client

What server do you want to connect to?localhost
Connected on port 1234
I will not hide behind the Fifth Amendment.
I will not hide behind the Fifth Amendment.
I will not hide behind the Fifth Amendment.
I will not hide behind the Fifth Amendment.
I will not hide behind the Fifth Amendment.
I will not hide behind the Fifth Amendment.
I will not hide behind the Fifth Amendment.
I will not hide behind the Fifth Amendment.
I will not hide behind the Fifth Amendment.
I will not hide behind the Fifth Amendment.
I will not hide behind the Fifth Amendment.
I will not hide behind the Fifth Amendment.
I will not hide behind the Fifth Amendment.
I will not hide behind the Fifth Amendment.
I will not hide behind the Fifth Amendment.
I will not hide behind the Fifth Amendment.
I will not hide behind the Fifth Amendment.
I will not hide behind the Fifth Amendment.
I will not hide behind the Fifth Amendment.
I will not hide behind the Fifth Amendment.
Press any key to continue . . .
```

Figure 2-1:
Running the
BartClient
program.

Listing 2-4:   The BartClient Program

```
import java.net.*;
import java.util.*;
import java.io.*;

public class BartClient
{
    public static void main(String[] args)
    {
        int port = 1234;

        System.out.println("Welcome to the Bart Client\n");

        Socket s = getSocket(port);                              →13

        try
        {
            System.out.println("Connected on port " + port);

            Scanner in =
                new Scanner(s.getInputStream());                 →20
            PrintWriter out;
            out = new PrintWriter(s.getOutputStream(),
                true);                                           →23

            // discard the welcome message
            in.nextLine();                                       →26

            // discard the exit instructions
            in.nextLine();                                       →29

            // get a quote
            out.println("get");                                  →32
            String quote = in.nextLine();                        →33

            // disconnect from the server
            out.println("bye");                                  →36
            s.close();                                           →37

            // write the quote on the chalkboard
            for (int i = 0; i < 20; i++)                         →41
                System.out.println(quote);
        }
        catch (Exception e)
        {
            e.printStackTrace();                                 →46
        }
    }

    private static Socket getSocket(int port)                    →50
    {
        Socket s;
        String host;
        InetAddress ip;

        Scanner sc = new Scanner(System.in);
        while (true)
        {
            System.out.print(
                "What server do you want to connect to?");
```

```
    host = sc.nextLine();                                          →62
    try
    {
        ip = InetAddress.getByName(host);                          →65
        s = new Socket(ip, port);                                  →66
        return s;                                                  →67
    }
    catch (UnknownHostException e)                                 →69
    {
        System.out.println("The host is unknown.");
    }
    catch (IOException e)
    {
        System.out.println("Network error.");
    }
    }
}
}
```

Here's an explanation of the more confusing aspects of this program:

→ **13**   Connecting to a server is a complicated enough procedure that I placed it in a separate method named `getSocket`. This method prompts the user for a host name and doesn't return until the user enters one that the program can connect to. The port number is passed as a parameter, and the return value is a `Socket` object that's connected to the server. (The nitty-gritty details about how this method works start with line 50.)

→ **20**   This statement gets a `Scanner` object that can be used to read data from the client via the socket's input stream.

→ **23**   This statement gets a `PrintWriter` object that can be used to send data to the client via the socket's output stream.

→ **26**   After it's connected, the server sends a welcome message. This message is helpful to users connected via telnet, but it isn't very useful to a client program such as this one. So this statement simply uses the `Scanner` object to read the line from the input stream and discards it.

Because the welcome message includes the version number for the server, the program could read the line and check it to make sure you're connected to a current version of the server. I don't think there will be much demand for additional features in `BartServer`, though, so you don't have to worry about version checking.

→ **29**   The server also sends a line of helpful instructions that you need to read from the stream and discard.

→ **32**   This line sends the word `get` to the server. That's how the client program asks the server to send back a randomly selected sentence.

→ **33**   After sending the `get` request, the client reads the next line of data from the socket input stream. Note that if delays occur because the network is slow, the `nextLine` method simply waits until the line has been sent.

→ 36   Having got what it came for (a blackboard sentence), the client program sends a `bye` command to the server. The server sends back a rude farewell message, but the client program isn't interested in it, so it doesn't even bother to read it.

→ 37   The connection to the server is closed.

→ 41   Now that the client program has its blackboard-sentence-writing assignment, it uses a `for` loop to write it on the board 20 times.

→ 46   Any of the `socket I/O` statements can throw exceptions. They are all caught here as a generic exception, and the diagnostic information is sent to the console so you can debug any problems that might arise.

→ 50   The `getSocket` method accepts a port number as a parameter and returns a socket that's connected via the specified port. This method doesn't give up until the user enters the name of a host that the program can connect to.

→ 62   The host name is read from the console.

→ 65   The static `getByName` method of the `InetAddress` class is called to get an IP address for the host name entered by the user. Note that if the user enters a host name that doesn't exist, `UnknownHostException` is thrown. This exception is caught in line 69.

→ 66   Now that you have an IP address, this line tries to create a `Socket` object using the specified address and port. This method throws `IOException` if it isn't able to connect to the IP address and port.

→ 67   If you make it to this line, you can assume the socket has been created and you're connected. So the `return` statement passes the socket back to the caller, in line 13.

Working with BartServer 2.0

The `BartServer` program presented in the previous section works fine, but it has one major deficiency: It handles connections for only one client. To make matters worse, it quits when that client disconnects. That's not much of a server.

So after much user feedback, I decided to release BartServer 2.0, with new and improved features. BartServer 2.0 uses threads to allow multiple clients to connect to the server at the same time. Each time a client connects, a thread is started to process any requests for that client. The main thread continues to run, waiting for other clients to connect. Figure 2-2 shows the multithreading features of BartServer 2.0 in action. Listing 2-5 shows the code for version 2.0 of BartServer.

Figure 2-2:
BartClients
galore!

Listing 2-5:   BartServer 2.0

```java
import java.net.*;
import java.io.*;
import java.util.*;

public class BartServer2
{
    public static void main(String[] args)
    {
        int port = 1234;

        BartQuote bart = new BartQuote();

        try
        {
            System.out.println("BartServer 2.0");
            System.out.println("Listening on port " + port);
            ServerSocket ss = new ServerSocket(port);

            while (true)                                        →19
            {
                Socket s = ss.accept();
                System.out.println(
                    "Connection established!");
                Thread t = new Thread(
                    new BartThread(s, bart));                   →25
                t.start();
            }
        }
```

(continued)

Listing 2-5 *(continued)*

```
            catch (Exception e)
            {
                System.out.println("System exception!");
            }
        }
    }
}


class BartThread implements Runnable                                →36
{
    private Socket s;
    private BartQuote bart;

    public BartThread(Socket socket, BartQuote bart)                →41
    {
        this.s = socket;
        this.bart = bart;
    }

    public void run()                                              →47
    {
        String client = s.getInetAddress().toString();
        System.out.println("Connected to " + client);
        try
        {
            Scanner in = new Scanner(s.getInputStream());
            PrintWriter out;
            out = new PrintWriter(s.getOutputStream(),
                true);

            out.println("Welcome to the Bart Server");
            out.println("Enter BYE to exit.");

            while (true)
            {
                String input = in.nextLine();
                if (input.equalsIgnoreCase("bye"))
                    break;
                else if (input.equalsIgnoreCase("get"))
                {
                    out.println(bart.getQuote());
                    System.out.println("Serving " + client);
                }
                else
                    out.println("Huh?");
            }
            out.println("So long, suckers!");
            s.close();
        }
        catch (Exception e)
        {
            e.printStackTrace();
        }

        System.out.println("Closed connection to " + client);
    }
}
```

Most of this code is the same as the code in version 1.0, so I just highlight the key changes:

→ 19   A `while` loop is used to service connection requests through the `accept` method of the `ServerSocket` object.

→ 25   Each time a new client connects, a thread is created using the `BartThread` class to create the thread's `Runnable` object. Then, this thread is started. In the meantime, the main thread stays in the `while` loop, waiting for other clients to connect.

If threading gives you a serious headache, you may want to turn back a chapter and review the information on programming with threads in Book V, Chapter 1.

→ 36   The `BartThread` handles the processing required for each connected client. This class implements `Runnable`, which means it must define a `run` method. The `run` method is called each time a new thread is created.

→ 41   The constructor for the `BartThread` class initializes the two class fields with values passed as parameters from the main thread. These parameters are the `Socket` object the client is connected to and a shared copy of the `BartQuote` object that was created by the main thread.

It isn't shown here, but the `getQuote` method of the `BartQuote` class used by this version of `BartServer` should be synchronized. That's because multiple threads access it. For more information, refer to Book V, Chapter 1.

→ 47   The `run` method services the requests for a single client connected to the BartServer. Most of the code in this method was simply copied straight from the previous version, so you shouldn't have any trouble understanding how this method works.

Chapter 3: Using Regular Expressions

In This Chapter

✔ Introducing regular expressions

✔ Trying out regular expressions with a helpful program

✔ Creating simple expressions that match patterns of characters

✔ Using regular expression features such as custom classes, quantifiers, and groups

✔ Using regular expressions with the String class

✔ Using the Pattern and Matcher classes for more-extensive regular expressions

Regular expressions are not expressions that have a lot of fiber in their diet. Instead, a *regular expression* is a special type of pattern-matching string that can be very useful for programs that do string manipulation. Regular expression strings contain special pattern-matching characters that can be matched against another string to see whether the other string fits the pattern. Regular expressions are very handy for doing complex data validation — for making sure that users enter properly formatted phone numbers, e-mail addresses, or Social Security numbers, for example.

Regular expressions are also useful for many other purposes, including searching text files to see whether they contain certain patterns (can you say, Google?), filtering e-mail based on its contents, or performing complicated search-and-replace functions.

In this chapter, you find out the basics of using regular expressions. I emphasize validation and focus on comparing strings entered by users against patterns specified by regular expressions to see whether they match up. For more complex uses of regular expressions, you have to turn to a more extensive regular expression reference. You can find several in-depth tutorials using a search engine such as Google; search for **regular expression tutorial**.

Regular expressions are constructed in a simple but powerful mini-language, so they're like little programs unto themselves. Unfortunately, this mini-language is terse — very terse — to the point of sometimes being downright arcane. Much of it depends on single characters packed with meaning that's

often obscure. So be warned — the syntax for regular expressions takes a little getting used to. After you get your mind around the basics, however, you'll find that simple regular expressions aren't that tough to create and can be very useful.

Also be aware that this chapter covers only a portion of all you can do with regular expressions. If you find that you need to use more complicated patterns, you can find plenty of helpful information on the Internet. Just search any search engine for *regular expression*.

A regular expression is often called a *regex*. Most people pronounce that with a soft *g*, as though it were spelled *rejex*, and some people pronounce it as though it were spelled *rejects*.

Creating a Program for Experimenting with Regular Expressions

Before I get into the details of putting together regular expressions, let me direct your attention to Listing 3-1, which presents a short program that can be very useful while you're learning how to create regular expressions. First, this program lets you enter a regular expression. Next, you can enter a string, and the program tests it against the regular expression and lets you know whether the string matches the regex. Then the program prompts you for another string to compare. You can keep entering strings to compare with the regex you've already entered. When you're done, just press the Enter key without entering a string. The program asks whether you want to enter another regular expression. If you answer yes (y), the whole process repeats. If you answer no (n), the program ends.

Listing 3-1:   The Regular Expression Test Program

```
import java.util.regex.*;
import java.util.Scanner;

public final class Reg {

    static String r, s;
    static Pattern pattern;
    static Matcher matcher;
    static boolean match, validRegex, doneMatching;

    private static Scanner sc =
        new Scanner(System.in);

    public static void main(String[] args)
    {
```

```java
System.out.println("Welcome to the "
    + "Regex Tester\n");
do
{
    do
    {
        System.out.print("\nEnter regex:   ");
        r = sc.nextLine();
        validRegex = true;
        try
        {
            pattern = Pattern.compile(r);
        }
        catch (Exception e)
        {
            System.out.println(e.getMessage());
            validRegex = false;
        }
    } while (!validRegex);

    doneMatching = false;
    while (!doneMatching)
    {
        System.out.print("Enter string: ");
        s = sc.nextLine();
        if (s.length() == 0)
            doneMatching = true;
        else
        {
            matcher = pattern.matcher(s);
            if (matcher.matches())
                System.out.println("Match.");
            else
                System.out.println(
                    "Does not match.");
        }
    }
} while (askAgain());
}

private static boolean askAgain()
{
    System.out.print("Another? (Y or N) ");
    String reply = sc.nextLine();
    if (reply.equalsIgnoreCase("Y"))
        return true;
    return false;
}
}
```

Here's a sample run of this program. For now, don't worry about the details of the regular expression string. Just note that it should match any three-letter word that begins with *f;* ends with *r;* and has *a, i,* or *o* in the middle.

```
Welcome to the Regex Tester

Enter regex:   f[aio]r
Enter string: for
Match.
Enter string: fir
Match.
Enter string: fur
Does not match.
Enter string: fod
Does not match.
Enter string:
Another? (Y or N) n
```

In this test, I entered the regular expression **f[aio]r**. Then I entered the string **for**. The program indicated that this string matched the expression and asked for another string. So I entered **fir**, which also matched. Then I entered **fur** and **fod**, which didn't match. Next, I entered a blank string, so the program asked whether I wanted to test another regex. I entered **n**, so the program ended.

This program uses the Pattern and Matcher classes, which I don't explain until the end of the chapter. I suggest that you use this program alongside this chapter, however. Regular expressions make a lot more sense if you actually try them out to see them in action. Also, you can learn a lot by trying simple variations as you go. (You can always download the source code for this program from this book's website at www.dummies.com/extras/javaaio if you don't want to enter it yourself.)

In fact, I use portions of console output from this program throughout the rest of this chapter to illustrate regular expressions. There's no better way to see how regular expressions work than to see an expression and some samples of strings that match and don't match the expression.

Performing Basic Character Matching

Most regular expressions simply match characters to see whether a string complies with a simple pattern. You can check a string to see whether it matches the format for Social Security numbers (xxx-xx-xxxx), phone numbers [(xxx) xxx-xxxx], or more complicated patterns such as e-mail addresses. (Well, actually, Social Security and phone numbers are more complicated than you may think — more on that in the section "Using predefined character classes," later in this chapter.) In the following sections, you find out how to create regex patterns for basic character matching.

Matching single characters

The simplest regex patterns match a string literal exactly, as in this example:

```
Enter regex:   abc
Enter string:  abc
Match.
Enter string:  abcd
Does not match.
```

Here the pattern abc matches the string abc but not abcd.

Using predefined character classes

A *character class* represents a particular type of character rather than a specific character. A regex pattern lets you use two types of character classes: predefined classes and custom classes. The predefined character classes are shown in Table 3-1.

Table 3-1	Character Classes
Regex	*Matches*
.	Any character
\d	Any digit (0–9)
\D	Any nondigit (anything other than 0–9)
\s	Any white-space character (space, tab, new line, return, or backspace)
\S	Any character other than a white-space character
\w	Any word character (a–z, A–Z, 0–9, or an underscore)
\W	Any character other than a word character

The period is like a wildcard that matches any character, as in this example:

```
Enter regex:   c.t
Enter string:  cat
Match.
Enter string:  cot
Match.
Enter string:  cart
Does not match.
```

Here c.t matches any three-letter string that starts with c and ends with t. In this example, the first two strings (cat and cot) match, but the third string (cart) doesn't because it's more than three characters.

The \d class represents a digit and is often used in regex patterns to validate input data. Here's a simple regex pattern that validates a U.S. Social Security number, which must be entered in the form xxx-xx-xxxx:

```
Enter regex:    \d\d\d-\d\d-\d\d\d\d
Enter string:  779-54-3994
Match.
Enter string:  550-403-004
Does not match.
```

Here the regex pattern specifies that the string must contain three digits, a hyphen, two digits, another hyphen, and four digits.

Note that this regex pattern isn't enough to validate real Social Security numbers because the government places more restrictions on these numbers than just the pattern xxx-xx-xxxx. No Social Security number can begin with 779, for example. Thus the number 779-54-3994 entered in the preceding example isn't a valid Social Security number.

Note that the \d class has a counterpart: \D. The \D class matches any character that is *not* a digit. Here's a first attempt at a regex for validating droid names:

```
Enter regex:    \D\d-\D\d
Enter string:  R2-D2
Match.
Enter string:  C2-D0
Match.
Enter string:  C-3PO
Does not match.
```

Here the pattern matches strings that begin with a character that isn't a digit, followed by a character that is a digit, followed by a hyphen, followed by another nondigit character, and ending with a digit. Thus, R2-D2 and C3-P0 match. Unfortunately, this regex is far from perfect, as any *Star Wars* fan can tell you, because the proper spelling of the shiny gold protocol droid's name is C-3PO, not C3-P0. Typical.

The \s class matches white-space characters including spaces, tabs, new-lines, returns, and backspaces. This class is useful when you want to allow the user to separate parts of a string in various ways, as in this example. (Note that in the fourth line, I use the Tab key to separate abc from def.)

```
Enter regex:    ...\s...
Enter string:  abc def
Match.
Enter string:  abc        def
Match.
```

Here the pattern specifies that the string can be two groups of any three characters separated by one white-space character. In the first string that's entered, the groups are separated by a space; in the second group, they're separated by a tab. The \s class also has a counterpart: \S. It matches any character that isn't a white-space character.

If you want to limit white space characters to actual spaces, use a space in the regex, like this:

```
Enter regex:   ... ...
Enter string: abc def
Match.
Enter string: abc        def
Does not match.
```

Here the regex specifies two groups of any character separated by a space. The first input string matches this pattern, but the second does not because the groups are separated by a tab.

The last set of predefined classes is \w and \W. The \w class identifies any character that's normally used in words, including uppercase and lowercase letters, digits, and underscores. An example shows how all that looks:

```
Enter regex:   \w\w\w\W\w\w\w
Enter string: abc def
Match.
Enter string: 123 456
Match.
Enter string: 123_456
Does not match.
```

Here the pattern calls for two groups of word characters separated by a nonword character.

Isn't it strange that underscores are considered to be word characters? I don't know of too many words in the English language (or any other language, for that matter) that have underscores in them. I guess that's the computer-nerd origins of regular expressions showing through.

Using custom character classes

To create a custom character class, you simply list all the characters that you want to include in the class within a set of brackets. Here's an example:

```
Enter regex:   b[aeiou]t
Enter string: bat
Match.
Enter string: bet
Match.
Enter string: bit
```

```
Match.
Enter string: bot
Match.
Enter string: but
Match.
Enter string: bmt
Does not match.
```

Here the pattern specifies that the string must start with the letter b, followed by a class that can include a, e, i, o, or u, followed by t. In other words, it accepts three-letter words that begin with *b,* end with *t,* and have a vowel in the middle.

If you want to let the pattern include uppercase letters as well as lowercase letters, you have to list them both:

```
Enter regex:  b[aAeEiIoOuU]t
Enter string: bat
Match.
Enter string: BAT
Does not match.
Enter string: bAt
Match.
```

You can use as many custom groups on a line as you want. Here's an example that defines classes for the first and last characters so that they too can be uppercase or lowercase:

```
Enter regex:  [bB][aAeEiIoOuU][tT]
Enter string: bat
Match.
Enter string: BAT
Match.
```

This pattern specifies three character classes. The first can be b or B, the second can be any uppercase or lowercase vowel, and the third can be t or T.

Using ranges

Custom character classes can also specify *ranges* of letters and numbers, like this:

```
Enter regex:  [a-z][0-5]
Enter string: r2
Match.
Enter string: b9
Does not match.
```

Here the string can be two characters long. The first must be a character from a–z, and the second must be 0–5.

You can also use more than one range in a class, like this:

```
Enter regex:  [a-zA-Z][0-5]
Enter string: r2
Match.
Enter string: R2
Match.
```

Here the first character can be lowercase a–z or uppercase A–Z.

You can use ranges to build a class that accepts only characters that appear in real words (as opposed to the \w class, which allows underscores):

```
Enter regex:  [a-zA-Z0-9]
Enter string: a
Match.
Enter string: N
Match.
Enter string: 9
Match.
```

Using negation

Regular expressions can include classes that match any character *but* the ones listed for the class. To do that, you start the class with a caret, like this:

```
Enter regex:  [^cf]at
Enter string: bat
Match.
Enter string: cat
Does not match.
Enter string: fat
Does not match.
```

Here the string must be a three-letter word that ends in at but isn't fat or cat.

Matching multiple characters

The regex patterns described so far in this chapter require that each position in the input string match a specific character class. The pattern \d\W[a-z], for example, requires a digit in the first position, a white-space character in the second position, and one of the letters a–z in the third position. These requirements are pretty rigid.

To create more flexible patterns, you can use any of the quantifiers listed in Table 3-2. *Quantifiers* let you create patterns that match a variable number of characters at a certain position in the string.

Table 3-2	Quantifiers
Regex	*Matches the Preceding Element*
?	Zero times or one time
*	Zero or more times
+	One or more times
{n}	Exactly *n* times
{n, }	At least *n* times
{n, m}	At least *n* times but no more than *m* times

To use a quantifier, you code it immediately after the element you want it to apply to. Here's a version of the Social Security number pattern that uses quantifiers:

```
Enter regex:  \d{3}-\d{2}-\d{4}
Enter string: 779-48-9955
Match.
Enter string: 483-488-9944
Does not match.
```

The pattern matches three digits, followed by a hyphen, followed by two digits, followed by another hyphen, followed by four digits.

Simply duplicating elements rather than using a quantifier is just as easy, if not easier. \d\d is just as easy as \d{2}.

The ? quantifier lets you create an optional element that may or may not be present in the string. Suppose you want to allow the user to enter Social Security numbers without the hyphens. You could use this pattern:

```
Enter regex:  \d{3}-?\d{2}-?\d{4}
Enter string: 779-48-9955
Match.
Enter string: 779489955
Match.
Enter string: 779-489955
Match.
Enter string: 77948995
Does not match.
```

The question marks indicate that the hyphens are optional. Notice that this pattern lets you include or omit either hyphen. The last string entered doesn't match because it has only eight digits, and the pattern requires nine.

Using escapes

In regular expressions, certain characters have special meaning. What if you want to search for one of those special characters? In that case, you *escape* the character by preceding it with a backslash. Here's an example:

```
Enter regex:  \(\d{3}\) \d{3}-\d{4}
Enter string: (559) 555-1234
Match.
Enter string: 559 555-1234
Does not match.
```

Here \(represents a left parenthesis, and \) represents a right parenthesis. Without the backslashes, the regular expression treats the parenthesis as a grouping element.

Here are a few additional points to ponder about escapes:

+ Strictly speaking, you need to use the backslash escape only for characters that have special meanings in regular expressions. I recommend, however, that you escape any punctuation character or symbol, just to be sure.

+ You can't escape alphabetic characters (letters) because a backslash followed by certain alphabetic characters represents a character, a class, or some other regex element.

+ To escape a backslash, code two slashes in a row. The regex \d\d\\\d\d, for example, accepts strings made up of two digits followed by a backslash and two more digits, such as 23\88 and 95\55.

Using parentheses to group characters

You can use parentheses to create groups of characters to apply other regex elements to, as in this example:

```
Enter regex:  (bla)+
Enter string: bla
Match.
Enter string: blabla
Match.
Enter string: blablabla
Match.
Enter string: bla bla bla
Does not match.
```

Here the parentheses treat bla as a group, so the + quantifier applies to the entire sequence. Thus, this pattern looks for one or more occurrences of the sequence bla.

Here's an example that finds U.S. phone numbers that can have an optional area code:

```
Enter regex:    (\(\d{3}\)\s?)?\d{3}-\d{4}
Enter string: 555-1234
Match.
Enter string: (559) 555-1234
Match.
Enter string: (559)555-1239
Match.
```

This regex pattern is a little complicated, but if you examine it element by element, you should be able to figure it out. It starts with a group that indicates the optional area code: `(\(\d{3}\)\s?)?`. This group begins with the left parenthesis, which marks the start of the group. The characters in the group consist of an escaped left parenthesis, three digits, an escaped right parenthesis, and an optional white-space character. Then a right parenthesis closes the group, and the question mark indicates that the entire group is optional. The rest of the regex pattern looks for three digits followed by a hyphen and four more digits.

When you mark a group of characters with parentheses, the text that matches that group is *captured* so that you can use it later in the pattern. The groups that are captured are called *capture groups* and are numbered beginning with 1. Then you can use a backslash followed by the capture-group number to indicate that the text must match the text that was captured for the specified capture group.

Suppose that droids named following the pattern \w\d-\w\d must have the same digit in the second and fifth characters. In other words, r2-d2 and b9-k9 are valid droid names, but r2-d4 and d3-r4 are not.

Here's an example that can validate that type of name:

```
Enter regex:    \w(\d)-\w\1
Enter string: r2-d2
Match.
Enter string: d3-r4
Does not match.
Enter string: b9-k9
Match.
```

Here \1 refers to the first capture group. Thus the last character in the string must be the same as the second character, which must be a digit.

Using the pipe symbol

The vertical bar (|) symbol defines an or operation, which lets you create patterns that accept any of two or more variations. Here's an improvement of the pattern for validating droid names:

```
Enter regex:   (\w\d-\w\d)|(\w-\d\w\w)
Enter string: r2-d2
Match.
Enter string: c-3po
Match.
```

The | character indicates that either the group on the left or the group on the right can be used to match the string. The group on the left matches a word character, a digit, a hyphen, a word character, and another digit. The group on the right matches a word character, a hyphen, a digit, and two word characters.

You may want to use an additional set of parentheses around the entire part of the pattern that the | applies to. Then you can add pattern elements before or after the | groups. What if you want to let a user enter the area code for a phone number with or without parentheses? Here's a regex pattern that does the trick:

```
Enter regex:   ((\d{3} )|(\(\d{3}\) ))?\d{3}-\d{4}
Enter string: (559) 555-1234
Match.
Enter string: 559 555-1234
Match.
Enter string: 555-1234
Match.
```

The first part of this pattern is a group that consists of two smaller groups separated by a | character. The first of these groups matches an area code without parentheses followed by a space, and the second matches an area code with parentheses followed by a space. So the outer group matches an area code with or without parentheses. This entire group is marked with a question mark as optional; then the pattern continues with three digits, a hyphen, and four digits.

Using Regular Expressions in Java Programs

So far, this chapter has shown you the basics of creating regular expressions. The following sections show you how to put them to use in Java programs.

Understanding the String problem

Before getting into the classes for working with regular expressions, I want to clue you in about a problem that Java has in dealing with strings that contain regular expressions. As you've seen throughout this chapter, regex patterns rely on the backslash character to mark different elements of a pattern. The bad news is that Java treats the backslash character in a string literal as an escape character. Thus, you can't just quote regular expressions in string literals, because Java steals the backslash characters before they get to the regular expression classes.

In most cases, the compiler simply complains that the string literal is not correct. The following line won't compile:

```
String regex = "\w\d-\w\d";    // error: won't compile
```

The compiler sees the backslashes in the string and expects to find a valid Java escape sequence, not a regular expression.

Unfortunately, the solution to this problem is ugly: You have to double the backslashes wherever they occur. Java treats two backslashes in a row as an escaped backslash and places a single backslash in the string. Thus you have to code the statement shown in the preceding example like this:

```
String regex = "\\w\\d-\\w\\d";    // now it will
                                   // compile
```

Here each backslash I want in the regular expression is coded as a pair of backslashes in the string literal.

If you're in doubt about whether you're coding your string literals right, just use `System.out.println` to print the resulting string. Then you can check the console output to make sure that you wrote the string literal right. If I followed the preceding statement with `System.out.println(regex)`, the following output would appear on the console:

```
\w\d-\w\d
```

Thus I know that I coded the string literal for the regular expression correctly.

Using regular expressions with the String class

If all you want to do with a regular expression is check whether a string matches a pattern, you can use the `matches` method of the `String` class. This method accepts a regular expression as a parameter and returns a boolean that indicates whether the string matches the pattern.

Here's a static method that validates droid names:

```
private static boolean validDroidName(String droid)
{
    String regex = "(\\w\\d-\\w\\d)|(\\w-\\d\\w\\w)";
    return droid.matches(regex);
}
```

Here the name of the droid is passed via a parameter, and the method returns a boolean that indicates whether the droid's name is valid. The method simply creates a regular expression from a string literal and then uses the `matches` method of the `droid` string to match the pattern.

You can also use the `split` method to split a string into an array of `String` objects based on delimiters that match a regular expression. One common way to do that is to simply create a custom class of characters that can be used for delimiters, as in this example:

```
String s = "One:Two;Three|Four\tFive";
String regex = "[:;|\\t]";
String strings[] = s.split(regex);
for (String word : strings)
    System.out.println(word);
```

Here a string is split into words marked by colons, semicolons, vertical bars, or tab characters. When you run this program, the following text is displayed on the console:

```
One
Two
Three
Four
Five
```

Using the Pattern and Matcher classes

The `matches` method is fine for occasional use of regular expressions, but if you want your program to do a lot of pattern matching, you should use the `Pattern` and `Matcher` classes instead. The `Pattern` class represents a regular expression that has been compiled into executable form. (Remember that regular expressions are like little programs.) Then you can use the compiled `Pattern` object to create a `Matcher` object, which you can use to match strings.

The `Pattern` class itself is pretty simple. Although it has about ten methods, you usually use just these two:

✦ **static Pattern compile(String *pattern*):** Compiles the specified pattern. This static method returns a `Pattern` object. It throws `PatternSyntaxException` if the pattern contains an error.

✦ **Matcher matcher(String input):** Creates a `Matcher` object to match this pattern against the specified string.

First, you use the `compile` method to create a `Pattern` object. (`Pattern` is one of those weird classes that doesn't have constructors. Instead, it relies on the static `compile` method to create instances.) Because the `compile` method throws `PatternSyntaxException`, you must use a `try/catch` statement to catch this exception when you compile a pattern.

After you have a `Pattern` instance, you use the `matcher` method to create an instance of the `Matcher` class. This class has more than 30 methods that let you do all sorts of things with regular expressions that aren't covered in this chapter, such as finding multiple occurrences of a pattern in an input string or replacing text that matches a pattern with a replacement string. For purposes of this book, I'm concerned only with the `matches` method: `static boolean matches()` returns a boolean that indicates whether the entire string matches the pattern.

To illustrate how to use these methods, here's an enhanced version of the `validDroidName` method that creates a pattern for the droid-validation regex and saves it in a static class field:

```
private static Pattern droidPattern;

private static boolean validDroidName(String droid)
{
    if (droidPattern == null)
    {
        String regex = "(\\w\\d-\\w\\d)|"
            + "(\\w-\\d\\w\\w)";
        droidPattern = Pattern.compile(regex);
    }
    Matcher m = droidPattern.matcher(droid);
    return m.matches();
}
```

Here the private class field `droidPattern` saves the compiled pattern for validating droids. The `if` statement in the `validDroidName` method checks whether the pattern has already been created. If not, the pattern is created by calling the static `compile` method of the `Pattern` class. Then the `matcher` method is used to create a `Matcher` object for the string passed as a parameter, and the string is validated by calling the `matches` method of the `Matcher` object.

Chapter 4: Using Recursion

In This Chapter

✔ Introducing recursion

✔ Calculating factors with recursion

✔ Listing directories with recursion

✔ Sorting with recursion

*R*ecursion is a basic programming technique in which a method calls itself to solve some problem. A method that uses this technique is called *recursive*. Many programming problems can be solved only by recursion, and some problems that can be solved by other techniques are better solved by recursion.

I'm not sure, but I think that the term *recursion* comes from the Latin *recurse, recurset, recursum,* which means to curse repeatedly. I do know that that's exactly what many programmers feel like doing when they're struggling with complex recursive programming problems.

True, the concept of recursion can get a little tricky. Many programmers steer clear of it, looking for other techniques to solve the problem at hand, and in many cases, a nonrecursive solution is best. Many problems just cry out for recursion, however.

Calculating the Classic Factorial Example

One of the classic problems for introducing recursion is calculating the factorial of an integer. The *factorial* of any given integer — I'll call it *n* so that I sound mathematical — is the product of all the integers from 1 to *n*. Thus the factorial of 5 is 120: $5 \times 4 \times 3 \times 2 \times 1$.

The nonrecursive solution

You don't have to use recursion to calculate factorials. Instead, you can use a simple for loop. Here's a method that accepts an int number and returns the number's factorial as a long:

```
private static long factorial(int n)
{
    long f = 1;
    for (int i = 1; i <=n; i++)
```

```
        f = f * i;
    return f;
}
```

This method uses a `for` loop to count from 1 to the number, keeping track of the product as it goes. Here's a snippet of code that calls this method and displays the result:

```
int n = 5;
long fact;
fact = factorial(n);
System.out.println("The factorial of "+ n + " is "
    + fact + ".");
```

If you run this code, the following line is displayed on the console:

```
The factorial of 5 is 120.
```

Factorials get big fast. You should use a `long` rather than an `int` to calculate the result. Also, you should use the `NumberFormat` class to format the result. If `int` is 20 instead of 5, the preceding code prints this on the console:

```
The factorial of 20 is 2432902008176640000.
```

If you use the `NumberFormat` class to format the result, the console output is more readable:

```
The factorial of 20 is 2,432,902,008,176,640,000.
```

The recursive solution

The nonrecursive solution to the factorial problem works, but it isn't much fun. The recursive solution is based on the notion that the factorial for any number *n* is equal to *n* times the factorial of *n* – 1, provided that *n* is greater than 1. If *n* is 1, the factorial of *n* is 1.

This definition of factorial is recursive because the definition includes the factorial method itself. It also includes the most important part of any recursive method: an end condition. The *end condition* indicates when the recursive method should stop calling itself. In this case, when n is 1, I just return 1. Without an end condition, the recursive method keeps calling itself forever.

Here's the recursive version of the factorial method:

```
private static long factorial(int n)
{
    if (n == 1)
        return 1;
    else
        return n * factorial(n-1);
}
```

This method returns exactly the same result as the version in the preceding section, but it uses recursion to calculate the factorial.

One way to visualize how recursion works is to imagine that you have five friends: Jordan, Jeremy, Jacob, Justin, and Bob. Your friends aren't very smart, but they're very much alike. In fact, they're clones of one another. Cloning isn't a perfect process yet, so these clones have limitations. Each can do only one multiplication problem and can ask one of its clones one question.

Now suppose that you walk up to Jordan and ask, "Jordan, what's the factorial of 5?"

Jordan says, "I don't know, but I do know it's 5 × the factorial of 4. Jeremy, what's the factorial of 4?"

Jeremy says, "I don't know, but I do know it's 4 × the factorial of 3. Jacob, what's the factorial of 3?"

Jacob says, "I don't know, but I do know it's 3 × the factorial of 2. Justin, what's the factorial of 2?"

Justin says, "I don't know, but I do know it's 2 × the factorial of 1. Hey, Bob! What's the factorial of 1?"

Bob, being the most intelligent of the bunch on account of not having a J-name, replies, "Why, *1,* of course." He tells Justin his answer.

Justin says, "Ah — 2 × 1 is 2." He tells Jacob his answer.

Jacob says, "Thanks — 3 × 2 is 6." Jacob tells Jeremy his answer.

Jeremy says, "Dude — 4 × 6 is 24." Jeremy tells Jordan his answer.

Jordan says, "Very good — 5 × 24 is 120." He tells you the answer.

That's pretty much how recursion works.

Displaying Directories

Recursion lends itself well to applications that have to navigate directory structures, such as a Windows or Unix file system. In a file system, a directory is a list of files and other directories. Each of those directories is itself a list of files and other directories, and so on. Directories can be snugly nestled inside other directories and have no limit in number.

Listing 4-1, at the end of this section, shows a program that uses a recursive method to list all the directories that are found starting from a given path. I use indentation to show the directory structure.

Here's the console output for the directories I used to organize the documents for this book:

```
Welcome to the Directory Lister
Enter a path: C:\Java AIO

Listing directory tree of:
C:\Java AIO
  Apps
    Book 1
    Book 2
    Book 3
    Book 4
    Book 5
  Manuscript
    Book 1
    Book 2
    Book 3
    Book 4
    Book 5
    Front
  Plans
Another? (Y or N) n
```

As you can see, I haven't done Books VI–IX yet. By the time you read this chapter, there will be even more directories to list!

Don't enter **c:** unless you're prepared to wait a long time for the program to finish listing *all* the directories on your hard drive. (Of course, you can always press Ctrl+C to stop the program, or just close the console window.)

The Directory Listing application is remarkably simple. Before I explain its details, though, I want to point out that this program uses the `File` class, which is part of the `java.io` package. The `File` class represents a single file or directory. You find out much more about this class in Book VIII. For now, you just need to know these five details:

✦ The constructor for this class accepts a directory path as a parameter and creates an object that represents the specified directory.

✦ You can use the `exists` method to find out whether the directory specified by the path parameter exists.

✦ The `listFiles` method returns an array of `File` objects that represent every file and directory in the current `File` object.

✦ The isDirectory method returns a boolean that indicates whether the current File object is a directory. If this method returns false, you can assume that the File object is a file.

✦ The getName method returns the name of the file.

Listing 4-1: The Directory Listing Application

```java
import java.io.File;                                              →1
import java.util.Scanner;

public class DirList
{
    static Scanner sc = new Scanner(System.in);

    public static void main(String[] args)
    {
        System.out.print(
            "Welcome to the Directory Lister");
        do
        {
            System.out.print("\nEnter a path: ");
            String path = sc.nextLine();                         →15

            File dir = new File(path);                           →17
            if (!dir.exists() || !dir.isDirectory())            →18
                System.out.println(
                    "\nThat directory doesn't exist.");
            else
            {
                System.out.println(
                    "\nListing directory tree of:");
                System.out.println(dir.getPath());               →25
                listDirectories(dir, "  ");                      →26
            }
        } while(askAgain());                                     →28
    }

    private static void listDirectories(                        →31
        File dir, String indent)
    {
        File[] dirs = dir.listFiles();                           →34
        for (File f : dirs)                                      →35
        {
            if (f.isDirectory())                                 →37
            {
                System.out.println(
                    indent + f.getName())                        →40
                listDirectories(f, indent + "  ");               →41
            }
        }
    }
```

(continued)

Listing 4-1 *(continued)*

```
private static boolean askAgain()
{
    System.out.print("Another? (Y or N) ");
    String reply = sc.nextLine();
    if (reply.equalsIgnoreCase("Y"))
        return true;
    return false;
}
}
```

The following paragraphs point out the highlights of how this program works:

→ **1**   This `import` statement is required to use the `File` class.

→ **15**   A `Scanner` object is used to get the pathname from the user.

→ **17**   The pathname is passed to the `File` class constructor to create a new `File` object for the directory entered by the user.

→ **18**   The `exists` and `isDirectory` methods are called to make sure that the path entered by the user exists and points to a directory rather than a file.

→ **25**   If the user entered a good path, the `getPath` method is called to display the name of the path represented by the `File` object. (I could just as easily have displayed the `path` variable here.)

→ **26**   The `listDirectories` method is called to list all the subdirectories in the directory specified by the user.

→ **28**   The user is asked whether he wants to list another directory, and the loop repeats if the user answers `Y`.

→ **31**   This line is the start of the `listDirectories` method. This method takes two parameters: a `File` object representing the directory to be listed and a `String` object that provides the spaces used to indent each line of the listing. When this method is first called from the `main` method, the indentation is set to two spaces by a string literal.

→ **34**   The `listFiles` method is called to get an array of all the `File` objects in this directory.

→ **35**   An enhanced `for` loop is used to process all the `File` objects in the array.

→ **37**   This `if` statement checks to see whether a file is a directory rather than a file.

→ **40**   If the `File` object is a directory, the indentation string is printed, followed by the name of the directory as returned by the `getName` method.

→ **41**   Next, the `listDirectories` method is called recursively to list the contents of the `f` directory. Two spaces are added to the indentation string, however, so that any directories in the `f` directory are indented two spaces to the right of the current directory.

If you're having trouble understanding how the recursion in this program works, think of it this way: The `listDirectory` method lists all the subdirectories in a single directory. For each directory, this method does two things: (1) prints the directory's name and (2) calls itself to print any subdirectories of that directory.

Earlier in this chapter, I mention that all recursive methods must have some type of condition test that causes the method to stop calling itself. In this program, the condition test may not be obvious. Eventually, however, the `listDirectories` method is passed a directory that doesn't have any subdirectories. When that happens, the recursion ends — at least for that branch of the directory tree.

Writing Your Own Sorting Routine

The world is full of computer science majors who don't know anything more about computers than you do, but they once attended a class in which the instructor explained how sorting algorithms worked. They may have received a C in that class, but it was good enough to graduate.

Now you have a chance to find out what you missed by not majoring in computer science. I'm going to show you how one of the most commonly used sorting techniques actually works. This technique is called *Quicksort*, and it's a very ingenious use of recursion. I even show you a simple Java implementation of it.

Quicksort is easily the most technical part of this entire book. If you never wanted to major in computer science (and if you don't even want to talk to people who did), you may want to skip the rest of this chapter now.

For most of us, figuring out how sorting algorithms such as Quicksort work is merely an intellectual exercise. The Java API has sorting already built in. (Check out the `Arrays.sort` method, for example.) Those sort routines are way better than any that you or I will ever write.

Understanding how Quicksort works

The Quicksort technique sorts an array of values by using recursion. Its basic steps are thus:

1. **Pick an arbitrary value that lies within the range of values in the array.**

This value is the *pivot point.* The most common way to choose the pivot point is to simply pick the first value in the array. Folks have written doctoral degrees on more-sophisticated ways to pick a pivot point that results in faster sorting. I like to stick with using the first element in the array.

2. **Rearrange the values in the array so that all the values that are less than the pivot point are on the left side of the array and all the values that are greater than or equal to the pivot point are on the right side of the array.**

   The *pivot value* indicates the boundary between the left side and the right side of the array. It probably won't be dead center, but that doesn't matter. This step is called *partitioning,* and the left and right sides of the arrays are *partitions.*

3. **Now treat each of the two sections of the array as a separate array, and start over with Step 1 for that section.**

   That's the recursive part of the algorithm.

The hardest part of the Quicksort algorithm is the partitioning step, which must rearrange the partition so that all values that are smaller than the pivot point are on the left and all elements that are larger than the pivot point are on the right. Suppose that the array has these ten values:

```
38 17 58 22 69 31 88 28 86 12
```

Here the pivot point is 38, and the task of the partitioning step is to rearrange the array to something like this:

```
17 12 22 28 31 38 88 69 86 58
```

Notice that the values are still out of order. The array, however, has been divided around the value 38: All values that are less than 38 are to the left of 38, and all values that are greater than 38 are to the right of 38.

Now you can divide the array into two partitions at the value 38 and repeat the process for each side. The pivot value itself goes with the left partition, so the left partition is this:

```
17 12 22 28 31 38
```

This time, the partitioning step picks 17 as the pivot point and rearranges the elements as follows:

```
12 17 22 28 31 38
```

As you can see, this portion of the array is sorted now. Unfortunately, Quicksort doesn't realize that at this point, so it takes a few more recursions to be sure. But that's the basic process.

Using the sort method

The actual code that drives a Quicksort routine is surprisingly simple:

```
public static void sort(int low, int high)
{
    if (low >= high)
        return;
    int p = partition(low, high);
    sort (low, p);
    sort (p+1, high);
}
```

This method sorts the portion of an array indicated by the low and high index values passed to it. Ignoring the `if` statement for now, the `sort` method works by calling a `partition` method. This method rearranges the array into two partitions so that all the values in the left partition are smaller than all the values in the right partition. The `partition` method returns the index of the end of the left partition. Then the `sort` method calls itself twice: once to sort the left partition and again to sort the right partition.

To get the `sort` method started, you call it with 0 as the low value and the array length and 1 as the high value. Thus the `sort` method begins by sorting the entire array. Each time the `sort` method executes, it calls itself twice to sort smaller partitions of the array.

The `if` statement at the beginning of the `sort` method compares the low value with the high value. If the low value is equal to or greater than the high value, the partition has only one element (or perhaps no elements) and therefore is already sorted. In that case, the `sort` method simply returns without calling itself again. That's the condition that ends the recursion.

Using the partition method

The `sort` method itself is the simple part of the Quicksort technique. The hard part is the `partition` method. This method accepts two parameters: the low and high indexes that mark the portion of the array that should be sorted. The basic outline of the `partition` method goes something like this:

1. **Pick a pivot point.**

2. **Move all elements that are less than the pivot point to the left side of the partition.**

3. **Move all elements that are greater than the pivot point to the right side of the partition.**

4. **Return the index of the pivot point.**

The most common technique for partitioning the array is to maintain two index variables, named i and j, that work from both ends of the array toward the center. First, i starts at the beginning of the array and moves forward until it encounters a value that's greater than the pivot value. Then j starts at the opposite end of the array and moves backward until it finds a value that's less than the pivot point. At that point, the `partition` method has a value that's greater than the pivot point on the left side of the array and a value that's less than the pivot point on the right side of the array. So it swaps them.

Next, the cycle repeats: i is incremented until it finds another value that's greater than the pivot value, j is decremented until it finds another value that's less than the pivot value, and the elements are swapped. This process repeats until j is less than i, which means that the indexes have crossed and the partitioning is done.

Here's some code that puts everything together:

```
public static int partition(int low, int high)
{
    int pivot = a[low];

    int i = low - 1;
    int j = high + 1;

    while (i < j)
    {
        for (i++; a[i] < pivot; i++);
        for (j--; a[j] > pivot; j--);
        if (i < j)
            swap(i, j);
    }
    return j;
}
```

Notice that in this code, the array being sorted is a static `int` array named a. The low and high ends of the partition to be partitioned are passed in as parameters, and the method starts by choosing the first element in the partition as the value for the pivot point. Next, it initializes the index variables i and j from the parameters. Notice that 1 is subtracted from the low value and that 1 is added to the high value. The index variables take one step back from the array before the looping starts so they can get a good start.

The `while` loop is used to indicate when the partitioning is finished. It repeats as long as i is less than j. After these index variables stop, the partitioning is done, and the value of j is returned to indicate the index point that divides the left partition from the right partition.

In the body of the `while` loop are two strange bodyless `for` loops. These `for` loops don't have bodies because their only purpose is to move their index values until they find a value that's either less than or greater than the pivot value.

The first `for` loop increments the `i` index variable until it finds a value that's greater than the pivot point. This `for` loop finds the first value that might need to be moved to the other side of the array.

Next, the second `for` loop decrements the `j` index variable until it finds a value that's less than the pivot point. So this loop finds a value that may need to be swapped with the value found by the first `for` loop.

Finally, the `if` statement checks whether the indexes have crossed. Assuming that they haven't, a `swap` method is called to swap the elements. The `swap` method is mercifully simple:

```
public static void swap(int i, int j)
{
    int temp = a[i];
    a[i] = a[j];
    a[j] = temp;
}
```

This method moves the `i` element to a temporary variable, moves the `j` element to the `i` element, and then moves the temporary variable to the `j` element.

Putting it all together

Now that you've seen the basic steps necessary to create a Quicksort program, Listing 4-2 shows a program that gives these methods a workout. This program creates an array of 100 randomly selected numbers with values from 1–100. It prints the array, uses the sorting methods shown in the previous sections to sort the array, and then prints the sorted array. Here's a sample run:

```
Unsorted array:

65 51 38 47 93 87 50 36 77 58 22 92 46 60 49 90 28 39 27  8
66 76 40 99 90 35 34 30  7 41 45 34 41 17 36 63 52 65 50 77
 2 93 48  6 91 67 34 69 33 47 50 12 88 15 65 40 29 74 34 14
55 37 28 25 98 66 69 88 66 27 29 88 29 87  9 29 77 32  4 11
68 40 17 61 50 90 24  1 59 91 69  5 82 69 51 45 29 38 61 86

Sorted array:

 1  2  4  5  6  7  8  9 11 12 14 15 17 17 22 24 25 27 27 28
28 29 29 29 29 29 30 32 33 34 34 34 34 35 36 36 37 38 38 39
40 40 40 41 41 45 45 46 47 47 48 49 50 50 50 50 51 51 52 55
58 59 60 61 61 63 65 65 65 66 66 66 67 68 69 69 69 69 74 76
77 77 77 82 86 87 87 88 88 88 90 90 90 91 91 92 93 93 98 99
```

As you can see, the first array is in random order, but the second array is nicely sorted. (Your results will vary, of course, because the unsorted array will be in a different order every time you run the program.)

Listing 4-2:   A Sorting Program

```java
public class QuickSortApp
{
    public static void main(String[] args)
    {
        int LEN = 100;
        int[] unsorted = new int[LEN];
        for (int i = 0; i<LEN; i++)                          →7
            unsorted[i] =
                (int)(Math.random() * 100) + 1;
        System.out.println("Unsorted array:");
        printArray(unsorted);                                →10
        int[] sorted = sort(unsorted);                       →11
        System.out.println("\n\nSorted array:");
        printArray(sorted);                                  →13
    }

    private static void printArray(int[] array)              →16
    {
        System.out.println();
        for (int i = 0; i < array.length; i++)
        {
            if (array[i] < 10)
                System.out.print(" ");
            System.out.print(array[i] + " ");
            if ((i+1) % 20 == 0)
                System.out.println();
        }
    }

    private static int[] a;                                  →29

    public static int[] sort(int[] array)                    →31
    {
        a = array;
        sort(0, a.length - 1);
        return a;
    }

    public static void sort(int low, int high)               →38
    {
        if (low >= high)
            return;
        int p = partition(low, high);
        sort (low, p);
        sort (p+1, high);
    }

    public static int partition(int low, int high)           →47
    {
        int pivot = a[low];
```

```
        int i = low - 1;
        int j = high + 1;

        while (i < j)
        {
            for (i++; a[i] < pivot; i++);
            for (j--; a[j] > pivot; j--);
            if (i < j)
                swap(i, j);
        }
        return j;
    }

    public static void swap(int i, int j)          →64
    {
        int temp = a[i];
        a[i] = a[j];
        a[j] = temp;
    }
}
```

Most of the code in this program has already been explained, so I just point out a few of the highlights here:

→ **7** This `for` loop assigns 100 random values to the array.

→ **10** The `printArray` method is called to print the unsorted array.

→ **11** The `sort` method is called to sort the array.

→ **13** The `printArray` method is called again to print the sorted array.

→ **16** The `printArray` method uses a `for` loop to print array elements. Each element is separated by two spaces. An additional space, however, is printed before each element if the element's value is less than `10`. That way, the values line up in columns. Also, the remainder operator (`%`) is used to call the `println` method every 20 elements. Thus this method prints 5 lines with 20 values on each line. (The last few values in the array won't line up exactly if they happen to be 100, but that's okay.)

→ **29** A static variable named `a` is used to hold the array while it is being sorted.

→ **31** The `sort` method has two versions. The first accepts an `int` array as a parameter and returns an `int` array with the sorted values. This method sets the static `a` variable to the array passed via the parameters, calls the second version of the `sort` method to sort the entire array, and then returns the sorted array.

→ **38** This line is the second `sort` method. It sorts the partition indicated by the parameters. (The operation of this method is explained in detail in the section "Using the sort method," earlier in this chapter.)

→ 47   The `partition` method is explained in detail in the preceding section.

→ 64   The `swap` method simply exchanges the two indicated values.

Remember the cool XOR technique for exchanging two integer values without the need for a temporary variable? You can improve the performance of your sort ever so slightly by replacing the swap method with this code:

```
public static void swap(int i, int j)
{
    a[i] ^= a[j];
    a[j] ^= a[i];
    a[i] ^= a[j];
}
```

Chapter 5: Working with Dates and Times

In This Chapter

✔ Understanding human and computer dates and times

✔ Using java.time classes to represent dates and times

✔ Comparing dates and times

✔ Performing calculations with dates and times

✔ Formatting dates and times

Does anybody really know what time it is? Does anybody really care about time?

So mused Robert Lamm of *The Chicago Transit Authority* (later known as simply *Chicago*) in 1969.

I'm not sure who cared much about time in 1969, but I do know that the people who designed the original version of Java in 1995 didn't care much about it, at least as evidenced by the weak classes they provided for working with times and dates in the Java.util package. Java programmers have long struggled with simple calculations involving dates and times, such as determining what the date will be 45 days from today or calculating the number of days between two given dates.

Java 8 changes all that. Java 8 provides an entirely new framework for working with dates and times, usually referred to as the Date-Time API. This new API is pretty complicated, involving about 50 new classes and interfaces and hundreds of new methods. In this chapter, I'll introduce you to just a few of the most important and useful classes of the new Date-Time API. Then you can explore the rest online via Oracle's documentation at `http://download.java.net/jdk8/docs/api/index.html`.

Pondering How Time is Represented

Before I launch into the details of the new Date-Time API's classes, let's review a few basic concepts about time. Probably the most important basic concept to understand about time (at least from a programming point of view) is that computers and humans use two entirely different methods of keeping track of time. Humans measure time using a system of progressively longer units, starting with seconds and increasing to minutes, hours, days, weeks, months, years, decades, and centuries.

Our human time units are intuitively familiar to us, but their precise definitions are more complicated than you might guess. All kinds of factors muck up the way we represent time: leap days, time zones, and daylight-saving time. And did you know that about once every 18 months, scientists pick a day (they usually choose June 30 or December 31) that they add one second to? This is necessary because the speed of the earth's rotation varies ever so slightly, throwing our clocks off.

In contrast, the way computers keep track of time is much simpler: Computers simply count the number of units (typically milliseconds or nanoseconds) that have elapsed since a given start time. Thus, to a computer, a time is just a number.

In Java, machine time is set as the number of nanoseconds that have elapsed since midnight, January 1, 1970. Why January 1, 1970? There's no particular reason other than historical: Java inherited that date from the Unix operating system, which was developed in the 1970s. (For more information, see the sidebar "And you thought Y2K was bad!")

The designers of Microsoft Windows decided to use January 1, 1601 as the start day for their clock. I guess that was a big year for William Shakespeare; in 1601 he was able to use the first version of Microsoft Word to write his plays.

The difference between how humans and computers keep track of time makes any computer program that deals with dates and times a bit tricky. For example, suppose you want to schedule a phone call between two

And you thought Y2K was bad!

Java counts time in nanoseconds starting with January 1, 1970. Why that particular date? It turns out that January 1, 1970 was the date the original designers of Unix chose as their origin time for the Unix operating system. That tradition was carried on into Linux, and then into Java.

The original Unix used a signed 32-bit number to count time, and counted time in full seconds rather than nanoseconds. Thus, in Unix time was represented as the number of seconds that have elapsed since January 1, 1970. Because the largest number that can be represented by a signed 32-bit number is relatively small, Unix time will come to an end on January 19, 2038.

Today, most Unix- and Linux-based systems have been upgraded to use 64-bit numbers to count time, so the world will not end in 2038 for those systems. But systems that still use old-style 32-bit time values will break in 2038.

I am already looking forward to the end-of-the-world party.

people, one in Los Angeles, the other in New York. Obviously, the time that you agree upon for the call must take into account the time zone of each participant. Thus you might agree to make the call at 1 p.m. local time for the West Coast participant and 4 p.m. local time for the east coast participant. So, how would you represent that appointment time in a database?

Or suppose you want to calculate the due date for an invoice that is dated January 27, 2015, when the payment due date is 45 days after the invoice date. The algorithm that calculates the due date must be aware that January has 31 days and that February has 28 days in 2015.

Fortunately, the new Date-Time API is designed to handle all those nuances for you. The Date-Time API includes all the classes you need to represent dates and times in just about any imaginable context, for performing calculations and comparisons between date and time objects, and for converting dates and times to string representations in just about any imaginable format.

Picking the Right Date and Time Class for Your Application

The first order of business when developing an application that must work with dates or times (or both) is picking the Date-Time class to represent your date and time values. The `java.time` package defines ten distinct classes used to represent different types of times and dates, as described in Table 5-1.

Table 5-1	Ten Date-Time Classes in `java.time`
Class	*What It Represents*
`LocalTime`	A time (hours, minutes, and seconds to nanosecond precision) without an associated time zone.
`LocalDate`	A date (year, month, and day) without an associated time zone.
`LocalDateTime`	A date and time without an associated time zone.
`OffsetTime`	A time and an offset from UTC (Coordinated Universal Time, also known as Greenwich Mean Time), such as 12:30:00-8.00, which means the time is 12:30 with an offset of -8 hours from UTC.
`OffsetDateTime`	A date and time with an offset value from UTC.
`ZonedDateTime`	A date and time with an associated time zone, such as `America/Los_Angeles`.
`MonthDay`	A month and day without an associated year. You can use a MonthDay object to represent a date such as a birthday, anniversary, or holiday.

(continued)

Table 5-1 *(continued)*

Class	What It Represents
YearMonth	A year and month, such as December, 2015. No day, time, or time zone values are associated with the year and month.
Year	A year, such as 2038. No month, day, time, or time zone values are associated with the year.
Instant	A single point of time, represented internally as the number of nanoseconds that have elapsed since midnight, January 1, 1970. The value assumes a UTC/GMT time offset of 0.

Each of these classes has many different methods that let you create date and time objects, perform calculations on them, compare them, and convert them to strings that can be displayed and read by humans. You can find complete documentation of the methods for each of these classes online at `http://download.java.net/jdk8/docs/api/`.

Using the now Method to Create a Date-Time Object

All Date-Time classes have a static `now` method, which creates an object representing the current date and/or time. For example, to get the current date, you would use code similar to this:

```
LocalDate date = LocalDate.now();
```

To get the current date and time with time zone, use this code:

```
ZonedDateTime datetime = ZonedDateTime.now();
```

The following program displays the current time using all ten classes, creating an object of each class using `now()` and printing it with `toString()`:

```java
import java.util.*;
import java.time.*;

public class TimeTester
{
    public static void main(String[] args)
    {
        System.out.println("\nLocalTime: "
            + LocalTime.now().toString());
        System.out.println("\nLocalDateTime: "
            + LocalDateTime.now().toString());
        System.out.println("\nZonedDateTime: "
            + ZonedDateTime.now().toString());
        System.out.println("\nOffsetTime: "
            + OffsetTime.now().toString());
        System.out.println("\nOffsetDateTime: "
            + OffsetDateTime.now().toString());
```

```
System.out.println("\nMonthDay: "
    + MonthDay.now().toString());
System.out.println("\nYearMonth: "
    + YearMonth.now().toString());
System.out.println("\nInstant: "
    + Instant.now().toString());
    }
}
```

If you compile and run this program, the output will appear something like this:

```
LocalTime: 20:56:26.325

LocalDateTime: 2013-10-07T20:56:26.388

ZonedDateTime: 2013-10-07T20:56:26.388-07:00[America/Los_Angeles]

OffsetTime: 20:56:26.388-07:00

OffsetDateTime: 2013-10-07T20:56:26.388-07:00

MonthDay: --10-07

YearMonth: 2013-10

Instant: 2013-10-08T03:56:26.388Z
```

From this output, you can get an idea of the information represented by the various Date-Time classes.

Using the parse Method to Create a Date-Time Object

Another way to create a Date-Time object is to use the static `parse` method, which creates a Date-Time object from a string that represents a specific date or time. For example, the following code creates a `LocalDate` object representing December 15, 2014:

```
LocalDate d = LocalDate.parse("2014-12-15");
```

To create a `LocalDateTime` object that represents a specific time on a specific date, use the `parse` method. Here's an example that sets the time to 3:45 p.m. on December 15, 2014:

```
LocalDateTime dt;
dt = LocalDateTime.parse("2014-12-15T15:45");
```

Note that the letter `T` separates the date from the time, and the time is expressed in 24-hour clock format. If you need to be more precise, you can also specify seconds, as in this example:

```
dt = LocalDateTime.parse("2014-12-15T15:45:13.5");
```

Here the time is set to 13.5 seconds after 2:45 p.m.

If the string is not in the correct format, the `parse` method throws a `DateTimeParseException`. Whenever you use the `parse` method, you should enclose it in a `try` block and catch this exception, as in this example:

```
LocalDateTime dt;
try
{
    dt = LocalDateTime.parse("2014-12-15T03:45PM");
}
catch (DateTimeParseException ex)
{
    System.out.println(ex.toString());
}
```

The `parse` method is especially useful for converting user input to a Date-Time object. For example, you might use it along with the `Scanner` class to read a date from the console, or you can use `parse` in a Swing application to read a date from a text box. When you do, you should prompt the user with the expected date format and catch `DateTimeParseException` in case the user enters the date in the wrong format.

Using the of Method to Create a Date-Time Object

A third way to create Date-Time objects is to use the static `of` method to create a Date-Time object from its constituent parts. For example, you can create a `LocalDate` object by supplying integers that represent the year, month, and day like this:

```
LocalDate date = LocalDate.of(2014,12,15);
```

Each of the Date-Time classes has one or more variations of the `of` method, as spelled out in Table 5-2.

Table 5-2	Date-Time of Methods
Class	*Method*
`LocalTime`	`of(int hour, int minute)`
	`of(int hour, int minute, int second)`
	`of(int hour, int minute, int second, int nanoOfSecond)`
`LocalDate`	`of(int year, int month, int dayOfMonth)`
	`of(int year, Month month, int dayOfMonth)`

Class	Method
LocalDateTime	of(int year, int month, int dayOfMonth, int hour, int minute)
	of(int year, int month, int dayOfMonth, int hour, int minute, int second)
	of(int year, int month, int dayOfMonth, int hour, int minute, int second, int nanoOfSecond)
	of(int year, Month month, int dayOfMonth, int hour, int minute)
	of(int year, Month month, int dayOfMonth, int hour, int minute, int second)
	of(int year, Month month, int dayOfMonth, int hour, int minute, int second, int nanoOfSecond)
	of(LocalDate date, LocalTime time)
OffsetTime	of(int hour, int minute, int second, int nanoOfSecond, ZoneOffset offset)
	of(LocalTime time, ZoneOffset offset)
OffsetDateTime	of(int year, int month, int dayOfMonth, int hour, int minute, int second, int nanoOfSecond, ZoneOffset offset)
	of(LocalDate date, LocalTime time, ZoneOffset offset)
	of(LocalDateTime dateTime, ZoneOffset offset)
MonthDay	of(int month, int dayOfMonth)
	of(Month month, int dayOfMonth)
YearMonth	of(int year, int month)
	of(int year, Month month)
Year	of(int year)

Note that several of the methods in Table 5-2 use the additional types Month, ZoneOffset, and ZoneId. These types are described in the following sections.

Using the Month enumeration

Several of the methods listed in Table 5-2 let you specify the month as a Month object. Month is an enumeration that represents the twelve months of the year, as follows:

Month.JANUARY	Month.MAY	Month.SEPTEMBER
Month.FEBRUARY	Month.JUNE	Month.OCTOBER
Month.MARCH	Month.JULY	Month.NOVEMBER
Month.APRIL	Month.AUGUST	Month.DECEMBER

Thus you can create a date like this:

```
LocalDate date = LocalDate.of(2014,Month.DECEMBER,15);
```

Interestingly, the Month enumeration has some interesting methods which you might find occasionally useful. For example, you can print the number of days in December like this:

```
System.out.println("December hath "
    + Month.DECEMBER.length(false) + " days.");
```

The boolean argument in the length method indicates whether the calculation should be for a leap year. Consult the online documentation for other useful methods of the Month enumeration.

Using the ZoneId class

To create a ZonedDateTime, you must first create a time zone object by using the ZoneId class. To create a time zone, you must know the standard name of the time zone you want to create. Unfortunately, there are more than 500 distinct zone IDs, and they periodically change. So listing them here would be impractical, but you can easily list them all by using this handy bit of code:

```
for (String id : ZoneId.getAvailableZoneIds())
    System.out.println(id);
```

This for loop will write the names of each ZoneId to the console.

Once you know the name of the ZoneId you want to use, you can create it using ZoneId.of , then use it to create a ZonedDateTime as in this example:

```
ZoneId z = ZoneId.of("America/Los_Angeles");
ZonedDateTime zdate;
zdate = ZonedDateTime.of(2014, 12, 15, 0, 0, 0, 0, z);
```

Or, if you prefer, you can create the ZoneId directly when you create the ZonedDateTime:

```
zdate = ZonedDateTime.of(2014, 12, 15, 0, 0, 0, 0,
    ZoneId.of("America/Los_Angeles"));
```

Using the ZoneOffset class

The of method OffsetTime and OffsetDateTime classes use an additional class named ZoneOffset to indicate the offset from UTC. You can create a ZoneOffset by using any of the following methods of the ZoneOffset class:

```
of(String offsetId)

ofHours(int hours)

ofHoursMinutes(int hours, int minutes)

ofHoursMinutesSeconds(int hours, int minutes, int
seconds)

ofTotalSeconds(int totalSeconds)
```

For example, you can create a ZoneOffset of -8 hours like this:

```
ZoneOffset z = ZoneOffset.ofHours(-8);
```

Alternatively, you could specify the offset as a string, as in this example:

```
ZoneOffset z = ZoneOffset.of("-08:00");
```

Note that when you use a string offset, you must provide two digits for the hours, minutes, and (optionally) seconds.

Once you have a ZoneOffset object, you can use it to create an OffsetTime, as in this example:

```
OffsetTime time = OffsetTime.of(10, 30, 0, 0, z);
```

Or if you prefer, you can create the ZoneOffset directly in the call to the OffsetTime's of method:

```
OffsetTime time = OffsetTime.of(10, 30, 0, 0,
    ZoneOffset.ofHours(-8));
```

Looking Closer at the LocalDate Class

The basic java.time classes are similar enough that once you learn how to use one of them, you'll find it easy to learn how to use the rest. Thus, for the rest of this chapter, I'll focus on just one: the LocalDate class. This class represents a date (year, month, and day) without an associated time. In this section and in the sections that follow, you'll learn how to use many of the methods of this class to extract information about a date, to compare two dates, and to perform calculations on a date.

Table 5-3 shows the most commonly used methods of the `LocalDate` class. For your convenience, this table includes the methods used to create `LocalDate` objects, even though those methods have already been covered earlier in this chapter.

Table 5-3	Methods of the LocalDate Class
Method	*Explanation*
Methods that create a `LocalDate` object	
`LocalDate now()`	Creates a `LocalDate` object that represents the current date.
`LocalDate of(int year, int month, int dayOfMonth)`	Creates a `LocalDate` object with a given year, month, and day.
`LocalDate of(int year, Month month, int dayOfMonth)`	Creates a `LocalDate` object with a given year, month, and day.
`LocalDate parse(String text)`	Creates a `LocalDate` object by parsing the text string.
Methods that extract information about a date	
`int getYear()`	Returns the year.
`Month getMonth()`	Returns the month as a `Month` object.
`int getMonthValue()`	Returns the month as an int from 1 through 12.
`int getDayOfMonth()`	Returns the day of the month.
`DayOfWeek getDayOfWeek()`	Returns the day of the week as a `DayOfWeek` object.
`int getDayOfYear()`	Returns the day of the year.
`int lengthOfMonth()`	Returns the number of days in this month.
`int lengthOfYear()`	Returns the number of days in this year.
Methods that compare dates	
`boolean isAfter(LocalDate other)`	Returns `true` if `other` occurs after this date.
`boolean isBefore(LocalDate other)`	Returns `true` if `other` occurs after this date.
`boolean isEqual(LocalDate other)`	Returns `true` if this date and `other` represent the same date.

Method	Explanation
Methods that perform date calculations	
LocalDate plusDays(long days)	Returns a copy of the LocalDate with the specified number of days added.
LocalDate plusNMonths(long days)	Returns a copy of the LocalDate with the specified number of months added.
LocalDate plusWeeks(long months)	Returns a copy of the LocalDate with the specified number of weeks added.
LocalDate plusYears(long days)	Returns a copy of the LocalDate with the specified number of years added.
LocalDate minusDays(long days)	Returns a copy of the LocalDate with the specified number of days subtracted.
LocalDate minusMonths(long months)	Returns a copy of the LocalDate with the specified number of months subtracted.
LocalDate minusWeeks(long months)	Returns a copy of the LocalDate with the specified number of weeks subtracted.
LocalDate minusYears(long years)	Returns a copy of the LocalDate with the specified number of years subtracted.
long until(LocalDate endDate, ChronoUnit unit)	Returns the difference between this date and the specified date measured in the specified units.

Extracting Information About a Date

Several methods of the LocalDate class let you extract useful information about a given date. For instance, the following example shows how you can extract the current year, month, and day:

```
LocalDate date = LocalDate.now();
int year = date.getYear();
int month = date.getMonthValue();
int day = date.getDayOfMonth();
```

If you need to know how many days into the year a particular date is, you can use this code:

```
LocalDate date = LocalDate.parse("2016-04-09");
System.out.println(date.getDayOfYear());
```

This example will print the number `100`, as April 9 is the 100th day of 2016.

The `getDayOfWeek` method returns a value of type `DayOfWeek`, which is an enumeration with the following values:

SUNDAY	THURSDAY
MONDAY	FRIDAY
TUESDAY	SATURDAY
WEDNESDAY	

Here's an example of how you might use this method:

```
LocalDate date = LocalDate.parse("2016-04-09");
System.out.println(date.getDayOfWeek());
```

In this example, the string `SATURDAY` will be printed because in 2016, April 9 falls on a Saturday.

The `lengthOfMonth` and `lengthOfYear` are useful if you want to know the number of days in the month or year represented by a `LocalDate`. Both methods take into account leap years.

Comparing Dates

You can't compare Date-Time objects using Java's standard comparison operators. Consider the following example:

```
if (LocalDate.now() == LocalDate.now())
    System.out.println("All is right in the universe.");
else
    System.out.println("There must be a disturbance " +
        "in the space-time continuum!");
```

If you run this code, `There must be a disturbance in the space-time continuum!` will be printed. That's because when used on objects, the equality operator tests whether two expressions refer to the same object, not to objects with the same value.

To test the equality of two dates, you must use the `isEqual` method, as in this example:

```
if (LocalDate.now().isEqual(LocalDate.now()))
    System.out.println("All is right in the universe.");
```

Similarly, you must use either the `isBefore` or the `isAfter` method to determine whether one date falls before or after another date.

Note that you *can* use built-in operators with methods that return integer results. Thus, the following code will work just as you would expect:

```
if (LocalDate.now().getDayOfMonth() < 15)
    System.out.println("It is not yet the 15th.");
```

Because the `getDayOfMonth` method returns an integer, you can use the `<` operator to determine if the 15th of the month has yet arrived.

Calculating with Dates

Just as you cannot use Java's built-in comparison operators with dates, you also may not use built-in mathematical operators. Instead, you can perform addition and subtraction on dates using the various `plus` and `minus` methods, and you can determine the difference between two dates by using the `until` method.

An important fact to consider when doing date and time calculations is that Date-Time objects are *immutable*. That means that once you create a Date-Time object, you cannot change its value. When you perform a calculation on a Date-Time object, the result is a new Date-Time object with a new value.

The `plus` and `minus` methods let you add various date and time units to a Date-Time object. Table 5-3 lists four variants of each for the `LocalDate` class, allowing you to add or subtract years, months, weeks, and days to a `LocalDate` object. The following code prints the current date, tomorrow's date, and the date one week, one month, and one year from now:

```
System.out.println("Today: " + LocalDate.now());
System.out.println("Tomorrow: " + LocalDate.now().plusDays(1));
System.out.println("Next week: " + LocalDate.now().plusWeeks(1));
System.out.println("Next month: " + LocalDate.now().plusMonths(1));
System.out.println("Next year: " + LocalDate.now().plusYears(1));
```

To determine the difference between two dates, use the `until` method. It calculates the difference between a date and the date passed as the first parameter, measured in the units indicated by the second parameter. For example, the following code determines the number of days between May 16, 2014 and December 15, 2014:

```
LocalDate date1 = LocalDate.parse("2014-05-16");
LocalDate date2 = LocalDate.parse("2014-12-15");
System.out.println(date1.until(date2, ChronoUnit.DAYS));
```

Some date calculations can be a bit more complex. For example, consider a business that prepares invoices on the 15th of each month. The following snippet of code displays the number of days from the current date until the next invoicing date:

```
LocalDate today = LocalDate.now();
LocalDate invDate = LocalDate.of(today.getYear(),
    today.getMonthValue(), 15);
if (today.getDayOfMonth() > 15)
    invDate = invDate.plusMonths(1);
long daysToInvoice = today.until(invDate,
    ChronoUnit.DAYS);
System.out.println(daysToInvoice
    + " until next invoice date.");
```

This example works by first getting the current date, then creating a new `LocalDate` object that represents the 15th of the current month. Then, if the current day of the month is greater than 15, it adds one month to the invoicing date. In other words, if it is the 16th or later, invoicing occurs on the 15th of the *following* month, not of this month. Then it uses the `until` method to determine the number of days between the current date and the next invoicing date.

`ChronoUnit` is an enumeration that defines the various units of time that can be used in date and time calculations. The possible values are:

CENTURIES	MILLENNIA
DAYS	MILLIS
DECADES	MINUTES
ERAS	MONTHS
FOREVER	NANOS
HALF-DAYS	SECONDS
HOURS	WEEKS
MICROS	YEARS

Most of these are self-explanatory, but two of them are a bit peculiar:

✦ ERA indicates whether the date refers to the Common Era (CE, also known as AD) or Before Era (BCE, also known as BC).

✦ FOREVER represents the largest value that can be represented as a duration. Sadly, Java won't let you live forever. The following code throws an exception:

```
LocalDate birthday = LocalDate.parse("1959-05-16");

birthday = birthday.plus(1,ChronoUnit.FOREVER);
```

Note that `ChronoUnit` is in the `java.time.temporal` package, so be sure to include the following statement at the top of any program that uses `ChronoUnit`:

```
import java.time.temporal.*;
```

Formatting Dates

If you use the `toString()` method to convert a `LocalDate` to a string, you get a string such as `2014-10-31`. What if you want to display the date in a different format, such as `10-31-2014` or `October 31, 2014`? To accomplish that, you can use the `format` method of the `LocalDate` class along with a custom formatter you create using the `DateTimeFormatter` class. To specify the format you want to use, you pass the `DateTimeFormatter` class a pattern string, using the formatting symbols listed in Table 5-4.

Table 5-4   Formatting Characters for the DateTimeFormatter Class

Format pattern	Explanation
y	Year (two or four digits)
M	Month (one or two digits or three or more letters)
d	Day of month (such as `1, 28`)
H	Hour
m	Minute
s	Second (`0 to 59`)
h	Clock hour (`1 to 12`)
a	AM or PM
V	Time zone ID (such as `America/Los_Angeles`)
z	Time zone name (such as `Pacific Daylight Time`)

The easiest way to create a `DateTimeFormatter` object is to use the static `ofPattern` method along with a pattern string. For example:

```
DateTimeFormatter formatter;
formatter = DateTimeFormatter.ofPattern("dd MMM YYYY");
```

This formatter produces dates formatted like `04 SEP 2014`. You can then use the formatter to produce a formatted `date` string like this:

```
LocalDate date = LocalDate.now();
String formattedDate = date.format(formatter);
```

Here's a simple program that prints the current date in several different formats:

```
import java.util.*;
import java.time.*;
import java.time.format.*;

public class FormatDateTime
{
    public static void main(String[] args)
    {
        LocalDateTime  now = LocalDateTime.now();
        printDate(now, "YYYY-MM-dd");
        printDate(now, "MM-dd-YYYY");
        printDate(now, "dd MMM YYYY");
        printDate(now, "MMMM d, YYYY");
        printDate(now, "HH:mm");
        printDate(now, "h:mm a");
    }

    public static void printDate(LocalDateTime date, String pattern)
    {
        DateTimeFormatter f;
        f = DateTimeFormatter.ofPattern(pattern);
        pattern = (pattern + "              ").substring(0, 14);
        System.out.println(pattern + " " + date.format(f));
    }
}
```

When you run this program, you'll get console output that resembles this:

```
YYYY-MM-dd      2013-10-09
MM-dd-YYYY      10-09-2013
dd MMM YYYY     09 Oct 2013
MMMM d, YYYY    October 9, 2013
HH:mm           20:29
h:mm a          8:29 PM
```

Did you notice the cool formatting trick I used? I forced the `System.out.println()` patterns to print 14-character long strings so all the dates would line up. The padding is accomplished by this slick line of code:

```
pattern = (pattern + "              ").substring(0, 14);
```

Here a string of 14 spaces is added to the `pattern` string, then a 14-character long substring is taken starting at the first character. I figured the nice spacing in the output would make it easier for you to see the effect of each of the pattern strings.

Looking at a Fun Birthday Calculator

Now that you've seen the techniques for working with Date-Time objects, it's time to look at a complete programming example. Listing 5-1 presents a program that prompts the user to enter his or her birthday and then prints a variety of interesting information deduced from the date, including:

+ The day of the week on which the user was born

+ The user's age in years

+ The date of the user's next birthday

+ The number of days until the user's next birthday

+ The user's half-birthday (six months from his or her birthday)

Here's an example of the `BirthdayFun` application in action:

```
Today is October 9, 2013.

Please enter your birthdate (yyyy-mm-dd): 1959-12-15

December 15, 1959 was a very good day!
You were born on a TUESDAY.
You are 53 years young.
Your next birthday is December 15, 2013.
That's just 67 days from now!
Your half-birthday is June 15.

Another? (Y or N) N
```

Listing 5-1: The BirthdayFun Application

```
import java.util.*;
import java.time.*;                                                    →2
import java.time.format.*;
import java.time.temporal.*;

public class BirthdayFun
{
    static Scanner sc = new Scanner(System.in);                        →8

    public static void main(String[] args)
    {
        do
        {
            LocalDate birthDate;                                       →14

            DateTimeFormatter fullFormat =                            →16
                DateTimeFormatter.ofPattern("MMMM d, YYYY");
            DateTimeFormatter monthDayFormat =
                DateTimeFormatter.ofPattern("MMMM d");
```

(continued)

Listing 5-1 *(continued)*

```
    System.out.println("Today is "                              →21
        + LocalDate.now().format(fullFormat) + ".");

    System.out.println();
    System.out.print("Please enter your birthdate "
        + "(yyyy-mm-dd): ");
    String input = sc.nextLine();
    try
    {
        birthDate = LocalDate.parse(input);                     →30

        if (birthDate.isAfter(LocalDate.now()))                 →32
        {
            System.out.println("You haven't been born yet!");
            continue;
        }

        System.out.println();

        System.out.println(birthDate.format(fullFormat)         →40
            + " was a very good day!");

        DayOfWeek birthDayOfWeek = birthDate.getDayOfWeek();    →42
        System.out.println("You were born on a "
            + birthDayOfWeek + ".");

        long years = birthDate.until(LocalDate.now(),           →46
            ChronoUnit.YEARS);
        System.out.println("You are " + years + " years young.");

        LocalDate nextBDay = birthDate.plusYears(years + 1);    →50
        System.out.println("Your next birthday is "
            + nextBDay.format(fullFormat) + ".");

        long wait = LocalDate.now().until(nextBDay,             →54
            ChronoUnit.DAYS);
        System.out.println("That's just " + wait
            + " days from now!");

        LocalDate halfBirthday = birthDate.plusMonths(6);       →59
        System.out.println("Your half-birthday is "
            + halfBirthday.format(monthDayFormat) + ".");
    }
    catch (DateTimeParseException ex)
    {
        System.out.println("Sorry, that is not a valid date.");
    }

    } while(askAgain());
}

private static boolean askAgain()
{
    System.out.println();
    System.out.print("Another? (Y or N) ");
    String reply = sc.nextLine();
```

```
        if (reply.equalsIgnoreCase("Y"))
        {
            return true;
        }
        return false;
    }
}
```

The following paragraphs explain the most important lines in this program:

→ **2**   The program uses classes from three packages: `java.time`, `java.time.format`, and `java.time.temporal`.

→ **8**   A `Scanner` is used to get the user input. The `Scanner` is defined as a class variable so that it can be accessed by both the `main` and the `askAgain` methods.

→ **14**   The `birthdate` variable is used to store the birthdate entered by the user.

→ **16**   The program uses two formatters: `fullFormat` formats the date in full-text format (such as December 15, 1959) and `monthDay Format` formats the date as just a month and day.

→ **21**   This line displays the current date.

→ **21**   This line displays the current date.

→ **31**   The string entered by the user is parsed.

→ **32**   The `if` statement ensures that the user has not entered a date in the future.

→ **40**   The date entered by the user is displayed.

→ **42**   The day of the week is calculated and displayed.

→ **46**   The person's age is calculated by determining the difference between the current date and the birthdate in years.

→ **50**   The date of the person's next birthday is calculated by adding the person's age plus 1 year to the original birthdate.

→ **54**   The number of days until the person's next birthday is calculated.

→ **59**   The person's half birthday is calculated by adding six months to the original birthdate.

Chapter 6: Using BigDecimals

In This Chapter

✔ Understanding the problem with double arithmetic in Java

✔ Solving the double problem with the BigDecimal class

✔ Creating objects with BigDecimal

✔ Doing arithmetic with BigDecimal objects

✔ Discovering other things to do with BigDecimal

*Y*ou would think that arithmetic would be one area in which any programming language would excel. After all, computers were conceived as enormous calculating machines.

Alas, Java doesn't always do arithmetic the way you'd like. In this chapter, you discover why. Then you work around Java's inherent arithmetic limitations by using a special class designed for just that purpose: the BigDecimal class. BigDecimal is a pain to use, but just about any program that does financial calculations should use it.

Seeing Why Java Can't Add

Every schoolboy (and schoolgirl) knows that ten pennies make a dime. You can write a Java program to prove this simple assertion. I created a double variable named dime and assigned it the value 0.10. Next, I created another double variable named penny and assigned it the value 0.01. Then I made a for loop that added the penny ten times to a third double variable named tenPennies. Finally, I used an if statement to see whether ten pennies really do equal a dime. The code for this program is shown in Listing 6-1.

Listing 6-1:   The New Math

```
public class TenPennies
{
    public static void main (String[] args)
    {
        System.out.println("Welcome to the New Math..."
            + "Or, Why Java Can't Add\n");
        double penny = 0.01;          // this is a penny
        double dime = 0.10;           // this is a dime
```

(continued)

Listing 6-1 *(continued)*

```
        double tenPennies = 0;
        for (int i = 0; i < 10; i++)   // add up 10 pennies
            tenPennies += penny;

        System.out.println("A dime is " + dime);
        System.out.println("Ten pennies is " +
            tenPennies);

        if (tenPennies == dime)
            System.out.println(
                "Ten Pennies is equal to a dime.");
        else
            System.out.println(
                "Ten pennies is NOT equal to a dime!");
    }
}
```

Place your bets now: Is 0.01 added ten times equal to 0.10? Here's the console output from this program:

```
Welcome to the New Math . . .Or, Why Java Can't Add

A dime is 0.1
Ten pennies is 0.09999999999999999
Ten pennies is NOT equal to a dime!
```

Apparently not. Somehow, Java came up with 0.09999999999999999 instead of 0.10, and although 0.09999999999999999 is *close* to 0.10, the two values aren't equal.

Double trouble

The root problem here is that Java's `double` type stores values in binary (base 2), not in decimal (base 10). The mathematicians among us know that in any counting system, certain fraction values can't be represented exactly. The best-known of these values in decimal is ⅓. Pull out a pocket calculator and divide 1 by 3, and then multiply the result by 3. You should end up with 1, but you get 0.999 . . . (with however many nines your calculator can display).

As it turns out, each counting system has a different combination of fractions that can't be represented exactly. In binary, one of the problem fractions is ¹⁄₁₀. Thus `double` and `float` types can't represent 0.1 accurately.

In most cases, you don't notice these errors because they're insignificant and are often hidden by rounding. Try this code:

```
float val = 0.1f;
System.out.println(val);
```

Here, Java's default behavior is to format the number so that the inaccuracy is hidden. Thus, the output from this program is simply 0.1. You can see the inaccuracy, however, if you use the NumberFormat class to format the number with ten significant digits, like this:

```
float val = 0.1f;
NumberFormat nf = NumberFormat.getNumberInstance();
nf.setMinimumFractionDigits(10);
System.out.println(nf.format(val));
```

If you run this code, the value displayed on the console is 0.1000000015.

Note that in this example, I used a float instead of a double to illustrate the problem. With a double, the value of 0.1 is much closer to 0.1 than it is with a float because a double has twice as many bits to work with. Trust me, though — the inaccuracy is still there.

Another example

The inaccuracy of double arithmetic is especially bad in programs that do financial calculations. Imagine trying to balance your checkbook if every once in a while, your calculator makes a 1¢ error while doing simple addition or subtraction. (Actually, I think that might happen at my house. Maybe my calculator uses an embedded Java program.)

Listing 6-2 shows a simple program that lets you enter a number, calculates 5 percent sales tax, and then displays the total and asks whether you want to enter another number. Here's a sample of its console:

```
Welcome to the sales tax calculator.

Enter subtotal: 19.95
Subtotal:    $19.95
Sales tax:   $1.00
Total:       $20.95

Again? (Y or N) y

Enter subtotal: 3.49
Subtotal:    $3.49
Sales tax:   $0.17
Total:       $3.66

Again? (Y or N) y

Enter subtotal: 0.70
Subtotal:    $0.70
Sales tax:   $0.03
Total:       $0.74

Again? (Y or N) n
```

All is well with the first two entries, but the third one has an embarrassing arithmetic error: 70 plus 3 is *not* 74.

Listing 6-2: Bad Tax!

```java
import java.text.*;
import java.util.*;

public class BadTax
{   static Scanner sc = new Scanner(System.in);
    static NumberFormat cf =
        NumberFormat.getCurrencyInstance();

    public static void main (String[] args)
    {
        double subTotal, salesTax, invoiceTotal;
        double taxRate = 0.05;

        System.out.println(
            "Welcome to the sales tax calculator.");
        do
        {
            System.out.print("\nEnter subtotal: ");
            subTotal = sc.nextDouble();
            sc.nextLine();

            salesTax = subTotal * taxRate;
            invoiceTotal = subTotal + salesTax;

            System.out.print("Subtotal:    ");
            System.out.println(cf.format(subTotal));
            System.out.print("Sales tax:   ");
            System.out.println(cf.format(salesTax));
            System.out.print("Total:       ");
            System.out.println(cf.format(invoiceTotal));
        } while (getAnother());
    }

    static boolean getAnother()
    {
        System.out.print("\nAgain? (Y or N) ");
        if (sc.nextLine().equalsIgnoreCase("Y"))
            return true;
        else
            return false;
    }
}
```

The moral of the story is that you should *never* use `double` to represent decimal values in any application that needs decimal arithmetic to be accurate. That caveat includes most applications that have anything to do with money. You don't want to send a customer an inaccurate invoice, do you?

BigDecimal to the Rescue!

If you can't use `double` for decimal values when you need accurate results, what can you use? Fortunately, the Java designers have provided a class that solves the problem for you. The `BigDecimal` class accurately represents a decimal number and provides methods you can use to perform arithmetic and do comparisons with the value.

Internally, the `BigDecimal` class represents decimal values by using integers. Because integer arithmetic isn't prone to the same conversion errors that floating-point arithmetic is, the `BigDecimal` class can provide accurate results. In addition, the `BigDecimal` class uses some fancy coding tricks to store numbers of virtually any size. In fact, the `BigDecimal` class is quite capable of representing the national debt down to the penny.

Like strings, `BigDecimal` objects are immutable. After you create one, you can't change its value. Many of the `BigDecimal` methods, however, perform some operation on the value (such as addition or subtraction) and return the result. Thus, you often find yourself writing statements like this one when you work with the `BigDecimal` class:

```
totalSales = totalSales.add(quarterlySales);
```

Here, the `add` method of the `BigDecimal` `totalSales` is called, and the return value, which is a new `BigDecimal` object, is assigned back to `totalSales`.

Creating BigDecimal Objects

To create a `BigDecimal` object, you call one of the constructors listed in Table 6-1. Each of these constructors takes a value and converts it to a `BigDecimal` object.

Table 6-1	Constructors BigDecimal Class
Constructor	*Explanation*
`BigDecimal(double val)`	Creates a `BigDecimal` from the `double` value.
`BigDecimal(float val)`	Creates a `BigDecimal` from the `float` value.
`BigDecimal(int val)`	Creates a `BigDecimal` from the `int` value.
`BigDecimal(long val)`	Creates a `BigDecimal` from the `long` value.
`BigDecimal(String val)`	Creates a `BigDecimal` from the `String` value. The string must contain a valid representation of a decimal number.

This round goes to C#

As you probably know, C# is Microsoft's answer to Java. If you take a casual look at C#, it looks a lot like Java, and if you take a *really* close look at C#, it still looks a lot like Java. The class libraries used by Java and C# are similar, but C#'s class library (called the .NET Framework) and Java's API have plenty of differences. The languages themselves are very similar, however.

Because C# is intended to compete with Java, computer prognosticators frequently compare the two languages. Java usually comes out on top, primarily because it's open-source, so you're not tied to one vendor if you use it.

C#, however, has a seemingly minor feature that Java really should have had from the start: a native `decimal` type. In C#, you can write code like this:

```
public decimal calculateOrderTax(decimal
        subTotal, decimal taxRate)
```

```
{
    decimal tax = subTotal * taxRate;
    return subTotal + tax
}
```

No matter how you slice it, that's much easier to code and understand than Java's `BigDecimal` class. Also, it's much more efficient, because decimal is a primitive type.

Unfortunately, there's little chance that we'll ever get a primitive decimal type in Java. Adding a new primitive type to the Java Virtual Machine would be a major undertaking. Perhaps in the next version of Java, we'll get the ability to overload mathematical operators for classes. Then `BigDecimal` can be enhanced to support the arithmetic operators directly instead of via cumbersome methods such as `add` and `subtract`.

Although you can create `BigDecimal` values from a `double` or `float` value, I recommend against it. The whole point of using `BigDecimal` is to avoid the accuracy errors that are inherent with `double` and `float` values, and the only way to do that is to avoid using `double` and `float` altogether. As the old computer saying reminds you, "Garbage In, Garbage Out."

Take these statements, for example:

```
BigDecimal value = new BigDecimal(0.01);
System.out.println(value);
```

Here's what gets printed on the console:

```
0.01000000000000000020816681711721685132943093776702880859375
```

The best way to create a `BigDecimal` object with an initial decimal value is via a string, like this:

```
BigDecimal value = new BigDecimal("0.01");
```

Here, `value` has a value of exactly `0.01`.

If the initial value is an integer, you can safely pass it to the constructor. Remember that integers don't have the same accuracy problems that `doubles` and `floats` do. Also, as you see later in the chapter, you can convert a `BigDecimal` to a `double` solely for the purpose of using the `NumberFormat` class to format the result. As long as you don't use the `double` in any calculations, you won't have to worry about floating-point inaccuracies.

Note: The `BigDecimal` class has no default constructor because you can't have a `BigDecimal` object without a value.

Doing BigDecimal Arithmetic

The worst part about using the `BigDecimal` class is that you can't use normal arithmetic operators with `BigDecimal` objects. The following code, for example, won't compile:

```
BigDecimal subTotal, taxRate, tax, total;
subTotal = new BigDecimal("32.50");
taxRate = new BigDecimal("0.05");
tax = subTotal * taxRate;   // error: won't compile
total = subTotal + tax      // this won't compile either
```

Instead, you have to call methods of the `BigDecimal` class to perform basic arithmetic. All these methods return the result of the calculation as `BigDecimal` objects. Here's how you can perform the preceding tax calculation:

```
BigDecimal subTotal, taxRate, tax, total;
subTotal = new BigDecimal("32.50");
taxRate = new BigDecimal("0.05");
tax = subTotal.multiply(taxRate);
total = subTotal.add(tax);
```

Table 6-2 lists all the arithmetic methods for the `BigDecimal` class. As you can see, the class has methods for basic operations such as add, subtract, multiply, and divide, as well as some additional operations such as abs (absolute power), pow (raising the number to a power), and negative (changes the sign of the number).

Table 6-2 **Arithmetic Methods of the BigDecimal Class**

Method	Explanation
`BigDecimal abs()`	Returns the absolute value of this `BigDecimal`.
`BigDecimal add`	Adds the specified `BigDecimal` to this `BigDecimal` and returns the result.

(continued)

Table 6-2 *(continued)*

Method	*Explanation*
`BigDecimal divide(BigDecimal val)`	Divides this `BigDecimal` by the specified `BigDecimal` and returns the result. The method may throw `ArithmeticException`.
`BigDecimal[] divideAndRemainder (BigDecimal val)`	Divides this `BigDecimal` by the specified `BigDecimal`. The result and the remainder are returned as a two-element `BigDecimal` array.
`BigDecimal[] divideToInteg ralValue(BigDecimal val)`	Divides this `BigDecimal` by the specified `BigDecimal` and returns the integer result.
`BigDecimal max(BigDecimal val)`	Returns the larger of this `BigDecimal` and the specified `BigDecimal`.
`BigDecimal min(BigDecimal val)`	Returns the smaller of this `BigDecimal` and the specified `BigDecimal`.
`BigDecimal multiply(BigDecimal val)`	Multiplies this `BigDecimal` by the specified `BigDecimal` and returns the result.
`BigDecimal negate()`	Negates this `BigDecimal` and returns the result.
`BigDecimal pow(int power)`	Raises this `BigDecimal` to the power specified by the `int` value and returns the result.
`BigDecimal remainder(BigDecimal val)`	Divides this `BigDecimal` by the specified `BigDecimal` and returns the remainder.
`BigDecimal subtract(BigDecimal val)`	Subtracts the specified `BigDecimal` from this `BigDecimal` and returns the result.

Notice that in addition to normal division, you can use the `divideTo IntegralValue` method to return the integer part of the result. Here's an example:

```
BigDecimal a = new BigDecimal("23.5");
BigDecimal b = new BigDecimal("7.0");
BigDecimal c;
c = a.divideToIntegralValue(b);
```

After these statements execute, the value of `c` is `3`.

You can also use the `remainder` method to get the remainder from a division:

```
c = a.remainder(b);
```

Here the value of `c` is `2.5`.

A common mistake among new users of the `BigDecimal` class is forgetting to assign the result of an arithmetic operation. You might stare at this code loop for hours, wondering why it doesn't seem to work:

```
BigDecimal totalWinnings = new BigDecimal("1000.00");
BigDecimal winningsThisGame = new BigDecimal("200.00");
totalWinnings.add(winningsThisGame);
System.out.println(totalWinnings);
```

The third statement adds `winningsThisGame` to `totalWinnings` but discards the result. What you probably meant was this:

```
totalWinnings = totalWinnings.add(winningsThisGame);
```

BigDecimal reminds me of COBOL

I hate to admit it, but long ago, in a galaxy far away, I was a COBOL programmer. Call me crazy, but something about the arithmetic methods of `BigDecimal` reminds me of COBOL.

COBOL had separate statements for doing basic arithmetic operations. Thus you could write statements like this:

```
MULTIPLY SUBTOTAL BY TAX-RATE GIVING TAX.
ADD TAX TO SUBTOTAL GIVING TOTAL.
```

Many COBOL programs had long sections with page after page of statements like that.

The fact that you can't use `BigDecimal` in arithmetic expressions makes you spell out calculations step by step, the way you had to in COBOL, as in this example:

```
tax = subTotal.multiply(taxRate);
total = subTotal.add(tax);
```

Sure, there are differences. COBOL was written in uppercase letters, and statements ended with periods; Java uses lowercase letters and semicolons. Oh, and there's the whole object-oriented thing, though I hear that the most recent versions of COBOL support it too.

Anyway, it takes me back to the days of *Welcome Back, Kotter* and disco. Sigh.

Rounding BigDecimal Values

Multiplication and division introduce the need for rounding. Suppose that your sales tax rate is 5 percent. The tax calculation on a sale of $32.55 would be $1.6275, but not too many people know how to make change for ¾ of a penny. As a result, this sales tax calculation should be rounded up to $1.63.

The NumberFormat class automatically rounds results when it converts numbers to strings. That's not real rounding, however, because it doesn't change the underlying values used in the calculations. In other words, you shouldn't leave the sales tax as $1.6275 and just print it as $1.63. Instead, you should actually *change* the sales tax to $1.63. That's the only way to avert the possibility of additional calculation errors down the line.

The fundamentals of scale

To use rounding with the BigDecimal class, you need to understand the idea of scale. The *scale* of a BigDecimal number is the number of digits that appear to the right of the decimal point. The BigDecimal classes provide several methods that let you work with the scale; they're shown in Table 6-3.

Table 6-3	Scaling Methods of the BigDecimal Class
Method	*Explanation*
int scale()	Returns the scale of this BigDecimal.
setScale(int scale)	Returns a new BigDecimal with the specified scale.
setScale(int scale, RoundingMode mode)	Returns a new BigDecimal with the specified scale and rounding mode. See Table 6-4 for RoundingMode values.
BigDecimal divide(BigDecimal val, int scale, RoundingMode mode)	Divides this BigDecimal by the specified BigDecimal and returns the result, using the specified scale and rounding mode. See Table 6-4 for rounding mode.

When you create a BigDecimal object, the starting value determines the object's scale. Look at this code:

```
BigDecimal num0 = new BigDecimal("1");
BigDecimal num1 = new BigDecimal("1.0");
BigDecimal num2 = new BigDecimal("1.00");
BigDecimal num3 = new BigDecimal("1.000");
```

```
int scale0 = num0.scale();
int scale1 = num1.scale();
int scale2 = num2.scale();
int scale3 = num3.scale();

System.out.println("Scale of " + num0 + " is " + scale0);
System.out.println("Scale of " + num1 + " is " + scale1);
System.out.println("Scale of " + num2 + " is " + scale2);
System.out.println("Scale of " + num3 + " is " + scale3);
```

When you run this code, the following lines appear on the console:

```
Scale of 1 is 0
Scale of 1.0 is 1
Scale of 1.00 is 2
Scale of 1.000 is 3
```

When you use addition and subtraction, the scale of the result is the largest scale between the two values that were added. If you add 25.0 to 1.625, the result is 26.625 with a scale of 3, because the result has three digits to the right of the decimal point.

With multiplication, the resulting scale is the sum of the scales of the two numbers. Thus 1.25 times 1.75 is 2.1875 with a scale of 4. Note that the scales are added even if the number ends with zeros. The result of 1.00 times 2.50, for example, is 2.5000 with a scale of 4.

With division, the scale is exactly what it needs to be to hold the result. The result of 25 divided by 5 is 5 with a scale of 0, but the result of 25 divided by 8 is 3.125 with a scale of 3.

The how-to of rounding

Now that you know about scale, you can see how it plays an important role in rounding. When you say that you want to round a number to two decimal places, what you mean is that you want the result to have a scale of 2 — and that any digits past the second decimal digit should be used to decide whether to round the result up or down.

The BigDecimal class accomplishes this task by using the setScale method. The name of this method is a little misleading, so don't be confused. Remember that BigDecimal objects are immutable, so calling the setScale method doesn't change the scale of an existing BigDecimal object; instead, it creates a new BigDecimal object whose scale is different from that of the original. Here's an example:

```
BigDecimal value1 = new BigDecimal("1.0000");
BigDecimal value2 = value1.setScale(2);
```

Here value2 is assigned the value 1.00 with the scale set to 2.

Reducing the scale with this version of the `setScale` method always runs the risk of cutting important digits. If `value1` had been set to `1.6125`, the last two digits would be cut off. The `BigDecimal` class doesn't like to let that happen, so it throws an `ArithmeticException` in that case.

You can use the other version of `setScale` to round the result to a specified scale, however. Then you have to specify one of the `RoundingMode` enumerations listed in Table 6-4. In almost all cases, you use `RoundingMode.HALF_UP`. The other rounding modes are strange. I include them here primarily for your enjoyment, so you can see what kinds of things mathematicians and computer scientists dream up while we're trying to figure out how to pay our bills.

Table 6-4	Members of the RoundingMode Enumeration
Rounding Mode	*Explanation*
`RoundingMode.HALF_UP`	This mode is the normal way to round things. Excess values that are 5 or greater are rounded up; values of 4 or less are rounded down. Thus, 5.2459 rounded to a scale of 2 is 5.25.
`RoundingMode.HALF_DOWN`	Excess values that are 5 or less are rounded down; values of 6 or greater are rounded up.
`RoundingMode.HALF_EVEN`	This mode is strange. Excess values of exactly 5 are rounded toward the nearest even number. Thus, 5.5 rounds up to 6, but 4.5 is rounded down to 4.
`RoundingMode.CEILING`	Numbers are always rounded up, regardless of the value of the excess digits.
`RoundingMode.FLOOR`	Numbers are always rounded down, regardless of the value of the excess digits.
`RoundingMode.DOWN`	Numbers are always rounded toward zero, regardless of the value of the excess digits. That means that positive numbers are rounded down and negative numbers are rounded up.
`RoundingMode.UP`	Numbers are always rounded away from zero, regardless of the value of the excess digits. That means that positive numbers are rounded up and negative numbers are rounded down.
`RoundingMode.UNNECESSARY`	Numbers are never rounded. The operation throws `ArithmeticException` if the scaling causes digits to be lost.

Getting back to the sales tax calculation, here's how you can avoid charging someone $1.6275 on a $32.55 purchase:

```
salesTax = subTotal.multiply(taxRate);
salesTax = salesTax.setScale(2, RoundingMode.HALF_UP);
invoiceTotal = subTotal.add(salesTax);
```

First, you multiply the subtotal by the tax rate. Assuming that the scale of both these `BigDecimal` objects is 2, the result has a scale of 4. Then you use the `setScale` method to change the scale of `salesTax` back to 2, with `HALF_UP` specified as the rounding mode. When that's done, you can continue with your other calculations.

If you're working with an application that does a lot of rounding, you may want to make a little helper method to save you some tedious coding. You can create a `round` method like this:

```
static BigDecimal round(BigDecimal d)
{
    return d.setScale(2, RoundingMode.HALF_UP);
}
```

Then you can change the second line in the example to this:

```
salesTax = round(salesTax);
```

Comparing BigDecimal Values

Another annoyance of using the `BigDecimal` class is that you can't use the equality operator (`==`) to compare values. The following code won't work:

```
BigDecimal big1 = new BigDecimal("1.0");
BigDecimal big2 = new BigDecimal("1.0");
if (big1 == big2)
    System.out.println("One equals one");
```

The reason it doesn't work is the same reason you can't compare strings in this way: The equals operator checks for reference equality, not value equality. Thus, it always returns `false` unless both variables point to the same instance of the `BigDecimal` class.

To test for value equality, you should use either the `equals` method or the `compareTo` method, as listed in Table 6-5. The `equals` method returns `true` if both `BigDecimal` objects have the same value and the same scale. The `compareTo` method returns an integer that indicates whether one `BigDecimal` is less than (returns –1), equal to (returns 0), or greater than (returns +1) another `BigDecimal`. You use this method in place of the < and > operators.

Table 6-5   Comparison Methods of the BigDecimal Class

Method	Explanation
`int compareTo(BigDecimal val)`	Compares this `BigDecimal` with the specified `BigDecimal`. Returns −1, 0, or +1 if this `BigDecimal` is less than, equal to, or greater than the specified `BigDecimal`.
`boolean equals(Object val)`	Returns a boolean that indicates whether this `BigDecimal` is equal to the specified object.

Consider the following snippet of code:

```
BigDecimal One1 = new BigDecimal("1.0");
BigDecimal One2 = new BigDecimal("1.00");

if (One1.equals(One2))
    System.out.println(
        "Scale doesn't matter with equals");
else
    System.out.println("Scale matters with equals");

if (One1.compareTo(One2) == 0)
    System.out.println(
        "Scale doesn't matter with compareTo");
else
    System.out.println("Scale matters with compareTo");
```

Here both `One1` and `One2` have a value of 1, but with different scales. When you run this code, the following lines are displayed on the console:

```
Scale matters with equals
Scale doesn't matter with compareTo
```

As you can see, the scale is considered when you compare values with the `equals` method. As a result, you should use `compareTo` if you aren't sure that the scale of the values will be the same.

Here's a little trick for using the `compareTo` method: You can perform the same comparisons provided by the regular relational operators (`<`, `<=`, `==`, `=>`, and `>`) by using these operators to compare the result of the `compareTo` method with 0. To check whether `value1` is greater than or equal to `value2`, use an `if` statement like this:

```
if (value1.compareTo(value2) >= 0)    // value1 >= value2
```

Here's a list of how these expressions match up:

Comparison You Want to Make	*Equivalent* `compareTo` *Expression*
`value 1 == value2`	`value1.compareTo(value2) == 0`
`value 1 != value2`	`value1.compareTo(value2) != 0`
`value 1 > value2`	`value1.compareTo(value2) > 0`
`value 1 >= value2`	`value1.compareTo(value2) >= 0`
`value 1 < value2`	`value1.compareTo(value2) < 0`
`value 1 <= value2`	`value1.compareTo(value2) <= 0`

Converting BigDecimals to Strings

The `BigDecimal` class has several methods that let you convert `BigDecimal` values to strings, doubles, or integers. Table 6-6 lists those methods.

Table 6-6	Conversion Methods of the BigDecimal Class
Method	*Explanation*
`double doubleValue()`	Returns the value of this `BigDecimal` as a double.
`int intValue()`	Returns the value of this `BigDecimal` as an int.
`long longValue()`	Returns the value of this `BigDecimal` as a long.
`String toPlainString()`	Returns a string representation of this `BigDecimal` that doesn't use scientific notation.
`String toString()`	Returns a string representation of this `BigDecimal` that uses scientific notation if necessary.

In most cases, the only reason to convert a `BigDecimal` to a `double` is so you can use the `double` with the `NumberFormat` class to format the value for output. As long as you don't do any intermediate calculations with the `double`, you won't encounter any accuracy errors unless the numbers are large. (You start to run into problems at about 13 digits, which is large enough even for Bill Gates's bank balance.)

Here's a snippet of code that converts a `BigDecimal` object named `salesTax` to a `double` and uses it with the `NumberFormat` class:

```
NumberFormat cf = NumberFormat.getCurrencyInstance();

double taxD = salesTax.doubleValue();
System.out.println(cf.format(taxD));
```

You can also use the `toString` method to format a `BigDecimal` as a string, but this method doesn't add commas or any other formatting niceties. Note also that this method sometimes switches to exponential notation if the number is large. To avoid that, you can use the `toPlainString` method instead.

Revisiting Sales Tax

Now that you've seen what you can do with the `BigDecimal` class, Listing 6-3 presents a `BigDecimal` version of the sales tax program from Listing 6-2. To prove that `BigDecimal` has solved the addition problems of the first version, here's a sample of the console output from this improved version:

```
Welcome to the sales tax calculator.

Enter subtotal: 19.95
Subtotal:    $19.95
Sales tax:   $1.00
Total:       $20.95

Again? (Y or N) y

Enter subtotal: 3.49
Subtotal:    $3.49
Sales tax:   $0.17
Total:       $3.66

Again? (Y or N) y

Enter subtotal: 0.70
Subtotal:    $0.70
Sales tax:   $0.04
Total:       $0.74

Again? (Y or N) n
```

As you can see, this version of the program properly calculates the tax on a $0.70 purchase at 4¢ and then adds the subtotal and tax correctly.

Listing 6-3: Good Tax!

```
import java.text.*;                                              →2
import java.math.*;
import java.util.*;

public class GoodTax
{    static Scanner sc = new Scanner(System.in);
    static NumberFormat cf
        = NumberFormat.getCurrencyInstance();

    public static void main (String[] args)
    {
        BigDecimal subTotal, salesTax, invoiceTotal;             →12
        BigDecimal taxRate = new BigDecimal("0.05");             →13

        double subD, taxD, totalD;                               →15

        System.out.println(
            "Welcome to the sales tax calculator.");
        do
        {
            System.out.print("\nEnter subtotal: ");

            subTotal = new BigDecimal(sc.nextLine());            →23
            salesTax = subTotal.multiply(taxRate);               →24
            salesTax = round(salesTax);                          →25
            invoiceTotal = subTotal.add(salesTax);               →26

            subD = subTotal.doubleValue();                       →28
            taxD = salesTax.doubleValue();
            totalD = invoiceTotal.doubleValue();

            System.out.print("Subtotal:    ");
            System.out.println(cf.format(subD));
            System.out.print("Sales tax:   ");
            System.out.println(cf.format(taxD));
            System.out.print("Total:       ");
            System.out.println(cf.format(totalD));
        } while (getAnother());
    }

    static BigDecimal round(BigDecimal d)                        →41
    {
        return d.setScale(2, RoundingMode.HALF_UP);
    }

    static boolean getAnother()
    {
        System.out.print("\nAgain? (Y or N) ");
        if (sc.nextLine().equalsIgnoreCase("Y"))
            return true;
        else
            return false;
    }
}
```

The following paragraphs describe some of the high points of this program:

→ 2   The BigDecimal class is in the java.math package, so this import statement is required to use it.

→ 12   This line declares three of the BigDecimal variables used by the program.

→ 13   This line declares the fourth BigDecimal variable and initializes it. (The other three are set inside the do loop.)

→ 15   These double variables are used only to format the BigDecimal values after the values have been calculated.

→ 23   The subtotal is obtained directly from the Scanner object's nextLine method. Note that this program throws an exception if you enter invalid data. In an actual program, you want to do some data validation here.

→ 24   The subtotal is multiplied by the tax rate to calculate the amount of sales tax for the order.

→ 25   The sales tax is rounded via a helper method named round.

→ 26   The sales tax is added to the subtotal, providing the total for the invoice.

→ 28   The BigDecimal values are converted to doubles so that they can be formatted with the NumberFormat class and printed on the console.

→ 41   The round method uses the setScale method to round any BigDecimal value to two places.

Whew! That's a lot of work for an extra penny, isn't it? The state tax board will be forever in your debt.

Book VI

Swing

You can find an interesting programming challenge that requires use of many of the programming techniques covered in this minibook at www.dummies.com/extras/javaaio. In this challenge, you enhance the Tic-Tac-Toe program you've created for several of the previous minibooks by adding a graphical user interface.

Contents at a Glance

Chapter 1: Swinging into Swing

In This Chapter

✔ **Examining some basic Swing concepts**

✔ **Fussing with frames**

✔ **Creating a simple Swing program**

✔ **Putting panels in your frames**

✔ **Looking at labels**

✔ **Beginning with buttons**

✔ **Leaping into layout**

So far in this book, all the programs have been console-based, like something right out of the 1980s. Console-based Java programs have their place, especially when you're just starting with Java. But eventually you'll want to create programs that work with a graphical user interface, also known as a GUI.

This chapter gets you started in that direction. You use a Java GUI package called *Swing* to create simple GUI applications that display simple buttons and text labels. Along the way, you find out about two key classes: JFrame and JPanel, which provide the visual containers that hold buttons, labels, and other components that I discuss in later chapters of Book VI.

Understanding Some Important Swing Concepts

Mastering Swing is one of the most complicated tasks in mastering Java — complicated enough, in fact, that I have to go over some conceptual information before I get into the nitty-gritty of writing GUI code. So put on your thinking cap for the next few sections.

Seeing what Swing does

Swing is a package that lets you create applications that use a flashy GUI instead of a dull console interface. Figure 1-1 shows a typical window created with Swing. As you can see, this window includes a variety of user-interface components, including labels, text fields, drop-down lists, and buttons.

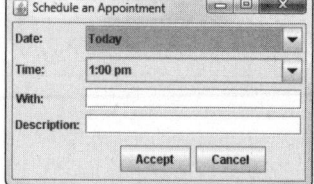

Figure 1-1:
A typical
Swing
window.

Viewing the Swing class hierarchy

The Swing API provides many classes for creating various types of user-interface elements. In this chapter, I look at three of those classes: JFrame, JPanel, and JLabel. These three classes are part of a larger collection of classes that are related through inheritance, as shown in Figure 1-2. The Swing family tree splits at the Component class, dividing into two groups of classes — one group derived from the JComponent class and another branch that descends from the Window class.

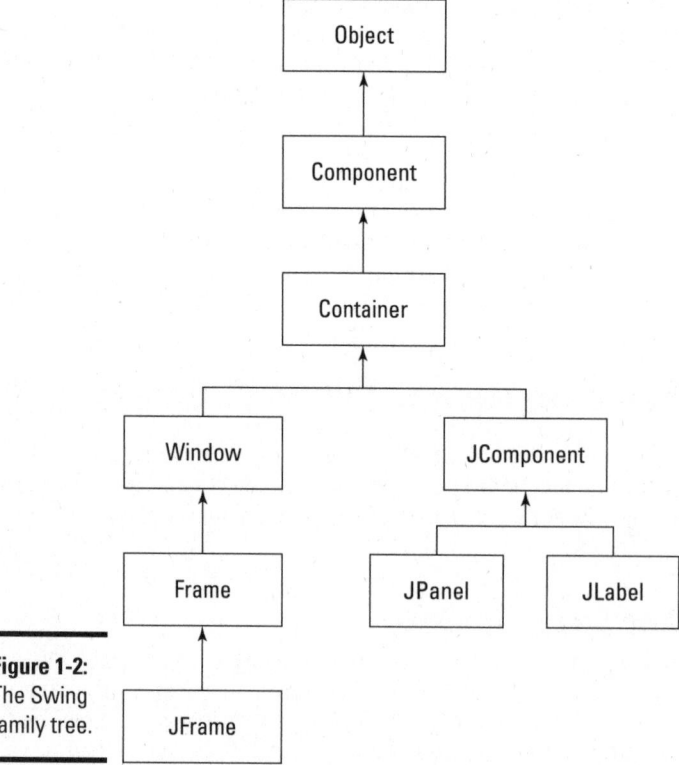

Figure 1-2:
The Swing
family tree.

The following paragraphs briefly describe the classes shown in this figure:

✦ **Object:** All classes ultimately derive from Object, so it's no surprise that this class is at the top of the tree.

✦ **Component:** The Component class represents an object that has a visual representation that can be shown onscreen and that can interact with users. This class defines some basic methods that are available to all Swing classes. The setVisible method determines whether a component is visible or hidden, for example, and the setBounds method sets the location and size of the component.

✦ **Container:** The Container class builds on the basic visual capabilities of the Component class by adding the capability to hold other containers. From the Container class, you get the add method, which lets you add components to a container. As you'll see, you use this method in almost all GUI programs.

✦ **Window:** This class defines a *window:* a specialized type of container object that has a border; a title bar; and buttons that minimize, maximize, and close it, and that the user can reposition (possibly even resize).

✦ **Frame:** A *frame* is a type of Window that serves as the basis for Java GUI applications.

✦ **JFrame:** JFrame is the Swing version of the older Frame class. Most of your Swing applications include at least one JFrame object.

✦ **JComponent:** The JComponent class is a Swing class that is the basis for all other Swing components except frames.

✦ **JPanel:** This class creates *panels,* which are containers used to organize and control the layout of components such as labels, buttons, and text fields. In most Swing applications, one or more panels are added to a frame. Then, when the frame is displayed, the components that were added to its panels are made visible.

✦ **JLabel:** This class creates a label that displays a simple text value.

As you work with Swing, you'll find that some of the classes you use are defined in the javax.swing package, so you need to start every Swing application with this line:

```
import javax.swing.*;
```

In addition, you'll find that some Swing features use classes in the java.awt and java.awt.event packages, so you may need to import those packages as well.

I've Been Framed!

The top-level component of most Swing-based applications is called a *frame* and is defined by the JFrame class. By itself, a frame doesn't do much, but to do anything else in Swing, you must first create a frame. Figure 1-3 shows a frame that does nothing but display the message Hello, World! in its title bar.

Figure 1-3:
The frame displayed by the Hello, World! program.

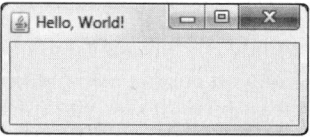

JFrame has about a bazillion methods, but only a few of them are useful in most programs. Table 1-1 lists the JFrame methods you use most, along with a couple of constructors.

Table 1-1	Useful JFrame Constructors and Methods
Constructor	*Description*
JFrame()	Creates a new frame with no title.
JFrame(String *title*)	Creates a new frame with the specified title.
Method	*Description*
void add(Component *c*)	Adds the specified component to the frame.
JMenuBar getJMenuBar()	Gets the menu for this frame.
void pack()	Adjusts the size of the frame to fit the components you've added to it.
void remove(Component c)	Removes the specified component from the frame.
void setDefaultCloseOperation	Sets the action taken when the user closes the frame. You should almost always specify JFrame.EXIT_ON_CLOSE.
void setIconImage(Icon image)	Sets the icon displayed when the frame is minimized.

Method	Description
`void setLayout (LayoutManager layout)`	Sets the layout manager used to control how components are arranged when the frame is displayed. The default is the `BorderLayout` manager.
`void setLocation (int x, int y)`	Sets the x and y positions of the frame onscreen. The top-left corner of the screen is 0, 0.
`void setLocationRelativeTo (Component c)`	Centers the frame onscreen if the parameter is `null`.
`void setResizeable (boolean value)`	Sets whether the size of the frame can be changed by the user. The default setting is `true` (the frame can be resized).
`void setSize(int width, int height)`	Sets the size of the frame to the specified width and height.
void setJMenuBar(JMenuBar menu)	Sets the menu for this frame.

At minimum, you want to set a title for a new frame, set the frame's size large enough for the user to see any components you add to it (by default, the frame is zero pixels wide and zero pixels high, so it isn't very useful), and call the `setVisible` method to make the frame visible. One way to do these three things is to create an instance of the `JFrame` class and set its properties by using statements like the following:

```
JFrame frame = new JFrame("This is the title");
frame.setSize(350, 260);
frame.setVisible(true);
```

A more common approach, however, is to create a frame by declaring a class that extends the `JFrame` class. Then you call these methods in the constructor, as I describe in the next section.

By default, the user can change the size of a frame. If you want to fix the size of your frame so that the user can't change it, just call `setResizeable(false)`.

Saying Hello, World! in Swing

To get you started with Swing, Listing 1-1 shows a Swing version of the classic `Hello, World!` program, using nothing but a frame. If you run this program, the frame shown in Figure 1-3 earlier in this chapter is displayed onscreen. As you can see in the figure, the frame's title bar contains the text `Hello, World!`

The purpose of this seemingly pointless little program is to illustrate one solution to the first problem you encounter when you work with Swing: The main method is a static method, but Swing frames are objects, so you have to figure out how to get your program out of a static context. This program does that by creating the application as a class that extends JFrame. Then the main method calls the class constructor, in effect creating an instance of itself. That's all that the main method does; the constructor does the real work of this application.

Listing 1-1:   The Swing Version of the Hello, World! Program

```
import javax.swing.*;                                        →1

public class HelloFrame extends JFrame                       →3
{
    public static void main(String[] args)                   →5
    {
        new HelloFrame();                                    →7
    }

    public HelloFrame()                                      →10
    {
        this.setSize(250,100);                               →12
        this.setDefaultCloseOperation(                       →13
            JFrame.EXIT_ON_CLOSE);
        this.setTitle("Hello World!");                       →15
        this.setVisible(true);                               →16
    }
}
```

The following paragraphs describe most of the features of this program:

→ 1   The program starts with an import statement that imports all the classes in the javax.swing package. Most of the Swing classes are defined in this package. You may have to import other classes, however, depending on what GUI features your program uses.

→ 3   The class for this application, named JFrame, extends a Swing class named JFrame. A class that extends JFrame is often called a *frame class*. The JFrame class defines a basic frame in which you can display GUI components, such as labels and text boxes. All Swing applications need at least one class that extends JFrame.

→ 5   Swing applications are still Java applications, and all Java applications need a static main method that starts the application, so the first method listed in this class is the main method.

→ 7   The first (and only) statement of the main method creates a new instance of the HelloFrame class. Unlike console applications, Swing applications can't run in a static context. As a result, the main purpose of the static main method in a Swing application is to create an instance of the application's frame class.

→ 10   When an instance of the HelloFrame class is created in line 7, the constructor that starts on this line is executed. The main job of the constructor for a frame class is to set the options for the frame and create any GUI components that are displayed in the frame.

→ 12   The first option that this constructor sets is the size of the frame. To do that, it calls the setSize method. The parameters specify that the frame should be 200 pixels wide and 100 pixels high. (A *pixel* is one of the little dots that make up the image on a computer screen. *Pixel* is short for *picture element,* but that won't be on the test.)

→ 13   The next option this constructor sets is what to do if the user closes the frame by clicking its Close button, which usually appears in the top-right corner of the frame. By default, clicking the Close button hides the frame but doesn't terminate the application. As a result, the application's main thread (the one that's still running in a static context via the main method) keeps running for a while. Eventually Java figures out that nothing's happening and shuts the application down. But the application exits more cleanly if you use setDefaultCloseOperation to set the close operation to JFrame.EXIT_ON_CLOSE. That code causes the program to terminate when the frame is closed.

→ 15   The next statement uses the setTitle method to set the title of the frame.

→ 16   The last statement in the constructor calls the setVisible method with a parameter value of true, which makes the frame visible onscreen. If you leave this statement out, the frame is created, but the user never sees it.

That's all there is to this program. Granted, it's a little more complicated than the console-based Hello, World! program from Book II, Chapter 1, but not by much. Just to make sure that its operation is clear to you, here's a recap of what happens when this program is run:

1. Java runs the static main method for the HelloWorld class.

2. The main method creates an instance of the HelloWorld class, which causes the constructor to be executed.

3. The constructor sets the frame size, the default close operation, and the title; then it displays the frame by setting the SetVisible property.

Positioning the frame onscreen

The JFrame class provides two methods that let you specify the position of the frame onscreen. If you want to place the frame at some arbitrary location onscreen, use the setLocation method. To put the frame at the top-left corner of the screen, for example, use this statement:

```
frame.setLocation(0,0);
```

If you want to center the frame onscreen, call the `setLocationRelativeTo` method and pass `null` as the parameter, like this:

```
frame.setLocationRelativeTo(null);
```

This method is designed to let you position a frame relative to some other component that's already displayed. But if you pass `null` as the parameter, the method centers the frame onscreen.

If you want to position a window at some location other than the top-left corner or dead center onscreen, you may need to know the width and height of the user's screen so that you can calculate a location for your frame. To determine the size of the user's screen, you can use a class named `Toolkit`. The `Toolkit` class has a bunch of methods, but you need to know two of them here:

- ✦ **`getDefaultToolkit:`** This static method creates a `Toolkit` object. You must use this method before you can use the `getScreenSize` method.

- ✦ **`getScreenSize:`** This method returns the size of the screen as a `Dimension` object. The `Dimension` class has two public fields that represent the size of the screen: `height` and `width`. Both fields are of type `int`.

Suppose that you want to position a frame so that its bottom-left corner is right in the center of the screen. The following code, placed in the frame's constructor, does the trick:

```
Toolkit tk = Toolkit.getDefaultToolkit();
Dimension d = tk.getScreenSize();
int x = d.width / 2;
int y = (d.height / 2) - this.getHeight();
this.setLocation(x, y);
```

This code first creates a `Toolkit` object and uses it to get the screen dimensions. It sets the x position to the horizontal center of the screen by dividing the screen width by 2. Then it sets the y position to the vertical center (the screen height divided by 2) less the width of the frame, which puts the *bottom* of the frame at the vertical midpoint.

Using the JPanel Class

A *panel* is a type of container that's designed to hold a group of components so they can be displayed in a frame. The normal way to display a group of controls — text fields, labels, buttons, and other GUI widgets — is to add those controls to a panel and then add the panel to the frame. You can bypass the panel and add the controls directly to the frame, if you want, but using a separate panel to hold the frame's controls is almost always a good idea.

Panels are defined by the JPanel class. Like the JFrame class, the JPanel class has a bevy of methods. Table 1-2 lists the most commonly used constructors and methods for the JPanel class.

Table 1-2   Interesting JPanel Constructors and Methods

Constructor	Description
JPanel()	Creates a new panel.
JPanel(boolean isDoubleBuffered)	Creates a new panel. If the parameter is true, the panel uses a technique called *double buffering,* which results in better display for graphics applications. This constructor is usually used for game programs or other panels that display animations.
JPanel(LayoutManager layout)	Creates a new panel with the specified layout manager. The default layout manager is FlowLayout.

Method	Description
void add(Component c)	Adds the specified component to the panel.
void remove(Component c)	Removes the specified component from the panel.
void setLayout (LayoutManager layout)	Sets the layout manager used to control how components are arranged when the panel is displayed. The default is the FlowLayout manager.
void setLocation(int x, int y)	Sets the x and y position of the frame onscreen. The top-left corner of the screen is 0, 0.
void setSize(int width, int height)	Sets the size of the frame to the specified width and height.
void setToolTipText (String text)	Sets the tooltip text that's displayed if the user rests the mouse cursor over an empty part of the panel.

You can use several techniques to create a panel and add it to a frame. One is to simply create a JPanel object and assign it to a variable in the JFrame constructor. Then you can add components to the panel and add the panel to the frame, as in this example:

```
// HelloFrame constructor
public HelloFrame()
```

```
{
    this.setSize(200,100);

    this.setDefaultCloseOperation(JFrame.EXIT_ON_CLOSE);
    this.setTitle("Hello, World!");

    JPanel panel = new JPanel();

    // code to add components to the panel goes here

    this.setVisible(true);
}
```

Another common technique involves creating a separate class for the panel. This class should extend `JPanel`. Then you can add any components the panel needs in the constructor, as follows:

```
class HelloPanel extends JPanel
{
    public HelloPanel()
    {
        // code to add components to the panel goes here
    }
}
```

Then, in the frame class constructor, you create a new instance of the panel class and add it to the panel, like this:

```
HelloPanel panel = new HelloPanel();
this.add(panel);
```

Alternatively, just this statement does the trick:

```
this.add(new HelloPanel());
```

Using Labels

Now that you know how to create frames and panels, you can create a useful component to add to a panel: a label, which is a component that simply displays text. Labels are used for a variety of purposes: to display captions for other controls (such as text fields or combo boxes), to display informational messages, or to show the results of a calculation or a database lookup.

A label can also display an image, or it can display both an image and some text. You have complete control of the appearance of the text, specifying the font, size, emphasis (bold, italic, or underlined), color, and so on. In this chapter, I discuss how to work with basic labels.

To create a label, you use the `JLabel` class. Table 1-3 shows its most commonly used constructors and methods.

Table 1-3   Tolerable JLabel Constructors and Methods

Constructor	Description
`JLabel()`	Creates a new label with no initial text.
`JLabel(String text)`	Creates a new label with the specified text.

Method	Description
`String getText()`	Returns the text displayed by the label.
`void setText(String text)`	Sets the text displayed by the label.
`void setToolTipText (String text)`	Sets the tooltip text that's displayed if the user rests the mouse cursor over the label for a few moments.
void setVisible(boolean value)	Shows or hides the label.

When you create a label, you can pass the text you want the label to display to the constructor, like this:

```
JLabel label1 = new JLabel("Hello, World!");
```

Or you can create the label first and then set its text later, as follows:

```
JLabel label1 = new JLabel();
label1.setText("Hello, World!");
```

A label won't be displayed until you add it to a panel that is (in turn) added to a frame. Here's an example of a constructor for a frame class that creates a panel, creates a label, adds the label to the panel, and adds the panel to the frame:

```
// HelloFrame constructor
public HelloFrame()
{
    this.setSize(300,150);

    this.setDefaultCloseOperation(JFrame.EXIT_ON_CLOSE);
    this.setTitle("Hello, World!");

    JPanel panel1 = new JPanel();
    JLabel label1 = new JLabel("Hello, World!");
    panel1.add(label1);
    this.add(panel1);

    this.setVisible(true);
}
```

Figure 1-4 shows what this frame looks like when the program is run.

Figure 1-4:
A frame
with a
panel,
which has a
label.

Creating Buttons

Next to labels, the Swing component you use most is the `JButton` component, which creates a button that the user can click. Figure 1-5 shows a frame with a single button.

Figure 1-5:
A frame
with a
panel,
which
includes a
button.

In Book VI, Chapter 2, you find out how to write the code that responds when the user clicks a button. Here I focus on how to create buttons and control their appearance. Table 1-4 lists the most commonly used constructors and methods that are available for the `JButton` class.

Table 1-4	Worthwhile JButton Constructors and Methods
Constructor	*Description*
`JButton()`	Creates a new button with no initial text.
`JButton(String text)`	Creates a new button with the specified text.
Method	*Description*
`doClick()`	Triggers an action event for the button as though the user clicked it. (I tell you why this method is useful sometimes in Book VI, Chapter 2.)

Method	Description
`String getText()`	Returns the text displayed by the button.
`void setBorderPainted (boolean value)`	Shows or hides the button's border. The default setting is `true` (the border is shown).
`void setContentAreaFilled (boolean value)`	Specifies whether the button's background should be filled or left empty. The default setting is `true` (the background is filled in).
`void setEnabled(boolean value)`	Enables or disables the button. The default setting is `true` (enabled).
`void setRolloverEnabled (boolean value)`	Enables or disables the rollover effect, which causes the border to get thicker when the mouse moves over the button. The default setting is `true` (rollover effect enabled).
`void setText(String text)`	Sets the text displayed by the button.
`void setToolTipText(String text)`	Sets the tooltip text that's displayed if the user lets the mouse rest over the button.
`void setVisible(boolean value)`	Shows or hides the button. The default setting is `true` (the button is visible).

As you can see, the constructors for the `JButton` class are similar to the constructors for the `JLabel` class: You can create either an empty button or a button with text. Here's the code that creates the button shown in Figure 1-5:

```
JButton button1 = new JButton("Click me!");
```

If you don't provide the button text when you call the constructor, you can supply it later via the `setText` method, like this:

```
JButton button1 = new JButton();
button1.setText("Click me!");
```

You may not think that you'd ever do that, but sometimes the meaning of a button changes depending on what the user is doing. A program that lets a user add, change, or delete records in a file, for example, might set the text of a button to `Add Record`, `Change Record`, or `Delete Record` depending on what the user happens to be doing at the time. In a program like that, you may need to use the `getText` method to find out what text is currently displayed on a button.

Most of the other methods listed in Table 1-4 simply affect how a button looks. To disable a button so that the user can't click it, call `setEnabled(false)`. To remove the dark border from the edges of a button, call `setBorderPainted(false)`. To remove the background from a button so all that's displayed is the text, call `setContentAreaFilled(false)`. Finally, to make a button disappear, call `setVisible(false)`.

Controlling the Layout of Components

Controlling the layout of components in a panel is one of the hardest things about using Swing — hard enough, in fact, that I devote Book VI, Chapter 5 to this topic. Until then, you need to know a few key points:

✦ The layout of components in a panel (or frame) is controlled by a *layout manager,* which determines the final placement of each component. The layout manager takes the size of the component, the size of the panel, and the position of other nearby components into account when it makes its decisions.

✦ Swing provides several layout managers you can choose among. Each has is own way of deciding where each component goes.

✦ The default layout manager for panels is called `FlowLayout`. It places components one after another in a row and starts a new row only when it gets to the end of the panel (or the frame that contains it).

✦ With `FlowLayout` (and the other layout managers, too), the layout changes if the user changes the size of the frame. The size of the frame makes a big difference in how `FlowLayout` arranges controls.

✦ You can always call the frame's `setResizeable(false)` method to prevent the user from resizing the frame.

✦ If you want to change the layout manager used for a panel, you call the panel's `setLayout` method.

✦ For many (if not most) Swing applications, you use more than one panel to display your components. Each panel can have a different layout manager. With this technique, you can create complex layouts with lots of components — all arranged just the way you want.

✦ If you need to, you can always turn off the layout manager altogether. To do that, you call the panel's `setLayout` method with `null` set as the parameter. Then you use *absolute positioning,* which lets you set the `x` and `y` positions and the size of each component by calling its `setBounds` method.

This list could go on and on. For more information about controlling layout, refer to Book VI, Chapter 5. For information about making menus, go to this book's companion website at `www.dummies.com/extras/javaio`.

Chapter 2: Handling Events

In This Chapter

✓ Understanding important event concepts

✓ Working with event-handling classes and interfaces

✓ Responding to button clicks

✓ Using inner classes for event handling

✓ Providing an Exit button

✓ Dealing with the Close button

✓ Taking another look at a button-click program

In Book VI, Chapter 1, I show you how to create Swing frames that include panels, labels, and buttons. Those frames don't do anything other than sit there, however. They look good, but they're completely unresponsive. Click them all you want, but they don't do anything. They're kind of like teenagers.

In this chapter, you get those buttons to do something. Specifically, you find out how to write code that's executed when a user clicks a button. The technique you use to do that is called *event listening*, and it's one of the most important aspects of writing Swing programs. It may seem a little complicated at first, but after you get the swing of it (sorry), event listening makes perfect sense.

 Although event listening is used mostly to respond to button clicks, it can also be used to respond to other types of user interactions. You can use event listening, for example, to write code that's executed when the user makes a selection from a combo box, moves the mouse over a label, or presses a key on the keyboard. The event-listening techniques in this chapter work for those events as well.

Examining Events

An *event* is an object that's generated when the user does something note-worthy with one of your user-interface components. Then this event object is passed to a special method you create, called an *event listener*. The event listener can examine the event object, determine exactly what type of event occurred, and respond accordingly. If the user clicks a button, the event listener might write any data entered by the user via text fields to a file. If the user passes the mouse cursor over a label, the event handler might change the text displayed by the label. And if the user selects an item from a combo box, the event handler might use the value that was selected to look up information in a database. The possibilities are endless!

Java provides several types of event objects, represented by various classes that inherit `AWTEvent`. Table 2-1 lists the most commonly used event classes. In addition, this table lists the listener interface for each event object. The *listener interface* is used to create an object that can listen for the event and handle it when it's generated.

Table 2-1	Commonly Used Event Classes	
Event Class	*Listener Interface*	*Description*
ActionEvent	ActionListener	Created when the user performs an action with a button or other component. Usually this means that the user clicked the button, but the user can also invoke a button action by tabbing to the button and pressing the Enter key.
ItemEvent	ItemListener	Created when the selected item in a list control, such as a combo box or list box, is changed.
DocumentEvent	DocumentListener	Created when the user changes the contents of a text component, such as a text field.
WindowEvent	WindowListener	Created when the status of the window (frame) changes.
KeyEvent	KeyListener	Created when the user presses a key on the keyboard. This event can be used to watch for specific keystrokes entered by the user.
MouseEvent	MouseListener	Created when the user does something interesting with the mouse, such as clicking one of the buttons, dragging the mouse, or simply moving the mouse cursor over another object.
FocusEvent	FocusListener	Created when a component receives or loses focus.

Most of these event classes are contained in the package `java.awt`. The only thing that's not in `java.awt` is `DocumentEvent` (which happens to be an interface, not a class, in the package `javax.swing.event`). Strictly speaking, event handling is provided by AWT, not by Swing.

The events listed in Table 2-1 can be divided into two categories. The first three — `ActionEvent`, `ItemEvent`, and `DocumentEvent` — are called *semantic events* because they're related to user interactions that usually have some specific meaning. When the user clicks a button, for example, he or she is trying to do something specific. By contrast, the other events are called *low-level event* because they refer to basic input events such as pressing a key or moving the mouse.

If you're cramming for the test, you absolutely need to know three important terms:

✦ **Event:** An object that's created when the user does something noteworthy with a component, such as clicking it.

✦ **Event source:** The component that generated the event object. Usually, the event source is a button or other component that the user can click, but any Swing component can be an event source.

✦ **Event listener:** The object that listens for events and handles them when they occur. The event-listener object must implement the interface appropriate for the event. These listener interfaces define the method or methods that the event source calls when the event occurs. Table 2-2 lists the methods that are defined by each of the interfaces listed in Table 2-1.

Book VI
Chapter 2

Handling Events

Table 2-2   Methods Defined by Event-Listener Interfaces

Listener Interface	Method	Description
`ActionListener` `(ActionEvent e)`	`void actionPerformed`	Called when an action event occurs.
`ItemListener`	`void itemStateChanged (ItemEvent e)`	Called when the selected item changes.
`DocumentListener`	`void changeUpdate (DocumentEvent e)`	Called when text is changed.
	`void insertUpdate (DocumentEvent e)`	Called when text is inserted.
	`void removeUpdate DocumentEvent e)`	Called when text is deleted.

(continued)

Table 2-2 *(continued)*

Listener Interface	Method	Description
`WindowListener`	`void windowActivated (WindowEvent e)`	Called when the window is activated.
	`void windowClosed (WindowEvent e)`	Called when the window has been closed.
	`void windowClosing (WindowEvent e)`	Called when the user attempts to close the window.
	`void windowDeactivated (WindowEvent e)`	Called when the window is deactivated.
	`void windowDeiconified (WindowEvent e)`	Called when the window is changed from icon to normal.
	`void windowIconified (WindowEvent e)`	Called when the window is minimized to an icon.
	`void windowOpened (WindowEvent e)`	Called when the window is opened.
`KeyListener`	`void keyPressed (KeyEvent e)`	Called when the user presses a key.
	`void keyReleased (KeyEvent e)`	Called when the user releases a key.
	`void keyTyped (KeyEvent e)`	Called when the user types a key (that is, presses and releases).
`MouseListener`	`void mouseClicked (MouseEvent e)`	Called when the user clicks the mouse.
	`void mouseEntered MouseEvent e)`	Called when the mouse cursor moves over a component.

Listener Interface	Method	Description
	`void mouseExited (MouseEvent e)`	Called when the mouse cursor leaves a component.
	`void mousePressed (MouseEvent e)`	Called when the user presses the mouse button.
	`void mouseReleased (MouseEvent e)`	Called when the user releases the mouse button.
`FocusListener`	`void focusGained (FocusEvent e)`	Called when the component gains focus.
`FocusListener`	`void focusLost (FocusEvent e)`	Called when the component loses focus.

Handling Events

Now that you know the basic objects that are used for event handling, you have to wire them up to create a program that responds to events.

To write Java code that responds to events, you have to do the following:

1. Create a component that can generate events.

You want to add buttons or other components that generate events to your frame so that it displays components the user can interact with. (Strictly speaking, all Swing components can generate some events. Even a label generates a `MouseEvent` when the user moves the mouse over it. But a frame that consists of nothing but labels isn't very useful.)

Usually, you declare the variable that refers to the event source as a private class field, outside the constructor for the frame or any other method, as in this example:

```
private JButton button1;
```

Then, in the constructor for the frame class, you can create the button. Here's code that creates a panel, creates a button, adds the button to a panel, and then adds the panel to the frame:

```
JPanel panel = new JPanel();
button1 = new JButton('Click me!");
panel.add(button1);
this.add(panel);
```

Note that this code appears in the constructor of the frame class, so in the last line, `this` refers to the frame.

2. **Create a class that implements the listener interface for the event you want to handle.**

To handle action events, for example, you should create a class that implements the `ActionListener` interface. The easiest way is to simply add `implements ActionListener` to the definition of the frame class. Thus, the frame class declaration looks something like this:

```
public class ClickMe
     extends JFrame implements ActionListener
```

Later in this chapter, I tell you about other ways to implement the event-listener interface.

3. **Write the code for any methods defined by the listener.**

When you implement a listener interface, you must provide an implementation of each method defined by the interface. Most listener interfaces define just one method, corresponding to the type of event the interface listens for. The `ActionListener` interface, for example, defines a method named `actionPerformed`, which is called whenever an action event is created. Thus the code you place inside the `actionPerformed` method is executed when an action event occurs.

Here's an `actionPerformed` method that responds to action events:

```
public void actionPerformed(ActionEvent e)
{
    if (e.getSource() == button1)
        button1.setText("You clicked!");
}
```

This code changes the text displayed by `button1` if the event source is `button1`.

4. **Register the listener with the source.**

The final step is registering the event listener with the event source. Every component that serves as an event source provides a method that lets you register event listeners to listen for the event. For `Action Event` sources, the method is `addActionListener`. Here's a modification to the frame constructor code that creates the `button1` button and registers the frame class as the action event listener:

```
JPanel panel = new JPanel();
button1 = new JButton("Click me!");
button1.addActionListener(this);
panel.add(button1);
this.add(panel);
```

Here you can specify `this` as the event listener because the frame class itself implements `ActionListener`.

Creating a ClickMe Program

To see how all these elements work together in a complete program, Figure 2-1 shows three incarnations of a frame created by a program called ClickMe. This program displays a frame with a single button that initially says Click Me! When the user clicks the button, the button's text changes to I've been clicked! (as shown in the second frame of the figure). Then, if the user clicks the button again, the text changes to I've been clicked 2 times! (as shown in the third frame). Thereafter, the count increases each time the button is clicked. Listing 2-1 shows the complete code for this program.

Figure 2-1:
The ClickMe
program in
action.

Listing 2-1:   The ClickMe Program

```
import javax.swing.*;
import java.awt.event.*;                              →2

public class ClickMe
    extends JFrame implements ActionListener          →5
{
    public static void main(String [] args)           →7
    {
        new ClickMe();
    }

    private JButton button1;                           →12

    public ClickMe()                                  →14
    {
        this.setSize(300,150);
```

(continued)

Listing 2-1 *(continued)*

```
        this.setDefaultCloseOperation
            (JFrame.EXIT_ON_CLOSE);
        this.setTitle("I'm Listening");

        JPanel panel1 = new JPanel();
        button1 = new JButton("Click Me!");                →21
        button1.addActionListener(this);                   →22
        panel1.add(button1);
        this.add(panel1);

        this.setVisible(true);
    }

    private int clickCount = 0;                            →29

    public void actionPerformed(ActionEvent e)             →31
    {
        if (e.getSource() == button1)                      →33
        {
            clickCount++;                                  →35
            if (clickCount == 1)                           →36
                button1.setText("I've been clicked!");
            else
                button1.setText("I've been clicked "
                    + clickCount + " times!");
        }
    }
}
```

The following paragraphs point out some key lines of the program:

→ 2   The program must import the `java.awt.event` package, which
        defines the `ActionEvent` class and the `ActionListener` interfaces.

→ 5   The `ClickMe` class extends the `JFrame` class and implements
        `ActionListener`. That way, this class does double duty: It defines
        the frame, and it listens for events generated by components added
        to the frame.

→ 7   The `main` method is required as usual. It simply creates an instance
        of the `ClickMe` class to get the frame started.

→ 12   The `button1` variable is defined as a private class field so that both
        the `ClickMe` constructor and the `actionPerformed` method can
        access it.

→ 14   The constructor does all the usual stuff that a constructor for a
        frame class does: It sets the frame size, default close operation, and
        title, and then it adds components to the frame. It ends by calling
        `setVisible` to make the frame visible onscreen.

→ 21   This line creates a button and assigns it to the `button1` field.

→ **22**   This line adds the current object as an action listener for the `button1` button.

→ **29**   A field named `clickCount` is used to keep track of how many times the button has been clicked. This field is initialized to zero when the object is created.

→ **31**   The `actionPerformed` method must be coded because the `ClickMe` class implements the `ActionListener` interface. This method is called by the `button1` object whenever the user clicks the button. The `ActionEvent` parameter is the event generated by the button click.

→ **33**   The getSource method of the ActionEvent parameter is called to determine the event source. In this program, this if statement really isn't required, because the program has only one event source. Most Swing programs have more than one event source, however, so you need to test the event source in the event listener.

→ **35**   This statement increments the click count to indicate that the button has been clicked.

→ **36**   This `if` statement tests the value of the `clickCount` field and changes the text displayed by the button accordingly.

Using Inner Classes to Listen for Events

An *inner class* is a class that's nested within another class. Inner classes are commonly used for event listeners. That way, the class that defines the frame doesn't also have to implement the event listener. Instead, it includes an inner class that handles the events. (I explain more about inner classes in Book III, Chapter 7.)

Listing 2-2 shows a version of the `ClickMe` program that uses an inner class to handle the action event for the button.

Listing 2-2:   The ClickMeInner Program with an Inner Class

```
import javax.swing.*;
import java.awt.event.*;

public class ClickMeInner extends JFrame                        →4
{
    public static void main(String [] args)
    {
        new ClickMeInner();
    }

    private JButton button1;                                     →11
```

(continued)

Listing 2-2 *(continued)*

```
    public ClickMeInner()
    {
        this.setSize(300,150);
        this.setDefaultCloseOperation(
            JFrame.EXIT_ON_CLOSE);
        this.setTitle("I'm Listening");

        ClickListener cl = new ClickListener();              →20

        JPanel panel1 = new JPanel();
        button1 = new JButton("Click Me!");
        button1.addActionListener(cl);                        →24
        panel1.add(button1);
        this.add(panel1);

        this.setVisible(true);
    }

    private class ClickListener
        implements ActionListener                            →32
    {
        private int clickCount = 0;                          →34

        public void actionPerformed(ActionEvent e)
        {
            if (e.getSource() == button1)                    →38
            {
                clickCount++;
                if (clickCount == 1)
                    button1.setText("I've been clicked!");
                else
                    button1.setText("I've been clicked "
                        + clickCount + " times!");
            }
        }
    }
}
```

This program works essentially the same way as the program shown in Listing 2-1, so I won't review every detail. Instead, I just point out some highlights:

→ **4**   The `ClickMeInner` class still extends `JFrame` but doesn't implement `ActionListener`.

→ **11**   The button that serves as the event source must be referenced by a class field so that the inner class can access it. This field can be private, because inner classes have access to private members of the class that contains them.

→ **20**   This statement creates an instance of the `ClickListener` class (the inner class) and assigns it to the variable `cl`.

→ **24**   This statement adds c1 as an action listener for the button. Note that because this frame has only one button, I could just as easily have omitted line 20 and coded line 24 like this:

```
button1.addActionListener(new ClickListener());
```

Because most real-world applications have more than one event source, however, creating an instance of the listener class first and then reusing that object as the listener for each event source is common.

→ **32**   The ClickListener class is declared as an inner class by placing its declaration completely within the ClickMeInner class. The ClickListener class implements the ActionListener interface so that it can handle action events.

→ **34**   The clickCount variable is declared as a class field in the inner class.

→ **38**   The button1 variable is available to the inner class here because inner classes can access private members of the class that contains them.

Book VI Chapter 2

Handling Events

Using Lambda Expressions to Handle Events

In Book III, Chapter 7, I show you how to use Lambda expressions to simply classes that implement interfaces that have just one method — that is, interfaces that qualify as functional interfaces. The ActionListener interface is such an interface: It has just one method, named ActionPerformed.

When you use a Lambda expression, you do not have to explicitly implement the ActionListener interface. Instead, you can use code such as the following to add an event listener:

```
button1.addActionListener(e -> button1Click() );
```

Then the method button1Click will be called whenever the user clicks button1.

Listing 2-3 shows a version of the ClickMe program that uses a Lambda expression to handle the button click event.

Listing 2-3:   The ClickMeLambda Program with an Inner Class

```
import javax.swing.*;
import java.awt.event.*;

public class ClickMeLambda
    extends JFrame
{
    public static void main(String [] args)
    {
        new ClickMeLambda();
```

(continued)

Listing 2-3 *(continued)*

```
    }

    private JButton button1;

    public ClickMeLambda()
    {
        this.setSize(300,150);
        this.setDefaultCloseOperation(JFrame.EXIT_ON_CLOSE);
        this.setTitle("I'm Listening");
        JPanel panel1 = new JPanel();
        button1 = new JButton("Click Me!");
        button1.addActionListener(e -> button1Click() );    →22
        panel1.add(button1);
        this.add(panel1);

        this.setVisible(true);
    }

    private int clickCount = 0;                              →29

    public void button1Click()                              →31
    {
        clickCount++;
        if (clickCount == 1)
            button1.setText("I've been clicked!");
        else
            button1.setText("I've been clicked "
                + clickCount + " times!");
    }
}
```

This program works essentially the same way as the program shown in
Listing 2-2, so I'll just point out the features directly related to the use of the
Lambda expression:

→ 22   This statement uses a Lambda expression to add an action lis-
       tener to handle button clicks. The Lambda expression simply calls
       the method button1Click whenever the user clicks the button.

→ 29   The clickCount variable is declared as a class field.

→ 11   The button1Click method is called whenever the user clicks
       the button. This method changes the text that's displayed on the
       button's label.

Note that I could have eliminated the button1Click method altogether,
and instead included its code directly in the Lambda expression, like this:

```
button1.addActionListener(e ->
    {
        clickCount++;
        if (clickCount == 1)
```

```
        button1.setText("I've been clicked!");
    else
        button1.setText("I've been clicked "
            + clickCount + " times!");
} );
```

However, this type of coding can quickly become unwieldy. So, as a rule, I prefer to always include the actual work done by an event handler in a separate method that's called via a Lambda expression when the event handler is set up.

Adding an Exit Button

In Book VI, Chapter 1, you find out how to create a frame that exits the application when the user clicks the frame's Exit button. To add an Exit button to your application, you must do three things:

1. **Create the Exit button and add it to the frame.**

Usually, you actually add the Exit button to a panel that is in turn added to the frame.

2. **Create a method that will be called when the user clicks the Exit button.**

In this method, you will call System.exit(0) to terminate the application.

3. **Call the method you created in Step 2 in the action event listener for the exit button.**

You can easily do that via a Lambda expression, like this:

```
exitButton.addActionListener(e -> exitButtonClick() );
```

In many applications, you don't want to indiscriminately terminate the application. Instead, you should make sure that the user has saved his or her data before ending. If not, you can either save the data automatically or require the user to save the data before allowing the program to end.

Suppose you want to change the ClickMeLambda application shown in Listing 2-3 so that it has an Exit button, but the Exit button won't let the user quit unless he or she has clicked the Click Me! button at least once. First, you change line 11 to declare an exitButton class field:

```
private JButton button1, exitButton;
```

Next, you add code to the constructor to create the button, register an event listener that calls a method named exitButtonClick, and add the button to the panel:

```
exitButton = new JButton("Exit");
```

```
exitButton.addActionListener(e -> exitButtonClick() );
panel1.add(exitButton);
```

Finally, you add the `exitButtonClick()` method:

```
public void exitButtonClick()
{
    if (clickCount > 0)
        System.exit(0);
    else
    {
        JOptionPane.showMessageDialog(
            ClickMe3.this,
            "You must click at least once!",
            "Not so fast, buddy",
            JOptionPane.ERROR_MESSAGE);
    }
}
```

Here an `if` statement checks to see whether the `clickCount` variable is greater than zero. If it is, `System.exit(0)` is called to end the application. Otherwise, `JOptionPane` is used to display an error message, and the application is not ended.

Unfortunately, just adding this logic to the Exit button isn't enough, because the user can bypass your Exit button by clicking the frame's Close button. What you want is for the frame's Close button to act exactly like the Exit button. To do that, you need to add a window event listener in addition to an action event listener, as I describe in the next section.

Catching the WindowClosing Event

Book VI, Chapter 1 shows you how to use the `setDefaultCloseOperation` method of the `JFrame` class to let the user quit the application by using the frame's Close button. If, however, your application checks to see whether data has been saved (or other conditions have been met) before allowing the user to exit, this approach won't work. In that case, you want to set up the Close button so that it works the same way as your Exit button.

To do that, you need to add a listener that listens for window events to the frame. When the user clicks the Close button, the frame generates a `window Closing` event, which you can handle by registering a `WindowListener` with the frame itself. Then, in the `windowClosing` method of the `Window Listener`, you can just call the Exit button's `doClick` event. Doing so triggers an action event for the Exit button as though the user had clicked it. Thus the Close button is handled exactly the same way as the Exit button.

The first step in setting up a window listener is getting rid of the default behavior that automatically exits the application when the user clicks the Close button. To do that, you must change the constant you use in `setDefaultCloseOperation` from EXIT_ON_CLOSE to DO_NOTHING_ON_ CLOSE, like this:

```
this.setDefaultCloseOperation(
    JFrame.DO_NOTHING_ON_CLOSE);
```

This way, the default action of the `JFrame` class is to ignore the Close button. Then you can install a window listener to handle the Close button any way you want.

Next, you can set up the `WindowListener` to listen for window events. One way to do that is to create an inner class that implements the `Window Listener` interface. Unfortunately, the `WindowListener` interface has a lot of methods, and you must provide an implementation for each method even if you don't want to do anything for that method. Thus your `WindowListener` looks something like this:

```
private class Closer implements WindowListener
{
    public void windowClosing(WindowEvent e)
    {
        exitButton.doClick();
    }

    public void windowActivated(WindowEvent e) {}
    public void windowClosed(WindowEvent e) {}
    public void windowDeactivated(WindowEvent e) {}
    public void windowDeiconified(WindowEvent e) {}
    public void windowIconified(WindowEvent e) {}
    public void windowOpened(WindowEvent e) {}
}
```

Finally, you register the `WindowListener` with the frame by calling its `addWindowListener` method in the frame class constructor, like so:

```
this.addWindowListener(new Closer());
```

If you find it annoying that you have to code all those dummy methods when you implement the `WindowListener` interface, you can use an *adapter class* instead. An adapter class is a class that implements an interface and provides dummy implementations for all the methods defined by the interface. Instead of implementing the interface, you extend the adapter class. Then you have to provide an implementation for only the method or methods you're interested in.

Many of Java's event-listener interfaces have corresponding adapter classes, which are listed in Table 2-3. Here's what the `Closer` class looks like if you extend `WindowAdapter` instead of implement `WindowListener`:

```
private class Closer extends WindowAdapter
{
```

```
        public void windowClosing(WindowEvent e)
        {
            exitButton.doClick();
        }
    }
```

Table 2-3	Adapter Classes for Event Listeners
Listener Interface	*Adapter Class*
WindowListener	WindowAdapter
KeyListener	KeyAdapter
MouseListener	MouseAdapter
FocusListener	FocusAdapter

That saves some code. You can save even more code by skipping the Closer class and handling the window closing event with an anonymous inner class instead. Then the statement in the frame constructor that registers the window event listener looks like this:

```
addWindowListener(new WindowAdapter()
    {
        public void windowClosing(WindowEvent e)
        {
            exitButton.doClick();
        }
    } );
```

Here the window listener is created as an anonymous inner class that extends WindowAdapter and defines the windowClosing method.

An *anonymous* inner class is simply a class that has no name, is used only once in the program, and is defined right at the spot where it's used. For a rundown of the weird syntax used to create an anonymous inner class, refer to Book III, Chapter 7.

It would be nice if you could avoid the crazy anonymous class syntax and use a simple Lambda expression as you do to set up a simple button event listener. No such luck. Unfortunately, because the WindowAdapter interface defines more than one method, it does not qualify as a functional interface. Thus you can't use it in a Lambda expression.

Revisiting the ClickMe Program

Now that you've mulled over the various techniques for creating an Exit button and handling the Close button, Listing 2-4 presents a third version of the ClickMe program that adds all these features so you can see how they work together. This version of the program adds an Exit button but doesn't allow the user to quit until he or she has clicked the Click Me! button at least once, and it treats the Close button as though the user had clicked Exit.

Listing 2-4:   The ClickMe Application with an Exit Button

```
import javax.swing.*;
import java.awt.event.*;

public class ClickMeExit extends JFrame
{
    public static void main(String [] args)
    {
        new ClickMeExit();
    }

    private JButton button1, exitButton;                    →11
    private int clickCount = 0;

    public ClickMeExit()
    {
        this.setSize(275,100);
        this.setTitle("I'm Listening");
        this.setDefaultCloseOperation(                      →18
            JFrame.DO_NOTHING_ON_CLOSE);

        JPanel panel1 = new JPanel();

        addWindowListener(new WindowAdapter()               →23
            {
                public void windowClosing(WindowEvent e)
                {
                    exitButton.doClick();                   →27
                }
            } );

        button1 = new JButton("Click Me!");
        button1.addActionListener(e -> button1Click() );
        panel1.add(button1);

        exitButton = new JButton("Exit");                   →35
        exitButton.addActionListener(e -> exitButtonClick()
);
        panel1.add(exitButton);
        this.add(panel1);

        this.setVisible(true);
    }

    public void button1Click()
```

Book VI
Chapter 2

Handling Events

(continued)

Listing 2-4 *(continued)*

```
    {
        clickCount++;
        if (clickCount == 1)
            button1.setText("I've been clicked!");
        else
            button1.setText("I've been clicked "
                + clickCount + " times!");
    }

    public void exitButtonClick()                              →53
    {
        if (clickCount > 0)
            System.exit(0);
        else
        {
            JOptionPane.showMessageDialog(
                ClickMeExit.this,
                "You must click at least once!",
                "Not so fast, buddy",
                JOptionPane.ERROR_MESSAGE);
        }
    }
}
}
```

The following paragraphs draw your attention to the key sections of this program:

→ **11** The `exitButton` variable is declared along with the `button1` variable as a class field so that it can be accessed from the inner classes.

→ **18** The `setDefaultCloseOperation` method tells the `JFrame` class that no default action is taken if the user closes the window.

→ **23** A window listener is installed on the frame to listen for window events. This listener is constructed from an anonymous inner class that extends the `WindowAdapter` class.

→ **27** In the `windowClosing` method, the `doClick` method of the Exit button is called. That way, the Close button is handled exactly as though the user had clicked the Exit button.

→ **35** This line and the next two lines create the Exit button, register its action event listener, and add it to the panel.

→ **53** In the `exitButtonClick` method, this `if` statement checks to see whether the user has clicked the Click Me! button at least once. If so, the application exits. Otherwise, a message is displayed, and the program refuses to budge.

Chapter 3: Getting Input from the User

In This Chapter

✔ Working with text fields and areas

✔ Creating check boxes

✔ Setting radio buttons

✔ Defining borders

✔ Playing with sliders

✔ Using some of these components in a sample program

*I*n the first two chapters of Book VI, I show you how to use two basic Swing user-interface components — labels and buttons — and how to handle events generated when the user clicks one of those buttons. If all you ever want to write are programs that display text when the user clicks a button, you can put the book down now. But if you want to write programs that actually do something worthwhile, you need to use other Swing components.

In this chapter, you find out how to use components that get information from the user. First, I cover two components that get text input from the user: text fields, which get a line of text, and text areas, which get multiple lines. Then I move on to two components that get either/or information from the user: radio buttons and check boxes.

Along the way, I tell you about some features that let you decorate these controls to make them more functional. Specifically, I look at scroll bars (which are commonly used with text areas), borders (which are used with radio buttons and check boxes), and sliders (volume).

Using Text Fields

A *text field* is a box that the user can type text in. You create text fields by using the JTextField class. Table 3-1 shows some of the more interesting and useful constructors and methods of this class.

Table 3-1	Handy JTextField Constructors and Methods
Constructor	**Description**
`JTextField()`	Creates a new text field.
`JTextField(int cols)`	Creates a new text field with the specified width.
`JTextField(String text, int cols)`	Creates a new text field with the specified width and initial text value.
Method	**Description**
`String getText()`	Gets the text value entered in the field.
`void requestFocus()`	Asks for the focus to be moved to this text field.
`void setColumns(int cols)`	Sets the size of the text field (but it's better to do this in the constructor, as described in this chapter).
`void setEditable(boolean value)`	If `false`, makes the field read-only.
`void setText(String text)`	Sets the field's text value.
`void setToolTipText(String text)`	Sets the tooltip text that's displayed if the user rests the mouse pointer over the text field for a few moments.

When you create a text field by calling a constructor of the `JTextField` class, you can specify the width of the text field and an initial text value, as in these examples:

```
JTextField text1 = new JTextField(15);
JTextField text2 = new JTextField("Initial Value", 20);
```

The width is specified in columns, which is a vague and imprecise measurement that's roughly equal to the width of the letter M in the font that the text field uses. You have to experiment a bit to get the text fields the right sizes.

The usual way to work with text fields is to create them in the frame constructor and then retrieve text entered by the user in the `actionPerformed` method of an action listener attached to one of the frame's buttons, using code like this:

```
String lastName = textLastName.getText();
```

Here the value entered by the user in the `textLastName` text field is assigned to the `String` variable `lastName`.

The following paragraphs describe a few additional details you need to know about using text fields:

✦ When you use a text field, you usually also want to place a label nearby to tell the user what type of text to enter in the field.

✦ You can create a read-only text field by calling the setEditable method with a value of false. This text field has a border around it, like a regular text field, but the background is gray instead of white, and the user can't change the text displayed by the control.

✦ In most programs, you want to make sure that the user enters acceptable data in text fields, especially if the user is supposed to enter numeric data in the text fields, as I describe in the section "Using text fields for numeric entry," later in this chapter.

Looking at a sample program

Figure 3-1 shows the operation of a simple program that uses a text field to ask for the user's name (top box in the figure). If the user enters a name, the program uses JOptionPane to say "Good morning" to the user by displaying the middle message box shown in Figure 3-1. If the user clicks the button without entering anything, however, the program displays the JOptionPane message shown at the bottom of the figure.

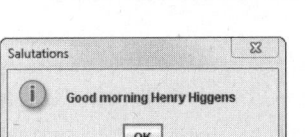

Figure 3-1:
The Namer application in action.

The code for this program is shown in Listing 3-1.

Listing 3-1: Saying "Good Morning" with a Text Field

```java
import javax.swing.*;
import java.awt.event.*;

public class Namer extends JFrame                               →4
{
    public static void main(String [] args)
    {
        new Namer();
    }

    private JButton buttonOK;
    private JTextField textName;                                 →13

    public Namer()
    {
        this.setSize(325,100);
        this.setTitle("Who Are You?");
        this.setDefaultCloseOperation(
            JFrame.EXIT_ON_CLOSE);

        JPanel panel1 = new JPanel();

        panel1.add(new JLabel("Enter your name: "));            →24

        textName = new JTextField(15);                          →26
        panel1.add(textName);

        buttonOK = new JButton("OK");
        buttonOK.addActionListener(e -> buttonOKClick() );
        panel1.add(buttonOK);

        this.add(panel1);

        this.setVisible(true);
    }

    public void buttonOKClick()
    {
        String name = textName.getText();                       →40
        if (name.length() == 0)                                 →41
        {
            JOptionPane.showMessageDialog(
                Namer.this,
                "You didn't enter anything!",
                "Moron",
                JOptionPane.INFORMATION_MESSAGE);
        }
```

```
        else
        {
            JOptionPane.showMessageDialog(
                Namer.this,
                "Good morning " + name,
                "Salutations",
                JOptionPane.INFORMATION_MESSAGE);
        }
        textName.requestFocus();                              →57
    }
}
```

This program isn't very complicated, so the following paragraphs just hit the highlights:

→ 4 The name of the frame class is `Namer`.

→ 13 A class variable is used to store a reference to the text field so that both the constructor and the action listener can access it.

→ 24 A label is created to tell the user what data to enter in the text field.

→ 26 The text field is created with a length of 15 columns and then added to the panel.

→ 40 This statement retrieves the value entered by the user and stores it in a `String` variable.

→ 41 This `if` statement checks to see whether the user entered anything by examining the length of the `String` variable created in line 40. If the length is 0, `JOptionPane` is used to display an error message. Otherwise `JOptionPane` is used to say "Good morning" to the user.

→ 63 The `requestFocus` method is called to move the focus back to the text field after the user clicks the button. If you don't do this, focus stays on the button, and the user has to use the Tab key to move the focus to the text field.

Using text fields for numeric entry

You need to take special care if you're using a text field to get numeric data from the user. The `getText` method returns a string value. You can pass this value to one of the `parse` methods of the wrapper classes for the primitive numeric types. To convert the value entered in a text box to an `int`, you use the `parseInt` method:

```
int count = Integer.parseInt(textCount.getText());
```

Here the result of the `getText` method is used as the parameter of the `parseInt` method.

Table 3-2 lists the `parse` methods for the various wrapper classes. Note that each of these methods throws `NumberFormatException` if the string can't be converted. As a result, you need to call the `parseInt` method in a `try/catch` block to catch this exception.

Table 3-2	**Methods That Convert Strings to Numbers**
Wrapper Class	*parse Method*
Integer	parseInt(String)
Short	parseShort(String)
Long	parseLong(String)
Byte	parseByte(String)
Float	parseFloat(String)
Double	parseDouble(String)

If your program uses more than one or two numeric-entry text fields, consider creating separate methods to validate the user's input. The following code snippet shows a method that accepts a text field and a string that provides an error message to be displayed if the data entered in the field can't be converted to an `int`. The method returns a Boolean value that indicates whether the field contains a valid integer:

```
private boolean isInt(JTextField f, String msg)
{
    try
    {
        Integer.parseInt(f.getText());
        return true;
    }
    catch (NumberFormatException e)
    {
        JOptionPane.showMessageDialog(f,
            "Entry Error", msg,
            JOptionPane.ERROR_MESSAGE);
        f.requestFocus();
        return false;
    }
}
```

You can call this method whenever you need to check to see whether a text field has a valid integer. Here's a method that gets the value entered in a `textCount` text field and displays it in a `JOptionPane` message box if the value entered is a valid integer:

```
public void buttonOKClick()
{
    if (isInt(textCount,
        "You must enter an integer."))
```

```
        {
            JOptionPane.showMessageDialog(Number.this,
                "You entered " +
                Integer.parseInt(textCount.getText()),
                "Your Number",
                JOptionPane.INFORMATION_MESSAGE);
        }
        textCount.requestFocus();
    }
```

Here the `isInt` method is called to make sure that the text entered by the user can be converted to an `int`. If so, the text is converted to an `int` and displayed in a message box. (In this example, the name of the outer class is `Number`, which is why the first parameter of the `showMessageDialog` method specifies `Number.this`.)

Creating a validation class

If you're feeling really ambitious, you can create a separate class to hold methods that do data validation. I suggest that you make the methods static so you don't have to create an instance of the validation class to use its methods. Also, to avoid parsing the data twice, write the validation methods so that they return two values: a boolean that indicates whether the data can be parsed and a primitive that provides the parsed value.

A method can return only one value, of course. The only way to coax a method to return two values is to return an object that contains both of the values, and to do that, you have to create a class that defines the object. Here's an example of a class you could use as the return value of a method that validates integers:

```
public class IntValidationResult
{
    public boolean isValid;
    public int value;
}
```

And here's a class that provides a static method named `isInt` that validates integer data and returns an `IntValidationResult` object:

```
public class Validation
{
    public static IntValidationResult isInt(
        JTextField f, String msg)
    {
        IntValidationResult result =
            new IntValidationResult();
        try
        {
            result.value =
                Integer.parseInt(f.getText());
```

```
                    result.isValid = true;
                    return result;
                }
                catch (NumberFormatException e)
                {
                    JOptionPane.showMessageDialog(f,
                        "Entry Error", msg,
                        JOptionPane.ERROR_MESSAGE);
                    f.requestFocus();
                    result.isValid = false;
                    result.value = 0;
                    return result;
                }
            }
        }
```

Here's a method that uses the isInt method of this class to validate the textCount field:

```
public void buttonOKClick()
{
    IntValidationResult ir;
    ir = Validation.isInt(textCount,
        "You must enter an integer.");
    if (ir.isValid)
    {
        JOptionPane.showMessageDialog(Number2.this,
            "You entered " + ir.value,
            "Your Number",
            JOptionPane.INFORMATION_MESSAGE);
    }
    textCount.requestFocus();
}
```

Using Text Areas

A *text area* is similar to a text field, but it lets the user enter more than one line of text. If the user enters more text in the text area than can be displayed at once, the text area can display a scroll bar to allow the user to see the entire text. Figure 3-2 shows a text area in action.

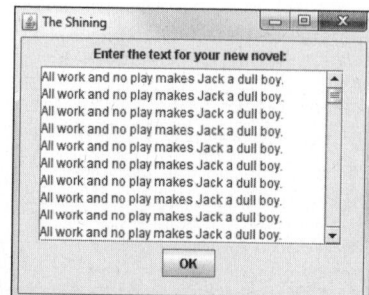

Figure 3-2:
A frame that
uses a text
area.

To create a text area like the one shown in Figure 3-2, you must actually use two classes. First, you use the `JTextArea` class to create the text area. Unfortunately, text areas by themselves don't have scroll bars, so you have to add the text area to a second component called a *scroll pane,* created by the `JScrollPane` class. Then you add the scroll pane — not the text area — to a panel so that it can be displayed.

Creating a text area isn't as hard as it sounds. Here's the code I used to create the text area shown in Figure 3-2, which I then added to a panel:

```
textNovel = new JTextArea(10, 25);
JScrollPane scroll = new JScrollPane(textNovel,
    JScrollPane.VERTICAL_SCROLLBAR_ALWAYS,
    JScrollPane.HORIZONTAL_SCROLLBAR_NEVER);
panel1.add(scroll);
```

Here the first statement creates a text area, giving it an initial size of 10 rows and 25 columns. Then the second statement creates a scroll pane. Notice that the text area object is passed as a parameter to the constructor for the `JScrollPane`, along with constants that indicate whether the scroll pane should include vertical or horizontal scroll bars (or both). Finally, the third statement adds the scroll pane to the panel named `panel1`.

The following sections describe the constructors and methods of the `JText Area` and `JScrollPane` classes in more detail.

Book VI
Chapter 3

Getting Input from
the User

The JTextArea class

Table 3-3 lists the most popular constructors and methods of the `JTextArea` class, which you use to create text areas. In most cases, you use the second constructor, which lets you set the number of rows and columns to display. The `rows` parameter governs the height of the text area, and the `cols` parameter sets the width.

Table 3-3	Clever JTextArea Constructors and Methods
Constructor	**Description**
`JTextArea()`	Creates a new text area.
`JTextArea(int rows, int cols)`	Creates a new text area large enough to display the specified number of rows and columns.
`JTextArea(String text, int rows, int cols)`	Creates a new text area with the specified initial text value, large enough to display the specified number of rows and columns.

(continued)

Table 3-3 *(continued)*

Method	Description
`void append(String text)`	Adds the specified text to the end of the text area's text value.
`int getLineCount()`	Gets the number of lines currently in the text value.
`String getText()`	Gets the text value entered in the field.
`void insert(String str, int pos)`	Inserts the specified text at the specified position.
`void requestFocus()`	Asks for the focus to be moved to this text field.
`void replaceRange(String str, int start, int end)`	Replaces text indicated by the start and end positions with the new specified text.
`void setColumns(int cols)`	Sets the width of the text area (but it's better to do this in the constructor).
`void setEditable(boolean value)`	If `false`, makes the field read-only.
`void setLineWrap(boolean value)`	If `true`, wraps lines if the text doesn't fit on one line.
`void setText(String text)`	Sets the field's text value.
`void setToolTipText(String text)`	Sets the tooltip text that's displayed if the user rests the mouse pointer over the text field for a few moments.
`void setWrapStyleWord()`	If `true`, wraps the text at word boundaries.

To retrieve the text that the user enters in a text area, you use the `getText` method. Here's a method from an action listener that retrieves text from a text area:

```
public void buttonOKClicked()
{
    String text = textNovel.getText();
    if (text.contains("All work and no play"))
    {
        JOptionPane.showMessageDialog(textNovel,
            "Can't you see I'm working?",
            "Going Crazy",
            JOptionPane.ERROR_MESSAGE);
    }
}
```

Here a message box is displayed if the text contains the string `All work and no play`.

Notice that in addition to the `getText` method, the `JTextArea` class has methods that let you add text to the end of the text area's current value (`append`), insert text into the middle of the value (`insert`), and replace text (`replace`). You use these methods to edit the value of the text area.

Two of the `JTextArea` methods are used to control how lines longer than the width of the text area are handled. If you call `setLineWrap` with a value of `true`, lines that are too long to display are automatically wrapped to the next line, and if you call `setWrapStyleWord` with a value of `true`, any lines that are wrapped split between words instead of in the middle of a word. You usually use these two methods together, as follows:

```
textItinerary = new JTextArea(10, 20);
textItinerary.setLineWrap(true);
textItinerary.setWrapStyleWord(true);
```

The JScrollPane class

Text areas aren't very useful without scroll bars. To create a text area with a scroll bar, you use the `JScrollPane` class, whose constructors and fields are listed in Table 3-4.

Note: This table doesn't show any methods for the `JScrollPane` class. The `JScrollPane` class does have methods (plenty of them, in fact), but none of them are particularly useful for ordinary programming, so I didn't include any of them in the table.

Table 3-4   Essential JScrollPane Constructors and Fields

Constructor	Description
`JScrollPane(Component view)`	Creates a scroll pane for the specified component.
`JScrollPane(Component, int vert, int hor)`	Creates a scroll pane for the specified component with the specified policy for the vertical and horizontal scroll bars.

Field	Description
`VERTICAL_SCROLLBAR_ALWAYS`	Always adds a vertical scroll bar.
`VERTICAL_SCROLLBAR_AS_NEEDED`	Adds a vertical scroll bar if necessary.
`VERTICAL_SCROLLBAR_NEVER`	Never adds a vertical scroll bar.
`HORIZONTAL_SCROLLBAR_ALWAYS`	Always adds a horizontal scroll bar.
`HORIZONTAL_SCROLLBAR_AS_NEEDED`	Adds a horizontal scroll bar if necessary.
`HORIZONTAL_SCROLLBAR_NEVER`	Never adds a horizontal scroll bar.

The usual way to create a scroll pane is to use the second constructor. You use the first parameter of this constructor to specify the component to which you want to add scroll bars. To add scroll bars to a `textNovel` text area, for example, you specify `textNovel` as the first parameter.

The second parameter tells the scroll pane whether to create a vertical scroll bar. The value you specify for this parameter should be one of the first three fields listed in Table 3-4:

✦ `VERTICAL_SCROLLBAR_ALWAYS`: Choose this field if you always want the scroll pane to show a vertical scroll bar.

✦ `VERTICAL_SCROLLBAR_AS_NEEDED`: Specify this field if you want to see the vertical scroll bar only when the text area contains more lines that can be displayed at once; the vertical scroll bar is shown only when it's needed.

✦ `VERTICAL_SCROLLBAR_NEVER`: Choose this field if you never want to see a vertical scroll bar onscreen.

The third parameter uses the three `HORIZONTAL_SCROLLBAR` constants to indicate whether the scroll pane includes a horizontal scroll bar always, never, or only when necessary.

Thus the following code adds scroll bars to a text area. The vertical scroll bar is always shown, but the horizontal scroll bar is shown only when needed:

```
JScrollPane scroll = new JScrollPane(textNovel,
    JScrollPane.VERTICAL_SCROLLBAR_ALWAYS,
    JScrollPane.HORIZONTAL_SCROLLBAR_AS_NEEDED);
```

Use the `JScrollPane` class with components other than text areas. As you see in Book VI, Chapter 4, scroll panes are often used with list controls as well.

Using Check Boxes

A *check box* is a control that the user can click to check or clear. Check boxes usually let the user specify a `Yes` or `No` setting for an option. Figure 3-3 shows a frame with three check boxes.

Figure 3-3:
A frame with three check boxes.

To create a check box, you use the `JCheckBox` class. Its favorite constructors and methods are shown in Table 3-5.

Table 3-5   Notable JCheckBox Constructors and Methods

Constructor	Description
`JCheckBox()`	Creates a new check box that is initially unchecked.
`JCheckBox(String text)`	Creates a new check box that displays the specified text.
`JCheckBox(String text, boolean selected)`	Creates a new check box with the specified text. The `boolean` parameter determines whether the check box is initially checked (`true`) or unchecked (`false`).

Method	Description
`void addActionListener (ActionListener listener)`	Adds an `ActionListener` to listen for action events.
`void addItemListener (ItemListener listener)`	Adds an `ItemListener` to listen for item events.
`String getText()`	Gets the text displayed by the check box.
`Boolean isSelected()`	Returns `true` if the check box is checked or `false` if the check box is not checked.
`void setSelected(boolean value)`	Checks the check box if the parameter is `true`; unchecks it if the parameter is `false`.
`void setText(String text)`	Sets the check box text.
`void setToolTipText(String text)`	Sets the tooltip text that's displayed if the user rests the mouse pointer over the check box for a few moments.

As with any Swing component, if you want to refer to the component in both the frame class constructor and a listener, you have to declare class variables to refer to the check box components, like this:

```
JCheckBox pepperoni, mushrooms, anchovies;
```

Then you can use statements like these in the frame constructor to create the check boxes and add them to a panel (in this case, `panel1`):

```
pepperoni = new JCheckBox("Pepperoni");
panel1.add(pepperoni);

mushrooms = new JCheckBox("Mushrooms");
panel1.add(mushrooms);
```

```
anchovies = new JCheckBox("Anchovies");
panel1.add(anchovies);
```

Notice that I didn't specify the initial state of these check boxes in the constructor. As a result, they're initially unchecked. If you want to create a check box that is initially checked, call the constructor like this:

```
Pepperoni = new JCheckBox("Pepperoni", true);
```

In an event listener, you can test the state of a check box by using the `is Selected` method, and you can set the state of a check box by calling its `set Selected` method. Here's a method that displays a message box and clears all three check boxes when the user clicks the OK button:

```
public void buttonOKClicked()
{
    String msg = "";
    if (pepperoni.isSelected())
        msg += "Pepperoni\n";
    if (mushrooms.isSelected())
        msg += "Mushrooms\n";
    if (anchovies.isSelected())
        msg += "Anchovies\n";
    if (msg.equals(""))
        msg = "You didn't order any toppings.";
    else
        msg = "You ordered these toppings:\n"
                + msg;
    JOptionPane.showMessageDialog(buttonOK,
        msg, "Your Order",
        JOptionPane.INFORMATION_MESSAGE);
    pepperoni.setSelected(false);
    mushrooms.setSelected(false);
    anchovies.setSelected(false);
```

Here, the name of each pizza topping selected by the user is added to a text string. If you select pepperoni and anchovies, for example, the following message is displayed:

```
You ordered these toppings:
Pepperoni
Anchovies
```

If you want, you can add event listeners to check boxes to respond to events generated when the user clicks those check boxes. Check boxes support both action listeners and item listeners. The difference between them is subtle:

✦ **Action event:** Generated whenever the user clicks a check box to change its state.

✦ **Item event:** Generated whenever the state of the check box is changed, whether as a result of being clicked by the user or because the program called the `setSelected` method.

Suppose that your restaurant has anchovies on the menu, but you refuse to actually make pizzas with anchovies on them. Here's a method you can call in an action listener to display a message if the user tries to check the Anchovies check box; after displaying the message, the method then clears the check box:

```
public void anchoviesChecked(){
    JOptionPane.showMessageDialog(anchovies,
        "We don't do anchovies here.",
        "Yuck!",
        JOptionPane.WARNING_MESSAGE);
    anchovies.setSelected(false);
}
```

**Book VI
Chapter 3**

Getting Input from
the User

Add a listener to a check box only if you need to provide immediate feedback to the user when he or she checks or unchecks the box. In most applications, you wait until the user clicks a button to examine the state of any check boxes in the frame.

Using Radio Buttons

Radio buttons are similar to check boxes, but with a crucial difference: They travel in groups, and a user can select only one radio button at a time in each group. When you click a radio button to select it, whatever radio button was previously selected is automatically deselected. Figure 3-4 shows a frame with three radio buttons.

Figure 3-4:
A frame
with three
radio
buttons.

To work with radio buttons, you use two classes. First, you create the radio buttons themselves with the `JRadioButton` class, whose constructors and methods are shown in Table 3-6. Then you create a group for the buttons with the `ButtonGroup` class. You must add the radio buttons themselves to a panel (so that they're displayed) and to a button group (so that they're grouped properly with other buttons).

Table 3-6   Various JRadioButton Constructors and Methods

Constructor	Description
JRadioButton()	Creates a new radio button with no text.
JRadioButton(String text)	Creates a new radio button with the specified text.

Method	Description
void addActionListener (ActionListener listener)	Adds an ActionListener to listen for action events.
void addItemListener (ItemListener listener)	Adds an ItemListener to listen for item events.
String getText()	Gets the text displayed by the radio button.
Boolean isSelected()	Returns true if the radio button is selected or false if the radio button is not selected.
void setSelected(boolean value)	Selects the radio button if the parameter is true.
void setText(String text)	Sets the radio-button text.
void setToolTipText(String text)	Sets the tooltip text that's displayed if the user rests the mouse pointer over the radio button for a few moments.

The usual way to create a radio button is to declare a variable to refer to the button as a class variable so that it can be accessed anywhere in the class, as in this example:

```
JRadioButton small, medium, large;
```

Then, in the frame constructor, you call the JRadioButton constructor to create the radio button:

```
small = new JRadioButton("Small");
```

Thereafter, you can add the radio button to a panel in the usual way.

To create a button group to group radio buttons that work together, just call the ButtonGroup class constructor:

```
ButtonGroup group1 = new ButtonGroup();
```

Then call the `add` method of the `ButtonGroup` to add each radio button to the group:

```
group1.add(small);
group1.add(medium);
group1.add(large);
```

Button groups have nothing to do with how radio buttons appear in the frame. The buttons can appear anywhere on the frame, even in different panels. (I show you how to use borders to group radio buttons and other components in the next section, cleverly named "Using Borders.")

Where button groups really come in handy is when you have more than one set of radio buttons in a form. Suppose that in addition to choosing the size of the pizza, the user can choose the style of crust: thin or thick. In that case, you use a total of five radio buttons and two button groups. The constructor code that creates the radio buttons might look something like this:

```
ButtonGroup size = new ButtonGroup();
ButtonGroup crust = new ButtonGroup();

small = new JRadioButton("Small");
medium = new JRadioButton("Medium");
large = new JRadioButton("Large");
size.add(small);
size.add(medium);
size.add(large);

thin = new JRadioButton("Thin Crust");
thick = new JRadioButton("Thick Crust");
crust.add(thin);
crust.add(thick);
```

(To keep this example simple, I omitted the statements that add the radio buttons to the panel.)

Strictly speaking, you don't have to create a button group if all the radio buttons in the frame are in the same group. In that case, Swing creates a default group and adds all the radio buttons to it. Because it requires only a few extra lines of code, however, I suggest that you always create a button group — even when you have only one group of radio buttons.

Using Borders

A *border* is a decorative element that groups components visually by drawing a line around them. The frame in Figure 3-5 shows some radio buttons and check boxes inside borders.

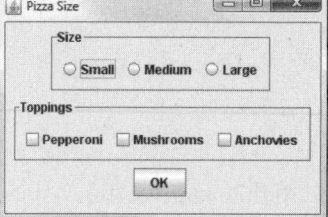

Figure 3-5:
A frame with
borders.

You can apply a border to any object that inherits JComponent, but the
usual technique is to apply the border to a panel and add to that panel any
components you want to appear within the border.

To create a border, call one of the static methods listed in Table 3-7.
Each of these methods creates a border with a slightly different visual
style. Then you apply the Border object to a panel by calling the panel's
setBorder method.

Table 3-7   **BorderFactory Methods for Creating Borders**

Method	*Description*
`Border createBevelBorder` `(int type)`	Creates a beveled border of the specified type. The type parameter can be `BevelBorder.LOWERED` or `BevelBorder.RAISED`.
`Border` `createEmptyBorder(int top, int left, int bottom, int right)`	Creates an empty border that occupies the space indicated by the parameters.
`Border` `createEtchedBorder()`	Creates an etched border.
`Border createLineBorder()`	Creates a line border.
`Border` `createLoweredBevelBorder()`	Creates a lowered beveled border.
`Border` `createRaisedBevelBorder()`	Creates a raised beveled border.
`Border createTitledBorder` `(String title)`	Creates a titled etched border.
`Border createTitledBorder` `(Border b, String title)`	Creates a titled border from the specified border.

DESIGN PATTERN

Book VI
Chapter 3

Getting Input from
the User

The Factory pattern

The `BorderFactory` class is an example of a very common design pattern called the *Factory pattern*. In short, when you use the Factory pattern, you don't use constructors to create objects. Instead, you use a *factory class* that has *factory methods* that create objects for you.

One benefit of the Factory pattern is that the users of the factory class don't need to know what type of object is actually created. Swing actually defines several classes for borders, for example, all of which implement the `Border` interface. If you have to use constructors to create border objects, you have to know about all the border classes. By creating a `BorderFactory` class that returns `Border` objects, you have to know only about the `BorderFactory` class and its methods.

The designers of the Java API could have created a `Border` class (instead of an interface) that lets you specify what type of border to create via a parameter passed to the constructor, but that approach would have many problems. For starters, the `Border` class would be complicated because it would have to implement every type of border. More important, adding a new type of border later is difficult. With the Factory pattern, you can create a new border type easily by (1) creating a class that implements the `Border` interface for the new border and (2) adding a method to the `BorderFactory` class to create the new border type.

The `BorderFactory` class is in the `javax.swing` package, but the `Border` interface that defines the resulting border objects is in `javax.swing.border`. Thus you need to include this `import` statement at the beginning of the class (in addition to importing `javax.swing.*`) if you plan to use borders:

```
import javax.swing.border.*;
```

All the methods listed in Table 3-7 are static methods. As a result, you don't have to create an instance of the `BorderFactory` class to call these methods.

Here's a snippet of code that creates a panel, creates a titled border, and applies the border to the panel:

```
JPanel sizePanel = new JPanel();
Border b1 = BorderFactory.createTitledBorder("Size");
sizePanel.setBorder(b1);
```

Any components you add to `sizePanel` appear within this border.

The last method listed in Table 3-7 needs a little explanation. It simply adds a title to a border created by any of the other created methods of the `BorderFactory` class. You can create a raised beveled border with the title `Options` like this:

```
Border b = BorderFactory.createRaisedBevelBorder();
b = BorderFactory.createTitledBorder(b, "Options");
```

Using Sliders

As Figure 3-6 shows, a *slider* is a component that lets a user pick a value from a set range (say, from 0 to 50) by moving a knob. A slider is a convenient way to get numeric input from the user when the input falls within a set range of values.

Figure 3-6:
A frame with a slider.

To create a slider control, you use the JSlider class. Table 3-8 shows its constructors and methods.

Table 3-8   Selected JSlider Constructors and Methods

Constructor	Description
JSlider()	Creates a new slider. The minimum and maximum values default to 0 and 100, and the initial value is set to 50.
JSlider(int min, int max)	Creates a new slider with the specified minimum and maximum values. The initial value is halfway between the minimum and maximum.
JSlider(int min, int max, int value)	Creates a new slider with the specified minimum, maximum, and initial values.
JSlider(int orientation, int min, int max, int value)	Creates a new slider with the specified minimum, maximum, and initial values. The orientation can be JSlider. HORIZONTAL or JSlider. VERTICAL.
Method	**Description**
void addChangeListener (ChangeListener listener)	Adds a ChangeListener to listen for change events.
int getValue()	Gets the value indicated by the current position of the knob.
void setFont()	Sets the font of the text associated with the slider.

Method	Description
void setInvert(boolean value)	If true, inverts the slider's direction so that the maximum value is on the left and the minimum value is on the right.
void setMajorTickSpacing (int value)	Sets the interval for major tick marks. The marks aren't shown unless setPaintTicks(true) is called.
void setMinimum(int value)	Sets the minimum value.
void setMaximum(int value)	Sets the maximum value.
void setMinorTickSpacing (int value)	Sets the interval for minor tick marks. The marks aren't shown unless setPaintTicks(true) is called.
setOrientation(int orientation)	Sets the orientation. Allowed values are JSlider.HORIZONTAL and JSlider.VERTICAL.
void setPaintLabels (boolean value)	If true, shows tick labels.
void setSnapToTicks (boolean value)	If true, rounds the value returned by the getValue method to the nearest tick mark.
void setToolTipText	Sets the tooltip text that's displayed if the user (String text) rests the mouse pointer over the slider for a few moments.

To create a bare-bones slider, just call the JSlider constructor. You can create a slider that ranges from 0 to 100 like this:

```
slider = new JSlider();
```

Here the slider variable is declared as a class variable of type JSlider.

If you want to specify the minimum and maximum values, use this constructor:

```
slider = new JSlider(0, 50);
```

The slider lets the user choose a value from 0 to 50. The initial position of the knob is 25, midway between the minimum and maximum values.

To set a different initial value, use this constructor:

```
slider = new JSlider(0, 0, 50);
```

Here the slider ranges from 0 to 50, and the initial value is 0.

You usually want to add at least some adornments to the slider to make it more usable. The slider shown in Figure 3-6 has minimum and maximum tick-mark values with labels visible. Here's the code used to create it:

```
slider = new JSlider(0, 50, 0);
slider.setMajorTickSpacing(10);
slider.setMinorTickSpacing(1);
slider.setPaintTicks(true);
slider.setPaintLabels(true);
panel1.add(slider);
```

Note: Even if you set the major and minor tick-spacing values, the tick marks won't appear onscreen unless you call setPaintTicks with the parameter set to true. The setPaintLabels method shows the labels along with the tick marks, and the setSnapToTicks method rounds the value to the nearest tick mark.

To get the value of the slider, you use the getValue method. Here's a method called from the action listener attached to the OK button in Figure 3-6:

```
public void buttonOKClick()
{
    int level = slider.getValue();
    JOptionPane.showMessageDialog(slider,
        "Remember, this is for posterity.\n"
            + "Tell me...how do you feel?",
        "Level " + level,
        JOptionPane.INFORMATION_MESSAGE);
}
```

Here a message box is displayed when the user clicks the OK button. The current setting of the slider component is retrieved and stored in an int variable named level, which is then used to create the title for the message box.

You can also add an event listener that reacts whenever the user changes the value of the slider. To do that, you use the addChangeListener method. The parameter must be an object that implements the ChangeListener interface, which defines a single method named stateChanged.

Because the ChangeListener interface has just one method, it qualifies as a functional interface and can be used in a Lambda expression. In most cases, the easiest way to implement a change listener is to create a method that contains the code you want executed when the slider control changes, then pass it via a Lambda expression to the slider control's `addChangeListener` method.

For more information about Lambda expressions, refer to Book III, Chapter 7.

Here's an example of a method you might call when the state of a slider is changed:

```
public void sliderChanged()
{
    if (slider.getValue() == 50)
    {
        JOptionPane.showMessageDialog(slider,
            "No! Not 50!",
            "The Machine",
            JOptionPane.WARNING_MESSAGE);
    }
}
```

To call this method in response to a change in the slider's state, call the slider's `addChangeListener` method with a a Lambda expression:

```
slider.addChangeListener(e -> sliderChanged() );
```

Then the `stateChanged` method is called whenever the user moves the knob to another position. It checks the value of the slider and displays a message box if the user has advanced the slider all the way to 50.

Designing a Pizza-Ordering Program

To give you an idea of how borders work together with radio buttons and check boxes, Listing 3-2 presents the complete code for the program that created the frame shown in Figure 3-5 earlier in this chapter. When the user clicks the OK button, this program displays a message box summarizing the user's order. For example, if the user orders a medium pizza with pepperoni and mushrooms, the following message is displayed:

```
You ordered a medium pizza with the following toppings:
Pepperoni
Mushrooms
```

If you order a pizza with no toppings, the message you get looks something like this:

```
You ordered a medium pizza with no toppings.
```

Listing 3-2:   The Pizza Order Program

```java
import javax.swing.*;
import java.awt.event.*;
import javax.swing.border.*;

public class Pizza extends JFrame
{
    public static void main(String [] args)
    {
        new Pizza();
    }

    private JButton buttonOK;                                    →12
    private JRadioButton small, medium, large;
    private JCheckBox pepperoni, mushrooms, anchovies;

    public Pizza()
    {
        this.setSize(320,200);
        this.setTitle("Order Your Pizza");
        this.setDefaultCloseOperation(
            JFrame.EXIT_ON_CLOSE);

        JPanel mainPanel = new JPanel();                        →23

        JPanel sizePanel = new JPanel();                        →25
        Border b1 =                                             →26
            BorderFactory.createTitledBorder("Size");
        sizePanel.setBorder(b1);                                →28

        ButtonGroup sizeGroup = new ButtonGroup();              →30

        small = new JRadioButton("Small");                      →32
        small.setSelected(true);
        sizePanel.add(small);
        sizeGroup.add(small);

        medium = new JRadioButton("Medium");                    →37
        sizePanel.add(medium);
        sizeGroup.add(medium);

        large = new JRadioButton("Large");                      →41
        sizePanel.add(large);
        sizeGroup.add(large);

        mainPanel.add(sizePanel);                               →45

        JPanel topPanel = new JPanel();
        Border b2 =
            BorderFactory.createTitledBorder(
                "Toppings");
        topPanel.setBorder(b2);
```

```
    pepperoni = new JCheckBox("Pepperoni");          →52
    topPanel.add(pepperoni);

    mushrooms = new JCheckBox("Mushrooms");
    topPanel.add(mushrooms);

    anchovies = new JCheckBox("Anchovies");
    topPanel.add(anchovies);

    mainPanel.add(topPanel);                         →61

    buttonOK = new JButton("OK");
    buttonOK.addActionListener(e -> buttonOKClick() );  →64
    mainPanel.add(buttonOK);

    this.add(mainPanel);                             →67

    this.setVisible(true);
}

public void buttonOKClick()
{
    String tops = "";                                →74
    if (pepperoni.isSelected())
        tops += "Pepperoni\n";
    if (mushrooms.isSelected())
        tops += "Mushrooms\n";
    if (anchovies.isSelected())
        tops += "Anchovies\n";

    String msg = "You ordered a ";                   →82
    if (small.isSelected())
        msg += "small pizza with ";
    if (medium.isSelected())
        msg += "medium pizza with ";
    if (large.isSelected())
        msg += "large pizza with ";

    if (tops.equals(""))                             →90
        msg += "no toppings.";
    else
        msg += "the following toppings:\n"
            + tops;
    JOptionPane.showMessageDialog(                    →95
        buttonOK, msg, "Your Order",
        JOptionPane.INFORMATION_MESSAGE);

    pepperoni.setSelected(false);                    →99
    mushrooms.setSelected(false);
    anchovies.setSelected(false);
    small.setSelected(true);
    }
}
```

**Book VI
Chapter 3**

Getting Input from
the User

Here are the highlights of how this program works:

→ 12　　The components that are added to the frame are declared as class variables.

→ 23　　This line creates `mainPanel`, the first of three panels that the program uses. This panel contains the other two panels, which use borders to group their components visually.

→ 25　　This line creates `sizePanel`, the panel used to hold the radio buttons that let the user pick the pizza's size.

→ 26　　The `BorderFactory` class is used to create a titled border with the word `Size` as its title.

→ 28　　The titled border is attached to the size panel.

→ 30　　A button group is created for the radio buttons.

→ 32　　The `Small` radio button is created. Notice that this button's `set Selected` method is called. As a result, Small is the default size for a pizza order. Notice also that the radio button is added to both the `sizePanel` panel and the `size` button group.

→ 37　　The `Medium` radio button is created and added to both the panel and the button group.

→ 41　　The `Large` radio button is created and added to both the panel and the button group.

→ 45　　The size panel is added to the main panel.

→ 47　　A new panel named `topPanel` is created to hold the topping check boxes. Like the size panel, this panel is given a titled border.

→ 52　　The Pepperoni, Mushrooms, and Anchovies check boxes are created and added to the panel.

→ 61　　The Toppings panel is added to the main panel.

→ 63　　The OK button is created and added directly to the main panel. Because this button isn't in a border, it doesn't need to be added to a separate panel, as the radio buttons and check boxes do.

→ 67　　The main panel is added to the frame. Now the frame is complete and can be made visible.

→ 74　　In the `buttonOKClicked` method, a string named `tops` is constructed with the toppings that the user selected.

→ 82　　Next, a string named `msg` is constructed with the pizza size. These lines build a string that says `You ordered a` *size* `pizza with` `,` where *size* is replaced by `small`, `medium`, or `large`, depending on which radio button the user selected.

→ 90   This `if` statement finishes the `msg` string by adding `no toppings` if the user didn't pick any toppings or the `tops` string if the user did pick toppings.

→ 95   This line uses `JOptionPane` to show a message box that displays the user's order.

→ 99   Finally, these lines reset the controls so that the application is ready to accept a new order.

Book VI
Chapter 3

Getting Input from
the User

Chapter 4: Choosing from a List

In This Chapter

✓ **Combo boxes**

✓ **Lists**

✓ **Spinners**

✓ **Trees**

A whole category of Swing components is designed to let the user choose one or more items from a list. This chapter presents four such controls. The first three — JList, JComboBox, and JSpinner — are straightforward. The fourth — JTree — is a bit more complicated but worth the effort.

WARNING!

If you put a JTree control in a frame, your friends will surely think you're some kind of guru. They'll start pestering you with questions and asking for your help. As a result, use this component only if your application really needs it — and if you feel up to the technical challenge of figuring out how it works.

Using Combo Boxes

A *combo box* is a combination of a text field and a drop-down list from which the user can choose a value. If the text-field portion of the control is editable, the user can enter a value in the field or edit a value retrieved from the drop-down list. Making the text field uneditable is common, however, and in that case the user must pick one of the values from the list. Figure 4-1 shows a frame with a simple combo box.

Figure 4-1:
A frame with a combo box.

You use the JComboBox class to create combo boxes. Table 4-1 lists the most frequently used constructors and methods of this class.

Table 4-1   Common JComboBox Constructors and Methods

Constructor	Description
`JComboBox()`	Creates an empty combo box.
`JComboBox(Object[] items)`	Creates a combo box and fills it with the values in the array.
`JComboBox(Vector[] items)`	Creates a combo box and fills it with the values in the vector.

Method	Description
`void addActionListener (ActionListener listener)`	Adds an action listener to the combo box.
`void addItem(Object item)`	Adds the item to the combo box.
`void addItemListener (ItemListener listener)`	Adds an item listener to the combo box.
`Object getItemAt(int index)`	Returns the item at the specified index.
`int getItemCount()`	Returns the number of items in the combo box.
`int getSelectedIndex()`	Returns the index of the selected item.
`Object getSelectedItem()`	Returns the selected item.
`void insertItemAt (Object item, int index)`	Inserts an item at a specified index.
`Boolean isEditable()`	Indicates whether the combo box's text field is editable.
`void removeAllItems()`	Removes all items from the combo box.
`void removeItem(Object item)`	Removes the specified item.
`void removeItemAt (int index)`	Removes the item at the specified index.
`void setEditable(boolean value)`	Specifies whether the combo box's text field is editable.
`void setMaximumRowCount (int count)`	Sets the number of rows displayed when the combo box list drops down.
`void setSelectedIndex (int index)`	Selects the item at the specified index. It throws `IllegalArgument Exception` if the index is less than `0` or greater than the number of items in the combo box.
`void setSelectedItem (Object item)`	Selects the specified item. It throws `IllegalArgumentException` if the item is not in the combo box.

Creating combo boxes

Creating a combo box is easy. You have three constructors to choose among, the first of which creates an empty combo box:

```
JComboBox combo1 = new JComboBox();
```

Then you can use the addItem to add items to the combo box:

```
combo1.addItem("Bashful");
combo1.addItem("Doc");
combo1.addItem("Dopey");
combo1.addItem("Grumpy");
combo1.addItem("Happy");
combo1.addItem("Sleepy");
combo1.addItem("Sneezy");
```

Alternatively, you can create a combo box and initialize its contents from an array, as in this example:

```
String[] theSeven = {"Bashful", "Doc", "Dopey",
                     "Grumpy", "Happy", "Sleepy",
                     "Sneezy"};
JComboBox combo1 = new JComboBox(theSeven);
```

Or if you have an existing Vector object with the data you want to display, you might use this code:

```
JComboBox combo1 = new JComboBox(vector1);
```

If the data you want to display is in an array list or another type of collection, use the toArray method to convert the collection to an array and then pass the array to the JComboBox constructor, like so:

```
JComboBox combo1 = new JComboBox(arraylist1.toArray());
```

You can add any kind of object you want to a combo box. The combo box calls the toString method of each item to determine the text to display in the drop-down list. Suppose that you have an array of Employee objects. If you create a combo box from this array, the string returned by each employee's toString method is displayed in the combo box.

By default, the user isn't allowed to edit the data in the text field portion of the combo box. If you want to allow the user to edit the text field, call setEditable(true). Then the user can type a value that's not in the combo box.

To remove items from the combo box, use one of the remove methods. If you know the index position of the item you want to remove, call the remove ItemAt method and pass the index number as a parameter. Otherwise, if you have the object you want to remove, call removeItem and pass the object.

To remove all the items in a combo box, call removeAllItems. Suppose that you have a combo box named custCombo that's filled with Customer objects read from a file, and you need to refresh this combo box periodically to make sure that it has all the current customers. Here's a method that does that:

```
private void fillCustomerCombo()
{
    ArrayList<Customer> customers = getCustomers();
    custCombo.removeAllItems();
    for (Customer c : customers)
        custCombo.addItem(c);
}
```

In this example, a method named getCustomers is called to get an ArrayList of customer objects from the file. Then all the items currently in the combo box are deleted, and an enhanced for loop is used to add the customers to the combo box.

Getting items from a combo box

To get the item selected by the user, you use the getSelectedItem method. Unfortunately, this method returns an Object type, so you must cast the returned value to the appropriate type before you can use it. Here's a method that created the combo box frame shown in Figure 4-1 earlier in this chapter:

```
public void buttonOK()
{
    String s = (String)combo1.getSelectedItem();
    JOptionPane.showMessageDialog(combo1,
        "You picked " + s,
        "Your Favorite",
        JOptionPane.INFORMATION_MESSAGE);
}
```

Here the getSelectedItem method retrieves the selected item, casts it to a String, and saves it in a String variable named s. Then a JOptionPane message box is shown, displaying the user's selection.

If you prefer, you can get the index of the selected item by calling the get SelectedIndex method. You might use this method if the combo box contains string values that correspond to objects stored in an array or a collection. Then you can use the retrieved index value to get the actual object from the collection.

Handling combo box events

When the user selects an item from a combo box, an action event is generated. In most applications, you simply ignore this event because you usually don't need to do anything immediately when the user selects an item. Instead, the selected item is processed when the user clicks a button.

If you want to provide immediate feedback when the user selects an item, you can set up an event handler by calling the combo box's addAction Listener method. In most cases, the easiest way to do that is to create a method that contains the code you want to execute when the user selects an item, and then pass this method to the addActionListener method via a Lambda expression.

For example, the following method displays a message box that says My favorite too! if the user picks Dopey:

```
private class combo1Changed()
{
    String s =
        (String)combo1.getSelectedItem();
    if (s.equals("Dopey"))
        JOptionPane.showMessageDialog(combo1,
            "He's my favorite too!",
            "Good Choice",
            JOptionPane.INFORMATION_MESSAGE);
}
```

Here's the code to call this method whenever the user changes the combo box selection:

```
combo1.addActionListener(e -> combo1Changed() );
```

Combo boxes also generate item events when the user selects an item. In fact, the combo box generates *two* item events when the user selects an item, which can be a little confusing. The first event is generated when the previously selected item is deselected. Then, when the new item is selected, another item event is generated. In most cases, you handle combo box action events rather than item events.

Using Lists

A *list* is a powerful Swing component that displays lists of objects within a box. Depending on how the list is configured, the user can be allowed to select one item in the list or multiple items. In addition, you have amazing control of how the items in the list are displayed.

Lists are almost always used in conjunction with scroll panes (covered in Book VI, Chapter 3) to allow the user to scroll the contents of the list. Figure 4-2 shows a sample frame with a list component.

Figure 4-2:
A frame with
a list.

Lists and combo boxes have several important differences:

✦ A list doesn't have a text field that lets the user edit the selected item. Instead, the user must select items directly from the list.

✦ The list doesn't drop down. Instead, the list items are displayed in a box whose size you can specify.

✦ The list doesn't provide a scroll bar, so you almost always add the list component to a scroll pane so that the user can scroll through the list.

✦ Lists allow users to select more than one item. By default, a list component lets users select any combination of items in the list. You can configure the list, however, to allow selection of a single value or a single range of adjacent values.

To select multiple items in a list, hold down the Ctrl key and click the items you want to select. To select a range of items, click the first item; then hold down the Shift key and click the last item.

✦ You can't directly change the values in a list after you create the list. If you want to create a list whose values you can change, you must take a few extra steps (as I describe in the section "Changing list items," later in this chapter).

You use the JList class to create combo boxes. Table 4-2 lists the most frequently used constructors and methods of this class.

Table 4-2	Routine JList Constructors and Methods
Constructor	**Description**
JList()	Creates an empty list.
JList(ListModel list)	Creates a list that uses the specified list model.

Constructor	Description
JList(Object[] items)	Creates a list and fills it with the values in the array.
JList(Vector[] items)	Creates a list and fills it with the values in the vector.
void clearSelection()	Clears all selections.

Method	Description
int getSelectedIndex()	Returns the index of the first selected item, or −1 if no items are selected.
int[] getSelectedIndexes()	Returns an array with the index of each selected item. The array is empty if no items are selected.
Object getSelectedValue()	Returns the first selected item or null if no items are selected.
Object[] getSelected Values()	Returns an array with all the selected items. The array is empty if no items are selected.
boolean isSelectedIndex (int index)	Returns true if the item at the specified index is selected.
boolean isSelectionEmpty()	Returns true if no items are selected.
void setFixedCellHeight (int height)	Sets the height of each row.
void setFixedCellWidth (int width)	Sets the width of each row.
void setSelectedIndex(int index)	Selects the item at the specified index.
void setSelectedIndices (int[] indices)	Selects the items at the indices specified in the array.
void setSelectionMode (int mode)	Sets the selection mode. Allowable values are ListSelectionModel. SINGLE_SELECTION, ListSelectionModel. SINGLE_INTERVAL_SELECTION, and ListSelectionModel. MULTIPLE_INTERVAL_SELECTION.
void setVisibleRowCount (int count)	Sets the number of rows displayed by the list.

Creating a list

To create a list and specify its items, you pass an array to the `JList` constructor. Then you call the `setVisibleRowCount` method to set the number of rows you want to be visible, add the list to a scroll pane, and add the scroll pane to a panel that you can later add to the frame. Here's an example:

```
String[] toppings = {"Pepperoni", "Sausage",
                     "Linguica", "Canadian Bacon",
                     "Salami", "Tuna", "Olives",
                     "Mushrooms", "Tomatoes",
                     "Pineapple", "Kiwi",
                     "Gummy Worms"};
list1 = new JList(toppings);
list1.setVisibleRowCount(5);
JScrollPane scroll = new JScrollPane(list1);
```

For more information about the `JScrollPane` class, including how to specify what scroll bars you want it to display, refer to Book VI, Chapter 3.

To control the type of selections the user can make, use the `setSelection Mode` method. You can pass this method in one of three fields defined by the `ListSelectionModel` class:

- ✦ **`ListSelectionModel.SINGLE_SELECTION`:** The user can select only one item at a time.

- ✦ **`ListSelectionModel.SINGLE_INTERVAL_SELECTION`:** The user can select multiple items, provided that all of them are within a single range.

- ✦ **`ListSelectionModel.MULTIPLE_INTERVAL_SELECTION`:** The user can select any combination of items.

This statement restricts the list to a single selection:

```
list1.setSelectionMode(ListSelectionModel.SINGLE_SELECTION);
```

Note that the default is to allow any combination of multiple selections.

Getting items from a list

For a list that allows only a single selection, you can retrieve the selected item by calling the `getSelectedValue` method. You have to cast the value to the appropriate type before you use it, as in this example:

```
String topping = (String)list1.getSelectedValue();
```

If the list allows multiple selections, the `getSelectedValue` method returns just the first selected item. To get all the selections, you have to use the `getSelectedValues` method instead. This method returns an array of objects that includes each item selected by the user. When you retrieve these objects, you have to cast each one to the appropriate type; Java doesn't provide any way to cast the entire array.

You can call the following method from an action listener for the list box shown in Figure 4-2 earlier in this chapter:

```
public void buttonOKClicked()
{
    String s = (String)combo1.getSelectedItem();
    JOptionPane.showMessageDialog(combo1,
        "You picked " + s,
        "Your Favorite",
        JOptionPane.INFORMATION_MESSAGE);
}
```

Here the `getSelectedItem` method retrieves the selected item, casts it to a `String`, and saves it in a `String` variable named `s`. Then a `JOptionPane` message box is shown to display the user's selection.

If you prefer, you can get the index of the selected item by calling the `get SelectedIndex` method. You might use this method if the combo box contains string values that correspond to objects stored in an array or a collection. Then you can use the retrieved index value to get the actual object from the collection, as in this example:

```
public void buttonOKClicked()
{
    Object[] toppings = list1.getSelectedValues();
    String msg =
        "You selected the following toppings:\n";
    for (Object topping : toppings)
        msg += (String)topping + "\n";
    JOptionPane.showMessageDialog(list1,
        msg,
        "Your Pizza",
        JOptionPane.INFORMATION_MESSAGE);
    list1.clearSelection();
}
```

Here the `getSelectedValues` method returns an array that contains the toppings selected by the user. Next, an enhanced `for` loop is used to build a string that lists each selected topping on a separate line. Then the `JOptionPane` class is used to display the `msg` string in a message box.

Changing list items

By default, the items in a `JList` component can't be changed after you create the list. If you want to create a list whose items can be changed, you must use another class — `DefaultListModel` — to create an object called a *list model* that contains the items you want to display in the `JList` component. Then you pass the list model object to the JList constructor. The list model is responsible for managing the list that's displayed by the JList component. As a result, you can use the list model's methods to add or remove items, and then the JList component automatically updates itself to reflect the list changes.

Table 4-3 shows the most commonly used constructors and methods of the DefaultListModel class.

Table 4-3   Useful DefaultListModel Constructors and Methods

Constructor	*Description*
DefaultListModel()	Creates a new list model object.
Method	*Description*
void add(Object element, int index)	Adds an element at the specified position.
void addElement(Object element))	Adds an element to the end of the list.
void clear()	Removes all elements from the list.
boolean Contains(Object element)	Returns true if the specified element is in the list.
Object firstElement()	Returns the first element in the list.
Object get(int index)	Returns the element at the specified location.
boolean isEmpty()	Returns true if the list is empty.
Object lastElement()	Returns the last element in the list.
void remove(int index)	Removes the element from the specified position in the list.
void removeElement(Object element)	Removes the specified element from the list.
int size()	Returns the number of elements in the list.
Object[] toArray()	Returns an array containing each element in the list.

When you create the default data model, it's empty, but you can call the add or addElement method to add elements to the list, as in this example:

```
String[] values = {"Pepperoni", "Sausage", "Linguica",
                   "Canadian Bacon", "Salami", "Tuna",
                   "Olives", "Mushrooms", "Tomatoes",
                   "Pineapple", "Kiwi", "Gummy Worms"};
DefaultListModel model = new DefaultListModel();
```

```
for (String value : values)
    model.addElement(value);
```

Here the elements from the `values` array are added to the list model. When you create the list control, pass the list model to the `JList` constructor, like so:

```
list = new JList(model);
```

You can remove an element from the list model by calling the `remove` or `removeElement` method. To remove all the elements from the model, call the `clear` method.

Using Spinners

A *spinner* is a text field that has two little arrows next to it. The user can click one of these arrows to increase or decrease the value in the text field. Usually the text field contains a number, so clicking one of the little arrows increments or decrements the number. You can also create a spinner that displays data taken from an array or a collection. Figure 4-3 shows a frame with three spinners arranged as a simple time picker.

Figure 4-3:
A frame
with three
spinners.

To create a spinner control, you use the `JSpinner` class, whose constructors and methods are shown in Table 4-4. Note that the second constructor accepts an object of type `SpinnerModel` as a parameter. This table also shows constructors for two classes that implement the `SpinnerModel` interface.

Table 4-4	JSpinner and Related Classes
Constructor	*Description*
`JSpinner()`	Creates a default spinner. The default spinner lets the user choose an integer that has an initial value of 0 and no minimum or maximum values.
`JSlider(SpinnerModel model)`	Creates a spinner using the specified `SpinnerModel` object.

(continued)

Table 4-4 *(continued)*

Method	Description
void addChangeListener (ChangeListener listener)	Adds a ChangeListener to listen for change events.
int getValue()	Gets the value.
void setToolTipText (String ext)	Sets the tooltip text that's displayed if the user rests the mouse over the slider for a few moments.

Constructors for SpinnerModel Classes	*Description*
SpinnerNumberModel (int init, int min, int max, int step)	Creates a number spinner model that lets the user select integer values ranging from min to max, with an increment of step. The initial value is set to init.
SpinnerNumberModel (double max, double step)	Creates a number spinner model that lets the user select double values ranging from min to max, with an increment of step. The initial value is set to init.
SpinnerListModel(Object[] values)	Creates a list spinner model using the values from the specified array.
SpinnerListModel (List collection)	Creates a list spinner model using the values from the specified collection. The collection must implement the List interface.

You can create a default spinner that lets the user select integer values, like this:

```
JSpinner spinner = new JSpinner();
```

This spinner starts with a value of 0 and increases or decreases the value by 1 each time the user clicks one of the spinner's arrows. You can retrieve the current value of the spinner at any time, like this:

```
int value = spinner.getValue();
```

For most spinners, you want to use the second constructor, which requires that you first create an object that implements the SpinnerModel interface.

Table 4-4 lists constructors for two classes that implement `Spinner`. The first, `SpinnerNumberModel`, creates numeric spinner controls that let you control the initial value, the minimum and maximum values, and the step value that's added or subtracted each time the user clicks one of the arrows.

Here's how you can use the `SpinnerNumberModel` to create the first spinner in Figure 4-3, which accepts integers from 1 to 12, starting with 1:

```
JSpinner hours = new JSpinner(
    new SpinnerNumberModel(1, 1, 12, 1));
```

Here's the code for the second spinner in Figure 4-3, which lets the user pick numbers from 0 to 59:

```
JSpinner minutes = new JSpinner(
    new SpinnerNumberModel(0, 0, 59, 1));
```

By using the `SpinnerListModel` class, you can also build a spinner control that lets users select values from a list. The constructor for this class accepts either an array or an object that implements the `List` interface. The `ArrayList` class implements this interface, which means you can use `SpinnerListModel` to create a spinner that lets users select items from an `ArrayList` object.

Here's the code for the third spinner in Figure 4-3, which lets the user specify a.m. or p.m.:

```
String[] ampmString = {"am", "pm"};
ampm = new JSpinner(
    new SpinnerListModel(ampmString));
```

In this example, the `SpinnerListModel` uses an array of strings with two elements: am and pm.

Using Trees

A *tree* is a fancy Swing component that displays hierarchical data in outline form, which we computer nerds refer to as a tree. The type of tree you're probably most familiar with is the directory structure of your disk drive. Trees are created from the `JTree` class.

Figure 4-4 shows a Swing frame that has a tree control in it. In this example, I use a tree control to represent a few of my favorite TV series, along with series that were spun off from them.

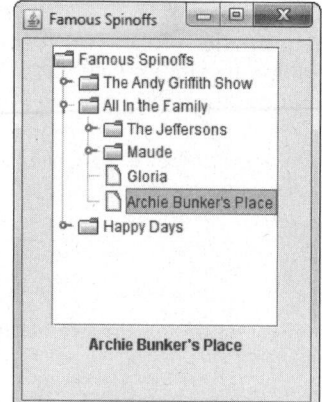

Figure 4-4:
A frame with
a tree.

Tree controls are probably the most difficult of all Swing controls to work with. To cover them completely, I'd have to devote a full chapter of 30 pages or more. In the few short pages that remain in this chapter, then, I'm just going to present the basics: how to create a tree component such as the one shown in Figure 4-4 and how to find out which element the user has selected.

Before I get into the mechanics of how to create a tree control, you need to know a few terms that describe the elements in the tree itself:

+ **Node:** Each element in the tree is called a *node*. Nodes in a tree must be created from a class that implements the `TreeNode` interface. If you want, you can create your own class that implements `TreeNode`. For most purposes, however, you can use the `DefaultMutableTreeNode` class. (Unfortunately, you have to type that class name a lot when you work with tree controls.)

+ **Root node:** A *root node* is the starting node for a tree. Every tree component must have one — and only one — root node. When you create a tree component, you pass the root node to the `JTree` constructor.

+ **Child node:** The nodes that appear immediately below a given node are called that node's *child nodes*. A node can have more than one child.

+ **Parent node:** The node immediately above a given node is called that node's *parent node*. Every node except the root node must have one — and only one — parent.

+ **Sibling nodes:** *Sibling nodes* are children of the same parent.

+ **Leaf node:** A *leaf node* is one that doesn't have any children.

+ **Path:** A path contains the node and all its ancestors — that is, its parent, its parent's parent, and so on — all the way back to the root.

+ **Expanded node:** An *expanded node* is one whose children are visible.

+ **Collapsed node:** A *collapsed node* is one whose children are hidden.

Building a tree

Before you can actually create a tree control, you must build the tree it displays. The easiest way to do that is to use the `DefaultMutableTreeNode` class, the details of which are shown in Table 4-5.

Table 4-5	The DefaultMutableTreeNode Class
Constructor	*Description*
`DefaultMutableTreeNode()`	Creates an empty tree node.
`DefaultMutableTreeNode (Object userObject)`	Creates a tree node with the specified user object.
Method	*Description*
`void add(TreeNode child)`	Adds a child node.
`TreeNode getFirstChild()`	Gets the first of this node's children.
`DefaultMutableTreeNode getNextSibling()`	Gets the next sibling.
`TreeNode getParent()`	Gets this node's parent.
`Object getUserObject()`	Gets the user object for this node.

**Book VI
Chapter 4**

Choosing from a List

The `DefaultMutableTreeNode` class implements the `TreeNode` interface. As a result, you can use `DefaultMutableTreeNode` objects for any of the methods listed in this table that call for `TreeNode` objects.

The `DefaultMutableTreeNode` class provides three basic characteristics for each node:

✦ The *user object,* which contains the data represented by the node. In my example, I use strings for the user objects, but you can use objects of any type you want for the user object. The tree control calls the user object's `toString` method to determine what text to display for each node. The easiest way to set the user object is to pass it via the `DefaultMutable TreeNode` constructor.

✦ The parent of this node, unless the node happens to be the root.

✦ Any children of this node, unless the node happens to be a leaf node. You create child nodes by calling the `add` method.

The `DefaultMutableTreeNode` class has many more methods for navigating the tree than the ones shown here. Given a root node, however, you can use the `getFirstChild` and `getNextSibling` methods to "walk" the entire tree and access each node.

In this section, I build a tree that lists spinoff shows from three popular television shows of the past:

✦ *The Andy Griffith Show,* which had two spinoffs: *Gomer Pyle, U.S.M.C.,* and *Mayberry R.F.D.*

✦ *All in the Family,* which directly spawned four spinoffs: *The Jeffersons, Maude, Gloria,* and *Archie Bunker's Place.* In addition, two of these spinoffs had spinoffs of their own involving the maids: The Jeffersons' maid became the topic of a show called *Checking In,* and Maude's maid became the main character in *Good Times.*

✦ *Happy Days,* which spun off *Mork and Mindy, Laverne and Shirley,* and *Joanie Loves Chachi.*

You can take many approaches to building trees, most of which involve some recursive programming. I'm going to avoid recursive programming in this section to keep things simple, but my avoidance means that you'll have to hard-code some of the details of the tree into the program. Most real programs that work with trees need some type of recursive programming to build the tree.

The first step in creating a tree is declaring a `DefaultMutableTreeNode` variable for each node that isn't a leaf node. For my TV series example, I start with the following code:

```
DefaultMutableTreeModel andy, archie, happy,
                        george, maude;
```

These variables can be local variables in the frame constructor because after you get the tree set up, you won't need these variables anymore. You see why you don't need variables for the leaf nodes in a moment.

Next, I create the root node:

```
DefaultMutableTreeNode root =
  new DefaultMutableTreeNode("Famous Spinoffs");
```

Now, to simplify the task of creating all the other nodes, I create a helper method called `makeShow`:

```
private DefaultMutableTreeNode makeShow(String title,
    DefaultMutableTreeNode parent)
{
    DefaultMutableTreeNode show;
    show = new DefaultMutableTreeNode(title);
    parent.add(show);
    return show;
}
```

This method accepts a string and another node as parameters, and returns a node whose user object is set to the String parameter. The returned node is also added to the parent node as a child. Thus you can call this method to both create a new node and place the node in the tree.

The next step is creating some nodes. Continuing my example, I start with the nodes for *The Andy Griffith Show* and its spinoffs:

```
andy = makeShow("The Andy Griffith Show", root);
makeShow("Gomer Pyle, U.S.M.C.", andy);
makeShow("Mayberry R.F.D.", andy);
```

Here, makeShow is called to create a node for *The Andy Griffith Show,* with the root node specified as its parent. The node returned by this method is saved in the andy variable. Then makeShow is called twice to create the spinoff shows, this time specifying andy as the parent node.

Because neither *Gomer Pyle, U.S.M.C.,* nor *Mayberry R.F.D.* had a spinoff show, I don't have to pass these nodes as the parent parameter to the makeShow method. That's why I don't bother to create a variable to reference these nodes.

Next in my example, I have to create nodes for *All in the Family* and its spinoffs:

```
archie = makeShow("All in the Family", root);
george = makeShow("The Jeffersons", archie);
makeShow("Checking In", george);
maude = makeShow("Maude", archie);
makeShow("Good Times", maude);
makeShow("Gloria", archie);
makeShow("Archie Bunker's Place", archie);
```

In this case, both *The Jeffersons* and *Maude* have child nodes of their own. As a result, variables are required for these two shows so that they can be passed as the parent parameter to makeShow when I create the nodes for *Checking In* and *Good Times.*

Finally, here's the code that creates the nodes for *Happy Days* and its spinoffs:

```
happy = makeShow("Happy Days", root);
makeShow("Mork and Mindy", happy);
makeShow("Laverne and Shirley", happy);
makeShow("Joanie Loves Chachi", happy);
```

The complete tree is successfully created in memory, so I can get on with the task of creating a JTree component to show off the tree.

Creating a JTree component

You use the JTree class to create a tree component that displays the nodes of a tree. Table 4-6 shows the key constructors and methods of this class.

Table 4-6   Ordinary Constructors and Methods of the JTree Class

Constructor	Description
void JTree()	Creates an empty tree (not very useful, if you ask me).
void JTree(TreeNode root)	Creates a tree that displays the tree that starts at the specified node.

Method	Description
void addTreeSelection Listener(TreeSelection Listener listener)	Adds the specified listener to listen for tree-selection events.
Object getLastSelected PathComponent()	Gets the node that is currently selected.
TreeSelectionModel getSelectionModel()	Gets the selection model for the tree. See this section for what you can do with the TreeSelectionModel object.
void setVisibleRowCount (int count)	Sets the number of rows visible in the display.

The first step in creating a JTree component is declaring a JTree variable as a class instance variable so that you can access the constructor and other methods, as follows:

```
JTree tree1;
```

Then, in the frame constructor, you call the JTree constructor to create the tree component, passing the root node of the tree you want it to display as a parameter:

```
tree1 = new JTree(root);
```

By default, the user is allowed to select multiple nodes from the tree. To restrict the user to a single selection, use this strange incantation:

```
tree1.getSelectionModel().setSelectionMode(
    TreeSelectionModel.SINGLE_TREE_SELECTION);
```

Here the `getSelectionModel` method is called to get a `TreeSelectionModel` object that determines how the user can select nodes in the tree. This class provides a method named `setSelectionMode` that lets you set the selection mode. To limit the tree to a single node selection, you must pass this method the `TreeSelectionModel.SINGLE_TREE_SELECTION` field. (I think Oracle could have saved us all a lot of work by providing `setSingleTreeSelection` method for the `JTree` class, but nobody asked me.)

You can control the size of the tree component by calling the `setVisibleRowCount` method, as in this example:

```
tree1.setVisibleRowCount(12);
```

Here the tree is just large enough to show 12 rows at a time.

Finally, you add the tree component to a scroll pane so that the user can scroll the tree if it doesn't fit in the space provided. Then you should add the scroll pane to a panel that is in turn added to the frame, like this:

```
JScrollPane scroll = new JScrollPane(tree1);
panel1.add(scroll);
```

That's it! Now the tree component looks like Figure 4-4 earlier in this chapter.

Getting the selected node

The easiest way to determine the currently selected node in a tree control is to call the `getLastSelectedPathComponent` method. This method returns an object, so you want to cast it to the correct type, as in this example:

```
Object o = tree1.getLastSelectedPathComponent();
DefaultMutableTreeNode show = (DefaultMutableTreeNode) o;
```

Here the selected node is retrieved and stored in the `Object` variable o. Then it's cast to a `DefaultMutableTreeNode` object.

You can use this method in an action event listener to retrieve the selected node when the user clicks a button. But what if your program must respond immediately when the user selects a node? To do that, you need to install a listener to listen for tree selection events.

The frame shown in Figure 4-4 earlier in this chapter has a label below the list box. The listener updates this label with the title of the selected show whenever the user selects a show in the tree.

To create a tree selection listener, you provide a class that implements the `TreeSelectionListener` interface. This interface provides a single method named `valueChanged`, which receives a `TreeSelectionEvent` object as a parameter. The easiest way to implement this interface is to use a Lambda expression to simply call a method that contains the code you want to run when the user selects a node.

Here's an example of such a method; it simply sets the value of a label named showName to the value of the user object of the selected item:

```java
public void tree1Changed()
{
    Object o = tree1.getLastSelectedPathComponent();
    DefaultMutableTreeNode show;
    show = (DefaultMutableTreeNode) o;
    String title = (String)show.getUserObject();
    showName.setText(title);
}
```

Then you can install an instance of this class to listen for tree selection events with this statement:

```java
tree1.addTreeSelectionListener(e -> tree1Changed() );
```

The JTree class provides many other methods for retrieving the nodes that are selected. In addition, you can add listeners that listen for tree selection events that are generated when the user selects nodes. These events let you create applications that display data for the selected node immediately when the user selects a node. If you want to use these features, check out the API documentation for the JTree class.

Looking at a complete program that uses a tree

Whew! That was a lot of information to digest. In this section, I put it all together.

Listing 4-1 shows the complete program that creates the frame shown in Figure 4-4. This program lets the user select a show from the tree and displays the title of the selected show in a label below the tree.

Listing 4-1:   The Spinoff Program

```java
import javax.swing.*;
import java.awt.event.*;
import javax.swing.tree.*;
import javax.swing.event.*;

public class SpinOffs extends JFrame
{
    public static void main(String [] args)
    {
        new SpinOffs();
    }
```

```
private JTree tree1;                                    →13
private DefaultTreeModel model;
private JLabel showName;

public SpinOffs()
{
    this.setSize(250,400);
    this.setTitle("Famous Spinoffs");
    this.setDefaultCloseOperation(
        JFrame.EXIT_ON_CLOSE);

    JPanel panel1 = new JPanel();

    DefaultMutableTreeNode root, andy, archie,          →25
                        happy, george, maude;

    root = new DefaultMutableTreeNode(                  →28
        "Famous Spin-offs");

    andy = makeShow(                                    →32
        "The Andy Griffith Show", root);
    makeShow("Gomer Pyle, U.S.M.C.", andy);
    makeShow("Mayberry R.F.D.", andy);

    archie = makeShow("All in the Family", root);       →36
    george = makeShow("The Jeffersons", archie);
    makeShow("Checking In", george);
    maude = makeShow("Maude", archie);
    makeShow("Good Times", maude);
    makeShow("Gloria", archie);
    makeShow("Archie Bunker's Place", archie);

    happy = makeShow("Happy Days", root);               →44
    makeShow("Mork and Mindy", happy);
    makeShow("Laverne and Shirley", happy);
    makeShow("Joanie Loves Chachi", happy);

    tree1 = new JTree(root);                            →49
    tree1.getSelectionModel().setSelectionMode(         →50
        TreeSelectionModel.SINGLE_TREE_SELECTION);
    tree1.setVisibleRowCount(12);
    tree1.addTreeSelectionListener(
        e -> tree1Changed() );

    JScrollPane scroll = new JScrollPane(tree1);        →56
    panel1.add(scroll);

    showName = new JLabel();
    panel1.add(showName);
    this.add(panel1);
    this.setVisible(true);
}
```

**Book VI
Chapter 4**

Choosing from a List

(continued)

Listing 4-1 *(continued)*

```
public DefaultMutableTreeNode makeShow(                    →65
    String title, DefaultMutableTreeNode parent)
{
    DefaultMutableTreeNode show;
    show = new DefaultMutableTreeNode(title);
    parent.add(show);
    return show;
}

public void tree1Changed()                                 →74
{
    Object o = tree1.
    getLastSelectedPathComponent();
    DefaultMutableTreeNode show;
    show = (DefaultMutableTreeNode) o;
    String title = (String)show.
        getUserObject();
    showName.setText(title);
}
}
```

All the code in this program has already been shown in this chapter, so I just
point out the highlights here:

→ 13   The tree and list models are defined as class instance variables.

→ 25   DefaultMutableTreeNode variables are defined for the root
                node and each show that has spinoff shows.

→ 28   The root node is created with the text Famous Spin-offs.

→ 32   These lines create the nodes for *The Andy Griffith Show* and its
                spinoffs.

→ 36   These lines create the nodes for *All in the Family* and its spinoffs.

→ 44   These lines create the nodes for *Happy Days* and its spinoffs.

→ 49   This line creates the JTree component, specifying root as the
                root node for the tree.

→ 50   These lines configure the JTree component so that it allows only
                a single selection, shows 12 rows at a time, and has a tree selec-
                tion listener.

→ 56   The JTree component is added to a scroll pane, which is then
                added to the frame.

→ 65   The makeShow method creates a node from a string and adds the
                node to the node passed as the parent parameter.

→ 74   The tree1Changed() method is called whenever the selected
                node changes. It simply displays the title of the selected show in
                the showName label.

Chapter 5: Using Layout Managers

In This Chapter

✓ Flow layout

✓ Border layout

✓ Box layout

✓ Grid layout

✓ GridBag layout

✓ Group layout

Controlling the layout of components in a frame is one of the most difficult aspects of working with Swing. In fact, it can be downright exasperating. Sometimes the components almost seem to have minds of their own. They get stubborn and refuse to budge. They line up on top of one another when you want them to be side by side. You make a slight change to a label or text field and the whole frame seems to rearrange itself. At times, you'll want to put your fist through the monitor.

I recommend against putting your fist through your monitor. You'll make a mess, cut your hand, and have to spend money on a new monitor — and when you get your computer working again, the components *still* won't line up the way you want them to be.

The problem isn't with the components; it's with the *layout managers,* which are responsible for determining where each component appears in its frame or panel.

In this chapter, you find out how to work with Swing's layout managers. This chapter takes the mystery out of Swing layout so that you have complete control of where components are placed.

Working with Layout Managers

Understanding layout managers is the key to creating Swing frames that are attractive and usable.

Introducing six Swing layout managers

Swing provides several layout managers for you to work with, including the following six, which I discuss in this chapter:

✦ **Flow:** This layout manager is the default for panels. It lays out components one after the other until it runs out of room; then it starts a new row of components.

✦ **Border:** This layout manager is the default for frames. It divides the container into five regions: North, South, East, West, and Center. When you add a component, you can specify which region you want to place the component in.

✦ **Box:** This layout manager arranges components in either a single row or a single column, depending on what alignment you specify when you create the layout manager.

✦ **Grid:** This layout manager is ideal when you want to create a grid of identically sized components.

✦ **GridBag:** This layout manager uses a more flexible grid than the Grid layout manager does. In GridBag layout, each row or column can be a different size; a component can span two or more rows or columns; and you can tell the layout manager what to do if the component is smaller or larger than the space allotted for it.

✦ **Group:** This layout manager works best with a visual tool for designing user applications. In Group layout, you describe an arrangement from two points of view: left to right and top to bottom.

Figure 5-1 shows frames arranged with each of these layout managers.

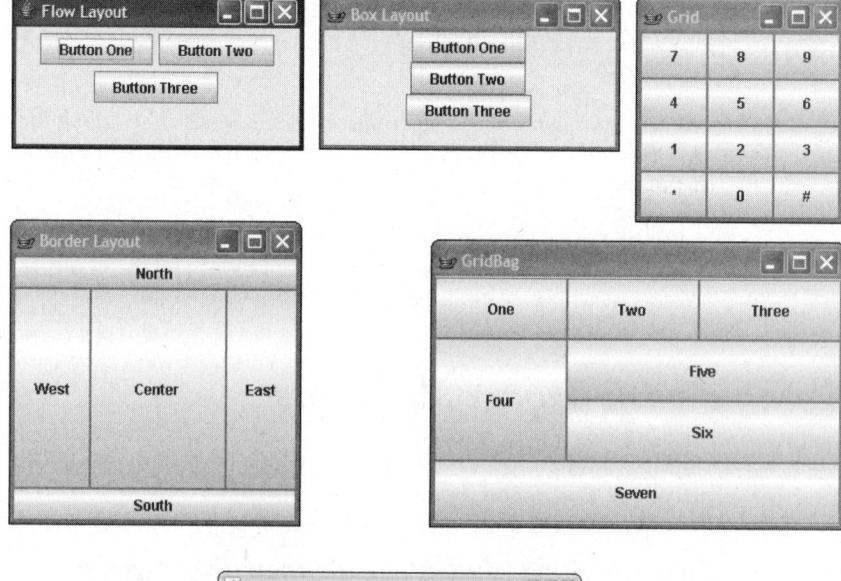

Figure 5-1:
The Flow,
Box, Grid,
Border,
GridBag,
and Group
layout
managers.

In addition to these six layout managers, Java provides a few others, including Card and Spring. The Card layout manager lets you create tabbed layouts, but it has been largely replaced by other components that do the same thing more effectively. The Spring layout manager uses a weird concept called *springs* to let you position components. This layout manager isn't intended to be hand-coded; instead, it's designed to be used by code generators that create graphic user interface (GUI) code for you. I don't cover either of these layout managers in this book. For more information on the Card and Spring layouts, refer to `http://docs.oracle.com/javase/tutorial/uiswing/layout/card.html` and `http://docs.oracle.com/javase/tutorial/uiswing/layout/spring.html`.

Applying layout managers

To set the layout manager for a panel or frame, you use the `setLayout` method. Here's how you create a panel and set GridBag as its layout manager:

```
JPanel panel1 = new JPanel();
panel1.setLayout(new GridBagLayout());
```

If you want to use Flow layout with a panel or Border layout with a frame, you don't have to do anything; those are the defaults.

In many cases, the best approach to creating complex frame layouts is using a combination of layout managers. You might create a panel with buttons that appear at the bottom of the frame. This panel would use Flow layout. Then you can add the panel to the South region of the frame, which uses Border layout by default.

Using Flow Layout

Because Flow layout is the default layout manager for panels, you're already familiar with how it works. The components are laid out in a single row, if possible. If a component doesn't fit on the current row, a new row is started.

By itself, the Flow layout manager isn't very useful. You'll probably use it mostly for small panels that consist of a few components, such as a row of buttons that is then added to a larger panel that uses one of the other layout managers.

Table 5-1 lists the constructors of the `FlowLayout` class, which you can use to create a new Flow layout manager.

Table 5-1	FlowLayout Constructors
Constructor	*Description*
`FlowLayout()`	Creates a Flow layout manager with centered alignment and no gaps.
`FlowLayout(int align)`	Creates a Flow layout manager with the specified alignment. The align parameter can be `FlowLayout.LEFT`, `FlowLayout.CENTER`, or `FlowLayout.RIGHT`.
`FlowLayout(int align, int hgap, int vgap)`	Creates a Flow layout manager with the specified alignment. The `int` parameters specify the size (in pixels) of gaps that are inserted between elements to space things out a bit.

By default, the rows are centered. You can specify left alignment for a panel like this:

```
JPanel panel1 = new JPanel();
panel1.setLayout(new FlowLayout(FlowLayout.LEFT));
```

To specify right alignment, use this statement instead:

```
panel1.setLayout(new FlowLayout(FlowLayout.RIGHT));
```

You can also specify gaps that are inserted between components. Here's an example:

```
panel1.setLayout(
    new FlowLayout(FlowLayout.LEFT, 20, 15));
```

Here the horizontal gap is set to 20, and the vertical gap is set to 15. Figure 5-2 shows a panel containing six buttons created with these settings.

Figure 5-2:
Flow layout with left alignment and gaps.

Using Border Layout

The Border layout manager carves a frame or panel into five regions: North, South, East, West, and Center, as shown in Figure 5-3. When you add a component to the frame or panel, you can specify which of these regions the component goes in.

```
┌─────────────────────────────────────────────┐
│                    North                      │
├──────────┬──────────────────┬────────────────┤
│          │                  │                │
│          │                  │                │
│          │                  │                │
│   West   │     Center       │     East       │
│          │                  │                │
│          │                  │                │
├──────────┴──────────────────┴────────────────┤
│                    South                      │
└─────────────────────────────────────────────┘
```

Figure 5-3:
How Border
layout
carves
things up.

Border layout is the default for frames. To create a panel with Border layout, use one of the constructors of the `BorderLayout` class that's shown in Table 5-2, as in this example:

```
JPanel panel1 = new JPanel();
panel1.setLayout(new BorderLayout());
```

Table 5-2   **Border Layout Constructors and Fields**

Constructor	Description
`BorderLayout()`	Creates a Border layout manager with no gaps.
`BorderLayout(int hgap, int vgap)`	Creates a Border layout manager with the specified horizontal and vertical gaps.

Field	Description
`NORTH`	Defines the North region (at the top of the container).

(continued)

Table 5-2 *(continued)*

Field	Description
SOUTH	Defines the South region (at the bottom of the container).
WEST	Defines the West region (on the left side of the container).
EAST	Defines the East region (on the right side of the container).
CENTER	Defines the Center region (in the middle of the container).

When you add a component to a panel or frame that uses the Border layout manager, you can specify the region to place the component in by using one of the BorderLayout fields, as in this example:

```
panel1.add(new JLabel("Welcome!"), BorderLayout.NORTH);
```

Here the label is added to the North region.

Here are a few additional important points to know about Border layout:

+ If you don't specify the region when you add a component, the component is placed in the center.

+ When the Border layout manager determines the size of each region, it first determines the size for the regions on the edges: North, South, East, and West. Then it gives whatever space remains to the center.

+ The Border layout manager automatically resizes the components in each region to completely fill the region. If you don't want that to happen, place the components in separate panels that use Flow layout and then add those panels to the Border layout regions.

+ If you add two or more components to the same region of a Border layout panel or frame, the last one in wins the fight for space; the others aren't visible at all. To add more than one component to a region, first add the components to a panel and then add the panel to the Border layout region.

Using Box Layout

You can use the Box layout manager to create a panel containing a single row or column of components. If the components are arranged in a single row, the box is called a *horizontal box*. If the components are stacked in a column, the box is a *vertical box*.

Although you can apply the Box layout directly to a panel, it's much more common to use the Box class, which is similar to a panel but defaults to Box layout rather than to Flow layout. In addition, the Box class has several static methods that are useful for laying out components in the box. Table 5-3 lists some methods of this class. (I define glue and struts after the table.)

Table 5-3   **The Box and Dimension Classes**

Box Methods	Description
`static Component createGlue()`	Creates a glue component. This component forces the components on any side of it as far away from one another as possible.
`static Box createHorizontalBox()`	Creates a horizontal box.
`static Component createHorizontalGlue()`	Creates a horizontal glue component. This component forces the components on either side of it as far away from one another as possible.
`static Component createHorizontalStrut(int width)`	Creates a horizontal strut component that places the specified amount of space between the components on either side of it.
`static createRigidArea(Dimension d)`	Creates an area of a fixed size.
`static Box createVerticalBox()`	Creates a vertical box.
`static Component createVerticalGlue ()`	Creates a vertical glue component. This component forces the components above and below it as far away from one another as possible.
`static Component createVerticalStrut(int width)`	Creates a vertical strut component that places the specified amount of space between the components above and below it.
Dimension Constructor	**Description**
`Dimension(int width, int height)`	Creates a new `Dimension` object with the specified width and height.

Here's an example that creates a horizontal box and adds three buttons to it:

```
Box box1 = Box.createHorizontalBox();
box1.add(new JButton("Accept"));
```

```
box1.add(new JButton("Cancel"));
box1.add(new JButton("Close"));
```

The real power of Box layouts is their use of struts, rigid areas, and glue:

+ **Struts:** A *strut* inserts a specified amount of space between components. You can create a strut by calling the `createHorizontalStrut` or `createVerticalStrut` method, depending on which type of strut you want to create.

  Suppose that you want the three buttons in the preceding example to be separated by 20 pixels, and you want 20 pixels of blank space on either end of the box as well. This code does the trick:

  ```
  Box box1 = Box.createHorizontalBox();

  box1.add(Box.createHorizontalStrut(20));
  box1.add(new JButton("Accept"));
  box1.add(Box.createHorizontalStrut(20));
  box1.add(new JButton("Cancel"));
  box1.add(Box.createHorizontalStrut(20));
  box1.add(new JButton("Close"));
  box1.add(Box.createHorizontalStrut(20));
  ```

+ **Rigid areas:** A *rigid area* is like a strut, but it spaces things out both horizontally and vertically, as in this example:

  ```
  box1.add(new JButton("Accept"));
  box1.add(Box.createRigidArea(new Dimension(20, 40)));
  box1.add(new JButton("Cancel"));
  ```

  Here I use a rigid area that's 20 by 40 pixels to separate the Accept button from the Cancel button. A side effect of this rigid area is that it increases the height of the box itself to 40 pixels. Empty space is left above and below the buttons.

+ **Glue:** *Glue* is similar to a strut, but it pushes components as far away from one another as possible within the bounds of the box itself. This code uses glue to move the third button as far away from the first two buttons as possible, based on the width of the box:

  ```
  Box box1 = Box.createHorizontalBox();

  box1.add(Box.createHorizontalStrut(20));
  box1.add(new JButton("Accept"));
  box1.add(Box.createRigidArea(new Dimension(20, 40)));
  box1.add(new JButton("Cancel"));

  box1.add(Box.createHorizontalGlue());
  box1.add(new JButton("Close"));
  box1.add(Box.createHorizontalStrut(20));
  ```

If you add this Box layout to the South region of a frame, the buttons appear as shown in Figure 5-4.

Figure 5-4:
Using Box
layout to
arrange
buttons.

Using Grid Layout

The Grid layout is designed for panels that need to have a set number of components all equally sized and arranged in a grid. You probably won't use Grid layout much, but if you need to create something that looks like a calculator or a phone, this layout manager is the one you need.

Table 5-4 lists the constructors of the GridLayout class, which you use to create a grid layout.

Table 5-4	GridLayout Constructors
Constructor	*Description*
GridLayout()	Creates a grid layout that arranges components in a single row. This construction is equivalent to GridLayout(1, 0).
GridLayout(int rows, int columns)	Creates a grid layout with the specified number of rows and columns. If one of the parameters is 0, the grid expands to fill as many rows or columns as necessary. (You can't specify 0 for both parameters.)
GridLayout(int rows, int columns, int hgap, int vgap)	Creates a grid layout with the specified number of rows and columns with gaps of the specified size between the rows and columns.

To create a panel with Grid layout, you call the GridLayout constructor to specify the size of the grid. One of the parameters can be 0 to allow the grid to expand to however many rows or columns are necessary to hold all the components you add to the panel.

The following code creates a Grid layout panel that resembles a phone (shown in Figure 5-1 earlier in this chapter):

```
JPanel panel1 = new JPanel();
panel1.setLayout(new GridLayout(0,3));

panel1.add(new JButton("7"));
panel1.add(new JButton("8"));
panel1.add(new JButton("9"));
panel1.add(new JButton("4"));
panel1.add(new JButton("5"));
panel1.add(new JButton("6"));
panel1.add(new JButton("1"));
panel1.add(new JButton("2"));
panel1.add(new JButton("3"));
panel1.add(new JButton("*"));
panel1.add(new JButton("0"));
panel1.add(new JButton("#"));
```

As you add components to a panel with Grid layout, the components are dropped into the grid's cells row by row, working across each row from left to right. As each row is filled, a new row is started.

Using GridBag Layout

The GridBag layout manager is the one you'll probably use most to lay out complicated panels. Like the Grid layout manager, GridBag lets you carve a panel into a grid, but the grid has the following special features:

✦ The rows and columns don't have to be the same size. Instead, GridBag automatically adjusts the width of each column and the height of each row based on the components you add to the panel.

✦ You can specify which cell you want each component to go in, and you can control each component's position in the panel.

✦ You can create components that span multiple rows or columns, such as a button two columns wide or a list box four rows high.

✦ You can tell GridBag to stretch a component to fill the entire space allotted to it if the component isn't already big enough to fill the entire area. You can specify that this stretching be done horizontally, vertically, or both.

✦ If a component doesn't fill its allotted area, you can tell the GridBag layout manager how you want the component to be positioned within the area — for example, left- or right-aligned.

The following sections describe the ins and outs of working with GridBag layouts.

Sketching out a plan

Before you create a GridBag panel, you should draw a sketch showing how you want the components to appear in the panel. Then slice the panel into rows and columns, and number the rows and columns starting with zero in the top-left corner. Figure 5-5 shows such a sketch, prepared in my own hand.

Figure 5-5: Sketching out a panel.

After you have the panel sketched out, list the components, their *x* and *y* coordinates on the grid, and their alignment, as well as whether each component spans more than one row or column. Here's an example:

Component	x	y	Alignment	Spans
Label "Name"	0	0	Right	
Label "Phone"	0	1	Right	
Label "Address"	0	2	Right	
Name text field	1	0	Left	2
Phone text field	1	1	Left	
Address text field	1	2	Left	
Size box	0	3	Left	
Style box	1	3	Left	
Toppings box	2	3	Left	
Button box	2	4	Right	

After you lay out the grid, you can write the code to put each component in its proper place.

Adding components to a GridBag layout

Before you can add components to a panel using GridBag layout, you must specify GridBag as the panel's layout manager. You do that by calling the `setLayout` method, passing a new `GridBagLayout` object as a parameter, as follows:

```
JPanel panel1 = new JPanel();
panel1.setLayout(new GridBagLayout());
```

When a panel uses the GridBag layout, the `add` method accepts two parameters: the component to add and a `GridBagConstraints` object that specifies where to place the component in the grid. The trick of using GridBag layout is figuring out how to set the `GridBagConstraints` values to get each component to go where you want it to go. Table 5-5 lists the fields of the `GridBagConstraints` class.

Table 5-5	The GridBagConstraints Class
Field	*Description*
`int gridx`	The *x* position of the component.
`int gridy`	The *y* position of the component.
`int gridwidth`	The number of columns spanned by the component. The default is `1`.
`int gridheight`	The number of rows spanned by the component. The default is `1`.
`double weightx`	A value that gives the grid layout a hint on how to apportion space for the component's width.
`double weighty`	A value that gives the grid layout a hint on how to apportion space for the component's height.
`Insets insets`	An `Insets` object that indicates how much space to use as padding around each component. The `Insets` class has a simple constructor: `Insets(int top, int left, int bottom, int right)`.
`int anchor`	A constant that indicates where to place the component if it doesn't fill the space. Values can be any of the following fields of the `GridBagConstraints` class: CENTER, NORTH, NORTHEAST, EAST, SOUTHEAST, SOUTH, SOUTHWEST, WEST, and NORTHWEST.
`int fill`	A constant that indicates whether to stretch the object to fill available space. Values can be any of the following fields of the `GridBagConstraints` class: NONE, HORIZONTAL, VERTICAL, or BOTH.

A few of these fields need some extra explanation:

✦ The `weightx` and `weighty` fields give the GridBag layout manager a hint about how to adjust the size of the columns and rows. If you set one of these values to 0, the size of the row or column remains fixed. A common technique is to set both of these parameters to 100 and then adjust them if you think the layout could benefit from some tweaking.

✦ The `insets` field lets you provide some padding around components. You set this field to an `Insets` object. Assuming that the `GridBag Constraints` object is named `gc`, this statement provides 5 pixels of space on each side of the component and sets the `insets` field like this:

```
gc.insets = new Insets(5, 5, 5, 5);
```

✦ By default, components are stretched to fill the cells of the grid. This effect is rarely what you want, so you usually want to set the fill field to change it.

✦ You also want to set the `anchor` field to indicate where you want the component to be placed if it doesn't fill the cell or cells allotted to it.

Working with GridBagConstraint constructors

To create a `GridBagConstraint` object, you call the `GridBagConstraint` constructor and then set any of the fields that you want to vary from the default values. Here's code that creates a `GridBagConstraint` object to add the Name text field shown in Figure 5-5 earlier in this chapter:

```
GridBagConstraints nameConstraints
    = new GridBagConstraints();
nameConstraints.gridx = 1;
nameConstraints.gridy = 0;
nameConstraints.gridwidth = 2;
nameConstraints.gridheight = 1;
nameConstraints.weightx = 100.0;
nameConstraints.weighty = 100.0;
nameConstraints.insets = new Insets(5, 5, 5, 5);
nameConstraints.anchor = GridBagConstraints.WEST;
nameConstraints.fill = GridBagConstraints.NONE;
```

Then you can call the `add` method to add the Name text field to the panel, as follows:

```
panel1.add(name, nameConstraints);
```

Obviously, this approach to controlling constraints is going to require a lot of coding. You have two common alternatives for creating a new constraint object for every component you add to the panel, as I explain in the following sections.

Method 1: Recycle a constraint object

The first method is to create a single constraint object and reuse it for all the components in the panel. Then you simply change the fields that need to be changed for each component. Here's code that adds all three text fields by using a single constraint object:

```
GridBagConstraints gc = new GridBagConstraints();
gc.gridx = 0;
gc.gridy = 0;
gc.gridwidth = 1;
gc.gridheight = 1;
gc.weightx = 100.0;
gc.weighty = 100.0;
gc.insets = new Insets(5, 5, 5, 5);
gc.anchor = GridBagConstraints.WEST;
gc.fill = GridBagConstraints.NONE;

gc.gridy = 0;
gc.gridwidth = 2;
add(name, gc);
gc.gridy = 1;
gc.gridwidth = 1;
add(phone, gc);
gc.gridy = 2;
gc.gridwidth = 2;
add(address, gc);
```

Here the first group of statements creates a `GridBagConstraints` object named `gc` and sets its values to the defaults that I want to apply to most of the components in the panel. Then the second group of statements sets the `gridy` and `gridwidth` fields before adding each text field to the panel.

Method 2: Use a helper

The second option is to create a *helper method* that you can call, passing just the values that vary for each component. Here's a method named `addItem` that adds a component and left-aligns it within the specified cells:

```
private void addItem(JPanel p, JComponent c, int x,
    int y, int width, int height, int align)
{
    GridBagConstraints gc = new GridBagConstraints();
    gc.gridx = x;
    gc.gridy = y;
    gc.gridwidth = width;
    gc.gridheight = height;
    gc.weightx = 100.0;
    gc.weighty = 100.0;
    gc.insets = new Insets(5, 5, 5, 5);
    gc.anchor = align;
    gc.fill = GridBagConstraints.NONE;
    p.add(c, gc);
}
```

Then you can call this method to add a component to the panel. You must pass the panel and the component, its *x* and *y* positions, and its width and height. Here's how you add the Name text field:

```
addItem(panel1, name, 0, 1, 2, 1,
    GridBagConstraints.WEST);
```

Viewing a GridBag layout example

Listing 5-1 shows the code for a program that displays the frame I drew for Figure 5-5, and Figure 5-6 shows how this frame appears when the program is run. As you can see, the final appearance of this frame is pretty close to the way I sketched it. I could probably fix a few minor variations with a little tweaking.

Figure 5-6:
The Pizza
Order appli-
cation in
action.

Listing 5-1:   The Pizza Order Application

```java
import javax.swing.*;
import java.awt.event.*;
import java.awt.*;

public class Pizza extends JFrame
{
    public static void main(String [] args)
    {
        new Pizza();
    }

    JTextField name, phone, address;
    JRadioButton small, medium, large, thick, thin;
    JCheckBox pepperoni, mushrooms, anchovies;
    JButton okButton, closeButton;

    public Pizza()
    {
        this.setTitle("Pizza Order");
        this.setDefaultCloseOperation(
            JFrame.EXIT_ON_CLOSE);
```

(continued)

Listing 5-1 *(continued)*

```
JPanel panel1 = new JPanel();
panel1.setLayout(new GridBagLayout());                    →23

addItem(panel1, new JLabel("Name:"),                      →25
    0, 0, 1, 1, GridBagConstraints.EAST);
addItem(panel1, new JLabel("Phone:"),
    0, 1, 1, 1, GridBagConstraints.EAST);
addItem(panel1, new JLabel("Address:"),
    0, 2, 1, 1, GridBagConstraints.EAST);

name = new JTextField(20);
phone = new JTextField(10);
address = new JTextField(20);

addItem(panel1, name, 1, 0, 2, 1,                         →36
    GridBagConstraints.WEST);
addItem(panel1, phone, 1, 1, 1, 1,
    GridBagConstraints.WEST);
addItem(panel1, address, 1, 2, 2, 1,
    GridBagConstraints.WEST);

Box sizeBox = Box.createVerticalBox();                    →43
small = new JRadioButton("Small");
medium = new JRadioButton("Medium");
large = new JRadioButton("Large");
ButtonGroup sizeGroup = new ButtonGroup();
sizeGroup.add(small);
sizeGroup.add(medium);
sizeGroup.add(large);
sizeBox.add(small);
sizeBox.add(medium);
sizeBox.add(large);
sizeBox.setBorder(
BorderFactory.createTitledBorder("Size"));
addItem(panel1, sizeBox, 0, 3, 1, 1,
    GridBagConstraints.NORTH);

Box styleBox = Box.createVerticalBox();                   →59
thin = new JRadioButton("Thin");
thick = new JRadioButton("Thick");
ButtonGroup styleGroup = new ButtonGroup();
styleGroup.add(thin);
styleGroup.add(thick);
styleBox.add(thin);
styleBox.add(thick);
styleBox.setBorder(BorderFactory.
    createTitledBorder("Style"));
addItem(panel1, styleBox, 1, 3, 1, 1,
    GridBagConstraints.NORTH);
```

```
        Box topBox = Box.createVerticalBox();                    →72
        pepperoni = new JCheckBox("Pepperoni");
        mushrooms = new JCheckBox("Mushrooms");
        anchovies = new JCheckBox("Anchovies");
        topBox.add(pepperoni);
        topBox.add(mushrooms);
        topBox.add(anchovies);
        topBox.setBorder(BorderFactory.
            createTitledBorder("Toppings"));
        addItem(panel1, topBox, 2, 3, 1, 1,
            GridBagConstraints.NORTH);

        Box buttonBox = Box.createHorizontalBox();               →84
        okButton = new JButton("OK");
        closeButton = new JButton("Close");
        buttonBox.add(okButton);
        buttonBox.add(Box.createHorizontalStrut(20));
        buttonBox.add(closeButton);
        addItem(panel1, buttonBox, 2, 4, 1, 1,
            GridBagConstraints.NORTH);

        this.add(panel1);
        this.pack();
        this.setVisible(true);
    }

    private void addItem(JPanel p, JComponent c,
        int x, int y, int width, int height,
        int align)
    {
        GridBagConstraints gc =
            new GridBagConstraints();
        gc.gridx = x;
        gc.gridy = y;
        gc.gridwidth = width;
        gc.gridheight = height;
        gc.weightx = 100.0;
        gc.weighty = 100.0;
        gc.insets = new Insets(5, 5, 5, 5);
        gc.anchor = align;
        gc.fill = GridBagConstraints.NONE;
        p.add(c, gc);
    }
}
```

Book VI
Chapter 5

Using Layout
Managers

The following paragraphs point out the highlights:

→ **23**   This line creates a GridBag layout manager for the panel.

→ **25**   These lines add the labels to the panel.

→ **36**   These lines add the text fields to the panel.

→ 43   These lines use a vertical `Box` object to create the radio buttons that let the user select the size.

→ 59   These lines use a vertical `Box` object to create the radio buttons that let the user select the crust style.

→ 72   These lines use a vertical `Box` object to create the check boxes that let the user select toppings.

→ 84   These lines use a horizontal `Box` object to hold the OK and Close buttons.

Note: This application doesn't include any event listeners, so the buttons don't do anything other than demonstrate how to use the GridBag layout.

Using Group Layout

Java 1.6 introduced a new Group layout manager. Group layout is most useful when you use it as part of a *visual editor* — an integrated development environment (IDE) in which you draw new buttons, text fields, and other components with your mouse. But this layout is also good for plain old code-writing.

The thing to remember about Group layout is that the layout describes an arrangement of components from two directions: left to right and from top to bottom. Imagine an ant crawling along a page. The page contains the five buttons shown in Figure 5-7. As the ant crawls from left to right, the ant sees three things:

✦ A button containing the letter *D*

✦ A column of three buttons (a group)

✦ A button containing the letter *Y*

Figure 5-7:
An arrangement of buttons created in Group layout.

The ant sees these three things one after another, so these items form a *sequential group.* In the middle of its journey, however, the ant sees the column of three buttons (R, O, and T) at the same time, so this column of three buttons is called a *parallel group.*

The ant encounters a parallel group within a sequential group. The code to describe the groups looks like this:

```
GroupLayout.SequentialGroup leftToRight =
         layout.createSequentialGroup();
   leftToRight.addComponent(buttonD);
   GroupLayout.ParallelGroup columnMiddle =
         layout.createParallelGroup();
      columnMiddle.addComponent(buttonR);
      columnMiddle.addComponent(buttonO);
      columnMiddle.addComponent(buttonT);
   leftToRight.addGroup(columnMiddle);
   leftToRight.addComponent(buttonY);
```

The code's indentation is highly irregular; I indent this way to help you see the group-within-group outline. Maybe the strange indentation helps; maybe it doesn't. You can indent the code any way you want. One way or another, the code describes a parallel group (the middle column of buttons) within a sequential group (the D button, the middle column, and the Y button).

To fully describe a Group layout, you need a second ant crawling from the top of Figure 5-7 downward. As the ant crawls downward, it sees the following things:

✦ A row of three buttons (a group)

✦ A button containing the letter *O*

✦ A button containing the letter *T*

The ant sees these three things one after another, so these three things form a sequential group. But at the start of its journey, the ant sees the row of three buttons (D, R, and Y) all at the same time, so this row of three buttons is a parallel group.

This downward-moving ant encounters a parallel group within a sequential group. The code to describe the groups looks like this:

```
GroupLayout.SequentialGroup topToBottom =
         layout.createSequentialGroup();
   GroupLayout.ParallelGroup rowTop =
         layout.createParallelGroup();
      rowTop.addComponent(buttonD);
      rowTop.addComponent(buttonR);
      rowTop.addComponent(buttonY);
   topToBottom.addGroup(rowTop);
   topToBottom.addComponent(buttonO);
   topToBottom.addComponent(buttonT);
```

When you put everything together, you get the code in Listing 5-2.

Listing 5-2:   A Frame with a Group Layout

```
import javax.swing.GroupLayout;
import javax.swing.JButton;
import javax.swing.JFrame;
import javax.swing.JPanel;

public class UseGroupLayout3
{

    public static void main(String[] args)
    {
        JFrame frame = new JFrame();
        JPanel panel = new JPanel();
        frame.setDefaultCloseOperation
            (JFrame.EXIT_ON_CLOSE);
        GroupLayout layout = new GroupLayout(panel);
        panel.setLayout(layout);

        JButton buttonD = new JButton("D");
        JButton buttonR = new JButton("R");
        JButton buttonY = new JButton("Y");
        JButton buttonO = new JButton("O");
        JButton buttonT = new JButton("T");

        GroupLayout.SequentialGroup leftToRight =
                layout.createSequentialGroup();
            leftToRight.addComponent(buttonD);
            GroupLayout.ParallelGroup columnMiddle =
                layout.createParallelGroup();
            columnMiddle.addComponent(buttonR);
            columnMiddle.addComponent(buttonO);
            columnMiddle.addComponent(buttonT);
            leftToRight.addGroup(columnMiddle);
            leftToRight.addComponent(buttonY);

        GroupLayout.SequentialGroup topToBottom =
                layout.createSequentialGroup();
            GroupLayout.ParallelGroup rowTop =
                layout.createParallelGroup();
            rowTop.addComponent(buttonD);
            rowTop.addComponent(buttonR);
            rowTop.addComponent(buttonY);
            topToBottom.addGroup(rowTop);
            topToBottom.addComponent(buttonO);
            topToBottom.addComponent(buttonT);

        layout.setHorizontalGroup(leftToRight);
        layout.setVerticalGroup(topToBottom);

        frame.add(panel);
        frame.pack();
        frame.setVisible(true);
    }
}
```

A reader from Minnesota asks: "What happens if you change the code in Listing 5-2? What if you modify one of the ants' descriptions so that the two descriptions don't agree?" The answer is: Nothing good happens. Yes, the two ants' descriptions seem to be redundant; but no, you can't eliminate one of the descriptions or make the descriptions inconsistent. If you do, your program exits prematurely with a nasty error message.

At first glance, Group layout seems to be quite complex. As with many programming techniques, Group layout makes some simple things difficult — but it also makes some complicated things easy. Check out some web-based tutorials on Group layout. When you learn more about it, you'll understand this layout's true power.

Book VII

Web Programming

You can find an interesting programming challenge that requires use of many of the programming techniques covered in this minibook at www.dummies.com/extras/javaaio. The challenge for this book is to enhance the Swing version of the Tic-Tac-Toe program created for previously so that it runs as an applet.

Contents at a Glance

Chapter 1: Creating Applets

A n *applet* is not a small piece of fruit. Rather, it's a Java application that's designed to run in a browser window on an Internet user's computer. When an Internet user visits a web page that contains an applet, the Java applet class is downloaded to the user's computer and run there. The applet takes over a portion of the page and, within that space, can do anything it wants.

Applets are Swing applications — at least, in most cases. As a result, everything that's covered in Book VI applies to applets.

In this chapter, you create applets that include Swing components. Then you add an applet to a web page so that anyone who views the page can use it.

Understanding Applets

An applet is similar to a Swing application, with several crucial differences:

✦ Instead of extending the `JFrame` class, applets extend the `JApplet` class. Both `JFrame` and `JApplet` provide a space for your Swing application to operate in:

- With `JFrame`, that space is a window that's managed by the host operating system's windowing system.

- With `JApplet`, the space is a rectangular area of a web page that's managed by a web browser.

✦ Standalone Swing applications are started when the Java Virtual Machine (JVM) calls the static `main` method. Thus a Swing application typically starts by creating an instance of the class that extends `JFrame`. By contrast, the browser automatically creates an instance of the class that extends `JApplet` when the applet is started, so applets don't have a static `main` method. Instead, a method named `init` is called to get the applet started. As a result, the `init` method is where you put the code that you'd put in the constructor for a class that extends `JFrame`.

✦ Standalone Swing methods need a way to let the user shut them down. Typically, Swing applications include an Exit button or an Exit menu command; applets don't. An applet remains alive as long as the page that contains it is displayed.

✦ Applets aren't displayed in windows; they're displayed in a region of a web page. As a result, you can't set the text for an applet's title bar, and you can't set the `DefaultCloseOperation`, because there's no Close button for the user to click. In addition, the user can't resize the applet.

✦ For security reasons, applets are prohibited from doing certain things. In particular, an applet is not allowed to do anything that affects the client computer's file system, including reading or writing files or running programs on the client computer.

Other than these differences and restrictions, an applet works pretty much the same way as a Swing application. In fact, the Swing components inside the applet look and behave *exactly* like they do in a stand-alone Swing application. Thus applets let you create Swing applications and run them on any computer anywhere in the world. Right?

Would that it were so. Unfortunately, the company that makes the world's most popular web browser, whose name I won't mention but whose initials are MICROSOFT, hasn't always played nice with Oracle. Or maybe Oracle hasn't always played nice with Microsoft. Who knows? Either way, the result has been a mess when it comes to whether users' computers can run applets — and, if they can, what version of Java they support. Users can download the Java plug-in from Oracle, but many users either don't want to take the time, don't understand the process, or don't trust it. (The main Java plug-in download site is `www.java.com`; when you get there, click the Free Java Download button to download the Java plugin.)

As a result, applets aren't the best way to create web-based applications that you expect to be used by the masses. The biggest sites on the Internet, such as eBay and Amazon, are *not* implemented with applets; instead, they're built with tools such as servlets and Java Server Pages, as described in the other chapters of Book VII. JavaBeans are covered at `www.dummies.com/extras/javaaio`.

Working with the JApplet Class

As I've already mentioned, an applet extends the `JApplet` class rather than the `JFrame` class. For the most part, the `JApplet` class works pretty much the same way as the `JFrame` class. As a result, you can add panels and other components to it, create menus, doodle on it, and so on. Table 1-1 lists the most commonly used methods of the `JApplet` class.

Table 1-1 **Useful JApplet Constructors and Methods**

Constructor	Description
JApplet()	Creates a new applet. You usually don't need to call the JApplet constructor because it's called automatically when the browser loads the applet.

Method	Description
void add(Component c)	Adds the specified component to the applet.
void destroy()	When called by the browser, informs the applet that its memory is about to be reclaimed by the JVM. Most applets don't need to override this method.
void init()	When called by the browser, informs the applet that it has been loaded. This method takes the place of the JFrame constructor for a Swing application.
void setLayout(LayoutManager layout)	Sets the layout manager used to control how components are arranged when the applet is displayed. The default is the Border Layout manager.
void setLocation(int x, int y)	Sets the x and y positions of the applet onscreen. The top-left corner of the screen is 0, 0.
void setLocationRelativeTo (Component c)	Centers the applet onscreen if the parameter is null.
void setSize(int width, int height)	Sets the size of the applet to the specified width and height.
void setJMenuBar (JMenuBar menu)	Sets the menu for this applet.
void start()	When called by the browser, informs the applet to start its execution.
void stop()	When the applet is hidden, the browser calls this method. Override this method if you need to stop activities while the applet is hidden.

**Book VII
Chapter 1**

Creating Applets

Looking at a Sample Applet

To see how a complete applet works, Listing 1-1 shows the complete code for an applet that lets the user order a pizza in one of three sizes (Small, Medium, and Large) with one of three toppings (Pepperoni, Mushrooms, and Anchovies). Figure 1-1 shows this applet in action on a web page.

Listing 1-1:   The Pizza Order Applet

```
import javax.swing.*;
import java.awt.event.*;
import javax.swing.border.*;

public class PizzaApplet extends JApplet                    →5
{
    private JButton buttonOK;
    private JRadioButton small, medium, large;

    private JCheckBox pepperoni, mushrooms, anchovies;

    public void init()                                      →12
    {
        this.setSize(320,200);                              →14
        JPanel mainPanel = new JPanel();

        JPanel sizePanel = new JPanel();
        Border b1 = BorderFactory.
            createTitledBorder("Size");
        sizePanel.setBorder(b1);

        ButtonGroup sizeGroup = new ButtonGroup();
        small = new JRadioButton("Small");
        small.setSelected(true);
        sizePanel.add(small);
        sizeGroup.add(small);

        medium = new JRadioButton("Medium");
        sizePanel.add(medium);
        sizeGroup.add(medium);

        large = new JRadioButton("Large");
        sizePanel.add(large);
        sizeGroup.add(large);

        mainPanel.add(sizePanel);

        JPanel topPanel = new JPanel();
        Border b2 = BorderFactory.
            createTitledBorder("Toppings");
        topPanel.setBorder(b2);
```

```
        pepperoni = new JCheckBox("Pepperoni");
        topPanel.add(pepperoni);

        mushrooms = new JCheckBox("Mushrooms");
        topPanel.add(mushrooms);

        anchovies = new JCheckBox("Anchovies");
        topPanel.add(anchovies);

        mainPanel.add(topPanel);

        buttonOK = new JButton("OK");
        buttonOK.addActionListener(e -> buttonOKClick() );
        mainPanel.add(buttonOK);

        this.add(mainPanel);

        this.setVisible(true);
    }

    public void buttonOKClick()
    {
        String tops = "";
        if (pepperoni.isSelected())
            tops += "Pepperoni\n";
        if (mushrooms.isSelected())
            tops += "Mushrooms\n";
        if (anchovies.isSelected())
            tops += "Anchovies\n";

        String msg = "You ordered a ";
        if (small.isSelected())
            msg += "small pizza with ";
        if (medium.isSelected())
            msg += "medium pizza with ";
        if (large.isSelected())
            msg += "large pizza with ";
        if (tops.equals(""))
            msg += "no toppings.";
        else
            msg += "the following toppings:\n" + tops;
        JOptionPane.showMessageDialog(buttonOK,
            msg, "Your Order",
            JOptionPane.INFORMATION_MESSAGE);

        pepperoni.setSelected(false);
        mushrooms.setSelected(false);
        anchovies.setSelected(false);
        small.setSelected(true);
    }
}
```

Figure 1-1:
The pizza applet in action.

This listing is an applet version of a Swing program presented in Book VI, Chapter 3. For the details on how the Swing components work, you can refer to that chapter. Here I just want to point out a few details that are specific to applets:

→ 5   The class extends `JApplet` instead of `JFrame`.

→ 12   The `init` method is overridden, and the code that ordinarily is in the constructor for the `JFrame` class is placed in the `init` method.

→ 14   The `setSize` method is called to set the size of the applet. Several methods that appeared in the Swing version of this program, however, are removed. In particular, the `setTitle` and `setDefaultCloseAction` methods are deleted because those methods don't apply to applets. From the rest of this method, however, you can see that most of this code is exactly the same as it is for a standalone Swing application.

Creating an HTML Page for an Applet

To run an applet, you must create an HTML page that includes an `APPLET` tag specifying the name of the applet and the size of the region you want to let the applet run inside. The `APPLET` tag also includes text that's displayed if the web browser isn't capable of running the applet.

The basic form of the `APPLET` tag is this:

```
<APPLET code="classname" width=width height=height>
    Text to display if applet can't be loaded
</APPLET>
```

Here's the HTML file that I used to display the page shown in Figure 1-1, earlier in this chapter:

```
<html>
  <head>
    <title>The Pizza Applet</title>
  </head>
  <body>
    <APPLET code="PizzaApplet" width="300" height="180">
    Sorry, your browser isn't able to run Java applets.
    </APPLET>
  </body>
</html>
```

Testing an Applet

Java comes with a special program called the *applet viewer* that lets you run an applet quickly after you compile it. Figure 1-2 shows the pizza applet displayed in the applet viewer.

Book VII Chapter 1

Creating Applets

Figure 1-2: The pizza applet displayed in the applet viewer.

If you're using TextPad, you can invoke the viewer by pressing Ctrl+3 after you compile the applet. From a command prompt, you must first create an HTML file, as described in the preceding section. Then navigate to the directory that contains the HTML file, and type this command:

```
appletviewer filename
```

To display the pizza applet with an HTML file named `PizzaApplet.html`, use this command:

```
appletviewer PizzaApplet.html
```

Chapter 2: Creating Servlets

In This Chapter

✔ Looking at servlets

✔ Downloading, installing, and configuring Tomcat

✔ Creating simple servlets

✔ Working with forms to get data from the user

Servlets are among the most popular ways to develop web applications today. Many of the best-known websites are powered by servlets, including Gmail, Amazon, Linkedin, and eBay. In this chapter, I give you just the basics: what a servlet is, how to set up your computer so that you can code and test servlets, and how to create a simple servlet. The next two chapters build on this topic, presenting additional web programming techniques.

Understanding Servlets

Before you can understand what a servlet is and how it works, you need to understand the basics of how web servers work. Web servers use a networking protocol called HTTP to send web pages to users. (*HTTP* stands for *Hypertext Transfer Protocol,* but that won't be on the test.) With HTTP, a client computer uses a uniform resource locator, or URL, to request a document that's located on the server computer. HTTP uses a *request/response model,* which means that client computers (web users) send request messages to HTTP servers, which in turn send response messages back to the clients.

A basic HTTP interaction works something like this:

1. Using a web-browser program running on a client computer, you specify the URL of a file that you want to access.

    In some cases, you actually type the URL of the address, but most of the time you click a link that specifies the URL.

2. Your web browser sends an HTTP request message to the server computer indicated by the URL.

    The request includes the name of the file that you want to retrieve.

3. The server computer receives the file request, retrieves the requested file, and sends the file back to you in the form of an HTTP response message.

4. The web browser receives the file, interprets the HTML that it contains, and displays the result onscreen.

The most important thing to note about normal web interactions is that they're static. By *static,* I mean that the content of the file sent to the user is always the same. If the user requests the same file 20 times in a row, the same page displays 20 times.

By contrast, a servlet provides a way for the content to be dynamic. A *servlet* is simply a Java program that extends the `javax.servlet.Servlet` class. The `Servlet` class enables the program to run on a web server in response to a user request, and output from the servlet is sent back to the web user as an HTML page.

When you use servlets, Steps 1, 2, and 4 of the preceding procedure are the same; the fateful third step is what sets servlets apart. If the URL specified by the user refers to a servlet rather than a file, Step 3 goes more like this:

3. The server computer receives the servlet request, locates the Java program indicated by the request, runs it, and returns the output from the program in the form of an HTTP response message.

In other words, instead of sending the contents of a file, the server sends the output generated by the servlet program. Typically, the servlet program generates some HTML that's displayed by the browser.

Servlets are designed to get their work done quickly and then end. Each time a servlet runs, it processes one request from a browser, generates one page that's sent back to the browser, and then ends. The next time that user or any other user requests the same servlet, the servlet runs again.

Using Tomcat

Unfortunately, you can't run servlet programs on any old computer. First, you have to install a special program called a *servlet engine* to turn your computer into a server that's capable of running servlets. The best-known servlet engine is Apache Tomcat, which is available free from the Apache Software Foundation at `http://tomcat.apache.org`. For this chapter, I used the early-release Tomcat version 8.

Tomcat can also work as a basic web server. In actual production environments, Tomcat is usually used in combination with a specialized web server, such as Apache's HTTP Server.

Installing and configuring Tomcat

Installing Tomcat isn't rocket science, but it's not as easy as making toast, either. Here are the steps you can follow to set up Tomcat 8:

1. **Download the Tomcat Zip file from the Apache website** (`http://tomcat.apache.org`).

Although Apache also offers an executable setup file for installing Tomcat, I suggest that you download the Zip file instead.

2. **Extract the contents of the Zip file by right-clicking the file and choosing Extract All; then specify `c:\` as the location to extract the files to.**

I know you don't want to clutter your root directory with a bunch of files, but the Tomcat Zip file contains a single folder named `apache-tomcat-8_0_0` (the version number may vary), so only this one folder is created. After all the files are extracted, give this folder a new name that's a little easier to type. I suggest `c:\tomcat`.

3. **Create an environment variable named `JAVA_HOME` that points to the location of your Java Development Kit (JDK).**

To create an environment variable, open Control Panel, double-click the System icon, and then click Advanced System Settings⇨Environment Variables⇨New, and create a variable named JAVA_HOME. The value of this variable needs to be the complete path to your JDK installation folder, such as `c:\Program Files\Java\jdk1.8.0`.

A common mistake is to set this variable to the `bin` directory or to the directory for the Java Runtime Environment (JRE), not the JDK. If Tomcat doesn't start up later, double-check the JAVA_HOME directory.

4. **Copy the `servlet-api.jar` file to the `jre\lib\ext` folder in your JDK root.**

If your JDK is installed in `c:\Program Files\Java\jdk1.8.0`, copy this file to `c:\Program Files\Java\jdk1.8.0\jre\lib\ext`. You find the `servlet-api.jar` file in `c:\tomcat\lib`, assuming that you extracted the Tomcat files to `c:\tomcat`.

If you skip this step or copy the `servlet-api.jar` file to the wrong place, you can't compile your servlet programs. If you get compiler messages complaining that the `javax.servlet` package doesn't exist, double-check this step to make sure you performed it right.

Starting and stopping Tomcat

After you install and configure Tomcat, you can start it by opening a command window, changing to the `c:\tomcat\bin` directory, and typing **startup**. A batch file runs, starting Tomcat. When Tomcat starts, it opens a second command window that displays various status messages. Figure 2-1 shows the status window in action.

Figure 2-1:
Starting
Tomcat.

You know that Tomcat has started when you see a line such as the following,
indicating how long the startup took:

```
INFO: Server startup in 1186 ms
```

If the Tomcat window appears for a few seconds, and then an exception
message flies by quickly and the window closes, the most likely problem is
that you already have a web server running on your system, and that
server has already laid claim to the port Tomcat wants to use for HTTP
communication. The solution to that problem is to edit the `server.xml`
file in `c:\tomcat\conf` and look for this tag:

```
<Connector port="8080"... />
```

Change the port number from 8080 to some other number, such as 18080.
Later, when you display servlets in a browser window, you have to specify
this number as the HTTP port number instead of 8080.

You don't need to shut down Tomcat after you start it unless you make a
change in one of its configuration files. If you do, you can shut down Tomcat
by running the `shutdown` batch file from the `c:\tomcat\bin` directory.
Then you can run the `startup` batch file to get Tomcat going again.

Testing Tomcat

To find out whether you installed Tomcat correctly, you can try running the
test servlets that are automatically installed when you install Tomcat. Open
a web-browser window, and type this address:

```
http://localhost:8080
```

(If you changed the port number by editing the `server.xml` file, as I discuss
in the preceding section, use the port number you specified instead of 8080.)

The page shown in Figure 2-2 appears. If it doesn't, refer to the section "Installing and configuring Tomcat," earlier in this chapter, and double-check each step to make sure you did it correctly.

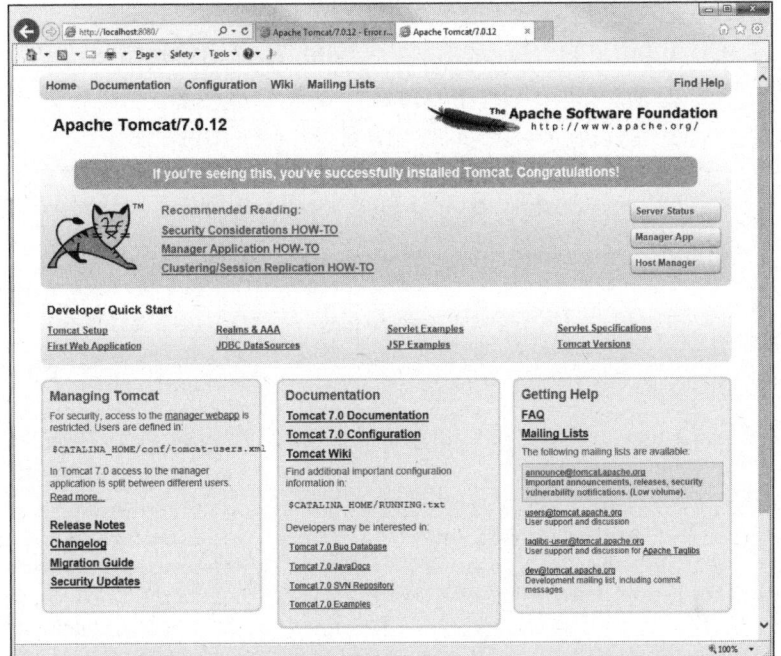

Figure 2-2:
Testing
Tomcat.

Creating a Simple Servlet

Okay, enough of the configuration stuff; now you can start writing some code. The following sections go over the basics of creating a simple `HelloWorld`–type servlet.

Importing the servlet packages

Most servlets need access to at least three packages: `javax.servlet`, `javax.servlet.http`, and `java.io`. As a result, you usually start with these `import` statements:

```
import java.io.*;
import javax.servlet.*;
import javax.servlet.http.*;
```

Depending on what other processing your servlet does, you may need additional `import` statements.

Extending the HttpServlet class

To create a servlet, you write a class that extends the `HttpServlet` class. Table 2-1 lists six methods you can override in your servlet class.

Table 2-1	The HttpServlet Class	
Method	*When Called*	*Signature*
doDelete	HTTP DELETE request	`public void doDelete(Http ServletRequest request, HttpServletResponse response) throws IOException, ServletException`
doGet	HTTP GET request	`public void doGet(HttpServlet Request request, HttpServlet Response response) throws IOException, ServletException`
doPost	HTTP POST request	`public void doPost(HttpServlet Request request, HttpServlet Response response) throws IOException, ServletException`
doPut	HTTP PUT request	`public void doPut(HttpServlet Request request, HttpServlet Response response) throws IOException, ServletException`
init()	First time servlet is run	`public void init() throws ServletException`
destroy()	Servlet is destroyed	`public void destroy()`

Most servlets override at least the `doGet` method. This method is called by the servlet engine when a user requests the servlet by typing its address in the browser's address bar or by clicking a link that leads to the servlet.

Two parameters are passed to the `doGet` method:

✦ An `HttpServletRequest` object representing the incoming request from the user. You use the `request` parameter primarily to retrieve data entered by the user in form fields. You find out how to do that later in this chapter, in the section "Getting Input from the User."

✦ An `HttpServletResponse` object representing the response that is sent back to the user. You use the `response` parameter to compose the output that is sent back to the user. You find out how to do that in the next section.

Printing to a web page

One of the main jobs of most servlets is writing HTML output that's sent back to the user's browser. To do that, you first call the `getWriter` method of the `HttpServletResponse` class, which returns a `PrintWriter` object that's connected to the response object. Thus, you can use the familiar `print` and `println` methods to write HTML text.

Here's a `doGet` method for a simple `HelloWorld` servlet:

```
public void doGet(HttpServletRequest request,
    HttpServletResponse response)
        throws IOException, ServletException
{
    PrintWriter out = response.getWriter();
    out.println("Hello, World!");
}
```

Here the `PrintWriter` object returned by `response.getWriter()` is used to send a simple text string back to the browser. If you run this servlet, the browser displays the text `Hello, World!`

Responding with HTML

In most cases, you don't want to send simple text back to the browser. Instead, you want to send formatted HTML. To do that, you must first tell the response object that the output is in HTML format. You can do that by calling the `set ContentType` method, passing the string `"text/html"` as the parameter. Then you can use the `PrintWriter` object to send HTML.

Listing 2-1 shows a basic `HelloWorld` servlet that sends an HTML response.

Listing 2-1:   The HelloWorld Servlet

```
import java.io.*;
import javax.servlet.*;
import javax.servlet.http.*;
import java.util.*;

public class HelloWorld extends HttpServlet
{
    public void doGet(HttpServletRequest request,
        HttpServletResponse response)
            throws IOException, ServletException
```

(continued)

Listing 2-1 *(continued)*

```
    {
        response.setContentType("text/html");
        PrintWriter out = response.getWriter();
        out.println("<html>");
        out.println("<head>");
        out.println("<title>HelloWorld</title>");
        out.println("</head>");
        out.println("<body>");
        out.println("<h1>Hello, World!</h1>");
        out.println("</body>");
        out.println("</html>");
    }
}
```

Here the following HTML is sent to the browser (I added indentation to show the HTML's structure):

```
<html>
  <head>
    <title>HelloWorld</title>
  </head>
  <body>
    <h1>Hello, World!</h1>
  </body>
</html>
```

When run, the `HelloWorld` servlet produces the page shown in Figure 2-3.

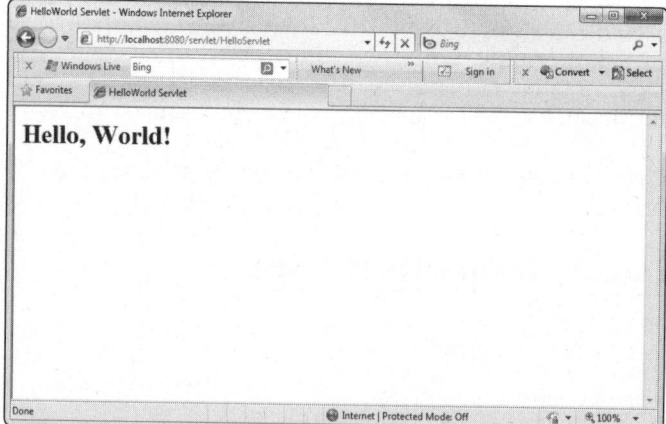

Figure 2-3:
The
HelloWorld
servlet
displayed in
a browser.

Obviously, you need a solid understanding of HTML to write servlets. If HTML is like a foreign language, you need to pick up a good HTML book, such as *HTML, XHTML, & CSS For Dummies,* 7th Edition, by Ed Tittel and Jeff Noble (Wiley), before you go much further.

For your reference, Table 2-2 summarizes all the HTML tags that I use in this book.

Table 2-2	Just Enough HTML to Get By
HTML tag	*Description*
`<html>`, `</html>`	Marks the start and end of an HTML document.
`<head>`, `</head>`	Marks the start and end of the head section of an HTML document.
`<title>`, `</title>`	Marks a title element. The text between the start and end tags is shown in the title bar of the browser window.
`<body>`, `</body>`	Marks the start and end of the body section of an HTML document. The content of the document is provided between these tags.
`<h1>`, `</h1>`	Formats the text between these tags as a level-1 heading.
`<h2>`, `</h2>`	Formats the text between these tags as a level-2 heading.
`<h3>`, `</h3>`	Formats the text between these tags as a level-3 heading.
`<form action="url", method="method">`	Marks the start of a form. The `action` attribute specifies the name of the page, servlet, or JavaServer Page (JSP) the form is posted to. The `method` attribute can be `GET` or `POST`; it indicates the type of HTTP request sent to the server.
`</form>`	Marks the end of a form.
`<input type="type", name="name">`	Creates an input field. Specify `type="text"` to create a text field or `type="submit"` to create a Submit button. The `name` attribute provides the name you use in the program to retrieve data entered by the user.
` `	Represents a nonbreaking space.

Running a Servlet

So exactly how do you run a servlet? First, you must compile the `.java` file to create a `.class` file; then you must move the `.class` file into a directory from which Tomcat can run the servlet. For testing purposes, you can move the servlet's class file to `c:\tomcat\webapps\Examples\WEB-INF\classes` and then type an address like this one in your browser's address bar:

`<http://localhost:8080/servlet/HelloWorld`

You may also want to override the `doPost` method, which is called if the user requests your servlet from a form. In many cases, you'll just call `doGet` from the `doPost` method, so that both get and post requests are processed in the same way.

As you know, the `doGet` method is called whenever the user enters the address of your servlet in the address bar or clicks a link that leads to your servlet. But many — if not most — servlets are associated with HTML forms, which provide fields in which the user can enter data. The normal way to send form data from the browser to the server is with an `HTTP POST` request, not a `GET` request.

If you want a servlet to respond to `POST` requests, you can override the `doPost` method instead of, or in addition to, the `doGet` method. Other than the method name, `doPost` has the same signature as `doGet`. In fact, it's not uncommon to see servlets in which the `doPost` method simply calls `doGet`, so that both `POST` and `GET` requests are processed identically. To do that, code the `doPost` method like this:

```
public void doPost(HttpServletRequest request,
    HttpServletResponse response)
        throws IOException, ServletException
{
    doGet(request, response);
}
```

Improving the HelloWorld Servlet

The `HelloWorld` servlet, shown in Listing 2-1 earlier in this chapter, isn't very interesting because it always sends the same text. Essentially, it's a static servlet — which pretty much defeats the purpose of using servlets in the first place. You could just as easily have provided a static HTML page.

Listing 2-2 shows the code for a more dynamic `HelloWorld` servlet. This version randomly displays one of six greetings. It uses the `random` method of the `Math` class to pick a random number from 1 to 6 and then uses this number to decide which greeting to display. It also overrides the `doPost` method as well as the `doGet` method, so posts and gets are handled identically.

Listing 2-2:   The HelloServlet Servlet

```java
import java.io.*;
import javax.servlet.*;
import javax.servlet.http.*;
import java.util.*;

public class HelloServlet extends HttpServlet
{
    public void doGet(HttpServletRequest request,
        HttpServletResponse response)
            throws IOException, ServletException
    {
        response.setContentType("text/html");
        PrintWriter out = response.getWriter();
        String msg = getGreeting();
        out.println("<html>");
        out.println("<head>");
        out.println(
            "<title>HelloWorld Servlet</title>");
        out.println("</head>");
        out.println("<body>");
        out.println("<h1>");
        out.println(msg);
        out.println("</h1>");
        out.println("</body>");
        out.println("</html>");
    }

    public void doPost(HttpServletRequest request,
        HttpServletResponse response)
            throws IOException, ServletException
    {
        doGet(request, response);
    }

    private String getGreeting()
    {
        String msg = "";
        int rand = (int)(Math.random() * (6)) + 1;
        switch (rand)
        {
            case 1:
                return "Hello, World!";
            case 2:
                return "Greetings!";
            case 3:
                return "Felicitations!";
            case 4:
                return "Yo, Dude!";
```

(continued)

Listing 2-2 *(continued)*

```
            case 5:
                return "Whasssuuuup?";
            case 6:
                return "Hark!";
        }
        return null;
    }
}
```

Getting Input from the User

If a servlet is called by an `HTTP GET` or `POST` request that came from a form, you can call the `getParameter` method of the `request` object to get the values entered by the user in each form field. Here's an example:

```
String name = request.getParameter("name"
```

Here the value entered in the form input field named `name` is retrieved and assigned to the `String` variable `name`.

Working with forms

As you can see, retrieving data entered by the user in a servlet is easy. The hard part is creating a form in which the user can enter the data. To do that, you create the form by using a separate HTML file. Listing 2-3 shows an HTML file named `InputServlet.html` that displays the form shown in Figure 2-4.

Listing 2-3:   The InputServlet.html File

```
<html>
  <head>
    <title>Input Servlet</title>
  </head>
  <body>
    <form action="/servlet/InputServlet"
        method="post">
      Enter your name: 
      <input type="text" name="Name">
      <br><br>
      <input type="submit" value="Submit">
    </form>
  </body>
</html>
```

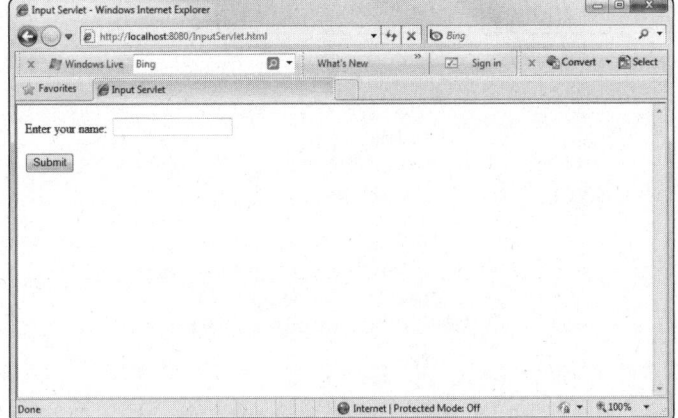

Figure 2-4:
A simple
input form.

The `action` attribute in the `form` tag of this form specifies that `/servlet/ InputServlet` is called when the form is submitted, and the `method` attribute indicates that the form is submitted via a `POST` rather than a `GET` request.

The form itself consists of an input text field named `name` and a Submit button. It's nothing fancy — just enough to get some text from the user and send it to a servlet.

Using the InputServlet servlet

Listing 2-4 shows a servlet that can retrieve the data from the form shown in Listing 2-3.

Listing 2-4:   The InputServlet Servlet

```
import java.io.*;
import javax.servlet.*;
import javax.servlet.http.*;

public class InputServlet extends HttpServlet
{
    public void doGet(HttpServletRequest request,
        HttpServletResponse response)
            throws IOException, ServletException
    {
        String name = request.getParameter("Name");

        response.setContentType("text/html");
        PrintWriter out = response.getWriter();
        out.println("<html>");
        out.println("<head>");
        out.println("<title>Input Servlet</title>");
        out.println("</head>");
```

(continued)

Listing 2-4 *(continued)*

```
        out.println("<body>");
        out.println("<h1>");
        out.println("Hello " + name);
        out.println("</h1>");
        out.println("</body>");
        out.println("</html>");
    }

    public void doPost(HttpServletRequest request,
        HttpServletResponse response)
            throws IOException, ServletException
    {
        doGet(request, response);
    }
}
```

As you can see, this servlet really isn't much different from the first `Hello World` servlet in Listing 2-1. The biggest difference is that it retrieves the value entered by the user in the `name` field and uses it in the HTML that's sent to the response `PrintWriter` object. If the user enters `Calvin Coolidge` in the `name` input field, for example, the following HTML is generated:

```
<html>
  <head>
    <title>HelloWorld</title>
  </head>
  <body>
    <h1>Hello Calvin Coolidge</h1>
  </body>
</html>
```

Thus the message `Hello Calvin Coolidge` is displayed on the page.

Although real-life servlets do a lot more than just parrot back information entered by the user, most of them follow this surprisingly simple structure — with a few variations, of course. Real-world servlets validate input data and display error messages if the user enters incorrect data or omits important data, and most real-world servlets retrieve or update data in files or databases. Even so, the basic structure is pretty much the same.

Using Classes in a Servlet

When you develop servlets, you often want to access other classes that you've created, such as input/output (I/O) classes that retrieve data from files or databases, utility or helper classes that provide common functions such as data validation, and perhaps even classes that represent business objects such as customers or products. To do that, all you have to do is save the class files in the `classes` directory of the servlet's home directory — which, for the purposes of this chapter, is `c:\tomcat\webapps\ROOT\WEB-INF\classes`.

To illustrate a servlet that uses several classes, Figure 2-5 shows the output from a servlet that lists movies read from a text file. This servlet uses three classes:

✦ **Movie:** A class that represents an individual movie.

✦ **MovieIO:** A class that has a static public method named `getMovies`. This method returns an `ArrayList` object that contains all the movies read from the file.

✦ **ListFiles:** The main servlet class. It calls the `MovieIO.getMovies` class to get an `ArrayList` of movies and then displays the movies on the page.

Figure 2-5: The ListMovies servlet.

Book VII
Chapter 2

Creating Servlets

The code for the `Movie` class is shown in Listing 2-5. As you can see, this class doesn't have much: It defines three public fields (`title`, `year`, and `price`) and a constructor that lets you create a new `Movie` object and initialize the three fields. Note that this servlet doesn't use the `price` field.

Listing 2-5: The Movie Class

```
public class Movie
{
    public String title;
    public int year;
    public double price;
    public Movie(String title, int year,
                 double price)
```

(continued)

Listing 2-5 *(continued)*

```
    {
        this.title = title;
        this.year = year;
        this.price = price;
    }
}
```

Listing 2-6 shows the `MovieIO` class. This class uses the file I/O features that are presented in Book VIII, Chapter 2 to read data from a text file. The text file uses tabs to separate the fields and contains these lines:

```
It's a Wonderful Life→1946→14.95
The Great Race→1965→12.95
Young Frankenstein→1974→16.95
The Return of the Pink Panther→1975→11.95
Star Wars→1977→17.95
The Princess Bride→1987→16.95
Glory→1989→14.95
Apollo 13→1995→19.95
The Game→1997→14.95
The Lord of the Rings: The Fellowship of the Ring→2001→19.95
```

Here the arrows represent tab characters in the file. I'm not going to go over the details of this class here, except to point out that `getMovies` is the only public method in the class, and it's static, so you don't have to create an instance of the `MovieIO` class to use it. For details on how this class works, turn to Book VIII, Chapter 2.

Listing 2-6:   The MovieIO Class

```java
import java.io.*;
import java.util.*;

public class MovieIO
{
    public static ArrayList<Movie> getMovies()
    {
        ArrayList<Movie> movies =
            new ArrayList<Movie>();
        BufferedReader in =
            getReader("c:\\data\\movies.txt");
        Movie movie = readMovie(in);
        while (movie != null)
        {
            movies.add(movie);
            movie = readMovie(in);
        }
        return movies;
    }
```

```
private static BufferedReader getReader(
    String name)
{
    BufferedReader in = null;
    try
    {
        File file = new File(name);
        in = new BufferedReader(
            new FileReader(file) );
    }
    catch (FileNotFoundException e)
    {
        System.out.println(
            "The file doesn't exist.");
        System.exit(0);
    }

    return in;
}

private static Movie readMovie(BufferedReader in)
{
    String title;
    int year;
    double price;
    String line = "";
    String[] data;

    try
    {
        line = in.readLine();
    }
    catch (IOException e)
    {
        System.out.println("I/O Error");
        System.exit(0);
    }
    if (line == null)
        return null;
    else
    {
        data = line.split("\t");
        title = data[0];
        year = Integer.parseInt(data[1]);
        price = Double.parseDouble(data[2]);
        return new Movie(title, year, price);
    }
}
}
```

Listing 2-7 shows the code for the ListMovie servlet class.

Listing 2-7:   The ListMovie Servlet Class

```
import java.io.*;
import javax.servlet.*;
import javax.servlet.http.*;
import java.util.*;

public class ListMovies extends HttpServlet
{
    public void doGet(HttpServletRequest request,                    →8
        HttpServletResponse response)
            throws IOException, ServletException
    {
        response.setContentType("text/html");
        PrintWriter out = response.getWriter();
        String msg = getMovieList();
        out.println("<html>");
        out.println("<head>");
        out.println(
            "<title>List Movies Servlet</title>");
        out.println("</head>");
        out.println("<body>");
        out.println("<h1>Some of My Favorites</h1>");
        out.println("<h3>");
        out.println(msg);
        out.println("</h3>");
        out.println("</body>");
        out.println("</html>");
    }

    public void doPost(HttpServletRequest request,                   →28
        HttpServletResponse response)
            throws IOException, ServletException
    {
        doGet(request, response);
    }

    private String getMovieList()                                    →35
    {
        String msg = "";
        ArrayList<Movie> movies = MovieIO.getMovies();
        for (Movie m : movies)
        {
            msg += m.year + ": ";
            msg += m.title + "<br>";
        }
        return msg;
    }
}
```

The following paragraphs describe what its methods do:

→ 8   The doGet method calls the getMovieList method to get a string that contains a list of all the movies, separated by break (<br>) tags. Then it uses a series of out.println statements to write HTML that displays this list.

→ 28   The doPost method simply calls the doGet method. That way, the servlet works whether it is invoked by a GET or a POST request.

→ 35   The getMovieList method calls the MovieIO.getMovies method to get an ArrayList that contains all the movies read from the file. Then it uses an enhanced for loop to retrieve each Movie object. Each movie's year and title is added to the msg string, separated by <br> tags.

Chapter 3: Using JavaServer Pages

In This Chapter

✔ Seeing how servlets work

✔ Dealing with page directives

✔ Trying out expressions

✔ Putting scriptlets to work

✔ Devising declarations

✔ Comprehending classes

In Book VII, Chapter 2, you discover how to create servlets that write HTML data directly to a page by using the `PrintWriter` object accessed through `response.out`. Although this technique works, it has one major drawback: You have to compose the HTML manually as a bunch of string literals. If the HTML has an error, you don't know about it until you run the servlet to see how it looks. Also, handcrafting HTML in `out.println` statements certainly isn't the most efficient way to create attractive web pages.

That's where JavaServer Pages (a technology usually called JSP for short) comes in. A *JavaServer Page* is an HTML file that has Java servlet code embedded in it in special tags. When you run a JSP, all the HTML is automatically sent as part of the response, along with any HTML that's created by the Java code you embed in the JSP file. As a result, JSP spares you the chore of writing all those `out.println` statements.

In this chapter, you find out how to create basic JavaServer Pages. At www. dummies.com/extras/javaaio, I show you how to incorporate special Java classes called *JavaBeans* into your JSP pages.

Note: To work with JavaServer Pages, you must first set up a working Tomcat environment. For information on how to do that, please refer to Book VII, Chapter 2.

Understanding JavaServer Pages

A JSP is an HTML document that's saved in a file with the extension `.jsp` instead of `.htm` or `.html`. Unlike servlet-class files, a JSP file can be stored in any directory that's available to the web server.

The first time a user requests a JSP file, the file is run through a translator program that converts the file to a Java servlet program and compiles it. All the HTML from the original JSP file is converted to `out.print` statements that send the HTML to the response, and the Java statements from the JSP file are incorporated into the servlet program. Then the servlet program is executed and the results sent back to the browser.

Note that this translation occurs only once: the first time someone requests the JSP. After that, the servlet itself is run directly whenever a user requests the JSP.

Enough of the concept — now on to the code. When you create a JSP, you mix special JSP elements into your normal HTML. You can include four types of JSP elements:

✦ **Directives:** A *directive* is an option setting that affects how the servlet is constructed from a JSP page. Directives let you do things such as specify what `import` statements the servlet requires, specify whether the servlet is thread-safe, and include other source files in the servlet. For example:

```
<%@ page import="java.util.*" %>
```

✦ **Expressions:** An *expression* can be any Java expression. The expression is evaluated and converted to a string (if necessary), and the result is inserted into the document. Expressions assume the following form:

```
<%= expression %>
```

✦ **Scriptlets:** A *scriptlet* is a sequence of Java statements inserted directly into the servlet code generated for the JSP. You can do just about anything you want in a scriptlet, including using `if` statements, looping, and calling other methods. You can even use `out.println` to add output to the page; the output is inserted into the page at the location where the scriptlet appears. Scriptlets have the following form:

```
<% statements %>
```

✦ **Declarations:** A *declaration* is Java code that is placed in the servlet class outside any methods. You use declarations to create class variables or define methods that can be called by scriptlets or expressions. Declarations take this form:

```
<%! statements %>
```

The remaining sections of this chapter show you how to create JSP pages that incorporate these elements.

Using Page Directives

A *page directive* is a JSP element that sets options that determine how the JSP is converted to a servlet. The basic format of a page directive is this:

```
<%@ page attribute=value %>
```

The *attribute* can be any of the attributes listed in Table 3-1. (A few attributes besides these are available, but they're rarely used.)

Table 3-1   **Commonly Used Page Directive Attributes**

Name	*Description*
`import="package.class"`	Adds an `import` statement to the servlet so that you can use classes in other JSP elements without having to qualify them fully.
`content-Type="MIME-type"`	Lets you specify the type of document created by the servlet. The default is `text/html`. You rarely need to change this setting.
`isThreadSafe="boolean"`	If `true`, the servlet is assumed to be thread-safe. If `false`, `implements SingleThreadModel` is added to the servlet class declaration so that the thread runs in the single-thread model. The default is `true`.
`session="boolean"`	If `true`, the servlet uses session management. The default is `true`.
`buffer="size"`	Specifies the size of the buffer used by the `out` variable. The default depends on the server but is never smaller than 8KB.
`errorPage="URL"`	Specifies the name of an error page that is displayed if this servlet throws an uncaught exception.
`isErrorPage="boolean"`	If `true`, this page is an error page for some other JSP page. The default is `false`.

The page directive you use most is `import`, as it lets you import the packages for API classes so that you can use them in expression, scriptlet, and declaration elements. Here's a page directive that imports the `java.util` package:

```
<%@ page import="java.util.*" %>
```

You can place page directives anywhere you want in a JSP document, but I suggest that you place them at or near the top so they will be easy to find.

Using Expressions

A JSP *expression* is any Java expression that evaluates to a string. Actually, the expression doesn't have to evaluate directly. Here's how you can use the `java.util.Date` class to display the current date and time:

```
<%=new java.util.Date()%>
```

This expression creates a new instance of the `java.util.Date()` class, which represents the current date and time. The `toString()` method is implicitly called to convert this object to a string.

If you include a `page import` directive, you can omit the qualification on this expression, as in this example:

```
<%@ page import="java.util" %>
<%=new Date()%>
```

To do more interesting things with expressions, you can use predefined variables, also known as *implicit objects* — Java variables that are available to expressions, scriptlets, or declarations throughout a JSP page. Table 3-2 lists the JSP implicit objects you use most often.

Table 3-2	Implicit Objects
Name	*Description*
out	Used to write data to the response; equivalent to `response.getWriter()` in a servlet.
request	Used as the request object; equivalent to the `request` parameter in the `doGet` or `doPost` method of a servlet.
response	Used as the response object; equivalent to the `response` parameter in the `doGet` or `doPost` method of a servlet.
session	Used to manage sessions; equivalent to `request.getSession()` in a servlet.

The implicit objects work the same way that their corresponding objects do in servlets. The `response` object, for example, is just the `response` parameter that's passed to the `doGet` or `doPost` method.

The implicit object you use most in expressions is `request`. In particular, you use its `getParameter` method to get values entered by the user in forms. Here's an expression that displays the value entered in an input field titled `Name`:

```
<%= request.getParameter("Name")%>
```

The value of the `Name` field is inserted wherever this expression occurs in the JSP file. Here's a simple JSP file named `InputJSP.jsp` that displays an input text box and a button. When the user clicks the button, whatever text he or she entered in the input field is displayed below the button, as follows:

```
<html>
  <head>
    <title>Input JSP</title>
  </head>
  <body>
    <form action="InputJSP.jsp" method="post">
      Enter some text: 
      <input type="text" name="Text">
      <br><br>
      <input type="submit" value="Submit">
    </form><br>
    <h3>You entered: 
    <%= request.getParameter("Text")%></h3>
  </body>
</html>
```

Book VII
Chapter 3

Using JavaServer Pages

The HTML for this JSP defines a form that contains an input text field named `Text` and a Submit button. When the user clicks the Submit button, an HTTP POST request is sent to the server to request `InputJSP.jsp`. Any text entered by the user is sent along with the request. When the servlet is run, the text is retrieved by the expression `request.getParameter("Text")` and displayed below the button. Figure 3-1 shows this servlet in action.

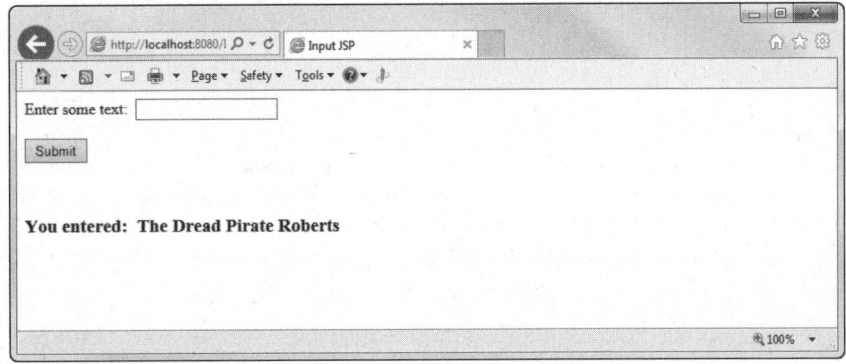

Figure 3-1:
`Input-`
`JSP.jsp`
in action.

Note: Expressions can also call methods that you add to the JSP with declaration elements. You see examples of how to do that in the section "Using Declarations," later in this chapter.

Using Scriptlets

As mentioned earlier in the chapter, a *scriptlet* is a statement or group of statements that's inserted directly into the servlet at the point where the out.print statements that create the surrounding HTML are generated. In short, scriptlets let you add your own code to the code that renders the page.

Scriptlets follow this basic form:

```
<% statements... %>
```

Here's a JSP named DateJSP.jsp that uses the DateFormat class to format the date and display it on the page:

```
<html>
  <%@ page import="java.text.*" %>
  <%@ page import="java.util.*" %>
  <head>
    <title>Date JSP</title>
  </head>
  <body>
    <h1>
      Today is
      <%
          DateFormat df = DateFormat.getDateInstance(
              DateFormat.FULL);
          Date today = new Date();
          String msg = df.format(today);
          out.println(msg);
      %>
    </h1>
    <h1>Have a nice day!</h1>
  </body>
</html>
```

This JSP begins with a pair of page import directives to import the java.text and java.util packages. Then the following Java statements are inserted right between the lines that generate the text Today is and Have a nice day!, like so:

```
DateFormat df
    = DateFormat.getDateInstance(DateFormat.FULL);
Date today = new Date();
String msg = df.format(today);
out.println(msg);
```

Scriptlets

Scriptlets don't have to add anything to the HTML output. In many cases, they perform functions such as writing information to a file. Suppose that you have a JSP that gets data from a form that includes input text fields named `FirstName` and `LastName`. Suppose also that you have a class named `CustFile` with a static method named `writeCustomer` that accepts a first and last name as parameters and writes them to a file. Here's a scriptlet that gets the first and last names and calls the `writeCustomer` method to write the name to the customer file:

```
<% String firstName = request.
   getParameter("FirstName");
   String lastName = request.
   getParameter("LastName");
   CustFile.
   writeCustomer(firstName,
   lastName);
%>
```

These lines create a string variable named `msg` and then use `out.println` to write the string to the response output. As a result, the formatted date is inserted between `<h1>Today is </h1>` and `<h1>Have a nice day!</h1>`. Figure 3-2 shows a page generated by this JSP.

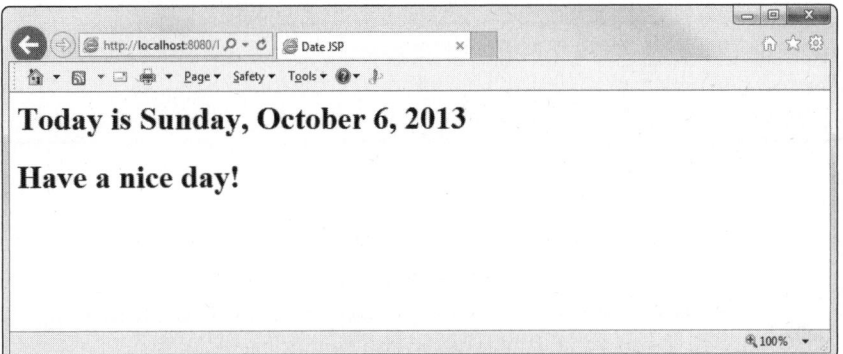

Book VII
Chapter 3

Using JavaServer
Pages

Figure 3-2:
`DateJSP.`
`jsp` in
action.

If you want, you can get pretty tricky with scriptlets. No rule says that you have to complete block statements such as `if` or `while` statements within a single scriptlet. If you leave a block open at the end of a scriptlet, any HTML that follows is generated by `out.print` statements that are included in the block. The only restriction is that you must eventually end the block with another scriptlet.

Here's a scriptlet named `LoopyJSP.jsp` that repeats a line 12 times on the page by including the line in the block of a `for` loop:

```
<html>
  <head>
    <title>Can't you see I'm trying to work here?</title>
  </head>
  <body>
    <% for (int i = 0; i < 12; i++)
       {
    %>
    All work and no play makes Jack a dull boy.<br>
    <%
       }
    %>
  </body>
</html>
```

If you run this scriptlet, the page appears as shown in Figure 3-3.

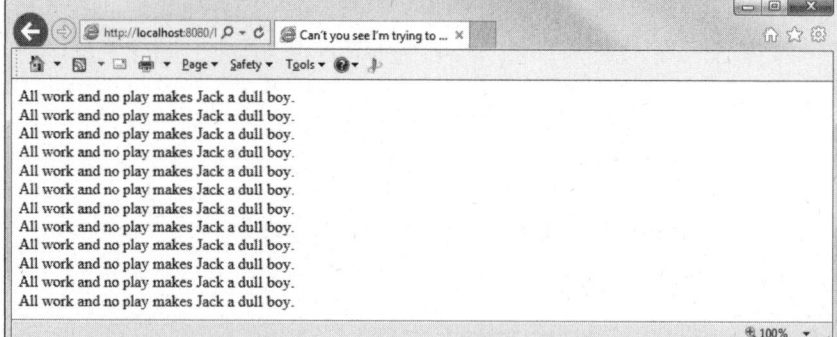

Figure 3-3: The LoopyJSP. jsp scriptlet doing its thing.

Obviously, this sort of programming structure is prone to error. I suggest that you avoid it whenever you can.

Using Declarations

A *declaration* is code that is included in the servlet but outside any method. Declarations are used to create class variables or methods that can be used in expressions, scriptlets, or other declarations. Declarations follow this format:

```
<%! statements... %>
```

You can place declarations anywhere you want in a JSP.

Here's a servlet that declares a static class field named `count` that's incremented each time the page is displayed:

```html
<html>
  <%@ page import="java.text.*" %>
  <%@ page import="java.util.*" %>

  <head>
    <title>Counter JSP</title>
  </head>
  <body>
    <h1>
      This JSP has been displayed <%= count++ %>
      time.</h1>
  </body>
</html>

<%!
private static int count = 1;
%>
```

In this servlet, the `count` variable is declared by the declaration element at the end of the JSP document, as follows:

```java
<%!
private static int count = 1;
%>
```

Then the expression in the body of the document displays and increments the `count` variable, like this:

```java
<%= count++ %>
```

When run, the JSP displays the number of times the page has been displayed since the server started.

Here's another example, this time declaring a method that's called in an expression:

```html
<html>
  <%@ page import="java.text.*" %>
  <%@ page import="java.util.*" %>
  <head>
    <title>Date JSP</title>
  </head>
  <body>
    <h1>
      Today is <%= getDate() %></h1>
    <h1>Have a nice day!</h1>
  </body>
</html>
```

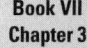

```
<%!
private String getDate()
{
    DateFormat df =
        DateFormat.getDateInstance(DateFormat.FULL);
    Date today = new Date();
    return df.format(today);
}
%>
```

The declaration at the end of this document declares a method that returns the current date as a string. Then the expression `<%= getDate() %>` is used to insert the date into the document.

Using Classes

Most JSP applications are complicated enough that they need additional classes to keep their code manageable. Maybe you want to create classes that handle the application's file or database I/O, and you want to create classes to represent business objects such as `Products` and `Customers`.

Setting up Tomcat to work with classes can be a little tricky, but it's easy if you follow these simple guidelines:

✦ **Contain all classes in packages.** Choose a nice package name for your application and then add a `package` statement to the beginning of each class file.

✦ **Store the class files (not necessarily the source files) in the** `WEB-INF\` `classes\`*package*`\` **directory below the directory in which the JSP pages are stored.** If the package name is `com.lowewriter.movie`, and you're storing your JSP pages in `c:\tomcat\webapps\ROOT`, save the class files in the following directory:

> `C:\tomcat\webapps\ROOT\WEB-INF\classes\com\lowewriter\movie`

✦ **In any JSP that uses one of your classes, include a page directive that imports the package.** Here's an example:

> `<%@ page import="com.lowewriter.movie.*" %>`

✦ **Add the directory in which you saved the packages to your `ClassPath` environment variable.** You want to add the directory that contains the packages, not the directory that contains the classes themselves, because the Java compiler uses the package name to find the package directory. So if you put your classes in the `webapps\ROOT\WIB-INF\classes` directory, you need to add `c:\tomcat\webapps\ROOT\WEB-INF\` `classes` to your `ClassPath`.

To illustrate how a JSP can use classes, Figure 3-4 shows a JSP that lists the movies in the `movies.txt` file. The JSP file that displays this page is shown in Listing 3-1. The JSP file itself is stored in `c:\tomcat\webapps\ROOT`.

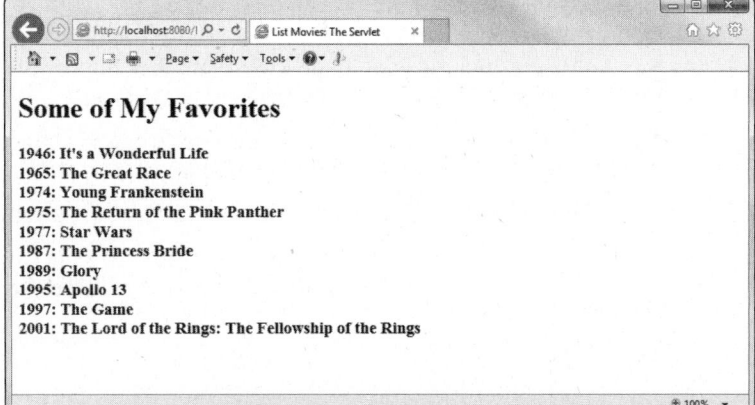

Figure 3-4:
The
ListMovies
JSP in
action.

Listing 3-1:   ListMovies.jsp

```
<!doctype html public "-//W3C//DTD HTML 4.0
Transitional//EN">
<%@ page import="com.lowewriter.movie.*" %>          →3
<%@ page import="java.util.*" %>
<html>
  <head>
    <title>List Movies: The Servlet</title>
  </head>
  <body>
    <h1>Some of My Favorites</h1>
    <h3>
      <%= getMovieList() %>                          →12
    </h3>
  </body>
</html>

<%!
private String getMovieList()                         →18
{
    String msg = "";
    ArrayList<Movie> movies = MovieIO.getMovies();    →21
    for (Movie m : movies)                            →22
    {
        msg += m.year + ": ";
        msg += m.title + "<br>";
    }
    return msg;                                        →28
}
%>
```

Following is an explanation of the key lines in this JSP:

→ **3**   The JSP includes two page directives that import the `com.lowewriter.movie` and `java.util` packages.

→ **12**   An expression is used to call the `getMovieList` method, which returns the list of movies to be displayed as a string.

→ **18**   The `getMovieList` method is defined in a declaration.

→ **21**   The `getMovies` method of the `MovieIO` class is called to retrieve an `ArrayList` that contains all the movies from the `movies.txt` file.

→ **22**   The `Movie` objects are retrieved from the `ArrayList`, and the year and title are added to the `msg` string.

→ **28**   The finished `msg` string is returned.

Listing 3-2 shows the `Movie` class. There's nothing special to note here other than the `package` statement that places the `Movie` class in the `com.lowewriter.movie` package. The class file that's compiled from this `.java` file is saved in `c:\tomcat\webaps\ROOT\WEB-INF\classes\com\lowewriter\movie`.

Listing 3-2:   Movie.java

```
package com.lowewriter.movie;

public class Movie
{
    public String title;
    public int year;
    public double price;
    public Movie(String title, int year,
                 double price)
    {
        this.title = title;
        this.year = year;
        this.price = price;
    }
}
```

Finally, the `MovieIO` class is shown in Listing 3-3. This class reads the movies from a text file. (For a detailed explanation of how this class works, jump forward to Book VIII, Chapter 2.) Notice that this class, like the `Movie` class, includes a `package` statement that dumps the `MovieIO` class into the movie package. The class file compiled from this `.java` file is saved in `c:\tomcat\webaps\ROOT\WEB-INF\classes\com\lowewriter\movie`.

Listing 3-3:   MovieIO.java

```java
package com.lowewriter.movie;

import java.io.*;
import java.util.*;

public class MovieIO
{
    public static ArrayList<Movie> getMovies()
    {
        ArrayList<Movie> movies =
            new ArrayList<Movie>();
        BufferedReader in =
            getReader("c:\\data\\movies.txt");
        Movie movie = readMovie(in);
        while (movie != null)
        {
            movies.add(movie);
            movie = readMovie(in);
        }
        return movies;
    }

    private static BufferedReader getReader(
        String name)
    {
        BufferedReader in = null;
        try
        {
            File file = new File(name);
            in = new BufferedReader(
                new FileReader(file) );
        }
        catch (FileNotFoundException e)
        {
            System.out.println(
                "The file doesn't exist.");
            System.exit(0);
        }
        return in;
    }

    private static Movie readMovie(BufferedReader in)
    {
        String title;
        int year;
        double price;
        String line = "";
        String[] data;
```

(continued)

Listing 3-3 *(continued)*

```java
        try
        {
            line = in.readLine();
        }
        catch (IOException e)
        {
            System.out.println("I/O Error");
            System.exit(0);
        }

        if (line == null)
            return null;
        else
        {
            data = line.split("\t");
            title = data[0];
            year = Integer.parseInt(data[1]);
            price = Double.parseDouble(data[2]);
            return new Movie(title, year, price);
        }
    }
}
```

Book VIII
Files and Databases

Contents at a Glance

Chapter 1: Working with Files

In This Chapter

✔ Examining the File class

✔ Understanding command-line parameters

✔ Introducing the JFileChooser class

*I*n this chapter, you discover the ins and outs of working with files and directories. I don't show you how to read or write files (for that info, you should flip to Book VIII, Chapter 2), but you do find out how to find files on the hard drive; create, delete, and rename files; and work with directories. You find out how to use the Swing file-chooser dialog box that lets you add filing capabilities to Swing applications. Finally, you find out how to retrieve parameters from the command line — a useful technique, because command-line parameters are often used to pass file information to console programs.

Beginning with Java 1.7, you have two choices for working with files and directories: You can use the original File class or you can use the new Path class, which is part of a new file-processing package called NIO.2. (*NIO.2* stands for *New I/O version 2.*) This chapter covers both of these classes.

Using the File Class

The File class is your key to processing files and directories. A File object represents a single file or directory. Note that the file or directory doesn't actually have to exist on your hard drive. Instead, the File object represents a file that may or may not actually exist.

Java uses a single class to represent both files and directories because a directory is actually nothing more than a special type of file. I suppose that the designers of Java could have created a separate Directory class to represent directories, but then you'd have to know how to use two classes instead of one.

The File class is in the java.io package, so any program that uses it should import java.io.File or java.io.*.

Java 1.7 introduces a new Path class, which is designed to replace the File class.

Knowing the class constructors and methods

Table 1-1 lists the main constructors and methods of the `File` class.

Table 1-1	The File Class
Constructor	*Description*
`File(String pathname)`	Creates a file with the specified pathname.
Field	*Description*
`String separator`	Separates components of a pathname on this system; usually is \ or /.
Method	*Description*
`boolean canRead()`	Determines whether the file can be read.
`boolean canWrite()`	Determines whether the file can be written.
`boolean createNewFile()`	Creates the file on the hard drive if it doesn't exist. The method returns `true` if the file was created or `false` if the file already existed.
`boolean delete()`	Deletes the file or directory. The method returns `true` if the file was deleted successfully.
`boolean exists()`	Returns `true` if the file exists on the hard drive and `false` if the file doesn't exist.
`String getCanonicalPath()`	Returns the complete path to the file, including the drive letter if run on a Windows system; throws `IOException`.
`String getName()`	Gets the name of this file.
`String getParent()`	Gets the name of the parent directory of this file or directory.
`File getParentFile()`	Gets a `File` object representing the parent directory of this file or directory.
`boolean isDirectory()`	Returns `true` if this `File` object is a directory or `false` if it is a file.
`boolean isFile()`	Returns `true` if this `File` object is a file or `false` if it is a directory.
`boolean isHidden()`	Returns `true` if this file or directory is marked by the operating system as hidden.

Method	Description
`long lastModified()`	Returns the time when the file was last modified, expressed in milliseconds since 0:00:00 a.m., January 1, 1970.
`long length()`	Returns the size of the file in bytes.
`String[] list()`	Returns an array of `String` objects with the name of each file and directory in this directory. Each string is a simple filename, not a complete path. If this `File` object is not a directory, the method returns `null`.
`File[] listFiles()`	Returns an array of `File` objects representing each file and directory in this directory. If this `File` object is not a directory, the method returns `null`.
`static File[] listRoots()`	Returns an array containing a `File` object for the root directory of every file system available on the Java runtime. Unix systems usually have just one root, but Windows systems have a root for each drive.
`boolean mkdir()`	Creates a directory on the hard drive from this `File` object. The method returns `true` if the directory was created successfully.
`boolean mkdirs()`	Creates a directory on the hard drive from this `File` object, including any parent directories that are listed in the directory path but don't already exist. The method returns `true` if the directory was created successfully.
`boolean renameTo(File dest)`	Renames the `File` object to the specified destination `File` object. The method returns `true` if the rename was successful.
`boolean setLastModified(long time)`	Sets the last modified time for the `File` object. The method returns `true` if the time was set successfully.
`boolean setReadOnly()`	Marks the file as read-only. The method returns `true` if the file was marked successfully.
`String toString()`	Returns the pathname for this file or directory as a string.

Creating a File object

To create a `File` object, you call the `File` constructor, passing a string representing the filename as a parameter. Here's an example:

```
File f = new File("hits.log");
```

Here the file's name is `hits.log,` and it lives in the current directory, which usually is the directory from which the Java Virtual Machine (JVM) was started.

If you don't want the file to live in the current directory, you can supply a complete pathname in the parameter string. You're now entering one of the few areas of Java that becomes system-dependent, however, because the way you write pathnames depends on the operating system you're using. The pathname `c:\logs\hits.log` is valid for Windows systems, for example, but not on Unix or Macintosh systems, which don't use drive letters and use forward slashes instead of backslashes to separate directories.

If you hard-code pathnames as string literals, the backslash character is the escape character for Java strings. Thus you must code two backslashes to get one backslash in the pathname. You must code the path `c:\logs\ hits.log` like this:

```
String path = "c:\\logs\\hits.log";
```

Creating a file

Creating a `File` object doesn't create a file on the hard drive. Instead, it creates an in-memory object that represents a file or directory that may or may not actually exist on the hard drive. To find out whether the file or directory exists, you can use the `exists` method, as in this example:

```
File f = new File(path);
if (!f.exists())
    System.out.println
        ("The input file does not exist!");
```

Here an error message is displayed on the console if the file doesn't exist.

To create a new file on the hard drive, create a `File` object with the filename you want to use and then use the `createNewFile` method, like this:

```
File f = new File(path);
if (f.createNewFile())
    System.out.println("File created.");
else
    System.out.println("File could not be created.");
```

Note that the `createNewFile` method returns a boolean that indicates whether the file was created successfully. If the file already exists, `create NewFile` returns `false`, so you don't have to use the `exists` method before you call `createNewFile`.

When you create a file with the `createNewFile` method, the file doesn't have anything in it. If you want the file to contain data, you can use the classes I describe in Book VIII, Chapter 2, to write information to the file.

Getting information about a file

Several of the methods of the `File` class simply return information about a file or directory. You can find out whether the `File` object represents a file or directory, for example, by calling its `isDirectory` or `isFile` method. Other methods let you find out whether a file is read-only or hidden, or retrieve the file's age and the time when it was last modified.

You can get the name of the file represented by a `File` object in several popular ways:

✦ To get just the filename, use the `getName` method. This method returns a string that includes just the filename, not the complete path.

✦ To get the path that was specified to create the `File` object (such as `\logs\hit.log`), use the `toString` method instead.

✦ To get the full path for a file — that is, the complete path including the drive letter (for Windows systems) and all the directories and subdirectories leading to the file — use the `getCannonicalPath` method. This method removes any system-dependent oddities such as relative paths, dots (which represent the current directory), and double dots (which represent the parent directory) to get the file's actual path.

Getting the contents of a directory

A *directory* is a file that contains a list of other files or directories. Because a directory is just a special type of file, it's represented by an object of the `File` class. You can tell whether a particular `File` object is a directory by calling its `isDirectory` method. If this method returns `true`, the `File` is a directory. Then you can get an array of all the files contained in the directory by calling the `listFiles` method.

The following code snippet lists the name of every file in a directory whose pathname is stored in the `String` variable path:

```
File dir = new File(path);
if (dir.isDirectory())
{
    File[] files = dir.listFiles();
    for (File f : files)
        System.out.println(f.getName());
}
```

Book VIII Chapter 1

Working with Files

The following snippet is a little more selective because it lists only files, not subdirectories, and doesn't list hidden files:

```
File dir = new File(path);
if (dir.isDirectory())
{
    File[] files = dir.listFiles();
    for (File f : files)
    {
        if (f.isFile() && !f.isHidden())
            System.out.println(f.getName());
    }
}
```

Directory listings are especially well suited to recursive programming, because each `File` object returned by the `listFiles` method may be another directory that itself has a list of files and directories. For an explanation of recursive programming and an example that lists directories recursively, see Book V, Chapter 4.

Renaming files

You can rename a file by using the `renameTo` method. This method uses another `File` object as a parameter that specifies the file you want to rename the current file to. It returns a `boolean` value that indicates whether the file was renamed successfully.

The following statements change the name of a file named `hits.log` to `savedhits.log`:

```
File f = new File("hits.log");
if (f.renameTo(new File("savedhits.log")))
    System.out.println("File renamed.");
else
    System.out.println("File not renamed.");
```

Depending on the capabilities of the operating system, the `renameTo` method can also move a file from one directory to another. This code moves the file `hits.log` from the folder `logs` to the folder `savedlogs`:

```
File f = new File("logs\\hits.log");
if (f.renameTo(new File("savedlogs\\hits.log")))
    System.out.println("File moved.");
else
    System.out.println("File not moved.");
```

Always test the return value of the `renameTo` method to make sure that the file was renamed successfully.

Deleting a file

To delete a file, create a `File` object for the file and then call the `delete` method, as in this example:

```
File f = new File("hits.log");
if (f.delete())
    System.out.println("File deleted.");
else
    System.out.println("File not deleted.");
```

If the file is a directory, the directory must be empty to be deleted.

With some recursive programming, you can create a method that deletes a nonempty directory — but be sure to heed the upcoming warning. The method looks something like this:

```
private static void deleteFile(File dir)
{
    File[] files = dir.listFiles();
    for (File f : files)
    {
    if (f.isDirectory())
        deleteFile(f);
    else
        f.delete();
    }
    dir.delete();
}
```

Then, to delete a folder named `folder1` along with all its files and subdirectories, call the `deleteFile` method:

```
deleteFile(new File("folder1");
```

This feature is extremely dangerous to add to a program. Don't use it without first testing it carefully. If you accidentally delete all the files on your hard drive, don't blame me!

Using Command-Line Parameters

Ever since Book I, Chapter 1, I've used this construction in every Java program presented so far:

```
public static void main(String[] args)
```

It's high time that you find out what the `args` parameter of the `main` method is used for. The `args` parameter is an array of strings that lets you access any command-line parameters that are specified by the user when he or she runs your program.

Suppose that you run a Java program named `Test` from a command program like this:

```
C:\>java Test the quick brown fox
```

In this case, the Java program is passed four parameters: `the`, `quick`, `brown`, and `fox`. You can access these parameters via the `args` array.

Suppose that the `main` method of the `Test` class is written like this:

```
public static void main(String[] args)
{
    for (String s : args)
        System.out.println(s);
}
```

Then the program displays the following output on the console when run with the command shown a few paragraphs back:

```
the
quick
brown
fox
```

Command-line parameters are useful in Java programs that work with files as a way to pass pathnames to the program. Here's a program that lists all the files in a directory passed to the program as a parameter:

```
import java.io.*;

public class ListDirectory
{
    public static void main(String[] args)
    {
        if (args.length > 0)
        {
            String path = args[0];
            File dir = new File(path);
            if (dir.isDirectory())
            {
                File[] files = dir.listFiles();
                for (File f : files)
                {
                    System.out.println(f.getName());
                }
            }
            else
                System.out.println("Not a directory.");
        }
    }
}
```

Choosing Files in a Swing Application

For the most part, you don't want to mess around with command-line parameters in Swing applications. Instead, you want to use the `JFileChooser` class to let users pick the files they want to work with. This class lets you display Open and Save dialog boxes similar to the ones you've seen in other graphic user interface (GUI) applications with just a few lines of code.

Figure 1-1 shows an Open dialog box created with just these two lines of code:

```
JFileChooser fc = new JFileChooser();
int result = fc.showOpenDialog(this);
```

Figure 1-1:
An Open
dialog box
displayed
by the
JFileChooser
class.

This code appears in a frame class that extends the `JFrame` class, so the `this` keyword in the `showOpenDialog` call refers to the parent frame.

The result returned by the `showOpenDialog` method indicates whether the user chose to open a file or click Cancel, and the `JFileChooser` class provides a handy `getSelectedFile` method that you can use to get a `File` object for the file selected by the user.

The important thing to know about the `JFileChooser` class is that it doesn't actually open or save the file selected by the user; instead, it returns a `File` object for the file the user selects. Your program has the task of opening or saving the file.

The JFileChooser class has many additional methods that you can use to tailor its appearance and behavior in just about any way imaginable. Table 1-2 lists the commonly used constructors and methods of this powerful class.

Table 1-2	The JFileChooser Class
Constructor	*Description*
JFileChooser()	Creates a file chooser that begins at the user's default directory. On Windows systems, this directory is usually My Documents.
JFileChooser(File file)	Creates a file chooser that begins at the location indicated by the file parameter.
JFileChooser(String path)	Creates a file chooser that begins at the location indicated by the path string.
Method	*Description*
void addChoosableFileFilter (FileFilter filter)	Adds a file filter to the chooser.
File getSelectedFile()	Returns a File object for the file selected by the user.
File[] getSelectedFiles()	Returns an array of File objects for the files selected by the user if the file chooser allows multiple selections.
void setAcceptAllFileFilter Used(boolean value)	If false, removes the All Files filter from the file chooser.
void setApproveButtonText(String text)	Sets the text for the Approve button.
void setDialogTitle(String title)	Sets the title displayed by the file-chooser dialog box.
void setFileHidingEnabled(boolean value)	Doesn't show hidden files if true.
void setMultiSelectionEnabl ed(boolean value)	Allows the user to select more than one file if true.
int showDialog(Component parent, String text)	Displays a custom dialog box with the specified text for the Accept button. The return values are JFileChooser.CANCEL_ OPTION, APPROVE_OPTION, and ERROR_OPTION.

Method	Description
`void setFileSelectionMode(int mode)`	Determines whether the user can select files, directories, or both. The parameter can be specified as `JFileChooser.FILES_ONLY`, `DIRECTORIES_ONLY`, or `FILES_AND_DIRECTORIES`.
`int showOpenDialog(Component parent)`	Displays an Open dialog box. The return values are the same as for the `showDialog` method.
`int showSaveDialog(Component parent)`	Displays a Save dialog box. The return values are the same as for the `showDialog` method.

Creating an Open dialog box

As you've just seen, you can create an Open dialog box with just a few lines of code. First, you call the `JFileChooser` constructor to create a `JFileChooser` instance; then you call the `showOpenDialog` method to display an Open dialog box.

If you don't pass a parameter to the constructor, the file chooser starts in the user's default directory, which on most systems is the operating system's current directory. If you want to start in some other directory, you have two options:

✦ Create a `File` object for the directory and then pass the `File` object to the constructor.

✦ Pass the pathname for the directory where you want to start to the constructor.

The `JFileChooser` class also includes methods that let you control the appearance of the chooser dialog box. You can use the `setDialogTitle` method to set the title (the default is `Open`), for example, and you can use the `setFileHidingEnabled` method to control whether hidden files are shown. If you want to allow the user to select more than one file, use the `setMultiSelectionEnabled` method.

A `setFileSelectionMode` method lets you specify whether users can select files, directories, or both. The options for this method need a little explanation:

✦ **`JFileChooser.FILES_ONLY`:** With this option (which is the default), the user can choose files only with the file-chooser dialog box. The user can navigate directories in the file-chooser dialog box but can't actually select a directory.

+ **JFileChooser.DIRECTORIES_ONLY:** With this option, the user can select only directories, not files. One common use for this option is to let the user choose a default location for files used by your application without actually opening a file.

+ **JFileChooser.FILES_AND_DIRECTORIES:** This option lets the user select either a file or a directory. For most applications, you want the user to pick either a file or a directory, but not both, so you probably won't use this option much.

In addition to an Open dialog box, you can display a Save dialog box by calling the showSaveDialog method. A Save dialog box is similar to an Open dialog box but has different default values for the title and the text shown on the Approve button. Otherwise these dialog boxes work pretty much the same way.

Getting the selected file

The file-chooser dialog box is a *modal* dialog box, which means that after you call the showOpenDialog method, your application is tied up until the user closes the file-chooser dialog box by clicking the Open or Cancel button.

You can find out which button the user clicked by inspecting the value returned by the showOpenDialog method:

+ If the user clicked Open, the return value is JFileChooser. APPROVE_OPTION.

+ If the user clicked Cancel, the return value is JFileChooser. CANCEL_OPTION.

+ If an I/O (input/output) or other error occurred, the return value is JFileChooser.ERROR_OPTION.

Assuming that the showOpenDialog method returns APPROVE_OPTION, you can use the getSelectedFile method to get a File object for the file selected by the user. Then you can use this File object elsewhere in the program to read or write data.

Putting it all together, then, here's a method that displays a file-chooser dialog box and returns a File object for the file selected by the user. If the user cancels or an error occurs, the method returns null.

```
private File getFile()
{
    JFileChooser fc = new JFileChooser();
    int result = fc.showOpenDialog(null);
    File file = null;
    if (result == JFileChooser.APPROVE_OPTION)
        file = fc.getSelectedFile();
    return file;
}
```

You can call this method from an action event handler when the user clicks a button, selects a menu command, or otherwise indicates that he or she wants to open a file.

Using file filters

The file-chooser dialog box includes a Files of Type drop-down list filter that the user can use to control what types of files are displayed by the chooser. By default, the only item available in this drop-down list is All Files, which doesn't filter the files at all. If you want to add another filter to this list, you must create a class that extends the `FileFilter` abstract class and then pass an instance of this class to the `addChoosableFileFilter` method.

Table 1-3 lists the methods of the `FileFilter` class. Fortunately, it has only two methods that you need to implement. This class is in the `javax.swing.filechooser` package.

For some reason, the Java designers gave this class the same name as an interface that's in the `java.io` package, which is also frequently used in applications that work with files. As a result, you need to fully qualify this class when you extend it, like this:

```
class JavaFilter
    extends javax.swing.filechooser.FileFilter
```

Table 1-3	The FileFilter Class
Method	*Description*
`public boolean abstract accept(File f)`	You must implement this method to return `true` if you want the file to be displayed in the chooser or `false` if you don't want the file to be displayed.
`public String abstract getDescription()`	You must implement this method to return the description string that is displayed in the Files of Type drop-down list in the chooser dialog box.

The `getDescription` method simply returns the text displayed in the Files of Type drop-down list. You usually implement it with a single return statement that returns the description. Here's an example:

```
public String getDescription()
{
    return "Java files (*.java)";
}
```

Here the string Java files (*.java) is displayed in the Files of Type drop-down list.

The accept method does the work of a file filter. The file chooser calls this method for every file it displays. The file is passed as a parameter. The accept method returns a boolean that indicates whether the file is displayed.

The accept method can use any criteria it wants to decide which files to accept and which files to reject. Most filters do this based on the file-extension part of the filename. Unfortunately, the File class doesn't have a method that returns the file extension, but you can get the name with the getName method and then use the matches method with a regular expression to determine whether the file is of the type you're looking for. Here's an if statement that determines whether the filename in the name variable is a .java file:

```
if (name.matches(".*\\.java"))
```

Here the regular expression matches strings that begin with any sequence of characters and end with .java. (For more information about regular expressions, refer to Book V, Chapter 3.)

Here's a FileFilter class that displays files with the extension .java:

```
private class javaFilter
    extends javax.swing.filechooser.FileFilter
{
    public boolean accept(File f)
    {
        if (f.isDirectory())
            return true;
        String name = f.getName();
        if (name.matches(".*\\.java"))
            return true;
        else
            return false;
    }
    public String getDescription()
    {
        return "Java files (*.java)";
    }
}
```

After you create a class that implements a file filter, you can add the file filter to the file chooser by calling the addChoosableFileFilter method, passing a new instance of the FileFilter class, like this:

```
fc.setChoosableFileFilter(new JavaFilter());
```

If you want, you can remove the All Files filter by calling the method `set AcceptAllFileFilterUsed`, like this:

`fc.setAcceptAllFileFilterUsed(false);`

Then only the file filters that you add to the file chooser appear in the Files of Type drop-down list.

Using Path Objects

Java 1.7 introduces a new type of object called a `Path` to address several weaknesses of the `File` class, which has been part of Java since version 1.0. The most egregious of the `File` class flaws addressed by `Path` objects is that many of the operations of the `File` class don't provide detailed error information when problems occur. The `delete` method of the `File` class, for example, returns a boolean value to indicate whether the file was deleted, but if the file could not be deleted, there's no way to find out why. `Path` objects correct this deficiency by throwing exceptions that contain detailed error information if an operation fails.

Note that `Path` is not actually a class; instead, it's an interface. That means you can't directly create a `Path` object by calling a constructor. Instead, you use a method of new class called `Paths` to create `Path` objects. The naming is confusing — `Path` versus `Paths`, interfaces versus classes — but after working with the `Paths` class to create `Path` objects, you get used to the distinction.

Both the `Path` interface and the `Paths` class are in the `java.nio.File` package, so any program that uses them should import `java.nio.file.*`.

Table 1-4 lists the constructor and methods of the `Path` class.

Table 1-4	Path Methods
Method	*Description*
`Path copyTo(Path target)`	Copies the file to the specified target file.
`Path moveTo(Path target)`	Moves the file to the target path and deletes the original file.
`Path createDirectory()`	Creates the directory on the hard drive if it doesn't already exist.
`Path createFile()`	Creates the file on the hard drive if it doesn't already exist.

(continued)

Table 1-4 *(continued)*

Method	Description
`void delete()`	Deletes the file or directory. The method throws an exception if the file or directory doesn't exist or couldn't be deleted.
`void deleteIfExists()`	Deletes the file or directory if it exists. The method doesn't throw an exception if the file or directory doesn't exist.
`boolean exists()`	Returns `true` if the file exists on the hard drive or `false` if the file doesn't exist on the hard drive.
`boolean notExists()`	Returns `true` if the file doesn't exist on the hard drive or `false` if the file does exist on the hard drive.
`String toAbsolutePath()`	Returns the full absolute path to the file, including the drive letter if run on a Windows system.
`DirectoryStream newDirectoryStream()`	Gets a `DirectoryStream` object that you can use to read the contents of the directory.
`DirectoryStream newDirectoryStream(String filter)`	Gets a `DirectoryStream` object that's filtered by the filter string, which can contain wildcards such as `*.txt` to retrieve just `.txt` files.
`boolean isFile()`	Returns `true` if this `File` object is a file or `false` if it is a directory.
`String toString()`	Returns the pathname for this file or directory as a string.

Creating files with the Paths class

One thing you may find confusing right off the bat is that the `Path` objects are created by calling a static method of the `Paths` class. `Path` and `Paths` are two distinct things: `Path` is an interface, and `Paths` is a class. To create a `Path` object, use the `get` method of the static `Paths` class, like this:

```
Path p = Paths.get("c:\\test.txt");
```

Here the file's name is `test.txt`, and it resides in the root directory of the `C:` drive.

Like a `File` object, a `Path` object represents a file that may or may not actually exist on the hard drive. You can test to see whether a file exists like this:

```
Path p = Paths.get(path);
if (!p.exists())
    System.out.println
        ("The input file does not exist!");
```

To create a new file, use the `createFile` method, like this:

```
Path p = Paths.get("c:\\test.txt");
try
{
    p.createFile();
    System.out.println ("File created!");
}
catch (Exception e)
{
    System.out.println ("Error: " + e.getMessage());
}
```

Note that the `createFile` method throws an exception if the file couldn't be created. The `getMessage` method of this exception returns a message that explains why the file couldn't be created.

Getting the contents of a directory

One of the weaknesses of the `File` class is that it doesn't deal well with large directories. In particular, methods such as `listFiles` that allow you to access the contents of a directory return an array of `File` objects. That's fine if the directory contains a few dozen or even a few hundred files, but what if the directory contains thousands or tens of thousands of files? In short, the `File` class is not scalable.

The `Path` class remedies this deficiency by letting you access the contents of a directory via a stream object defined by `DirectoryStream`. I say more about working with streams in Book VIII, Chapter 2, but for now, suffice it to say that a stream provides a simple way to access a large number of data items one at a time. You can retrieve the items in a directory stream easily by using an enhanced `for` statement, as in this example:

```
Path c = Paths.get("C:\\");
try
{
    DirectoryStream<Path> stream
        = c.newDirectoryStream();
    for (Path entry: stream)
        System.out.println(entry.toString());
}
catch (Exception e)
{
    System.out.println("Error: " + e.getMessage());
}
```

This example displays a listing of the contents of the C:\ directory, much as typing DIR C:\ at a command prompt would.

You could change the preceding example to list just the text files (files with the extension .txt) by changing the first statement after the try statement to this:

```
DirectoryStream<Path> stream
    = c.newDirectoryStream("*.txt");
```

Using a File Visitor to Walk a File Tree

In the section "Getting the contents of a directory," earlier in this chapter, I mention that processing subdirectories of a main directory by using the File class requires fancy recursive programming. With Java 1.7 (and later versions), you can use a new feature that does the difficult recursive part of the programming for you. It does this by *walking* the file tree — visiting every file in the tree and calling one or more methods defined by a special class you create, called a *file visitor*. Here are the basic details of how this magic works:

1. **Create a file-visitor class, which is extended from FileVisitor or, more often, SimpleFileVisitor.**

The SimpleFileVisitor class defines several methods that are called for every file in the file tree, as shown in Table 1-5.

Table 1-5	The SimpleFileVisitor Class
Method	*Description*
FileVisitResult visitFile(T file, BasicFileAttributes attr)	Called once for every file in the file tree.
FileVisitResult visitFileFailed(T file, IOException e)	Called if the file couldn't be accessed.
FileVisitResult preVisitDirectory(T dir)	Called once for every directory in the file tree. This method is called before any of the files in the directory are visited.
FileVisitResult preVisitDirectoryFailed (T dir, IOException e)	Called once for every directory in the file tree that couldn't be accessed.
FileVisitResult postVisitDirectory(T dir)	Called once for every directory in the file tree. This method is called after all the files in the directory are visited.

2. **In the file visitor, override one or more methods that are defined by the `SimpleFileVisitor` class.**

These methods are where you write the code that you want to execute for every file visited when the directory tree is walked. You always want to override at least three of the methods listed in Table 1-5:

- `visitFile`, which is called for every file in the file tree

- `visitFileFailed`, which is called for every file that can't be accessed (usually due to permissions issues)

- `preVisitDirectoryFailed`, which is called for every directory that couldn't be accessed

3. **Create a `Path` object that indicates the starting point (that is, the root) of the file tree you want to walk.**

If you want to visit all the files on your `C:` drive, for example, this path should point to `C:\`.

4. **Call the `walkFileTree` method of the static `Files` class to process the files.**

This method takes just two arguments: the `Path` object (which identifies the root of your file tree) and an instance of your file-visitor class.

Confusing enough? An example should clear things up. Listing 1-1 shows just about the simplest example of a file visitor I can come up with. This program lists all the files in `C:\Windows\System32`, including all its subfolders.

Listing 1-1:   Simple File Visitor

```
import java.nio.file.*;
import java.io.*;
import java.nio.file.attribute.*;

public class FileVisitorDemo
{
    public static void main(String[] args)
    {
        Path start = Paths.get("c:\\Windows\\System32");      #9
        MyFileVisitor visitor = new MyFileVisitor();          #10
        try
        {
            Files.walkFileTree(start, visitor);               #13
        }
        catch (Exception e)
        {
            System.out.println(e.getMessage());
        }
    }
    private static class MyFileVisitor extends SimpleFileVisitor <Path>    #21
    {
```

(continued)

Listing 1-1 *(continued)*

```
public FileVisitResult visitFile(Path file,                      #23
    BasicFileAttributes attr)
{
    System.out.println(file.toString());
    return FileVisitResult.CONTINUE;                            #27
}

public FileVisitResult visitFileFailed(Path file,              #30
    BasicFileAttributes attr)
{
    System.out.println(file.toString() + " COULD NOT ACCESS!");
    return FileVisitResult.CONTINUE;
}

public FileVisitResult preVisitDirectoryFailed                 #36
    (Path dir, IOException e)
{
    System.out.println(dir.toString() + " COULD NOT ACCESS!");
    return FileVisitResult.CONTINUE;
}
    }
}
```

Here are the highlights of how this program works:

→ 9   Creates an instance of the Path class that starts the file tree at
       C:\Windows\System32. You could substitute any directory you
       want for this path.

→ 10   Creates an instance of the MyFileVisitor class, which is defined
       later in the program (at line 21).

→ 13   Walks the file tree, starting at the directory indicated by start,
       using the MyFileVisitor object created in line 10.

→ 21   Defines the MyFileVisitor class, which extends the Simple
       FileVisitor class. SimpleFileVisitor is a generic class, so
       you must specify a type. Usually you specify the Path type so
       that SimpleFileVisitor processes Path objects.

→ 23   Overrides the visitFile method, which is called once for each
       file that is accessed as the file tree is walked. This method simply
       prints the name of the file to the console. In a more realistic pro-
       gram, you would perform some more significant action on the file,
       such as copying it or opening the file and reading its contents.

→ 27   Produces the return value of the visitFile method, which is of
       type FileVisitResult. The most commonly returned value is
       CONTINUE, which indicates that the file-tree walker should con-
       tinue processing files. Other options include TERMINATE, SKIP_
       SIBLINGS, and SKIP_SUBTREE.

→ 30   Overrides the `visitFileFailed` method, which is called whenever a file can't be accessed. In this program, the `visitFile Failed` method simply prints an error message.

→ 36   Overrides the `preVisitDirectoryFailed` method, which is called whenever a directory can't be accessed. Like the `visitFile Failed` method, the `preVisitDirectoryFailed` method simply prints an error message.

Chapter 2: Working with File Streams

In This Chapter

✔ Knowing your Java streams

✔ Reading and writing text streams

✔ Reading and writing binary streams

I/O, I/O, it's off to work I go.

Or so goes the classic song, which pretty much sums up the whole purpose of computers. Without I/O (input/output), computers — and the programs that run on them — would be worthless.

Imagining any useful computer program that doesn't do some form of I/O is hard. Even the very first program presented in this book — the classic `Hello, World!` program — does I/O; it displays a simple message onscreen.

In this chapter, you find out about Java's most fundamental technique for getting data into and out of programs: streams. You've been working with streams all along in this book. When you use the `System.out.print` or `System.out.println` method to display text on the console, you're actually sending data to an output stream, and when you use a `Scanner` object to get data from `System.in`, you're reading data from an input stream.

In this chapter, you build on what you already know about stream I/O and see how it can be used to read and write data to hard-drive files.

Understanding Streams

A *stream* is simply a flow of characters to and from a program. The other end of the stream can be anything that can accept or generate a stream of characters, including a console window, a printer, a file on a disk drive, or even another program.

Streams have no idea of the structure or meaning of your data; a stream is just a sequence of characters. In later chapters of Book VIII, you find out how to work with data at a higher level by using databases and XML.

You can roughly divide the world of Java stream I/O into two camps:

✦ **Character streams:** *Character streams* read and write text characters that represent strings. You can connect a character stream to a text file to store text data on a hard drive. Typically, text files use special characters called *delimiters* to separate elements of the file. For example:

- A *comma-delimited file* uses commas to separate individual fields of data.

- A *tab-delimited file* uses tabs to separate fields.

Usually you can display a text file in a text editor and make some sense of its contents.

✦ **Binary streams:** *Binary streams* read and write individual bytes that represent primitive data types. You can connect a binary stream to a *binary file* to store binary data on a hard drive. The contents of binary files make perfect sense to the programs that read and write them, but if you try to open a binary file in a text editor, the file's contents look like gibberish.

Conceptually, the trickiest part of understanding how streams work is getting your mind around all the different classes. Java has nearly 100 classes for working with streams. Fortunately, you need to know about only a few of them for most file I/O applications. In the rest of this chapter, I tell you about the most important classes for working with character and binary streams. (For a complete list of file I/O classes, browse to `http://download.java.net/jdk8/docs/api/` and click java.io in the list of packages near the top left of the page.)

All the classes in this chapter are in the `java.io` package, so programs that work with file streams include an `import java.io.*` statement.

Reading Character Streams

To read a text file through a character stream, you usually work with the following classes:

✦ `File`: The `File` class (which I cover in detail in Book VIII, Chapter 1) represents a file on a hard drive. In file I/O applications, the main purpose of the `File` class is to identify the file you want to read from or write to.

✦ `FileReader`: The `FileReader` class provides basic methods for reading data from a character stream that originates from a file. It provides methods that let you read data one character at a time. Usually, you don't work with this class directly. Instead, you create a `FileReader` object to connect your program to a file and then pass that object to the constructor of the BufferedReader class, which provides more efficient access to the file. (This class extends the abstract class Reader, which is the base class for a variety of classes that can read character data from a stream.)

✦ **BufferedReader:** This class "wraps" around the FileReader class to provide more efficient input. This class adds a *buffer* to the input stream that allows the input to be read from the hard drive in large chunks rather than a byte at a time, which can result in a huge improvement in performance. The BufferedReader class lets you read data one character at a time or a line at a time. In most programs, you read data one line at a time and then use Java's string-handling features to break the line into individual fields.

Table 2-1 lists the most important constructors and methods of these classes.

Table 2-1   The BufferedReader and FileReader Classes

Constructor	Description
BufferedReader(Reader in)	Creates a buffered reader from any object that extends the Reader class. Typically you pass this constructor a FileReader object.
FileReader(File file)	Creates a file reader from the specified File object. It throws FileNotFoundException if the file doesn't exist or if it's a directory rather than a file.
FileReader(String path)	Creates a file reader from the specified pathname. It throws FileNotFoundException if the file doesn't exist or if it's a directory rather than a file.

Method	Description
void close()	Closes the file and throws IOException.
int read()	Reads a single character from the file and returns it as an integer. The method returns −1 if the end of the file has been reached. It throws IOException.
String readLine()	Reads an entire line and returns it as a string. The method returns null if the end of the file has been reached. It throws IOException.
void skip(long num)	Skips ahead the specified number of characters.

In the following sections, you find out how to read a file named movies.txt that contains one line each for ten of my favorite movies. Each line of the file contains the title of the movie, a tab, the year when the movie was released, another tab, and the price I paid for it. Here are the contents of the file:

```
It's a Wonderful Life→1946→14.95
Young Frankenstein→1974→16.95
Star Wars→1977→17.95
The Princess Bride→1987→16.95
Glory→1989→14.95
The Game→1997→14.95
Shakespeare in Love→1998→19.95
Zombieland→2009→18.95
The King's Speech→2010→17.85
Star Trek: Into Darkness→2013→19.95
```

(In this list, the arrows represent tab characters.) Later in this chapter, I show you a program that writes data to this file.

If you create this file with a text editor, make sure that your text editor preserves the tabs correctly.

Creating a BufferedReader

The normal way to connect a character stream to a file is to create a File object for the file, using one of the techniques presented in Book VIII, Chapter 1. Then you can call the FileReader constructor to create a FileReader object and pass this object to the BufferedReader constructor to create a BufferedReader object, as in this example:

```
File f = new File("movies.txt");
BufferedReader in = new BufferedReader(
                new FileReader(f));
```

Here a BufferedReader object is created to read the movies.txt file.

Reading from a character stream

To read a line from the file, you use the readLine method of the Buffered Reader class. This method returns null when the end of the file is reached. As a result, testing the string returned by the readLine method in a while loop to process all the lines in the file is common.

This code snippet reads each line from the file and prints it to the console:

```
String line = in.readLine();
while (line != null)
{
    System.out.println(line);
    line = in.readLine();
}
```

After you read a line of data from the file, you can use Java's string-handling features to pull individual bits of data out of the line. In particular, you can use the split method to separate the line into the individual strings that are separated by tabs. Then you can use the appropriate parse methods (such as parseInt and parseDouble) to convert each string to its correct data type.

Here's a routine that converts a line read from the movies.txt file to the title (a string), year (an int), and price (a double):

```
String[] data = line.split("\t");
String title = data[0];
int year = Integer.parseInt(data[1]);
double price = Double.parseDouble(data[2]);
```

After the entire file is read, you can close the stream by calling the close method, like so:

```
in.close();
```

Reading the movies.txt file

Listing 2-1 shows a complete, albeit simple, program that reads the movies.txt file and prints the contents of the file to the console.

Listing 2-1:   Reading from a Text File

```
import java.io.*;                                           →1
import java.text.NumberFormat;

public class ReadFile
{
    public static void main(String[] args)
    {
        NumberFormat cf = NumberFormat.getCurrencyInstance();

        BufferedReader in = getReader("movies.txt");        →10

        Movie movie = readMovie(in);                        →12
        while (movie != null)                               →13
        {
            String msg = Integer.toString(movie.year);
            msg += ": " + movie.title;
            msg += " (" + cf.format(movie.price) + ")";
            System.out.println(msg);
            movie = readMovie(in);
        }
    }                                                        →21

    private static BufferedReader getReader(String name)    →23
    {
        BufferedReader in = null;
        try
```

Book VIII
Chapter 2

Working with
File Streams

(continued)

Listing 2-1 *(continued)*

```
        {
            File file = new File(name);
            in = new BufferedReader(
                new FileReader(file) );
        }
        catch (FileNotFoundException e)
        {
            System.out.println(
                "The file doesn't exist.");
            System.exit(0);
        }
        return in;
    }
    private static Movie readMovie(BufferedReader in)      →40
    {
        String title;
        int year;
        double price;
        String line = "";
        String[] data;
        try
        {
            line = in.readLine();
        }
        catch (IOException e)
        {
            System.out.println("I/O Error");
            System.exit(0);
        }
        if (line == null)
            return null;
        else
        {
            data = line.split("\t");
            title = data[0];
            year = Integer.parseInt(data[1]);
            price = Double.parseDouble(data[2]);
            return new Movie(title, year, price);
        }
    }

    private static class Movie                             →70
    {
        public String title;
        public int year;
        public double price;

        public Movie(String title, int year, double price)
        {
            this.title = title;
            this.year = year;
```

```
            this.price = price;
        }
    }
}
```

If you run this program, the following output is displayed on the console:

```
1946: It's a Wonderful Life ($14.95)
1974: Young Frankenstein ($16.95)
1977: Star Wars ($17.95)
1987: The Princess Bride ($16.95)
1989: Glory ($14.95)
1997: The Game ($14.95)
1998: Shakespeare in Love ($19.95)
2009: Zombieland ($18.95)
2010: The King's Speech ($17.85)
2013: Star Trek Into Darkness ($19.95)
```

Because I've already explained most of this code, the following paragraphs provide just a road map to this program:

→ **1**   The program begins with `import java.io.*` to import all the Java I/O classes used by the program.

→ **10**   The program uses a method named `getReader` to create a `BufferedReader` object that can read the file. The name of the file is passed to this method as a parameter. Note that in a real program, you'd probably get this filename from the user via a `JFileChooser` dialog box or some other means. In any event, the `BufferedReader` object returned by the `getReader` method is saved in a variable named `in`.

→ **12**   Another method, named `readMovie`, is used to read each movie from the file. This method returns a `Movie` object. (`Movie` is a private class that's defined later in the program.) If the end of the file has been reached, this method returns `null`.

→ **13**   A `while` loop is used to process each movie. This loop simply builds a message string from the `Movie` object, displays it on the console, and then calls `readMovie` to read the next movie in the file.

→ **21**   The program ends without closing the file. That's okay, though, because the file is closed automatically when the program that opened it ends. If the program were to go on with other processing after it finished with the file, you'd want to close the file first.

→ **23**   The `getReader` method creates a `BufferedReader` object for the filename passed as a parameter. If any exceptions are thrown during creation of the `BufferedReader` object, the program exits.

→ **40**   The `readMovie` method reads a line from the reader passed as a parameter, parses the data in the line, creates a `Movie` object from the data, and returns the `Movie` object. If the end of the file

Book VIII
Chapter 2

Working with File Streams

is reached, this method returns `null`. The statement that reads the line from the file is enclosed in a `try/catch` block that exits the program if an I/O error occurs.

→ 70   The `Movie` class is a private inner class that defines the movie objects. To keep the class simple, it uses public fields and a single constructor that initializes the fields.

Writing Character Streams

The usual way to write data to a text file is to use the `PrintWriter` class — which, as luck would have it, you're already familiar with. It's the same class that provides the `print` and `println` methods used to write console output. As a result, the only real trick to writing output to a text file is figuring out how to connect a print writer to a text file. To do that, you work with three classes:

✦ **FileWriter:** The `FileWriter` class connects to a `File` object but provides only rudimentary writing ability.

✦ **BufferedWriter:** This class connects to a `FileWriter` and provides output buffering. Without the buffer, data is written to the hard drive one character at a time. This class lets the program accumulate data in a buffer and writes the data only when the buffer is filled or when the program requests that the data be written.

✦ **PrintWriter:** This class connects to a `Writer`, which can be a `BufferedWriter`, a `FileWriter`, or any other object that extends the abstract `Writer` class. Most often, you connect this class to a `Buffered Writer`.

The `PrintWriter` class is the only one of these classes whose methods you usually use when you write data to a file. Table 2-2 lists the most important constructors and methods of this class.

Table 2-2	The PrintWriter, BufferedWriter, and FileWriter Classes	
Constructor	*Description*
`PrintWriter(Writer out)`	Creates a print writer for the specified output writer.
`PrintWriter(Writer out, boolean flush)`	Creates a print writer for the specified output writer. If the second parameter is `true`, the buffer is automatically flushed whenever the `println` method is called.

Constructor	Description
BufferedWriter(Writer out)	Creates a buffered writer from the specified writer. Typically, you pass this constructor a FileWriter object.
FileWriter(File file)	Creates a file writer from the specified File object and throws IOException if an error occurs.
FileWriter(File file, boolean append)	Creates a file writer from the specified File object and throws IOException if an error occurs. If the second parameter is true, data is added to the end of the file if the file already exists.
FileWriter(String path)	Creates a file writer from the specified pathname and throws IOException if an error occurs.
FileWriter(String path, boolean append)	Creates a file writer from the specified pathname and throws IOException if an error occurs. If the second parameter is true, data is added to the end of the file if the file already exists.

PrintWriter Method	Description
void close()	Closes the file.
void flush()	Writes the contents of the buffer to the hard drive.
int read()	Reads a single character from the file and returns it as an integer. The method returns −1 if the end of the file has been reached. It throws IOException.
void print(value)	Writes the value, which can be any primitive type or any object. If the value is an object, the object's toString() method is called.
void println(value)	Writes the value, which can be any primitive type or any object. If the value is an object, the object's toString() method is called. A line break is written following the value.

Connecting a PrintWriter to a text file

To connect a character stream to an output file, you first create a `File` object for the file, as I describe in Book VIII, Chapter 1. Then you call the `PrintWriter` constructor to create a `PrintWriter` object that you can use to write to the file. This constructor wraps around a `BufferedWriter` object, which in turn wraps around a `FileWriter` object like this:

```
File file = new File("movies.txt");
PrintWriter out =
    new PrintWriter(
        new BufferedWriter(
            new FileWriter(file) ) );
```

If you find this arrangement a little confusing, that's good! That makes me feel a little better, because I find it a little confusing too. The basic idea going on here is that each of the classes is adding a capability to the class it wraps. At the bottom is the `FileWriter` class, which has the ability to write characters to a file. The `BufferedWriter` class adds buffering to the mix, saving data in a buffer until it makes sense to write it all out to the file in one big spurt. The `PrintWriter` class adds basic formatting capabilities, such as adding a line ending at the end of each line and converting primitive types to strings.

Both the `FileWriter` and the `PrintWriter` classes have an optional `boolean` parameter you can use to add extra capabilities to the file stream. If you specify `true` in the `FileWriter` constructor, the file is appended if it exists. *Appended* simply means that any data in the file is retained; data that you write to the file in your program is simply added to the end of the file. Here's a `PrintWriter` constructor that appends data to its file:

```
File file = new File("movies.txt");
PrintWriter out =
    new PrintWriter(
        new BufferedWriter(
            new FileWriter(file, true )))// append mode
```

If you specify `false` instead of `true`, or if you leave this parameter out, an existing file is deleted, and its data is lost.

The `boolean` parameter in the `PrintWriter` class has less dire consequences. It simply tells the `PrintWriter` class that it should tell the `BufferedWriter` class to flush its buffer whenever you use the `println` method to write a line of data. Although this option may decrease the efficiency of your program by a small amount, it also makes the program a little more reliable, because it reduces the odds of losing data if your program or the whole computer crashes while unwritten data is in the buffer.

Unfortunately, the code for specifying this option looks a little goofy because of the way that the constructors for the `BufferedWriter` and `FileWriter` classes are nested:

```
File file = new File("movies.txt");
PrintWriter out =
    new PrintWriter(
        new BufferedWriter(
            new FileWriter(file) ), true); ////mode flush
```

If all these nested constructors make your head spin, you can always construct each object separately and use variables to keep track of them. Here's an example that does just that, and also turns on append mode for `FileWriter` and flush mode for `PrintWriter`:

```
FileWriter fw = new FileWriter(file, true);
BufferedWriter bw = new BufferedWriter(fw);
PrintWriter out = new PrintWriter(bw, true);
```

If you find this coding technique easier to understand, by all means use it.

Writing to a character stream

After you successfully connect a character stream to a file, writing data to it is as easy as writing text to the console. You just use the `print` and `println` methods exactly as though you were writing to the console.

One minor complication is that if you're writing data to a text file in a delimited format, you have to include statements that write the delimiter characters to the file. Suppose (for example) that the title and year of a movie that you want to write to the text file are stored in `String` variables named `title` and `year`. This snippet of code writes these fields with a tab delimiter between them:

```
System.out.print(title);
System.out.print("\t");
System.out.println(year);
```

Here the last item to be written is written with the `println` method rather than the `print` method. That ends the current line.

If you prefer to be a little more efficient, you can build a string representing the entire line and then write the line all at once, as follows:

```
String line = title + "\t" + year;
System.out.println(line);
```

This method is a little more efficient than the preceding version, but not as much as you'd think. In most cases, `BufferedWriter` holds your text in a buffer until the `println` method is called anyway.

If you didn't specify the `flush` option when you created the `PrintWriter` object, you can still periodically force any data in the buffer to be written to the hard drive by calling the `flush` method, as follows:

```
out.flush();
```

Also, when you're finished writing data to the file, you can close the file by calling the `close` method, like this:

```
out.close();
```

Writing the movies.txt file

Listing 2-2 shows a complete program that writes lines to a text file. The data written is taken from an array that's hard-coded into the file, but you can easily imagine how to obtain the data from the user by prompting for console input or using text fields in a Swing application. (For full coverage of Swing, see Book VI.)

Listing 2-2:   Writing to a Text File

```java
import java.io.*;

public class WriteFile
{
    public static void main(String[] args)                      →5
    {
        Movie[] movies = getMovies();

        PrintWriter out = openWriter("movies2.txt");
        for (Movie m : movies)
            writeMovie(m, out);
        out.close();
    }

    private static Movie[] getMovies()                          →15
    {
        Movie[] movies = new Movie[10];

        movies[0] = new Movie("It's a Wonderful Life",
            1946, 14.95);
        movies[1] = new Movie("Young Frankenstein",
            1974, 16.95);
        movies[2] = new Movie("Star Wars",
            1977, 17.95);
        movies[3] = new Movie("The Princess Bride",
            1987, 16.95);
        movies[4] = new Movie("Glory",
            1989, 14.95);
        movies[5] = new Movie("The Game",
            1997, 14.95);
        movies[6] = new Movie("Shakespeare in Love",
            1998, 19.95);
        movies[7] = new Movie("Zombieland",
            1997, 18.95);
        movies[8] = new Movie("The King's Speech",
            1997, 19.95);
```

```
        movies[9] = new Movie("Star Trek Into Darkness",
            1997, 19.95);

        return movies;
    }

    private static PrintWriter openWriter(String name)        →43
    {
        try
        {
            File file = new File(name);
            PrintWriter out =
                new PrintWriter(
                    new BufferedWriter(
                        new FileWriter(file) ), true );
            return out;
        }
        catch (IOException e)
        {
            System.out.println("I/O Error");
            System.exit(0);
        }
        return null;
    }

    private static void writeMovie(Movie m,                   →61
        PrintWriter out)
    {
        String line = m.title;
        line += "\t" + Integer.toString(m.year);
        line += "\t" + Double.toString(m.price);
        out.println(line);
    }

    private static class Movie                                →70
    {
        public String title;
        public int year;
        public double price;

        public Movie(String title, int year, double price)
        {
            this.title = title;
            this.year = year;
            this.price = price;
        }
    }
}
```

Because all the coding elements in this program have already been explained in this chapter, the following paragraphs just provide a road map to the major part of the program:

→ **5**   The `main` method begins by calling a method named `getMovies`, which returns an array of `Movie` objects to be written to the file. (The `Movie` class is defined as an inner class later in the program.) Then it calls `openWriter`, which creates a `PrintWriter` object that the program can use to write data to the file. Next, it uses an enhanced `for` loop to call the `writeMovie` method for each movie in the array. This method accepts a `Movie` object that contains the movie to be written and a `PrintWriter` object to write the movie to. Finally, the `PrintWriter` is closed.

→ **15**   The `getMovies` method returns an array of `Movie` objects that are written to a file. In a real-life program, you'd probably do something other than hard-code the movie information in this method. You might prompt the user to enter the data, for example, or use a Swing frame to get the data.

→ **43**   The `openWriter` method creates a `PrintWriter` object for the filename passed to it as a parameter. The `PrintWriter` uses a buffer that's flushed each time `println` is called.

→ **61**   The `writeMovie` method accepts as parameters a `Movie` object to be written and the `PrintWriter` to which the movie should be written. It creates a string that includes the title, a tab, the year, another tab, and the price; then it writes the string to the file.

→ **70**   The `Movie` class is an inner class that defines a movie object. This class simply consists of three public fields (title, year, and price) and a constructor that initializes the fields.

Reading Binary Streams

Binary streams, used to store data in raw binary format rather than in text format, are a bit tougher to read than character streams. The biggest obstacle to pass when you're reading a binary stream is that you need to know exactly the type of each item that was written to the file. If any incorrect data is in the file, the program won't work, so you need to ensure that the file contains the data your program expects it to contain.

To read a binary file, you usually work with the following classes:

◆ **`File`:** Once again, you use the `File` class to represent the file itself.

◆ **`FileInputStream`:** `FileInputStream` is what connects the input stream to a file.

◆ **`BufferedInputStream`:** This class adds buffering to the basic `FileInputStream`, which improves the stream's efficiency and gives it a moist and chewy texture.

✦ **DataInputStream:** This class is the one you actually work with to read data from the stream. The other `Stream` classes read a byte at a time. This class knows how to read basic data types, including primitive types and strings.

Table 2-3 lists the vital constructors and methods of these classes.

Table 2-3	Classes for Reading Binary Streams
Constructors	*Description*
`BufferedInputStream (InputStream in)`	Creates a buffered input stream from any object that extends the `InputStream` class. Typically you pass this constructor a `FileInputStream` object.
`DataInputStream (InputStream in)`	Creates a data input stream from any object that extends the `InputStream` class. Typically you pass this constructor a `BufferedInputStream` object.
`FileInputStream File (File file)`	Creates a file input stream from the specified object. It throws `FileNotFoundException` if the file doesn't exist or if it's a directory rather than a file.
`FileInputStream(String path)`	Creates a file input stream from the specified pathname. It throws `FileNotFoundException` if the file doesn't exist or if it's a directory rather than a file.
DataInputStream Methods	*Description*
`boolean readBoolean()`	Reads a `boolean` value from the input stream. It throws `EOFException` and `IOException`.
`byte readByte()`	Reads a `byte` value from the input stream. It throws `EOFException` and `IOException`.
`char readChar()`	Reads a `char` value from the input stream. It throws `EOFException` and `IOException`.

(continued)

Book VIII
Chapter 2

Working with
File Streams

Table 2-3 *(continued)*

Constructors	Description
double readDouble()	Reads a double value from the input stream. It throws EOFException and IOException.
float readFloat()	Reads a float value from the input stream. It throws EOFException and IOException.
int readInt()	Reads an int value from the input stream. It throws EOFException and IOException.
long readLong()	Reads a long value from the input stream. It throws EOFException and IOException.
short readShort()	Reads a short value from the input stream. It throws EOFException and IOException.
String readUTF()	Reads a string stored in UTF format from the input stream. It throws EOFException, IOException, and UTFDataFormatException.

The following sections present programs that read and write data in a binary file named movies.dat that contains information about movies. Each record in this file consists of a UTF string containing the movie's title, an int representing the year when the movie was released, and a double representing the price I paid for the movie at my local discount video store. Although the format of this file is different from that of the movies.txt file shown earlier in this chapter, the file contains the same data. Refer to the section "Reading Character Streams," earlier in this chapter, to see a list of the movies in this file.

If you're unfamiliar with UTF, it is a standardized way of encoding characters in text files. The most commonly used forms of UTF are UTF-8, which encodes each character as a single byte, and UTF-16, which encodes each character as a 2-byte sequence. For more information, use your favorite search engine to search for **UTF**.

Creating a DataInputStream

To read data from a binary file, you want to connect a DataInputStream object to an input file. To do that, you use a File object to represent the file, a FileInputStream object that represents the file as an input stream, a BufferedInputStream object that adds buffering to the mix, and finally a `DataInputStream` object to provide the methods that read various data types. The constructor for such a beast looks like this:

```
File file = new File("movies.dat");
DataInputStream in = new DataInputStream(
        new BufferedInputStream(
            new FileInputStream(file) ) );
```

If all this nesting makes you nauseous, you can use this format instead:

```
File file = new File("movies.dat");
FileInputStream fs = new FileInputStream(file);
BufferedInputStream bs = new BufferedInputStream(fs);
DataInputStream in = new DataInputStream(bs);
```

Either way, the effect is the same.

Reading from a data input stream

With binary files, you don't read an entire line into the program and parse it into individual fields. Instead, you use the various `read` methods of the `DataInputStream` class to read the fields one at a time. To do that, you have to know the exact sequence in which data values appear in the file.

Here's a code snippet that reads the information for a single movie and stores the data in variables:

```
String title = in.readUTF();
int year = in.readInt();
double price = in.readDouble();
```

All of the read methods throw `EOFException` if the end of the file is reached and `IOException` if an I/O error occurs, so you need to call these methods inside a `try`/`catch` block that catches these exceptions. The `readUTF` method also throws `UTFDataFormatException`, but that exception is a type of `IOException`, so you probably don't need to catch it separately.

The `read` methods usually are used in a `while` loop to read all the data from the file. When the end of the file is reached, `EOFException` is thrown. Then you can catch this exception and stop the loop. One way to do that is to use a `boolean` variable to control the loop, as follows:

```
boolean eof = false;
while (!eof)
{
    try
    {
        String title = in.readUTF();
        int year = in.readInt();
        double price = in.readDouble();
        // do something with the data here
    }
```

```
        catch (EOFException e)
        {
            eof = true;
        }
        catch (IOException e)
        {
            System.out.println("An I/O error "
                + "has occurred!");
            System.exit(0);
        }
}
```

Here the `boolean` variable `eof` is set to `true` when `EOFException` is thrown, and the loop continues to execute as long as `eof` is `false`.

After you read a line of data from the file, you can use Java's string-handling features to pull individual bits of data out of the line. In particular, you can use the `split` method to separate the line into the individual strings that are separated by tabs. Then you can use the appropriate `parse` methods to parse each string to its correct data type.

Here's a routine that converts a line read from the `movies.txt` file to the title (a string), year (an `int`), and price (a `double`):

```
String[] data = line.split("\t");
String title = data[0];
int year = Integer.parseInt(data[1]);
double price = Double.parseDouble(data[2]);
```

After the entire file has been read, you can close the stream by calling the `close` method, like this:

```
in.close();
```

This method also throws `IOException`, so you want to place it inside a `try/catch` block.

Reading the movies.dat file

Now that you've seen the individual elements of reading data from a binary file, Listing 2-3 presents a complete program that uses these techniques. This program reads the `movies.dat` file; creates a `Movie` object for each title, year, and price value; and prints a line on the console for each movie. If you run this program, the output looks exactly like the output from the text-file version presented in the section "Reading the `movies.txt` file," earlier in this chapter. (Note that you must first create the `movies.dat` file before you can run this program. The program that creates the movies.dat file is found later in this chapter, in Listing 2-4.)

Listing 2-3:   Reading from a Binary File

```java
import java.io.*;
import java.text.NumberFormat;

public class ReadBinaryFile
{
    public static void main(String[] args)                      →6
    {
        NumberFormat cf =
    NumberFormat.getCurrencyInstance();

        DataInputStream in = getStream("movies.dat");

        boolean eof = false;
        while (!eof)
        {
            Movie movie = readMovie(in);
            if (movie == null)
                eof = true;
            else
            {
                String msg = Integer.toString(movie.year);
                msg += ": " + movie.title;
                msg += " (" + cf.format(movie.price) + ")";
                System.out.println(msg);
            }
        }
        closeFile(in);
    }

    private static DataInputStream getStream(String name) →28
    {
        DataInputStream in = null;
        try
        {
            File file = new File(name);
            in = new DataInputStream(
                    new BufferedInputStream(
                      new FileInputStream(file) ) );
        }
        catch (FileNotFoundException e)
        {
            System.out.println("The file doesn't exist.");
            System.exit(0);
        }
        return in;
    }

    private static Movie readMovie(DataInputStream in)      →46
    {
        String title = "";
        int year = 0;;
        double price = 0.0;;
```

(continued)

Listing 2-3 *(continued)*

```
    try
    {
        title = in.readUTF();
        year = in.readInt();
        price = in.readDouble();
    }
    catch (EOFException e)
    {
        return null;
    }
    catch (IOException e)
    {
        System.out.println("I/O Error");
        System.exit(0);
    }
    return new Movie(title, year, price);
}

private static void closeFile(DataInputStream in)        →71
{
    try
    {
        in.close();
    }
    catch(IOException e)
    {
        System.out.println("I/O Error closing file.");
        System.out.println();
    }
}

private static class Movie                               →84
{
    public String title;
    public int year;
    public double price;

    public Movie(String title, int year, double price)
    {
        this.title = title;
        this.year = year;
        this.price = price;
    }
}
}
```

The following paragraphs describe what each method in this program does:

→ 6   The `main` method is intentionally kept simple so that it can focus
       on controlling the flow of the program rather than doing the detail
       work of accessing the file. As a result, it calls a method named
       `getStream` to get a data input stream object to read the file. Then

it uses a `while` loop to call a method named `readMovie` to get a movie object. If the `Movie` object isn't `null`, the movie's data is printed to the console. Finally, when the loop ends, a method named `closeFile` is called to close the file.

→ **28**   The `getStream` method creates a `DataInputStream` object for the filename passed as a parameter. If any exceptions are thrown, the program exits.

→ **46**   The `readMovie` method reads the data for a single movie and creates a `Movie` object. If the end of the file is reached, the method returns `null`.

→ **71**   The `closeFile` method closes the input stream.

→ **84**   As in the other programs in this chapter, the `Movie` class is defined as a private inner class.

Writing Binary Streams

To write data to a binary file, you use the following classes:

✦ **FileOutputStream:** The `FileOutputStream` class connects to a `File` object and creates an output stream that can write to the file. This output stream is limited in its capabilities, however, in that it can write only raw bytes to the file. In other words, it doesn't know how to write values such as `int`s, `double`s, or strings.

✦ **BufferedOutputStream:** This class connects to a `FileOutputStream` and adds output buffering.

✦ **DataOutputStream:** This class adds the ability to write primitive data types and strings to a stream.

Table 2-4 lists the essential constructors and methods of these classes.

Table 2-4   The DataOutputStream, BufferedOutputStream, and FileOutputStream Classes

Constructor	Description
`DataOutputStream(Output Stream out)`	Creates a data output stream for the specified output stream.
`BufferedIOutputStream(Output Stream out)`	Creates a buffered output stream for the specified stream. Typically you pass this constructor a `FileOutputStream` object.

(continued)

Table 2-4 *(continued)*

Constructor	Description
`FileOutputStream(File file)`	Creates a file writer from the file. It throws `FileNotFoundException` if an error occurs.
`FileOutputStream(File file, boolean append)`	Creates a file writer from the file. It throws `FileNotFoundException` if an error occurs. If the second parameter is `true`, data is added to the end of the file if the file already exists.
`FileOutputStream(String path)`	Creates a file writer from the specified pathname. It throws `FileNotFoundException` if an error occurs.
`FileOutputStream(String path, boolean append)`	Creates a file writer from the specified pathname. It throws `FileNotFoundException` if an error occurs. If the second parameter is `true`, data is added to the end of the file if the file already exists.

DataInputStream Method	Description
`void close()`	Closes the file.
`void flush()`	Writes the contents of the buffer to the hard drive.
`int size()`	Returns the number of bytes written to the file.
`void writeBoolean(boolean value)`	Writes a `boolean` value to the output stream. It throws `IOException`.
`void writeByte(byte value)`	Writes a `byte` value to the output stream. It throws `IOException`.
`void writeChar(char value)`	Writes a `char` value to the output stream. It throws `IOException`.
`void writeDouble(double value)`	Writes a `double` value to the output stream. It throws `IOException`.
`void writeFloat(float value)`	Writes a `float` value to the output stream. It throws `IOException`.

Constructor	Description
void writeInt(int value)	Writes an int value to the output stream. It throws IOException.
void writeLong(long value)	Writes a long value to the output stream. It throws IOException.
void writeShort(short value)	Writes a short value to the output stream. It throws IOException.
void writeUTF(String value)	Writes a string stored in UTF format to the output stream. It throws EOFException, IOException, and UTFDataFormatException.

Creating a DataOutputStream

Creating a DataOutputStream object requires yet another one of those crazy nested constructor things:

```
File file = new File(name);
DataOutputStream out = new DataOutputStream(
      new BufferedOutputStream(
        new FileOutputStream(file) ) );
```

If you prefer, you can unravel the constructors like this:

```
File file = new File(name);
FileOutputStream fos = new FileOutputStream(file);
BufferedOutputStream bos = new BufferedOutputStream(fos);
DataOutputStream out = new DataOutputStream(bos);
```

The FileOutputStream class has an optional boolean parameter that you can use to indicate that the file should be appended if it exists. To use this feature, call the constructors like this:

```
File file = new File(name);
DataOutputStream out = new DataOutputStream(
      new BufferedOutputStream(
        new FileOutputStream(file, true) ) );
```

If you specify false instead of true or leave the parameter out, an existing file is deleted, and its data is lost.

Writing to a binary stream

After you successfully connect a `DataOutputStream` to a file, writing data to it is simply a matter of calling the various `write` methods to write different data types to the file. The following code writes the data for a `Movie` object to the file:

```
out.writeUTF(movie.title);
out.writeInt(movie.year);
out.writeDouble(movie.price);
```

These methods throw `IOException`, of course. As a result, you have to enclose them in a `try/catch` block.

If you included the `BufferedOutputStream` class in the stream, it accumulates data in its buffer until it decides to write the data to the hard drive. If you want, you can force the buffer to be written to the hard drive by calling the `flush` method, like this:

```
out.flush();
```

Also, when you finish writing data to the file, close the file by calling the `close` method, like this:

```
out.close();
```

The `flush` and `close` methods also throw `IOException`, so you need a `try/catch` block to catch the exception.

Writing the movies.dat file

Listing 2-4 presents a program that writes the `movies.dat` file from an array of `Movie` objects whose values are hard-coded into the program.

Listing 2-4:   Writing to a Binary File

```
import java.io.*;

public class WriteBinaryFile
{
    public static void main(String[] args)                          →5
    {
        Movie[] movies = getMovies();
        DataOutputStream out = openOutputStream("movies.dat");
        for (Movie m : movies)
            writeMovie(m, out);
        closeFile(out);
    }

    private static Movie[] getMovies()                              →14
    {
        Movie[] movies = new Movie[10];
```

```
        movies[0] = new Movie("It's a Wonderful Life",
            1946, 14.95);
        movies[1] = new Movie("Young Frankenstein",
            1974, 16.95);
        movies[2] = new Movie("Star Wars",
            1977, 17.95);
        movies[3] = new Movie("The Princess Bride",
            1987, 16.95);
        movies[4] = new Movie("Glory",
            1989, 14.95);
        movies[5] = new Movie("The Game",
            1997, 14.95);
        movies[6] = new Movie("Shakespeare in Love",
            1998, 19.95);
        movies[7] = new Movie("Zombieland",
            1997, 18.95);
        movies[8] = new Movie("The King's Speech",
            1997, 19.95);
        movies[9] = new Movie("Star Trek Into Darkness",
            1997, 19.95);
        return movies;
    }

    private static DataOutputStream
        openOutputStream(String name)                           →42
    {
        DataOutputStream out = null;
        try
        {
            File file = new File(name);
            out = new DataOutputStream(
                    new BufferedOutputStream(
                        new FileOutputStream(file) ) );
            return out;
        }
        catch (IOException e)
        {
            System.out.println(
                "I/O Exception opening file.");
            System.exit(0);
        }
        return out;
    }

    private static void writeMovie(Movie m,                     →62
        DataOutputStream out)
    {
        try
        {
            out.writeUTF(m.title);
            out.writeInt(m.year);
            out.writeDouble(m.price);
        }
        catch (IOException e)
        {
            System.out.println(
                "I/O Exception writing data.");
            System.exit(0);
        }
    }

    private static void closeFile(DataOutputStream out)         →79
    {
```

Book VIII
Chapter 2

**Working with
File Streams**

(continued)

Listing 2-4 *(continued)*

```
        try
        {
            out.close();
        }
        catch (IOException e)
        {
            System.out.println("I/O Exception closing file.");
            System.exit(0);
        }
    }

    private static class Movie                                    →92
    {
        public String title;
        public int year;
        public double price;

        public Movie(String title, int year, double price)
        {
            this.title = title;
            this.year = year;
            this.price = price;
        }
    }
}
```

Because this chapter explains all the coding elements in this program, the following paragraphs just provide a road map to the major parts of the program:

→ 5   The main method calls getMovies to get an array of Movie objects. Next, it calls openOutputStream to get an output stream to write data to the file. Then an enhanced for loop calls writeMovie to write the movies to the file. Finally, the method calls closeFile to close the file.

→ 14   The getMovies method creates an array of movies to be written to the file.

→ 42   The openOutputStream method creates a DataOutputStream object so that the program can write data to the file.

→ 62   The writeMovie method accepts two parameters: the movie to be written and the output stream to write the data to.

→ 79   The closeFile method closes the file.

→ 92   Once again, the Movie class is included as an inner class.

Chapter 3: Database for $100, Please

In This Chapter

✔ Understanding some basic database concepts

✔ Taking a quick look at SQL

✔ Creating tables

✔ Selecting data

✔ Joining data

✔ Updating and deleting data

SQL stands for *Structured Query Language.* SQL is the lingua franca (that's not a type of pasta but a type of tongue) of relational databases. It's the standard language used for creating and accessing relational databases and is the foundation of database processing in Java.

Java provides *Java Database Connectivity (JDBC),* which lets you formulate SQL statements, send them off to a database server, and process the results. To use JDBC, however, you need to know some basic concepts of SQL databases and at least enough SQL to formulate some sensible SQL statements.

This chapter won't make you a database guru or an expert on SQL — a complicated language that's the subject of many entire books, including *SQL For Dummies,* 8th Edition, by Allen G. Taylor (Wiley). This chapter covers just enough SQL to get you going with JDBC.

Also, this chapter doesn't cover JDBC. I decided to save that topic for Book VIII, Chapter 4, so if you already know SQL, you can skip this chapter.

Defining a Relational Database

The term *relational database* is one of the most used and abused buzzwords in all of computerdom. A relational database can be

✦ **A database in which data is stored in tables:** Relationships can be established between tables based on common information. A table of customers and a table of invoices, for example, might both contain a customer-number column. This column can serve as the basis for a relationship between the tables.

✦ **A database that is accessed via SQL:** IBM invented SQL to provide a practical way to access data stored in relational databases.

✦ **Any database system developed since about 1980, with the exception of a few cutting-edge object-oriented databases:** Marketers quickly figured out that the way to sell database programs was to advertise them as relational. Thus just about every database program ever made has *claimed* to be relational, whether it really is or not.

From a Java programmer's perspective, the second definition is the only one that matters. If you can use SQL to access the database, the database is relational.

Understanding (and Pronouncing) SQL

SQL is a *query language,* which means that it's designed to extract, organize, and update information in relational databases. Way back in the 1970s, when it was invented (SQL is old enough to be Java's grandfather), SQL was supposed to be an English-like query language that untrained users could employ to access and update relational database data without the need for programming. That didn't happen, of course. SQL is nothing like English. It's way too complicated and esoteric for untrained users to figure out. But it has become the overwhelming favorite among programmers.

Ever since you first saw the acronym *SQL,* you've probably been wondering how to pronounce it. (If not, humor me.) Two schools of thought exist on this subject:

✦ Spell out the letters: *Ess-Queue-El.*

✦ Pronounce it like the word *sequel.*

Either one does the job, but be warned: Some people are adamant that it must be pronounced one way or the other. Those people also tend to hold the opinion that anyone who pronounces it the "wrong" way (in their opinion) is an illiterate dweeb.

Introducing SQL Statements

Unlike Java, SQL is *not* object-oriented. Remember, SQL was invented during the Nixon administration. Like Java, however, SQL uses statements to get work done. Table 3-1 lists the SQL statements you use most often.

Table 3-1	Common SQL Statements
SQL Statement	*Description*
Data Manipulation	
select	Retrieves data from one or more tables. This statement is the one you use most often.
insert	Inserts one or more rows into a table.
delete	Deletes one or more rows from a table.
update	Updates existing rows in a table.
Data Definition	
create	Creates tables and other database objects.
alter	Changes the definitions of a table or other database object.
drop	Deletes a table or other database object.
use	In scripts, indicates what database subsequent statements apply to.

Unlike Java statements, statements in SQL aren't case-sensitive, which means that you can write select, Select, or SELECT. You can even write sElEcT for kicks, if you want.

Creating a SQL Database

Before you can store data in a relational database, you must create the database. Normally you don't do that from a Java program. Instead, you do it by writing a script file that contains the Create statements necessary to create the table and then running the script through the database server's administration program. (Some database servers also let you define databases interactively, but the script approach is preferred because you often need to delete and re-create a database while testing your applications.)

The scripts shown in this section (and in the rest of this chapter) are for version 5.5 of MySQL. MySQL is a free SQL database server that you can download from dev.mysql.com/downloads/mysql. The complete MySQL download includes both the server and a handy program called the MySQL Command Line Client, which lets you enter SQL commands from a prompt and see the results immediately. (To install MySQL, go to the website mentioned at the start of this paragraph, click the link for the installer that's appropriate for your Windows version, and then follow the onscreen instructions.)

Script statements end with semicolons, which is about the only thing that SQL scripts have in common with Java scripts. Be aware, however, that the semicolon isn't required when you use SQL statements in a Java program. The semicolon is required only when you use SQL statements in a script or interactively from the MySQL Command Line Client program.

I don't have room in this book to provide a complete tutorial on writing scripts that create SQL databases. Instead, I present Listing 3-1 — a sample script that creates a database named `movies`, which I use in the rest of this chapter and the next one — and walk you through its most important lines.

Listing 3-1:   A Database Creation Script

```
drop database movies;                                          →1
create database movies;                                        →2
use movies;                                                    →3
create table movie (                                           →4
    id int not null auto_increment,                            →5
    title varchar(50),                                         →6
    year int,                                                  →7
    price decimal(8,2),                                        →8
    primary key(id)                                            →9
);

insert into movie (title, year, price)                         →12
    values ("It's a Wonderful Life", 1946, 14.95);
insert into movie (title, year, price)
    values ("Young Frankenstein", 1974, 16.95);
insert into movie (title, year, price)
    values ("Star Wars", 1977, 17.95);
insert into movie (title, year, price)
    values ("The Princess Bride", 1987, 16.95);
insert into movie (title, year, price)
    values ("Glory", 1989, 14.95);
insert into movie (title, year, price)
    values("The Game",1997,14.95);
insert into movie (title, year, price)
    values("Shakespeare in Love",1998,19.95);
insert into movie (title, year, price)
    values("Zombieland",2009,18.95);
insert into movie (title, year, price)
    values("The King's Speech",2010,17.85);
insert into movie (title, year, price)
    values("Star Trek Into Darkness",2013,19.95);
```

The following paragraphs describe the important lines of this script:

→ 1   It's common for a script that creates a database to begin with a `drop database` statement to delete any existing database with the same name. During testing, it's common to delete and re-create the database, so you want to include this statement in your scripts.

→ 2   This statement creates a new database named `movies`.

→ 3   The `use` statement indicates that the script statements that follow apply to the newly created `movies` database.

→ 4   This `create table` statement creates a table named `movie` with columns named `id`, `title`, `year`, and `price`. This statement also specifies that the primary key for the table is the `id` column.

→ 5   The `id` column's data type is `int`, which corresponds to Java's `int` type. This column also specifies `not null`, which means that it must have a value for every row, and it specifies `auto increment`, which means that the database server itself provides values for this column. Each time a new row is added to the table, the value for the `id` column is incremented automatically.

→ 6   The `title` column's data type is `varchar`, which is like a Java `String`.

→ 7   The `year` column's data type is `int`.

→ 8   The `price` column's data type is `decimal`. Java doesn't have a `decimal` type, so the values from this column are converted to `double`.

→ 9   The `create table` statement specifies that the `id` column is the table's primary key. A *primary key* is a column (or a combination of columns) containing a unique value for each row in a table. Every table should have a primary key.

→ 12   The `insert` statements add data to the database. Each of these ten statements adds a row to the movie table. The syntax of the `insert` statements is weird, because you first list all the columns that you want to insert data for and then list the actual data. Each of the `insert` statements, for example, inserts data for three columns: `title`, `year`, and `price`. The first `insert` statement (the one in line 12) inserts the values `"It's a Wonderful Life"`, `1946`, and `14.95`.

To run this script in MySQL, start the MySQL Command Line Client from the Start menu and then use a `source` command that names the script, as in this example:

```
mysql> source c:\data\create.sql
```

Note that the first time you run this script, you see an error message indicating that the `movies` database can't be dropped because it doesn't exist. You can safely ignore this error.

Querying a Database

As the name *Structured Query Language* suggests, queries are what SQL is all about. A *query* is an operation performed against one or more SQL tables; it extracts data from the tables and creates a *result set,* which contains the selected rows and columns.

A crucial point to understand is that the result set is itself a table consisting of rows and columns. When you query a database from a Java program, the result set is returned to the program in an object created from the `ResultSet` class. This class has methods that let you extract the data from each column of each row in the result set.

Using a basic select statement

To query a database, you use the `select` statement. In this statement, you list the table or tables from which you want to retrieve the data; the specific table columns you want to retrieve (you may not be interested in everything that's in the table); and other clauses that indicate which rows to retrieve, what order to present the rows in, and so on. Here's a simple `select` statement that lists all the movies in the `movie` table:

```
select title, year
    from movie
    order by year;
```

In the following list, I take this statement apart piece by piece:

- ✦ `select title, year` names the columns you want to include in the query result.

- ✦ `from movie` names the table from which you want to retrieve the rows.

- ✦ `order by year` indicates that the result is sorted by the `year` column so that the oldest movie appears first.

In other words, this `select` statement retrieves the `title` and `year` for all the rows in the `movie` table and sorts them in `year` sequence. You can run this query by typing it directly in the Command Line Client. Here's what you get:

```
mysql> select title, year from movie order by year;
+------------------------+------+
| title                  | year |
+------------------------+------+
| It's a Wonderful Life  | 1946 |
| Young Frankenstein     | 1974 |
| Star Wars              | 1977 |
| The Princess Bride     | 1987 |
| Glory                  | 1989 |
| The Game               | 1997 |
| Shakespeare in Love    | 1998 |
| Zombieland             | 2009 |
| The King's Speech      | 2010 |
| Star Trek Into Darkness| 2013 |
+------------------------+------+
10 rows in set (0.00 sec)
```

As you can see, the Command Line Client displays the rows returned by the `select` statement. This feature can be very handy when you're planning the `select` statements that your program needs, or when you're testing a program that updates a table and want to make sure that the updates are made correctly.

If you want the query to retrieve all the columns in each row, you can use an asterisk instead of naming the individual columns, like so:

```
select * from movie order by year;
```

Using an asterisk in this manner isn't a good idea, however, because the columns that make up the table may change. If you use an asterisk, your program can't deal with changes in the table's structure.

Both examples so far include an `order by` clause. In a SQL database, the rows stored in a table aren't assumed to be in any particular sequence. As a result, if you want to display the results of a query in sequence, you must include an `order by` in the `select` statement.

Narrowing the query

Suppose that you want to find information about one particular video title. To select certain rows from a table, use the `where` clause in a `select` statement, as in this example:

```
mysql> select title, year from movie
    ->     where year <= 1980
    ->     order by year;
+------------------------+------+
| title                  | year |
+------------------------+------+
| It's a Wonderful Life  | 1946 |
| Young Frankenstein     | 1974 |
| Star Wars              | 1977 |
+------------------------+------+
3 rows in set (0.00 sec)
```

Here the `select` statement selects all the rows in which the `year` column is less than or equal to `1980`. The results are ordered by the `year` column.

Excluding rows

Perhaps you want to retrieve all rows except those that match certain criteria. Here's a query that ignores movies made in the 1970s (which is probably a good idea):

```
mysql> select title, year from movie
    ->     where year < 1970 or year > 1979
    ->     order by year;
+-------------------------+------+
| title                   | year |
+-------------------------+------+
| It's a Wonderful Life   | 1946 |
| The Princess Bride      | 1987 |
| Glory                   | 1989 |
| The Game                | 1997 |
| Shakespeare in Love     | 1998 |
| Zombieland              | 2009 |
| The King's Speech       | 2010 |
| Star Trek Into Darkness | 2013 |
+-------------------------+------+
8 rows in set (0.01 sec)
```

Using singleton selects

When you want to retrieve information for a specific row, mention the primary key column in the `where` clause, like this:

```
mysql> select title, year from movie where id = 7;
+---------------------+------+
| title               | year |
+---------------------+------+
| Shakespeare in Love | 1998 |
+---------------------+------+
1 row in set (0.49 sec)
```

Here the `where` clause selects the row whose `id` column equals 7. This type of `select` statement is called a *singleton select* because it retrieves only one row. Singleton selects are commonly used in Java programs to allow users to access or update a specific database row.

Finding what something sounds like

Suppose that you want to retrieve information about a movie and can't quite remember the name, but you know that it includes the word *princess*. One of the most interesting variations of the `where` clause throws in the word `like`, which lets you search rows using wildcards. Here's an example in which the percent sign (%) is a wildcard character:

```
mysql> select title, year from movie
    ->     where title like "%princess%";
```

```
+------------------------+--------+
| title                  | year   |
+------------------------+--------+
| The Princess Bride     | 1987   |
+------------------------+--------+
1 row in set (0.01 sec)
```

Using column functions

What if you want a count of the total number of movies in the `movie` table or a count of the number of movies that were made before 1970? To do that, you use a column function. SQL's column functions let you make calculations on columns. You can calculate the sum, average, or largest or smallest value, or count the number of values for an entire column.

Table 3-2 summarizes these functions. *Note:* The functions operate on the values returned in a result set, which isn't necessarily the entire table.

Table 3-2	Column Functions
Function	*Description*
sum(*column-name*)	Adds the values in the column.
avg(*column-name*)	Calculates the average value for the column. Null values aren't included in the calculation.
min(*column-name*)	Determines the lowest value in the column.
max(*column-name*)	Determines the highest value in the column.
count(*column-name*)	Counts the number of rows that have data values for the column.
countDistinct (*column-name*)	Counts the number of distinct values for the column.
count(*)	Counts the number of rows in the result set.

To use one of these functions, specify the function rather than a column name in a `select` statement. The following `select` statement calculates the number of rows in the table and the year of the oldest movie:

```
mysql> select count(*), min(year) from movie;
+----------+-----------+
| count(*) | min(year) |
+----------+-----------+
|       10 |      1946 |
+----------+-----------+
1 row in set (0.00 sec)
```

As you can see, ten movies are in the table, and the oldest was made in 1946.

If the `select` statement includes a `where` clause, only the rows that match the criteria are included in the calculation. This statement finds out how many movies in the table were made before 1970:

```
mysql> select count(*) from movie where year < 1970;
+----------+
| count(*) |
+----------+
|        1 |
+----------+
1 row in set (0.00 sec)
```

The result is 2.

Selecting data from more than one table

In the real world, most `select` statements retrieve data from two or more tables. Suppose that you want a list of all the movies you've currently loaned out to friends. To do that, you have to create another table in your database that lists your friends' names and the `ids` of any movies they've borrowed. Here's a `create table` statement that creates just such a table:

```
create table friend (
    lastname varchar(50),
    firstname varchar(50),
    movieid int
);
```

Now load it up with some data, like so:

```
insert into friend (lastname, firstname, movieid)
    values ("Haskell", "Eddie", 3);
insert into friend (lastname, firstname, movieid)
    values ("Haskell", "Eddie", 5);
insert into friend (lastname, firstname, movieid)
    values ("Cleaver", "Wally", 9);
insert into friend (lastname, firstname, movieid)
    values ("Mondello", "Lumpy", 2);
insert into friend (lastname, firstname, movieid)
    values ("Cleaver", "Wally", 3);
```

With that out of the way, you can get to the business of using both the `friend` and `movie` tables in a single `select` statement. All you have to do is list both tables in the `from` clause and then provide a condition in the `where` clause that correlates the tables, as follows:

```
mysql> select lastname, firstname, title
    ->     from movie, friend
    ->     where movie.id = friend.movieid;
```

```
+-----------+-----------+--------------------+
| lastname  | firstname | title              |
+-----------+-----------+--------------------+
| Haskell   | Eddie     | Star Wars          |
| Haskell   | Eddie     | Glory              |
| Cleaver   | Wally     | The King's Speech  |
| Mondello  | Lumpy     | Young Frankenstein |
| Cleaver   | Wally     | Star Wars          |
+-----------+-----------+--------------------+
5 rows in set (0.00 sec)
```

Here you can see which movies have been loaned out and who has them.
Notice that the id and movieid columns in the where clause are qualified
with the name of the table the column belongs to.

Here's a select statement that lists all the movies Eddie Haskell has
borrowed:

```
mysql> select title from movie, friend
    ->      where movie.id = friend.movieid
    ->      and lastname = "Haskell";
+-----------+
| title     |
+-----------+
| Star Wars |
| Glory     |
+-----------+
2 rows in set (0.00 sec)
```

That rat has two of your best movies!

Notice in this example that you can refer to the friend table in the where
clause, even though you're not actually retrieving any of its columns. You
must still mention both tables in the from clause, however.

Eliminating duplicates

If you want to know just the names of all your friends who have a movie
checked out, you can do a simple select from the friend table, like this:

```
mysql> select lastname, firstname from friend;
+-----------+-----------+
| lastname  | firstname |
+-----------+-----------+
| Haskell   | Eddie     |
| Haskell   | Eddie     |
| Cleaver   | Wally     |
| Mondello  | Lumpy     |
| Cleaver   | Wally     |
+-----------+-----------+
5 rows in set (0.00 sec)
```

This result set has a problem, however: Eddie Haskell and Wally Cleaver are listed twice. Wouldn't it be nice if you could eliminate the duplicate rows? Your wish is granted in the next paragraph.

You can eliminate duplicate rows by adding the distinct keyword in the select statement, as follows:

```
mysql> select distinct lastname, firstname from friend;
+----------+-----------+
| lastname | firstname |
+----------+-----------+
| Haskell  | Eddie     |
| Cleaver  | Wally     |
| Mondello | Lumpy     |
+----------+-----------+
3 rows in set (0.07 sec)
```

Notice that no duplicates appear; each distinct name appears only once in the result set.

Updating and Deleting Rows

You've already seen how to create databases, insert rows, and retrieve result sets. All that remains now is updating and deleting data in a table. For that, you use the update and delete statements, as described in the following sections. I explain the delete statement first because its syntax is simpler.

Using the delete statement

The basic syntax of the delete statement is

```
delete from table-name where condition;
```

Here's a statement that deletes the movie whose id is 10:

```
mysql> delete from movie where id = 10;
Query OK, 1 row affected (0.44 sec)
```

Notice that the Command Line Client shows that this statement affected one line. You can confirm that the movie was deleted by following up with a select statement, like so:

```
mysql> select * from movie;
+----+-----------------------+------+-------+
| id | title                 | year | price |
+----+-----------------------+------+-------+
|  1 | It's a Wonderful Life | 1946 | 14.95 |
|  2 | Young Frankenstein    | 1974 | 16.95 |
|  3 | Star Wars             | 1977 | 17.95 |
|  4 | The Princess Bride    | 1987 | 16.95 |
```

```
|  5 | Glory                   | 1989 | 14.95 |
|  6 | The Game                | 1997 | 14.95 |
|  7 | Shakespeare in Love     | 1998 | 19.95 |
|  8 | Zombieland              | 2009 | 18.95 |
|  9 | The King's Speech       | 2010 | 17.85 |
+----+-------------------------+------+-------+
9 rows in set (0.00 sec)
```

As you can see, movie 10 is gone.

If the `where` clause selects more than one row, all the selected rows are deleted, as in this example:

```
mysql> delete from friend where lastname = "Haskell";
Query OK, 2 rows affected (0.45 sec)
```

A quick query of the `friend` table shows that both records for Eddie Haskell are deleted, like so:

```
mysql> select * from friend;
+----------+-----------+---------+
| lastname | firstname | movieid |
+----------+-----------+---------+
| Cleaver  | Wally     |       9 |
| Mondello | Lumpy     |       2 |
| Cleaver  | Wally     |       3 |
+----------+-----------+---------+
3 rows in set (0.00 sec)
```

If you don't include a `where` clause, the entire table is deleted. This statement deletes all the rows in the `movie` table:

```
mysql> delete from movie;
Query OK, 9 rows affected (0.44 sec)
```

A quick `select` of the `movie` table confirms that it is now empty, as follows:

```
mysql> select * from movie;
Empty set (0.00 sec)
```

Fortunately, you can just run the `create.sql` script again to create the table.

Using the update statement

The `update` statement selects one or more rows in a table and then modifies the value of one or more columns in the selected rows. Its syntax is this:

```
update table-name
    set expressions...
    where condition;
```

The `set` expressions resemble Java assignment statements. Here's a statement that changes the price of movie 8 to 18.95:

```
mysql> update movie set price = 18.95 where id = 8;
Query OK, 1 row affected (0.44 sec)
Rows matched: 1  Changed: 1  Warnings: 0
```

You can use a quick `select` statement to verify that the price was changed, as follows:

```
mysql> select id, price from movie;
+----+-------+
| id | price |
+----+-------+
|  1 | 14.95 |
|  2 | 16.95 |
|  3 | 17.95 |
|  4 | 16.95 |
|  5 | 14.95 |
|  6 | 14.95 |
|  7 | 19.95 |
|  8 | 18.95 |
|  9 | 17.85 |
+----+-------+
9 rows in set (0.00 sec)
```

To update more than one column, use commas to separate the expressions. Here's a statement that changes Eddie Haskell's name in the `friend` table:

```
mysql> update friend set lastname = "Bully",
    ->       firstname = "Big"
    ->       where lastname = "Haskell";
Query OK, 2 rows affected (0.46 sec)
Rows matched: 2  Changed: 2  Warnings: 0
```

Again, a quick `select` shows that the rows are properly updated, as follows:

```
mysql> select firstname, lastname from friend;
+-----------+----------+
| firstname | lastname |
+-----------+----------+
| Big       | Bully    |
| Big       | Bully    |
| Wally     | Cleaver  |
| Lumpy     | Mondello |
| Wally     | Cleaver  |
+-----------+----------+
5 rows in set (0.00 sec)
```

One final trick with the `update` statement you should know about is that the `set` expressions can include calculations. The following statement increases the prices of all the movies by 10 percent:

```
mysql> update movie set price = price * 1.1;
Query OK, 10 rows affected (0.46 sec)
Rows matched: 10  Changed: 10  Warnings: 0
```

Here's a `select` statement to verify that this update worked:

```
mysql> select id, price from movie;
+----+-------+
| id | price |
+----+-------+
|  1 | 16.45 |
|  2 | 18.65 |
|  3 | 19.75 |
|  4 | 18.65 |
|  5 | 16.45 |
|  6 | 16.45 |
|  7 | 21.95 |
|  8 | 20.85 |
|  9 | 19.64 |
| 10 | 21.95 |
+----+-------+
10 rows in set (0.01 sec)
```

Chapter 4: Using JDBC to Connect to a Database

In This Chapter

✔ Configuring JDBC drivers

✔ Creating a connection

✔ Executing SQL statements

✔ Retrieving result data

✔ Updating and deleting data

*J*DBC — *Java Database Connectivity* — is a Java feature that lets you connect to almost any relational database system, execute SQL commands, and process the results, all from within a Java program. In this chapter, you set up JDBC and use it to access data in a MySQL database.

If you aren't familiar with the basics of SQL, read the previous chapter before tackling this chapter.

Setting Up a Driver

Before you can write a Java program to access a database via JDBC, you must first install a driver that links Java's database API classes to an actual database. Correctly setting up the driver can be tricky, but once you get it working, accessing the database is easy.

To install the JDBC driver for MySQL, browse to `www.mysql.com/products/connector` and click the link for *JDBC Driver for MySQL (Connector/J)*. After you download it from MySQL's website, run it to install the driver.

That's all you have to do. You can now connect to MySQL from a Java program.

Connecting to a Database

Before you can use JDBC to access a SQL database, you must first establish a connection to the database. The first step to establishing a connection involves *registering* the driver class so the class is available.

To do that, use the `forName` method of the `Class` class, specifying the package and class name of the driver. To register the MySQL connector, use this statement:

```
Class.forName("com.mysql.jdbc.Driver");
```

To register the standard ODBC driver, use this statement instead:

```
Class.forName("sun.jdbc.odbc.JdbcOdbcDriver");
```

Note that the `forName` method throws `ClassNotFoundException`, so you have to enclose this statement in a `try/catch` block that catches `ClassNotFoundException`.

After you register the driver class, you can call the static `getConnection` method of the `DriverManager` class to open the connection. This method takes three `String` parameters: the database URL, the username, and a password. Here's an example:

```
String url = "jdbc:mysql://localhost/Movies";
String user = "root";
String pw = "pw";
con = DriverManager.getConnection(url, user, pw);
```

The URL parameter has the following syntax:

```
jdbc:subprotocol:subname
```

where *subprotocol* is `mysql` for a MySQL database and `odbc` for an ODBC driver. The *subname* is the database name. For a MySQL database, this can be a complete URL, but for a database on your own computer, just specify `//localhost/` plus the name of the database.

For ODBC, you use the name you used when you created the data source. For example:

```
String url = "jdbc:odbc:Movies";
```

The user and password parameters must also be valid for the database server you're using. For testing purposes on a MySQL database, you can use `root` and the password you created when you installed MySQL.

Note: In the examples that follow, I assume the root password is `PassWord`, but you should use whatever password you created when you installed MySQL. For ODBC, use `admin` with no password for testing.

Note that the `getConnection` method throws `SQLException`, so you need to enclose it in a `try/catch` block statement that catches this exception.

Putting it all together, here's a method that returns a Connection object that connects to the movies database in MySQL:

```
private static Connection getConnection()
{
    Connection con = null;
    try
    {
        Class.forName("com.mysql.jdbc.Driver");
        String url = "jdbc:mysql://localhost/Movies";
        String user = "root";
        String pw = "PassWord";
        con = DriverManager.getConnection(url, user, pw);
    }
    catch (ClassNotFoundException e)
    {
        System.out.println(e.getMessage());
        System.exit(0);
    }
    catch (SQLException e)
    {
        System.out.println(e.getMessage());
        System.exit(0);
    }
    return con;
}
```

You can find these classes — and the other classes for working with SQL databases — in the java.sql package. As a result, you have to include an import statement that specifies this package in any program that uses JDBC.

Querying a Database

After you establish a connection to a database, you can execute select statements to retrieve data. To do so, you have to use several classes and interfaces:

✦ **Connection:** The Connection class has two methods you're likely to use. The close method closes the connection, and the createStatement method returns a Statement object, which you then use to execute statements.

✦ **Statement:** The Statement interface contains the methods necessary to send statements to the database for execution and return the results. In particular, you use the executeQuery method to execute a select statement or the executeUpdate method to execute an insert, update, or delete statement.

✦ **ResultSet:** The ResultSet interface represents rows returned from a query. It provides methods you can use to move from row to row and to get the data for a column.

Table 4-1 lists the methods of the `Connection` class and the `Statement` interface you use to execute queries. (You find out about the many methods of the `ResultSet` interface later in this chapter, in the section "Navigating through the result set.")

Table 4-1	**Connection and Statement Methods**
Connection Class Method	*Description*
`void close()`	Closes the connection.
`Statement createStatement()`	Creates a `Statement` object that can execute a SQL statement on the database connected by the connection.
`Statement createStatement(int type, int concur)`	Creates a `Statement` object that can execute a SQL statement on the database connected by the connection.
Statement Interface Methods	*Description*
`ResultSet executeQuery(String sql)`	Executes the `select` statement contained in the string parameter and returns the result data as a `ResultSet` object.
`ResultSet executeQuery(String sql)`	Executes the `select` statement contained in the string parameter and returns the result data as a `ResultSet` object.
`int executeUpdate (String sql)`	Executes the `insert`, `update`, or `delete` statements contained in the string parameter and returns the result data as a `ResultSet` object.

The first parameter of the `createStatement` method specifies the type of result set that is created, and can be one of the following:

```
ResultSet.TYPE_FORWARD_ONLY
ResultSet.TYPE_SCROLL_INSENSITIVE
ResultSet.TYPE_SCROLL_SENSITIVE
```

The second parameter indicates whether the result set is read-only or updatable, and can be one of the following:

```
ResultSet.CONCUR_READ_ONLY
ResultSet.CONCUR_UPDATABLE
```

Executing a select statement

The following snippet executes a `select` statement and gets the result set:

```
Statement s = con.createStatement();
String select = "Select title, year, price "
    + "from movie order by year";
ResultSet rows = s.executeQuery(select);
```

Here the result set is stored in the `rows` variable.

Navigating through the result set

The `ResultSet` object returned by the `executeQuery` statement contains all the rows that are retrieved by the `select` statement. You can access only one of those rows at a time. The result set maintains a pointer called a *cursor* to keep track of the current row. You can use the methods shown in Table 4-2 to move the cursor through a result set.

Table 4-2	Navigation Methods of the ResultSet Interface
Method	*Description*
`void close()`	Closes the result set.
`void last()`	Moves the cursor to the last row.
`int getRow()`	Gets the current row number.
`boolean next()`	Moves to the next row.

The following snippet shows how you can structure code that processes each row in a result set:

```
while(rows.next())
{
    // process the current row
}
```

All you have to do is replace the comment with statements that retrieve data from the result set and process it, as described in the next section.

Getting data from a result set

Table 4-3 lists the methods of the `ResultSet` interface you can use to retrieve data from the current row. As you can see, each of these methods comes in two versions: One specifies the column by name, the other by index number. If you know the index number, using it to access the column values is more efficient than using the column names.

Table 4-3	Get Methods of the ResultSet Interface
Method	*Description*
BigDecimal getBigDecimal(String columnName)	Gets the value of the specified column as a BigDecimal.
BigDecimal getBigDecimal(int columnIndex)	Gets the value of the specified column as a BigDecimal.
boolean getBoolean(String columnName)	Gets the value of the specified column as a boolean.
boolean getBoolean(int columnIndex)	Gets the value of the specified column as a boolean.
Date getDate(String columnName)	Gets the value of the specified column as a Date.
Date getDate(int columnIndex)	Gets the value of the specified column as a Date.
double getDouble(String columnName)	Gets the value of the specified column as a double.
double getDouble(int columnIndex)	Gets the value of the specified column as a double.
float getFloat(String columnName)	Gets the value of the specified column as a float.
float getFloat(int columnIndex)	Gets the value of the specified column as a float.
int getInt(String columnName)	Gets the value of the specified column as an int.
int getInt(int columnIndex)	Gets the value of the specified column as an int.
long getLong(String columnName)	Gets the value of the specified column as a long.
long getLong(int columnIndex)	Gets the value of the specified column as a long.
short getShort(String columnName)	Gets the value of the specified column as a short.
short getShort(int columnIndex)	Gets the value of the specified column as a short.
String getString(String columnName)	Gets the value of the specified column as a String.
String getString(int columnIndex)	Gets the value of the specified column as a String.

Here's a bit of code that gets the title, year, and price for the current row:

```
String title = row.getString("title");
int year = row.getInt("year");
double price = row.getDouble("price");
```

The following code does the same thing, assuming the columns appear in order:

```
String title = row.getString(1);
int year = row.getInt(2);
double price = row.getDouble(3);
```

Note that unlike almost every other index in Java, column indexes start with 1, not 0.

Putting it all together: A program that reads from a database

Now that you've seen the various elements that make up a program that uses JDBC to query a database, Listing 4-1 shows a program that reads data from the movies database and lists it on the console. When you run this program, the following appears on the console:

```
1946: It's a Wonderful Life ($16.45)
1974: Young Frankenstein ($18.65)
1977: Star Wars ($19.75)
1987: The Princess Bride ($18.65)
1989: Glory ($16.45)
1997: The Game ($16.45)
1998: Shakespeare in Love ($21.95)
2009: Zombieland ($20.85)
2010: The King's Speech ($19.64)
2013: Star Trek Into Darkness ($21.95)
```

Listing 4-1: The Movie Listing Program

```
import java.sql.*;
import java.text.NumberFormat;

public class ListMovies
{
    public static void main(String[] args)                    →6
    {
        NumberFormat cf = NumberFormat.getCurrencyInstance();

        ResultSet movies = getMovies();
        try
        {
            while (movies.next())
```

(continued)

Listing 4-1 *(continued)*

```
        {
            Movie m = getMovie(movies);
            String msg = Integer.toString(m.year);
            msg += ": " + m.title;
            msg += " (" + cf.format(m.price) + ")";
            System.out.println(msg);
        }
    }
    catch (SQLException e)
    {
        System.out.println(e.getMessage());
    }
}


private static ResultSet getMovies()                    →28
{
    Connection con = getConnection();
    try
    {
        Statement s = con.createStatement();
        String select = "Select title, year, price "
            + "from movie order by year";
        ResultSet rows;
        rows = s.executeQuery(select);
        return rows;
    }
    catch (SQLException e)
    {
        System.out.println(e.getMessage());
    }
    return null;
}


private static Connection getConnection()               →46
{
    Connection con = null;
    try
    {
        Class.forName("com.mysql.jdbc.Driver");
        String url = "jdbc:mysql://localhost/Movies";
        String user = "root";
        String pw = "PassWord";
        con = DriverManager.getConnection(url, user, pw);
    }
    catch (ClassNotFoundException e)
    {
        System.out.println(e.getMessage());
        System.exit(0);
    }
    catch (SQLException e)
    {
        System.out.println(e.getMessage());
        System.exit(0);
    }
}
```

```
        return con;
    }

    private static Movie getMovie(ResultSet movies)        →70
    {
        try
        {
            String title = movies.getString("Title");
            int year = movies.getInt("Year");
            double price = movies.getDouble("Price");
            return new Movie(title, year, price);
        }
        catch (SQLException e)
        {
            System.out.println(e.getMessage());
        }
        return null;
    }

    private static class Movie                              →86
    {
        public String title;
        public int year;
        public double price;
        public Movie(String title, int year, double price)
        {
            this.title = title;
            this.year = year;
            this.price = price;
        }
    }
}
```

The following paragraphs describe the basics of how this program works:

→ 6   The `main` method begins by calling the `getMovies` method to get a `ResultSet` object that contains the movies to be listed. Then a `while` loop reads each row of the result set. The `getMovie` method is called to create a `Movie` object from the data in the current row. Then an output string is created and sent to the console. The loop is contained in a `try/catch` statement because the `next` method may throw `SQLException`.

→ 28   The `getMovies` method is responsible for getting a database connection, and then querying the database to get the movies. The first task is delegated to the `getConnection` method. Then a `Statement` is created and executed with the following `select` statement:

```
select title, year, price from movie order by year
```

Then the result set is returned to the main method.

→ 46   The getConnection method creates a Connection object to the database. Note that the user ID and password are hard-coded into this method. In a real application, you get this information from the user or from a configuration file.

→ 70   The getMovie method extracts the title, year, and price from the current row and uses these values to create a Movie object.

→ 86   The Movie class is created as an inner class. To keep this application simple, this class uses public fields and a single constructor that initializes the fields with the values passed as parameters.

Updating SQL Data

Besides executing select statements, you can also use a Statement object to execute insert, update, or delete statements as well. To do that, call the executeUpdate method instead of the executeQuery method. This method returns an int value that indicates how many rows were updated. You can test the return value to determine whether the data was properly updated.

Here's a method that accepts a movie ID, a last name, and a first name, and then inserts a row into the friend table:

```
private static void loanMovie(int id, String lastName,
    String firstName)
{
    Connection con = getConnection();
    try
    {
        Statement stmt = con.createStatement();
        String insert = "insert into friend "
            + "(lastname, firstname, movieid) "
            + "values ("
            + "\"" + lastName + "\", \""
            + firstName + "\", " +
            + id + ")";
        int i = stmt.executeUpdate(insert);
        if (i == 1)
            System.out.println("Loan recorded.");
        else
            System.out.println("Loan not recorded.");
    }
    catch (SQLException e)
    {
        System.out.println(e.getMessage());
        System.exit(0);
    }
}
```

The getConnection method called at the start of this method is the same getConnection method in Listing 4-1. After a connection is created, a Statement object is created, and an insert statement is constructed using the values passed via the parameters. For example, if you pass id 3, last name Haskell, and first name Eddie, the following insert statement is built:

```
Insert into friend (lastname, firstname, movieid)
    Values ("Haskell", "Eddie", 3)
```

Then the executeUpdate method is called to execute the insert statement. An if statement is used to determine whether the row is inserted.

You can execute update or delete statements in the same manner.

While you're testing database code that executes SQL statements constructed from strings like this, throw in a System.out.println call to print the statement to the console. That way, you can verify that the statement is being created properly.

Using an Updatable RowSet Object

If you're using a newer JDBC driver (one that supports JDBC 2.0 or later), you have another option for updating data: with an updatable result set. With an updatable result set, you can change data in a result set row, add a row to the result set, or delete a row from the result set. When you do, the updates are automatically written back to the underlying database.

To create an updatable result set, you must specify the ResultSet. CONCUR_UPDATABLE field on the createStatement method when you create the Statement object, like this:

```
Statement stmt = con.createStatement(
    ResultSet.TYPE_SCROLL_SENSITIVE,
    ResultSet.TYPE_CONCUR_UPDATABLE);
```

The first parameter indicates that the result set is scrollable, which means you can move the cursor backward and forward through the result set. You can use the methods listed in Table 4-4 to scroll the result set. This parameter also indicates that the result set can be synchronized with the database so that any changes made by other users are reflected in the result set.

Table 4-4	Methods for Scrollable Result Sets
Method	*Description*
`boolean absolute (int row)`	Moves the cursor to the given row number in this `ResultSet` object.
`void afterLast()`	Moves the cursor to the end of this `ResultSet` object, just after the last row.
`void beforeFirst()`	Moves the cursor to the front of this `ResultSet` object, just before the first row.
`boolean first()`	Moves the cursor to the first row in this `ResultSet` object.
`boolean last()`	Moves the cursor to the last row in this `ResultSet` object.
`boolean next()`	Moves the cursor down one row from its current position.
`boolean previous()`	Moves the cursor to the previous row in this `ResultSet` object.
`boolean relative (int rows)`	Moves the cursor a relative number of rows, either positive or negative.

The second parameter indicates that the result set is updatable, and any changes you make to the result set are automatically written back to the database. You can use any of the methods listed in Table 4-5 to update the result set, and thus update the underlying database.

Table 4-5	Methods for Updatable Result Sets
Method	*Description*
`void cancelRowUpdates()`	Cancels the updates made to the current row in this `ResultSet` object.
`void deleteRow()`	Deletes the current row from this `ResultSet` object and from the underlying database.
`void insertRow()`	Inserts the contents of the insert row into this `ResultSet` object and into the database.
`void moveToCurrentRow()`	Moves the cursor to the remembered cursor position, usually the current row.
`void moveToInsertRow()`	Moves the cursor to the insert row.
`void refreshRow()`	Refreshes the current row with its most recent value in the database.
`void updateRow()`	Updates the underlying database with the new contents of the current row of this `ResultSet` object.

Deleting a row

To delete a row from a result set, use one of the navigation methods in Table 4-4 to move to the row you want to delete, and then use the deleteRow method to delete the row. Here's code that deletes the third row in the result set:

```
try
{
    rs.absolute(3);
    rs.deleteRow();
}
catch (SQLException e)
{
    System.out.println(e.getMessage());
    System.exit(0);
}
```

Updating the value of a row column

To update the value of a row column, navigate to the row you want to update, and then use one of the updater methods listed in Table 4-6 to change one or more column values. Finally, call updateRow to apply the changes. For example:

```
try
{
    rs.absolute(6);
    rs.updateInt("year", 1975);
    rs.updateRow();
}
catch (SQLException e)
{
    System.out.println(e.getMessage());
    System.exit(0);
}
```

Here the year column of the sixth row in the result set is changed to 1975.

**Book VIII
Chapter 4**

**Using JDBC to
Connect to a
Database**

Table 4-6	Update Methods of the ResultSet Interface
Update by Column Name	*Update by Column Index*
void updateBigDecimal(String columnName, BigDecimal value)	void updateBigDecimal(int columnIndex, BigDecimal value)
void updateBoolean(String columnName, boolean value)	void updateBoolean(int columnIndex, boolean value)

(continued)

Table 4-6 *(continued)*

Update by Column Name	Update by Column Index
void updateDate(String columnName, Date value)	void updateDate(int columnIndex, Date value)
void updateDouble(String columnName, double value)	void updateDouble(int columnIndex, double value)
void updateFloat(String columnName, float value)	void updateFloat(int columnIndex, float value)
void updateInt(String columnName, int value)	void updateInt(int columnIndex, int value)
void updateLong(String columnName, long value)	void updateLong(int columnIndex, long value)
void updateShort(String columnName, short value)	void updateShort(int columnIndex, short value)
void updateString(String columnName, String value)	void updateString(int columnIndex, String value)

Inserting a row

To insert a row, you use a special row in the result set called the *insert row*. First, call the moveToInsertRow method to move the cursor to the insert row. Then use update methods to set the value for each column in the insert row. You then call the insertRow method to copy the insert row into the result set, which in turn writes a new row to the database. And finally, call moveToCurrentRow to move back to the previous position in the result set.

Here's an example:

```
try
{
    rs.moveToInsertRow();
    rs.updateString("title",
        "Monty Python and the Holy Grail");
    rs.updateInt("year", 1975);
    rs.updateDouble("price", 13.95);
    rs.insertRow();
    rs.moveToCurrentRow();
}
catch (SQLException e)
{
    System.out.println(e.getMessage());
    System.exit(0);
}
```

Chapter 5: Working with XML

*I*n this chapter, you find out how to work with *Extensible Markup Language (XML)* — the best thing to happen to computing since the invention of the vacuum tube (at least, according to some overenthusiastic prognosticators).

This chapter focuses on the basics of reading an XML document into memory and extracting data from it. With the background in this chapter, you shouldn't have much trouble studying the API documentation on your own to find out more about XML programming.

Defining XML

Most computer-industry pundits agree that XML will completely change the way you work with computers. Here are just some of the ways XML will revolutionize the world of computers:

✦ Unlock the vast warehouses of data that are locked up in the vaults of corporate mainframe computers

✦ Enable every electronic device on the planet, from the most complex supercomputers to desktop computers to cellphones to wristwatches, to communicate with one another

✦ Allow every computer program ever written to exchange data with every other computer program ever written

✦ Probably cure cancer and solve the budget deficit, too

Yawn.

So what is XML, really? Simply put, XML is a way to store and exchange information in a standardized way that's easy to create, retrieve, and transfer between different types of computer systems or programs.

When XML is stored in a file, the file is usually given the extension .xml.

Tags

Like Hypertext Markup Language (HTML), XML uses tags to mark the data. Here's a bit of XML that describes a book:

```
<Book>
  <Title>Java All-In-One For Dummies</Title>
  <Author>Lowe</Author>
</Book>
```

This chunk of XML defines an *element* called Book, which contains information for a single book. The Book element in turn contains two subordinate elements: Title and Author.

Notice that each element begins with a tag that lists the element's name. This tag is called the *start tag*. The element ends with an element that repeats the element name, preceded by a slash — an *end tag*.

Everything that appears between the start tag and the end tag is the element's *content,* which can consist of text data or of one or more additional elements. In the latter case, the additional elements nested within an element are called *child elements,* and the element that contains them is called the *parent element.*

The highest-level element in an XML document is called the *root element.* A properly formed XML document consists of a single root element, which can contain elements nested within it. Suppose that you want to create an XML document with information about two movies. The XML document might look something like this:

```
<Movies>
  <Movie>
    <Title>It's a Wonderful Life</Title>
    <Year>1946</Year>
    <Price>14.95</Price>
  </Movie>
  <Movie>
    <Title>Young Frankenstein</Title>
    <Year>1974</Year>
    <Price>16.95</Price>
  </Movie>
</Movies>
```

Here the root element named Movies contains two Movie elements, each of which contains Title, Year, and Price elements.

Although XML superficially resembles HTML, you find two key differences:

✦ The tags used in HTML indicate the format of data that displays, whereas tags in an XML document indicate the meaning of the data. HTML has tags such as `<B>` and `<I>` that indicate whether data is bold or italic, for example. By contrast, an XML document that holds information about books may have tags such as `<Title>` and `<Author>` that provide the title and author of the book.

✦ The tags used in an HTML document are set in stone, whereas you can make up any tags you want to use in an XML document. If you're creating an XML document about cars, you may use tags such as `<Make>`, `<Model>`, and `<Year>`. But if you're creating an XML document about classes taught at a university, you may use tags such as `<Course>`, `<Title>`, `<Instructor>`, `<Room>`, and `<Schedule>`.

Attributes

Instead of using child elements, you can use attributes to provide data for an element. An *attribute* is a name-and-value pair that's written inside the start tag for an element. Here's a `Movie` element that uses an attribute instead of a child element to record the year:

```
<Movie year="1946">
  <Title>It's a Wonderful Life</Title>
  <Price>14.95</Price>
</Movie>
```

Whether you use attributes or child elements is largely a matter of personal preference. Many XML purists say that you should avoid using attributes or use them only to identify data such as identification numbers or codes; others suggest using attributes freely. In my experience, a few attributes here and there don't hurt, but for the most part I avoid using them.

The XML declaration

Every XML file should begin with an XML declaration that identifies the version of XML being used. For most XML documents, the declaration should look like this:

```
<?xml version='1.0'?>
```

Note that the XML declaration does not require an end tag. The XML declaration should be the first line in the file.

The movies.xml file

For your reference, Listing 5-1 shows the `movies.xml` file, which the programs that appear later in this chapter use.

Listing 5-1:   The movies.xml File

```
<?xml version='1.0'?>
<Movies>
  <Movie year="1946">
    <Title>It's a Wonderful Life</Title>
    <Price>14.95</Price>
  </Movie>
  <Movie year="1974">
    <Title>Young Frankenstein</Title>
    <Price>16.95</Price>
  </Movie>
  <Movie year="1977">
    <Title>Star Wars</Title>
    <Price>17.95</Price>
  </Movie>
  <Movie year="1987">
    <Title>The Princess Bride</Title>
    <Price>16.95</Price>
  </Movie>
  <Movie year="1989">
    <Title>Glory</Title>
    <Price>14.95</Price>
  </Movie>
  <Movie year="1997">
    <Title>The Game</Title>
    <Price>14.95</Price>
  </Movie>
  <Movie year="1998">
    <Title>Shakespeare in Love</Title>
    <Price>19.95</Price>
  </Movie>
  <Movie year="2009">
    <Title>Zombieland</Title>
    <Price>18.95</Price>
  </Movie>
  <Movie year="2010">
    <Title>The King's Speech</Title>
    <Price>17.95</Price>
  </Movie>
  <Movie year="2013">
    <Title>Star Trek Into Darkness</Title>
    <Price>19.95</Price>
  </Movie>
</Movies>
```

Using a DTD

An XML document can have a *DTD*, which spells out exactly what elements can appear in an XML document and in what order the elements can appear. *DTD* stands for *Document Type Definition,* but that won't be on the test.

A DTD for an XML document about movies, for example, may specify that each Movie element must have Title and Price subelements and an attribute named year. It can also specify that the root element must be named Movies and consist of any number of Movie elements.

The main purpose of the DTD is to spell out the structure of an XML document so that users of the document know how to interpret it. Another, equally important use of the DTD is to *validate* the document to make sure that it doesn't have any structural errors. If you create a Movies XML document that has two titles for a movie, for example, you can use the DTD to detect the error.

You can store the DTD for an XML document in the same file as the XML data, but more often, you store the DTD in a separate file. That way, you can use a DTD to govern the format of several XML documents of the same type. To indicate the name of the file that contains the DTD, you add a <!DOCTYPE> declaration to the XML document. Here's an example:

```
<!DOCTYPE Movies SYSTEM "movies.dtd">
```

Here the XML file is identified as a Movies document, whose DTD you can find in the file movies.dtd. Add this tag near the beginning of the movies. xml file, right after the <?xml> tag.

Listing 5-2 shows a DTD file for the movies.xml file that was shown in Listing 5-1.

Listing 5-2:   A DTD File for the movies.xml File

```
<?xml version="1.0" encoding="UTF-8"?>
<!ELEMENT Movies (Movie*)>
<!ELEMENT Movie (Title, Price)>
<!ATTLIST Movie year CDATA #REQUIRED>
<!ELEMENT Title (#PCDATA)>
<!ELEMENT Price (#PCDATA)>
```

Each of the ELEMENT tags in a DTD defines a type of element that can appear in the document and indicates what can appear as the content for that element type. The general form of the ELEMENT tag is this:

```
<!ELEMENT element (content)>
```

Use the rules listed in Table 5-1 to express the content.

Table 5-1	Specifying Element Content
Content	*Description*
element*	The specified element can occur 0 or more times.
element+	The specified element can occur 1 or more times.
element?	The specified element can occur 0 or 1 time.
element1|element2	Either element1 or element2 can appear.
element1,element2	element1 appears, followed by element2.

(continued)

Table 5-1 *(continued)*

Content	Description
#PCDATA	Text data is allowed.
ANY	Any child elements are allowed.
EMPTY	No child elements of any type are allowed.

The first ELEMENT tag in the DTD I show in Listing 5-2, for example, says that a Movies element consists of zero or more Movie elements. The second ELEMENT tag says that a Movie element consists of a Title element followed by a Price element. The third and fourth ELEMENT tags say that the Title and Price elements consist of text data.

TIP

If this notation looks vaguely familiar, that's because it's derived from regular expressions.

The ATTLIST tag provides the name of each attribute. Its general form is this:

```
<!ATTLIST element attribute type default-value>
```

Here's a breakdown of this tag:

✦ *element* names the element whose tag the attribute can appear in.

✦ *attribute* provides the name of the attribute.

✦ *type* specifies what can appear as the attribute's value. The *type* can be any of the items listed in Table 5-2.

✦ *default* provides a default value and indicates whether the attribute is required or optional. *default* can be any of the items listed in Table 5-3.

Table 5-2 — Attribute Types

Element	The Attribute Value . . .
CDATA	Can be any character string.
(string1|string2...)	Can be one of the listed strings.
NMTOKEN	Must be a *name token*, which is a string made up of letters and numbers.
NMTOKENS	Must be one or more name tokens separated by white space.
ID	Is a name token that must be unique. In other words, no other element in the document can have the same value for this attribute.

(continued)

Table 5-2 (continued)

Element	The Attribute Value . . .
IDREF	Must be the same as an ID value used elsewhere in the document.
IDREFS	Is a list of IDREF values separated by white space.

Table 5-3   Attribute Defaults

Default	Optional or Required?
#REQUIRED	Required.
#IMPLIED	Optional.
value	Optional. This value is used if the attribute is omitted.
#FIXED value	Optional. If included, however, it must be this value, and if omitted, this value is used by default.

Here's the ATTLIST tag declaration from movies.dtd:

```
<!ATTLIST Movie year CDATA #REQUIRED>
```

This declaration indicates that the attribute goes with the Movie element, is named year, can be any kind of data, and is required.

Here's an ATTLIST tag that specifies a list of possible values along with a default:

```
<!ATTLIST Movie genre (SciFi|Action|Comedy|Drama) Comedy>
```

This form of the ATTLIST tag lets you create an attribute that's similar to an enumeration, with a list of acceptable values.

Processing XML in Two Ways: DOM and SAX

In general, you can use either of two approaches to process XML documents in a Java program:

✦ **DOM:** Stands for Document Object Model. The basic idea of DOM is that you read an entire XML document from a file into memory, where the document is stored as a collection of objects that are structured as a tree. Then you can process the elements of the tree (called *nodes*) however you want. If you change any of the nodes, you can write the document back to a file.

✦ **SAX:** Stands for Simple API for XML. SAX is a read-only technique for processing XML that lets you read the elements of an XML document from a file and react to them as they come. Because SAX doesn't require you to store an entire XML document in memory at one time, it's often used for very large XML documents.

In this section, I cover the basics of using DOM to retrieve information from an XML document. DOM represents an XML document in memory as a tree of `Node` objects. Figure 5-1 shows a simplified DOM tree for an XML document that has two `Movie` elements. Notice that the root element (`Movies`) is a node, each `Movie` element is a node, and each `Title` and `Price` element is a node. In addition, text values are stored as child nodes of the elements they belong to. Thus, the `Title` and `Price` elements each have a child node that contains the text for these elements.

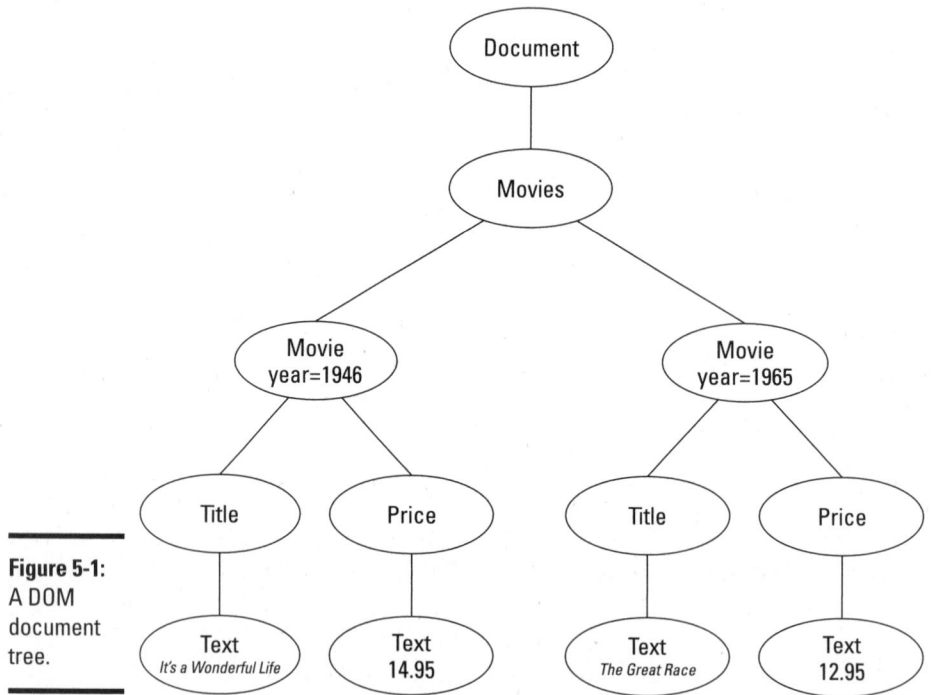

Figure 5-1:
A DOM document tree.

Reading a DOM Document

Before you can process a DOM document, you have to read the document into memory from an XML file. You'd think that this would be a fairly straightforward proposition, but unfortunately, it involves some pretty strange incantations. Rather than go through all the classes and methods you have to use, I just look at the finished code for a complete method that accepts a `String` containing a filename as a parameter and returns a document object as its return value. Along the way, you find out what each class and method does.

Here's a method that reads an XML file into a DOM document:

```
private static Document getDocument(String name)
{
    try
    {
        DocumentBuilderFactory factory =
            DocumentBuilderFactory.newInstance();
        factory.setIgnoringComments(true);
        factory.setIgnoringElementContentWhitespace(true);
        factory.setValidating(true);
        DocumentBuilder builder =
            factory.newDocumentBuilder();
        return builder.parse(new InputSource(name));
    }
    catch (Exception e)
    {
        System.out.println(e.getMessage());
    }
    return null;
}
```

Creating a DocumentBuilderFactory

The first statement of the preceding example calls the `newInstance` method of the `DocumentBuilderFactory` class to create a new `DocumentBuilder Factory` object. The job of the `DocumentBuilderFactory` is to create `DocumentBuilder` objects that can read XML input and create DOM documents in memory.

Why not just call the `DocumentBuilderFactory` constructor? It turns out that `DocumentBuilderFactory` is an abstract class, so it doesn't have a constructor. `newInstance` is a static method that determines which class to create an instance of based on the way your system is configured.

Configuring the DocumentBuilderFactory

After you get a `DocumentBuilderFactory`, you can configure it to read the document the way you want. The next three statements configure three options that are applied to document builders created by this factory object:

```
factory.setIgnoringComments(true);
factory.setIgnoringElementContentWhitespace(true);
factory.setValidating(true);
```

Here's a closer look at these statements:

✦ **The `setIgnoringComments` method tells the document builder not to create nodes for comments in the XML file.** Most XML files don't contain comments, but if they do, they're not part of the data represented by the document, so they can be safely ignored. Setting this option causes them to be ignored automatically. (If you don't set this option, a node is created for each comment in the document, and because you can't predict when or where comments appear, your program has to check every node it processes to make sure that the node isn't a comment.)

✦ **The `setIgnoringElementContentWhitespace` method causes the document builder to ignore any white space that isn't part of a text value.** If you don't include this option, the DOM document includes nodes that represent white space. The only thing that these white space nodes are good for is making the DOM document harder to process, so you should always set this option.

✦ **The `setValidating` method tells the document builder to validate the input XML if it specifies a DTD.** Validating the input can also dramatically simplify your program, because you know that the DOM document conforms to the requirements of the DTD. If you're processing the `movies.xml` file shown in Listing 5-1 earlier in this chapter, you know for certain that the first child of a `Movie` element is a `Title` element and that the second child is a `Price` element. Without the validation, all you know is that the first child of a `Movie` element *should be* a `Title` element, but you have to check it to make sure.

Creating a document builder and the document

After you set the options, you can call the `newDocumentBuilder` method to create a document builder, as follows:

```
DocumentBuilder builder =
    factory.newDocumentBuilder();
```

Here the document builder is referenced by a variable named `builder`.

Finally, you can create the DOM document by calling the `parse` method of the document builder. This method accepts an `InputSource` object as a parameter. Fortunately, the `InputSource` class has a constructor that takes a filename parameter and returns an input source linked to the file. So you can create the input source, parse the XML file, create a DOM document, and return the DOM document to the caller, all in one statement:

```
return builder.parse(new InputSource(name));
```

Note that several of these methods throw exceptions. In particular, `new DocumentBuilder` throws `ParserConfigurationException`, and `parse` throws `IOException` and `SAXException`. To keep this example simple, I caught all exceptions in one `catch` clause and printed the exception message to the console.

Using the getDocument method

By adding the `getDocument` method, you can create a DOM document from a file with a single statement, like this:

```
Document doc = getDocument("movies.xml");
```

Here the `movies.xml` file is read, and a DOM document is created and assigned to the `doc` variable.

Also note that you must provide three `import` statements to use the `getDocument` method, as follows:

```
import javax.xml.parsers.*;
import org.w3c.dom.*;
import org.xml.sax.*;
```

`DocumentBuilder` and `DocumentBuilderFactory` are in the `javax. xml.parsers` package, `Document` is in `org.w3c.dom`, and `InputSource` is in `org.xml.sax`.

Reading DOM Nodes

After you have a DOM document in memory, you can easily retrieve data from the document's nodes. The DOM API is based on interfaces rather than classes, so each node of the DOM document is represented by an object that implements one or more DOM interfaces. The following paragraphs give you an overview of the interfaces you need to work with:

✦ **Document:** The entire document is represented by an object that implements the `Document` interface. The method you use most from this interface is `getDocumentElement`, which returns an `Element` object that represents the document's root node. After you have the root node, you can navigate to other nodes in the document to get the information you're looking for.

✦ **Node:** The `Node` interface represents a node in the DOM document. This interface provides methods that are common to all nodes. Table 5-4 lists the most useful of these methods. This table also lists some of the field values that the `getNodeType` method can return.

Table 5-4	The Node Interface
Method	*Description*
`NodeList getChildNodes()`	Gets a `NodeList` object that contains all this node's child nodes.
`Node getFirstChild()`	Gets the first child of this node.

(continued)

Table 5-4 *(continued)*

`Node getLastChild()`	Gets the last child of this node.
`int getNodeType()`	Gets an `int` that indicates the type of the node. The value can be one of the fields listed later in this table.
`String getNodeValue()`	Gets the value of this node, if the node has a value.
`Node getNextSibling()`	Gets the next sibling node.
`Node getPrevSibling()`	Gets the preceding sibling node.
`boolean hasChildNodes()`	Determines whether the node has any child nodes.

Field	*Description*
`ATTRIBUTE_NODE`	The node is an attribute node.
`CDATA_SECTION_NODE`	The node has content data.
`COMMENT_NODE`	The node is a comment.
`DOCUMENT_NODE`	The node is a document node.
`ELEMENT_NODE`	The node is an element node.
`TEXT_NODE`	The node is a text node.

✦ **Element:** The `Element` interface represents nodes that correspond to elements in the XML document. `Element` extends `Node`, so any object that implements `Element` is also a `Node`. Table 5-5 lists some of the most useful methods of this interface.

Table 5-5   The Element Interface

Method	*Description*
`String getAttribute(String name)`	Gets the value of the specified attribute.
`NodeList getElementsBy TagName(String name)`	Gets a `NodeList` object that contains all the element nodes that are contained within this element and have the specified name.
`boolean hasAttribute(String name)`	Determines whether the element has the specified attribute.

✦ **Text:** The text content of an element isn't contained in the element itself, but in a `Text` node that's stored as a child of the element. The `Text` interface has a few interesting methods you may want to look up, but for most applications, you just use the `getNodeValue` method inherited from the `Node` interface to retrieve the text stored by a text node.

✦ **NodeList:** A `NodeList` is a collection of nodes that's returned by methods such as the `getChildNodes` method of the `Node` interface or the `getElementsByTagName` of the `Element` interface. `NodeList` has just two methods: `item(int i)`, which returns the node at the specified index, and `getLength()`, which returns the number of items in the list. (As with *almost* every other index in Java, the first node is index 0, not 1.)

Processing elements

Assuming that you use a DTD to validate the XML file when you build the document, you can usually navigate the document to pick up the information you need without resorting to `NodeList` objects. Here's a routine that simply counts all the `Movie` elements in the `movies.xml` file (shown in Listing 5-1 earlier in this chapter) after it's been parsed into a `Document` object named `doc`:

```
int count = 0;
Element root = doc.getDocumentElement();
Node movie = root.getFirstChild();
while (movie != null)
{
    count++;
    movie = movie.getNextSibling();
}
System.out.println("There are " + count + " movies.");
```

This method first calls the `getFirstChild` method to get the first child of the root element. Then it uses each child element's `getNextSibling` method to get the next element that's also a child of the root element.

If you run a program that contains these lines, the following line appears on the console:

```
There are 10 movies.
```

This program doesn't do anything with the `Movie` elements other than count them, but in the next section ("Getting attribute values"), you see how to extract data from the `Movie` elements.

An alternative way to process all the elements in the `movies.xml` file is to use the `getChildNodes` method to return a `NodeList` object that contains all the elements. Then you can use a `for` loop to access each element individually. Here's a snippet of code that lists the name of each element:

```
Element root = doc.getDocumentElement();
NodeList movies = root.getChildNodes();
for (int i = 0; i < movies.getLength(); i++)
{
    Node movie = movies.item(i);
    System.out.println(movie.getNodeName());
}
```

Here the `item` method is used in the `for` loop to retrieve each `Movie` element. If you run a program that contains these lines, ten lines with the word `Movie` are displayed on the console.

Getting attribute values

To get the value of an element's attribute, call the `getAttribute` method and pass the name of the attribute as the parameter. This code returns the string value of the attribute. Then you can convert this value to another type if necessary. Note that the value may include some white space, so you should run the value through the `trim` method to get rid of any superfluous white space.

Here's an example that gets the `year` attribute from each movie in the `movies.xml` file and determines the year of the oldest movie in the collection:

```
Element root = doc.getDocumentElement();
Element movie = (Element)root.getFirstChild();
int oldest = 9999;
while (movie != null)
{
    String s = movie.getAttribute("year");
    int year = Integer.parseInt(s);
    if (year < oldest)
        oldest = year;
    movie = (Element)movie.getNextSibling();
}
System.out.println("The oldest movie in the file "
    + "is from " + oldest + ".");
```

The `year` attribute is extracted with these two lines of code:

```
String s = movie.getAttribute("year");
int year = Integer.parseInt(s);
```

The first line gets the string value of the `year` attribute, and the second line converts it to an `int`.

Notice the extra casting that's done in this method. It's necessary because the `movie` variable has to be an `Element` type so that you can call the getAttribute method. The getNextSibling method returns a Node, however, not an Element. As a result, the compiler doesn't let you assign the node to the movie variable unless you first cast it to an Element.

Getting child element values

You may be surprised to find that the text content of an element isn't stored with the element. Instead, it's stored in a child node of type Text. Consider the following XML:

```
<Title>The Princess Bride</Title>
```

This element results in two nodes in the XML document: an Element node named Title and a Text node that contains the text The Princess Bride.

Thus, if you have a Title element in hand, you must get the Text element before you can get the text content, as in this example:

```
Node textElement = titleElement.getFirstChild();
String title = textElement.getNodeValue();
```

If you prefer to write your code a little more tersely, you can use a single statement like this:

```
String title =
    titleElement.getFirstChild().getNodeValue();
```

If you find this incantation to be a little tedious, and you're doing a lot of it in your program, write yourself a little helper method, like this one:

```
private static String getTextValue(Node n)
{
    return n.getFirstChild().getNodeValue();
}
```

Then you can get the text content for an element by calling the getTextValue method, like this:

```
String title = getTextValue(titleElement);
```

After you get the text content, you can parse it to a numeric type if you need to.

Putting It All Together: A Program That Lists Movies

Now that you've seen the various interfaces and classes you use to get data from an XML file, Listing 5-3 shows a complete program that reads the movies.xml file (shown in Listing 5-1 earlier in this chapter) and lists the title, year, and price of each movie on the console. When you run this program, the following appears on the console:

```
1946: It's a Wonderful Life ($14.95)
1974: Young Frankenstein ($16.95)
1977: Star Wars ($17.95)
1987: The Princess Bride ($16.95)
1989: Glory ($14.95)
1997: The Game ($14.95)
1998: Shakespeare in Love ($19.95)
2009: Zombieland ($18.95)
2010: The Kings Speech ($17.95)
2013: Star Trek Into Darkness ($19.95)
```

Listing 5-3:   Reading an XML Document

```
import javax.xml.parsers.*;                                →1
import org.xml.sax.*;
import org.w3c.dom.*;
import java.text.*;

public class ListMoviesXML
{
    private static NumberFormat cf =
        NumberFormat.getCurrencyInstance();

    public static void main(String[] args)                 →11
    {

        Document doc = getDocument("movies.xml");

        Element root = doc.getDocumentElement();

        Element movieElement = (Element)root.getFirstChild();
        Movie m;
        while (movieElement != null)
        {
            m = getMovie(movieElement);
            String msg = Integer.toString(m.year);
            msg += ": " + m.title;
            msg += " (" + cf.format(m.price) + ")";
            System.out.println(msg);
            movieElement =
                (Element)movieElement.getNextSibling();
        }
    }

    private static Document getDocument(String name)        →29
    {
        try
        {
            DocumentBuilderFactory factory =
                DocumentBuilderFactory.newInstance();
            factory.setIgnoringComments(true);
```

```
factory.setIgnoringElementContentWhitespace(true);
        factory.setValidating(true);
        DocumentBuilder builder =
            factory.newDocumentBuilder();
        return builder.parse(new InputSource(name));
    }
    catch (Exception e)
    {
        System.out.println(e.getMessage());
    }
    return null;
}

private static Movie getMovie(Element e)                      →49
{
    // get the year attribute
    String yearString = e.getAttribute("year");
    int year = Integer.parseInt(yearString);

    // get the Title element
    Element tElement = (Element)e.getFirstChild();
    String title = getTextValue(tElement).trim();

    // get the Price element
    Element pElement =
        (Element)tElement.getNextSibling();
    String pString = getTextValue(pElement).trim();
    double price = Double.parseDouble(pString);

    return new Movie(title, year, price);
}

private static String getTextValue(Node n)                   →65
{
    return n.getFirstChild().getNodeValue();
}

private static class Movie                                   →70
{
    public String title;
    public int year;
    public double price;

    public Movie(String title, int year, double price)
    {
        this.title = title;
        this.year = year;
        this.price = price;
    }
}
}
```

Because all the code in this program appears elsewhere in this chapter, the following paragraphs just provide a simple description of what each method in this program does:

→ 1   Wow, that's a lot of packages to import. Too bad that Java's designers couldn't have put all these XML classes in one *big* package.

→ 11   The main method starts by calling the getDocument method to get a Document object from the file movies.xml. Then it gets the root element and uses a while loop to spin through all the child elements, which you know to be Movie elements because the document was validated when it was parsed. As each Movie element is processed, it's passed to the getMovie method, which extracts the year attribute and the title and price elements, and returns a Movie object. Then the movie is printed on the console.

→ 29   The getDocument method accepts a filename as a parameter and returns a Document object. Before it creates the DocumentBuilder object, it sets the configuration options so that comments and white space are ignored and the XML file is validated. Because the XML file is validated, you must create a DTD file (like the file in Listing 5-2 earlier in this chapter). Also, you must begin the XML file with a DOCTYPE declaration (such as <!DOCTYPE Movies SYSTEM "movies.dtd">).

→ 49   The getMovie method is passed an Element object that represents a Movie element. It extracts the year attribute, gets the text value of the title element, and parses the text value of the price element to a double. Then it uses these values to create a new Movie object, which is returned to the caller.

→ 65   The getTextValue method is simply a little helper method that gets the text content from a node. This method assumes that the node has a child node containing the text value, so you shouldn't call this method unless you know that to be the case. (Because the XML document was validated, you do.)

→ 70   The Movie class is a private inner class that represents a single movie. It uses public fields to hold the title, year, and price data, and it provides a simple constructor that initializes these fields.

Book IX
Fun and Games

Contents at a Glance

Chapter 1: Fun with Fonts and Colors

In This Chapter

✓ **Setting the font of a text control**

✓ **Finding out what fonts are available**

✓ **Playing with colors**

✓ **Working with system colors**

✓ **Setting foreground and background colors**

I n this chapter, I look at ways of dressing up the text that appears in Swing controls. In particular, I show you how to change the font that text is displayed in — including bold, italic, and size — as well as how to change the color of your text.

Most of the examples work with labels, but the methods you call to set the font and color are available to all Swing components because they're defined by the `Component` class, which all Swing components inherit.

Also, the information about fonts and colors that I present in this chapter applies to graphics created with the methods of the `Graphics2D` class, which I discuss in Book IX, Chapter 2.

For a full discussion of Swing, see Book VI.

Working with Fonts

In Java, a font is represented by the `Font` class. Each `Font` object has three basic characteristics: the font name, a style identifier (plain, bold, italic, or bold italic), and a point size.

Although the `Font` class has a ton of methods, you probably won't use them unless you're writing a desktop publishing program in Java. Instead, you can get by with the basic constructor, which has this form:

```
Font(String name, int style, int size)
```

This statement creates a `Font` object for a font named Papyrus:

```
Font("Papyrus", Font.PLAIN, 14)
```

Here, the font style is plain, and the size is 14 points.

Realizing that the `Font` class constructor doesn't really create a font is important. Instead, this constructor creates a `Font` object that represents a font installed on your computer. Creating a `Font` object with the name `Comic Strip`, for example, doesn't create a font named Comic Strip unless that font is already installed on the computer.

Using font names

The `name` parameter specifies the name of the installed font you want to use. If you specify `Times New Roman`, for example, the Times New Roman font is used.

Coding string literals for specific fonts usually isn't a good idea, because you have no way to guarantee that every computer has the font you specify. You can get around that problem in two ways:

✦ **Let the user configure the fonts by picking them from a list of available fonts.** For details, see the section "Getting a list of available fonts," later in this chapter.

✦ **Use one of several logical font names that Java provides in an attempt to let you specify fonts generically.** By *logical,* Java simply means that the font names are generic font types rather than the names of specific fonts. Table 1-1 lists the logical font names. You don't get much choice when you use logical font names, but at least you can choose among a basic serif font, a sans-serif font, and a monospace font. Also, you can use the `Dialog` and `Dialog Input` fonts to set the font used in dialog boxes.

Table 1-1	Logical Font Names
Logical Font	*Description*
Serif	A basic serif font — Times New Roman in Windows and usually Times Roman in non-Windows systems
SansSerif	A sans-serif font — Arial in Windows and usually Helvetica in non-Windows systems
Monospaced	A monospace font — Courier New in Windows and usually Courier in non-Windows systems
Dialog	The font used to display text in system dialog boxes
DialogInput	The font used for text input in system dialog boxes

Using font styles

Fonts can have one of four styles: plain, bold, italic, and bold italic. To set the font style, use the following three constants as the second parameter of the Font class constructor:

```
Font.BOLD
Font.ITALIC
Font.PLAIN
```

Here's how you create a Font object for 24-point JSL Ancient Bold:

```
Font("JSL Ancient", Font.BOLD, 24)
```

You may have noticed that bold italic has no constant. To create a bold italic font, you combine the Font.BOLD and Font.ITALIC constants with a | operator, like this:

```
Font("Garamond", Font.BOLD | Font.ITALIC, 12)
```

Here the Font object is Garamond, bold italic, and 12 points.

Setting a component's font

To set the font used to display a component, just call the component's setFont method and pass it a Font object, as in this example:

```
JLabel textLabel = new JLabel("Arghh, Matey");
Font f = new Font("JSL Ancient", Font.PLAIN, 16);
textLabel.setFont(f);
```

Here the font of the label named textLabel is set to 16-point JSL Ancient. (JSL Ancient is one of my personal favorites; it's used in the Pirates of the Caribbean ride at Disneyland.)

If the font is used for only one component, you can just create the component right in the setFont method call, like this:

```
textLabel.setFont(new Font("JSL Ancient", Font.PLAIN, 16));
```

If you want a component to inherit the font used by the container that holds it (such as a panel), call the component's setFont method with the parameter set to null. Here's code that sets the font for a pair of buttons in a panel named panel1 to JSL Ancient:

```
JPanel panel1 = new JPanel();
panel1.setFont(new Font("JSL Ancient", Font.PLAIN, 16));
```

```
JButton b1 = new JButton("Jolly");
b1.setFont(null);
panel1.add(b1);

JButton b2 = new JButton("Roger");
b2.setFont(null);
panel1.add(b2);
```

In this example, both buttons have their fonts set to `null`, so they both pick up the font of their parent, `panel1`.

Getting a list of available fonts

If you want to let the user pick a font, get a list of all the available fonts on the system so that you can put the font names in a combo box. To do that, you first have to get a `GraphicsEnvironment` object that represents the graphics environment the program is running in. The `GraphicsEnvironment` class has a static method called `getLocalGraphicsEnvironment` that does the job for you, as follows:

```
GraphicsEnvironment g;
g = GraphicsEnvironment.getLocalGraphicsEnvironment();
```

Note that the `GraphicsEnvironment` class is in the `java.awt` package, so you need to provide an `import` statement to import that package.

After you have a `GraphicsEnvironment` object, you can call its `getAvailableFontFamilyNames` method, which returns an array of strings containing all the font names that are available on the system, as in this example:

```
String[] fonts;
fonts = g.getAvailableFontFamilyNames();
```

You can use this array in the constructor of a combo box, like this:

```
JComboBox fontComboBox = new JComboBox(fonts);
```

Then you can create a font from the name selected by the user with code similar to this:

```
String name = (String) fontComboBox.getSelectedItem();
Font f = new Font(name, Font.PLAIN, 12);
```

Viewing a program that plays with fonts

So that you can see how these elements work together, Listing 1-1 presents a simple program that lets the user choose a font, style, and size for the sample text that's displayed. Figure 1-1 shows this program in action. Whenever the user chooses a font or size from one of the combo boxes or selects or clears one of the check boxes, the font used to display the text at the top of the form changes accordingly.

Figure 1-1:
The Fonts
program in
action.

Listing 1-1: A Program That Plays with Fonts

```java
import javax.swing.*;
import java.awt.event.*;
import java.awt.*;

public class Fonts extends JFrame
{
    public static void main(String [] args)
    {
        new Fonts();
    }

    private JLabel sampleText;

    private JComboBox fontComboBox;
    private JComboBox sizeComboBox;
    private JCheckBox boldCheck, italCheck;

    private String[] fonts;

    public Fonts()
    {
        this.setSize(500,150);
        this.setTitle("Fun with Fonts ");
        this.setDefaultCloseOperation(JFrame.EXIT_ON_CLOSE);

        sampleText = new JLabel(
            "All work and no play makes Jack a dull boy");
        this.add(sampleText, BorderLayout.NORTH);

        GraphicsEnvironment g;
        g = GraphicsEnvironment
                .getLocalGraphicsEnvironment();
        fonts = g.getAvailableFontFamilyNames();

        JPanel controlPanel = new JPanel();

        fontComboBox = new JComboBox<String>(fonts);
        fontComboBox.addActionListener(e -> updateText());
        controlPanel.add(new JLabel("Family: "));
        controlPanel.add(fontComboBox);

        Integer[] sizes = {7, 8, 9, 10, 11, 12,
                            14, 18, 20, 22, 24, 36};
        sizeComboBox = new JComboBox<Integer>(sizes);
        sizeComboBox.setSelectedIndex(5);
        sizeComboBox.addActionListener(e -> updateText() );
        controlPanel.add(new JLabel("Size: "));
        controlPanel.add(sizeComboBox);
```

→12

→14

→18

→28

→30

→35

→37

→42

(continued)

Listing 1-1 *(continued)*

```
    boldCheck = new JCheckBox("Bold");                              →50
    boldCheck.addActionListener(e -> updateText());
    controlPanel.add(boldCheck);

    italCheck = new JCheckBox("Ital");                              →54
    italCheck.addActionListener(e -> updateText() );
    controlPanel.add(italCheck);

    this.add(controlPanel, BorderLayout.SOUTH);                    →58
    updateText();

    this.setVisible(true);
}

public void updateText()                                           →64
{
    String name
        = (String) fontComboBox.getSelectedItem();

    Integer size
        = (Integer)sizeComboBox.getSelectedItem();

    int style;
    if (boldCheck.isSelected()
        && italCheck.isSelected())
        style = Font.BOLD | Font.ITALIC;
    else if (boldCheck.isSelected())
        style = Font.BOLD;
    else if (italCheck.isSelected())
        style = Font.ITALIC;
    else
        style = Font.PLAIN;

    Font f = new Font(name, style,
        size.intValue());
    sampleText.setFont(f);
}
}
```

The following paragraphs hit the high points of this program:

→ **12** This line creates the label whose font changes when the user makes a selection.

→ **14** These lines create the controls that the user works with to pick the font, size, and style.

→ **18** The `fonts` variable is an array of strings that's used to hold the name of each font available in the system.

→ **38** The label that contains the sample text is added to the North region of the frame.

→ **30** These lines get the `GraphicsEnvironment` object and then use it to populate the `fonts` array with the names of the fonts available in the system.

→ **35**   A panel is used to hold the two combo-box and two check box controls.

→ **37**   These lines create the font combo box (called Family) and add it to the panel.

→ **42**   These lines create the Size combo box and add it to the panel. The combo box is filled from an array of integers that lists commonly used point sizes. If you want to, you can call `setEditable(true)` to make this combo box editable; then the user can type any desired font size in the combo box. To keep the application simple, I didn't make the combo box editable.

→ **50**   These lines create the Bold check box and add it to the panel.

→ **54**   These lines create the Ital (italic) check box and add it to the panel.

→ **58**   The panel is added to the South region of the frame. The next line calls the action listener's `updateText` method, which applies the selected font, style, and size to the label. (If you don't call this method here, the label is displayed initially with the default font, not with the font indicated by the initial value of the Family combo box.)

→ **64**   The `updateText` method changes the font of the `sampleText` label to the font selected by the user. First, it gets the name selected in the Family combo box. Then it gets the size selected by the user in the Size combo box. Because combo boxes return objects, the selected item is cast to an `Integer`. Next, the settings of the two check boxes are evaluated to determine how to set the `style` variable. Finally, a new `Font` object is created and assigned to the `sampleText` label.

Working with Color

In Java, a particular color is represented by an instance of the `Color` class. The `Color` class breaks color down into its three basic component colors: red, green, and blue. Every color that can be represented by the `Color` class is simply a mixture of different amounts of red, green, and blue. The amount of each component color (red, green, or blue) is represented by an integer that ranges from 0 to 255.

In the following sections, you discover how to use the `Color` class to create color objects and how to use standard predefined colors. Then you apply colors to Swing components. Finally, you use a handy Swing dialog box: Choose a Color.

Creating colors

One way to create a `Color` object is to call the `Color` constructor, passing it the red, green, and blue values you want to use, as in this example:

```
Color c = new Color(255, 255, 0);
```

Here a color with full red, full green, and no blue is created, resulting in bright yellow.

If all three constituent colors are 0, the resulting color is black. If all three are 255, the result is white. And if all three values are the same, falling somewhere between 0 and 255, the result is a shade of gray.

Because color numbers can be confusing to work with and hard to remember, the Color class provides several static constants that give you predefined colors:

+ BLACK   + WHITE

+ GRAY   + CYAN

+ MAGENTA   + LIGHT_GRAY

+ RED   + PINK

+ BLUE   + YELLOW

+ GREEN   + DARK_GRAY

+ ORANGE

Here's a statement that creates a Color object that represents the color red:

```
Color c = Color.RED;
```

Colors also have a characteristic called *alpha,* which indicates the color transparency. By default, alpha is set to 255; therefore, the color isn't transparent. If you want to set a different alpha value, you can call a second Color constructor that accepts the alpha value as a fourth parameter, as in this example:

```
Color c = new Color(255, 0, 0, 128);
```

Here the color is semitransparent.

The following paragraphs describe a few additional details worth knowing about the Color class:

+ Color objects are immutable; no set methods let you change a color.

+ You can get the red, green, blue, and alpha values by using the getRed, getGreen, getBlue, and getAlpha methods.

+ You can use the brighter method to create a color that's brighter than the current color. Likewise, the darker method returns a Color object that's a little darker than the current color. These methods work by increasing the red, green, and blue values but keeping them in proportion to one another.

✦ If you call the `Color` constructor with a parameter that's less than 0 or greater than 255, `IllegalArgumentException` is thrown. As a result, check the `parameter` values before calling the constructor.

✦ The `Color` class provides an alternative constructor that lets you set the constituent colors by using `float` values between 0.0 and 1.0.

✦ The `Color` class is in the `java.awt` package, so you need an `import` statement that specifies either `java.awt.Color` or `java.awt.*`.

Using system colors

You can use the `SystemColor` class to get colors that correspond to the colors configured by the underlying operating system for various elements of the graphical user interface (GUI), such as menu text or the desktop background. Note that the `SystemColor` class extends the `Color` class, so you can use `SystemColor` objects with the `setForeground` and `setBackground` methods or with any other methods that call for `Color` objects.

The `SystemColor` class has a bevy of static methods that return `System Color` objects for the colors used by different parts of the system's GUI, as listed in Table 1-2.

Table 1-2	SystemColor Methods
Field	*Description*
`static SystemColor activeCaption`	Background color of the active window's title bar
`static SystemColor activeCaptionBorder`	Border color of the active window's title bar
`static SystemColor activeCaptionText`	Text color of the active window's title bar
`static SystemColor control`	Background color used for controls
`static SystemColor controlText`	Text color used for controls
`static SystemColor desktop`	Background color used for the desktop
`static SystemColor inactiveCaption`	Background color used for the title bar of inactive windows
`static SystemColor inactiveCaptionBorder`	Border color used for the title bar of inactive windows
`static SystemColor inactiveCaptionText`	Text color used for the title bar of inactive windows

(continued)

Table 1-2 *(continued)*

Field	Description
static SystemColor info	Background color used for tooltips
static SystemColor infoText	Text color used for tooltips
static SystemColor menu	Background color used for menus
static SystemColor menuText	Text color used for menus
static SystemColor textHighlight	Background color used for highlighted text
static SystemColor textHighlightText	Text color used for highlighted text
static SystemColor textInactiveText	Text color used for inactive text
static SystemColor textText	Text color used for text boxes and other text controls
static SystemColor textHighlight	Background color used for highlighted text
static SystemColor window	Background color used for windows
static SystemColor windowBorder	Border color used for windows
static SystemColor windowText	Text color used for windows

Here's a statement that sets the background color of a button to the color used as the background for tooltips:

```
button1.setBackground(SystemColor.info);
```

Setting the colors of Swing components

Every Swing component has two methods that let you set the colors used to draw the component: setForeground and setBackground. The setForeground method sets the color used to draw the component's text, and the setBackground method sets the color that fills in behind the text.

Here's code that sets the foreground color of a label to red:

```
JLabel errorMessage = new JLabel("Oops!");
errorMessage.setForeground(Color.RED);
```

As with fonts, you can force a component to use the color of its container by setting the color to `null`, like this:

```
textLabel.setForeground(null);
```

Then if you add `textLabel` to a panel, the label uses the panel's foreground color.

Using a color chooser

The `JColorChooser` class creates a standardized dialog box, shown in Figure 1-2, that lets the user pick a color.

Figure 1-2:
The Choose
a Color
dialog box.

Picking colors with a color chooser

The Choose a Color dialog box includes five tabs that let the user select one of three methods to pick a color:

✦ The Swatches tab, which is open in Figure 1-2, provides 279 predefined color choices.

✦ The HSV tab lets the user select the color by specifying the *hue* (that is, the base color); *saturation* (the amount of the color); and *value,* which indicates the brightness of the color.

✦ The HSL tab is similar to the HSV tab but lets the user select the color based on *hue, saturation,* and *lightness.*

The difference between HSV and HSL is subtle. To get white in HSV, you set the saturation to 0 percent, but to get white in HSL, you set lightness to 100 percent.

✦ The RGB tab lets the user specify the red, green, and blue values for the color.

✦ The CMYK tab lets the user specify color as a combination of cyan, magenta, yellow, and black.

Note: Before Java 1.7, the Choose a Color dialog box had just three tabs for choosing colors: Swatches, HSB, and RGB. (The HSB tab was the same as the HSV tab in the 1.7 version of the Choose a Color dialog box.)

Coding a color chooser

All you need to display a Choose a Color dialog box is one line of code. Just call the static `showDialog` method, which takes three parameters:

✦ The parent component to use for the dialog box (`null` to center the dialog box onscreen)

✦ The text to display in the title bar

✦ The initial color

The `showDialog` method returns the color selected by the user or `null` if the user cancels without selecting a color.

Here's an example:

```
Color c = JColorChooser.showDialog(null, "Choose a Color",
    sampleText.getForeground());
```

Just to prove how easy it is to use a color chooser, Listing 1-2 shows the complete code for a program that uses a color chooser. This program displays the frame shown in Figure 1-3. When the user clicks the Choose Color button, a color chooser just like the one shown in Figure 1-2 earlier in this chapter appears. Then, when the user selects a color and clicks OK, the color selected by the user is applied to the label.

Figure 1-3:
The Color Chooser dialog box.

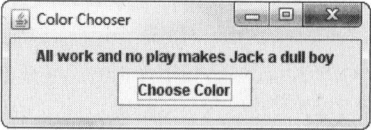

Listing 1-2:   A Program That Uses a Color Chooser

```
import javax.swing.*;
import java.awt.event.*;
import java.awt.*;
```

```
public class ColorChooser extends JFrame
{
    public static void main(String [] args)
    {
        new ColorChooser();
    }

    private JLabel sampleText;                              →12
    private JButton chooseButton;

    public ColorChooser()
    {
        this.setSize(300,100);
        this.setTitle("Color Chooser");
        this.setDefaultCloseOperation(JFrame.EXIT_ON_CLOSE);

        JPanel panel1 = new JPanel();

        sampleText = new JLabel(
            "All work and no play makes Jack a dull boy");
        sampleText.setBackground(null);
        panel1.add(sampleText);

        chooseButton = new JButton("Choose Color");
        chooseButton.addActionListener(
            e -> chooseButtonClick() );
        panel1.add(chooseButton);

        this.add(panel1);
        this.setVisible(true);
    }

    public void chooseButtonClick()
    {
        Color c = JColorChooser.showDialog(null,             →39
            "Choose a Color",
            sampleText.getForeground());
        if (c != null)                                       →42
            sampleText.setForeground(c);
    }
}
```

Here are the key points to note while you peruse this program:

→ **12**   This label's color is set to the value chosen by the user.

→ **39**   In the `chooseButtonClick` method, this statement calls the static
`showDialog` method of the `JColorChooser` class to display a
Color Chooser dialog box. The color selected by the user is saved
in the variable c.

→ **43**   If c is `null`, the user canceled out of the Color Chooser dialog
box, so the label's foreground color is unchanged. Otherwise, the
label's `setForeground` method is called to set the label's color to
the color chosen by the user.

Chapter 2: Drawing Shapes

In This Chapter

✔ Creating basic shapes such as lines, rectangles, and ellipses

✔ Setting the fill color and stroke thickness

✔ Creating shapes you can see through

✔ Creating gradient fills

✔ Rotating shapes

✔ Drawing text onscreen

*W*ere you one of those kids who, way back in school, passed away the boring hours of algebra class by doodling in the margins of the book? If so, you're in luck. Now that you're a grownup and you're mastering Java programming, you don't have to doodle in the book. Instead, you can write programs that doodle onscreen.

This chapter is a gentle introduction to the fascinating world of drawing in Java. The designers of Java call this feature *Java 2D*. With Java 2D, you can draw basic shapes: lines, arcs, rectangles, ellipses, and so on. You can set the style used to draw the shape's outline, and you can fill the shape with a solid color, a gradient fill, or text that's created from an image. You can make your shapes solid or transparent, and you can rotate, clip, skew, and do all sorts of other unspeakable things to them.

Getting a Graphics Context

Before you can do any drawing with Java 2D, you have to get yourself an object called a *graphics context*. The best way to do that is to place all the code that does your drawing in the `paint` method of a component that's added to a frame or panel so that it can be displayed. The `paint` method receives the graphics context for the component as a parameter.

Swing calls the `paint` method whenever a component needs to be repainted for any reason. That happens when the component is first displayed, but it can happen again if the user minimizes the window that displays the component and then restores it — or if the user moves another window over it and then moves that window out of the way. In addition, you can cause the `paint` method to be called at any time by calling the component's `repaint` method. You should do this whenever something happens that affects the appearance of the component.

The graphics context object is created from a class called `Graphics2D`. Just to be ornery, however, the `paint` method is passed an object of the `Graphics` class, from which `Graphics2D` is derived. As a result, the very first thing you need to do in your `paint` method is cast the `Graphics` parameter to a `Graphics2D` object, like this:

```
public void paint(Graphics g)
{
    Graphics2D g2 = (Graphics2D)g;

    // more to come...
}
```

The `Graphics2D` class has a `setRenderingHint` method that lets you set a variety of *hints* that influence how your drawings are rendered to the component. Most of these hints are pretty esoteric, but one — the antialiasing hint — can give you dramatically better-looking graphics. To apply it, use this statement:

```
g2.setRenderingHint(
    RenderingHints.KEY_ANTIALIASING,
    RenderingHints.VALUE_ANTIALIAS_ON);
```

Drawing Shapes

To draw a shape, you must first create a `Shape` object that represents the shape you want to draw. Java 2D provides several classes that implement the `Shape` interface. I have more to say about those classes later in this chapter, but to get you started, I create a basic rectangle, like this:

```
Shape rect = new Rectangle2D.Float(10, 20, 120, 150);
```

This statement creates a rectangle whose top-left corner is at (10, 20), whose width is 120, and whose height is 150. The top-left corner of a component is (0, 0), so this rectangle appears in the top-left part of the component's display area.

Never mind about the strange incantation `Rectangle2D.Float`. I explain it in the section "Creating Shapes," later in this chapter.

After you have a shape in hand, you can draw it by calling the `draw` method of the graphics context, like this:

```
g2.draw(rect);
```

This method draws an outline of the shape, using the current color.

Tweaking a drawn shape

Here are some ways to tweak a shape:

+ **Change the color before you draw the shape.** Call the `setColor` method, like this:

```
g2.setColor(Color.RED);
```

Here the color is changed to `RED`.

+ **Change the thickness of the line used to draw the shape.** Call `setStroke`, and pass it a new instance of the `BasicStroke` class, as in this example:

```
g2.setStroke(new BasicStroke(4));
```

Here the stroke thickness is set to 4.

+ **Fill a shape with color.** Call the `fill` method, like this:

```
g2.fill(rect);
```

+ **Create a shape with both an outline and a fill color.** Call both `draw` and `fill`, and change the color in between, as in this example:

```
g2.setColor(Color.BLACK);
g2.draw(rect);
g2.setColor(Color.MAGENTA);
g2.fill(rect);
```

Here the rectangle is drawn with a black outline and then filled with magenta.

Seeing how a graphics program creates shapes

To give you an idea of how graphics programs are usually constructed, Listing 2-1 shows a simple program that displays an ellipse. Figure 2-1 shows the frame displayed by this program. It's not very exciting, but I promise that things get more interesting by the end of this chapter.

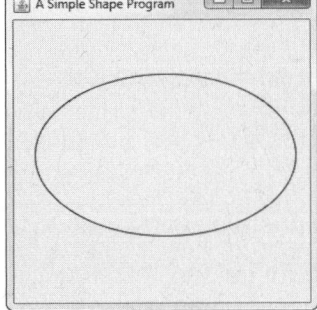

Figure 2-1:
The frame displayed by the program in Listing 2-1.

I use the basic structure of this program throughout this chapter to illustrate how graphics programming works. In particular, whenever you see code examples that call methods on an object named g2, you can assume that the code appears inside a paint method, such as the one shown in this listing.

Listing 2-1: The SimpleShape Program

```
import javax.swing.*;                                        →1
import java.awt.*;
import java.awt.geom.*;

public class SimpleShape extends JFrame                      →5
{
    public static void main(String [] args)                  →7
    {
        new SimpleShape();
    }

    public SimpleShape()                                     →12
    {
        this.setSize(300, 300);
        this.setTitle("A Simple Shape Program");
        this.setDefaultCloseOperation(JFrame.EXIT_ON_CLOSE);

        this.add(new PaintSurface(), BorderLayout.CENTER);

        this.setVisible(true);
    }

    private class PaintSurface extends JComponent             →23
    {
        public void paint(Graphics g)                        →25
        {
            Graphics2D g2 = (Graphics2D)g;

            g2.setRenderingHint(                             →29
                RenderingHints.KEY_ANTIALIASING,
                RenderingHints.VALUE_ANTIALIAS_ON);

            Shape s = new Ellipse2D.Float(                   →33
                20, 50, 250, 150);
            g2.setPaint(Color.BLACK);
            g2.draw(s);
        }
    }
}
```

The following paragraphs hit the important points of this program:

→ **1**   The program imports three packages: `java.swing`, `java.awt`, and `java.geom`. Most programs that draw graphics need at least these three classes, and some features may require you to import additional classes.

→ **5**   The `SimpleShape` class extends `JFrame`. It works just as well as an applet by extending `JApplet` instead, provided that you remove the constructor statements that call methods that aren't defined by `JApplet` (in particular, `setTitle` and `setDefaultClose Operation`).

→ **7**   The `main` method simply creates a new instance of the `Simple Shape` class to get things going.

→ **12**   The `SimpleShape` constructor does the normal frame housekeeping duties. Then it adds an instance of the `PaintSurface` class to the frame just before making the frame visible.

→ **23**   The `PaintSurface` class extends `JComponent`.

→ **25**   The `paint` method is overridden here. It receives a single parameter of type `Graphics`, named g. Notice that the first thing this method does is cast the `Graphics` parameter to a `Graphics2D` variable. This parameter allows you to use features of the `Graphics2D` class that aren't available if the graphics context is treated as a `Graphics` object.

→ **29**   After casting the graphics context object, the program sets the rendering hint to use antialiasing, which results in much smoother output.

→ **33**   After setting the rendering hint, the program creates a shape (an ellipse), sets the painting color to black, and draws the shape on the component.

Creating Shapes

All the various shapes you can draw with Java 2D are created with classes that implement the `Shape` interface. Although the `Shape` interface has some interesting methods of its own, for now I focus on the various classes that implement the `Shape` interface, listed in Table 2-1.

Table 2-1	Classes That Represent Basic Shapes
Class Constructor	*Description*
`Arc2D.Float(float x, float y, float w, float h, float start, float extent, int type)`	Creates an *arc,* which is a segment of an ellipse defined by the first four parameters. `start` is the starting angle of the arc in degrees, `extent` is the angular extent of the arc, and `type` is the type of arc to draw. Type can be OPEN, CHORD, or PIE.
`Ellipse2D.Float(float x, float y, float w, float h)`	Creates an ellipse that fits within the rectangle whose top-left corner is at (x, y), whose width is w, and whose height is h. To create a circle, specify the same value for w and h.
`Line2D.Float(float x1, float y1, float x2, float y2)`	Creates a line from (x1, y1) to (x2, y2).
`Line2D.Float(Point2D p1, Point2D p2)`	Creates a line from p1 to p2.
`Rectangle2D.Float(float x, float y, float w, float h)`	Creates a rectangle whose top-left corner is at (x, y), whose width is w, and whose height is h.
`RoundRectangle2D.Float(float x, float y, float w, float h, float arcw, float arch)`	Creates a rounded rectangle whose top-left corner is at (x, y), whose width is w, and whose height is h. The arcw and arch parameters specify the width and height of the corner arcs.

One complication that you'll notice immediately is that the class names are weird. The class for creating a rectangle, for example, is `Rectangle2D.Float`. Here's why: The `Float` class is actually an inner class of the `Rectangle2D` class, which is abstract. What Table 2-1 doesn't show is that each of these classes also has an inner class named `Double`, which lets you represent shapes with more precision. For most purposes, `float` precision is adequate, but you may need to use the `Double` classes if you're working on an application that requires high precision to represent shapes.

Figure 2-2 shows several of these shapes drawn in a frame. The code that created this figure is shown in Listing 2-2, later in the chapter. Before examining the code in detail, however, I describe how you use each of the constructors listed in Table 2-1 to create these shapes.

Figure 2-2:
A bunch of
shapes.

Creating lines

The most basic type of shape is a line, created with the `Line2D.Float`
class. To create a line, you specify the x and y coordinates of the start and
end of the line, as in this example:

```
Shape line1 = new Line2D.Float(0, 0, 100, 200);
```

This code creates a line that goes from (0, 0) to (100, 200).

The `Line2D.Float` class has an alternative constructor that accepts
`Point2D` objects for its parameters. `Point2D` is also an abstract class with
inner classes named `Float` and `Double`, so you must use `Point2D.Float` or
`Point2D.Double` to create a `Point2D` object. Here's the same line created
with `Point2D` objects:

```
Point2D start = new Point2D.Float(0, 0);
Point2D end = new Point2D.Float (100, 200);
Shape line1 = new Line2D.Float(start, end);
```

The grid lines in Figure 2-2 were drawn by line shapes inside `for` loops,
like this:

```
for (int i = 0; i < getSize().width; i += 10)
    g2.draw(new Line2D.Float(i, 0, i, getSize().height));
for (int i = 0; i < getSize().height; i += 10)
    g2.draw(new Line2D.Float(0, i, getSize().width, i));
```

The first `for` loop draws the vertical lines, and the second draws the horizontal
lines.

Creating rectangles

A rectangle requires an (x, y) starting point, a width, and a height. Here's the
code that creates the first rectangle shown in Figure 2-2 earlier in this chapter:

```
Shape rect1 = new Rectangle2D.Float(10, 10, 60, 80);
```

Here the rectangle starts at (10, 10). Its width is 60, and its height is 80.

Java 2D also provides a RoundRectangle2D class that lets you create rectangles with rounded corners. The constructor for this class takes two additional parameters that specify the width and height of the arc used to draw the corners. Here's the rounded rectangle in the middle of the first row of shapes shown in Figure 2-2:

```
Shape round1 = new RoundRectangle2D.Float
                    (110, 10, 80, 80, 10, 10);
```

Here, the corners are rounded with an arc whose height and width are both 10.

You can create some interesting shapes by using unequal values for the arc's width and height. Here's the code for the third shape in the first row of Figure 2-2:

```
Shape round2 = new RoundRectangle2D.Float(210, 10, 60,
                    80, 50, 75);
```

Here the arc's width is 50 and its height is 75.

Creating ellipses

An *ellipse* is a round shape that fits within a rectangular area. Thus, the constructor for the Ellipse2D.Float class is similar to the Rectangle2D.Float constructor. Here's an example that creates an ellipse where the bounding rectangle is a square:

```
Shape ellipse1 = new Ellipse2D.Float(10, 110, 80, 80);
```

Note that if the bounding rectangle happens to be a square, the ellipse is a circle. This one is the first shape shown in the second row of Figure 2-2.

Here's the code for the second ellipse in the figure:

```
Shape ellipse2 = new Ellipse2D.Float(110, 110, 80, 40);
```

This ellipse fits inside a rectangle whose width is 80 and height is 40. Thus the ellipse is short and wide, kind of like me. If I ate a little less and exercised a little more, maybe I'd look more like the third ellipse, created with this code:

```
Shape ellipse3 = new Ellipse2D.Float(210, 110, 40, 80);
```

Creating arcs

Another useful type of shape is an *arc,* which is a segment of an ellipse. To create an arc, you supply the bounding rectangle that contains the ellipse. Here are the parameters you need to specify:

✦ **The starting angle for the arc:** This angle is expressed in degrees. 0 is due east (or 3:00 o'clock high, as they say in the movies).

✦ **The extent:** The *extent* is an angle that represents how much of the ellipse the arc spans. This angle, too, is specified in degrees.

The important thing to know is that the arc travels counterclockwise from the starting point. If you specify 0 as the starting point and 90 as the extent, the arc travels from 3:00 o'clock to 12:00 o'clock high.

✦ **The arc type:** Choose one of the following:

- `Arc2D.OPEN` indicates that you want to draw just the arc itself.

- `Arc2D.CHORD` means that you want to draw the arc and then connect the ends with a straight line to create a closed shape.

- `Arc2D.PIE` means that you want to use straight lines to connect the ends to the center of the ellipse, thereby creating a shape that looks like a piece of pie.

Here's an example that creates the first arc shown in Figure 2-2:

```
Shape arc1 = new Arc2D.Float(10, 210, 80, 80, 90, 90,
                Arc2D.OPEN);
```

The second arc is created with this statement:

```
Shape arc1 = new Arc2D.Float(110, 210, 80, 80, 0, 180,
                Arc2D.CHORD);
```

Finally, the third arc (the pie slice) is created by this statement:

```
Shape arc1 = new Arc2D.Float(210, 210, 45, 180, 45, 90,
                Arc2D.PIE);
```

Looking at the ShapeMaker program

Now that you've seen how to create a variety of shapes, you're ready to take a glance at Listing 2-2, which draws the shapes shown in Figure 2-2 earlier in this chapter.

This program relies on a very useful technique for any program that works with more than a few shapes. Instead of creating and drawing each shape separately in the `paint` method, the program stores the shapes in an `ArrayList` object of type `Shape`. The shapes are created in the `PaintComponent` constructor, so the code that creates the shapes is executed only once. Then, in the paint method, an enhanced for loop is used to draw each shape in the ArrayList. This technique is especially handy for programs that let the user draw shapes. Each time the user draws a new shape, you just add the shape to the ArrayList. Then, whenever the paint method is called, all the shapes are drawn.

Listing 2-2:   The ShapeMaker Program

```java
import javax.swing.*;
import java.awt.event.*;
import java.awt.*;
import java.awt.geom.*;
import java.util.*;

public class ShapeMaker extends JFrame
{
    public static void main(String [] args)
    {
        new ShapeMaker();
    }

    public ShapeMaker()
    {
        this.setSize(300, 300);
        this.setTitle("Shape Maker");
        this.setDefaultCloseOperation(JFrame.EXIT_ON_CLOSE);
        this.add(new PaintSurface(), BorderLayout.CENTER);

        this.setVisible(true);
    }

    private class PaintSurface extends JComponent
    {
        ArrayList<Shape> shapes = new ArrayList<Shape>();
        Point startDrag, endDrag;
        Shape found = null;

        public PaintSurface()
        {
            Shape s;

            // a rectangle
            s = new Rectangle2D.Float(10, 10, 60, 80);
            shapes.add(s);

            // a rounded rectangle
            s = new RoundRectangle2D.Float(110, 10, 80, 80, 10, 10);
            shapes.add(s);

            // a rounded rectangle
            s = new RoundRectangle2D.Float(210, 10, 60, 80, 50, 75);
            shapes.add(s);

            // a circle
            s = new Ellipse2D.Float(10, 110, 80, 80);
            shapes.add(s);
```

```
    // an ellipse
    s = new Ellipse2D.Float(110, 110, 80, 40);
    shapes.add(s);

    // another ellipse
    s = new Ellipse2D.Float(210, 110, 40, 80);
    shapes.add(s);

    // an arc
    s = new Arc2D.Float(10, 210, 80, 80, 90, 90, Arc2D.OPEN);
    shapes.add(s);

    // another arc
    s = new Arc2D.Float(110, 210, 80, 80, 0, 180, Arc2D.CHORD);
    shapes.add(s);

    // another arc
    s = new Arc2D.Float(210, 210, 80, 80, 45, 90, Arc2D.PIE);
    shapes.add(s);
}

public void paint(Graphics g)
{
    Graphics2D g2 = (Graphics2D)g;

    // turn on antialiasing
    g2.setRenderingHint(
        RenderingHints.KEY_ANTIALIASING,
        RenderingHints.VALUE_ANTIALIAS_ON);

    // draw background grid
    g2.setPaint(Color.LIGHT_GRAY);
    for (int i = 0; i < getSize().width; i += 10)
        g2.draw(new Line2D.Float(i, 0, i, getSize().height));
    for (int i = 0; i < getSize().height; i += 10)
        g2.draw(new Line2D.Float(0, i, getSize().width, i));

    // draw all the shapes in the array list
    g2.setColor(Color.BLACK);
    g2.setStroke(new BasicStroke(2));
    for (Shape s : shapes)
        g2.draw(s);
    }
  }
}
```

Filling Shapes

To fill a shape with a solid color, first call the setColor method to set the fill color. Then call the fill method to fill the shape, as in this example:

```
g2.setColor(Color.RED);
g2.fill(rect1);
```

Here the fill color is set to RED, and then the shape named rect1 is filled.

There's more to filling than solid colors, however. In the following sections, you find out how to create fills that are partially transparent and fills that gradually fade from one color to another.

Drawing transparently

Java 2D lets you create transparent shapes by specifying a compositing rule. A compositing rule can do more than just set the transparency, but its other uses are more advanced than this chapter allows. Rather than go into all the gory details, let me just ask you to accept my word that to set the transparency, you must use this odd incantation:

```
g2.setComposite(AlphaComposite.getInstance
    (AlphaComposite.SRC_OVER, 0.50F));
```

The key here is the `float` parameter value, which must range from `0.0` to `1.0`. In this case, the transparency is set to `0.50F`, which means that the shapes are 50 percent transparent. As a result, whatever is under the shape when it is drawn partially shows through.

Using a gradient fill

Instead of using a solid color, you can specify a *gradient fill,* which blends two colors by using the `GradientPaint` class, whose constructors are shown in Table 2-2. A gradient fill is created from two color points. Imagine a line drawn between these two points. The gradient fill varies the color smoothly from the color that's set at the first point to the color set at the second point. Then it extends the colors on this line at 90-degree angles to the line to fill an entire area.

Table 2-2	Constructors of the GradientPaint Class
Constructor	*Description*
`GradientPaint(float x1, floaty1, Color c1, float x2, float y2, Color c2)`	Creates a gradient in which the color at point `x1, y1` is `color1`; the color at point `x2, y2` is `color2`; and points in between are blended smoothly. All points beyond the `x1, y1` point have `color1`, and all points beyond the `x2, y2` point have `color2`.
`GradientPaint(Point2D p1, Color c1, Point2D p2 Color c2)`	Creates a gradient in which the color at point `p1` is `color1`, the color at point `p2` is `color2`, and points in between are blended smoothly. All points beyond `p1` have `color1`, and all points beyond `p2` have `color2`.

Constructor	Description
GradientPaint(float x1, float y1, Color c1, float x2, float y2, Color c2, boolean cyclic)	Creates the same gradient as the first constructor, but if the cyclic parameter is true, the gradient pattern repeats infinitely beyond the two points.
GradientPaint(Point2D p1, Color c1, Point2D p2 Color c2, boolean cyclic)	Creates the same gradient as the second constructor, but if the cyclic parameter is true, the gradient pattern repeats infinitely beyond the two points.

This example sets a gradient fill that varies the color from magenta to yellow:

```
GradientPaint gp =
    new GradientPaint(0, 0, Color.MAGENTA,
                    0, 100, Color.YELLOW);
```

Table 2-3 shows four examples of gradient fills created with the Gradient Paint class. Each of the rectangles is 100 × 100 pixels. The table also shows the locations of the points for each fill relative to x, y, width, and height. For each fill, the color for point 1 is black; for point 2, it's white.

Table 2-3   **Four Gradient Fill Examples**

Gradient Fill	Name	Point 1 (Black)	Point 2 (White)
	gp1	x, y	x, y + height-
	gp2	x, y	x + width, y-
	gp3	x, y+35	x, y + height + 35-
	gp4	x+35, y+35	x+width-35, y+height-35-

Here's the code that creates these four gradient fills:

```
GradientPaint gp1 = new GradientPaint(x, y, Color.BLACK,
    x, y + h, Color.WHITE);
GradientPaint gp2 = new GradientPaint(x, y, Color.BLACK,
    x + w, y, Color.WHITE);
GradientPaint gp3 = new GradientPaint(x, y+35,
```

```
        Color.BLACK, x, y+h-35, Color.WHITE, true);
    GradientPaint gp4 = new GradientPaint(x+35, y+35,
        Color.BLACK, x+w-35, y+h-35, Color.WHITE, true);
```

Using this code as a starting point, you can devise many variations to create your own fills.

Rotating and Translating

This section describes two methods of the `Graphics2D` class that modify how a shape is drawn:

✦ The `translate` method moves the `(0, 0)` point from the top-left corner to any arbitrary point.

✦ The `rotate` method rotates the component's coordinate system so that shapes are drawn at an angle.

TIP

Choosing color points

Here are some suggestions for choosing the locations of the two color points:

✔ The points are relative to the top-left corner of the component, not to the shape you're filling. You usually want both points to lie at or near the edges of the shape you're drawing.

✔ The easiest way to keep the number straight is to create variables named `x`, `y`, `width`, and `height`, and use these variables to create both the shapes and the gradient fills.

✔ If you want to have the first color at the top and the second color at the bottom, use `(x, y)` as the first point and `(x, y+height)` as the second point.

✔ If you want to have the first color at the left and the second color at the right, use `(x, y)` as the first point and `(x+width, y)` as the second point.

✔ Each point is painted with the full color that you specify. If you want a band of solid color on the edges of the object before the gradient begins, choose points that are somewhat inside the object. You could use `(10, 10)` and `(width-10, height-10)`, for example.

✔ If you use the third or fourth constructors and specify `true` for the `cyclic` parameter, the gradient pattern repeats itself. Then you want to pick points that are closer together so that you can see the repetition within your object. If the width of the object is `150`, for example, pick points such as `(0, 0)` and `(0, 50)` to see the cycle repeat three times within the object.

The translate method

The `translate` method takes two parameters — namely, the x and y coordinates of the point you want to designate as the center of the universe. For many graphics applications, translating to the center of the component is useful, so (0, 0) is in the middle of the component. Accordingly, points with a negative x value appear to the left of center, and points with a negative y value appear above center. Here's a code snippet that does that task, regardless of the size of the component:

```
int cx = getSize().width / 2;      // center X;
int cy = getSize().height / 2;     // center Y;
g2.translate(cx, cy);
```

The rotate method

Rotation is a little more complicated. The `rotate` method itself is simple enough; it takes a single parameter that rotates the coordinate system by the angle you specify. Here's an example:

```
g2.rotate(angle);
```

The angle isn't measured in degrees. Instead, it's measured in *radians,* a unit that (if you remember your high school math) is the length of the arc subtended by the angle (assuming that the radius is 1). Java's `Math` class has a handy `toRadians` method that automatically converts degrees to radians. So to rotate the coordinate space by 45 degrees, you use this statement:

```
g2.rotate(Math.toRadians(45));
```

Note that the `rotate` method rotates the entire coordinate space for the component you're painting on, not just a single shape. As a result, to draw a shape rotated around its center, you translate to the center of the shape you want to rotate, call the `rotate` method, and then draw the shape. The `Graphics2D` class provides a convenient version of the `rotate` method that does that for you automatically. It takes three parameters: the rotation angle and the x and y coordinates of the point around which you want to rotate, as in this example:

```
g2.rotate(Math.toRadians(45), 100, 150);
```

Here the coordinate space is rotated 45 degrees around point 100, 150. (The translation is only temporary; the `rotate` method restores the preceding translation after it does the rotation.)

Here's an example from a `paint` method that creates an ellipse and then draws it several times at different rotations:

```
int x = 50;
int y = 75;
int width = 200;
int height = 100;
Shape r1 = new Ellipse2D.Float(x, y, width, height);
for (int angle = 0; angle <= 360; angle += 45)
{
    g2.rotate(Math.toRadians(angle),
        x + width/2, y + height/2);
    g2.setPaint(Color.YELLOW);
    g2.fill(r1);
    g2.setStroke(new BasicStroke(4));
    g2.setPaint(Color.BLACK);
    g2.draw(r1);
}
```

Here the `rotate` method is called inside a `for` loop that varies the angle from 0 degrees through 360 degrees in 45-degree increments. Assuming that the `paint` method has set antialiasing and 50 percent transparency, and has drawn the grid lines shown in the preceding examples, Figure 2-3 shows how the shapes drawn by these statements appear.

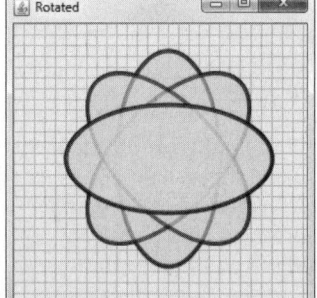

Figure 2-3:
Rotated
shapes.

Drawing Text

You can use the `drawString` method to draw the text contained in a string. This method accepts three parameters: the string to be drawn and the x and y coordinates of the bottom-left corner of the first character to be drawn (technically speaking, the start of the *baseline* for the text). Here's an example:

```
g2.drawString("This is some text!", 100, 50);
```

Here the string `"This is some text!"` is drawn at point `(100, 50)`.

The current stroke, color, translation, and rotation apply to the text that's drawn, as well as to the current font that you specify via the `setFont` method. This method accepts a `Font` object, like this:

```
g2.setFont(new Font("Times New Roman", Font.PLAIN, 36));
```

Here the font is set to 36-point Times New Roman. For more information about creating fonts, refer to Book IX, Chapter 1.

Letting the User Draw on a Component

In many applications, you need to let the user doodle directly on a panel. To do that, you need to create listeners that listen for mouse events such as clicks, drags, or just basic movements. Then you need to coordinate those listeners with the `paint` method so that the mouse events generated by the user are translated into shapes that are drawn on the component.

Two interfaces are involved in listening to mouse events. The first, `Mouse Listener`, provides several methods that are called when the user clicks a mouse button or moves the mouse into or out of a component. The second, `MouseMotionListener`, provides methods that are called when the user moves or drags the mouse. Table 2-4 lists the methods for these two interfaces, plus the `MouseEvent` interface which provides details about the mouse events.

Table 2-4	**Mouse Events and Listeners**
MouseListener Method	*Description*
`void mouseClicked(MouseEvent e)`	The user clicked a mouse button.
`void mouseEntered(MouseEvent e)`	The mouse entered a component.
`void mouseExited(MouseEvent e)`	The mouse exited a component.
`void mousePressed(MouseEvent e)`	The user pressed a mouse button.
`void mouseReleased(MouseEvent e)`	The user released a mouse button.
MouseMotionListener Method	*Description*
`void mouseMoved (MouseEvent e)`	The user moved the mouse without pressing a button.
`void mouseDragged(MouseEvent e)`	The user moved the mouse while a button was pressed.

(continued)

Table 2-4 *(continued)*

MouseEvent Method	Description
int getButton()	This method gets the mouse button that has been clicked, pressed, or released. The result can be BUTTON1, BUTTON2, BUTTON3, or NOBUTTON.
int getClickCount()	This method gets the number of clicks to determine whether the user double- or triple-clicked.
Point getPoint()	This method gets the mouse position as a Point object.
int getX()	This method gets the x position.
int getY()	This method gets the y position.

Note that both the MouseListener and MouseMotionListener interfaces have corresponding adapter classes named MouseAdapter and MouseMotionAdapter. If you use one or both of these adapter classes, you have to override the methods for only the events you want to respond to. (For more information about adapter classes and listeners, refer to Book VI, Chapter 2.)

To see how mouse events can be used to create programs that let the user draw onscreen, take a look at a simple program that lets the user draw rectangles. The basic technique used by the program goes something like this:

✦ When the user presses the mouse button, you make a note of the location to use as the starting point of the rectangle to be drawn.

✦ When mouse movement is detected, you make a note of the mouse location and call repaint to force the component to be repainted. Then, in the paint method, you draw a temporary rectangle from the original starting position to the current mouse position to give the user a visual clue while he or she is drawing the rectangle. This rectangle is drawn with a light gray line and isn't filled. Each time the user moves the mouse, this rectangle is redrawn according to the current mouse position. As a result, the rectangle appears to grow and shrink with the mouse movements.

✦ When the user releases the mouse button, you create a new Rectangle 2D.Float object, using the original starting location and the mouse location when the button was released. Then you add the rectangle to an ArrayList of Shape objects and call repaint to force the component to be repainted. This code causes all the rectangles in the ArrayList to be drawn in the order in which the user created them.

✦ Also when the user releases the mouse button, you clear the two mouse locations that were saved while the user was drawing the rectangle. That way, the `paint` method knows not to draw the temporary rectangle.

Here are a few other points to know about this program before I dive into the code:

✦ Rectangles created with the `Rectangle2D` class are always specified with the (x, y) coordinates of the top-left corner, a width, and a height. Users don't always draw rectangles starting with the top-left corner, however. They might press the mouse button to anchor the rectangle and then draw the mouse up and to the left, so that the original position is the bottom-right corner instead of the top-left corner. To facilitate this action, the program includes a helper method that creates a rectangle from any two arbitrary points that mark opposite corners. This method uses these points to determine the location of the top-left corner and the width and height.

✦ To make the rectangles visually interesting, the program uses an array to fill each rectangle with a different color. Also, each rectangle is filled with 50-percent transparency so that rectangles underneath it are visible.

✦ The component surface also shows a grid drawn with `Line2D` shapes.

Figure 2-4 shows this program in action, after the user has drawn several rectangles. Listing 2-3 provides the complete code for the program.

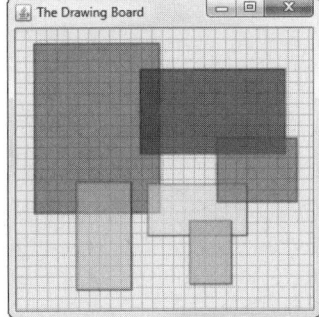

Figure 2-4:
The Drawing Board program in action.

Listing 2-3: The DrawingBoard Program

```
import javax.swing.*;
import java.awt.event.*;
import java.awt.*;
import java.awt.geom.*;
import java.util.*;
```

(continued)

```
public class DrawingBoard extends JFrame
{
    public static void main(String [] args)                              →8
    {
        new DrawingBoard();
    }

    public DrawingBoard()                                                →13
    {
        this.setSize(300, 300);
        this.setTitle("The Drawing Board");
        this.setDefaultCloseOperation(JFrame.EXIT_ON_CLOSE);
        this.add(new PaintSurface(), BorderLayout.CENTER);
        this.setVisible(true);
    }

    private class PaintSurface extends JComponent
    {
        ArrayList<Shape> shapes = new ArrayList<Shape>();                →24
        Point startDrag, endDrag;

        public PaintSurface()
        {
            this.addMouseListener(new MouseAdapter()
            {
                public void mousePressed(MouseEvent e)                  →31
                {
                    startDrag = new Point(e.getX(), e.getY());
                    endDrag = startDrag;
                    repaint();
                }

                public void mouseReleased(MouseEvent e)                 →38
                {
                    Shape r = makeRectangle(
                                    startDrag.x, startDrag.y,
                                    e.getX(), e.getY());
                    shapes.add(r);
                    startDrag = null;
                    endDrag = null;
                    repaint();
                }
            } );

            this.addMouseMotionListener(new MouseMotionAdapter()
            {
                public void mouseDragged(MouseEvent e)                  →52
                {
                    endDrag = new Point(e.getX(), e.getY());
                    repaint();
                }
            } );
        }

        public void paint(Graphics g)                                   →59
        {
            Graphics2D g2 = (Graphics2D)g;

            // turn on antialiasing
            g2.setRenderingHint(
```

```
        RenderingHints.KEY_ANTIALIASING,
        RenderingHints.VALUE_ANTIALIAS_ON);

    // draw background grid
    g2.setPaint(Color.LIGHT_GRAY);
    for (int i = 0; i < getSize().width; i += 10)
    {
        Shape line = new Line2D.Float(
            i, 0, i, getSize().height);
        g2.draw(line);
    }

    for (int i = 0; i < getSize().height; i += 10)
    {
        Shape line = new Line2D.Float(
            0, i, getSize().width, i);
        g2.draw(line);
    }

    // draw the shapes
    Color[] colors = {Color.RED, Color.BLUE,                    →85
                    Color.PINK, Color.YELLOW,
                    Color.MAGENTA, Color.CYAN };
    int colorIndex = 0;

    g2.setStroke(new BasicStroke(2));                           →90
    g2.setComposite(AlphaComposite.getInstance(
        AlphaComposite.SRC_OVER, 0.50f));

    for (Shape s : shapes)                                      →94
    {
        g2.setPaint(Color.BLACK);
        g2.draw(s);
        g2.setPaint(colors[(colorIndex++)%6]);
        g2.fill(s);
    }

    // paint the temporary rectangle
    if (startDrag != null && endDrag != null)                  →103
    {
        g2.setPaint(Color.LIGHT_GRAY);
        Shape r = makeRectangle(
            startDrag.x, startDrag.y,
            endDrag.x, endDrag.y);
        g2.draw(r);
    }
}

private Rectangle2D.Float makeRectangle(                       →113
    int x1, int y1, int x2, int y2)
{
    int x = Math.min(x1, x2);
    int y = Math.min(y1, y2);
    int width = Math.abs(x1 - x2);
    int height = Math.abs(y1 - y2);
    return new Rectangle2D.Float(
        x, y, width, height);
}
    }
}
```

The following paragraphs provide a road map through this program:

→ **8**   The `main` method creates an instance of the `DrawingBoard` class.

→ **13**   The constructor for the `DrawingBoard` class initializes the frame in the usual way, adding a new instance of a `JComponent` class named `PaintSurface`.

→ **24**   The `PaintSurface` class begins by defining three instance variables. The first, named `shapes`, is an `ArrayList` object that holds the shapes drawn by the user. The next two variables are `Point` objects that represent the start and end points for the rectangle currently being drawn by the user.

→ **31**   The `PaintSurface` constructor uses anonymous inner classes to create the mouse listeners. The `mousePressed` method is invoked when the user presses a mouse button. It sets the `startDrag` and `endDrag` variables to the current position of the mouse and then calls `repaint` to force the component to be repainted.

→ **38**   The `mouseReleased` method is called when the user releases the mouse, indicating that a rectangle has been drawn. It calls the `makeRectangle` method to create a rectangle from the starting x and y values and the current x and y values. Then it adds this rectangle to the `shapes` collection, clears the `startDrag` and `endDrag` points, and calls `repaint` to force the component to be repainted.

→ **52**   The `mouseDragged` method in the `MouseMotionAdapter` anonymous class is called when the mouse moves while the button is held down. This method simply sets the `endDrag` variable to the new mouse location and calls `repaint` to repaint the component.

→ **59**   The `paint` method is where the good stuff happens in this program. It begins by casting the `Graphics` object to a `Graphics2D` object, turning on antialiasing, and drawing the background grid. Then it draws the shapes from the `shapes` collection.

→ **85**   To fill each rectangle with a different color, the program creates an array of `Color` objects that specifies six colors. Then it defines a variable named `colorIndex` to index the array. Each time a rectangle is drawn, this index is incremented.

→ **90**   The stroke thickness is set to 2, and the `setComposite` method is used to set the transparency to 50 percent.

→ **94**   An enhanced `for` loop is used to draw each rectangle. First, the color is set to black, and the rectangle is drawn. Then the color is set, and the rectangle is filled. The modulo division operator (`%`) is used to constrain the index from 0 through 5, and the index is incremented so that the next rectangle uses the next color in the array.

→ 103   This `if` statement draws the temporary rectangle while the user is dragging the mouse. If either `startDrag` or `endDrag` is `null`, the rectangle isn't drawn.

→ 113   `makeRectangle` is a helper method that creates a `Rectangle2D.Float` object, given the points of two opposite corners. It sets the starting point to the smaller of the two x values and the smaller of the two y values, and it sets the width and height to the absolute value of the difference between the two x values and the two y values.

Chapter 3: Using Images and Sound

In This Chapter

✔ **Displaying images in Swing components**

✔ **Drawing images directly on a panel**

✔ **Scaling images**

✔ **Using a file chooser to pick an image**

✔ **Adding annoying sound effects and music to your programs**

*S*o far in this book, all the Swing applications have been pretty boring. They've had plenty of labels, text fields, combo boxes, and the like, but no pictures!

This chapter remedies that situation. You find out how to incorporate graphic images (that is, pictures — not necessarily images of a graphic nature) into your Swing applications. Just to make things interesting, I show you how to throw in sound effects and music, too.

Java's support for images and sound is designed assuming that you're going to use them in applets that run over a slow Internet connection. As a result, Java goes to great lengths to accommodate large files that can take a long time to download. It includes a special class called `MediaTracker` that lets you monitor the progress of a long download so that you can display a progress bar, display the image, or play the sound piece by piece as it arrives. Fortunately, Java also includes some shortcut methods that let you just load an image or sound file and use it without worrying about the `MediaTracker` details.

I'm a big believer in shortcuts, except on family vacations. I took a shortcut once on a family trip to see Mount Lassen. It turned out that the shortcut involved about an hour of driving five miles on a windy dirt road. We would have arrived a half hour sooner had we gone the long way. But trust me: This isn't that kind of shortcut. You really get there faster if you skip the `MediaTracker` details until the end.

Using Images

An *image* is a file that contains a picture. Java supports pictures in several formats, including these:

✦ **GIF:** *GIF* is *Graphics Interchange Format*, commonly used for small images such as those used as button icons and the like.

✦ **JPEG:** The Joint Photographic Experts Group (hence the name *JPEG*) devised this format to store photographic images in compressed form. JPEG is the preferred form for larger images. Note that when images are compressed with JPEG, some of the image data is lost, resulting in a small decrease in quality.

✦ **PNG:** *PNG* is *Portable Network Graphics* format, which was designed specifically for portability and network access. You'd think that this format would be the most common in Java applications because Java, too, was designed for portability and network access. Although Java does indeed support PNG, the more popular choices are GIF and JPEG.

Java does *not* directly support other common graphics-file formats, such as BMP (Windows bitmap), PCX (PC Paintbrush bitmap), and WMF (Windows Metafile Format). The easiest way to deal with this limitation is to simply convert your images to GIF, JPEG, or PNG. Programs that can do that conversion are readily available. If you insist on using images in those formats, you can get third-party packages that do support other graphic file formats. Hop on the Internet, cruise to your favorite search service, and search for "Java" and the format you want to support.

Using the ImageIcon Class

The easiest way to work with images is to use the `ImageIcon` class, which lets you load an image from a file by using a filename or URL. Then you can display it by attaching it to a label or button component or by painting it directly. The `ImageIcon` class shelters you from the details of using the `MediaTracker` class by automatically waiting for the entire image to load.

Icons typically are small images used to provide visual cues about what a button does, but the `ImageIcon` class isn't just for small images. You can use it to display large images as well, as long as you're willing to hold up your program while the image loads. For Swing applications, the wait usually isn't a problem. For applets, though, you may want to consider alternatives to large image files.

Table 3-1 lists the most important constructors and methods of the classes that you use to work with `ImageIcon` objects. I describe these constructors and methods in the following sections.

Table 3-1   Classes for Working with ImageIcon Objects

ImageIcon Constructor and Method	*Description*
ImageIcon(String filename)	Creates an ImageIcon object from the file indicated by the specified filename.
ImageIcon(URL url)	Creates an ImageIcon object from the file indicated by the specified URL.
Image getImage()	Gets the Image object associated with this ImageIcon.

JLabel and JButton Constructor	*Description*
JLabel (Icon image)	Creates a label with the specified image. (Note that ImageIcon implements the Icon interface.)
JButton(Icon image)	Creates a button with the specified image.
JButton(String text, Icon image)	Creates a button with the specified text and image.

Using ImageIcon in a Swing application

In a Swing application, you can load an image directly into an ImageIcon object by specifying the filename in the ImageIcon constructor, like this:

```
ImageIcon pic = new ImageIcon("HalfDome.jpg");
```

Here an ImageIcon object is created from a file named HalfDome.jpg. This file must live in the same directory as the class file. You can just as easily provide a path in the String parameter, however, like this:

```
ImageIcon pic = new ImageIcon("c:\\HalfDome.jpg");
```

Here the file is in the root directory of the C: drive. (Remember that you have to use two backslashes to get a single backslash in a Java string literal.) Then you can attach the image to a Swing component, such as a label or button, to display the image.

Many Swing components can display icons directly, including JLabel, JButton, JCheckBox, and JRadioButton. If you simply want to display the image, use a JLabel component and specify the ImageIcon object in its constructor, like this:

```
JLabel picLabel = new JLabel(pic);
```

Here a label is created from the previously created ImageIcon object named pic. When you add this label to a panel or frame, the image is displayed.

To put everything together, here's a complete application that displays the HalfDome.jpg image in a frame:

```java
import javax.swing.*;

public class PictureApp extends JFrame
{
    public static void main(String [] args)
    {
        new PictureApp();
    }

    public PictureApp()
    {
        this.setTitle("Picture Application");
        this.setDefaultCloseOperation(
            JFrame.EXIT_ON_CLOSE);
        JPanel panel1 = new JPanel();
        ImageIcon pic = new ImageIcon("HalfDome.jpg");
        panel1.add(new JLabel(pic));
        this.add(panel1);
        this.pack();
        this.setVisible(true);
    }
}
```

Figure 3-1 shows the frame that's displayed when this program is run.

Figure 3-1:
Displaying
an image
in a Swing
application.

Although this example shows how to display a large JPEG file, the ImageIcon class is also commonly used to attach smaller GIF images as icons for various types of buttons. To do that, you simply pass the ImageIcon object to the button constructor.

The following code produces the button shown in the margin:

```
JButton openButton;
ImageIcon openIcon = new ImageIcon("OpenIcon.gif");
openButton = new JButton(openIcon);
```

You can also create buttons with both text and an icon. I created the button shown in the margin with this code:

```
openButton = new JButton("Open", openIcon);
```

Using ImageIcon in an applet

If the program is an applet, use a URL instead of a filename to identify the image file. The only trick is figuring out how to get a URL for a file that lives in the same location as the applet itself. To do that, you can use this strange but functional incantation:

```
URL url = PictureApplet.class.getResource("HalfDome.jpg");
```

Here you use the `class` property of the class that defines your applet (in this case, `PictureApplet`) to get its `Class` object and then call the `getResource` method, which returns a `URL` object for the specified file. After you have the URL of the image file, you can create an `ImageIcon` from it, like this:

```
pic = new ImageIcon(url);
```

Then you can use the `ImageIcon` object in a label or button component, or you can use the `getImage` method to get the underlying `Image` object so that you can paint it directly to the screen.

Using the Image Class

If you want to paint an image directly to a graphics context (from the `paintComponent` method of a panel, for example), you need to use the `Image` class to represent the image. You want to create the `Image` object in the panel constructor but paint it in the `paintComponent` method. As a result, you need to declare the variable that references the image as an instance variable so that you can refer to it from both the constructor and the `paintComponent` method. The declaration for the instance variable looks something like this:

```
Image img;
```

Table 3-2 lists the most important constructors and methods of the classes that you use to work with `Image` objects. I describe these constructors and methods in the following sections.

Table 3-2	Classes for Working with Image Objects
Image Class Method and Field	*Description*
`Image getScaledInstance (int x, int x, int hints)`	Gets an `Image` object that has been scaled according to the x and y parameters. If either x or y is negative, the aspect ratio of the image is preserved. The `hints` parameter can be one of these fields: DEFAULT, SPEED, or SMOOTH.
`int SCALE_DEFAULT`	Gets a constant that represents the default scaling method.
`int SCALE_SPEED`	Gets a constant that represents a scaling method that favors speed over smoothness.
`int SCALE_SMOOTH`	Gets a constant that represents a scaling method that favors smoothness over speed.
Toolkit Class Method	*Description*
`static Toolkit getDefaultToolkit()`	Gets a `Toolkit` object.
`Image getImage(String filename)`	Gets an `Image` object from the specified filename.
Graphics Class Method	*Description*
`void drawImage(Image img, int x, int y, ImageObserver observer)`	Draws the specified image at the position indicated by the x and y parameters. The `observer` parameter specifies the object that listens for image update events.
`void drawImage(Image img, int x, int y, int width, int height, ImageObserver observer)`	Draws the specified image at the position indicated by the x and y parameters, using the size specified by the `width` and `height` parameters. The `observer` parameter specifies the object that listens for image update events.

Creating an Image object

`Image` is an abstract class, so it doesn't have a handy constructor you can use to create an image from a file or URL. You can create an `Image` object from a file, however, in two fairly simple ways: by using the `ImageIcon` class in the section "Using the ImageIcon Class" earlier in this chapter, or by using the `Toolkit` class.

To create an image from an `ImageIcon` object, you first create an `ImageIcon` object as described in the preceding section. Then you can use the `getImage` method to extract the `Image` from the `ImageIcon`, as in this example:

```
ImageIcon picIcon = new ImageIcon("c:\\HalfDome.jpg");
Image picImage = picIcon.getImage();
```

You want to put this code in the panel constructor so that it's executed only once.

To use the `getImage` method of the `Toolkit` class, first use the static `get DefaultToolkit` method to get a `Toolkit` object and then call `getImage` to load an image from a file, as in this example:

```
Toolkit kit = Toolkit.getDefaultToolkit();
img = kit.getImage("HalfDome.jpg");
```

Again, this code goes in the panel constructor so that the image isn't reloaded every time it needs to be painted.

 If you're loading a single small image, either technique is suitable. If you're loading a lot of images or a large image, the `Toolkit` technique is a better choice for two reasons: It doesn't make you create a bunch of unnecessary `ImageIcon` objects, and it doesn't tie up the application until the entire image is loaded.

Drawing an Image object

After you load an image and create an `Image` object, you can draw it by adding code in the `paint` method, like this:

```
g.drawImage(img, 0, 0, this);
```

The `drawImage` method takes four parameters. The first three are easy enough to understand: They're the image to be painted and the x and y coordinates where you want the image to appear. The fourth parameter is an object that implements the `ImageObserver` interface. This interface includes a method called `imageUpdate` that's called whenever the status of the image has changed. For small images or for applications that load the image from a local file, this method is probably called only once: when the image has finished loading. If you load a large image over the Internet (in an applet, for example), the `imageUpdate` method is likely to be called every time a chunk of the image is received.

Fortunately, it turns out that all Swing components, including `JPanel`, implement the `ImageObserver` interface, and their default implementation of the `imageUpdate` method simply calls `repaint`. This method in turn calls the `paint` method, so the image is automatically drawn again.

Scaling options

Placing an image in a fixed-size rectangle can distort the appearance of the image. Suppose you display an image whose original size is 400 x 600 in a 200 x 200 area. The image is one-half of its original width but one-third of its original height, making all the elements look short and fat. A better way to scale the image is to call the image's `getScaledInstance` method, as follows:

```
img = img.getScaledInstance
    (200, -1, Image.
    SCALE_DEFAULT);
```

The first two parameters of this method specify the desired width and height. If you set one of these parameters to a negative value, the `getScaledInstance` method calculates the appropriate value while preserving the original image's aspect ratio. The third parameter is a constant that indicates what scaling method to use. The three choices you use most are `SCALE_DEFAULT`, which uses the default method; `SCALE_SPEED`, which favors speed over smoothness; and `SCALE_SMOOTH`, which favors smoothness over speed.

Another form of the `drawImage` method lets you set the size at which you want the image to be drawn, like this:

```
g.drawImage(img, 0, 0, 200, 200, this);
```

Here the image is drawn in a 200 × 200–pixel rectangle starting in the top-left corner of the panel.

Viewing an Image example

To show how the elements presented in the preceding two sections work together, Listing 3-1 shows a complete program that uses the `Image` class to display an image in a panel.

To add a little interest, this application uses a `JFileChooser` dialog box to let the user select the image to be displayed, as shown in Figure 3-2. The file chooser includes a filter so that only JPEG, GIF, and PNG files are listed. For more information about the `JFileChooser` class, see Book VIII, Chapter 1.

Figure 3-2:
The Picture-
Frame
application
in action.

Listing 3-1:   The PictureFrame Application

```java
import javax.swing.*;
import java.awt.event.*;
import java.awt.*;
import java.io.*;

public class PictureFrame extends JFrame
{
    Image img;                                                          →8
    JButton getPictureButton;

    public static void main(String [] args)
    {
        new PictureFrame();
    }

    public PictureFrame()
    {
        this.setSize(300, 300);
        this.setTitle("Picture Frame Application");
        this.setDefaultCloseOperation(JFrame.EXIT_ON_CLOSE);

        JPanel picPanel = new PicturePanel();                           →22
        this.add(picPanel, BorderLayout.CENTER);

        JPanel buttonPanel = new JPanel();                              →25
        getPictureButton = new JButton("Get Picture");
        getPictureButton.addActionListener(e -> getPictureButtonClick() );
        buttonPanel.add(getPictureButton);
        this.add(buttonPanel, BorderLayout.SOUTH);

        this.setVisible(true);
    }

    public void getPictureButtonClick()                                →34
    {
        String file = getImageFile();
        if (file != null)
```

(continued)

Listing 3-1 *(continued)*

```
    {
        Toolkit kit = Toolkit.getDefaultToolkit();
        img = kit.getImage(file);
        img = img.getScaledInstance(
            300, -1, Image.SCALE_SMOOTH);
        this.repaint();
    }
}

private String getImageFile()                                    →47
{
    JFileChooser fc = new JFileChooser();
    fc.setFileFilter(new ImageFilter());
    int result = fc.showOpenDialog(null);
    File file = null;
    if (result == JFileChooser.APPROVE_OPTION)
    {
        file = fc.getSelectedFile();
        return file.getPath();
    }
    else
        return null;
}

private class PicturePanel extends JPanel                        →62
{
    public void paint(Graphics g)
    {
        g.drawImage(img, 0, 0, this);
    }
}

private class ImageFilter                                        →70
    extends javax.swing.filechooser.FileFilter
{
    public boolean accept(File f)
    {
        if (f.isDirectory())
            return true;
        String name = f.getName();
        if (name.matches(".*((.jpg)|(.gif)|(.png))"))
            return true;
        else
            return false;
    }

    public String getDescription()
    {
        return "Image files (*.jpg, *.gif, *.png)";
    }
}
}
```

The following paragraphs hit the highlights of this program:

→ **8**   The `img` variable is declared here so that the class can access it.

→ **22**   In the frame class constructor, a new instance of the `PicturePanel` class is created and added to the center of the frame.

→ **25**   Next, a panel is created to hold the button the user clicks to open an image file. The button specifies `this` for the action listener, and the panel is added to the South region of the frame.

→ **36**   The `getPictureButtonClick` method is invoked when the user clicks the Get Picture button. It calls the `getImageFile` method, which displays the file chooser and returns the name of the file selected by the user. Then, assuming that the filename returned is not `null`, the `Toolkit` class is used to load the image. The image is scaled so it is 300 pixels wide while preserving the aspect ratio, and the frame is repainted.

→ **48**   The `getImageFile` method creates and displays a file-chooser dialog box that shows only JPG, GIF, and PNG files. If the user selected a file, the complete path of the file chosen by the user is returned; otherwise, `null` is returned.

→ **63**   The `PicturePanel` class defines the panel that displays the picture. It consists of just one method: `paint`, which uses the `drawImage` method to draw the image.

→ **71**   The `ImageFilter` class is used to limit the file-chooser display to JPG, GIF, and PNG files. It uses the following regular expression to do so:

```
.*((.jpg)|(.gif)|(.png))
```

For more information about file filters, refer to Book VIII, Chapter 1. To get more information about regular expressions, turn to Book V, Chapter 3.

Playing Sounds and Making Music

Java provides built-in support for playing sound and music files. You can play sound and music files in a variety of formats, including wave files in several formats (WAV, AU, RMF, and AIFF, as well as MIDI files). Wave files are usually used to add specific sound effects to your application, such as chimes, explosions, or drumrolls. MIDI files let you play music while your application is running.

An audio file is represented by an object that implements the AudioClip interface, whose methods are listed in Table 3-3. As you can see, this interface is simple: You can play a sound once, play it in a loop, and stop playing the sound. Note that when you play or loop a sound, your program doesn't wait for the sound to finish playing. Instead, the sound is played in a separate thread so that your program can continue with its other chores.

Table 3-3	The AudioClip Interface
Method	*Description*
void play()	Plays the clip once.
void loop()	Plays the clip in a loop.
void stop()	Stops playing the clip.

Interestingly enough, the easiest way to create an AudioClip object is to use a static method of the Applet class called newAudioClip. This is a little confusing; because newAudioClip is a static method, you can use it in nonapplet programs as easily as you can use it in applets. Go figure.

Anyway, the newAudioClip method requires a URL, not a simple filename, so first you must figure out how to get a URL for the sound file you want to play.

Here's a snippet of code that creates an AudioClip from a file named hit.wav and plays it:

```
URL url = MyApp.class.getResource("hit.wav");
click = Applet.newAudioClip(url);
click.play();
```

The first line gets the Class object for the current class (assumed here to be MyApp) and then uses the getResource method to get a URL object for the specified file, which must be in the same directory as the MyApp class. Next, the newAudioClip method is called to create an AudioClip object. Finally, the play method is called to play it.

To make things a little more interesting, Listing 3-2 shows a program that plays the hit.wav sound every time you click the mouse in the program's frame. This program displays an empty frame that has a MouseListener installed. Each time the mouseClicked method is called, the sound is played.

Listing 3-2:   The MouseClicker Program

```java
import javax.swing.*;
import java.awt.event.*;
import java.awt.*;
import java.applet.*;
import java.net.URL;

public class MouseClicker extends JFrame
{
    AudioClip click;

    public static void main(String [] args)
    {
        new MouseClicker();
    }

    public MouseClicker()
    {
        this.setSize(400, 400);
        this.setTitle("Mouse Clicker");
        this.addMouseListener(new Clicker());

        URL urlClick = MouseClicker.class.getResource("hit.wav");
        click = Applet.newAudioClip(urlClick);

        this.setVisible(true);
    }

    private class Clicker extends MouseAdapter
    {
        public void mouseClicked(MouseEvent e)
        {
            click.play();
        }
    }
}
```

Chapter 4: Animation and Game Programming

In This Chapter

✔ Using threads to control animation

✔ Creating a bouncing ball

✔ Creating a whole room full of bouncing balls

✔ Devising a simple Pong-like game

*B*ecause of its powerful drawing capabilities, Java lends itself especially well to creating game programs — especially games that are created as applets so they can be played over the Internet. Game programming is a huge subject, big enough for a whole shelf of books. In this chapter, I just scratch the surface of creating basic animations and playing simple games. Specifically, you find out how to get a ball bouncing in an applet, how to create a paddle to hit the ball, and how to find out when you miss.

In other words, welcome to the 1970s! You're going to create an applet that plays Pong!

This chapter combines features that are presented in several chapters throughout this book. Specifically, you find information about drawing shapes in Book IX, Chapter 2. For information about working with threads, refer to Book V, Chapter 1. For information creating event listeners, see Book VI, Chapter 2. Finally, for details about creating and running applets, see Book VII, Chapter 1. (The easiest way to code and test the applets presented in this chapter is to use TextPad, since its handy shortcut makes it easy to run applets: Ctrl+3.)

Working with Sprites

In animation and game programming, an object that moves around the screen is usually called a *sprite*. The sprite itself can be drawn by various means. If the sprite is a simple geometric shape such as a circle, you can just create an `Ellipse2D` object and use the `draw` or `fill` method to render it. More commonly, the sprite is represented by a small image. Then you use the `drawImage` method to render the sprite.

In some cases, the sprite may have a series of images associated with it. If the sprite is a little person who walks around in your game world, you might have several images representing him walking left and right or moving in various stages of his little stride. Then you can put these images in an array and use an index variable to keep track of which image to draw.

Animating a sprite

No matter what a sprite looks like, the basic technique for animating it in Java is the same:

1. **Repaints the drawing component periodically.**

2. **Each time you repaint the drawing component, calculate a new position for the sprite and draw the sprite in its new position.**

There are several ways to handle Step 1 of this procedure. The easiest is to use the `Timer` class, which you learned about in Chapter 5 of Book III. The `Timer` class lets you create a `Timer` object that generates events at regular intervals and lets you set up a listener to handle those events.

Suppose you want to create a ball that travels across a component, starting at the left side of the component and traveling across to the right side. Here's an outline of how you can do that using the `Timer` class:

1. **Create the component that the ball is drawn on.**

   Usually this component can just extend `JComponent`.

2. **In the `paint` method, recalculate the position of each shape being animated and then draw it.**

3. **Create an instance of the drawing component and add it to a frame or applet.**

4. **Create a `Timer` object that calls the drawing component's `repaint` method at periodic intervals.**

   Typically, you set the timer to run 10 or 20 milliseconds. The drawing component's `repaint` method automatically calls the `paint` method, which repaints the ball in its new location.

5. **To get the animation going, call the `Timer` object's `start` method.**

Creating an animation applet

Sound simple enough? Listing 4-1 shows the first of several versions of an applet program that animates a moving ball. Figure 4-1 shows this applet in action when run in the applet viewer.

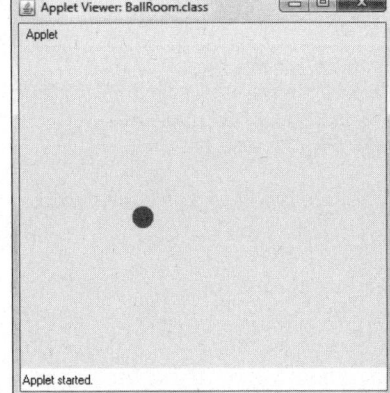

Figure 4-1:
The
BallRoom
applet in
action.

Listing 4-1: The BallRoom Applet

```
import java.applet.*;
import java.awt.*;
import javax.swing.*;
import java.awt.geom.*;

public class BallRoom extends JApplet                →6
{
    public static final int WIDTH = 350;
    public static final int HEIGHT = 300;

    private PaintSurface canvas;

    public void init()                               →13
    {
        this.setSize(WIDTH, HEIGHT);
        canvas = new PaintSurface();
        this.add(canvas, BorderLayout.CENTER);

        Timer t = new Timer(20,
            e -> {canvas.repaint();} );
        t.start();
    }

}

class PaintSurface extends JComponent                →26
{
    int x_pos = 0;      // the starting X position
    int y_pos = 150;    // the starting Y position
    int d = 20;         // the diameter of the ball

    public void paint(Graphics g)                    →32
```
(continued)

Listing 4-1 *(continued)*

```
    {
        Graphics2D g2 = (Graphics2D)g;
        g2.setRenderingHint(
            RenderingHints.KEY_ANTIALIASING,
            RenderingHints.VALUE_ANTIALIAS_ON);

        x_pos += 1;    // move ball right one pixel

        Shape ball = new Ellipse2D.Float(
            x_pos, y_pos, d, d);
        g2.setColor(Color.RED);
        g2.fill(ball);
    }
}
```

The following paragraphs describe the key portions of this program:

→ 6   The `BallRoom` class extends `JApplet` and defines two public
       static constants, named `WIDTH` and `HEIGHT`. These constants are
       used to set the size of the component the ball is animated within.
       It also defines a `PaintSurface` variable named `canvas` that's
       used as the canvas on which the animated ball is drawn.

→ 13   The `init` method is called when the applet starts. It sets the
       size of the applet, creates a new instance of the `PaintSurface`
       class on which the ball is animated, and adds that instance to
       the applet. Next, it creates a `Timer` object that calls the `canvas`
       object's `paint` method every 20 milliseconds.

→ 26   The `PaintSurface` class extends `JComponent`. The instance
       variables defined for this class define the characteristics of the
       ball that is animated: its x and y positions on the component and
       the ball's diameter.

→ 32   The `paint` method is called whenever the `PaintSurface` com-
       ponent needs to be redrawn (every 20 milliseconds). The `paint`
       method begins by casting the graphics context to a `Graphics2D`
       object and setting antialiasing on. Next, it calculates a new posi-
       tion for the ball by adding 1 to the x position. Then it creates a
       `Shape` object to represent the ball as an ellipse at the current
       `x_pos` and `y_pos` positions, using the width and height specified
       by the d variable. Finally, it sets the color and draws the ball by
       calling the `fill` method.

Understanding Double Buffering

If you've looked into animation and game programming before, you may have
heard of a technique called *double buffering,* which is required to produce
smooth, flicker-free animation. When you use double buffering, you don't

draw shapes directly to the component. Instead, you create an offscreen image object called a *buffer* and draw the shapes to it. Then, when all the shapes are drawn, you transfer the entire buffer image to the component.

Fortunately, any drawing you do on a Swing component is automatically double-buffered. Before Swing, you had to do double buffering manually by creating an `Image` object and then creating a graphics context so that you could write to the `Image`. With Swing, however, you don't have to do anything special to use double buffering.

If you want to turn double buffering off for some reason (maybe just to see how much it improves the animation for your application), you can do so by calling the `setDoubleBuffered` method of the component you're drawing to, like this:

```
this.setDoubleBuffered(false);
```

Bouncing the Ball

The program shown in Listing 4-1 illustrates the basic framework of a program that animates sprites. The ball that it animates isn't very interesting, however: It just flies across the screen in a straight line and disappears off the right edge, never to be seen again. To be more interesting, the ball should travel in different directions and bounce off the edges of the component so that it stays visible.

The trick of animating the ball so that it travels in other than horizontal (or vertical) lines and bounces off the walls is calculating the ball's new (x, y) position for each animation cycle. This problem has at least two basic approaches:

✦ The most realistic approach is to keep track of two variables for the ball: the angle in which it's traveling and its speed. Then you can use high school trigonometry to calculate the new (x, y) position of the ball for each cycle. If the ball hits one of the edges, you have to calculate the ball's new angle. (You probably need some sines and cosines, and maybe a square root or a logarithm or something. I'm not sure; I didn't do so well in math.)

✦ The easier way is to store two variables — call them x_speed and y_speed — that represent the distance the ball travels horizontally and vertically for each animation cycle. This technique is much easier because it doesn't require any math more complicated than addition. For each animation cycle, just add x_speed to the x position and add y_speed to the y position. If the ball hits the left or right edge, negate x_speed to reverse the ball's horizontal direction, and if the ball hits the top or bottom edge, negate y_speed so that the ball reverses its vertical direction. The result is a pretty convincing bounce off the wall.

To add capability for the ball to bounce, you need to add some instance variables and modify the `paint` method a bit. The resulting `PaintSurface` class is shown in Listing 4-2. (This class works with the `BallRoom` class shown in Listing 4-1. Because the `BallRoom` class is unchanged, I've omitted it here so you can focus on the changes to the `PaintSurface` class.)

Listing 4-2: A Bouncing Version of the PaintSurface Class

```
class PaintSurface extends JComponent
{
    int x_pos = 0;                                                  →3
    int y_pos = 0;
    int x_speed = 1;
    int y_speed = 2;
    int d = 20;
    int width = BallRoom.WIDTH;
    int height = BallRoom.HEIGHT;

    public void paint(Graphics g)
    {
        Graphics2D g2 = (Graphics2D)g;
        g2.setRenderingHint(
            RenderingHints.KEY_ANTIALIASING,
            RenderingHints.VALUE_ANTIALIAS_ON);
        if (x_pos < 0 || x_pos > width - d)                         →17
            x_speed = -x_speed;
        if (y_pos < 0 || y_pos > height - d)                        →19
            y_speed = -y_speed;
        x_pos += x_speed;                                           →21
        y_pos += y_speed;

        Shape ball = new Ellipse2D.Float(                           →24
            x_pos, y_pos, d, d);
        g2.setColor(Color.RED);
        g2.fill(ball);
    }
}
```

The following paragraphs describe the key elements of this class:

→ 3   For this version of the `PaintSurface` class, the instance variables keep track of the ball's x and y positions and speed, as well as its diameter and the height and width of the drawing surface.

→ 17   This `if` statement checks to see whether the ball has hit the left wall (the x position is less than 0) or the right wall (the x position is greater than the width of the component less the diameter of the ball). If so, the x speed is reversed. (You must take the diameter of the ball into account on the right wall because the x position indicates the position of the *left* side of the ball, and you want the ball to bounce when its *right* side hits the right wall.)

→ 19   This `if` statement applies the same logic to the y speed to see whether the ball has hit the top or bottom wall.

→ 21   After the x and y speed values are adjusted for bounces, the next two statements move the ball. If x_speed is a positive number, the ball moves right; if it's negative, the ball moves left. Similarly, if y_speed is positive, the ball moves down; if it's negative, the ball moves up.

→ 24   These lines draw the ball at its new location.

Bouncing a Bunch of Balls

Most games require you to animate more than one sprite. More than one ball may be onscreen at one time, for example, or the game may have sprites other than balls. Thus the paint method needs to be able to move — and draw — multiple sprites.

One way to do that is to create a class for the sprites to be animated and add instances of that class to an array list or other collection. Then the paint method can use a loop to move and draw each sprite in the collection.

Creating a Ball class

To add the ability to animate more than one ball, start by adding a class that represents a single ball, as shown in Listing 4-3.

Listing 4-3:   A Ball Class

```
class Ball extends Ellipse2D.Float                              →1
{
    private int x_speed, y_speed;                               →3
    private int d;
    private int width = BallRoom.WIDTH;
    private int height = BallRoom.HEIGHT;

    public Ball(int diameter)                                   →8
    {
        super((int)(Math.random() * (BallRoom.WIDTH - 20) +
1),
                (int)(Math.random() * (BallRoom.HEIGHT - 20) +
1),
                diameter, diameter);
        this.d = diameter;
        this.x_speed = (int)(Math.random() * 5 + 1);
        this.y_speed = (int)(Math.random() * 5 + 1);
    }

    public void move()                                          →18
    {
        if (super.x < 0 || super.x > width - d)
            x_speed = -x_speed;
```

(continued)

Listing 4-3 *(continued)*

```
        if (super.y < 0 || super.y > height - d)
            y_speed = -y_speed;
        super.x += x_speed;
        super.y += y_speed;
    }
}
```

The following paragraphs point out the highlights of this program:

→ 1   Because a ball is essentially an ellipse with a few additional characteristics, this class extends the `Ellipse2D.Float` class. An advantage of implementing the `Ball` class this way is that you can pass a `Ball` object directly to the `draw` and `fill` methods to paint the ball.

→ 3   The `Ball` class defines five private instance variables, representing the x and y speeds, the diameter of the ball, and the width and height of the component the balls are animated within. Notice that the x and y positions of the ball have no instance variables. Because the `Ellipse2D.Float` class already keeps track of its x and y positions, you just use the x and y fields of the superclass when you need those values.

→ 8   The `Ball` class defines a single constructor that accepts the diameter of the ball to create as a parameter but calculates the other values at random. As a result, you can call the `Ball` constructor several times to create several balls, each ball having a different starting position and trajectory.

→ 18   The `Ball` class also has a `move` method, which can be called to move the ball. First, this method adjusts the ball's trajectory if it has hit one of the edges. Then it simply adds the `x_speed` and `y_speed` values to the x and y fields of the superclass.

Animating random balls

With the `Ball` class in hand, Listing 4-4 shows a version of the `Paint Component` class that creates an array list with ten randomly placed balls and then draws each one in the `paint` method.

Listing 4-4:   The PaintSurface Class for Bouncing Balls

```
import java.util.ArrayList;

class PaintSurface extends JComponent
{
    public ArrayList<Ball> balls = new ArrayList<Ball>();

    public PaintSurface()
```

```
    {
        for (int i = 0; i < 10; i++)
            balls.add(new Ball(20));
    }

    public void paint(Graphics g)
    {
        Graphics2D g2 = (Graphics2D)g;
        g2.setRenderingHint(
            RenderingHints.KEY_ANTIALIASING,
            RenderingHints.VALUE_ANTIALIAS_ON);
        g2.setColor(Color.RED);
        for (Ball ball : balls)
        {
            ball.move();
            g2.fill(ball);
        }
    }
}
```

This class starts by declaring an instance variable named `balls` that holds
the balls to be animated. Then, in the constructor, it uses a `for` loop to
create ten balls and add them to the collection. In the `paint` method, which
is called once every 20 milliseconds, a `for` loop is used to call each ball's
`move` method and then pass the ball to the `fill` method to paint it on the
component.

Figure 4-2 shows this program in action, with 10 balls bouncing around
randomly onscreen. If you feel daring, try changing the `for` statement in the
`PaintComponent` constructor so that it creates 100 balls instead of 10. The
little applet window gets pretty crowded!

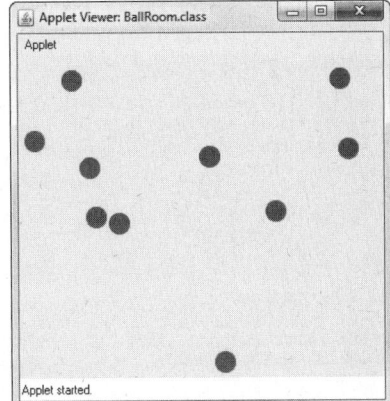

Figure 4-2:
A room full
of bouncing
balls.

Creating Collidable Balls

The balls created by the `Ball` class shown earlier in this chapter have one slightly unrealistic behavior: They're transparent to one another. If two balls happen to arrive at the same place at the same time, they simply pass right through each other without noticing.

If you want to create balls that bounce off one another as well as off the walls, all you have to do is modify the `move` method of the `Ball` class. Just get a reference to the collection that contains all the other balls, and check each ball to see whether the current ball has hit any of the other balls. If so, adjust the trajectory of each ball accordingly.

Listing 4-5 shows a version of the `Ball` class in which the balls bounce off one another.

Listing 4-5:   A Ball Class That Handles Collisions

```
class Ball extends Ellipse2D.Float
{
    public int x_speed, y_speed;
    private int d;
    private int width = BallRoom.WIDTH;
    private int height = BallRoom.HEIGHT;
    private ArrayList<Ball> balls;

    public Ball(int diameter, ArrayList<Ball> balls)              →9
    {
        super((int)(Math.random() * (BallRoom.WIDTH - 20) + 1),
            (int)(Math.random() * (BallRoom.HEIGHT - 20) + 1),
            diameter, diameter);
        this.d = diameter;
        this.x_speed = (int)(Math.random() * 5 + 1);
        this.y_speed = (int)(Math.random() * 5 + 1);
        this.balls = balls;
    }

    public void move()                                            →20
    {
        // detect collision with other balls
        Rectangle2D r = new Rectangle2D.Float(
            super.x, super.y, d, d);
        for (Ball b : balls)
        {
            if (b != this &&                                      →27
                b.intersects(r))
            {
                // on collision, the balls swap speeds            →30
                int tempx = x_speed;
                int tempy = y_speed;
                x_speed = b.x_speed;
                y_speed = b.y_speed;
                b.x_speed = tempx;
                b.y_speed = tempy;
                break;                                            →37
            }
        }
    }
```

```
        if (super.x < 0)
        {
            super.x = 0;
            x_speed = Math.abs(x_speed);
        }
        else if (super.x > width - d)
        {
            super.x = width - d;
            x_speed = -Math.abs(x_speed);
        }
        if (super.y < 0)
        {
            super.y = 0;
            y_speed = Math.abs(y_speed);
        }
        else if (super.y > height - d)
        {
            super.y = height - d;
            y_speed = -Math.abs(y_speed);
        }
        super.x += x_speed;
        super.y += y_speed;
    }
}
```

→40

The following lines describe the high points of this version of the Ball class:

→ 9   The constructor accepts a reference to the array list that holds the balls. The Ball class needs this list so that each ball can determine whether it has struck any other balls. The reference to the array list is saved in an instance variable named balls.

     Note that because of this change to the constructor, you'll have to modify one line in the PaintSurface class as well. Specifically, you'll need to change line 10 in Listing 4-4 to read:

```
balls.add(new Ball(20, balls));
```

→ 20   The move method begins by creating a rectangle from the current ball. (You see how this rectangle is used in a moment.) Then it uses a for loop to check for a collision with each of the balls in the balls array list.

→ 27   For each ball, an if statement tests two conditions. First, it eliminates the current ball by checking b != this. If you allowed balls to collide with themselves, the balls would be in constant collision and would never be able to move.

     Next, the if statement checks to see whether the current ball has collided with the other ball by calling intersects, a method defined by the Shape interface. This method accepts a rectangle object and returns true if the shape intersects any part of the specified rectangle. The rectangle object created before the for loop began is used as the parameter of this method. (Note that this collision test isn't perfect; it sometimes treats near misses as collisions. But it's close enough.)

→ 30   If a collision is detected, the x and y speed values of the two
balls are swapped. Not only do the balls bounce away from each
other, but also the slower ball picks up speed and the faster ball
slows down.

→ 37   A break statement is executed if a collision is detected to prevent
detecting collisions with more than one ball. Without this break
statement, collisions that involve more than two balls usually
result in pretty strange behavior. Try removing the break statement to see what happens. (Even with this break statement, the
balls sometimes behave in unexpected ways. I think it's kind of fun
to watch, but then again, I'm pretty easily entertained.)

→ 40   The rest of this method is different from the previous version, primarily because when you check for collisions with both the edges
of the component and other balls, the ball always has a chance
to collide with both the edge and another ball. Thus the if statements that check for edge collisions force the x and y speed
values to be appropriate negative or positive numbers.

Playing Games

The key to turning an animation program into a game program is adding
user interaction via the mouse or keyboard. Either way, the technique is the
same: You add event listeners to handle keyboard or mouse events. Then,
in the event listeners, you make appropriate changes to the game's sprites
according to the user's actions.

Suppose you want to create a paddle that the user can move back and forth
by dragging the mouse. To do that, just add a listener for mouse motion and
save the mouse pointer's x position in an instance variable that represents the
top-left corner of the paddle. Here's code to do this, written as an anonymous
inner class:

```
addMouseMotionListener(new MouseMotionAdapter()
{
    public void mouseMoved(MouseEvent e)
    {
        paddle_x = e.getX() - 30;
    }
} );
```

Place this code in the constructor for the component the animation is drawn
on. (Notice that here, I'm subtracting 30 from the x position. I do that because
the width of the paddle is 60, and I want the mouse position to be the center
of the paddle, not the left edge.)

Having stored the mouse pointer's position in an instance variable, you can
use it to draw the paddle in the paint method. Here's an example:

```
Shape paddle = new Rectangle2D.Float(
                      paddle_x, 360, 60, 8);
g2.setColor(Color.BLACK);
g2.fill(paddle);
```

The paddle is drawn as a 60 × 8–pixel black rectangle. When the user moves the mouse pointer over the applet, the paddle moves along with the mouse pointer.

To show how you can incorporate this technique into a program that plays a simple game, Listing 4-6 shows the complete code for a simple Pong-like game, in which a ball bounces around and the user tries to hit it with the paddle. Each time the user hits the ball, he or she gets points based on how fast the ball is moving at the time. If the user misses the ball, 1,000 points are deducted, and the ball is replaced by a new ball with a random speed and trajectory.

To add a small amount of interest to this admittedly boring game, the player can put English on the ball by moving the mouse pointer quickly at the moment it hits the ball. When the program detects this movement, the ball changes color, and its x velocity is increased by 50 percent. Thus, the ball bounces off the paddle at a skewed angle and increases its speed. The player scores more points with each hit, but of course, the ball is harder to hit when it's traveling faster.

Figure 4-3 shows this program in action. As you can see, I'm getting pretty good at it.

Figure 4-3:
The
NotPong
game in
action.

Listing 4-6:   The NotPong Program

```
import java.applet.*;
import java.awt.*;
import java.awt.event.*;
import javax.swing.*;
import java.awt.geom.*;
import java.util.concurrent.*;

public class NotPong extends JApplet                              →8
{
    public static final int WIDTH = 400;
    public static final int HEIGHT = 400;

    private PaintSurface canvas;

    public void init()                                           →16
    {
        this.setSize(WIDTH, HEIGHT);
        canvas = new PaintSurface();
        this.add(canvas, BorderLayout.CENTER);
        ScheduledThreadPoolExecutor executor =
            new ScheduledThreadPoolExecutor(3);
        executor.scheduleAtFixedRate(new AnimationThread(this),
            0L, 20L, TimeUnit.MILLISECONDS);
    }
}

class AnimationThread implements Runnable                        →27
{
    JApplet c;

        public AnimationThread(JApplet c)
    {
        this.c = c;
    }

        public void run()
    {
        c.repaint();
    }
}

class PaintSurface extends JComponent                            →42
{
    int paddle_x = 0;                                           →44
    int paddle_y = 360;

    int score = 0;                                              →47
    float english = 1.0f;

    Ball ball;                                                  →50

    Color[] color = {Color.RED, Color.ORANGE,                  →52
                     Color.MAGENTA, Color.ORANGE,
                     Color.CYAN, Color.BLUE};
    int colorIndex;

    public PaintSurface()                                       →57
    {
        addMouseMotionListener(new MouseMotionAdapter()
```

```
            {
                public void mouseMoved(MouseEvent e)
                {
                    if (e.getX() - 30 - paddle_x > 5)
                        english = 1.5f;
                    else if (e.getX() - 30 - paddle_x < -5)
                        english = -1.5f;
                    else
                        english = 1.0f;
                    paddle_x = e.getX() - 30;
                }
            } );
        ball = new Ball(20);
    }

    public void paint(Graphics g)
    {
        Graphics2D g2 = (Graphics2D)g;
        g2.setRenderingHint(
            RenderingHints.KEY_ANTIALIASING,
            RenderingHints.VALUE_ANTIALIAS_ON);
        Shape paddle = new Rectangle2D.Float(
            paddle_x, paddle_y, 60, 8);

        g2.setColor(color[colorIndex % 6]);

        if (ball.intersects(paddle_x, paddle_y, 60, 8)
            && ball.y_speed > 0)
        {
            ball.y_speed = -ball.y_speed;
            ball.x_speed = (int)(ball.x_speed * english);
            if (english != 1.0f)
                colorIndex++;
            score += Math.abs(ball.x_speed * 10);
        }

        if (ball.getY() + ball.getHeight()
            >= NotPong.HEIGHT)
        {
            ball = new Ball(20);
            score -= 1000;
            colorIndex = 0;
        }
        ball.move();
        g2.fill(ball);

        g2.setColor(Color.BLACK);
        g2.fill(paddle);
        g2.drawString("Score:" + score, 250, 20);

    }
}

class Ball extends Ellipse2D.Float
{
```

→75

→81

→84

→86

→96

→103

→106

→108

→113

(continued)

Listing 4-6 *(continued)*

```
public int x_speed, y_speed;
private int d;
private int width = NotPong.WIDTH;
private int height = NotPong.HEIGHT;

public Ball(int diameter)
{
    super((int)(Math.random() * (NotPong.WIDTH - 20) + 1),
        0, diameter, diameter);
    this.d = diameter;
    this.x_speed = (int)(Math.random() * 5 + 5);
    this.y_speed = (int)(Math.random() * 5 + 5);
}

public void move()
{
    if (super.x < 0 || super.x > width - d)
        x_speed = -x_speed;
    if (super.y < 0 || super.y > height - d)
        y_speed = -y_speed;
    super.x += x_speed;
    super.y += y_speed;
}
}
```

The following paragraphs explain the gory details of how this program works:

→ 8   Like the other examples in this chapter, the NotPong class extends JApplet. You can get the program to run as a standalone Swing application, however, with just a few minor changes.

→ 16   The init method is called when the applet is started. It sets the size of the applet, creates a new PaintSurface object and adds it to the applet, and then creates and starts the thread that controls the animation.

→ 27   The AnimationThread class in this program is the same as in the other programs in this chapter. The thread is scheduled to execute every 20 milliseconds. Inside the thread's run method, the repaint method forces the animation to update itself.

→ 42   The PaintSurface class extends JComponent. It provides the surface on which the animations are drawn.

→ 44   These instance variables define the initial position of the paddle.

→ 47   These instance variables keep track of the score and the English applied to the ball. The English is initially set to 1.0, but (as you see later) it changes to -1.5 or 1.5 if the user moves the paddle quickly as the ball is hit.

→ 50   This instance variable represents the ball.

→ 52   An array of `Color` objects and an index variable are used so that the ball can be drawn with several colors. Each time the user hits the ball with English applied, the index variable is incremented so that the ball is drawn with a different color.

→ 57   The constructor for the `PaintSurface` class adds a mouse motion listener that extends the `MouseMotionAdapter` class. In this anonymous class, the `mouseMoved` method simply updates the paddle's x position. After the listener is added, a new `ball` object is created.

→ 75   The `paint` method is called each time the component is repainted, which happens approximately every 20 milliseconds. This method begins by casting the graphics context object to `Graphics2D` and enabling antialiasing to eliminate flicker.

→ 81   This statement creates the `Shape` object that represents the paddle.

→ 84   This statement sets the color used to draw the ball. Note that the remainder division operator is used to provide an index value that's always between 0 and 6.

→ 86   This `if` statement determines whether the ball has struck the paddle by calling the `intersects` method of the ball. (The `Ball` class inherits this method from its base class `Rectangle2D.Float`.) The second part of the `if` condition makes sure that the ball is traveling downward when it hits; a hit isn't registered if the ball is traveling up (which happens on occasion, especially when the ball is moving fast).

       If the ball has hit the paddle, the y speed is reversed (to make the ball travel up instead of down), and the x speed is multiplied by the English amount. Then, if the English amount is other than 1.0, the color-index variable is incremented. Finally, the player's score is increased by ten times the ball's x speed. Thus the user scores more if he or she hits a fast-moving ball.

→ 96   This `if` statement checks to see whether the ball has hit the south wall. If so, a new ball is created, the color index is reset to 0, and 1,000 points are deducted from the score.

→ 103   These statements move the ball and draw it in its new position.

→ 106   These statements draw the paddle after setting the color to black.

→ 108   This statement draws the score near the top-right corner of the playing area.

→ 113   This class defines the ball. As it turns out, this class is nearly identical to the `Ball` class shown in the section "Creating a Ball class," earlier in this chapter. For an explanation of how it works, refer to that section.

Index

B

F

O

S

U

V

W

X

Y

Z

About the Author

Doug Lowe has been writing computer programming books since the guys who invented Java were in high school. He's written books on COBOL, FORTRAN, Visual Basic, IBM mainframe computers, mid-range systems, PCs, web programming, and probably a few he's long forgotten about. He's the author of more than 30 *For Dummies* books, including *Networking For Dummies,* 10th Edition, *Networking All-In-One For Dummies,* 4th Edition, *PowerPoint 2013 For Dummies,* and *Electronics All-In-One For Dummies*. He lives in that sunny all-American city Fresno, California, where the motto is "Yes, We Have Bad Air, But It's Not Our Fault!"

Dedication

To my beautiful wife, Kristen Gearhart.

Author's Acknowledgments

I'd like to thank everyone at Wiley who was involved in the creation of this book, starting with project editor Heidi Unger, who did a great job of managing all the editorial work required to put this book together in spite of the fact that the book was delayed by the long development cycle of Java 8, and that I disappeared for a bit in the middle of the process to get married. I'd also like to thank acquisitions editor Connie Santisteban for making the whole project possible, John Meuller for his excellent and thorough technical review, and copy editor Barry Childs-Helton for crossing all my i's and dotting all my t's — wait, reverse that!

Publisher's Acknowledgments

Acquisitions Editor: Connie Santisteban

Project Editor: Heidi Unger

Copy Editor: Barry Childs-Helton

Technical Editor: John Mueller

Editorial Assistant: Annie Sullivan

Sr. Editorial Assistant: Cherie Case

Project Coordinator: Phil Midkiff

Supervising Producer: Richard Graves

Cover Image: ©budgetstockphoto/
iStockphoto.com